The Scientific Study

of Foreign Policy

JAMES N. ROSENAU

The Scientific Study of Foreign Policy

Revised and Enlarged Edition

Frances Pinter (Publishers) Ltd, London

Nichols Publishing Company, New York

Library of Congress Cataloging in Publication Data

Rosenau, James N
    The scientific study of foreign policy.

    1. International relations — Addresses,
essays, lectures. I. Title.
JX1395.R573   1980   327.1   79-25453
ISBN 0-89397-074-3
ISBN 0-89397-075-1 pbk.

Copyright © James N. Rosenau

First Published in Great Britain by
Frances Pinter (Publishers) Limited
5 Dryden Street, London WC2E 9NW

ISBN 0-903804-56-5 Hardback
ISBN 0-903804-57-3 Paperback

Published in the U.S.A. by
Nichols Publishing Company
P.O. Box 96, New York, N.Y. 10024

Printed in Great Britain by A. Wheaton & Co. Ltd., Exeter

For Heidi

An Autobiographical Extension: Preface to the Revised and Enlarged Edition

Since a number of people expressed regret when the original publishers of this book let the original edition go out of print, it seemed an opportunity to assess whether the growth of the field and my own intellectual development in the intervening decade warranted the compilation of a revised and enlarged edition. Though this assessment was not easy to make, its results are self evident: the reader now holds a heavier, costlier, more varied, and—I like to think—a more useful volume.

If growth in the field of foreign policy studies was the only criterion for determining whether a new edition would be compiled, the decision could have been reached quickly. As indicated in the brief evaluation of its growth that I made in the mid-1970s (see pages 133–146), the scientific study of foreign policy can reasonably be described as having exploded over the past ten years. A welter of empirical studies as well as a number of theoretical formulations have flowed into the field, many building on each other even as many also broke new ground. Indeed, the growth of the field has been so extensive as to yield major efforts to synthesize and summarize many of its findings.[1]

---

[1] See, for example, Maurce A. East, Stephen A. Salmore, Charles R. Hermann (eds.), *Why Nations Act*: *Theoretical Perspectives for Comparative Foreign Policy Studies* (Beverly Hills: Sage Publications, 1978), and Patrick J. McGowan and Howard B. Shapiro, *The Comparative Study of Foreign Policy* (Beverly Hills: Saga Publications, 1973).

Yet the decision to compile a revised and enlarged edition was not simple. My own development since the original edition had taken enough turns to raise the question of whether I had anything further to contribute to the field. While not rejecting the many reasons offered in the original edition for studying foreign policy scientifically, my interests took two major turns, each of which led to preoccupations that rivaled my concern for foreign policy phenomena. Largely because the 1970s were marked by a rapid mounting of the interdependence of world affairs and a discernable decline in the capacity of governments to sustain effective foreign policies, but perhaps also because of a chronic inability to stay put intellectually, I became progressively more preoccupied with the nongovernmental dynamics underlying the swift transformation of the global system in recent years. The first turn along these lines led me to the concept of adaptation and to treating nation-states as adapting entities that must reconcile their internal tensions and their external needs in order to survive and prosper. As a result, I developed an organizing "theory of national adaptation" which, in turn, stimulated and guided the authorship of a series of papers in which different aspects of the adaptive process were subjected to close scrutiny. The second turn took a more systems-wide perspective and focused on the transnational forces that seem to be hastening the interdependence of peoples and their institutions. This focus has yet to yield an organizing theoretical formulation, but it did lead to another series of papers in which I offered several neglected concepts, such as aggregation and authority structures, as a basis for more thoroughly comprehending the processes and repercussions of transnationalization.

Neither the adaptive nor the transitional perspectives preclude a concern for foreign policy phenomena. In both perspectives governments and their policies are among the central actors, in the former serving as the mechanisms through which national adaptation is sustained and in the latter acting to promote, contain, or otherwise effect the mounting interdependence. Yet, each perspective also encompasses so many phenomena only tangentially related to foreign policy that using the two series of papers as the basis for a revised and enlarged edition of this volume hardly seemed justified, a conclusion which led directly to the question of whether I had made further contributions to the scientific study of foreign policy.

The answer is mixed. On the one hand, in recent years I have come to wonder whether my work in the foreign policy field was founded on the wrong questions and was therefore misleading those inclined to take cues from it. Nor was I alone in expressing doubts about my work. One analyst, for example, observed that "for a theoretician Rosenau has been too coy."[2] On the other hand, since the original edition of this book. I co-authored two empirical analyses that derive from my pre-theories of foreign policy and that yielded some provocative findings. Furthermore, despite my misgivings about whether the questions posed in the original edition were sound, it did go out of print and appears to have been sufficiently useful to occasion expressions of regret over its unavailability.

After pondering these contradictory answers at some length, it proved impossible to resolve them by not compiling and publishing the more important essays I have written in the last decade. To choose such a course would be to withhold ideas from the marketplace and that, I am convinced, is unthinkable for anyone committed to scientific inquiry. Our work may be "too coy", and it may prove to be misleading, but we have an obligation as scientists to disseminate our findings and interpretations. Knowledge-building is a social process, an exposing of ideas to peers so that expansion, revision, and/or rejection of them can ensue and knowledge thereby be fashioned. To withhold ideas from whatever may be their rightful place in the marketplace is thus to undermine the dynamics whereby knowledge is established and cumulated.

The very openness of the marketplace, moreover, means that those who shop in it must decide for themselves whether the opportunities are worth the risks. Accordingly, if others eventually come to view any of my ideas that they plucked out of the marketplace as having misled them, such an outcome is their problem and not mine. As long as one maintains high standards and does not knowingly contribute erroneous data to the marketplace, one cannot be responsible for the way in which others respond to and use the materials. This is especially so if one's contributions are accompanied with appropriate qualifications and indications of their tentative and speculative nature, a theme to which I have tried to adhere in all my writings.

Once the decision to compile a new edition of this book was made, its implementation proved easier than expected, thanks to Frances Pinter. She agreed to publish in separate volumes those of my essays that focus on the processes of national adaptation and the dynamics of transnationalization. These can be found, respectively, in *The Study of Political Adaptation* and *The Study of Global Interdependence*: *Essays on the Transnationalization of World Affairs*, both scheduled for publication by Frances Pinter, Ltd., in 1980.

At the same time, in order to allow for those points where overlap occurs among the foreign policy, adaptive, and transnational perspec-

[2] Ralph Pettman, *Human Behavior and World Politics*: *An Introduction to International Relations* (New York: St. Martin's Press, 1975), p. 56.

tives, I have included in this revised edition the organizing theory I developed on national adaptation (Chapter 18) and an essay on interdependence in which I outlined the potential uses of the concept of aggregation (Chapter 19). Likewise, so as to remain true to the skeptical spirit that underlies scientific inquiry, I have also included here a recent essay in which I most succinctly raised the question of whether my work is founded on the wrong questions (Chapter 9).

Three other new essays have been included in this revised edition. One (Chapter 3) is a recent effort to return to fundamentals and assess what it is we do when we undertake to theorize about international phenomena. The second (Chapter 8) consists of the later of the two empirical articles on foreign policy I co-authored subsequent to the publication of the original edition of this book.[3] The third (Chapter 14) is an attempt to explore conceptually how variables external to a nation-state operate to underlie its foreign policies.

Besides enlarging the book to include six new essays, the process of revision also led to the dropping of one chapter (14) from the original work. This was done, not because that chapter's 1958 data on U.S. foreign policy elites have been rendered obsolete by the events of the 1970s (in fact, quite the opposite is the case), but rather because, given space limitations, they are of lesser general relevance than the data presented here in the chapters (7 and 8) designed to exemplify how the scientific study of foreign policy is practiced when the hypothesis-testing side of the enterprise is undertaken. Also for space reasons, I have dropped the appendix to Chapter 18 in which the key variables are operationalized. Readers interested in this appendix will find an appropriate citation indicating where it can be obtained.

Aside from these deletions and a few involving unnecessary repetition, I have not altered or revised the contents of any of the chapters. As indicated in my original preface that follows, there are good reasons to forego the temptation to up-date or otherwise change any of the articles and to collect them together exactly as they were originally published.

Finally, this revised edition also includes a bibliography of my own writings to date. Such an inclusion may seem inappropriate or unnecessary, but it is offered in the spirit of intellectual autobiography with which I have prefaced both editions. The bibliography is, as it were, an autobiographical appendix that those who find some merit in my formulations may want to examine for articles not included in the three

---

[3] The earlier of these is not included here because its central findings are adequately summarized in Chapter 8, albeit the reader may want to consult the former (as cited in Chapter 8) for details pertaining to how the key variables were operationalized and countries assigned to the categories of the resulting classification scheme.

collections of essays. As the very least the bibliography provides an insight into the peregrinations of a scientist across the varied and irregular landscape of world affairs.

As one's intellectual growth lengthens and expands, so does one's associations and support base. This is especially so in my case, as I left Rutgers University only a few weeks after completing the original edition and subsequently spent three years at Ohio State University and seven at the University of Southern California. Thus, in addition to those whose nourishment and help I have acknowledged at the end of the earlier preface, mention must be made of the several individuals and institutions whose assistance was invaluable in making possible the preparation of this revised edition and the six additions that have enlarged it.

The institutional support came from several sources. The Research Foundation of Ohio State University and the National Science Foundation (through its Grant GS-3117) provided support that facilitated completion of the papers presented here as Chapters 8, 13, and 15, while the Institute for Transnational Studies and the School of International relations at the University of Southern California supplied the support necessary to prepare Chapters 3, 9, and 19. The role in the knowledge-building process of such research organisations is too often taken for granted, and so I am pleased to be able to acknowledge that without their support preparing these papers would have been a much harder task than was otherwise the case.

As already noted, I am enormously grateful to Frances Pinter for her support. If all publishers proceeded as she does, the knowledge-building process would unfold in a much smoother and less halting fashion.

It is also a pleasure to record my indebtedness to Gary Gartin, Edwin P. McClain, and George H. Ramsey, all three of whom moved with me from Ohio to California in 1973 and each of whom contributed far more than was required of them as research assistants. (In addition, George co-authored Chapter 8 with me and I am grateful for his permission to include it in this collection.) Much the same can be said about Thomas M. Johnson, who subsequently provided useful assistance on several projects. All of these gentlemen are humane and yet rigorous social scientists. They are my friends, and I shall always be indebted to them for the creative and patient way in which they filled in as critics of the early drafts of my recent papers.

First Kay Neves and later Louise Marks helped greatly through the secretarial skills and wisdom they brought to managing the multiplicity of tasks that initiate and sustain a research program. They are also my good friends as well as colleagues, and I cannot say enough in appreciation of all they have done.

As one's support base expands through time, so does it also contract. This autobiographical extension would thus not be complete without noting that Norah Rosenau died on July 5, 1974. Much of what I wrote about her in the earlier preface still obtains, but her absence has deprived me of a vital source of ideas and energy, to put it mildly.

Of course, none of the foregoing is responsible for the additions of this enlarged edition. Again many have helped, but the responsibility for the final result is solely mine.

JAMES N. ROSENAU

Pacific Palisades, California
November 2, 1979

Preface to an Intellectual Autobiography

So much about this volume—its title, its format, and its contents—seems presumptuous. Its title suggests that the same methods that unraveled the mysteries of atomic structure can reveal the dynamics of societal behavior. Its format a collection of my essays over a ten-year period—implies an exaggerated sense of self-importance. And its contents—long, involved, and occasionally contradictory essays—answer fewer questions than they raise.

Yet reflection about these initial feelings yielded a conviction that apologies were unnecessary, that whatever the faults of the volume, its title, format, and contents can be justified on intellectual grounds. It may well be that in taking the study of foreign policy seriously and in attempting to delineate the boundaries of a field, these essays appear self-righteous or arrogant. However, this ought not to obscure the intellectual bases for bringing a decade of work together.

Notwithstanding the conclusion that there was intellectual value in bringing my essays together, doubts about the endeavor persisted. The one that proved most difficult to overcome concerned the format of the volume. Having always associated the publication of collected works with great literary or public figures, I found it hard to perceive my papers as worthy of juxtaposition in a single volume. If you are interested in evaluating the scientific study of foreign policy, I kept saying to myself, why not do so directly through a new effort? Instead of subjecting the reader to unintegrated, overlapping, contradictory, and hesitant essays written for different purposes at different times, why not write a fresh and coherent monograph that confidently depicts how the methods of science clarify the external behavior of societies? On rereading the essays, however, it became increasingly clear that their juxtaposition, and even their contradiction and overlap, provided important lessons. Both the recurrent preoccupations of the essays and the contradictions to which they give rise reflect the problems that confront anyone who seeks to comprehend the enduring dimensions of foreign policy behavior. A newly written volume might succinctly outline the conceptual equipment available for analyzing the convergence of national and international systems, but in so doing it might also suggest that this equipment was serviceable and did not present serious theoretical and research problems. In these essays, however, it is clear that such equipment is still a long way from being appropriate, much less free of problems. The restless preoccupation with boundaries—between societies and their environments, between one type of issue and another, between politics and nonpolitics—and the resulting shifts from one conceptual formulation to another—from penetrated systems to linkages to undertakings to issue-areas —are relevant indicators of the substantive difficulties with which a science of foreign policy must contend. Such restlessness may stem partly from certain personality factors—a need to be different and a reluctance to adhere to a particular approach—but I am persuaded that it also represents a stage in the emergence of a field and that therefore it is worthy of preservation.

For this reason I have kept the editing of the volume to a minimum, allowing the contradictions and overlaps to stand exposed. Aside from the updating of several citations, the deletion of a few examples that have lost their relevance, the relabeling of one basic term (see footnote 42 of Chapter 6), and the alteration of footnotes in order to achieve a uniform style, the essays are reproduced exactly as they originally appeared. I was often tempted to alter them and achieve a more unified volume. Yet it seemed preferable to resist the temptation and provide a more realistic indication of the analytic problems with which the study of foreign policy is beset.

Stated differently, the juxtaposition of the essays may also be viewed as an intellectual autobiography. Their order is not chronological, but neither does intellectual development always proceed in an orderly sequence. Partly because most of the essays were written in response to invitations in which specific foci were requested, and partly because of a belief that different theoretical and empirical concerns serve each other and should be pursued simultaneously, a chronological arrangement of the chapters would not give an accurate picture of how the problems of different intellectual stages come into being and get resolved. By arranging the chapters in terms of five recurrent themes, however, the outlines of an intellectual autobiography become clear. First (Part One) there is the preoccupation with one's self as the observer. Then (Part Two) there follows an intensive search for the methodological procedures which will render one's findings independent of oneself. Subsequently (Part Three) an effort is made to assess and perfect the basic conceptual equipment that one can employ to construct theory and generate findings. Finally there ensue the attempts to theorize and to undertake empirical research, tasks which in the study of foreign policy must be subdivided (Part Four) between the international and domestic contexts out of which the external behavior of societies emanates.

Like a personal autobiography, an intellectual autobiography is also filled with the fears and hopes that have moved its author and the idiosyncrasies that have characterized him. The pages that follow reveal an obsessive concern with the limits of case studies, an insistent aspiration to generate theory that is enduring, and a pervasive fear of becoming the prisoner of analytic habit—of becoming so wedded to a way of thinking that familiar relationships are distorted and new ones are overlooked.

Reflecting on the intellectual underpinning of these themes, it seems clear that they arise out of an overwhelming sense of the rapidity with which conventional wisdom about foreign affairs becomes obsolete. Today's acute crisis is tomorrow's vague memory, and the content of the memory usually offers little guidance in comprehending either tomorrow's crisis or the cumulative thrust of history. I became acutely aware of this rapid obsolescence early in my teaching career, which began on a part-time basis the day Harry S. Truman announced that the Russians had exploded an atomic device and moved into a full-time occupation as the Korean war became protracted. I can still recall how the initial feeling of satisfaction that I had served my students well by leading a "relevant" discussion of the whys and wherefores of Korea gave way to a sense that I had misled them terribly. Of what use would my analyses of the Korean war be to those students five or ten years after their graduation? The question could not be quelled. Increasingly I had to admit that they would be of no use, that I had provided no intellectual equipment with which they could probe the international scene long after Korea had moved off the public stage. A sense of obligation about equipping students with durable analytic tools thus began to emerge, and was continuously reinforced as the various episodes of the 1950s, seemingly so earth-shaking at their height, faded one after another into oblivion. By the time my dissertation was completed (see Chapter I) and I turned to communicating in the pages of journals, the preoccupation with intellectual obsolescence became a basis of my writing as well as my teaching. Indeed, in this era when the flow of ideas through journals is denounced as a mechanism for academic survival, it is useful to note that many of the ideas and concepts developed herein originated in the classroom in response to the need to clarify a complex process for inquisitive sophomores. In effect, teaching and research are part of the same process and stem from the same need—communication. For the most part "publish or perish" is an irrelevant cliché. "Communicate or perish" is a far more accurate characterization of why research gets undertaken and essays get written.

Once the initial doubts about the format and contents of the volume were resolved, those pertaining to its title dissipated. A rereading of the juxtaposed essays made it clear that they were all part of an attempt to study foreign policy phenomena scientifically. Several of the essays make this orientation explicit, but its implicit presence in the remainder is unmistakable. Viewed autobiographically, it is clear in retrospect that, as my concern about analytic obsolescence intensified, the assumptions and methods of science became increasingly attractive as a means to overcome it. Movement in this direction was spurred significantly by two fortuitous events, the publication of David Easton's *The Political System** and my wife's graduate education. The former, which was published shortly after I began teaching, crystallized my uneasiness about the absence of durable analytic equipment in the ideas I presented to students. Easton's discussion of "hyperfactualism" and his plea for theory gave meaning and legitimacy to my discontent and I still derive encouragement from returning to that seminal volume on occasion.

If Easton started me down the scientific road, my wife guided the way and gave coherence and substance to the task it entailed. From the very start of her training in psychology, a discipline that had long since evolved a commitment to experimental methods and thus to the philosophy of science, she would come home with ideas about the study of human behavior that were at once shocking and exciting. The notion of operational variables was new and so were the premises of statistics and the idea that one sought to comprehend reality intersubjectively with other observers rather than to recreate its objective nature. Such conceptions, now so much a part of the study of politics, had not even been hinted at in my own graduate education and, supported by the enthusiasm and camaraderie of a young marriage, they thus became a subject of continuous discussion and occasional contention. "Human beings are different," I would say. "They are irrational and each one is unlike every other: how can you predict what a person will do?" "You don't attempt to predict the specific behavior of

---

* New York: Alfred A. Knopf, 1953.

a single individual," my wife would respond, "any more than the physicist tries to predict the behavior of a single atom. You deal with people in general, or with certain types of people in general. The only goal that is attainable is to explain how most individuals who have given characteristics will behave under specific conditions."

So, haltingly and painfully, yet with a sense of liberation and accomplishment, the turn to science gained momentum, achieving a firm intellectual footing in 1963 and 1964 when I dared to set forth in writing (Chapter 6) the bases of a pre-theory of foreign policy that I had long been working out in the classroom. Once the pre-theory conception made its way into mimeograph, my commitment to the scientific study of foreign policy was no longer a source of qualms and its presence in all the subsequent chapters is quite explicit. Indeed, three of the essays (Chapters 14, 16, and 17) contain hypotheses that were designed to apply and extend the pre-theory and I am presently writing a monograph that tries to move it closer to the realm of theory by explicating the components of the clusters of variables it comprises.

Some readers may nevertheless be offended by the book's title, feeling that while it may be possible to study individuals scientifically, large societal aggregates are too complex for investigation through the tools of science. Hopefully such readers will suspend judgment until they have read the essays (and particularly Chapters 2 and 4). While they may continue to reject it as a basis for their own analyses of foreign policy phenomena, hopefully they will also conclude that the title of the volume is an accurate description of its contents. In any event, it is worth reiterating here what is elaborated at a number of points in the volume, that no claim is being made that the scientific approach is the only way to study foreign policy phenomena or that it is the best method for analyzing the external behavior of nations. I would contend only that it is a legitimate method for certain purposes and that, for those whose intellectual development has followed a course similar to mine, its employment is bound to prove compelling and satisfying.

All of this is not to say that the publication of this book means that I see myself as having resolved, either for myself or for others, the intellectual problems inherent in the analysis of foreign policy. It may well be that as I continue to work much of what follows will have to be modified or rejected.

It is not possible to enumerate all the persons and books that contributed to my development as a student of politics. Besides those already cited, however, two other figures loom large in my intellectual autobiography. One is Neil A. McDonald, whose wisdom and guidance as a colleague and friend for twenty years have been an unending source of enrichment and strength. Throughout the 1950s he and I were the entire Political Science Department of Douglass College, and in the daily contact and joint seminars through which we sustained the life of the Department I learned more about the dynamics, nuances, and limits of politics, as well as about the nature of integrity, humanity, generosity, and humility, than I will ever be capable of translating into words. My most specific debt to him is for the conception of politics as a process of calculated control over the more remote environment (see Chapter 10), a conception which he developed * and which still serves as my point of departure whenever I think about public and international affairs. If this were all that I learned from him, it would be a very great debt indeed. But my indebtedness to him goes so much further that nothing I write here can fully express my gratitude.

As indicated in Chapter 12, Richard C. Snyder was also a major source of intellectual nourishment. His contribution to my training at Princeton, especially his uninhibited readiness to challenge long-standing habits of thought and his contagious enthusiasm for the search for new and meaningful ways of organizing foreign policy phenomena continues to influence my thinking. That I am no longer an uncritical adherent of the decision-making framework to which he exposed me during 1950–52 is due in large measure to the fact that he provided me with the conceptual equipment and intellectual motivation to move on to my own formulations.

Of course, the development of one's mind requires not only intellectual nourishment, but also the help of persons and institutions who facilitate the formulation of theory and the accumulation, analysis, and presentation of data. My debts in this regard are numerous. Two institutions, the Center of International Studies of Princeton University and the Research Council of Rutgers University, have provided the material support which enabled me to gather the data presented in Chapter 7. But it is hard to thank institutions as distinguished from the individuals who serve as their leaders. Special mention must be made of Klaus Knorr, who as chief administrator of the Center of International Studies provided encouragement and counsel throughout the period when these essays were written. Professor Knorr was not always comfortable with my formulations, but he never wavered in either his support or his readiness to criticize.

In addition to thanking several generations of students at Douglass College for the never-ending feedback that they provided in the classroom, a number of them gave unstintingly of their time, in summers and in off hours during the school year, to the task of processing the materials pre-

* Neil A. McDonald, *Politics: A Study of Control Behavior* (New Brunswick, N.J.: Rutgers University Press, 1965).

sented in the two empirical chapters. In particular, I am happy to register my appreciation for the assistance of Elizabeth M. James, Bette Misdom, Linda Alfonso, Paulette Kellner, Marilyn Gechtman, Marilyn Ayres, Linda Robinson, Dorothy Stefanik, and Marilyn Falik. Mrs. Esther Rosenblum, a former student, and Maureen Berman, a present one, have served as able research assistants for the past few years and their help in preparing this volume for publication has been especially valuable. For the support of my secretary, Mrs. Roberta Weber, who not only typed early and final drafts of virtually all the chapters but who has been helpful in so many other ways over the years, I owe more than can ever be adequately repaid.

Nor does intellectual development occur without emotional support. The essays are impersonal and intellectual, but they could never have been written without the aid, criticism, encouragement, and love of my wife, Norah. Her intellectual contribution to my development as a scientist has already been noted, but this is perhaps insignificant in comparison to her role as a companion and critic. It is not easy to be both loving wife and harsh critic, especially when it requires responding to the writing of a person who prizes his phrases and who sometimes clings to ideas that have not been fully worked out. Yet Norah has never backed away from the role of critic in order to preserve marital harmony, and in her persistence I have seen the meaning of true devotion. Every word in this book has been sub-jected to her close scrutiny and reflection and virtually every paragraph is more coherent and precise because of her efforts. Nor is this all: when doubts were paralyzing and the feeling that meaning would never come prevailed, Norah would give up endless hours listening and encouraging. She has never let me down.

Of course, none of the foregoing is responsible for the ideas presented herein. Many have helped, but for the final result I alone am responsible.

JAMES N. ROSENAU

New Brunswick, New Jersey
April 16, 1970

Table of Contents

Part One: The Scientist

For all its emphasis on objectivity and on rendering findings independent of the individual observer, science is an intensely personal enterprise. Both at the theoretical and empirical levels the rules of science compel those who practice it to be constantly aware of themselves in relation to their subject matter. Since they know that their theorizing must ultimately be subjected to the test of empirical verification, they must continuously face the challenge of their basic talents and creativity. Do they comprehend the subject well enough to be vindicated when the data are gathered? Similarly, they can never avoid the challenge to their ingenuity and integrity at the empirical level. Have they gathered the appropriate materials? Have they unknowingly succumbed to the temptation to process them in such a way as to insure the confirmation of their theories? Precisely because science is based on explicit stanards of evidence rather than on aesthetic tastes, intuitive feelings, or moral criteria, these questions press endlessly upon scientists and heighten their sensitivity to their own presence in the quest for understanding.

Nor is this personal dimension of the scientific enterprise confined to those sciences that have yet to build up a wide range of verified findings. Physical and biological scientists intimately experience the objectivity that they practice. The fact that they have accumulated an impressive body of "established" knowledge about the physical and biological realms does not make them more immune to the intimate challenge of theory and research than the social scientist whose subject is still elusive and far from established. One need only read Watson's recent account of how he discovered the structure of DNA to appreciate the intensity with which the challenge of theory can be experienced by physical scientists.*

The three chapters that follow elaborate on the ways in which the very objectivity of science provides a never ending subjective experience. The first was written at the outset of a career, the second a decade later, and the third still another decade later, but together they indicate the large extent to which the subsequent chapters of this volume constitute an intellectual autobiography as well as a scientific inquiry.

---

* James Watson, *The Double Helix* (New York: Atheneum, 1968).

1 The Birth of a Political Scientist *

Here, on a quiet lakefront in Maine, recurring thoughts about a dissertation just completed intrude rudely upon a vacation that was expected to be wonderfully free of that which hung so heavily for five long years. But at least this is an ideal spot for reflection: across the water, where the nearby woods blend into the distant mountains, one can see both the trees and the forest, an unaccustomed sight to the tired possessor of a new Ph.D.

I

In retrospect, it is astonishing how much psychic energy can be invested in a doctoral candidacy. One hears a great deal about the long hours, the stiff exams, and the intense competition which mark the training of medical and law students. But who has ever heard of a fledgling doctor or lawyer who postponed taking his exams or dawdled over completing his requirements? Yet such behavior seems to be commonplace among aspiring academicians. The number of graduate students who sail easily and quickly through their graduate career is probably very small compared to those who either fail to complete their studies or who do so after considerable procrastination, hesitation, and self-laceration. Moreover, the fears and frustrations of graduate students are ordinarily impervious to the friendly assurances of their teachers and advisers. I doubt whether the

* Written in the summer of 1957, "The Birth of a Political Scientist" is reprinted from PROD (now *The American Behavioral Scientist*), Vol. III, No. 5 (January 1960), pp. 19–21, by permission of the publisher, Sage Publications, Inc.

elders of any profession provide new recruits with as much encouragement and sympathy as do instructors of graduate courses. Indeed, one occasionally hears of an adviser who practically guarantees passage of prelims in order to get a gifted and troubled student over the hurdle. Some graduate programs have even adopted institutional devices intended to reduce the tensions that hinder effective study. More than a few now require new students to attend a series of lectures that acquaint them with the psychological hazards as well as the formal requirements which lie ahead.

But, alas, the difficulties lie in the students and not in a heartless system that makes rigorous and excessive demands. Considerate and kindly paternalism is apparently no match for the self-doubt (and perhaps self-pity) that the graduate student thrusts in his own way. Why is this? And why is it so unique to an academic career? Some psychoanalysts contend that acquiring a Ph.D. stands for the attainment of adulthood, a condition of life that the troubled graduate student subconsciously wishes to avoid for a variety of reasons. To be an adult is to be on a par with his parents, to possess status, to have a title, to incur obligations—circumstances that are all very awesome and threatening to the person whose childhood fostered fears of competition and responsibility. And these are the very circumstances that attend the earning of a doctorate. The new Ph.D. can no longer fall back on the security of being a student, of having others determine how he should spend his time and what he should learn. Henceforth others will view him as a grownup, as learned and responsible, and sometimes they may even call him "doctor." Even worse, his professors will no longer be his seniors, becoming instead his colleagues (brothers rather than fathers), and it could be that someday he will find himself surpassing them. It is successful competition against one's father: an exciting thought, and a dreadful thought ("Better not take prelims this time—I might pass them").

It might be argued that this interpretation does not explain why the graduate student seems so much more susceptible to psychological difficulties than his medical and legal counterparts. Surely the M.D. and the LL.B. also symbolize adulthood and entrance upon a professional life. Why, then, do not unresolved childhood fears haunt the schools of medicine and law? I imagine the psychoanalyst would reply that the latter provide much more definite and precise channels to a career, that the medical or law student has already made the transition to adulthood and thus defines himself as acquiring technical training pursuant to the fulfillment of goals already decided upon. The graduate student, on the other hand, has not had to decide what he will be doing ten or fifteen years later. Thus he may still possess those childhood fears that certainty about the future could resolve. And, if he wants, he can further postpone adulthood by reminding himself that, despite his age, he is still attending school, just as he always has since the age of five.

There is still another, equally crucial, factor that renders preparation for an academic career psychologically more hazardous than the training for any. other profession: namely, the dissertation. To take courses is to *consume* knowledge, which is then inventoried through examinations. Although it varies in pace and skill from student to student, this consumption process is essentially a technical matter, involving the mastery of new data and patterns of thought. To write a thesis, on the other hand, is to *produce* knowledge. Even if it is based on secondary sources or is merely a translation or interpretation of someone else's work, a dissertation is a creation that derives its substance from within the student. Unlike his contemporaries in medical or law school, then, the graduate student is thrust back upon his own resources. He is a producer as well as a consumer. He is required to contribute, to originate, to create. Little wonder that he becomes so intimately and emotionally involved in his dissertation, viewing it with the same ambivalent mixture of tenderness and awe that mark parental attitudes toward children. And little wonder that no amount of advice or encouragement can get him to finish and submit his thesis if he is not satisfied with every dimension of the product he has fashioned. For, in a fundamental sense, the graduate student posits himself as the major judge of his thesis. He is his own worst critic, demanding of himself a perfection that neither his adviser nor his dissertation committee would dare ask of even a senior colleague in the field.

The meaning of a dissertation for its creator is also wide open to psychoanalytic interpretation. Some might even say that it represents the ninth month in the birth of an adult. (Perhaps more than random imagery was operative when a colleague, upon hearing that I had been granted a degree, congratulated me for "having emerged from the long, dark tunnel.") Whatever its deeper psychological meanings, however, surely the dissertation constitutes a unique experience. Aside from the arts, what other profession requires of its new recruits a creative innovation as the mark of fitness to enter the field? Businessmen are expected to be innovative and productive in their forties and fifties, as are doctors, lawyers, engineers, civil servants, and so on. But the scholar is required, in his early twenties, to make an original contribution to his profession. Whatever the wisdom of such an arrangement (and I do not question it), surely the graduate student is entitled to founder a bit, to doubt himself, to advance at an uneven pace. I rather suspect that the medical or law schools would have a considerably higher proportion of troubled students if an original contribution to medical or legal studies were a prerequisite of graduation.

There are, of course, concrete intellectual consequences of the emotional energy that is invested in a dissertation. One of the most important results is the persistency of the question, "How do I know this?" At least in my case all the fears of completing a successful thesis forced me to challenge and rechallenge the validity of each sentence I wrote. I became acutely sensitive to the nature of proof, to tests of reliability, to the distinctions between fact and inference, and to the impossibility of obtaining neat and final conclusions about complex phenomena. It is one thing to comprehend in a general fashion the necessity of employing sound procedures. All graduate students develop a certain sophistication along these lines, and derive not a little excitement from a newly found capacity to demonstrate the methodological flaws of major works in their field. But it is quite another thing to experience at first hand the dilemma of accumulating reliable knowledge—that is, knowledge which, within its own limits, facilitates accurate prediction. A dissertation not only provides such an experience, but, given its deeper meaning for the graduate student, it also compels a kind of soul-searching about reliability that, I am certain, leaves a permanent mark upon the course of subsequent research.

This is not to ignore the considerable falderal that accompanies each day's bout with the thesis. It is impossible to be unaffected by the warnings and rumors, real or imagined, that each generation of graduate students passes on to its successors and upon which so many coffee breaks thrive. Thus one is ever alert to the idiosyncrasies, real or imagined, of his adviser, just as the predilections of key members of the dissertation committee are an ever-present consideration. Thus one is ever aware of the "Department" and its unwritten regulations about the length, format, and subject matter of an acceptable thesis. And thus one pays respect to a variety of traditions which are said to lessen the risks of nonacceptance—an appropriate number of footnotes, perhaps a table or two of imposing statistics, not to mention an elaborate bibliography that lists the standard works in the field regardless of their utility.

But even as one makes all the necessary obeisances to the folklore of dissertation writing, the large question of "how do I know this" persists. And it does so not only because of a gnawing fear that somehow a member of the orals board might ask precisely such a question; it also endures because the graduate student has to live with himself. His thesis is too important to him to permit of a casual approach to the question of reliability. It is a matter of earning, rather than falsifying, his way into adulthood. Even if others are impressed by imaginative insights, varied footnotes, elaborate graphs, and tight organization, he knows that this is only the appearance of reliability, not the substance of it. And so he embarks on a search for certainty, only to find that it lies in such phrases as "apparently," "presumably," and "it would seem as if." It turns out, however, that these phrases are even more meaningful possessions than the three new letters that will soon follow his name. For these phrases reflect a self-discipline, a modesty, and an integrity that are not easily achieved—traits that, in effect, separate the man from the boy and thereby signify his coming of age.

2 Games International Relations Scholars Play *

Sometimes it seems as if international relations scholars have nothing better to do with their time than to argue about the proper way to study their subject. With almost clocklike regularity, the journals of the field publish claims and counterclaims as to the virtue of one approach over another. Prodded by a need for intellectual identity and by editors who seek to enliven their journals with controversy, "schools" are pitted against each other, "cases" for particular methods are made, old "frameworks" are contrasted, and new ones are offered. As a result commitments deepen, differences widen, assertions harshen, and the argument becomes so heated that a "crisis" is said to exist.[1] At this point, fatigued by their efforts at combat—though no less entrenched in their positions—scholars break off the dispute for a time and return to the tasks of research. The dynamics of international phenomena, rather than the operations of scholars, once again become the focus of inquiry.

Despite their intensity and their residues of bitterness, these periodic excursions into self-examination should not be denigrated. As noted below, they occur for good reasons. If the argument sometimes gets out of hand, this may be a small price to pay for the greater self-consciousness that subsequently infuses research. Those entering the field may question the

* Copyright by the Board of Editors of the JOURNAL OF INTERNATIONAL AFFAIRS, reprinted from Volume XXI, Number 2, Pages 293–303, 1967. Permission to reprint is gratefully acknowledged to the Editors of the JOURNAL.

[1] For a recent example, see John Hanessian, Jr., "The Study and Teaching of International Relations: Some Comments on the Current Crisis," *SAIS Review*, X (Summer 1966), pp. 27–39.

tolerance and maturity of their elders, but let them not forget that no less than the "truth" about international relations is at stake. If the fledgling in the field can avoid the controversy and find his own intellectual identity, so much the better; but if he cannot, let him not be dismayed. No field of study can progress unless there is agreement over the basic rules that researchers must follow, and this agreement cannot evolve unless and until alternative approaches are tested and contrasted.

I. THE UNIVERSE OF INTERNATIONAL PHENOMENA

There is no question, however, that progress would occur more rapidly if a sense of perspective could be achieved with respect to the argument. The best antidote for crisis is perspective, and in this case the best means to achieve perspective is to recognize that, though scholars differ in their purposes and approaches, they are all attempting to develop or maintain a posture with respect to the phenomena of international relations. The clearer one's own posture becomes, of course, the more difficult it is to recognize that it is only a posture and that it is not inherently superior to the postures adopted by others. Hence, maintaining a sense of perspective requires the self-conscious adoption of techniques to prevent mistaking postures toward international phenomena for the phenomena themselves. I have found two techniques to be especially useful in this regard. One involves a simple mental diagram and the other an analogy with sports. If these techniques seem to devalue scholarly effort, then they are serving their purpose well. For the scholar who feels demeaned by being placed in a diagram and equated to a sports enthusiast needs to be reminded that he has lost his sense of perspective and is equating his conception of reality with reality itself.

The diagrammatic technique is simple indeed. One draws a circle to represent the universe of international phenomena. If one's purpose is to comprehend this universe, one then draws an x outside the circle to represent one's location with respect to it. If one's purpose is to alter and reform this universe, the x is located within the circle, indicating that one is an actor in the processes whereby international politics unfold. If one's purpose is to comprehend the universe in order to reform it, the location of the x moves from outside to inside the circle whenever the shift from observer to actor occurs. One cannot be both observer and actor simultaneously. If one tries to occupy both roles at once by placing the x on the circle itself, then one's location is peripheral to the central action of world politics and at the same time lacks sufficient distance from the action to comprehend it. Here we are concerned with international relations scholars *qua* scholars. The ensuing discussion thus focuses on their location outside the universe of international phenomena.

A major virtue of this simple diagram is that it compels thought about one's relation to one's subject matter. For the contents of the circle must be filled in by the observer from wherever he has located himself outside it. The universe of international phenomena does not acquire structure on its own; it must be structured. No matter how far back he stands, the observer cannot perceive this universe in its entirety. He has neither the time, the resources, nor the capacity to assess and describe every phenomenon. An assessment of a single moment in history would require years to complete if none of its aspects were omitted. A complete geographic description of a country would require a life-size map and create a storage problem. Unable to perceive and depict the universe of international phenomena in its entirety, the observer is forced to select some of its dimensions as important and in need of close examination, while dismissing others as trivial and unworthy of further analysis. With regard to the moment in history, for example, the observer is likely to find that a full account of what the chief of state ate for lunch and what happened during his cabinet's deliberations over lunch is neither possible nor desirable, with the result that he distorts reality by concentrating on the deliberative aspects of the phenomena and ignoring their digestive aspects. Likewise, faced with the dilemma of not being able to account for everything, the geographer is likely to select mountains and rivers as important and treat hills and brooks as unimportant, thus yielding a map that is manageable and storable even as it is also a distortion of reality.

It follows, therefore, that whatever the "true" structure of the universe of international phenomena may be, the structure that is described and assessed is the one the observer imposes upon it. Stated in terms of our diagram, the circle can be filled with polka dots, horizontal dashes, shaded squares, vertical lines, or smaller circles. Or all these elements, along with the many others one might imagine, can be introduced into different areas of the circle. Stated substantively, the universe of international phenomena can be seen to consist of large aggregates called nations, of even larger units called international organizations, of roles occupied by different people in different generations, or of particular individuals active in a particular era. Or all these actors, along with the many others one might conceptualize, can be included in the international universe. Then, needing more detail to work with, the international relations scholar is likely to enrich his universe of phenomena by identifying certain factors as relevant to the motives of actors, by selecting some of their actions as consequential, by differentiating among the objects of their actions—continuing in this manner to distort reality until his subject matter has a manageable and comprehensible structure.

In other words, use of the diagrammatic technique serves as a reminder that though there may be an objective truth about world politics, the observer can never know it. He must select in order to know reality, and in so doing he must distort it. He must use some method to comprehend the truth of world politics, thus inevitably rendering it subjective. The "established facts" of world politics are, in effect, no more than widespread agreement—what I shall call an "intersubjective consensus"—among actors and experts as to the existence and relevance of particular phenomena. Thus the truths of world politics are only as true as the intersubjective consensus that supports them. The wider the consensus, the more "real" the reality.

The second technique for maintaining a sense of perspective with respect to the intersubjective nature of international reality, that of analogizing to sports, is perhaps even more effective.[2] It is based on a view that posits the gathering of data and the structuring of concepts as a game one plays in order to move ever nearer to the truth. The game has its rules. They are sometimes codified and sometimes implicit but always operative. Usually the rules are inhibiting, and only rarely do they allow unrestrained action. The play is often dull as the opponent, elusive and stubborn, brings action to a standstill. Yet tense and exciting moments, full of the drama of forward movement, do occur as the opponent gives way in the face of a breakthrough. And who is the opponent? He is Man, both individually and collectively, acting in unexpected and complex ways that constantly challenge the researcher's ingenuity, resist his classifications, elude his disciplined procedures, and refuse to be arrayed in simple and clear-cut patterns.

We can, it must quickly be added, play a variety of games with international phenomena. Since we can never grasp these phenomena in their entirety and must select among them, our contests can take all kinds of forms. We can play the scientific game or the historical game, the game of the journalist or the game of the preacher. We can abide by strict rules of evidence, heed our consciences, or rely on informed impressions. We can derive our findings from quantitative data, from the lessons of a single case, or from the values we espouse.

Furthermore, whatever the game, we can play it in a number of different ball parks. In the world-politics league, our contests with human behavior are scheduled in a few supranational parks, many national sites, some conference rooms, and occasional foreign offices. Our opponent, in other words,

2 I first outlined this sports analogy in "Transforming the International System: Small Increments Along a Vast Periphery," *World Politics, XVIII* (April 1966), pp. 525–28, and I am grateful to the editors for permission to reprint here several passages from that article.

is Man in a variety of guises—as international organization, national society, diplomatic situation, bureaucracy, or individual decision-maker.

Finally, whatever game we play and wherever we play it, we can adopt a seemingly infinite range of styles and strategies. We can subject the opponent to the rigors of realism, to the tenets of idealism, to the precepts of decision-making analysis, to the assumptions of general-systems theory, and so on through all the concepts, approaches, and schools that researchers have used to guide their play.

Let us carry the analogy one step further and emphasize that although it may be possible to rank the ball parks according to their elegance, and the strategies of play according to their effectiveness, we cannot do the same with the games themselves. Baseball is not better than football or worse than golf. They are different games that appeal to different people, require different skills, and serve different interests. If a person is small and prefers to compete against himself, then he plays golf, whereas football appeals to those who are large and like to engage in contact sports. So it is with the various games through which truth is acquired. If a person is temperamentally uneasy with ambiguity and reluctant to generalize without repeated observations, then he plays the scientific game, whereas the historical game appeals to those whose temperaments are less discomforted by ambiguity and more content with single observations. Each game can be played well or poorly, and each can be won or lost or stalemated; but none can be judged as inherently better or worse than any other. Each is played for different reasons and to attain different kinds of truth. The adequacy of the truth in each game is measured against the rules of that game, not against the truths achieved in other games. The assessments of world politics made by the journalist who depends on informed judgment are neither more nor less accurate than those asserted by the preacher who relies on spiritual perceptions or those developed by the scholar who employs systematic analysis. These are simply three different sets of truth, derived from the play of three very different games. Likewise, the findings of the historian who uses the case method to search for meaning in a single instance of world politics are neither better nor worse than those of the political scientist who applies quantitative techniques in order to discern the patterns that emerge from a number of situations. Again these are different kinds of truth, answering different kinds of questions that stem from different kinds of scholarly interests.

While it is thus inappropriate to pass judgment on the value of the game a scholar plays in order to acquire and interpret data, the question of how he scores against his opponent must always be a matter of concern. Distinguished performance in the various games of scholarship is marked by a processing of data that, within the rules of the researcher's own game, is so imaginative or persuasive as to fashion a wide intersubjective consensus among those who play the same game. A record-setting performance is achieved when a researcher's findings are so striking and so clearly a consequence of opportunities provided by the rules of his game that the scope of the resulting consensus is widened to include not only all the devotees of his game, but also a number of people who ordinarily prefer other sports. Contrariwise, low or losing scores will be recorded by researchers who either process their data in a pedestrian fashion or fail to live up to the rules of their game. Such performances are not likely to attract large crowds, and those few who do attend are likely to drift away before the play is over.

II.   GAMES SCHOLARS PLAY

If students of world politics could come to accept the idea that each is playing a game that can be assessed only in terms of its own rules, progress in the field would surely occur more rapidly. For it is precisely here that the lack of perspective is most conspicuous and the argument is least constructive. Reluctant to acknowledge the intersubjective nature of truth, persuaded that objective reality can be discerned, many analysts are inclined to rank the various ways of structuring the universe of international phenomena and then to view the game they play as the best. Hence, instead of assessing a colleague's performance in terms of the game he is playing, international relations scholars will often criticize him for not playing another game and dismiss his findings on the grounds that he would have come to different conclusions if he had played the game he ought to have played. Energy that could go into the building of intersubjective consensuses about the nature of international phenomena is thus diverted to the unattainable goal of achieving an intersubjective consensus as to the most worthwhile method of studying international phenomena.

So as to minimize the energy expended in this fruitless way, it is perhaps useful to restate the basic aims and rules of the games that international relations scholars play. Although a host of variations is possible, the games that are played can be reduced to two major types, the classical and the scientific.[3] The classicist and the scientist share a location external to

---

[3] These designations are meant to be descriptive and should not be construed as evaluative. The label "classical" is not intended to imply that the players of this game are old-fashioned in their orientations, but is used to denote all those methods of inquiry, from the historical to the philosophical, that are employed by recognized scholars other than scientists. Labels other than classical—such as traditional, historical, and intuitional—are sometimes used to refer to the nonscientific methods, but this designation seems preferable because it is the most neutral. In addition to the classical and the scientific, still other types of games are played by journalists,

the universe of international phenomena and an aspiration to comprehend it on the basis of observation, but otherwise their aims are sharply divergent. The former seeks meaning through tracing the behavior of identifiable actors in particular situations at specific moments in time, whereas the latter attempts to structure the universe of international phenomena in terms of recurring patterns that span generations and situations. For the player of the classical game, victory is achieved whenever he is satisfied that some aspect or problem of world politics is adequately revealed by the richness of his data and the clarity of his description and explanation. The goal of the scientist, on the other hand, is to move up the ladder of generalization and construct theories that encompass and explain more and more of the phenomena that make up the universe of world politics. This specificity-generality distinction regarding aims gives rise to another difference between the goals of the two types of games. The specificity orientation of the classicist leads him to aspire to statements of what is or was the case with respect to the aspect of world politics on which he focuses. The scientist's concern with recurring patterns, however, leads him to aspire to probability statements about the aspect that interests him. For the scientist, the truth of world politics is always a matter of how many times out of, say, one hundred a pattern of behavior is likely to occur. The greater the probability of its occurrence, the more is it considered to reveal about the structure of the universe of international phenomena. Probability statements are not among the goals of the classicist. Concerned as he is with observations about particular sequences of events that are fixed in time and that either did or did not occur, the challenge of his game is that of ascertaining how and why the events happened as they did rather than of deriving and testing probabilistic predictions.

It follows that the rules of the classical game are far less stringent than those of the scientific game. In classical analysis the researcher may roam freely over the universe of international phenomena in order to select those that best account for the situations that interest him. He scores well if his account is coherent and full of insight; but however high his score, the account is always his; its findings never become independent of the coherence and insight with which he organizes and analyzes his materials. To be sure, the rules oblige him to indicate where he obtained each component of his account and prohibit his misrepresenting the nature of his data. Beyond this, however, he is free to draw on archival materials for one part of the account, to cite a historical example in another, to quote

politicians, citizens, preachers, and the many other actors who have occasion to discern and assess the international scene. Here, of course, we are concerned only with scholarly games, which are assumed to be distinguished from all other types by their goal of understanding *why* the course of events unfolds as it does.

respected authorities in still another, and to use common knowledge, anecdotal wisdom, rigorous logic, and sustained reflection to link the various parts to each other. If the resulting composite impresses players of the classical game as yielding new comprehension about some aspect of world politics, then it will form the basis of an intersubjective consensus and assume a conspicuous place in the literature of the field.

The rules of the scientific game, on the other hand, are not nearly so flexible. The scientist must also piece together a coherent and insightful account out of his data, but, unlike a player in any other game, he must do so in a way that renders his findings independent of himself. The distinguishing feature of the scientist's "truths" is that they must be susceptible to confirmation by independent observers. Thus the rules of his game require him to make explicit the assumptions, concepts, and procedures that he used when he made his selections among all the phenomena in the international universe. More accurately, these assumptions, concepts, and procedures must be sufficiently explicit to permit any researcher to arrive at the same conclusions by gathering the same data and processing them in the same way. The scientist is free to employ the views of respected authorities in developing his probabilistic statements, and there is nothing to prevent his constructing statements out of historical example, anecdotal wisdom, or indeed, sheer hunch. Once he proceeds to test the statements, however, the rules of the game become stringent because, if they are not followed, the findings can never be dissociated from the finder.

The rules governing the processing and interpretation of data are equally stringent. The researcher must indicate each operation performed in gathering the data, specify the boundaries of the categories used to classify the data, and note each step, both conceptual and statistical, taken in discerning patterns in the data. Further, he must explicate the criteria used to interpret quantitative differences in the distributions of the data and must indicate clearly how the relationships that emerge confirm or negate his probability statements. Adherence to both sets of rules is necessary to achieve distinction in the game of science. If the player abides by the "process" rules but is lax in using the interpretation rules, then the same data will mean different things to different observers and intersubjective consensus will not develop. Similarly, fidelity to the "interpretation" rules will not offset laxity in those pertaining to process for the obvious reason that different observers will produce different data, which are bound to mean different things even if common criteria of interpretation are employed.

Let us indicate the stringency of the scientific game in another way. If the scientist does not make explicit his bases for selecting among the universe of international phenomena, there is no way of knowing whether the behavior predicted by his probability statements was found to occur many times out of one hundred because of his biases or because of factors at work in the international universe. Indeed, in order to minimize the possibility of attaching meaning to extraneous processes, the rules of the scientific game require its players to use a cutoff point (or, in statistical terms, a test of significance) that distinguishes between the relative frequency of occurrence that is best attributed to random factors and the frequency that may reasonably be presumed to reflect recurring patterns of international behavior. The scientific game is thus the only one with rules that allow for the defeat of its players. The predicted behavior can prove to be improbable. If the tests of the probability statements do not produce frequencies in excess of the previously established cutoff point, the scientist is a loser even before he submits his findings as a basis for intersubjective consensus. If he somehow fails to recognize he has lost and submits his findings for consideration, the rules of the game are such that others can point out that his play has been less successful than he realizes. For the scientific game is also the only one that permits checks to be made on the findings of its players. One cannot check up on the accuracy of the classicist's conclusions. What he finds may be impressive or it may be unimpressive, but in either case it must be accepted or rejected in terms of one's respect for him and the strength of his argument. There are no independent procedures that can satisfactorily answer the questions of whether his findings are due to chance or to substantive factors, or whether his interpretations stemmed from bias or from objectivity. In the case of the scientist, on the other hand, even if he was dead drunk when he derived his findings and developed his interpretations, their validity can be assessed. He has made his bases of selection among international phenomena explicit, and his results can thus be independently checked.

That these differences in the rules of the games international relations scholars play provide a perspective from which to avoid unnecessary argument can be readily demonstrated. Consider the charge against the scientists often made by players of other games that, despite its mathematical and quantitative apparatus, scientific inquiry has thus far generated only marginal data and has yet to yield findings that are relevant to the great problems of our time.[4] Such a criticism provokes needless controversy because it has little relevance to the tasks the scientist has set for himself. From his point of view the great problems are composites of innumerable interrelated lesser problems and processes that must be analyzed and comprehended separately before the pieces of the larger picture can be put together. For the scientist, therefore, his findings are not irrelevant. His game requires

---

[4] For a recent example of this criticism, see Charles Burton Marshall, "Waiting for the Curtain," *SAIS Review*, X (Summer 1966), pp. 21–26.

him to start at the bottom of the ladder of generalization, and to criticize him for not beginning at or near the top rung is to ask him to play a different game. Much the same can be said about the charge that scientists are preoccupied with the quantification and measurement of phenomena at the expense of "the more fruitful parts of the subject" that are to be found "in the qualitative judgments they are able to bring to bear on history and contemporary affairs." [5] This criticism generates unnecessary debate because, in effect, it asks the scientist to forego his commitment to probabilistic statements based on recurring patterns discerned and assessed through means independent of the observer and to accept instead conclusions substantiated by the observer's thoughts and opinions on how and why international phenomena are structured as they are. As previously indicated, scientists have no aversion to qualitative judgments. Indeed, they cannot play their game without heavy reliance on them. More often than not such judgments form the basis of the probabilistic statements that they subject to quantitative measurement. To demand that the scientist not proceed from judgment to measurement is thus like demanding that the golfer go on the course with his driver but without his putter.

Similarly, a great deal of the criticism of those who play the classical game appears irrelevant from the perspective of the sports analogy. Consider the charge that the classicists compile "a great mass of detail to which absurdly broad and often falsifiable generalizations are applied." [6] Classicists choose to structure aspects of the international universe in great detail because their game calls for specificity. For them comprehension can be achieved only when the minute dimensions of a problem have been exposed, and to criticize them for not being more selective is thus to ask them to break the rules of their game and attach importance to fewer aspects of the international universe than those rules allow. Similarly, to criticize their willingness to draw broad generalizations from a welter of data is to request that they forego their commitment to informed reflection. Moreover, the falsifiability of the classicist's generalizations can be measured only by the degree to which an intersubjective consensus evolves among other players of the classical game. To conclude that they are false because they do not meet the scientist's test of significance is like condemning the high jumper for not having pole vaulted. The classical game requires that evidence be used to support conclusions; but the criteria of evidence are very different from those used in the scientific game, and one set of criteria is not inherently better than the other. To repeat, it all depends on which game one is playing.

[5] Hedley Bull, "International Theory: The Case for a Classical Approach," *World Politics*, XVIII (April 1966), p. 374.

[6] Morton A. Kaplan, "The New Great Debate: Traditionalism vs. Science in International Relations," *World Politics*, XIX (Oct. 1966), p. 15.

The question arises of how to proceed if the scientist and the classicist develop contrary findings about the same aspect of the international universe. Is not one finding true and the other false? And therefore is not one game superior to the other as a means of comprehending international phenomena? The answer to these questions must be in the negative. To assume that only one of the findings is correct is to posit an objective reality that is more discoverable by one method than another. Undoubtedly there is such a reality, but, as I have said, it can never be known. Thus there is no way of determining which finding more closely approximates the way events actually unfold in the international system. Does this mean that the observer must view the contradictory findings as equally valid? Not at all. He applauds the results of the game he prefers and becomes part of only one of the two intersubjective consensuses that form around the contradictory findings. If the finding yielded by the game he prefers somehow seems less persuasive than the one developed in the other contest, he may alter his preferences as to which game is the most satisfying. In this way, one intersubjective consensus may come to be more extensive than another; but such changes are a measure of shifts in tastes and not of discoveries in the objective world. The fact that one sport plays to large crowds at every performance while another barely fills the grandstands does not make the former superior to the latter. It only means that one is more pleasing to more people than the other and, as recent attendance figures for professional baseball and football indicate, that tastes in the games people prefer constantly change.

Because it is an essential rule of the game I prefer to play, let me conclude by making explicit my preference for contesting international phenomena through the methods of science. So that my conclusions can be fully assessed and checked, it should also be made clear that my record at avoiding controversy over what constitutes the most desirable game is not unblemished. The temptation to engage in such controversy is often irresistible; but as one becomes a hardened sportsman one also becomes magnanimous, and it now seems obvious to me that the contest over which is the best game is the one game that can never be won. Thus, although somewhat moralistic, it is worth asserting that international relations scholars would be well advised to perfect their skills at the game they prefer instead of worrying about its value relative to other contests in which they could alternatively engage.

3 Thinking Theory
Thoroughly *

It rarely happens, but now and again in academic life one is
jolted into returning to fundamentals, into ascertaining whether one has
unknowingly strayed from one's organizing premises. This happened
to me recently when a graduate student inquired whether she could take
an "independent reading" course under my direction. Noting that my
competence was limited, I responded by asking what topics or problems
she planned to investigate. Her answer startled me, perhaps partly
because it was ungrammatical but mainly because I found it pedagogi-
cally challenging. Her answer was simple: "I would like you to teach
me to think theory!" I agreed to take on the role of advisor.

At this writing, some eleven weeks, many conversations and much
reflection later, I still find the assignment challenging, though now I
am beginning to wonder whether the capacity to think theoretically, the
inclination to perceive and assess the course of events as suggestive
or expressive of larger forces, is a talent that can be taught. It may
be, instead, a cast of mind, a personality trait, or a philosophical
perspective that some acquire early in life and others do not.

If this is so, there is not much that a professor can do to teach
students how to think theoretically. They can be introduced to the nature
of theories, taught the various purposes theories can serve, exposed to
the controversies over the relative worth of different theories, and
instructed on the steps required for the construction of viable theories.

* An earlier version of this chapter was presented
to the Conference on International Relations Theory organized by the Centre of Inter-
national Politics and Organizations, School of International Studies, Jawaharlal Nehru
University, New Delhi, India, May 14-17, 1979, and published in K. P. Misra and
Richard Smith Beal (eds.), *International Relations Theory: Western and Non-Western
Perspectives* (New Delhi: Vikas Publishing House Pvt. Ltd., 1979), Chapter 1.

And, to solidify the learning of these lessons, they can then be given assignments in which they have to formulate concrete hypotheses and tie them together into an actual theoretical framework. The learning of these skills underlying the design of theories is not, however, the equivalent of learning how to think theoretically. Or, more accurately, it is not the equivalent of what I understood my student as wanting me to teach her. In fact, she may only have been asking instruction on the dos and don'ts of theoretical design. But because of the way she worded her request I interpreted her as seeking more than an intro- duction to the procedures and techniques essential to creative theorizing. It seemed to me she was looking to acquire not a set of skills, but rather a set of predispositions, a cluster of habits, a way of thinking, a mental lifestyle—or whatever may be the appropriate label for that level of intellectual existence that governs the use of skills and the application of values—that she did not possess and that she thought she valued enough to want to make part of her orientation toward international phenomena. It is this more fundamental dimension of the life of the mind that I now suspect may not be teachable or learnable, a caveat that needs emphasis at the outset because the ensuing analysis amounts to nothing less than a pronouncement on how to think theoreti- cally.

NINE PRE-CONDITIONS FOR CREATIVE THEORIZING

It follows that the task of disciplining ourselves and our students to think theoretically consists, first, of identifying the cognitive inclina- tions and perceptual impulses from which creative theory springs and, second, of then forming intellectual habits which assure the prevalence of these inclinations and impulses whenever we turn to theory-building endeavors. The central question examined in this paper follows: what are the mental qualities that best enable one to "think theory" and how can their acquisition be best assured? Nine such qualities strike me as especially conducive to the development of good theorists. Each of the nine seem equally important and there is some overlap among them. Accordingly, the sequence of their elaboration here should not be interpreted as implying a rank ordering.

> *To think thoretically one has to avoid treating the task as that of formulating an appropriate definition of theory.*

So as to clarify what is involved in thinking theoretically, let me start with the proposition that the task is not one of developing a clear-cut definition of theory. On balance, it is probably preferable to have a precise conception of the nature of theory rather than a vague one, but definitional exactness is not the only criterion of thinking theoretically and it may not even be a necessary requirement for such thought. I can readily imagine a young student thinking theoretically about international phenomena well before his or her first course on the subject turns to the question of what constitutes theory and the various uses to which it can be put. Indeed, I have had the good fortune of encountering a few students who were, so to speak, born theoreticians. From their very first comments in class as freshmen it was clear that they thought theoretically even though they have never had any methodological training or any exposure to the history of international relations.

Most of us are not so lucky. Most of us have to be trained to think theoretically and then we have to engage in the activity continuously in order to achieve and sustain a genuinely theoretical perspective. Hence, the fact that a few among us can maintain such a perspective without training and practice is a useful reminder that definitional clarity is not a prerequisite to creative theorizing.

The reminder is important because many of us tend to exaggerate the importance of exact definitions. To be clear about the nature of theory is not to guarantee the formulation of meaningful theory. Such clarity can be misleading. It can provide a false sense of security, a misguided confidence that one needs only to organize one's empirical materials in the proper way if one is equipped with a clear-cut definition of theory. It is my impression that much of the writing in our field derives from this premise that good definitions automatically yield good theories, as if the definitions somehow relieve the observer of the need to apply imagination and maintain philosophical discipline.

To be sure, much of the writing also suffers from loose and ambiguous conceptions of theory or from a confusion between theory and method. Such research would, obviously, be more valuable if it proceeded from a tighter and clearer notion of what the theoretical enterprise entails. So, to repeat, I am not arguing against definitional clarity. On the contrary, I believe it is highly appropriate to help students achieve such clarity by introducing them to the vast array of articles and books now available on the dynamics, boundaries, uses, and abuses of theory in the international field. But I am arguing for more than definitional clarity. I am arguing for caution and restraint in the use of definitions: in digesting the literature on theory and building a more elaborate conception of what it involves, one has to be careful not to lean too heavily on definitions and guidance. Also needed is a cast of mind, a mental set that focuses application of the definitions and facilitates creative theorizing.

> *To think theoretically one has to be clear as to whether one aspires to empirical theory or value theory.*

Progress in the study of international affairs depends on advances in both empirical and value theory. But the two are not the same. They may overlap; they can focus on the same problem; and values always underlie the selection of the problems to which empirical theories are addressed. Yet they differ in one overriding way: empirical theory deals essentially with the "is" of international phenomena, with things as they are if and when they are subjected to observation, while value theory deals essentially with the "ought" of international phenomena, with things as they should be if and when they could be subjected to manipulation. This distinction underlies, in turn, entirely different modes of reasoning, a different rhetoric, and different types of evidence.

The habit of making the necessary analytic, rhetorical, and evidential distinctions between empirical and value theory can be difficult for young students to develop. Indeed, it can be weak and elusive for any of us who have strong value commitments and a deep concern for certain moral questions. The more intensive are our values, the more are we tempted to allow our empirical inquiries to be guided by our beliefs rather than by our concern for observation. For this reason I have found that helping students become habituated to the is-ought distinction is among the most difficult pedagogical tasks. They can understand the distinction intellectually and they can even explain and defend it when pressed; but practicing it is another matter and often their empirical analyses slip into moral judgments without their being aware of it. It is as if they somehow fear that their values and the policy goals they want to promote will be undermined if they allow themselves to focus on observable phenomena. Such, of course, is not the case. On the contrary, moral values and policy goals can be well served, even best served, by putting them aside and proceeding detachedly long enough to enlarge empirical understanding of the obstacles that hinder realization of the values and progress toward the goals.

This is the one line of reasoning on behalf of thinking theoretically that my most value-committed students find persuasive. If empirical theory is posited as a tool of moral theory, they can approach it instrumentally and see virtue in habituating themselves to distinguishing between the two. It takes awhile, however, before the perceived virtues of habituation are translated into actual habits and, in fact, some never manage to make the transition, hard as they may try. Impatient with the need for change, convinced that time is too scarce to afford the slow pace of empirical inquiry, many simply give up and dismiss the is-ought distinction as one of those picayune obsessions to which some academics fall prey.

It is my impression that impatience with empirical theorizing is likely to be especially intense among Third World students of international relations. The newly-developed consciousness of the long-standing injustices built into First World-Third World relationships, the lure of dependency theory, and perhaps a frustration over the central tendencies of social science in the First World have made Third World theorists particularly resistant to detached empirical theorizing. Their resistance gives a First World scholar pause: is his insistence on habituating oneself to the is-ought distinction yet another instance of false superiority, of projecting onto the developing world practices that have worked in industrial societies? It could be. Of late I have become keenly aware of the biases that may underlie my intellectual endeavors and thus I am not prepared merely to brush aside the idea that the is-ought distinction may be inappropriate to theorizing in much of the world. In this particular instance, however, I cannot even begin to break the habit. The relevance of the distinction strikes me as global, as independent of any national biases, as necessary to thinking theoretically wherever and whenever enlarged comprehension is sought. Empirical theory is not superior to moral theory; it is simply preferable for certain purposes, and one of these is the end of deepening our grasp of why international processes unfold as they do.

Aware that my own expertise, such as it may be, lies in the realm of empirical theory, the ensuing discussion makes no pretense of being relevant to thinking theoretically in the moral context. All the precepts that follow are concerned only with those mental qualities that may render us more thoroughgoing in our empirical theorizing.

> *To think theoretically one must be able*
> *to assume that human affairs are founded*
> *on an underlying order.*

A prime task of empirical theory is to explain why international phenomena are structured as they are and/or behave as they do. To perform this task one must assume that each and every international phenomenon is theoretically explicable, that deeper understanding of its dynamics could be achieved if appropriate instruments for measuring it were available. To assume that everything is potentially explicable is to presume that nothing happens by chance, capriciously, at random, that for every effect there must be a cause. That is, there must be an underlying order out of which international relations springs. If this were not the case, if events could occur for no reason, there would be little point in theorizing. If some events are inherently inexplicable, efforts to build creative theory are bound to fall short to the extent that they embrace phenomena that may occur at random. Indeed, in the absence of the assumption of an underlying order, attempts to fashion theory are futile, pointless exercises, a waste of time that could be better spent writing poetry, playing tennis, or tending the garden.

This is *not* to say that thought only acquires the status of theory when it purports to account for every event. As indicated below, theory is also founded on the laws of probability. Hence it only purports to account for central tendencies, but this claim is unwarranted if an assumption of underlying order is not made. That is, to think theoretically one must presume that there is a cause for every effect even though one does not seek to explain every effect.

I have found that most students have a difficult time becoming habituated to the assumption of an underlying order. They see it as a denial of their own freedom. To presume there is a cause for everything, they reason, is to deprive people of free will, perhaps even to relieve them of responsibility for their actions. The assumption of an underlying order does not, of course, have such implications. One's freedom of choice is not lessened by the fact that the choices made are not random and, instead, derive from some source. Yet, fearful about compromising their own integrity, many students cannot accept this subtlety and insist on the premise that people have the capacity to cut themselves off from all prior experience and to act as they please for no reason whatsoever. To support their resistance to the assumption of an underlying order, they will often cite instances of international history when the unexpected occurred or when a highly deviant, impetuous, and irrational action was undertaken, as if somehow irrationality and impetuosity are capricious and do not stem from any sources.

Besides patiently reassuring dubious students that there are no insidious threats in the assumption of an underlying order, resistance to the idea can be lessened, even broken in some instances, by pointing out how the assumption offers hope for greater understanding and deeper comprehension. To presume that there is a cause of every effect is to assume that everything is potentially knowable, that inquiry can pay off, that one is not necessarily destined to go down an intellectual path that dead ends, leads nowhere. The assumption of an underlying order, in other words, is pervaded with hope. We do not make it to allow ourselves to be hopeful, but it has that consequence. It enables us to view ourselves as totally in charge of our own investigations, limited only by our imaginations and the resources at our disposal.

It allows us to approach the chaos we perceive in the world around us as a challenge, as an orderliness that has yet to be identified and traced. It permits us to dare to think theory thoroughly because the affairs of people are patterned and the patterns are susceptible to being uncovered.

> *To think theoretically one must be predisposed to ask about every event, every situation, or every observed phenomenon, "Of what is it an instance?"*

Of all the habits one must develop to think theoretically, perhaps none is more central than the inclination to ask this question at every opportunity. It must be a constant refrain, a melody that haunts every lurch forward in the process of moving from observations to conclusions. For to see every event as an instance of a more encompassing class of phenomena is to sustain the search for patterns and to avoid treating any phenomenon as inherently unique. To think theoretically is to be at home with abstractions, to generalize, to discern the underlying order that links otherwise discrete incidents, and such a mode of thinking cannot be achieved and maintained unless every observed phenomenon is approached as merely one instance of a recurring sequence.

Again students appear to have a hard time building up this habit. They are inclined to probe for the special meaning of an event, to explore it for what sets it apart from all other events, rather than to treat it as an instance of a larger pattern. They want to understand the Iranian revolution, not revolutions as a social process, and to the extent this is their preference, to that extent do they resist building up the impulse to always reach for more general theoretical insights. Indeed, I have had many students who simply do not know where to begin when asked to indicate of what pattern some event they regard as important is an instance. Their faces turn blank and their tongues turn silent. They are paralyzed. They do not know what it means to treat the event as merely an instance of something, as just part of a larger category. And so they stumble, mumble, or otherwise resist thinking in those elementary terms out of which theorizing springs.

My response here is twofold. First, I try to portray the pleasure, the sheer joy, to be had from taking steps up the ladder of abstraction. Fitting pieces into larger wholes offers, I believe, a special sense of satisfaction, a feeling of accomplishment not unlike that which accompanies solving a puzzle or resolving a mystery. Indeed, theory building can readily be viewed as puzzle solving, as uncovering the dynamics embedded deep in the interstices of human relationships, and there are few students who are not intrigued by the challenge of solving puzzles.

If appealing thus to the curiosity of students does not succeed in getting them to ask habitually "Of what is this an instance?" (and often it is not a sufficient incentive), I revert to a second line of reasoning which, in effect, amounts to an attempt to shame them into the habit. This involves pointing out the implications of stumbling and mumbling, of not being able to discern any larger class of phenomena of which the observed phenomenon is an instance. The implications are unmistakable: to be paralyzed by the question "Of what is this an instance?" is not to know what one is interested in, to be lacking questions that generate and guide one's inquiry, to be confused by the phenomena one claims to be worthy of investigation. Based on the presumption of an underlying order, I believe that no phenomenon exists in isolation, unique only unto itself, and thus I believe that we always have an answer to the of-what-is-this-an-instance question, whether we know it or not. Accordingly, the task is not one of figuring out an answer presently unknown to us; it is rather that of explicating an answer that we have already acquired but have yet to surface. I am arguing, in other words, that we do not get interested in an international phenomenon for no reason, that our interest in it stems from a concern about a more encompassing set of phenomena, and that there is therefore no need to be paralyzed by the question if we press ourselves to move up the ladder of abstraction on which our intellectuality is founded. Once shamed into acknowledging that their concerns are not confined to the lowest rung on the ladder, most students are willing to begin to venture forth and approach the phenomena they observe as mere instances of something else.

> *To think theoretically one must be ready to*
> *appreciate and accept the need to sacrifice*
> *detailed descriptions for broad observations*

One cannot begin to mount the rungs of the ladder of abstraction if one is unable to forego the detailed account, the elaborated event, the specific minutia. As indicated, the theoretical enterprise is committed to the teasing out of central tendencies, to encompassing ever greater numbers of phenomena, to moving up the ladder of abstraction as parsimoniously as possible. Thus theory involves generalizing rather than particularizing and, in so doing, it requires relinquishing, subordinating, and/or not demonstrating much of one's impulse to expound everything one knows. It means, in effect, that one must discipline one's self to accept simple explanations over complex ones.

These are not easy tasks. Most of us find comfort in detail. The more details we know, the more are we likely to feel we have mastered our subject. To forego much of the detail, on the other hand, is to opt for uncertainties, to expose ourselves to the criticisms of those who would pick away at our generalizations wih exceptions. The temptations to fall back on details are thus considerable and much concentration on the upper rungs of the ladder of abstraction is required if the temptations are to be resisted.

Happily this is less of a problem for beginning students than more mature ones who are introduced late to the theoretical enterprise. The former have yet to acquire extensive familiarity with details and they are therefore not likely to feel threatened by the loss of their knowledge base. They want to focus on the unique, to be sure, but at least it is possible to expose them to the case of theorizing before they find security in endless minutiae. Exactly how more mature scholars accustomed to the comforts of detail can be persuaded to be theoretically venturesome is, I confess, a problem for which I have yet to find anything resembling a solution.

To think theoretically one must be tolerant
of ambiguity, concerned about probabilities,
and distrustful of absolutes.

To be concerned about central tendencies one needs to be accepting of exceptions, deviations, anomalies, and other phenomena that, taken by themselves, run counter to the anticipated or prevailing pattern. Anomalies ought not be ignored and often explorations of them can lead to valuable, path-breaking insights; but neither can anomalies be allowed to undermine one's focus on central tendencies. Empirical theories deal only with probabilities and not with absolutes, with how most phenomena are likely to respond to a stimulus and not with how each and every phenomenon responds. Theorists simply do not aspire to account for every phenomenon. They know there will be anomalies and exceptions; indeed, they are suspicious on those unlikely occasions when no exceptions are manifest. Rather their goal is to build theories in which the central tendencies encompass the highest possible degree of probability, with certainties and absolutes being left for ideologues and zealots to expound.

Although they engage in it continuously in their daily lives, students tend to be resistant to the necessity of thinking probabilistically when they turn to theorizing. More accurately, they tend to be reluctant to ignore the ambiguity, to be restless with anything less than perfect certainty, as if any exception to the anticipated central tendencies constitute a negation of their reasoning. I have found this low tolerance of ambiguity difficult to contest. Many students, fearful of uncertainty, seem to get fixated on the exception, and it is very hard at that point to recapture their interest in central tendencies. The very rhetoric of their everyday language—that things are "completely" the case or that an observation is "absolutely" accurate—reinforces their inclinations to be intolerant of deviations. In this mood they recognize only the "whole truth" as valid and regard central tendencies as a partial rather than a legitimate form of knowledge.

I confess to perplexity over how to handle this obstacle to theorizing on the part of students. I have tried elaborating on the many ways in which probabilistic thinking underlies their daily lives. I have tried making analogies between the physicist and the political scientist, pointing out that the former does not aspire to account for the behavior of every atom any more than the latter aspires to accounting for every voter. I have tried sarcasm, stressing the noxious values that derive from a concern with absolutes. Neither alone nor in combination, however, do such techniques seem to have any effect on many students. Whatever its sources, their intolerance of ambiguity is apparently too deep-seated to yield to reasoning or persuasion. So, reluctantly, I have concluded that students with a low tolerance of ambiguity and a high need for certainty are unlikely to ever think theory thoroughly and that it is probably wasted energy to try to teach them to do so.

> *To think theoretically one must be playful*
> *about international phenomena.*

At the core of the theorizing process is a creative imagination. The underlying order of world affairs is too obscure and too complex to yield to pedestrian, constricted, or conventional minds. Only deep penetration into a problem, discerning relationships that are not self-evident and might even be the opposite of what seems readily apparent, can produce incisive and creative theory. Thus to think theoretically one must allow one's mind to run freely, to be playful, to toy around with what might seem absurd, to posit seemingly unrealistic circumstances and speculate what would follow if they were ever to come to pass. Stated differently, one must develop the habit of playing and enjoying the game of "as if"—that is, specifying unlikely unconditions and analyzing them *as if* they prevailed.

Put in still another way, it has always seemed to me that good theory ought never be embarrassed by surprises, by unanticipated events that have major consequences for the system on which the theory focuses. A Hitler-Stalin pact, a Nixon resignation, or a Sadat peace initiative should not catch the creative theorist unawares because part of his or her creativity involves imagining the unimaginable. One imagines the unimaginable by allowing one's variables to vary across the entire range of a continuum even if some of its extreme points seem so unlikely as to be absurd. To push one's thinking beyond previously imagined extremes of a continuum is to play the game of "as if", and it involves a playfulness of mind that mitigates against surprises as well as facilitates incisive theorizing.

How one teaches playfulness is, of course, another matter. In some important sense it is an intellectual quality that cannot be taught. One acquires—or perhaps inherits—creativity early in life and no amount of subsequent training can greatly enhance the imaginative powers of those with tunnel vision and inhibited mentalities. On the other hand, encouragement to playfulness can bring out previously untapped talents in some students. Many have become so used to being told what to think that their creative impulses have never been legitimated and, accordingly, they have never even heard of the existence of the "as if" game. So no harm can be done by pressing our students (not to mention ourselves) to be playful and flexible in their thinking, and just conceivably such an emphasis may produce some unexpected results.

> *To think theoretically one must be genuinely*
> *puzzled by international phenomena.*

Creative use of the imagination requires humility toward international phenomena. One must be as concerned about asking the right questions about the order underlying world affairs as finding the right answers. To focus only on answers is to be sure about the questions one wants to probe and this, in turn, is to impose unnecessary limits on one's capacity to discern and integrate the deeper structures of global politics. If, on the other hand, one is genuinely puzzled by why events unfold as they do, one is committed to always asking why they occur in one way rather than another and, in so doing, pressing one's theoretical impulses as far as possible.

I do not use the notion of "genuine puzzles" casually. They are not simply open-ended questions, but refer rather to perplexity over specific and patterned outcomes. To be genuinely puzzled about the declining capacity of governments to govern effectively, for example, one does not ask, "Why do governments do what they do?" Rather one asks, say, "Why are most governments unable to control inflation?" or "Why do they alter their alliance commitments under specified conditions?" Genuine puzzles, in other words, are not idle, ill-framed, or impetuous speculations. They encompass specified dependent variables for which adequate explanations are lacking.[1] I do not see how one can begin to think theoretically if one does not discern recurrent outcomes that evoke one's curiosity and puzzlement. Some analysts

---

[1] This point is elaborated in Chapter 9.

believe they are starting down the road to theory when they start asking what the outcomes are, but such a line of inquiry leads only to dead-ends, or worse, to endless mazes, because one never knows when one has come upon a relevant outcome. Genuine puzzles can lead us down creative paths, however, because they discipline us to focus on particular patterns.

One cannot teach others to be puzzled. Again it is very much a matter of whether curiosity has been repressed or allowed to flourish at an early age. It is possible, however, to keep after students and colleagues with the simple question, "What genuinely puzzles you about international affairs?" Hopefully repetition of the question will prove to be sufficiently challenging to facilitate a maximum expression of whatever may be the curiosity potential students may possess.

> *To think theoretically one must be constantly ready to be proven wrong.*

Perhaps nothing inhibits the ability to be intellectually puzzled and playful than the fear of being embarrassed by the inaccuracies of one's theorizing. Many of us have fragile egos that are so sensitive to error as to lead us to prefer sticking close to conventional wisdom than risking speculation which may be erroneous. It is as if our stature as students depends upon the soundness of our observations.

Fragile egos are not readily bolstered and some students may never be capable of venturing forth. In my experience, however, there is one line of reasoning that some students find sufficiently persuasive to lessen their fears of appearing ridiculous. It involves the thought that our comprehension of international phenomena can be substantially advanced even if our theories about them prove to be woefully wrong. Such progress can occur in two ways. One is that falsified theory has the virtue of indicating avenues of inquiry which no longer need be traversed. Doubtless egos are best served by theoretical breakthroughs; but if one presumes that knowledge is at least partly developed through a process of elimination, there is some satisfaction to be gained from having narrowed the range of inquiry through theory that subsequently proves fallacious.

Secondly, unsound theory can facilitate progress by provoking others into demonstrating its falsity and attempting to show how and why it went astray. Indeed, assuming that the erroneous theory focuses on significant matters, often the more outrageous the theory is, the more it is likely to provoke further investigation. Thus even if one cannot negotiate a theoretical breakthrough on one's own, one can serve one's ego by the possibility that one's errors may sustain the knowledge-building process. This is surely what one astute analyst had in mind when he observed, "It is important to err importantly." [2]

CONCLUSION: BRINGING IT ALL TOGETHER

Plainly, there is no easy way to evolve the habit of thinking theoretically. Indeed, if the foregoing nine precepts are well founded, it can be readily argued that theorizing is the hardest of intellectual tasks. Clearing away the confusion of day-to-day events and teasing out their underlying patterns is not merely a matter of applying one's mental skills. Sustained, disciplined, and uninhibited work is required, and even then theory can be elusive, puzzles difficult to identify, details hard to ignore, and probabilities tough to estimate. And the lures and practices of non-theoretical thinking are always present, tempting us to forego the insecurities and ambiguities of high levels of abstraction in favor of the comfortable precision available at low levels.

Yet the payoffs for not yielding to the temptations and persisting to think theoretically are considerable. There is an exhilaration, an exquisiteness, to be enjoyed in the theoretical enterprise that virtually defies description. Stimulated by the rarified atmosphere, energized by the freedom to roam uninhibitedly across diverse realms of human experience, one gets giddy at high levels of abstraction. It is that special kind of giddiness that comes from the feeling that one is employing all the resources and talents at one's command, moving beyond anything one has done before. And if one should be so fortunate as actually to achieve a theoretical breakthrough, then the exhilaration, the excitement, and the sense of accomplishment can approach the thrill of discovery that Darwin, Einstein, Freud, and the other great explorers of underlying order must have experienced at their moments of breakthrough.

For all the difficulties it entails, then, thinking theoretically is, on balance, worth the effort. And so, therefore, is the effort to teach others to think thoroughly in this way. The habits of theoretical thinking may not always be teachable, and they may not even be teachable at all; but if our efforts successfully manage to reach only a few students, they are worth undertaking. And it is even conceivable that in trying to teach others to think theoretically, we may refine and enlarge our own capacities for comprehending the underlying order that sustains and alters the human condition.

---

[2] Marion J. Levy, " 'Does It Matter If He's Naked?' Bawled the Child," in Klaus Knorr and James N. Rosenau (eds.), *Contending Approaches to International Relations* (Princeton: Princeton University Press, 1969), p. 93.

Part Two: The Science

The popular tendency to use the word "science" as a designation for both a method of inquiry and a body of knowledge is a persistent source of controversy in the study of international affairs. Many people, accustomed to regarding the findings of chemistry, physics, or biology as science, find it difficult to accept the idea of extending the scientific enterprise to the phenomena of foreign policy. The physical sciences, they contend, are sciences because they have accumulated a vast storehouse of reliable knowledge, whereas knowledge about foreign policy phenomena is so scant and transitory that it is premature and presumptuous to approach them in a scientific manner. Such a contention is based on a confusion of science-as-method and science-as-subject. While the paucity of knowledge in this field is indisputable, it does not mean that the behavior of nations cannot be subjected to the data-gathering procedures and criteria of evidence that are the hallmark of the scientific method. As a focus of study, the nation-state is no different from the atom or the single cell organism. Its patterns of behavior, idiosyncratic traits, and internal structure are as amenable to the process of formulating and testing hypotheses as are the characteristics of the electron or the molecule.

To be sure, the behavior of atoms may be more easily assessed than that of nation-states, with the result that an enormous discrepancy exists between physics and foreign policy from a science-as-subject perspective. In terms of science-as-method, however, the two are essentially the same. Both require the analyst to specify units of analysis, to identify relevant variables, to operationalize key concepts, to frame testable propositions, to gather quantified data, to evaluate the patterns formed by the data, and to revise the propositions in the light of the findings.

Viewed collectively, the six chapters that follow constitute an effort to bring all these dimensions of the scientific method to bear on foreign policy phenomena. Only two of the six actually carry out the task of operationalizing hypotheses and putting them to the test of empirical data, but the others wrestle with the many problems that must be overcome before the data-gathering stage of science can be carried out. Most notably, the other four chapters reflect a continuing preoccupation with the problem of specifying the key independent, intervening, and dependent variables of foreign policy analysis. While the net result is far from a thorough analysis of the problem, at least the outlines of a science do emerge from the juxtaposition of the chapters.

4 Moral Fervor, Systematic Analysis, and Scientific Consciousness in Foreign Policy Research *

[The best route to enhanced credibility in the Soviet-American relationship,] if one may speak most directly, is to stop lying, faking, and posturing.[1]

[In the modern era] the scope for wrong-doing in foreign policy has greatly expanded; and of its expansion governments have not been reluctant to take advantage. In their dealings with other governments, and with other people, their behavior is characteristically bad. It is deceitful. It is treacherous. It is cruel.[2]

These are not the exhortations of office-seekers or the exclamations of aroused citizens. They are the observations of two distinguished scholars

* Earlier versions of this chapter were presented to the Conference on Political Science and the Study of Public Policy, sponsored by the Committee on Governmental and Legal Processes of the Social Science Research Council at Cape Newagen, Maine in August, 1967, and published in Austin Ranney (ed.), *Political Science and Public Policy* (Chicago: Markham Publishing Company, 1968), pp. 197–236. Reprinted by permission of the publisher. Copyright © 1968 by Markham Publishing Company.

[1] Milton J. Rosenberg, "Attitude Change and Foreign Policy in the Cold War Era," in James N. Rosenau (ed.), *Domestic Sources of Foreign Policy* (New York: Free Press, 1967), p. 135.

[2] James Eayrs, *Right and Wrong in Foreign Policy* (Toronto: University of Toronto Press, 1966), p. 32.

who have earned a reputation for careful and detached inquiry and who wrote these lines as parts of serious attempts to apply their expertise to problems of foreign policy. The discrepancy between the bewildered simplicity and moral fervor of these excerpts and the complex qualifications and cautious conclusions that usually mark their research is, I would contend, typical of what happens when scholars turn their attention to foreign policy phenomena.[3] Such phenomena seem to invite the abandonment of scholarly inclinations.[4] Ask almost any scholar what is possible and desirable with respect to urban redevelopment and he is likely to avoid a direct answer, responding that the problem is complicated, that a host of variables are operative, and that the causal connections are difficult to trace. Ask almost any scholar what is possible and desirable with respect to Vietnam or the Middle East and he is likely to give an unqualified answer—one that derives from moral judgment, assumes motivation, and simplifies causation. Consciousness of scientific method, so evident elsewhere in the study of human behavior today, has yet to become predominant in the analysis of foreign policy.

Much the same can be said of those political scientists whose professional concern with foreign policy phenomena leads them in analytic rather than normative directions. Although the work of specialists in the field may not be pervaded with moral fervor, neither is it characterized by scientific consciousness. Rare is the inquiry that specifies the independent and dependent variables that are being investigated, that sets forth explicit hypotheses in which the relationship of the variables is posited, and that then generates data designed to test the hypotheses. Hardly less rare than testable propositions are propositions that can be rendered testable, that identify discrete units of action which can be observed with sufficient frequency to allow variations in their structure and in the sources and consequences of their behavior to become evident.

Stated differently, most inquiries into foreign policy phenomena do not contain variables that vary, that increase or decrease under different conditions. To be sure, specified causes and effects may be recognized as capable of operating in other ways and thus are often called "variables." However, the nature of these other ways and the range across which the variation can occur—what shall be called here, for purposes of emphasis,

---

[3] For a number of other examples of this discrepancy, see my "Behavioral Science, Behavioral Scientists, and the Study of International Phenomena," *Journal of Conflict Resolution*, 9 (December 1965), pp. 509–20.

[4] Even historians are apparently capable of responding favorably to the invitation. For a cogent discussion along these lines, see Francis L. Loewenheim, "A Legacy of Hope and a Legacy of Doubt: Reflections on the Role of History and Historians in American Foreign Policy since the Eighteenth Century," in F. L. Loewenheim (ed.), *The Historian and the Diplomat: The Role of History and Historians in American Foreign Policy* (New York: Harper & Row, 1967), pp. 1–71.

the "variance" of variables—is conspicuously absent from most inquiries. Instead variables are usually analyzed exclusively in terms of the way they operate in the particular situation being examined. Consequently, they are rarely seen to vary—to slacken or intensify, widen or narrow, rise or fall, grow or diminish, strengthen or weaken. The words "more" and "less" do not pervade the literature of the field. Foreign policy actors are not conceived in terms of behavior that would be more in one direction and less in another if more of a particular circumstance prevailed and less of another. Rather, most of the research into foreign policy phenomena is problem-oriented and consists of data and conclusions derived either from descriptive case histories or from broader assessments in which the variance of the variables is limited to the problem being considered.

1. SYSTEMATIC VERSUS SCIENTIFIC INQUIRY

More often than not, to be sure, both the cases and the broad assessments are systematic. The cases systematically analyze the evolution of conflicts and the actions taken to resolve them. The broader accounts systematically cluster together a number of situations with which a nation has coped in the past or must cope in the present and then systematically generalize about the factors and goals that seem to be relevant to the nation's behavior in all the situations. To be systematic, however, is not in itself to be scientific, a point that is succinctly illustrated by the old analogy to the telephone book, which is surely one of the most systematic documents ever produced, and also one of the least scientific. For all their systematic reconstruction of decision and action through time, most case histories neither test nor yield propositions that are applicable beyond the specific situation considered. When the events subjected to systematic examination run their course, the case is treated as complete, and even if the analyst draws "some lessons for the future" from it, these are virtually never cast in the form of hypotheses that are testable when comparable problems subsequently arise.

Likewise, for all their systematic treatment of the factors underlying a nation's foreign policy, the broader assessments are not usually compiled through a process of hypothesis testing, but rather are derived from an informed and careful piecing together of a generalized pattern out of those events and trends that strike the analyst as relevant. Having thus identified the pattern, the analyst has no reason to speculate about how it might be differently structured if different events and trends had unfolded. Hence he has no need to cast his conclusions as to the pattern's importance and consequences in hypothetical terms, or even to indicate a range within which the main variables that comprise it are likely to vary. Like the case histories, therefore, the broad assessments do not in themselves provide a basis for further inquiry. They are concerned with a specific problem and, having examined the sources and solutions of it, they simply come to an end.

Several consequences follow from the disjunction of systematic analysis and scientific consciousness in the study of foreign policy. The most crucial of these is that knowledge about foreign policy behavior does not cumulate. Since the case histories and the broad assessments neither test nor yield hypotheses, their conclusions cannot be placed in a larger context. Thus no "established" findings or propositions can be gleaned from the vast literature on foreign policy that would be comparable to the twenty-nine major propositions and their many corollaries uncovered in the research on domestic political institutions.[5] At any moment in time there is considerable knowledge available about the prevailing international scene, but virtually all of it becomes obsolete when conditions change. At that point the case writer may write a new case and the generalizer may develop new generalizations, but while monographs may thereby cumulate, knowledge does not. Not having allowed for variations within a larger context, the cases and the broad assessments are time- and problem-bound.

A second consequence of the lack of scientific consciousness, and one that is closely related to the noncumulative nature of foreign policy knowledge, is the paucity of rewards for self-sustained inquiry. The inclination to cast problems in the form of hypotheses practically guarantees that the researcher will be confronted with an endless series of intriguing questions. Human behavior being as complex as it is, hypotheses are rarely confirmed in their entirety. Even when a hypothesis approaches full confirmation, questions arise as to the scope of its application, pressing the researcher to carry his tests of its validity to the point where eventually the hypothesis is disproved and new ones are framed to account for the discrepant behavior. In the case of the systematic but nonscientific modes of research, however, the incentives to probe further are not so intense. Even as the case histories and broad assessments satisfy one's curiosity about the particular foreign policy episode or problem investigated, so do they tend to dampen one's imagination with respect to the dynamics of foreign policy. There are no questions left over. All the relevant circumstances have been described, assessed, and put into place. There is no built-in predisposition to ask what would happen if variables were differently structured. Hence, having grasped the particular moments in history recounted by the cases or having comprehended the particular dimensions of the problem explored by the broad assessments, the mind tends to come to rest.

And since foreign policy analysts do not set out to test explicit hypo-

[5] Bernard Berelson and Gary A. Steiner, *Human Behavior: An Inventory of Scientific Findings* (New York: Harcourt, 1964), pp. 417–36.

theses, they can never be wrong. Their analyses might be inappropriate, superficial, or out of date, but they cannot be wrong. A researcher might fail to anticipate a major event such as the ouster of Khrushchev or the sudden collapse of the Arab armies and thus be embarrassed by the conclusions reached in his assessment, but such embarrassment need not last long. Not having started with a hypothesis that the unanticipated event reveals to be unsound, the researcher need not concede or even recognize that his reasoning was ill founded and that a new formulation is in order.[6] The analyst with a scientific consciousness, on the other hand, cannot ignore his errors. By casting his expectations in if-then terms, he has made explicit the conditions under which he would be shown to be wrong. Either his hypotheses are confirmed or they are not. The latter outcome points to flaws in his comprehension of the subject, provokes thought as to where his reasoning went astray, and thus challenges his scientific consciousness even further.

It might be argued that the deadening effect of case histories and broad assessments is not the fault of their authors, that the authors have fulfilled their responsibilities by carefully depicting a historic sequence of events or cogently analyzing the dynamics of a situation, and that it is up to others to exploit the cases or the assessments for any more general hypotheses they may contain. Such an argument, however, runs counter to experience. The fact is that case histories and broad assessments rarely generate further research. If a case writer does not test or derive explicit hypotheses from his materials, others are seldom provoked to apply and extend the comprehension gleaned from them. If the author of the broad assessment does not offer if-then propositions, others are disinclined to pursue the implications of his reasoning in more than a casual fashion. Hence, to repeat, nothing cumulates.

Elsewhere a colleague and the present writer have stressed that there is no inherent reason why this must be so. Both systematic and scientific analyses aspire to greater understanding, and while they do not use the same methods to realize their common goal, neither are their methods mutually exclusive. Theoretically, therefore, it is possible for the scientific researcher to glean relevant findings and insights from case histories and broad assessments and then cast them into hypotheses to be tested by new materials.[7]

---

[6] If need be, he can always resort to humor in the form of an antiscience quip to alleviate the embarrassment. As Zbigniew K. Brzezinski is reported to have observed when events in October of 1964 negated his published expectation that Khrushchev would have a long tenure in office, "If Khrushchev couldn't predict his downfall, how would you expect *me* to do it?" See William H. Honan, "They Live in the Year 2000," *New York Times Magazine,* April 9, 1967, p. 64.

[7] Klaus Knorr and James N. Rosenau (eds.), *Contending Approaches to International Politics* (Princeton, N.J.: Princeton University Press, 1969), Chap. 1.

Self-evident as this may be, however, it does not accord with experience. Whatever the theoretical possibilities may be, researchers in the field simply do not get aroused to transform the findings of case histories and the insights of broad assessments into the bases for further inquiry. The reasons for this discontinuity are doubtless many and varied, but the lack of cumulation and the existence of the discontinuity seem incontestable.

The seven case histories summarized in the Appendix to this chapter illustrate this point. None of the findings of any of the cases is cited by subsequent researchers. None of them has served as the basis for other inquiries into comparable phenomena. None has even stimulated other cases. No one has written a case history of the 1961 Berlin crisis or the 1964 foreign aid program, to mention two obvious situations to which case writers might reasonably have been expected to be attracted as a result of the existence of dramatic accounts of the 1948 blockade of Berlin and the 1957 effort to expand the foreign aid program.[8] Case histories, in short, are short-lived. As curiosity gets aroused by more recent episodes, a case passes into oblivion, serving only the occasional historian who chances upon it and uses it to get a "feel" for the era he is studying.

The broad assessments are similarly fated. Most of those written in the 1950s, for example, now serve merely as background reading for historians. The literature on limited war fostered by the Korean conflict is not central to the research monographs generated by the Vietnam war. Nor does the arms-control literature of the 1960s appear to be rooted in the spate of serious inquiries into strategic problems that were published in the previous decade. To be sure, the more recent analyses are not oblivious of the work done in the earlier periods. Frequent references to the pioneering efforts of, say, Brodie, Bull, Kahn, Kissinger, Osgood, and Schelling can be found in the more recent writings on limited war and arms control. More often than not, however, the earlier inquiries are cited by way of pointing out how circumstances have changed and how new interpretations are therefore necessary. Each researcher and each generation of foreign policy analysts, it would seem, starts afresh, interpreting the prevailing scene in terms of the problems it presents and thus offering nothing on which to build when the set is changed and the curtain goes up on new actors playing different roles.[9]

[8] See W. Phillips Davison, *The Berlin Blockade: A Study in Cold War Politics* (Princeton: Princeton University Press, 1958), and H. Field Haviland, Jr., "Foreign Aid and the Policy Process: 1957," *American Political Science Review*, 52 (September 1958), pp. 689–724.

[9] There are, of course, exceptions. We are describing a central tendency and do not wish to imply that the literature is completely barren of enduring research. A few broad assessments (but hardly any case histories) stand out as sources on which new generations of researchers depend. Morton A. Kaplan's *System and Process in International Politics* (New York: Wiley, 1957) comes readily to mind as a work

One other consequence of the nonscientific character of foreign policy research needs to be noted, namely, that it commands little respect among those in positions to apply its concepts and findings to the actual conduct of world affairs.[10] While the advice of foreign policy specialists is sought by and provided to the agencies and personnel of government, the resulting interaction would not seem to be a typical client-expert relationship. It derives less from the client's dependence on the expert's expertise than from the official's need to clarify and check out his thinking with detached and knowledgeable observers. Certainly it does not involve the kind of dependence on expertise that characterizes officialdom's relationships with many other types of specialists on human behavior. Plainly, neither officials nor nongovernmental leaders defer to the foreign policy expert's judgment on the adequacy of an international posture to the same extent that they do, say, to the economist's views on the soundness of a fiscal policy or the psychiatrist's assessment of the mental state of an accused murderer. Indeed, the assessments of the foreign policy scholar hardly even enjoy the respect of family and friends.   Anyone who has ever done research on foreign affairs can testify that nonprofessional acquaintances never hesitate to dispute and reject offhandedly the conclusions derived from months of painstaking inquiry. Most people, officials and ordinary citizens alike, consider themselves to be as qualified or as unqualified as the next person in international affairs, and thus those who specialize in such matters are not viewed as experts. While there are no doubt many reasons for this, surely an important one is that such "experts" have no expertise. Lacking a scientific consciousness, they have not built up a body of rigorously tested knowledge or even a coherent set of testable propositions that specify what is likely to happen over a range of diverse circumstances. The economist offers elaborate theories and supporting data as to what happens to supply when demand increases, and the psychiatrist can refer to a vast storehouse of empirical material to support his diagnosis of what form of mental illness is likely to result in particular symptoms. The political scientist who

that continues to be cited as a basis for inquiry even though it was published more than a decade ago. Such exceptions, however, support the point about the research-provoking nature of inquiries that are infused with a scientific consciousness. Almost invariably the exceptions are works that offer hypotheses, that cast political processes in terms of variance that is greater under certain conditions and less under others. Similarly, an important part of the research employing simulation techniques, especially the studies conducted or stimulated by Harold Guetzkow, can be fairly described as cumulative. But again the exception seems to prove the rule. Many of the simulation runs reported by Guetzkow and his colleagues are designed to test and extend the findings of previous runs. See Harold Guetzkow et al., Simulation in International Relations: Developments for Research and Training (Englewood Cliffs, N.J.: Prentice-Hall, 1963), passim.

   10 See Louis Morton, "The Cold War and American Scholarship," in Historian and Diplomat, pp. 123–69.

specializes in foreign policy, however, can provide only illustrations from past experience and informed impressions of present practice. So why should anyone defer to him? The knowledge he offers can be acquired just as easily by reading a good newspaper or conversing with knowledgeable friends. He may bring to bear a richer variety of data and a more refined capacity for seeing interrelationships, but like the journalist and the intelligent citizen, he bases his foreign policy assessments and recommendations on untested impressions rather than on a rigorously substantiated body of knowledge.

To assert that foreign policy research is not cumulative, that, indeed, it tends to stifle questioning and thought, and that its gatherers hardly differ from journalists and informed citizens is a strong indictment that, in all fairness, needs to be documented. As it stands, the indictment is only an impression. Although it is based on a long acquaintance with the literature of the field, it may well be skewed by a preference for the scientific mode. Certainly there are those who make quite the opposite indictment and contend that research in the field is too scientific."[11] Thus it is possible that a systematic content analysis of the literature would reveal more sensitivity to the variance of variables and a greater incidence of explicit hypotheses than it is claimed here exist. An inventory of research practices might show that the recent trends toward aggregate data analysis and simulation involve more than a small minority of the researchers in the field. However, in the absence of an elaborate inventory of the literature—and plainly one ought to be compiled—we can only proceed on the assumption that our indictment is essentially valid and that it is sufficient to present some sample evidence indicating that the foregoing is not simply a product of bias (see the Appendix to this chapter).

Before we turn to the main purpose of this chapter, however, one aspect of the indictment does need to be clarified. Lest it create false issues, conjuring up images of complex formulas, quantified data, and statistical manipulations, emphasis must be given to the fact that foreign policy researchers are not being indicted for failing to employ elaborate procedures and mathematical computations. It is the implications of the initial premise with which researchers approach foreign policy phenomena that are at issue, not the refinements of their methodology—the consciousness of scientific

---

11 For an expression of this viewpoint, see Kenneth W. Thompson, "Normative Theory in International Relations," *Journal of International Affairs*, 21 (1967), p. 289. On the other hand, there are those who would agree with the judgment made here. For example, although he did not classify it as an indictment, Henry Kissinger has recently noted that "American writing on foreign policy has generally tended to fall into three categories: analyses of specific cases or historical episodes, exhortations justifying or resisting greater participation in international affairs, and investigations of the legal bases of world order" (*The New York Times*, February 12, 1967, sec. 7, p. 3).

method, not its detailed application. Stated most succinctly, a scientific consciousness involves an automatic tendency to ask, "Of what larger pattern is this behavior an instance?" Analysts continuously motivated by this question cannot be content just to derive a conclusion from their observations. Their initial premise is that each conclusion must serve as the basis for new observations, that the function of data is not only to test prior expectations, but also to generate new ones. Because it treats every observation as an instance of a more general class of events, a scientific consciousness also impels speculation about the conditions under which the observed behavior would not have occurred or would have occurred in a different form. Such speculation in turn leads researchers, virtually without forethought, to infuse their variables with variance and to cast them in the form of hypotheses whose testing will either affirm or negate their conclusions about the more general class of events.

Systematic but nonscientific analysis, on the other hand, does not give rise to consideration of the ways in which changing conditions might foster varying behavior. Once the antecedents of the observed behavior have been thoroughly examined and other possible interpretations have been carefully considered, the conclusions that the behavior seems to suggest can be accepted. The search is not for a larger pattern, but for inherent meaning. The analyst asks, "What are the sources of this observed behavior and what are its consequences?" The issue for him is whether a sufficient number of factors have been examined to justify the answer to the question. Hence, although informed and systematically developed, this answer need not be relevant to other situations in the past, present, or future. Inevitably, therefore, the analyst must rely on his impressions of the interconnections among situations if he offers generalizations that span two or more of them. The generalizations may well stem from much thought and long experience in the study of foreign policy situations, but they will perforce be impressionistic. Since conclusions about each situation are not structured so that they can be verified in other situations, systematic but nonscientific analyses provide no cumulated body of confirmed findings that the researcher can fall back on when he registers observations about the similarities and differences among several situations. It is in this sense that the journalist or the knowledgeable friend have as much to offer as the foreign policy specialist if the latter does not have a consciousness of scientific method.

It follows that the crucial distinction between scientific inquiry and that which is systematic but not scientific lies in the manner in which data are used and not in the amount or even the kind of data gathered. If the initial premise that the researcher brings to his data is rooted in a scientific consciousness, it does not matter whether he has made a single observation or a multitude, since he will treat both the single event and the many events of policy-oriented researchers will then be held in greater esteem than is presently the case.

Assuming that it is essentially válid to conclude that foreign policy research is at present long on systematic analysis and short on scientific consciousness, the question arises as to why this should be so. What is it about foreign policy phenomena that renders them so conducive to non-scientific inquiry? And how might they be made more susceptible to the derivation and testing of explicit hypotheses?

II. THE PROBLEM OF URGENCY

Two of the reasons for the present state of foreign policy research are self-evident and require only brief comment. One of these is the vital importance of the problems posed by the subject. The growing destructive capacity of modern weapons and the ever-present possibility of a nuclear holocaust add a dimension of urgency to foreign policy problems that leads many analysts to compromise their research standards and forego the patience and detachment they normally bring to their work. The notion that foreign policy phenomena are simply data to be explained is for many students of the subject a betrayal of responsibility. "The problems have to be solved now," they seem to say. "If we take the time to treat a foreign policy event as an instance of a larger pattern, none of us will be around to discern that larger pattern!" Thus reinforced with moral and seemingly practical reasons for not being overly concerned about the cumulation of findings that extend beyond particular situations, many researchers feel no impulse to allow for the variance of their variables and to cast their conclusions in terms of hypotheses that can be subjected to further exploration.[14]

The trouble with such reasoning is that it posits a false dichotomy between scientific inquiry and policy-oriented solutions. The fact that specific policy recommendations emerge from an investigation does not preclude the derivation of hypotheses from the materials examined. As has already been indicated, the maintenance of a scientific consciousness requires a

[14] It must be noted, however, that moral fervor and fear that the arms race may eventuate in nuclear holocaust do not necessarily lead to a curbing of scientific consciousness. Curiously, some of those who feel most strongly about such matters, i.e., those who call themselves "peace researchers," can often be found among the small minority of foreign policy analysts who are sensitive to the variance of variables and the derivation of testable hypotheses. A perusal of the recently founded *Journal of Peace Research* and the annual volumes of the Peace Research Society (International) will reveal a much greater scientific consciousness than a comparable survey of such older and more established journals as *Foreign Affairs, Orbis, World Politics,* and *International Affairs.*

as part of a more general class of phenomena. The essence of scientific inquiry is thus not to be found in complex formulas or neatly arrayed tables of data. The case history can be a scientific document if its data are used as a basis for anticipating how other, as yet unexamined, data might be arrayed. Likewise, the broad assessment can be essentially scientific if the impressions it sets forth are cast in hypothetical terms that are susceptible to further exploration.   Consider, for example, the propostion that "As societies enter the phase when integration tends to take precedence over development as a main problem, there is greater concern for international order and less interest in foreign adventures that might lead to war." [12] It appears in a broad historical analysis, and yet this particular work gives rise to an urge to engage in new research precisely because it is filled with conclusions cast in such a fashion.

On the other hand, a plethora of quantitative data depicting a nation's recurrent foreign policy behavior can be subjected to nonscientific techniques of analysis. The presence of tables of data is no guarantee that a scientific consciousness has been at work. Many a work can be found that contains a number of systematic tabulations but no hypotheses. In his investigation of the 1951 Japanese peace treaty, for example, Cohen presents twenty-nine elaborate tables, which range from presentations of press coverage to content analyses of John Foster Dulles' speeches and the central themes of Senate debate.[13] Yet, as indicated below in the Appendix to this chapter, this case history does not employ its quantitative data for other than descriptive purposes and thus fails to manifest a scientific consciousness.

In short, the indictment of the foreign policy field set forth here does not amount to a call for all researchers to abandon their present modes of inquiry for new ones. There is no implication that every analyst should be required to undergo retooling in mathematics and training in statistics. Nor does it imply that a policy-oriented concern with current problems needs to be replaced by an aspiration to construct general theory. Rather, it calls on researchers to supplement their efforts, whatever the purposes of these may be and however many data they may encompass, with a sensitivity to the variance of any variables that are used and to the larger relevance of any conclusions that are reached.   Such a sensitivity in no way hinders policy-oriented research and it does not require sophistication in quantitative procedures. It does hold forth the hope that a cumulative body of reliable findings on foreign policy may emerge and that the recommendations

[12] C. E. Black, *The Dynamics of Modernization: A Study in Comparative History* (New York: Harper & Row, 1966), p. 135.

[13] Bernard C. Cohen, *The Political Process and Foreign Policy: The Making of the Japanese Peace Settlement* (Princeton: Princeton University Press, 1957).

perspective and not a procedure with respect to the processing of data. If the researcher is unable to await the outcome of quantitative tests of complex propositions, he can still place the results of his inquiry in a larger context without undermining their immediate applicability. Nothing is lost, except perhaps some succinctness, if in urging a certain course of action upon the policy-maker the researcher indicates the more general class of behavior from which his recommendations are drawn. If, for example, he is urging American policy-makers to take a firm stand in the face of China's emerging nuclear capabilities, little would be sacrificed if he made it clear why he thinks firm stands are more likely to induce international actors to accept arms-control measures than accommodative stands.[15] If it is true that at present his recommendations are necessarily rooted in impressions and have no more reliability than those of a thoughtful journalist or an informed citizen, the question arises whether he can afford *not* to supplement his specific conclusions with disciplined speculation about the larger patterns into which they fit.

III. THE PROBLEM OF COMPLEXITY

Another obvious deterrent to scientific consciousness in foreign policy research is the complexity of the subject. The number of variables that may underlie the impact and success of a policy is so astronomical that many researchers regard foreign policy phenomena as inherently not susceptible to scientific treatment. As two distinguished analysts have put it, "When it comes to studying foreign policy in its various manifestations . . . the social scientist is . . . asked to explain and predict attitudes whose complexity makes a mockery of the few 'scientific' tools we have. . . . To attempt generalizations and construction of models that will give us a rigorous scientific understanding and prediction of foreign policy is a hopeless task." [16] Without in the least denying the complexity of foreign policy phenomena, it must be emphasized that this line of reasoning is profoundly fallacious and a major obstacle to cumulative research in the field. It is based on an erroneous conception of science. As has already been indicated, science implies only a certain method of handling data and nothing about their particular nature. If the relevance of science were limited only to simple phenomena,

15 For an illustration of the fact that it is possible not to place recommendations on this subject in a larger context, see Morton H. Halperin, *China and the Bomb* (New York: Praeger, 1965), the last three chapters of which contain no such hypotheses, although they present thirteen recommendations of what the United States "must" do and sixty-four courses of action that it "should" follow.

16 Kenneth W. Thompson and Roy C. Macridis, "The Comparative Study of Foreign Policy," in R. C. Macridis (ed.), *Foreign Policy in World Politics*, (Englewood Cliffs, N.J.: Prentice-Hall, 1962), pp. 26–27.

the great explosion of knowledge that marks the twentieth century would not have occurred. Physics, chemistry, economics, psychology, and the many other areas of inquiry that have advanced so rapidly in recent decades would still be intuitive enterprises if those who investigated such matters held the attitude quoted above. Indeed, it is reasonable to argue that these advances occurred precisely because researchers did not stand in awe of their subject matter and turned to the scientific method in order to untangle its complexity.

However, to reject the argument that foreign policy phenomena are too complex to be analyzed scientifically is not to deny their extraordinary multitude and variability. On the contrary, in view of the analytic innovations suggested below, it is extremely important that their complexity be fully recognized. In order to ensure this recognition and facilitate the subsequent analysis, an example of the scale of complexity with which foreign policy researchers must contend can usefully be outlined. Consider Latin America and the number and variety of specific policy situations that comprise the foreign policy of any nation toward that region. Figured conservatively, what is summarily called a nation's "Latin-American policy" involves attention to 89,100 continuing situations and several hundred thousand items of data. These figures were derived by positing "Latin America" as consisting of five basic types of units, each of which possesses three basic characteristics. Three of the units are to be found in nations, namely, their publics, their nongovernmental elites, and their officials. The other two units are of an international kind, one consisting of international organizations in which formalized interaction between nations takes place and the other of the unformalized interaction that comprises international relationships. The three characteristics of each unit are its attitudes, its behavior patterns, and its structure; attitudes refer to tendencies to act in a certain way, behavior patterns to the way attitudes are expressed in the form of concrete action, and structure to the patterns of interaction among the component parts of a unit or between one unit and other units in its environment.

If we now combine the units and their characteristics into a three-by-five matrix (see Table III–1), we can identify fifteen basic types of si⁺   ⸱s toward which policy-makers outside Latin America may have to act in attempting either to preserve prevailing attitudinal, behavioral, and structural patterns or to promote desired changes in them. Obviously, however, these 15 types are only the beginning of an adequate classification. If we make the simplifying assumption that the public of each nation consists of 4 elements—the active modernist, the passive modernist, the active traditionalist, and the passive traditionalist—then the first column of the matrix must be treated as 4 columns, giving rise to 12 types of situations involving publics. Assuming that each nation has 4 elite groups, the business, labor, religious, and military elites, each of which in turn is composed of traditionalists and modernists, then the second column of the matrix emerges as actually 8 columns, which, when combined with the 3 rows, result in 24 types of situations involving elites. Assuming further that it is meaningful to distinguish between the executive and the legislative officials of each nation, then we end up with 6 types of situations involving officials. If it is also presumed that as a minimum the activities of 3 individuals within each elite group and each segment of officialdom are particularly crucial to the course of events, then ninety "individual" situations must be included in the total.

If account is then taken of the fact that the 12 public situations, the 24 elite situations, the 6 official situations, and the 90 individual situations are to be found in 20 countries, it turns out that 2,640 national situations have constantly to be monitored by those who formulate and conduct a nation's policies toward Latin America. And to these 2,640 national situations must be added a wide variety of international ones. For illustrative purposes let us say that 10 international organizations, such as the Organization of American States, the World Bank, and the Alliance for Progress, are active in the region, and that each of the 20 nations has a discernible and significant unformalized relationship with 5 other nations in the hemisphere, thus giving rise to 100 international relationships in the region. In turn the 10 organizations and 100 relationships must be seen as having attitudinal, behavioral, and structural dimensions, so that 330 international situations must be added to the 2,640 national situations in order to get a more complete picture of the specific policy situations that are unfolding at any one time. Nor do these 2,970 situations tell the full story. At least one more simplifying assumption must be made—that all human affairs can be divided into 3 functional areas, the social, the economic, and the political— with the result that as a minimum "Latin America" consists of 8,910 basic situations that may be of concern to policy-makers abroad at any moment in time, and over which they must therefore attempt to exert influence.

Even the total of 8,910 situations, however, does not adequately describe the region as it appears to officials outside Latin America. For each

Table 4 – 1

	Publics	Elites	Officials	International Relationships	International Organizations
Attitudes					
Behavior					
Structure					

of these situations tends to overlap with a number of others. A riot in Venezuela can precipitate protests in Colombia. An election result in Chile can have consequences for Bolivia. Public unrest in Argentina can give rise to major changes in the foreign policies pursued by Argentine officialdom. A coup d'état in Peru can contribute to friction among the elites of Guatemala. Action against Cuba can drastically alter attitudes in the OAS. Inflation in Brazil can have structural implications for the Alliance for Progress. Indeed, if one makes the not unreasonable assumption that each of the 8,910 situations overlaps with at least 5 others, and if these overlapping situations are in themselves treated as situations, the total amounts to 44,550 situations.

And there is more. Whether or not officials outside Latin America regard their own actions as variables, certainly foreign policy analysts cannot ignore the feedback consequences of international behavior. Each situation at one moment in time has the potential of being altered at the next moment as a result of the foreign policy action directed toward it, so that if the analyst's concern extends across at least two moments in time, the 44,550 policy situations appear as 89,100 situations. Further complexity arises when it is recognized that three or four nations outside Latin America may seek to preserve or alter any of the situations within it, and that the degree of preservation or alteration can vary considerably depending upon whether political, economic, or military policies are directed at the situations. Consequently, from the perspective of the analyst examining the Latin American policy of one of the three or four nations during, say, a major era of international life, the 89,100 situations may actually consist of several hundred thousand data to be taken into account.

But one need not be overwhelmed by so much complexity. For the analyst who possesses a scientific consciousness, such complexity becomes an opportunity, and the existence of hundreds or thousands of data serves as a source of motivation and not of despair. He assumes they rest on an underlying order and regards discernment of this order as an endless challenge. He does not see the many data as capricious and beyond comprehension. He starts with the faith that none of them occurred by chance, but that all of them were brought into being by events that are at least theoretically knowable.[17] He can thus proceed with his attempts to move to higher

---

[17] By allowing for events that are "theoretically knowable," the scientist avoids being bound by the technology for testing hypotheses that may be available at a given time. Like other technologies, those of observation and measurement are not stagnant. Propositions that are unverifiable today may well be testable tomorrow (as those who once made forecasts about the far side of the moon will now happily affirm). Thus the foreign policy analyst need not be paralyzed by the fact that so many of the events in which he is interested occur in places to which he presently does not have access. He needs only to be certain that the data he seeks to predict

and higher levels of generalization, both supported and urged on by the firm belief that the multitude of reasons for the multitude of data can be subsumed under more encompassing explanations. In short, an analyst with a scientific orientation, far from being aghast at complexity such as that posed by the Latin American example, views it as a chance to trace larger patterns and build cumulative knowledge.

Yet there is no magic in science. Complexity does not automatically yield to an analyst's scientific approach. Unlike those who are not interested in going beyond impressionistic and broad assessments of what all the data appear to add up to, the scientist is committed to adhering to rigorous rules of procedure that require him to break the complexity down into its component parts before proceeding step by step up the ladder of generalization. He starts by asking what a few data are instances of, hoping thus to cumulate answers that will eventually reveal the pattern of which all the data are instances. Hence the analyst who proceeds scientifically as well as systematically resists the temptation to explain a nation's "Latin-American policy." For him Latin America poses not one but many research problems, each of which must be solved before all-encompassing generalizations can be offered.

The development of a scientific consciousness and acceptance of its philosophical underpinnings are not simple steps and require more than an acknowledgment of the complexity of foreign policy phenomena. Obviously, this acknowledgment must be accompanied by confidence that the complexity is surmountable, and this in turn depends on the availability of the basic ingredients of a scientific approach, namely, independent and dependent variables that are clearly differentiated, that have specified forms of variance, and that are, when brought together in testable hypotheses, appropriate to the questions that sustain the curiosity of researchers. If these fundamentals are lacking, it is difficult for researchers to maintain a scientific consciousness even if they recognize that the scientific approach does not preclude a concern for urgent policy problems and accept the fact that their subject matter is extremely complex. For the absence of clarity at this basic level hinders the derivation and accumulation of reliable findings that foster confidence in the potentialities of scientific inquiry and that discourage a return to case histories and broad assessments. Hindrances of this sort, it would seem, are a major cause of the present state of foreign policy research. There is little clarity about the prime variables of the field, and thus it is to an elucidation of these more subtle obstacles to the development of scientific consciousness that we now turn.

---

are theoretically capable of being observed, rather than being dependent on, say, divine revelation for confirmation.

IV. PROBLEMS OF THE DEPENDENT VARIABLE

The core of any hypothesis about human phenomena is the behavior that the researcher is seeking to comprehend and that is predicted to undergo change as conditions vary. This behavior constitutes the dependent variable of his hypotheses, and as such it not only must undergo changes that are capable of being observed and measured, but it must also be appropriate to the kind of knowledge being sought. If the behavior is too narrowly conceived, the observation and measurement of its variation under different conditions will yield findings that can never provide more than partial answers to the questions being asked. For example, the psychologist interested in social behavior is not likely to develop findings appropriate to his concerns if neurological reactions constitute the behavior he observes and measures. Such reactions may indeed vary in different individuals exposed to different social situations, but to increase comprehension of them is not to satisfy curiosity about interpersonal activity. Likewise, if the behavior is too broadly conceived, its observable variations will be so gross that the researcher will not be able to develop answers to his specific queries. The psychologist who casts all social behavior in terms of a cordial-hostile continuum is not likely to uncover many differentiated findings. Doubtless every social behavior could be located at some point along this continuum, but findings that depict how different people shift their location on it in response to various stimuli will also fail to alleviate the researcher's curiosity about the nuances of interpersonal activity.

The two prime dependent variables used in foreign policy research, decisions and policies, present problems of this order. The authoritative efforts of a national society to maintain control over its external environment through the preservation of desired situations abroad and the modification of undesired ones can be viewed as the central concern of foreign policy research,[18] and neither decisions nor policies appear to be appropriate forms of behavior in terms of which to develop knowledge about these authoritative efforts. Stated most succinctly, hypotheses that seek to predict decisional behavior are too narrow to provide more than partial comprehension of these efforts, and hypotheses that seek to predict policy behavior are too broad to provide incisive understanding of them. The limitations inherent in decisions as dependent variables can be readily grasped by noting that ordinarily a society must engage in a series of behaviors and not in a single behavior in order to preserve or alter a situation abroad. Other factors besides the society's efforts are at work in the situation, and many of these generate resistance to its efforts. Hence, not only must the

[18] For an extended formulation of this view of the nature of foreign policy, see Chapter 10.

behavior that initiated the effort be sustained through time, but new behaviors are needed in order to cope with the resistance it encounters as well as with other unexpected developments that occur as the situation evolves. The preservation or modification of situations abroad ordinarily does not depend on a single choice among alternative courses of action, but is a consquence of a series of decisions, each of which is in part a function of the outcomes of the previous decisions. However, as the concept of decision-making has developed in foreign policy research, it refers to activity at a particular moment in time and does not allow for the sequential nature of the behavior that initiates, sustains, and terminates foreign policy efforts. To be sure, decisions are not posited as instantaneous and allowance is made for the welter of activity and passage of time that precede choice, but once a decision is made, the dependent variable is presumed to have been observed and the analysis comes to an end. This is not to deny, of course, that the implementation of a decision will ordinarily produce effects requiring new decisions. Decision-making analysts acknowledge the relevance of outcomes by including the expected consequences of decisions among the independent variables that shape the choices made. But such a procedure is not the same as taking into account the ways in which the actual consequences abroad feed back into the foreign policy effort as it is unfolding. Usually these consequences are postponed for consideration in relation to a subsequent decision. As has already been indicated, however, the difficulty with such postponements is that researchers are seldom provoked to investigate the subsequent decisions of a sequence. It is thus hardly surprising that the cumulated findings generated by the decision-making approach to foreign policy have never been very substantial.[19] Confined to a single behavior and unconcerned with outcomes, findings based on decisions as variables can provide only partial answers to the questions that perplex foreign policy researchers.

Events in Vietnam after February 1965, when the United States decided to alter the situation through the use of bombers, provide a vivid illustration of the insufficiency of decisions as dependent variables What is analytically challenging about American behavior in that situation is not the bombing decision and the unwillingness of the North Vietnamese to alter their attitudes and behavior. The original bombing decision appears to have heightened this unwillingness and thereby necessitated a series of new choices, each of which further escalated the conflict and occasioned the necessity of another decision. An analysis in which any one of these decisions constitutes the dependent variable is thus ill designed to fulfill the aims of the foreign policy researcher. He is interested in explaining the

[19] For an elaboration of this point, see Chapter 12.

entire sequence of American behavior in the situation and thus needs dependent variables that are appropriate to such a concern.

Much the same can be said about the Latin-American example. Suppose the researcher is interested in predicting the behavior of a nation that, for the sake of its own security as well as for humanitarian reasons, aspires to the construction of stable polities and economies in Latin America. Assuming that the nation translates this aspiration into a decision to try to bring about such conditions, plainly the researcher would not be encompassing the phenomena of interest to him if he concentrated solely upon this decision. Nor would it be sufficient if the nation sought to alter or preserve the 89,100 situations in Latin America through one one-hundredth as many implementing decisions and the researcher were able to gather complete information on all of these. The cumulated findings derived from the 891 data would still be inappropriate to the hypotheses he wished to test. For again many of the implementing decisions would have a significant impact on many of the situations in Latin America and would thus create new conditions toward which new foreign policy efforts would have to be directed. Tempting as it might be for the researcher simply to project movement toward the original aspiration on the basis of the 891 data he had accumulated, not very much time would elapse before he realized that the bases of his projections no longer obtained and that his dependent variable failed to yield data adequate to explain the full sequence of behavior that engaged his interest in the first place. To be sure, some of his data might prove relevant to the understanding of future decisions, but he could not be sure which of the original decisions reflected firm commitments that would be reiterated as new situations evolved and which would be revised as a consequence of their own impact.

Perhaps out of recognition of the inherent limitations of decisions as dependent variables, many foreign policy researchers focus on policies as the behavior central to their inquiry. Conceived narrowly as the goals that a national society sets for itself with respect to aspects of its external environment and the actions that it has taken or will take in order to realize or maintain these goals, policies have the advantage of subsuming both decisions that initiate behavior and those that implement it. In this narrow sense, moreover, a focus on policies does not preclude analysis of the feedback of decisional outcomes and does not confine attention to activity at a single moment in time. Unfortunately, however, these possibilities are often overlooked when policies are actually used as dependent variables and a much broader conception tends to dominate their usage in research. In this conception, a policy designates a variety of unrelated goals and, consequently, a wide range of unrelated action sequences. This broader construction prevails because researchers tend to organize their inquiry around the aspect of a nation's external environment that interests them rather than around a goal it seeks to realize or a situation it seeks to alter or preserve. In part they do so because many of the environmental aspects are constants in a rapidly changing world. Unlike the goals and behavior that underlie foreign policy efforts, at least the environmental aspects have a location in geographic space and often have finite boundaries in time. Hence they seem to offer parameters within which the researcher can organize his inquiry. In fact, of course, this constancy is misleading in that it predisposes researchers to treat any and all actions that may be or are directed at a particular environmental aspect in the same context and as thus reflecting essentially the same policy. If, for example, Venezuela is the aspect of the United States' external environment that interests a researcher, then no matter how many U.S. pronouncements about or involvements in Venezuelan affairs he has investigated, he is likely to presume that the conclusions derived therefrom govern American goals and behavior with respect to any situations that may arise in Venezuela and that the United States may wish to preserve or alter. The result is likely to be an article entitled "United States Foreign Policy toward Venezuela," which purports (at least implicitly) to encompass the totality of American relations with that country and tends to discount the variance in those relations. If the researcher's interests are continental in scope, then he presents his findings in a volume on "United States Foreign Policy toward Latin America," which moves even further from empirical phenomena and collapses unrelated goals and behavior sequences into an even more general totality. Nor does this exhaust the possibilities in the broad construction of the concept. A number of researchers have interests that are global in scope, and have filled many library shelves with treatises on, simply, "United States Foreign Policy," which offer relatively few examples in support of a broad discussion of the values and behavorial norms that guide American efforts toward any situation abroad that requires preservation or alteration.

In short, in their most common usage as dependent variables, policies have no fixed behavioral boundaries and are so variable, amorphous, and all-encompassing that the findings they yield obscure variance and defy cumulation. While it is at least logically (if not empirically) possible to identify decisions in terms of the activity that initiates, sustains, and terminates them, such is not the case with policies broadly conceived. The basic structure of the behavior they subsume cannot be inferred from findings descriptive of them. Indeed, behavior is not even a necessary component of policy variables. Often analysts refer to policies that consist not of concrete action, but of commitments or attitudes that might be translated into action if new situations arise abroad which warrant it. Clearly a scientific consciousness is difficult to develop if the phenomena one is inclined to predict have no empirical referents. If researchers are to acquire the habit of hypothesizing, they ought to have available dependent variables that have at least a theoretically observable structure, that are not as limiting as decisions and not as encompassing as policies, and that can cumulatively provide the kind of findings appropriate to the testing of hypotheses and to the questions that stimulate foreign policy researchers.

One obvious solution to the need for more appropriate dependent variables is to insist that hypotheses be founded upon the narrow conception of a policy. As previously noted, this narrow construction has a number of advantages and it does seem to be suitable to the interests of researchers. Such a solution, however, would quickly founder. The broad conception of policy is too deeply ingrained in the terminology and analytic habits of the field to be simply put aside. The distinction between the narrow and broad conception could thus not be maintained for long, and the present state of inquiry would soon be reestablished. Hence, while recognizing that analytic habit is not necessarily altered by terminological innovation, the last section of this chapter offers the *undertaking* as a variable that meets the needs of foreign policy research.

V. PROBLEMS OF THE INDEPENDENT VARIABLE

If the behaviors through which national societies initiate, sustain, and terminate efforts to preserve or alter situations constitute the dependent variables of foreign policy research, the independent variables are all those factors that shape these behaviors and determine the variance. Elsewhere we have suggested that these can be usefully subdivided into five main types—individual, role, governmental, societal, and systemic—and that an assessment of the relative potency or causal strength of each type is necessary to hypothesizing about the foreign policy behavior that is likely to occur under specific conditions.[20] The step from the identification of relevant types of independent variables to the specification of those within each type and the operationalization of their variance is not an easy one to take. A host of problems must be solved, and appropriateness and clarity are again important criteria. Variables must be appropriate in the sense that they account for enough of the foreign policy behavior to justify the researcher's efforts, and they must be marked by clarity in the sense that their variance is ranged along meaningful and observable dimensions. There is some evidence, for example, that foreign policy behavior is more

20 See Chapter 6.

likely to occur in the summer than at other times of the year,[21] but the relative potency of the seasonal variable is probably so low that further efforts to refine it would be inappropriate.[22] Similarly, the nature of a society's political structure is presumably highly relevant to its external behavior, but such a presumption must be translated into clear-cut degrees or kinds of relevance before political structure can be used as an independent variable in researchable hypotheses.

While the task of identifying and operationalizing the more "robust" of the independent variables is an urgent one, an effort to carry it forward requires more time than is available here.[23] Two problems that will probably prove especially difficult to solve, however, can usefully be flagged. One of them in particular seems so insurmountable that it is no doubt a major barrier to the development of a scientific consciousness in foreign policy research. This is what might be called the feedback problem. It stems from the fact that foreign policy research is concerned with independent variables that unfold through time and it arises most acutely in the case of societal and systemic variables. Both within and outside the society that initiates a foreign policy undertaking, events occur or situations emerge as it unfolds that are sufficiently potent to feed back into the undertaking as determinants of its future course. These feedback variables can be reactions to the undertaking or they can occur quite independently of it. An undertaking may precipitate the fall of a cabinet abroad or stimulate the rise of an opposition party at home; or it may be in progress when a U-2 is downed, a Stalin dies, a Middle Eastern war erupts, a common market is formed, or a new president is elected. These are typical of the many types of developments that can operate as potent independent variables after the undertaking has been initiated. The goals of the undertaking remain essentially the same, but the path of action toward them may be altered as a consequence of feedback. In effect, therefore, the foreign policy researcher must look at independent variables that are operative during as well as prior to the behavior he seeks to explain. Stated in still another way, some of the independent and dependent varia-

---

[21] Johan Galtung, "Summit Meetings and International Relations," *Journal of Peace Research*, 1 (1964), pp. 36–54.

[22] The location of the cutoff between an appropriate and inappropriate variable could be derived on the basis of statistical criteria. Correlations over .30 or .40 are usually regarded as significant by those who employ statistical methods. Since correlations of this order account for roughly 10 or 12 percent of the variance, it is reasonable to view any variable that accounts for less than this amount of the observed foreign policy behavior as inappropriate. Surely seasonal variables do not exceed the cutoff point.

[23] For an account of a collective effort to operationalize key variables, see James N. Rosenau, Philip M. Burgess, and Charles F. Hermann, "The Adaptation of Foreign Policy Research: A Case Study of an Anti-Case Study Project," *International Studies Quarterly*, Vol. 17 (March 1973), pp. 119-44.

bles are concurrent in time even though it is necessary for the researcher to treat them as analytically separable.[24]

Plainly feedback processes greatly complicate foreign policy research. They require that the analyst be able not only to predict how the national society of interest to him will respond to stimuli, but also to anticipate internal and external reactions to its behavior in order to know what feedback processes will be operative as independent variables. Stated in terms of the Latin American example, the researcher must not only comprehend the decision-making dynamics of the society whose undertakings toward Latin America he seeks to explain and predict, but also have some knowledge about decision-making phenomena in the twenty national societies of that region in order to allow for new events or trends that will significantly deflect, slow, or otherwise affect the undertakings as they unfold.

Yet the complexity introduced by feedback variables is not as awesome as it might appear.[25] While there can be no doubt that the tasks of foreign policy research are made more difficult by the need to account for independent variables of this sort, there are several mitigating considerations. One is the aforementioned point that the researcher need be concerned only with robust variables. Many phenomena can therefore be ignored. To take on the task of tracing feedback is not to be required to account for every response that a foreign policy undertaking is likely to generate or for every development abroad or at home that may occur as it unfolds. Only those responses or events that may significantly affect the path of action followed by the undertaking need be the focus of concern. Presumably these will not be so great in number and variety as to make the problem unmanageable. Not every cabinet that falls abroad or every opposition party that arises at home can deflect, slow, or otherwise affect an undertaking. All twenty societies of Latin America may react to a particular aspect of an undertaking, but this does not mean that the analyst has to investigate all twenty situations. Conceivably none of the twenty reactions will be sufficient to have a major impact upon the undertaking.

24 For an extended discussion of the operation and analysis of feedback processes in political systems, see Karl W. Deutsch, *The Nerves of Government: Models of Political Communication and Control* (New York: Free Press, 1963), Chap. 11.

25 For an account of procedures that further reduce the awesomeness of tracing and assessing feedback processes in political research, see Herbert A. Simon, "Political Research: The Decision-Making Framework," in David Easton (ed.), *Varieties of Political Theory* (Englewood Cliffs, N.J.: Prentice-Hall, 1966), pp. 22–23. For a rare work that demonstrates that feedback variables in foreign policy can be empirically analyzed, see Charles A. McClelland, "Decisional Opportunity and Political Controversy: The Quemoy Case," *Journal of Conflict Resolution,* 6 (September 1962), pp. 201–213.

Or perhaps the reactions of only two or three of the larger Latin American societies will serve as significant feedbacks.

Second, and relatedly, it must be remembered that much of the knowledge required to anticipate and account for feedback processes has to be acquired anyway. The very societal and systemic variables that are likely to be significant during an undertaking are also likely to be among those that would be deemed sufficiently robust to warrant investigation prior to its initiation. The stability of the governments in the region toward which an undertaking is directed, for example, is likely to be treated as a potent systemic variable under any circumstances, so the fact that one or more of them may fall as the undertaking unfolds does not introduce a new analytic dimension into the researcher's inquiry. He has already allowed for the processes represented by the cabinet collapse and thus is prepared to handle it as an independent variable at any stage of the undertaking. Similarly, public sentiments and political processes at home will undoubtedly be regarded as potent societal variables underlying the initiation of any foreign policy undertaking. Hence the emergence of an opposition party as a response to a particular undertaking ought not to introduce independent variables that the researcher is not equipped to analyze. In terms of the Latin American example, if an undertaking designed to generate viable politics and economies in that region is significantly deflected and slowed because of the resistance to change of nongovernmental elites in all twenty countries, it is highly unlikely that the researcher will be caught unaware. Doubtless he will have already operationalized elite attitudes as a potent independent variable and ranged them along a resistant-receptive continuum. Consequently, if he has based his original hypotheses on essentially receptive attitudes, he does not need to develop new knowledge or conceptualize new variables to take the feedback into account. All that is required are revised hypotheses in which the resistant end of the elite attitude scale is accorded greater potency.

Nor need improbable developments—such as the downing of a U-2 or the death of a Stalin—which are entirely unrelated to undertakings, but which nevertheless operate as potent independent variables, be viewed as an unmanageable feedback problem. The death of a leader and the collapse of a spy mission may not be predictable in their precise historical form, but their consequences can be included in the range across which the researcher's dependent variables are conceived to be operative. Some leadership deaths and some exposed spy missions will profoundly affect the character of an undertaking, whereas others will have no impact upon its path and pace whatsoever. In order to ensure that these polar consequences of improbable events are included in the variance of the variables, the researcher can at least pose a kind of null hypothesis by asking, "Under what circumstances will an undertaking be substantially set back?" or, pressing nullity still further, "What unforeseen developments can lead to its abandonment?" and then take account of even the seemingly absurd answers in the framing of his variables.[26]

Another noteworthy problem of the independent variable, and one made especially acute by the analytic recognition given to feedback processes, concerns the phenomena that are often called "policy contents" and that seem more precisely designated as "issue-area" phenomena. Stated most succinctly, these refer to the kind of values over which an issue is waged and toward which a policy is directed. Evidence is mounting that the values at stake in a conflict operate as sources of the behavior of the parties to it; that individuals, officials, and groups behave differently in different issue areas; and that therefore the dynamics of political processes and political systems vary from one issue area to another. In short, the contents of a policy, or, in the terminology used below, the goals of an undertaking, are in themselves independent variables, both as they stimulate initial behavior on the part of officials and publics and as they feed back into the ensuing actions.[27]

Although much remains to be done by way of identifying and exploring the kinds of domestic policy issues that can be clustered together into empirically meaningful discrete areas, the task has not even been launched with respect to foreign policy issues. There is a widespread assumption that foreign policy questions evoke different forms and degrees of behavior than do domestic ones, but the common elements of the former type and the ways in which they might be fruitfully subdivided have been the subject of only the most impressionistic speculation.[28] Whereas elaborate typologies of the values that may be at work in domestic situations are available,[29] no equivalent materials have been developed for the classification and analysis of foreign policy undertakings.[30] Not even such commonplace categories as left, center, and right, or radical and conservative, appear usable as an initial basis for thinking along these lines. Whereas the char-

26 To recur to an earlier example (see note 6 above), Khrushchev may not have known he was going to be ousted, but Brzezinski could have operationalized the variance of his variables in a way that allowed for such a development.

27 For a general formulation of the issue-area concept, see Chapters 6 and 17.

28 A recent example is provided in Chapter 17.

29 See, for example, Ernest A. T. Barth and Stuart D. Johnson, "Community Power and a Typology of Social Issues," Social Forces, 38 (October 1959), pp. 29–32; Seymour Martin Lipset, "The Value Patterns of Democracy: A Case Study in Comparative Analysis," American Sociological Review, 28 (August 1963), pp. 515–31; Robin M. Williams, Jr., "Individual and Group Values," Annals of the American Academy of Political and Social Science, 371 (May 1967), pp. 20–37; Lewis A. Froman, "The Categorization of Policy Contents," in Austin Ranney (ed.), Political Science and Public Policy (Chicago: Markham, 1968), Chap. 3.

30 However, Harold Sprout is presently engaged in an attempt to classify

acterization of domestic policies in terms of these distinctions conveys at least a modicum of meaning, their application to foreign policies invariably is more confounding than clarifying, and it is a measure of both the neglect and the complexity of the problem that no better distinctions of this crude sort have been developed.

To be sure, researchers have not totally ignored the content dimension of foreign policy behavior. Classifications of policies do exist, but they usually consist of the means employed to satisfy values rather than the values themselves. Often, for example, distinctions are made among economic, military, and diplomatic means, and their utilization is presumed to connote the operation of similarly separable values. Indeed, it would seem that military policy has evolved into a separate field of research, with courses taught and texts written on the subject, but without any effort to test empirically the underlying assumption that all undertakings founded on the use or threat of military instruments have common characteristics that operate in similar and significant ways.[31] Such assumptions, however, are clearly premature. Values do attach to the means employed in foreign policy, and these may be sufficiently potent to have a significant impact on behavior, but there is no evidence that distinctions based on the instruments of policy subsume meaningful differences in international behavior. A nation can either fight for or negotiate over the same value, and the question is thus one of differentiating between the values that elicit fighting and those that foster negotiating behavior. Posing the problem more explicitly, do foreign policy undertakings directed at, say, disarmament matters have certain common dimensions that are not shared by undertakings concerned with recognition of geographic boundaries? Are the latter in turn differentiable from issues pertaining to the population explosion or to the building of viable political institutions? At what level or levels of generalization, in other words, should issues be clustered together and treated as independent variables?

Answers to questions such as these are urgently needed not only because issue areas seem likely to be robust independent variables. A greater comprehension of such matters also appears central to the development of scientific consciousness. At least it seems reasonable to assert that the lack of even the crudest categories for classifying foreign policy issues greatly inhibits the inclination to search for underlying patterns in international behavior. At present there is a tendency for researchers to think in terms of issues rather than issue areas, and to assume that each issue

---

"national goals in foreign policy and international politics," using a distinction between substantive (or core) and instrumental values as the point of departure.

[31] For a lonely exception, see Bernard C. Cohen, "The Military Policy Public," *Public Opinion Quarterly*, 30 (Summer 1966), pp. 200–11.

is different from every other issue, an assumption that negates the possibility of asking, "Of what is this an instance?" and that inevitably leads to the idiographic case study.

VI. THE CONCEPT OF THE UNDERTAKING

Let us conclude on an innovative note. We have criticized the present state of research for lacking hypotheses or even analytic tools that would foster a readiness to frame, test, and revise hypotheses. Yet identifying problems is not the same as solving them. To decry the shortage of conceptual equipment that permits foreign policy behavior to be treated as sequential through time and that allows for the operation of feedback processes is not to offer a constructive suggestion for developing such equipment. Most notably, it is not to offer a behavioral entity that has a temporal dimension, that subsumes independent feedback variables even as it also serves as an adequate dependent variable, and that recurs with sufficient frequency to be cumulated and yield (or fail to yield) patterns that confirm (or fail to confirm) hypotheses. In order to demonstrate that such tools of science can be fashioned and manipulated by the foreign policy researcher, therefore, the remainder of this paper outlines what appears to be an appropriate behavioral entity and indicates how it might be used.[32]

We shall refer to this basic entity as the *undertaking,* since this label connotes the serial, purposeful, and coordinative nature of foreign policy behavior. To anticipate the presentation that follows, undertakings are what foreign policy researchers observe, what they trace in case histories and measure in quantitative studies, what they attempt to analyze and explain, what they represent in their models and predict in their hypotheses.

---

[32] An initial hesitation about the wisdom of suggesting the addition of yet another concept to the field was overcome when it was learned that understanding, if not research, had been advanced by the introduction of similar concepts into another discipline that was—and still is—faced with problems comparable to those confronting foreign policy research. Indeed, although developed independently, the formulation presented here closely parallels the essays of two psychologists, Murray and Sears, who argued that the single action (or S-R) was an inappropriate entity for the study of social behavior, that it failed to account for the interactive and temporal dimensions of an individual's comportment, and that therefore new conceptual entities had to be developed. Murray called his entity the "interpersonal proceeding" and Sears referred to his as the "dyadic unit," and taken together their essays make a persuasive case for the procedure of using fresh terminology and concepts to rethink the stubborn and enduring problems of a field. See Henry A. Murray, "Toward a Classification of Interaction," and Robert R. Sears, "Social Behavior and Personality Development," in Talcott Parsons and Edward A. Shils (eds.), *Toward a General Theory of Action* (Cambridge, Mass.: Harvard University Press, 1952), pp. 434–78.

An undertaking is conceived to be a course of action that the duly constituted officials of a national society pursue in order to preserve or alter a situation in the international system in such a way that it is consistent with a goal or goals decided upon by them or their predecessors.[33] An undertaking begins when a situation arises abroad that officials seek to maintain or change. It is sustained as long as the resources of the society mobilized and directed by the officials continue to be applied to the situation. It terminates either when the situation comes to an end and obviates the need for further action or when officials conclude that their action cannot alter or preserve the situation and abandon their efforts. Undertakings thus can be small scale or large scale. They can require the negotiations of a single ambassador, the activities of a vast bureaucracy, or the endeavors of a mobile army. They can extend across months or years, countries or continents, crises or stalemates. They can be directed at individuals or groups, political parties or social structures, nations or regions, enemies or allies. They can be sustained through continued activity or intermittent involvement, through conflict or cooperation, through military threat or diplomatic overture.

In other words, undertakings, unlike policies and decisions, encompass goals *and* their implementation. Their distinctive quality is that they focus on what government does, not on how it decides to do it or on what it commits itself to do. Whereas it is possible for the student of policies to find the phenomena that interest him exclusively in a speech or statute, the single document can never suffice as evidence for the student of undertakings. The commitment to action reflected in the speech and the decision reflected in the statute may bear little resemblance to what in fact transpires as governments undertake to alter or preserve their external environments, and it is this analytic gap that a focus on undertakings seeks to bridge. In effect, by examining a bounded sequence of actions and reactions across a span of time and in a situational context, undertakings fuse commitments with their enactment, decisions with their outcomes, resources with their utilization.

Although undertakings involve varied types of activity, they have specifiable analytic boundaries. These are defined in terms of the behavior, decisional and implementive, associated with the pursuit of goals in concrete situations. The key to the operational identification of undertakings lies not in their goals, but in the situations they are designed to affect.

---

[33] Although cast in terms of foreign policy, obviously the concept is equally applicable to the analysis of domestic policy. Whether officials seek to preserve or alter situations abroad or at home, they engage in sequences of behavior that are here regarded as undertakings. Indeed, given the greater availability of data on domestic decisional and feedback processes, it could be argued that the concept is especially suitable to internal "policy" phenomena.

The empirical referents of situations, conflicts over the prevailing structure of relationships, are readily recognizable. The actors who are parties to a situation, the time at which the actors begin to dispute and seek change in the prevailing structure, the geographic space in which the structure is located, and the point at which action ends and the conflict ceases are all manifest phenomena and thus accessible to the researcher. Tracing the temporal, spatial, and functional boundaries of a war in Vietnam, a coup d'état in Peru, the establishment of new missile sites in Cuba, a worsening balance of payments, restlessness on the part of Jordanian refugees, a blockade in Berlin—to mention but a few obvious examples—is not an insurmountable problem even though the time, location, and behavior encompassed by the various situations differ considerably. Goals, on the other hand, pose an enormously complex challenge to the empiricist. Frequently they are cast in highly abstract terms. At other times they are not articulated by the actors and have to be inferred from behavior. Sometimes the articulated goals are not the true ones and are designed to mislead. Almost always, moreover, goals undergo modification as the situations toward which they are directed evolve. The overall commitment to preserving or altering a situation is not likely to change, but the dynamics of the situation will usually require acceptance of greater or lesser degrees of preservation or alteration than were anticipated. Thus it would seem that as long as undertakings are defined in terms of situational rather than goal referents, the danger that they will come to be used in the broad and amorphous way that marks the usage of the policy concept will be minimized.

To be sure, the danger is never eliminated. The empirical referents are not always mutually exclusive and unmistakable. Undertakings do overlap and situations are interdependent, so that to a certain extent the delineation of their boundaries is necessarily arbitrary. Hence there will always be the temptation to define situations and undertakings in such a general way that their temporal, spatial, and functional referents are obscure and ambiguous. From one perspective, for example, it might seem useful to regard the state of world order as a single situation and to treat all the diverse activities designed to preserve or promote peace as one grand undertaking. Plainly such a formulation renders the undertaking as unusable as the policy. A major purpose of adopting the undertaking as a unit of analysis is to facilitate the cumulation of numerous and discrete data, each consisting of meaningful and comparable sequences of behavior. To generate such data, therefore, the researcher must err in the direction of specificity rather than generality when exercising the arbitrariness that is inherent in the delineation of the boundaries of situations and undertakings. This means that he must maximize precision with respect to all three types of empirical referents—temporal, spatial, and functional. If, for example, he is precise only about the spatial referents, but ignores the temporal and functional ones, the danger of excessive generality looms large and the ability to differentiate dependent variables that can be subjected to hypothesis testing is correspondingly reduced. Viewed spatially, Latin America can be seen as one situation and efforts to promote its stability can constitute a single undertaking. Viewed functionally as well as spatially, it can approach 44,550 situations and, as noted, this figure can rise to 89,100 when the temporal dimension is introduced. Or take the example of postwar Berlin. Its spatial referent is unmistakable, but temporally it has been the scene of several international conflicts separated by many years during which a prevailing structure was accepted by the parties to the conflicts. Hence, to ignore the temporal dimension and treat postwar Berlin as one continuous situation is to obfuscate variability in foreign policy behavior. When the Soviet Union undertook to alter, and the United States to preserve, the arrangements of that beleaguered city in 1948–49, both societies framed goals, developed strategies, mobilized resources, applied pressures, and reacted to countermoves in ways that differed substantially from their behavior in the Berlin conflict of 1961–62. The latter constituted a new undertaking for both societies, in part because the 1948–49 episode added a historical precedent that had not existed in the earlier conflict. Similarly, opportunities to cumulate findings and observe variance will be missed if precision is maintained with respect to the temporal dimension but not with respect to the other two. If, for example, the "Camp David" period of Soviet-American relations, running from the Khrushchev-Eisenhower meeting of September 1959 to the U-2 incident of May 1960, is treated as a single situation, then a variety of functionally unrelated efforts to preserve or alter arrangements in diverse parts of the world that were undertaken during the eight-month period might be falsely subsumed under the larger effort to maintain a cordial relationship and thus overlooked as discrete data.

If we assume that the operational utility of undertakings can be maintained by the rule of erring on the side of specificity, the question arises of how they are to be used as dependent variables. What variance in undertakings, that is, is the student of foreign policy interested in? Suppose that the researcher has gathered data on a thousand foreign policy undertakings of each of sixteen national societies: what aspects of these data should his hypotheses seek to predict? Suppose further that the sixteen societies consisted of eight that were large and eight that were small, with four of each of the eight having open polities and four having closed polities, and with two of each of the clusters of four having developed economies and two having underdeveloped economies: what patterns within the thousand undertakings of each society would the researcher want to identify in order to make comparisons among the societies and thereby assess the role of such independent variables as physical size, political structure, and economic development? While an elaborate attempt to answer questions such as these cannot be essayed here, the need for a clear specification of dependent variables is so essential to the fostering of a scientific consciousness that it seems useful to suggest a few aspects of undertakings that may be worth pursuing as dependent variables.

Perhaps the most easily measured dependent variable is the *duration* of an undertaking. The time that elapses from the inception to the conclusion or abandonment of an effort to alter or preserve a situation abroad can be established without too much difficulty and readily lends itself to comparative analysis. To a certain extent, of course, duration is a function of the nature of the situation that officials undertake to affect. It took much less time to get missiles out of Cuba than it has taken to build political institutions in Vietnam, partly because the scope and dynamics of the situation were much less complex in Cuba than they are in Vietnam. Nevertheless, presumably variance in the duration of undertakings is also a function of some of the independent variables of interest to foreign policy researchers. In part, for example, it may be a reflection of capabilities, of the ability of a society to cope with its external environment. If one has data on a thousand undertakings in each of sixteen societies, it seems reasonable to assume that the impact of situational differences will be greatly reduced, thus allowing one to hypothesize that the average duration of undertakings will be appreciably less in large developed societies than in large underdeveloped societies, and that both types of large societies, being able to draw upon more resources, will be able to conclude their undertakings significantly more quickly than small underdeveloped societies. The duration of undertakings may also reflect political structure and political style. It might be hypothesized that closed polities have greater flexibility in foreign policy than open ones and can thus abandon their undertakings more swiftly, a proposition that is readily testable through the duration variable and our hypothesized data bank. Similarly, researchers who have notions about how certain societies differ in their style of statecraft might treat the duration variable as a measure of foreign policy skill and hypothesize that large developed societies with a cumbersome style will record a pattern of significantly longer undertakings than will similar societies with a polished style.

Another dependent variable that presents a minimum of measurement difficulties is what might be called the *undertaking potential:* the number of undertakings that a society is capable of launching and sustaining at any one time. It would be a simple matter, given the data on a thousand undertakings of sixteen societies, to calculate a rate of undertakings per month (UPM) for each society and thereby to test propositions about the potency of certain independent variables. A number of hypotheses along this line readily come to mind. Presumably, for example, geographic position affects the UPM; the more landlocked a national society is and the more neighbors it has, the greater its UPM. A small insular society would thus be hypothesized to have a significantly lower UPM than a small continental one. Even more provocative are the possibilities of using the UPM to measure, compare, and trace the changing position of societies in the international system, the basic hypothesis being that the more a society exercises leadership in the system, the more situations it will be inclined to become involved in, and thus the higher its UPM at any point in time and the greater the increase in its UPM through time. Still another use of the UPM might be to assess the potency of industrialization as an independent variable. It seems reasonable to hypothesize that the more industrialized a society is, the more complex will be its governmental bureaucracy and, consequently, the greater will be its capacity to sustain a high number of undertakings simultaneously. In operational terms, it appears reasonable to predict a very high correlation between the UPM and, say, the per capita income figures for the sixteen societies.

Although somewhat more difficult to operationalize, a third dependent variable that seems worthy of investigation is what might be called the *direction* of undertakings. Here we have in mind a dichotomous variable that distinguishes between those undertakings designed to preserve and those designed to alter existing situations abroad. If we assume that a satisfactory method could be devised to classify every undertaking as either essentially preservative or essentially promotive—an assumption that does not seem unwarranted—the directional variable could be used to probe the potency of societal factors as a source of foreign policy behavior. For example, it seems reasonable to hypothesize that dynamic societies—those undergoing rapid social change—are likely to engage in significantly more promotive undertakings than preservative ones, whereas exactly the opposite prediction could reasonably be made for static societies. Likewise, the relative strength of ideology and the "national interest" as independent variables might be explored through hypotheses that linked the former to promotive undertakings and the latter to preservative ones.

Other aspects of undertakings that might be pursued as dependent variables are their *scope* (are they directed at individuals, groups, nations, or regions?), their *stability* (do they exhibit constancy of purpose?), their *cost* (how extensive are the human and nonhuman resources they employ?), and their *contents* (are they concerned with the disposition of goods, territory, status, or welfare?). Variables such as these, of course, are based on less tangible phenomena. They would thus be considerably more difficult to operationalize, and the classification of undertakings in these terms would probably not result in as high a degree of intercoder reliability as would the use of the dependent variables outlined in the previous three paragraphs. But, at this stage, all that is needed is a satisfactory level of reliability — say, 75 percent or better — to provide confidence that the characteristics of phenomena rather than the quirks of coders are being measured. If such a level could be achieved in the case of these less tangible variables, many other stimulating hypotheses could be developed and tested.

Our task here, however, is not that of specifying and perfecting variables. Rather it is to show how their use might lead to the accumulation of knowledge about foreign policy that will satisfy both the curiosity of the researcher and the needs of the policy-maker. Hopefully the foregoing is sufficient to show that, if time and energy are invested in the development of appropriate variables, the predominance of a scientific consciousness can pay off as handsomely in foreign policy research as it has in other fields.

APPENDIX: AN ANALYSIS OF SEVEN CASE STUDIES

Although this chapter does not test, with a systematic content analysis of the extant literature, the impressions it presents of the state of foreign policy research, in all fairness some evidence needs to be provided to support the charge that the available materials are not cumulative and are conspicuously lacking in a consciousness of scientific method. What follows is a brief analysis of seven case studies in the field. These may not constitute a representative sample, but each case is a thorough, recent, and widely read study. If a scientific consciousness is more prevalent than alleged here, presumably it should be apparent in these cases. Our procedure is to examine the concluding sections of each case to determine whether the described sequence of events was viewed as an instance of a more general class of phenomena and, if so, whether normative propositions, instrumental policy recommendations, and/or empirical hypotheses were derived from it. If our indictment is excessive, this procedure should yield at the very least a few empirical hypotheses.

Being lengthy and thorough, Van Dyke's account of the evolution of the United States space program serves as a good point of departure.[34] Stressing that neither the rational-comprehensive nor the successful limited-

[34] Vernon Van Dyke, *Pride and Power: The Rationale of the Space Program* (Urbana: University of Illinois Press, 1964).

comparison method of decision-making [35] is depicted by his account, Van Dyke's final chapter suggests rather that the space program corresponds to those rare but important situations (such as Pearl Harbor or Korea) in which the end values are so crucial that they overwhelm and replace a rational or incremental approach to the choices that have to be made. Van Dyke posits three values, national security, national prestige, and national pride, as values that are powerful enough to govern behavior in this way and, in the final five pages of the book, addresses himself to the question of which of the three his case history is an instance. His answer, based mainly on his "reading of events" associated with the May 1961 decision greatly to enlarge the space program, is that the last of them was the crucial one: "As I reconstruct the situation, there was no call for rational-comprehensive analysis, and not much call for a comparison of possible ends or values. A few values of very great importance were at stake, pride above all." [36] Van Dyke does not moralize about the legitimacy of pride as a basis for a policy or make recommendations for the improvement of the space program. Neither does he speculate about the operation of pride as an independent variable in other situations or in relation to the other variables that he discounts as inadequate to explain the space program. The concluding chapter does not claim to have tested any explicit hypotheses and offers no new ones derived from the inquiry. It simply provides an overall assessment of why the behavior and events unfolded as they did. To be sure, having earlier noted that "a value provides motivation mainly when it is in jeopardy," [37] in the very last paragraph of the book Van Dyke implicitly hypothesizes that the more national pride achieves satisfaction, the less potent will it be as a source of behavior. Explicitly, however, he only correlates the success of the space probes with diminution of enthusiasm for the program, a correlation that says nothing about the kind of situations in which pride is likely to be a governing value or the consequences that different degrees of jeopardy to it are likely to have for the decision-making process. In effect, although Van Dyke's scientific consciousness was sufficient to lead him to ask of what larger pattern the 1961 space decision was an instance—as a result making us more aware of values as a source of behavior and more appreciative of the possibility that pride can be a powerful variable—it was not enough to stimulate him to take the next step and make his findings testable in other situations and thus capable of being integrated into a larger research enterprise.

[35] As described in Charles E. Lindblom, "The Science of 'Muddling Through,'" *Public Administration Review*, 19 (Spring 1959), pp. 79–88.

[36] Van Dyke, *Pride and Power*, p. 272.

[37] *Ibid.*, p. 179.

Since it focuses on matters that recur annually, any case history in which the U.S. appropriations process figures prominently should perhaps be especially conducive to the generation of hypotheses and the operation of a scientific consciousness. Hence let us now examine two cases with this characteristic—Schilling's extensive inquiry into the making of the 1950 defense budget [38] and Haviland's detailed account of the foreign aid program in 1957.[39] Certainly the former is not lacking in speculation. In a fifty-two-page concluding chapter Schilling undertakes to analyze and explain what he regards as the main finding revealed by his case history, namely, that the defense budget exercises a " 'gyroscopic' effect . . . on the content of foreign policy," since "Congress and Executive alike have tended to spin along at the same general level of expenditure year after year in spite of rather startling developments elsewhere in the nation's security position." [40] Two sets of independent variables are posited as the sources of the "gyroscopic tendencies" in 1950. One is "the structure of the policy process," with its "tendency . . . to be leaderless," and the resulting need for bargaining and consensus building. The other is the content of the ideas that comprised "the prevailing climate of opinion" with respect to defense budgeting. Although Schilling evidences some degree of scientific consciousness by devoting a number of pages to speculation about how changes in the structure of the policy process and in the four main ideas constituting the climate of opinion would have altered "the kind of choices made in the fiscal 1950 budget," he does not bring the analysis to a scientific conclusion with hypotheses that take advantage of his analysis and predict the outcome of budget-making in subsequent years. Rather the purpose of the inquiry turns out to be an evaluation of the adequacy of the policy-making process, and the only hypotheses to emerge are essentially normative propositions about the desirability of maximizing rationality and reducing the influence of the military over budgetary decisions. To be sure, by suggesting that both the structure of the policy-making process and the climate of opinion in which it unfolds are essentially resistant to change, Schilling's interpretation contains the empirical prediction that it is "unrealistic to expect" subsequent defense budgets to be any more responsive to the requirements of foreign policy than was the case in 1950.[41] Such a prediction, however, does not constitute a fruitful scientific hypothesis inasmuch as it treats the variables as constants. Having

[38] Warner R. Schilling, "The Politics of National Defense: Fiscal 1950," in Warner R. Schilling, Paul Y. Hammond, and Glenn H. Snyder, *Strategy, Politics, and Defense Budgets* (New York: Columbia University Press, 1962), pp. 1–266.

[39] H. Field Haviland, Jr., "Foreign Aid and the Policy Process: 1957," *American Political Science Review*, 52 (September 1958), pp. 689–724.

[40] Schilling, "Politics of National Defense," p. 220.

[41] *Ibid.*, p. 239.

concluded that the determinants of the gyroscopic effect are resistant to change, Schilling does not allow for variance in their potencies and thus does not speculate about the extent to which differential budgetary responses would result from structural or opinion changes within the policy-making process or from profound shifts in the structure of the international system. Hence, while his case history raises a number of interesting questions and provides insightful glimpses into the dynamics of foreign policy, it offers little guidance for interpreting or anticipating, say, the budgetary episodes of the 1960s, by which time a substantial streamlining of the structure of the National Security Council and the Department of Defense had been accomplished, a thoroughgoing revision in attitudes toward budget-making and most of the other major foci of the climate of opinion had taken place, and a wholesale alteration of conditions abroad, including the balance of nuclear weapons and the coherence of the two great alliance systems, had occurred. Even in terms of its own purpose of assessing the adequacy of the policy-making process, in other words, Schilling's case is now obsolete. It is good, even superior, history and as such serves to heighten one's sense of the problems that arise in a political system marked by a wide dispersion of responsibility, but instrumentally and scientifically it can only be regarded as obsolete—not because it deals with events that occurred long ago or because the world has changed since 1950, but because in interpreting the events it did not place them in the larger context of a range of possibilities that could take the changes since 1950 into account.

Although explicitly inclined to treat his case as an instance of a larger pattern and to assess the consistency of his findings with those uncovered by other researchers, Haviland's inquiry into the 1957 foreign aid debate also lacks the essentials of an analytical approach that is scientific as well as systematic. He recognizes that "the annually recurring debate over foreign aid" permits the holding of "a stethoscope . . . to the heart of the United States foreign policy process," and accordingly indicates that his purpose in recounting what happened in 1957 includes shedding "some light . . . on the foreign policy process in general." [42] Carrying through on this commitment, Haviland devotes most of his concluding section to systematically comparing the 1957 episode "with the results of other analyses." [43] In particular, three findings are posited as confirming "conclusions reached in other studies." One finding concerns the role of the public. Haviland views the events he describes as affirming again "that the great majority of the public are not very well informed about foreign affairs, that their interest in the subject is likely to follow the fever chart of world crises

[42] Haviland, "Foreign Aid," p. 689.
[43] *Ibid.*, p. 716.

in the news, and that it is a small educated minority who keep themselves
the best informed and are the most internationally minded." [44] A second
finding derived from the 1957 foreign aid experience deals with the role
of party loyalty in legislative voting, which Haviland found to be consistent
with the general conclusion of some other researchers "that the parts have
a collective interest in the welfare of the whole party and that what happens
to the whole affects all of the parts, some more than others." [45] Thirdly,
with respect to bipartisanship Haviland notes that "On the whole, this
study confirms the conclusion that the development of consultation, confidence, and cooperation between the leadership of the two parties is a
necessary means of surmounting serious conflicts within each of the parties
in order to mobilize a broad base of consensus to support major foreign
policy positions." [46] Yet, notwithstanding the larger context of substantive
process and research in which Haviland locates the events he recounts,
from a scientific perspective his case has little utility. Once again the key
variables are treated as constants. None of the three findings is presented
as reflecting a factor in the policy-making process which, depending on how
it is constituted in a particular year, can have different consequences for
the structure and success of the foreign aid program at that moment in
time. To what extent, for example, would the amount of funds appropriated
for the program be likely to increase (or decrease) if the proportion of the
public uninformed about foreign affairs declined (or rose) and the small
educated minority that is internationally minded grew (or shrank)? To
what extent does a larger (or smaller) legislative majority conduce to greater
(or lesser) party support for (or opposition to) foreign aid appropriations?
If the degree of consultation, confidence, and cooperation between the
leadership of the two parties rises (or falls) substantially, somewhat, or
minimally, is the foreign aid consensus likely to expand (or contract) substantially, somewhat, or minimally? Questions such as these are neither
discussed by Haviland nor posed in the form of hypotheses to be tested
in subsequent foreign aid debates. Consequently, his account offers little
guidance for interpreting and anticipating the outcome of foreign aid controversies in which the proposed expenditures and the efforts to promote
them are considerably more (or less) than was the case in 1957. In this
instance, moreover, the lack of a scientific consciousness has had practical
political consequences. In the years subsequent to 1957 a wide variety of
techniques, from White House-sponsored conferences to prestigeful com-
missions to new legislative strategies, have been employed by supporters
of the foreign aid program to obtain higher appropriations,[47] and each

[44] *Ibid.*, p. 717.
[45] *Ibid.*, p. 719.
[46] *Ibid.*, p. 721.
[47] *Cf.* Rosenau, *National Leadership and Foreign Policy: A Case Study in the*

year advocates of the program are mystified by the outcome of their efforts and increasingly dissatisfied with findings such as Haviland's. One wonders whether knowledge of the subject would not be much more extensive if these findings had been cast in the form of testable hypotheses that could be revised and expanded as each year's foreign aid episode was completed.

Perhaps no case study of foreign policy formulation in the United States is more thorough and self-conscious than Cohen's elaborate account of the international negotiations and national politics that culminated in the 1951 peace settlement with Japan.[48] Unlike the other cases noted above, Cohen's account eschews concentration on a particular aspect or agency of the policy-making process, and instead covers "all the major elements that might help to shape policy," including the public, the press, interest groups, the chief negotiators, and the executive-legislative relationship. Furthermore, Cohen's study has the advantage of being highly sensitive to the idea that "it is a far from simple task . . . to build up a useful body of relevant knowledge about over-all processes." [49] More than most case writers, Cohen is thus concerned about the larger relevance of his inquiry and expresses hope that it will generate other case histories that, taken together, will "ultimately . . . turn up a large body of related and comparable data on the various processes of [foreign] policy development." [50] Indeed, he argues that "it does not seem beyond the bounds of reason that there may be a time when enough will be known about the various types of foreign policy-making processes as a result of studies of this kind so that the probable processes awaiting new policy issues can be predicted from a brief analysis of only a few of the attendant factors and their relationships and of some of the other variables involved."[51] In the end, however, Cohen backs away from the implications of this commitment to comparability and prediction. After twelve chapters and 280 pages of detailed analysis he refuses to advance hypotheses that assess the relative potency of key variables and to predict the likely outcome when different potencies attach to them in other types of policy-making situations:

It is . . . premature, on the basis of just one study of this type, to attach orders of importance to the many variables in the process of policy-making. It would seem, by way of example, that the nature of the policy issue itself has an important effect on the character of the political process that attends it; but it is too early to say if it is a controlling effect, or in what circumstances

Mobilization of Public Support (Princeton, N.J.: Princeton University Press, 1963), Chap. 1.

[48] Bernard C. Cohen, *The Political Process and Foreign Policy: The Making of the Japanese Peace Settlement* (Princeton, N.J.: Princeton University Press, 1957).
[49] *Ibid.*, pp. 5–6.
[50] *Ibid.*, p. 287.
[51] *Ibid.*, p. 8.

it may be a controlling effect, or even to make definite statements about the range of types of issues that have any effects at all.[52]

Evaluated in terms of a scientific consciousness, the response to such a quotation can only be that it is never too early to make statements about what affects what under specified conditions. As long as such statements are derived from past experience (i.e., at least one case study) and can be tested in a future one, the more definite they are, the better. Their definiteness will undoubtedly have to be qualified after other cases are examined, but how else can comprehension be refined and nuance be developed? Certainly not by waiting for an unspecified number of comparable cases to accumulate and then hoping that somehow their recurrent features will be self-evident. Patterns do not present themselves. They must be generated, and this cannot happen unless researchers are willing to hypothesize on the basis of their findings.

Curiously, while Cohen's concluding chapter is consistent with his disinclination to assess the potency of variables and to assert definite propositions, the rhetoric of the chapter suggests scientific predispositions. Arguing that his case history "has been productive of hypotheses that have some bearing not on the case alone but also on the larger study of the political process," [53] Cohen devotes the chapter to a consideration of several of the "more important of these." The first to be considered started as "a useful assumption in organizing this study [and] emerges from it with the somewhat higher status of an unrefined hypothesis: that the climate of public opinion in the body politic, organized and unorganized political interest groups, and the media of mass communication are integral and important parts of the political processes of foreign policy-making." [54] Again we have a formulation lacking variables that vary. It is more of an assertion than a hypothesis. It asserts that the variables are "integral and important," but gives no hint of how different climates of opinion, different degrees of interest-group activity, and different emphases by the mass media might alter the character and products of the policy-making process. The "second major proposition—or set of propositions, to be more exact"—to emerge from Cohen's case history is even less scientifically adequate. For all practical purposes it contains no variables and merely asserts that the foreign policy-making process "is one in which there is a constant meshing of interests and attitudes, actions and reactions, of different, frequently competing groups in a more or less orderly fashion."[55] If, as seems reasonable, a proposition is considered to be a statement in

---

52 *Ibid.*, p. 281.
53 *Ibid.*, pp. 281–82.
54 *Ibid.*, p. 282.
55 *Ibid.*, p. 285.

which the structure, characteristics, or behavior of identifiable factors are alleged to vary in specific ways as a consequence of interacting with each other, plainly this is not a proposition. At best it is a summary and at worst it is a tautology that does no more than "reflect," as Cohen himself notes, "the inordinate complexity of the patterns of influence" that comprise the policy-making process.[56]

Nor can it be said that it is American policy-making processes in particular that are especially conducive to unscientific, even if systematic, analysis. Case histories of foreign policy processes in other societies are similarly devoid of explicit hypotheses in which the key variables are specified and their range of variation indicated. Epstein's impressive account of Britain's participation in the Suez crisis of 1956 is a good illustration.[57] Epstein concedes that "the difficulties in the way of suggesting generalizations from a case study seem so great that one might be tempted to forgo the effort altogether and simply tell the story of what happened in Britain during the Suez crisis." Yet his scientific consciousness is sufficient to lead him to assert at the outset that such a procedure "would not be enough to satisfy a political scientist," that the latter "is ambitious to understand how a political system works in more than a given situation." Indeed, noting that the political scientist's "purpose must always be comparative," Epstein extends his aspirations for his case study to other systems as well as other situations: ". . . the objective is not just to learn, from the Suez crisis, something about *Britain's* Parliament and parties, but hopefully also something about types of parliamentary and party systems."[58] However, eight chapters and some two hundred pages later, after he has recounted what various British cabinet officials, parliamentary groups, constituency organizations, the press, interest groups, and the general public thought and did before, during, and after the climactic events of early November 1956, Epstein's scientific consciousness has faded and the commitments set forth at the outset are hardly discernible in his concluding chapter. The latter consists largely of summary estimates of the various institutions and processes described, and while as a result it does offer some generalizations about the functioning of the British political system, none of these are presented in the form of testable hypotheses or even in such a way that testable hypotheses can be derived from them. Party cohesion, party competition, executive stability, and parliamentary debate are among the variables assessed, but Epstein's assessments do not include any indication of the range within which each of these can or might vary

---

[56] *Ibid.*
[57] Leon D. Epstein, *British Politics in the Suez Crisis* (Urbana: University of Illinois Press, 1964).
[58] *Ibid.*, p. 3.

under different conditions. There is no attempt to differentiate between high and low party cohesion, between intense and weak party competition, between more and less executive stability, and between wide and narrow parliamentary debate. The reader is thus perplexed as to what to do with the generalizations. In the absence of variability, he can apply them only to circumstances similar to the Suez crisis, and since the latter is more of an extreme than a typical event in British political life, the generalizations are for all practical purposes useless.

Epstein's scientific consciousness deserts him even more fully with regard to his commitment to comparison. To be sure, his concluding chapter contains a few sentences in which the capacity of the British Prime Minister to engage in foreign policy undertakings without legislative consultation or approval is compared with that of the American President (and there is one brief reference to this capacity in the Third and Fourth Republics of France), but these are all offered in passing and do not, as they easily might have, consist of propositions that other researchers can verify with respect to U.S. behavior in foreign policy crises. Presidential initiatives undertaken without legislative approval in the Vietnam situation offer obvious parallels to the Suez crisis. Unfortunately, however, Epstein's concluding chapter provides virtually no observations that might be transformed into propositions applicable to Vietnam. Conceivably one might hypothesize about the Vietnam situation on the basis of his conclusion that the Suez episode does not "prove that overwhelming popular support, perhaps determined in advance, is essential for the successful prosecution of a foreign policy involving a military commitment," [59] but this is about the only link that can be established between Epstein's general conclusions and subsequent research into other political systems. For the most part the few comparisons that he draws are so all-encompassing that they defy application to other systems. His final observation is illustrative of this defiance: "At the end, then, of this case study, it can be fairly concluded that Britain's Suez experience displayed a rigidly partisan political mold that appears to be a response of the parliamentary system to problems facing a major democratic nation in the first half of the twentieth century."[60] Epstein hoped at the outset that his readers might learn "something about other types of parliamentary and party systems," but it seems fair to say that he did not take advantage of the opportunity to fulfill this aspiration that his data made possible.

Let us turn now to a case history in which the dependent variables include the outcome of foreign policy behavior abroad. Despite its broader scope, however, the particular case under review, Davison's lengthy account

[59] *Ibid.*, p. 203.
[60] *Ibid.*, p. 209.

of the Soviet Union's 1948 attempt to seal off Berlin by cutting its overland communications to West Germany,[61] does not reflect a scientific consciousness any more than do those in which the sequence of events is
limited to the outcome of the policy-making process at home. Indeed,
Davison's concluding chapter makes no effort whatsoever to treat the
Berlin blockade as an instance of a larger pattern; rather it is devoted to
emphasizing the importance of the last of the "four major factors" that
enabled Berlin to overcome the blockade. The decision of the Western
powers to defend their position in the city, the strong democratic leadership of the city, and the effective instruments of leadership available to the
city's elite comprise the first three factors, but all of these are posited as
having been highly dependent on the fourth factor, the resistance morale
of the West Berliners. The sources and dynamics of this morale are com-
pellingly explored by Davison, and the reader completes the case history
fully in agreement with his conclusion that the breaking of the blockade
was a triumph of heroic proportions. Yet no generalizations emerge from
the analysis. Four main variables are specified and the interaction
among them is stressed, but how they might vary and interact in subsequent
Berlin crises is not a subject of speculation on Davison's part. In effect,
his analysis comes to an end with the lifting of the blockade on May 12,
1949. To be sure, as a result of acquaintance with Davison's account any
estimates one makes about other Berlin crises are likely to be much more
sensitive to the significance of public opinion and political structure in
that beleaguered city, but in disciplining this sensitivity the reader gets
no help from Davison. He only notes that the variables were crucial in
1948–49, and since his analysis of them is so completely time-bound, their
subsequent relevance in an era of nuclear stalemate cannot be hypothetically
deduced from the case itself.

Finally, let us examine a case that recounts the events in 1953 that
led to the selection of a new U.S. ambassador to the Soviet Union.[62] It is
neither as complex nor as lengthy a case as the others, but it does deal
with an important aspect of foreign policy and its inclusion here helps
to demonstrate that the development of a commitment to a scientific consciousness need not start early in a professional career; for the absence
of a readiness to move to higher levels of generalization is even more
conspicuous in this case than in any of the others. Indeed, the case does
not even state a general purpose at the outset. It merely begins with the
advent of the vacancy in the ambassadorship and describes the problem

---

[61] W. Phillips Davison, *The Berlin Blockade: A Study of Cold War Politics*
(Princeton, N.J.: Princeton University Press, 1958).

[62] James N. Rosenau, *The Nomination of "Chip" Bohlen* (New York: Holt,
1958.)

this situation posed for the incoming Eisenhower administration. Further-more, not only does the case fail to derive any hypotheses from the sequence of events; it does not even offer any conclusions. After describing the posture toward the ambassador-designate taken by the relevant execu-tive and legislative officials and then recounting the clash that followed from the conflicting postures, the case simply comes to an end with a tally of the Senate vote on the nomination.

The case concludes with a very brief section of "Afterthoughts" in which some questions about the immediate implications of the nomination are raised, but no effort is made to suggest possible answers to them, much less to query the general meaning of the episode. A central theme of the case, for example, concerns the dilemma faced by Republican senators who had long complained about the "betrayal" of U.S. interests at Yalta, and who now were asked by a Republican President to approve the nomination of the man who had been Franklin D. Roosevelt's translator at that wartime conference with the Russians. Yet no attempt was made to apply the way in which the senators resolved this attitudinal conflict to other types of foreign policy actors, much less to other foreign policy situations in which senatorial behavior is relevant. What might have served as an ideal opportunity to formulate propositions about the relative potency of idiosyncratic and role variables was treated as nothing more than a dramatic moment of personal truth for several persons who happened to be members of the Senate in 1953. As such, to be sure, the case reconstructs a climactic episode in American politics, and, through lengthy excerpts from official documents, does so in a compelling fashion. Looking back over the case a decade later, however, what stands out is not its dramatic content, but its lack of significance. Not having identified and assessed any general implications, the case now seems somewhat trivial.

In sum, all seven of these case histories of foreign policy behavior are long on systematic analysis and short on scientific consciousness. None of them yielded a single hypothesis about what foreign policy behavior would be likely to occur under a specified set of conditions. Our indictment of the state of research in the field may be exaggerated, but the foregoing evidence provides no basis for revising it.[63]

---

[63] Happily, however, a reason to revise the indictment slightly has arisen since the completion of this chapter. In early 1968 a lengthy case history of an important foreign policy episode was published that so fully reflects a scientific consciousness that a fifty-page concluding chapter is devoted to the discussion of forty-nine general propositions derived from the preceding narrative. See Glenn D. Paige, *The Korean Decision: June 24–30, 1950* (New York: Free Press, 1968), Chap. 11.

5 Comparative Foreign Policy: One-time Fad, Realized Fantasy, and Normal Field *

This chapter was originally written early in 1967, and the invitation to update it provides a useful opportunity to assess progress in the comparative study of foreign policy. In order to facilitate such an assessment, I have left the original version intact, adding this initial paragraph and a postscript which revises some of the observations made eight years ago and answers some of the questions then posed in the light of subsequent developments. The reader can thus compare the current state of inquiry with that of eight years ago and evaluate whether or not the intervening period has been one of progress. My own evaluation, presented in the postscript, is summarized in the alterations in the original title of the article.

All signs are pointing in the same direction: as a television commercial might describe it, "Comparative Foreign Policy is coming on"

* This chapter was originally published as "Comparative Foreign Policy: Fad, Fantasy, or Field?" in *International Studies Quarterly* 12 (September 1968): 296-329. Copyright © 1968 by Sage Publications, Inc., Beverly Hills, Calif. An introductory paragraph and a postscript were added to the original version and published under the above, revised title in Charles W. Kegley, Jr., Gregory A. Raymond, Robert M. Rood, Richard A. Skinner (eds.), *International Events and the Comparative Analysis of Foreign Policy* (Columbia, S.C.: University of South Carolina Press, 1975), pp. 3-38. The revised version is reprinted with the permission of the publishers of both versions.

Recent lists of dissertations in progress reveals that other research findings along this line are soon to become available.[5] Then there is perhaps the surest sign of all: textbook publishers, those astute students of trends in Academe, have discerned a stirring in this direction and are busily drumming up manuscripts that can be adopted as texts when the trend achieves discipline-wide acceptance by political scientists.[6]

In sum, it seems more than likely that in the coming years something called "Comparative Foreign Policy" will occupy a prominent place in the teaching of political science and in the research of political scientists. But is such a development desirable? Is the phrase "comparative foreign policy" a contentless symbol to which students of international politics pay lip service in order to remain *au courant* with their colleagues elsewhere in the discipline? Does it stand for a scientific impulse that can never be realized because foreign policy phenomena do not lend themselves to comparative analysis? Or does it designate an important and distinguishable set of empirical phenomena that can usefully be subjected to extended examination? Is comparative foreign policy, in short, a fad, a fantasy, or a field?

In some respects it is all of these and the purpose of this paper is to identify the fad and fantasy dimensions in order to minimize confusion and contradiction as the field evolves. Although the field is barely in its infancy, hopefully an assessment of its inception and an attempt to identify its boundaries and problems will, even at this early stage, lessen the growing pains that lie ahead.

I. THE SOURCES OF REORIENTATION

That the fad, the fantasy, and the field are all of recent origin can be readily demonstrated. Traditionally, the analysis of foreign policy phenomena has consisted of a policy-oriented concern with particular situations faced by specific nations. Thus the single case, limited in time by its importance to the relevant actors and in scope by the immediacy of its manifest repercussions, has dominated the literature for decades.[7] Attempts to contrast two or more empirical cases have been distinct exceptions and have been narrowly confined to the problem of whether democracies or

5 In the 1966 listing (*American Political Science Review*, 60, pp. 786–91), nine dissertations carried titles that suggested research on topics involving the comparative study of foreign policy.

6 During a recent two-week period the present writer received such invitations from three different publishers, each of whom was unaware of what the others were doing.

7 For an elaboration of this point, see Chapters 4 and 6.

dictatorships are likely to conduct themselves more effectively in the international arena.[8] Even those political scientists in the early postwar era who explicitly sought to render foreign policy analysis more systematic by focusing on decision-making processes did not move in a comparative direction. The decision-making approach to foreign policy called attention to a host of important variables and greatly diminished the long-standing tendency to posit national actors as abstract entities endowed with human capacities and qualities. But, in demanding that foreign policy be analyzed from the perspective of concrete and identifiable decision-makers, the approach also tended to preclude examination of the possibility that the perspectives of decision-makers in different societies might be similar, or at least comparable. Thus, throughout the 1950s and well into the 1960s, the newly discovered decision-making variables served to improve the quality of the case histories rather than to replace them with new modes of analysis.[9]

To be sure, the immediate postwar period did not lack attempts to generalize about the processes whereby any society formulates and conducts its foreign policy. In addition to the efforts of Richard C. Snyder and others who pioneered in decision-making analysis,[10] several more eclectic observers sought to specify the variables that operate wherever foreign policy phenomena are found,[11] and a few textbook editors also undertook to bring together in one volume analyses of how different countries made and sustained their external relations.[12] In none of the more abstract

[8] See, for example, Carl Joachim Friedrich, *Foreign Policy in the Making* (New York: Norton, 1938), Chaps. 1–4.

[9] For an extended attempt to assess the impact of the decision-making approach on the study of foreign policy, see Chapter IX.

[10] Cf. Karl W. Deutsch, "Mass Communications and the Loss of Freedom in National Decision-Making: A Possible Research Approach to Interstate Conflicts," *Journal of Conflict Resolution*, 1 (1957), pp. 200–11; Joseph Frankel, "Towards a Decision-Making Model in Foreign Policy," *Political Studies*, 7 (1959), pp. 1–11; Edgar S. Furniss, Jr., *The Office of Premier in French Foreign Policy-Making: An Application of Decision-Making Analysis* (Princeton: Foreign Policy Analysis Project, Princeton University, 1954); Richard C. Snyder, H. W. Bruck, Burton M. Sapin, *Decision-Making as an Approach to the Study of International Politics* (Princeton, N.J.: Foreign Policy Analysis Project, Princeton University, 1954).

[11] However, the list of works of this nature is not a long one. The main entries are Feliks Gross, *Foreign Policy Analysis* (New York: Philosophical Library, 1954); Louis J. Halle, *Civilization and Foreign Policy: An Inquiry for Americans* (New York: Harper, 1952); Kurt London, *How Foreign Policy Is Made* (New York: D. Van Nostrand, 1949); Charles Burton Marshall, *The Limits of Foreign Policy* (New York: Henry Holt, 1954); and George Modelski, *A Theoretical Analysis of the Formation of Foreign Policy* (London: University of London, 1954), later published as *A Theory of Foreign Policy* (New York: Praeger, 1962).

[12] The only textbooks with such a focus published prior to the 1960s were Roy C. Macridis (ed.), *Foreign Policy in World Politics* (Englewood Cliffs, N.J.: Prentice-Hall, 1958), and Philips W. Buck and Martin Travis, Jr. (eds.), *Control of Foreign Relations in Modern Nations* (New York: Norton, 1957).

formulations, however, was the possibility of engaging in comparative analysis seriously considered. Foreign policy variables were identified and discussed as if they operated in identical ways in all societies and the hypothetical society abstracted therefrom was described in terms of a multiplicity of examples drawn largely from the "lessons" of modern international history.[13] The appeasement at Munich, the betrayal at Pearl Harbor, the success of the Marshall Plan—these are but a few of the incidents that served as the empirical basis for the traditional model in which nations were posited as serving (or failing to serve) their national interests through foreign policies that balance ends with means and commitments with capabilities. That the lessons of history might be variously experienced by different policy-making systems was not accounted for in the abstract models and thus, to repeat, they were no more oriented toward comparative analysis than were the case histories that constituted the mainstream of foreign policy research.

Nor did the textbook editors take advantage of the opportunity afforded by the accumulation of materials about the external behavior of different countries and present concluding chapters that attempted to identify the similarities and differences uncovered by the separate, but juxtaposed, analyses of several policy-making systems. Ironically, in fact, the one text that used the word "comparative" in connection with the study of a foreign policy also explicitly raised doubts about the applicability of this form of analysis: in the first edition of this work the introductory chapter on the "Comparative Study of Foreign Policy" was written by Gabriel A. Almond, who noted the "lack of the most elementary knowledge" about foreign policy phenomena and concluded that therefore "it will be some time before rigorous and systematic comparison becomes possible."[14] Even more ironically, the comparable chapter of the second edition of the same text, written four years later by Kenneth W. Thompson and Roy C. Macridis, went even further and rejected the premises of comparative analysis on the grounds that foreign policy variables involve a "complexity [that] makes a mockery of the few 'scientific' tools we have," thereby rendering any attempt to generalize on the basis of comparative assessments "a hopeless task."[15]

The existence of this attitude of hopelessness and of the traditional inclination toward case histories raises the question of why pronounced signs of a major reorientation have appeared with increasing frequency

[13] London also presented separate descriptions of policy-making in Washington, London, Paris, Berlin, and Moscow, but these were not then subjected to comparative analysis (London, *How Policy Is Made,* pp. 99–153).

[14] Macridis, *op. cit.,* pp. 5–6.

[15] Roy C. Macridis (ed.), *Foreign Policy in World Politics* (Englewood Cliffs, N.J.: Prentice-Hall, 1962, Second Edition), pp. 26–27.

in the mid-1960s? The answer would seem to be that two unrelated but major trends, one historical and the other intellectual, have converged at this point, and while neither alone would have stimulated the impulse to compare foreign policy phenomena, their coincidence in time has served to generate strong pressures in this direction.

Let us look first at the intellectual factors. It seems clear, in retrospect, that the rapid emergence of a heavy emphasis upon comparison in the analysis of domestic politics served as a potent impetus to reorientation in the study of foreign policy. The turning point for the field of comparative politics can be traced to the mid 1950s, when structural-functional analysis was first applied to political phenomena,[16] an event that in turn led to the formation of the Committee on Comparative Politics of the Social Science Research Council[17] and the publication of its many pioneering volumes.[18] These works highlighted the idea, explicitly set forth in the first chapter of the first volume, that certain key functions must be performed if a political system is to persist, and that these functions can be performed by a wide variety of structures.[19] Whatever the limitations of structural-functional analysis—and there are many [20]—this central premise provided a way for students of domestic processes to compare seemingly dissimilar phenomena. Until structural-functional analysis was made part of the conceptual equipment of the field, the most salient dimensions of political systems were their unique characteristics and there seemed to be little reason to engage in comparison, except perhaps to show how different governmental forms give rise to dissimilar consequences. Indeed, prior to the mid-1950s it was quite commonplace to show that even similar governmental forms can give rise to dissimilar consequences: "Look at this

[16] Cf. Gabriel A. Almond, "Comparative Political Systems," *Journal of Politics*, 18 (1956), pp. 391–409.

[17] Gabriel A. Almond, "Research in Comparative Politics: Plans of a New Council Committee," *Items*, VIII (March 1954), pp. 1–4.

[18] Gabriel A. Almond and James S. Coleman (eds.), *The Politics of the Developing Areas* (Princeton: Princeton University Press, 1960); Lucian W. Pye (ed.), *Communications and Political Development* (Princeton: Princeton University Press, 1963); Joseph LaPalombara (ed.), *Bureaucracy and Political Development* (Princeton: Princeton University Press, 1963); Robert E. Ward and Dankwart A. Rustow (eds.), *Political Modernization in Japan and Turkey* (Princeton: Princeton University Press, 1964); James S. Coleman (ed.), *Education and Political Development* (Princeton: Princeton University Press, 1965); Lucian W. Pye and Sidney Verba (eds.), *Political Culture and Political Development* (Princeton: Princeton University Press, 1965); Joseph LaPalombara and Myron Weiner (eds.), *Political Parties and Political Development* (Princeton: Princeton University Press, 1966).

[19] Cf. Gabriel A. Almond, "A Functional Approach to Comparative Politics," in Almond and Coleman, *op. cit.*, pp. 3–64.

[20] For a succinct review and assessment of these limitations, see Ernest Nagel, *The Structure of Science: Problems in the Logic of Scientific Explanation* (New York: Harcourt, 1961), pp. 520–535. Also see Robert E. Dowse, "A Functionalist's Logic," *World Politics*, 18 (1966), pp. 607–622.

Western parliament and contrast it with that non-Western legislature," a student at that time would observe with a sense of satisfaction. "They both go through the same procedures, but how diverse are the results!"

Then the breakthrough occurred. Structural-functional analysis lifted sights to a higher level of generalization and put all political systems on an analytic par. Thereafter, tracing differences was much less exhilarating than probing for functional equivalents, and students of domestic politics were quick to respond to the challenge and reorient their efforts. Since the mid-1950s political scientists have turned out a seemingly endless series of articles and books committed to comparative analysis—to a delineation of similarities and differences upon which empirically based models of the political process could be founded. A spate of comparative materials on governance in underdeveloped polities was the vanguard of this analytic upheaval, but its repercussions were by no means confined to Africa, Asia, and Latin America. No type of system or area of the world was viewed as an inappropriate subject for comparative analysis. Even the two systems which an earlier generation of political scientists viewed as polar extremes, the United States and the Soviet Union, were considered as fit for comparison and as apt subjects to test a "theory of convergence."[21] Similarly, while the West–nonWest distinction had been regarded as representing mutually exclusive categories, it was now treated as descriptive of two segments of the *same* continuum of whatever class of political phenomena was being examined.[22] Nor was there any reluctance to break systems down and look at only one of their component parts: political parties were compared,[23] and so were political cultures,[24] oppositions,[25] revolutionary movements,[26] Communist regimes,[27] bureaucracies,[28] constitutional subsystems,[29] military elites,[30] and so on, through all the major institutions, processes, and personnel of polities. As the comparative movement gained

[21] Zbigniew Brzezinski and Samuel P. Huntington, *Political Power: USA/USSR* (New York: Viking, 1964), pp. 3–14 and *passim*.

[22] For example, see Samuel P. Huntington, "Political Development and Political Decay," *World Politics*, 17 (1965), pp. 386–430.

[23] LaPalombara and Weiner, *op. cit.*

[24] Gabriel A. Almond and Sidney Verba, *The Civic Culture: Political Attitudes and Democracy in Five Nations* (Princeton: Princeton University Press, 1963).

[25] Robert A. Dahl (ed.), *Political Oppositions in Western Democracies* (New Haven: Yale University Press, 1966).

[26] Chalmers Johnson, *Revolutionary Change* (Boston: Little, Brown, 1966).

[27] Robert C. Tucker, "On the Comparative Study of Communism," *World Politics*, 19 (1967), pp. 242–257.

[28] LaPalombara, *op cit.;* and Ferrel Heady, *Public Administration: A Comparative Perspective* (Englewood Cliffs, N.J.: Prentice-Hall, 1966).

[29] Herbert Jacob and Kenneth N. Vines (eds.), *Politics in the American States: A Comparative Analysis* (Boston: Little, Brown, 1965); Frank Munger (ed.), *American State Politics: Readings for Comparative Analysis* (New York: Crowell, 1966);

momentum, moreover, it generated efforts to clarify the methodological problems posed by the new orientation[31] and, more importantly, to provide comparable data for most or all of the polities extant.[32] Like all major movements, the trend toward comparative analysis also evoked protests and denunciations of its legitimacy.[33]

If the ultimate purpose of political inquiry is the generation of tested and/or testable theory, then this upheaval in comparative politics had already begun to yield solid results by the mid-1960s. One could look only with wonderment upon the progress that had occurred in a decade's time: not only were data being gathered and processed in entirely new ways, but a variety of stimulating, broad-gauged, systematic, and empirically based models of domestic political processes in generalized types of polities had made their way into the literature.[34] Curiously, however, foreign policy phenomena were not caught up in these tides of change. None of the new empirical findings, much less any of the new conceptual formulations, dealt with the responses of polities and their institutions, processes, and personnel to international events and trends. For reasons suggested else-

---

and Lewis A. Froman, Jr., "An Analysis of Public Policies in Cities," *Journal of Politics,* 29 (1967), pp. 94–108.

[30] Morris Janowitz, *The Military in the Political Development of New Nations: An Essay in Comparative Analysis* (Chicago: University of Chicago Press, 1964); John J. Johnson (ed.), *The Role of the Military in Underdeveloped Countries* (Princeton: Princeton University Press, 1962); and Sydney Nettleton Fisher (ed.), *The Military in the Middle East: Problems in Society and Government* (Columbus: Ohio State University Press, 1963).

[31] Cf. Richard L. Merritt and Stein Rokkan (eds.), *Comparing Nations: The Use of Quantitative Data in Cross-National Research* (New Haven: Yale University Press, 1966), *passim;* Arthur K. Kalleburg, "The Logic of Comparison: A Methodological Note on the Comparative Study of Political Systems," *World Politics,* 19 (1966), pp. 69–82; Sigmund Neumann, "Comparative Politics: A Half-Century Appraisal," *Journal of Politics,* 19 (1957), pp. 369–390; Sigmund Neumann, "The Comparative Study of Politics," *Comparative Studies in Society and History,* 1 (January 1959), pp. 105–112; Michael Haas, "Comparative Analysis," *Western Political Quarterly,* 15 (1962), pp. 294–303; and Harry Eckstein, "A Perspective on Comparative Politics, Past and Present," in Harry Eckstein and David E. Apter (eds.), *Comparative Politics: A Reader* (New York: Free Press, 1964), pp. 3–32.

[32] See Arthur S. Banks and Robert B. Textor, *A Cross-Polity Survey* (Cambridge: The M.I.T. Press, 1963), and Bruce M. Russett, Hayward R. Alker, Jr., Karl W. Deutsch, and Harold D. Lasswell, *World Handbook of Political and Social Indicators* (New Haven: Yale University Press, 1964).

[33] Leslie Wolf-Phillips, "Metapolitics: Reflections on a 'Methodological Revolution,'" *Political Studies,* 12 (1964), 352–369.

[34] For example, see Gabriel A. Almond and G. Bingham Powell, Jr., *Comparative Politics: A Developmental Approach* (Boston: Little, Brown, 1966); David E. Apter, *The Politics of Modernization* (Chicago: University of Chicago Press, 1965); Louis Hartz, *et al,* *The Founding of New Societies* (New York: Harcourt, 1964); Robert T. Holt and John E. Turner, *The Political Bases of Economic Development: An Exploration in Comparative Analysis* (Princeton: Van Nostrand, 1966); and A. F. K. Organski, *The Stages of Political Development* (New York: Knopf, 1965).

where,[35] everything was compared but foreign policy phenomena, and only belatedly have students of comparative politics even acknowledged the need to make conceptual allowance for the impact of international variables upon domestic processes.[36]

The recent signs of interest in comparative foreign policy, in other words, arise out of the work of students of international politics and foreign policy and not from an extension of the models and inquiries of those who focus on national or subnational phenomena. As indicated, however, it seems doubtful whether the former would have become interested in comparative analysis if the latter had not successfully weathered a decade of upheaval. This spillover thus constitutes the prime intellectual source of the reorientation toward comparative foreign policy; in large measure the reorientation stemmed from the desire of students of international processes to enjoy success similar to that of their colleagues in an adjoining field.[37]

The other major source of the reorientation is to be found in certain postwar historical circumstances that coincided with the upheaval in the field of comparative politics. At least two trends in world politics would appear to have attracted the attention of students of foreign policy to the virtues of comparative analysis. Perhaps the most important of these involves the proliferation of national actors that occurred during the

---

[35] See Chapter 15.

[36] The conference that occasioned this chapter, along with the one that led to the volume edited by R. Barry Farrell (*op. cit.*), is one of the few efforts to examine national-international relationships organized by students of domestic political systems. For another belated acknowledgment of the relevance of international variables, see Almond and Powell (*op. cit.*), pp. 9, 203–204. Actually, in all fairness it should be noted that some years ago Almond did acknowledge that studies of "the functioning of the domestic political system . . . have commonly neglected the importance of the international situation in affecting the form of the political process and the content of domestic public policy. . . . We do not know until this day whether the differences in the functioning of the multiparty systems of the Scandinavian countries and those of France and Italy are to be attributed to internal differences in culture, economics, and political and governmental structure, or whether they are attributable to the differences in the 'loading' of these systems with difficult and costly foreign policy problems, or whether both and in what proportions" (in Macridis, *op. cit.*, 1958, pp. 4–5). In his ensuing pioneering works on domestic systems, however, Almond did not follow the line of his own reasoning. Not even his highly general structural-functional model of the political process, presented two years later in *The Politics of the Developing Areas,* made conceptual room for the impact of international variables or the functions served by political activities oriented toward a system's external environment.

[37] For evidence that the foreign policy field was not the only one to experience the spillover from the comparative movement initiated by students of national and subnational politics, see John Useem and Allen D. Grimshaw, "Comparative Sociology," *Items,* 20 (December 1966), pp. 46–51, which outlines developments that have recently culminated in the appointment of a new committee on comparative sociology by the Social Science Research Council.

1955–1965 decade as a result of the withdrawal of colonial powers from Africa and Asia. Not only did foreign policy phenomena also proliferate at a comparable rate during this period (there being more actors engaging in foreign policy actions), but, more importantly, the recurrence of similar patterns was far more discernible and impressive in a world of some 120 nations than it had been when half this number of actors comprised the international system. Conversely, the more the international system grew in size, the less did concentration upon unique patterns seem likely to un-ravel the mysteries of international life. Stated differently, as more and more nations acquired independence and sought to come to terms with neighbors and great powers, the more did contrasts among two or more of them loom as the route to comprehension of world politics. The de-colonization of sub-Sahara Africa was especially crucial in this respect. The resulting national actors were so similar in size, cultural heritage, social composition, political structure, and stage of economic development, and the problems they faced in the international system were thus so parallel, that the analysis of their foreign policies virtually compelled comparison. At least this would seem to be the most logical explanation for the fact that many of the early efforts to derive theoretical proposi-tions about foreign policy from the comparative analysis of empirical materials focused on Africa in particular [38] and underdeveloped polities in general. [39]

The advent of the thermonuclear era and the emergence of Red China as a budding and recalcitrant superpower are illustrative of another historical trend that has fostered a reorientation in foreign policy analysis, namely, the emergence of problems that are worldwide in scope. As more and more situations have arisen toward which all national actors must necessarily take a position, analysts with a policy-oriented concern have become increasingly inclined to juxtapose and contrast the reactions and policies of nations that they previously treated as single cases. Many analyses of the 1963 nuclear test ban treaty, the continuing problem of nuclear proliferation, and the Chinese acquisition of a nuclear capability are obvious examples. Indeed, the worldwide implications of China's emergence recently resulted in what is probably the first work to focus on an immediate policy problem by analyzing how a number of different national actors are inclined to respond to it. [40]

[38] See, for example, McKay, *op. cit.*, and Doudou Thiam, *The Foreign Policy of African States: Ideological Bases, Present Realities, Future Prospects* (New York: Praeger, 1965).

[39] For a particularly stimulating effort of this kind, see Henry A. Kissinger, "Domestic Structure and Foreign Policy," *Daedalus*, 95 (Spring 1966), pp. 503–529.

[40] A. M. Halpern (ed.), *Policies Toward China: Views from Six Continents* (New York: McGraw-Hill, 1965).

II. THE STUDY OF COMPARATIVE FOREIGN POLICY AND THE COMPARATIVE STUDY OF FOREIGN POLICY

Reorientation of analytic modes never occurs without a period of transition and adjustment that is often slow and difficult. Apparently the study of foreign policy is not to be an exception. Some of the early changes suggest that the reorientation is based partly upon a headlong and ill-considered rush to get aboard the comparative bandwagon. Perhaps because the intellectual and historic factors that have fostered change converged and reinforced each other in such a short span of time, little thought has been given to what comparison entails in relation to foreign policy phenomena. "After all," some students of foreign policy seem to say, "the comparative people are doing it, why shouldn't we?" What "it" is in this context, however, is rarely examined and is often assumed to involve no more than the juxtaposition of the foreign policy phenomena of two or more systems. What aspects of foreign policy should be compared, how they should be compared, why they should be compared, whether they can be compared—questions such as these are not raised. Rather, having presumed that simply by juxtaposing such phenomena an endeavor called "comparative foreign policy" is established, many analysts proceed in the accustomed manner and examine each unit of the juxtaposed materials separately as a case history.

A good illustration of the continuing predisposition to settle for juxtaposition without comparison is provided by the aforementioned work on how more than sixteen different national actors are inclined to respond to Communist China.[41] Despite the abundance of comparable material made available by the common focus of the various chapters, neither the editor nor the authors saw fit to contrast systematically the relative potencies of the variables underlying responses to China. Instead, each of the sixteen substantive chapters deals with the policies of a different country or region toward China, and the editor's introductory and concluding chapters are concerned, respectively, with presenting an overview of China itself and summarizing all the differences that were revealed to underlie policies toward it. In effect, the work consists of sixteen separate studies conveniently brought together in one place.[42]

In short, comparative foreign policy has to some extent become a new label for an old practice. It is in this sense—in the sense that reference is made to comparative analysis without adherence to the procedures it requires—that some of the recent signs of reorientation are essentially

---

[41] *Ibid.*

[42] For an elaboration of this assessment, see my review of the book in *The Journal of Asian Studies,* 26 (1967), pp. 287–288.

no more than a passing fad, an emulation of form rather than of substance. Even worse, to the extent that the label is more than an empty symbol of modernity, it has been invested with misleading connotations. An unfortunate tendency, perhaps also stemming from ill-considered emulation, has developed whereby comparative foreign policy is viewed as a body of knowledge, as a subject to be explored, as a field of inquiry. Scholars and textbook publishers alike tend to refer to the study of comparative foreign policy as if there existed in the real world a set of phenomena that could be so labeled. Scholars speak of engaging in research on comparative foreign policy and publishers talk of issuing eight or ten paperbacks as their comparative foreign policy series. Such nomenclature is unfortunate because the benefits of comparative analysis cannot be enjoyed if it is conceived in terms of subject matter rather than in methodological terms. Comparison is a method, not a body of knowledge. Foreign policy phenomena—and not comparative foreign policy phenomena—comprise the subject matter to be probed and these can be studied in a variety of ways, all of them useful for certain purposes and irrelevant to other purposes. The comparative method is only one of these ways and it is not necessarily the best method for all purposes. It is most useful with respect to the generation and testing of propositions about foreign policy behavior that apply to two or more political systems. Only by identifying similarities and differences in the external behavior of more than one national actor can analysis move beyond the particular case to higher levels of generalization.[43] On the other hand, if the researcher is concerned with the processes of only a single system, then the comparative method may not be as valuable as the case history.[44]

Strictly speaking, therefore, it makes a difference whether one defines oneself as engaged in the comparative study of foreign policy or in the study of comparative foreign policy. The former, it is argued here, is a legitimate and worthwhile enterprise that may well lead to the formation of a disciplined field of inquiry, whereas the latter is an ambiguous label that serves to perpetuate a fad rather than to establish a field.

Still another kind of confusion has arisen out of the initial burst of enthusiasm for a more systematic approach to the analysis of foreign policy phenomena, namely, a tendency to posit such phenomena as encompassing

[43] For a discussion of the different levels of generalization at which the comparative analysis of political systems can be undertaken, see Tucker, *op. cit.,* pp. 246–254.

[44] Under special circumstances, however, it is possible to apply the comparative method to a single system. If certain conditions remain constant from one point in time to another, then variables pertinent to the one system can be contrasted and assessed in terms of their operation at different historical junctures. For an extended discussion and application of this procedure, which has been designated as "quantitative historical comparison," see Chapter 7.

the entire range of actions and interactions through which the interdependence of nations is sustained. Just as this ever-increasing interdependence has stimulated analysts to look more carefully at foreign policy, so has it spurred a greater concern with linkages between national and international political systems. Also referred to as "transnational politics" or "national-international interdependencies," these linkages are seen as comprising all the ways in which the functioning of each type of political system is a consequence of the other.[45] While the foreign policy and linkage approaches overlap in important ways, they are not identical. The latter is broader than the former and can be viewed as subsuming it. Foreign policy phenomena comprise certain kinds of linkages, those in which governments relate themselves to all or part of the international system through the adoption of purposeful stances toward it, but there are other major kinds in which the links may be fashioned by nongovernmental actors or by the unintentional consequences of governmental action. These other kinds of linkages can, of course, be highly relevant to the formulation, conduct, and consequences of foreign policy, but they emanate from and are sustained by a set of processes that are analytically separable from the processes of foreign policy. Yet, impressed by the extent to which national systems have become pervaded by external stimuli, some analysts tend to emphasize the fact that in responding to these stimuli the national system is responding to elements "foreign" to it, an emphasis which leads to the erroneous equation of national-international linkages with foreign policy phenomena.[46]

III. TRACING THE OUTLINES OF A FIELD

To note that foreign policy phenomena involve governmental undertakings directed toward the external environment neither justifies treating them as a separate field of inquiry nor indicates where the boundaries of such a field lie. While it is possible to argue that the comparative study of foreign policy is a subfield of political science because many political scientists research such matters and see themselves as engaged in a common enterprise when they do so, plainly a field must have an intellectual identity apart from the activities of its practitioners. For a field to exist, presumably it must have its own discipline—its own subject matter, its own point of view, and its own theory. In the absence of a subject matter with an internal coherence of its own, of a viewpoint that structures the subject

[45] For an elaboration of this conception, see Chapter 15.
[46] See Hanrieder, op. cit., and my critique of this article, *American Political Science Review*, 59 (1967), pp. 983-988.

matter in unique ways, and of a body of theoretical propositions that have not been or cannot be derived from any other way of structuring the subject, researchers can never be sure whether in fact they are engaging in a common enterprise. Under such circumstances, they may actually be working on highly diverse problems that share only the labels that are attached to them. What is regarded as "the field" may be no more than a composite of several different enterprises that overlap in some respects but that have distinctive subject matters, viewpoints, and propositions of their own.

Thus it is conceivable that the comparative study of foreign policy is not a field at all. Perhaps the search for its subject matter, viewpoint, and propositions will yield the conclusion that it is best viewed as a composite of national and international politics—as the appropriate concern of two fields, one treating foreign policy phenomena as dependent variables in the operation of national political systems and the other as independent variables in the operation of international political systems. Needless to say, it would make matters much easier if a separate field could not be delineated and comparative studies of foreign policy could be assessed in terms of the concepts and standards of either the national or international politics fields. Much preliminary conceptualization and argumentation could thereby be avoided and analysts could push on to the main task of gathering data and advancing comprehension.

Tempting as such a conclusion may be, however, it must be rejected. The fact is that the national and international fields do not encompass all the phenomena to which the label of "foreign policy" might be attached. No matter how much the viewpoints of these fields may be stretched, some phenomena remain unexplained. Reflection about the nature of these phenomena, moreover, reveals a subject matter that is internally coherent, that is distinctive in its point of view, and that is at least capable of generating its own unique body of theory.

Stated most succinctly, the phenomena that are not otherwise accounted for, and that we shall henceforth regard as the subject matter of the field of foreign policy, are those that reflect an association between variations in the behavior of national actors and variations in their external environments. The distinctive point of view of this field is that inquiry must focus on the association between the two sets of variations and that this association can only be comprehended if it is examined and assessed under a variety of conditions. The theoretical propositions unique to the field are those that predict the association between the two sets of variations rather than only the behavior of the national actor or only the events in its environment.

Let us first look more closely at the subject matter of the field and indicate those aspects which render it internally coherent. Thus far we have loosely referred to foreign policy phenomena as if their nature was self-evident. Obviously, an enumeration of the major phenomena encompassed by this loose terminology is necessary if an assessment is to be made of whether they constitute a coherent body of data. Such an enumeration seems best begun with the premise that at the heart of foreign policy analysis is a concern with sequences of interaction, perceptual or behavioral, which span national boundaries and which unfold in three basic stages. The first, or *initiatory*, stage involves the activities, conditions, and influences—human and nonhuman—that stimulate national actors to undertake efforts to modify circumstances in their external environments. The second, or *implementive*, stage consists of the activities, conditions, and influences through which the stimuli of the initiatory stage are translated into purposeful actions directed at modifying objects in the external environment. The third, or *responsive*, stage denotes the activities, conditions, and influences that comprise the reactions of the objects of the modification attempts.[47] The three stages so defined encompass, respectively, the independent, intervening, and dependent variables of foreign policy analysis.

The independent variables can be usefully divided into two major types, those that are internal to the actor that initiates a foreign policy undertaking[48] and those that are external to it. The former include any human or nonhuman activities, conditions, and influences operative on the domestic scene that stimulate governmental officials to seek, on behalf of the national actor, to preserve or alter some aspect of the international system. Examples of internal independent variables are elections, group conflicts, depleted oil reserves, geographic insularity, demands for higher tariffs, historic value orientations, a lack of societal unity, executive-legislative frictions, and so on, through all the diverse factors that contribute to national life and that can thereby serve as sources of foreign policy. External independent variables also include human and nonhuman activities, conditions, and influences, but these occur abroad and operate as foreign policy stimuli by serving as the objects that officials seek to preserve or alter through their undertakings. Diplomatic incidents, deteriorating

[47] This three-stage formulation of foreign policy sequences derives from a conception, elaborated in Chapter 10, which posits certain kinds of efforts to modify behavior, together with the modifications that do or do not subsequently ensue, as the essence of political behavior.

[48] As indicated in Chapter 4, the use of the word "undertaking" throughout is intended to emphasize that by "foreign policy" is meant considerably more than mere pronouncements indicating present or future lines of action. Such a designation helps to remind us that foreign policy can arise out of complex sources and require the mobilization of complex resources as well as lengthy and continuous efforts to bring about modifications of situations and conditions in the external environment.

economies, crop failures, military buildups, elections, and historic enmities are but a few of the many diverse circumstances abroad that might stimulate official action. Obviously, foreign policy undertakings cannot be completely divorced from either the society out of which they emanate or the circumstances abroad toward which they are directed, so that some external and internal independent variables will be present in every undertaking, albeit the mix of the two types may vary considerably from one undertaking to the next.

The intervening variables in foreign policy analysis are hardly less extensive. They include not only any attitudes, procedures, capabilities, and conflicts that shape the way in which governmental decision-makers and agencies assess the initiatory stimuli and decide how to cope with them, but they also embrace any and all of the resources, techniques, and actions that may affect the way in which the decisions designed to preserve or modify circumstances in the international system are carried out. The priority of values held by officials; their tolerance for ambiguous information; their capacity for admitting past errors; their training and analytic skills; the hierarchical structure of their decision-making practices; the rivalry of agencies for money, power, and prestige; the administrative procedures employed in the field; the readiness to threaten the use of military force and the availability of men and material to back up the threats; the appropriateness of propaganda techniques; and the flexibility of foreign aid programs are examples of the many intervening variables that can operate in foreign policy undertakings.

The dependent variables comprising the responsive stage are equally complex and extensive. They include the activities, attitudes, relationships, institutions, capacities, and conditions in the international system that are altered (or not altered) or preserved (or not preserved) as a result of the foreign policy undertakings directed toward them. As in the case of independent variables, the dependent variables can be divided into two major types, those that involve an alteration or preservation of behavior internal to the object of the foreign policy undertaking and those that pertain to the object's changed or unchanged external behavior. Again a number of obvious examples can be cited. The readiness of another actor to enter into and/or conclude negotiations, the inclination to comply with or resist demands for support on issues in the United Nations, and the strengthening or weakening of an alliance exemplify external dependent variables. The ability or inability to put armies into the field as a consequence of military assistance, the continuance or downfall of a hostile government, and the emergence of a new social structure or the persistence of an old one as a result of a multifaceted foreign aid program are illustrative of circumstances that would be treated as internal dependent variables whenever they become the focus of foreign policy undertakings.

The field of foreign policy is thus seen to cover a vast range of phenomena. Circumstances can arise whereby virtually every aspect of local, national, and international politics may be part of the initiatory or responsive stage of the foreign policy process. Indeed, the foregoing examples indicate that students of foreign policy may often be led by their subject matter to move beyond political science to investigate phenomena in the other social sciences. They may even find themselves investigating phenomena in the physical sciences. This might occur, for example, if the foreign policy undertakings of interest aim to modify the external environment by compensating for depleted oil reserves. To comprehend the behavior of the national actor and the resistance or compliance of the actors abroad whose oil deposits make them the objects of modification attempts, investigators must acquire some familiarity with the geology, technology, and economy of discovering, mining, and transporting oil.[49]

Yet, despite its breadth of coverage, the subject matter of the foreign policy field is internally coherent. All the phenomena of interest to foreign policy analysts acquire structure and coherence through their concern with the three stages of the interaction process through which national actors purposefully relate themselves to the international system. If individual, group, organizational, or societal phenomena are not relevant to one of the stages of a particular foreign policy undertaking, then the analyst does not investigate them. A vast range of phenomena may fall within the scope of his concerns, but they always do so in a specific context—that of whether variations in the initiatory and implementive stages can be related to variations in the responsive stage. Often, to be sure, the analyst may find that the two sets of variations are unrelated to each other. Some, perhaps many, foreign policy undertakings are totally ineffective and thus do not reflect an association in the two sets of variations. However, the internal coherence of the subject matter of a field derives from logical possibilities and not from empirical realities. It is the legitimacy of the search for, not the fact of, association between the two sets of variations that renders foreign policy phenomena internally coherent.

This is not to deny that the subject matter of the foreign policy field

[49] Of course, all of this is not to say that the individual student of foreign policy should or can be so broad-gauged as to be able to handle all the phenomena that fall within his purview. We have been tracing the outlines of a field to be probed by many persons and not of a research design to be implemented by one. Plainly the diversity and range of materials encompassed by the field are too great for one analyst to master fully. On the other hand, presumably the individual researcher must be capable of communicating with the many types of specialists to whom he may have to turn for guidance on those aspects of undertakings that lie outside his competence.

overlaps many other fields at many points. As already indicated, the phenomena encompassed by the initiatory and implementive stages can be of considerable concern to students of national politics, just as those comprising the responsive stage can be highly relevant to the analysis of international politics. Furthermore, variations in any one of the stages may also be related to variations in sequences of behavior that span national boundaries but are not part of either of the other two stages. Foreign policy undertakings do have unintended consequences for social, economic, and political life, and, to the extent that they do, the phenomena of the field become central to these other disciplines. Yet notwithstanding such overlap, the foreign policy analyst structures his subject matter in such a way as to distinguish it from that of any other field. He is interested in the entire relationship that national actors establish with their external environments and not in only a segment of it. None of the three stages has any meaning for him by itself. The characteristics of each stage hold his attention only insofar as they may be associated with the characteristics of the other two. For him foreign policy becomes intelligible only to the extent that its sources, contents, and consequences are considered jointly. This is the distinctive viewpoint of the field. No other field concerns itself with the association between variables on both sides of national boundaries. The phenomena embraced by this association are the ones that always remain unexplained even after the fields of national and international politics are stretched to their limits. Students of national (or comparative) politics have no theoretical justification for sustaining an interest in foreign policy once the behavioral sequences it initiates are extended into the external environment. Although slow to make theoretical allowance for the point, they do have a vital concern with the internal consequences of the processes of foreign policy formulation and with the feedback effects that may result from the alterations which foreign policy undertakings bring about in the external environment. The responsive stage itself, however, lies outside of the scope of their field. Similarly, nothing in the theoretical foundations of international politics provides students of that field with justification for probing the sources of foreign policy that are located within national actors or the response to foreign policy undertakings that are confined to the target society and do not become foreign policy initiatives on the part of that society. Theories of international politics focus on the interactions of national actors and not on the sources or consequences of interaction which are not part of prior or subsequent interactions.

Although the problems posed by the third requirement for the existence of a field, a unique body of theoretical propositions, are discussed at greater length in a later section, it can be seen from the foregoing that the study of foreign policy also meets this condition. Propositions about the association between variations in the behavior of national actors and variations in their external environments cannot be derived from any other field of inquiry. Foreign policy theory necessarily borrows from theories of local and national politics in order to manipulate properly the internal independent variables of the initiatory stage, the intervening variables of the implementive stage, and the internal dependent variables of the responsive stage. It must also rely on theories of international politics for guidance in manipulating the external independent and dependent variables of the initiatory and responsive stages. Yet, by virtue of combining theory about domestic and international processes, foreign policy theory is neither domestic nor international theory. It bears the same relationship to these allied fields as social psychological theory does to psychology on the one hand and sociology on the other.[50] Like social psychology, it alone consists of propositions that relate the behavior of an actor both to its own functioning and to its environment. The list of foreign policy theorists is not long and contains no names comparable to Lewin, Hovland, Newcomb, Asch, or Festinger in social psychology, but presumably this is due to the fact that the reorientation toward the comparative analysis of foreign policy has just begun rather than to an inherent inability of the field to support its own unique body of theory.

IV. SOME UNDERLYING ASSUMPTIONS

Having traced in bold strokes the outline of the field, some finer touches are in order. A number of problems require further discussion. Perhaps the most important of these is the question of why the responsive stage must be part of foreign policy analysis. Why not treat governmental decisions as the dependent variables and bypass the responsive stage? After all, it might be argued, aspects of the international system are being taken into account as external independent variables—why must they also be regarded as dependent variables? If the focus is on the national actor in relation to its environment, why is it necessary to investigate the consequences of foreign policy undertakings for other actors? Furthermore, how is one to know whether the presumed or modified behavior that constitutes the responsive stage is in fact a response to the foreign policy undertaking being examined? Are there not insurmountable methodological

50 For a discussion of how the distinctiveness of social psychology is not diminished despite the large extent to which it borrows from psychology and sociology, see Theodore M. Newcomb, *Social Psychology* (New York: Dryden, 1950), Chap. 1; and Morton Deutsch and Robert M. Krauss, *Theories in Social Psychology* (New York: Basic Books, 1965), Chap. 1.

problems inherent in the task of separating responses to external influences from behavior generated by other factors?

A similar line of questioning can be pursued with respect to the initiatory and implementive stages. Since foreign policy undertakings are being treated as purposeful, why not regard the governmental decisions that launch them as the independent variables and bypass the initiatory stage? Why not focus on the purposeful behavior directly, rather than positing it as an intervening process? If the interaction of national actors and their environments constitutes the subject matter of the field, why does not its scope include unplanned actions as well as purposeful ones? How does one assess the relative potencies of all the independent variables that may be operative as a source of a foreign policy undertaking? Indeed, how does one determine whether the undertaking is a consequence of the external and internal independent variables being examined rather than of the decision-making process that launched it?

Another set of problems posed by the suggested outline concerns the nature of foreign policy theory. What are the main questions that such theory is designed to answer? Are not all the uninteresting questions answered by other fields? Do not national and international political theory, respectively, cope with the ways in which foreign policy phenomena are functional or dysfunctional for national and international systems? Posed differently, theories of national and international politics deal with the fascinating questions of why systems endure or collapse and how they do or do not achieve equilibria—but what kinds of systemic questions can be asked about foreign policy phenomena? If foreign policy analysis does not pose functional and systemic questions, what theoretical challenges does it have to offer? To repeat, is it a fantasy to aspire to the construction of generalized theories of foreign policy that are viable and relevant? If so, why compare? Why not simply examine the particular relationship that particular national actors establish with their particular environments?

Obviously this is not the place to develop full answers to all these questions. However, an explication of some of the basic assumptions underlying our delineation of the foreign policy field should clarify some of these problems and point the way to a more formal and extended attempt to resolve all of them.

The centrality of the responsive stage is unquestionably the most radical conclusion of our effort to trace the outlines of the foreign policy field. Probably because of the enormous methodological difficulties they pose, responses to foreign policy are usually examined with much less care than are the variables comprising the initiatory and implementive stages. Ordinarily analysts tend to settle for a brief account of the international environment in which the national actor is located, noting any limitations and opportunities that the environment may impose and offer, and then moving on to examine what the actor seeks to accomplish in this environment and why.[51] The problem of sorting out the consequences of foreign policy undertakings from the events that would have occurred anyway is so awesome that, in effect, the responsive stage is ordinarily viewed as consisting of constants rather than variables. Yet, here we are insisting that it cannot be bypassed, that it is a central aspect of the field, and that the methodological obstacles must be confronted and surmounted.

Several reasons and one assumption underlie this insistence. The assumption—perhaps better called an article of faith—is that the methodological problem is at least theoretically solvable. Differentiating between responses intended by political actors and those that would have occurred anyway is the central problem of political analysis and haunts research in all areas of the discipline. Yet it has not deterred inquiry into the responses of voters to candidates, of legislatures to interest groups, of bureaucracies to leaders. Why, then, should it block the analysis of attempts to modify behavior that span national boundaries? To be sure, the crossing of national boundaries renders foreign policy situations more complex than other types, but this is a difference in degree and not in kind. More variables may have to be examined in foreign policy analysis, but the problem remains that of identifying behavior that would not have occurred in the absence of a specified stimulus. The fact that the methodological equipment presently available rarely permits a satisfactory solution of the problem does not mean that it can never be solved. For political scientists to abandon inquiry on these grounds would be the equivalent of astronomers having long ago ceased theorizing about the far side of the moon because it could not be observed through telescopes. Old methodological techniques do get perfected and new types of equipment do get developed in political science as well as in astronomy. Political science is still a long way from having the equivalent of the space capsule, but recent progress with simulation and other procedures for tracing the flow of influence indicates that methodological innovation is far from over. Hence what is

---

[51] Interestingly, and perhaps significantly, works concerned with national actors passing through periods of dynamic readjustment to the international system stand out as exceptions to this general tendency. Recent works on postwar Germany, for example, are notable for the equal attention that they pay to the interaction of all three of the stages comprising the foreign policy field. Cf. Karl W. Deutsch and Lewis J. Edinger, *Germany Rejoins the Powers: Mass Opinion, Interest Groups, and Elites in* Contemporary German Foreign Policy (Stanford, Cal.: Stanford University Press, 1959); James L. Richardson, *Germany and the Atlantic Alliance: The Interaction of Strategy and Politics* (Cambridge, Mass.: Harvard University Press, 1966); and Wolfram F. Hanrieder, *West German Foreign Policy, 1949–1963: International Pressure and Domestic Response* (Stanford, Cal.: Stanford University Press, 1967).

important is whether it is at least theoretically possible to translate responses to foreign policy undertakings into observable behavior. The answer seems to be clearly in the affirmative and is the basis for the assumption that the methodological obstacles to treating the responsive stage as a set of dependent variables can be surmounted.

As for the substantive reasons for insisting that the responsive stage cannot be bypassed, one is the simple fact that a concern for foreign policy cannot be sustained without the question of its effectiveness and consequences arising. Some conception of the receptivity of the international system to the behavior of the national actor being examined is necessary even if the degree of receptivity is treated as a constant rather than a variable. Whether their research is oriented toward the solution of practical policy problems or the building of theoretical models, foreign policy analysts cannot avoid assessing the likelihood of one or another type of undertaking bringing about the desired modifications in the structure of the external environment. All their conceptual tools lead to such assessments. If one examines any of the standard concepts of the field, it soon becomes clear that what we have called the responsive stage is a central element. To refer, say, to "foreign policy attitudes" is to denote judgments about general or specific conditions abroad that ought to be preserved or altered; to describe "foreign policy issues" is to depict either conflicts at home about what constitutes effective action abroad or conflicts abroad that may have adverse consequences at home if attempts to modify them are not undertaken; to study "foreign policy decision-making" is to analyze what officials hope to preserve or alter through their external behavior. Since the responsive stage thus cannot be bypassed, it seems only prudent to treat its variability as a central aspect of the field.

But there is an even more important reason for placing the responsive stage on an analytic par with the initiatory and implementive stages. Not only do the responses that unfold in the environment provide a means of assessing the effectiveness of foreign policy undertakings, but they also lead the analyst to treat the foreign policy process as dynamic rather than static, since many of the dependent variables that comprise the responsive stage of one undertaking operate as independent variables in the initiatory stage of a subsequent undertaking. For example, having fostered viable social and political institutions abroad through an effective foreign aid program, the aid-giving nation may then be faced with a changing alliance system as the newly strengthened recipient societies are able to follow more independent foreign policy lines of their own. Neither the national actor nor its environment, in other words, ever remains constant. Both are in a state of flux, altering in response to each other in a dynamic fashion that serves to maintain the distinction between the actor and its environment.

The foreign policy process is thus marked by continuity, and it is only for analytic convenience that undertakings are examined separately. The ultimate goal is comparison across many undertakings, since only then can higher levels of generalization about national actors in their environments be attained. Treating each undertaking as an analytic unit facilitates movement toward this goal, while the inclusion of the responsive stage serves as a means of bridging the artificial discontinuity to which such a procedure gives rise.

There is another important advantage in the notion that the dependent variables of the responsive stage may operate as independent variables in the initiatory stage of subsequent undertakings. It provides a basis for drawing a boundary beyond which the student of foreign policy no longer needs to analyze the consequences of attempts to modify behavior abroad. If the foreign policy analyst were to examine all the repercussions of an undertaking, eventually he would become, in effect, a student of the society toward which the undertaking was directed. Such a transformation from foreign policy analyst to national politics specialist, however, is prevented by utilizing the distinction between those dependent variables that are and those that are not likely to serve as independent variables in subsequent undertakings. That is, having examined the responsive stage with a view to establishing whether it is associated with variations in the initiatory and implementive stages, the foreign policy analyst loses interest in the responses if they do not emerge as stimuli to further action on the part of the national actor whose undertakings are the focus of his attention.

Much the same line of reasoning underlies the inclusion of the initiatory stage as a major aspect of the field. While the analysis of foreign policy would be greatly simplified if pre-decisional determinants were treated as constants and governmental policymaking processes as independent variables, such a procedure would omit from consideration an important body of phenomena of interest to students of the field. As in the case of the responsive stage, both policy-oriented and theory-building analysts have substantive concerns that lead them to inquire into the factors that give rise to foreign policy undertakings and to assess the relative potencies of the factors they identify. In his effort to improve the quality and direction of undertakings, the policy-oriented analyst must examine their sources or he cannot account for the variation in their degrees of success and failure. Likewise, his theoretically oriented colleague must differentiate among the many domestic and foreign influences acting upon decision-makers in order to construct models that are both susceptible to empirical proof and capable of explaining an even wider body of phenomena. To be sure, both types of analysts could follow the precepts of the decision-making approach and analyze the pre-decisional determinants in terms of the stimuli to which government officials see themselves as reacting.[52] In doing so, however, they would nevertheless be treating the antecedents of decision as independent variables. They would still be asking whether variations that occurred prior to decision were associated with those that occurred subsequently. Hence it seems preferable to examine the initiatory stage directly rather than indirectly through the perceptions of officialdom. That is, since assessing the strength of causal factors is at best extremely difficult, it seems unnecessarily complicating to make the task that of first determining how others (officials) assess the relevant factors and then assessing these assessments.[53] Besides, officials may not reconstruct the world in such a way as to highlight the variations in the initiatory stage that the analyst is interested in correlating with variations in the responsive stage, in which case he would have to forego the decision-making approach anyway. The procedure of focusing on the initiatory stage directly does not, however, neglect the fact that the way officials perceive and experience the world is crucial to the action they take. It will be recalled that the dimensions of purpose, timing, and style given to undertakings by the way in which decision-makers experience the initiatory stimuli, are treated as intervening variables in the implementive stage. Furthermore, those aspects of the decision-making process itself that operate as initiatory stimuli (e.g. competition for prestige, power, or appropriations among agencies and their personnel) are regarded as independent variables and analyzed accordingly.

Turning to the question of why purposeful behavior serves as an organizing focus of the foreign field, it must first be emphasized that by "purpose" is meant nothing more than the fact that officials do not act at random. They always have some goal in mind, some notion of how the action they take will help to preserve or modify one or more aspects of the international environment. The goals need not be highly concrete or rational. Nor need they be integral parts of an overall plan. On the contrary, our conception of goals allows for them to be ambiguous, tentative and not fully formed. They might amount to no more than "stalling for time" or be no clearer than an effort to "muddle through."[54] They might well be unrealistic goals and give rise to a host of unintended and undesir-

---

[52] Snyder, Bruck, and Sapin, *op. cit.*, p. 37.

[53] For an elaboration of this point, see Chapter 12.

[54] Although policy-making designed to "muddle through" situations is here conceived to be goal-oriented behavior, some analysts tend to posit it as lacking this characteristic. (Cf. Charles E. Lindblom, "The Science of 'Muddling Through,'" *Public Administration Review*, 29 [1959], pp. 79–88.) The latter position arises out of the unnecessarily narrow view that only behavior directed toward long-range, well planned, and duly considered ends can be goal-oriented. Ends may be short-range, poorly planned, and impetuously considered, but action designed to serve them is nonetheless goal-oriented. Even the "muddler" hopes to get "through" and thus it is difficult to conceive of his behavior as purposeless.

able consequences. Imprecise, ineffective, and counterproductive as they may be, however, foreign policy undertakings are launched for some reason. They do envision some future state of affairs as being served and it is in this sense that they are regarded as purposeful.

The emphasis on the purposefulness of foreign policy undertakings serves two needs. One is obvious. Without the presumption of goal-oriented behavior, there would be no basis for knowing which variations in the external environment should be examined in order to determine whether they are associated with variations in the behavior of foreign policy actors. The variable circumstances in the environment are so numerous that many are bound to be associated merely by chance with the foreign policy undertakings being considered. The student of foreign policy, however, is interested in systematic associations and not in those founded on happenstance. The goal-oriented nature of foreign policy provides the analyst with a reference point for selecting associations around which to organize his inquiry. To be sure, he may be interested in associations involving variations in the initiatory stage that officials do not formally include among their purposes; and he may also wish to probe associations involving variations in the responsive stage that are unintended consequences of the purposeful undertakings. But, even in cases where his focus extends beyond the goal-oriented nature of foreign policy, such orientations still serve as a baseline for his assessments.

A second reason for emphasizing the purposefulness of undertakings is that it helps to distinguish foreign policy from the total set of interactions that occur betwen a society and its environment. As previously indicated, foreign policy phenomena constitute only one kind of linkage that a society establishes with its environment. Others are established by businessmen, scientists, artists, and tourists, to name but a few of the many types of private individuals and groups whose interactions span national boundaries. These cultural, social, economic, and scientific linkages can be so relevant to the processes of foreign policy that the analyst may often find it appropriate to treat them as independent and/or dependent variables operative in undertakings. In themselves, however, such linkages are not of interest to the foreign policy analyst. He is interested in the national actor, not in subnational actors—in public individuals or groups, not in private ones. Stated in another way, the foreign policy analyst is concerned with the linkages that the entire society, rather than segments of it, establishes with the external environment. Only governments can link the personnel and resources of the entire society to situations abroad and this, to repeat, governments always do for some purpose. On the other hand, whether nongovernmental linkages are or are not intended by those who sustain them, there is a limit beyond which they cannot be controlled by governmental purposes. Up to a point travel can be forbidden, and so can trade and scientific and other types of exchange. But, if only because some of the interaction is perceptual, government cannot arrogate to itself total control over external ties. Hence, from the perspective of the national actor, the linkages established by subnational groups or by individuals are not purposeful. From this perspective, the actions of governments are the only goal-oriented external undertakings of the entire society. This characteristic distinguishes foreign policy from all other national-international linkages.

V. THE CHALLENGE OF THEORY

There remains the problem of what questions foreign policy theory is designed to answer. As implied earlier, the foreign policy analyst is not faced with the kinds of systemic and functional challenges that impress his counterparts in the national and international fields. Foreign policy theory can never in itself explain why and how a national system manages to persist or why and how it collapses. Such theory can shed light on one of the functional requirements of all national systems—the necessity of adapting to the environment—but it does not pretend to deal with the full range of integrative mechanisms through which national systems maintain their internal coherence. Thus it can never provide more than partial answers to the intriguing questions of systemic persistence. Similarly, the endurance or deterioration of international systems lies outside the competence of the foreign policy theorist. By explaining why and how one or more national actors interact with their environments, foreign policy theory provides some of the material needed for a functional analysis of international systems, but it does not address itself to the sum of the separate patterns of interaction maintained by different actors and thus the student of foreign policy must again stand aside when the fascinating questions of systemic stability and change are posed by his colleagues in the international field.

It is exactly at this point that foreign policy theorists run the risk of engaging in unrealistic fantasy. Those whose aspirations for foreign policy theory include the capacity to explain and predict systemic coherence and collapse are bound to be thwarted. The fantasy is enticing and the aspiration is worthy, but neither can ever be realized. Foreign policy is the only field that relates the behavior of a national actor both to its environment and to its own functioning, but the price of such a focus is that the boundaries of the field do not correspond to those of any empirical political system. While a foreign policy undertaking can be judged as functional or dysfunctional for the national system that undertakes it and functional or dysfunctional for the international system with respect to which it has consequences, there is no concrete "foreign policy system" for which its functionality can be assessed.

What, then, are the theoretical challenges posed by the foreign policy field? The answer is that the challenges are endless if aspirations are scaled down to the level of middle-range theory and not cast in systemic terms at the highest level of generalization.[55] The question is paralyzing only if the foreign policy analyst wants to construct broad-gauged models that account for the dynamics of concrete systems of action whose boundaries are rooted in historical experience and political authority. Once he accepts the fact that his subject matter does not permit emulation of colleagues in allied fields who employ functional analysis and systems theory, a host of theoretical tasks come into view that enliven thought and compel inquiry.

Before identifying these tasks, it is useful to note that the act of identification is itself important. Too many first-rate theorists have forsaken the foreign policy field because of its failure to excite their imaginations. For example, two of the most distinguished empirical theorists in the modern era of political science, Almond and Dahl, started their careers with important works dealing with foreign policy [56] and subsequently turned their talents to phenomena that originate and unfold within national boundaries. Neither ever returned to the study of foreign policy, apparently finding the construction of theory about units bounded by a common system of authority more challenging. Hence the drama of foreign policy undertakings, of national actors coping with their environments, needs to be emphasized if the field is to recruit and keep theorists capable of exploiting the re-orientation toward comparative analysis.

The many challenges inherent in foreign policy phenomena are most succinctly identified by calling attention to two main types, those that derive from the truly political quality of the field's unit of analysis, the undertaking, and those that are posed by the adaptive function of national systems. The former set of challenges are rarely appreciated. Many political scientists do not seem to recognize that while comprehension of foreign policy undertakings may not explain or anticipate systemic stability and

[55] The distinction between middle-range and general theories is best described by Robert K. Merton, who notes that the former are "intermediate to the minor working hypotheses evolved in abundance during the day-by-day routines of research, and the all-inclusive speculations comprising a master conceptual scheme from which it is hoped to derive a very large number of empirically observed uniformities of social behavior," in *Social Theory and Social Structure* (Glencoe, Ill.: Free Press, 1957, revised edition), pp. 5–6.

[56] Gabriel A. Almond, *The American People and Foreign Policy* (New York: Harcourt, 1950), and Robert A. Dahl, *Congress and Foreign Policy* (New York: Harcourt, 1950).

change, it will provide fundamental insights into the dynamics of politics. For the attempt to modify behavior across national boundaries is perhaps the purest of all political acts. Unlike their domestic counterparts, foreign policy officials cannot appeal to the common ties of culture and history to secure the compliance of those whose behavior they are attempting to modify. Unlike domestic officials, they cannot merely rely on the structures from which their own authority is derived to induce compliance. The foreign policy official is the only politician whose actions are directed toward persons and situations that are normally responsive to cultural standards, historical aspirations, and sources of authority that are different from his own. Hence the foreign policy undertaking is the most delicate of political actions and the most fragile of political relationships. It involves a degree of manipulation of symbols that is unmatched in any other political situation. It requires a balance between the use of persuasion on the one hand and the use or threat of force on the other that is more precarious than it is in any other kind of politics. It reveals the limits of legitimacy, the sources of loyalty, and the dynamics of bargaining. It demonstrates the inertia of habit as well as the continuities to which habitual behavior gives rise. It exposes the universality of resistance to change and, correspondingly, the large extent to which change can be introduced only in small increments at the margins of organized life.

In short, the field of foreign policy contains the promise that virtually every dimension of politics will be examined in its purest form. In a profound sense the challenge of foreign policy theory is at the middle-range level hardly less than that of empirical political theory itself. There is no problem that the empirical political theorist confronts—whether it be that of authority, law, influence, responsibility, federalism, rationality, order, sovereignty, community, leadership, communications, or revolution—that cannot be fruitfully investigated in the foreign policy field.[57]

The other clearly identifiable set of theoretical challenges arises out of the aforementioned notion that foreign policy undertakings perform an adaptive function for national systems. General systems analysis may be beyond the scope of the foreign policy theorist, but the functional problems posed within the area of his concern are nonetheless compelling. Even though national systems may collapse for strictly internal reasons, they cannot persist without coping with their environments and this never-ending effort to maintain boundaries and achieve an accommodation with the environment commands attention and provokes inquiry. It is just as dramatic as a newborn child's efforts to make the transition to an oxygen-filled world, an adolescent's search for identity in a world that seems

[57] For an elaboration of the notion that the quintessence of politics can be found in the foreign policy field, see Chapter 10.

to engulf independence and demand acquiescence, a marriage's endeavor to survive in a world of possessive relatives and tempting lovers, a business firm's struggle to keep up with technological change and a world of aggressive competitors, a minority group's fight to bring about a world of fair and equal treatment, a political party's striving to expand its popularity and create a world that it can govern. For none of these—or for any of the many other actors that could be listed—is accommodation with the environment easy or predetermined. At any moment the boundaries separating a system from its environment can give way and suffer drastic revision, if not elimination. At no point can an actor assume that a permanent accommodation has been attained. Performance of the adaptive function is never completed. It must be continuously serviced. Thus foreign policy undertakings are inherently intriguing, both in the basic emotional sense that they are rooted in human efforts to survive and prosper and in the theoretical sense that it is no simple matter to fathom why and how national systems manage to remain differentiated from their environments.

But why compare? Granting the challenges inherent in the study of foreign policy undertakings, why is it also necessary to reorient the field toward comparative analysis? Although a full discussion of the reasons would constitute an essay in itself, they can be asserted simply and concisely here. Comparison is necessary because the two major theoretical challenges we have identified cannot otherwise be met. Comprehension of the external activities undertaken by one national system is not sufficient to answer the questions of systemic adaptation and political process that are inherent in foreign policy phenomena. The repeated experiences of two or more systems must be carefully contrasted for an answer to such questions to begin to emerge. Only in this way can the theorist begin to satisfy his curiosity and the policy analyst begin to accumulate reliable knowledge on which sound recommendations and choices are made. Only in this way will it be possible to move beyond historical circumstances and comprehend the continuities of national life in a world of other nations.

Postscript

The prediction made eight years ago that the comparative study of foreign policy would become a major preoccupation in the 1970s has already been confirmed. A trend that was described in 1967 as an "occasional" paper, book, dissertation, or text on the subject can now be fairly characterized as an incessant outpouring of research and teaching materials. This outpouring has been so great, in fact, that it can only be highlighted here; the important task of compiling a full bibliographic essay must be postponed to another time or left to others.

That the prediction has been upheld in the realm of teaching is perhaps most clearly indicated by the publication of a separate volume of twenty syllabi (out of "approximately" forty submitted) for courses in which some kind of comparative approach to foreign policy phenomena was undertaken.[58] Moreover, the prescience of textbook publishers has resulted in such a proliferation of texts and books of reading that the number of courses presently being given on the subject is probably much greater than it was when the anthology of syllabi was compiled. Or at least it is now possible to organize such a course around a few basic works rather than relying on fugitive papers or noncomparable treatments. To be sure, the latter treatments are still available, both in the form of innumerable texts on American foreign policy and in compendia of single-country analyses. Macridis's compendium, for example, is now in its fourth edition and it still characterizes efforts to compare foreign policy phenomena rigorously as a "hopeless task." [59] But a pronounced trend in this proliferation of teaching materials has been the use of a comparative context. This has been done both in single-author texts [60] and in books of readings,[61] of which this volume is still another instance. Indeed, even selected dimensions of foreign policy phenomena, such as conflict behavior and reactions to crisis, have become the focus of comparative treatment in texts.[62] No less indicative, teaching packages that allow students to work out problems in the comparative analysis of foreign policy [63] or to engage in foreign policy simulations [64] have also become readily available. Equally indicative

[58] Charles F. Hermann and Kenneth N. Waltz (eds.), *Basic Courses in Foreign Policy: An Anthology of Syllabi* (Beverly Hills: Sage Publications, 1970).

[59] Roy C. Macridis (ed.), *Foreign Policy in World Politics* (Englewood Cliffs, N.J.: Prentice-Hall, 1972), p. 25.

[60] Roy E. Jones, *Analyzing Foreign Policy: An Introduction to Some Conceptual Problems* (London: Routledge and Kegan-Paul, 1970); John P. Lovell, *Foreign Policy in Perspective.: Strategy, Adaptation, Decision Making* (New York: Holt, Rinehart and Winston, 1970); and David O. Wilkinson, *Comparative Foreign Relations: Framework and Methods* (Belmont, Calif.: Dickenson, 1969).

[61] William O. Chittick, *The Analysis of Foreign Policy Outputs* (Columbus, Ohio: Merrill, 1974); Harold K. Jacobson and William Zimmerman (eds.), *The Shaping of Foreign Policy* (New York: Atherton, 1969); Wolfram F. Hanrieder (ed.), *Comparative Foreign Policy* (New York: David McKay, 1971); and James N. Rosenau (ed.), *Comparing Foreign Policies* (Berverly Hills: Sage Publishing, 1974).

[62] Cf. Alexander L. George, David K. Hall and William E. Simons, *The Limits of Coercive Diplomacy* (Boston: Little, Brown, 1971); T. Halper, *Foreign Policy Crisis: Appearance and Reality in Decision Making* (Columbus, Ohio: Merrill, 1971); and Jonathan Wilkenfeld (ed.), *Conflict Behavior and Linkage Politics* (New York: David McKay, 1973).

[63] Patrick J. McGowan and Michael K. O'Leary, "Methods and Data for the Comparative Analysis of Foreign Policy," in C. W. Kegley, Jr., G. A. Raymond, R. M. Rood and R. A. Skinner (eds.), *International Events and the Comparative Analysis of Foreign Policy* (Columbia, University of South Carolina Press, 1975).

[64] For example, see Charles P. Schleicher, *Participant's Manual for Real-Nation Gaming* (Columbus, Ohio: Merrill, 1973).

are signs that highly analytic examples may be replacing historical narratives as the means used by teachers to expose their students to real-world events. At least the popularity of monographs such as Allison's analysis of how three different models might be used to explain U.S. behavior in the Cuban missile crisis suggest that even single-country case studies are being treated comparatively in the classroom.[65] Finally, for teachers who prefer to open or close courses on an abstract note, short essays elaborating and extolling the virtues of a comparative approach to foreign policy can be assigned.[66]

On the research side, too, the prediction has been confirmed. The proliferation of comparative studies has been nothing short of astonishing over the past seven years. Now dissertations in this vein are not only in progress,[67] but a number of important ones have also been completed that compare, both theoretically and empirically, selected aspects of the external behavior of either all the nations in the world or some analytic subsample of them.[68] Collaborative research efforts spanning several universities have been launched, and in one case, at least temporarily completed.[69] Attempts to generate quantitative materials that will facilitate analysis of the sources of foreign policy behavior have mushroomed, and many data sets have been created with substantial financial support from federal sources.[70] The resulting flow of articles and monographs devoted to the comparative analysis of foreign policy is too great even to begin to enumerate, but the appear-

[65] Graham T. Allison, *Essence of Decision* (Boston: Little, Brown, 1971).

[66] See, for example, Hanrieder (ed.), *op. cit.*; and J. David Singer, *The Scientific Study of Politics: An Approach to Foreign Policy Analysis* (Morristown, N.J.: General Learning, 1972).

[67] See Rona B. Hitlin, "Doctoral Dissertations in Political Science, 1972," *PS*, 5 (Fall, 1972), pp. 513-74.

[68] For example, see Clair K. Blong, "A Comparative Study of the Foreign Policy Behavior of Political Systems Exhibiting High Versus Low Levels of External Penetration," Ph.D. dissertation, University of Maryland, 1973; Charles W. Kegley, Jr., "Toward the Construction of an Empirically Grounded Typology of Foreign Policy Output Behavior," Ph.D. dissertation, Syracuse University, 1971; Patrick J. McGowan, "Theoretical Approaches to the Comparative Study of Foreign Policy," Ph.D. dissertation, Northwestern University, 1970; David W. Moore, "Governmental and Societal Influences of Foreign Policy: a Partial Examination of Rosenau's adaptation Model," Ph.D. dissertation, Ohio State University, 1970; and Steven A. Salmore, "Foreign Policy and National Attributes: a Multivariate Analysis," Ph.D. dissertation, Princeton University, 1972.

[69] James N. Rosenau, Philip M. Burgess and Charles F. Hermann, "The Adaptation of Foreign Policy Research: A Case Study of an Anti-Case Study Project," *International Studies Quarterly*, 17 (March 1973), pp. 119-44.

[70] Cf. Edward E. Azar, "Analysis of International Events," *Peace Research Reviews*, 4 (November, 1970), pp. 1-106; Philip M. Burgess, "The Comparative Analysis of Policy Environments: a Report on the CAPE Project," Behavioral Sciences Laboratory, Ohio State University (mimeo., 1970); William R. Corson, "Measuring Conflict and Cooperation Intensity in International Relations," a paper presented at the Michigan State University International Events Data Conference, East Lansing, 1969; Charles F. Hermann, "Bureaucratic Politics and Foreign Policy: a Theoretical Framework

ance of a yearbook designed to provide an outlet for the increase is a good indication of their number.[71]

But the original questions remain: Does all this activity add up to more than a fad? Does it still express an unrealized fantasy? Does it reflect the characteristics of a field? My own answers are resoundingly negative to the second question and even more emphatically positive to the first and last.

It might be argued that fads are by definition momentary and that any mode of inquiry that has persisted for nearly a decade has passed the test of being more than mere craze. There are, however, more persuasive reasons for judging these eight years of effort as more than a passing phase. The vast research output it has spawned does more than pay lip service to the comparative method. It reveals an intense, restless, and creative use of models, variables, and methodologies in which comparisons are hypothesized or made. The complexities of foreign policy phenomena have yielded to the scientific mode, and increasingly parsimonious conceptions that are not bound by time and place have been built, extended, and revised. Descriptions have been supplemented by analyses, implicit assumptions have given way to explicit propositions, unrelated examples have been replaced by recurring patterns, and noncomparable case studies have been complemented by careful replications. Where past investigations focused on either concrete single countries (such as England or China) or concrete clusters of countries based on geographic location (such as those in Europe or the Far East), now the nations to be examined are chosen on the basis of analytic categories as well, with small ones being perhaps most intensely probed [72] but with comparisons between large and small nations, between open and closed ones, and between developed and underdeveloped ones by no means being neglected.[73] Indeed, a rich

Using Events Data," a paper presented at the Annual Meeting of the International Studies Association, New York, 1973; and Charles A. McClelland, R. G. Tomlinson, R. G. Sherwin, G. A. Hill, H. L. Colhoun, P. H. Fenn, and J. D. Martin, *The Management and Analysis of International Event Data: A Computerized System for Monitoring and Projecting Event Flows* (Los Angeles: University of Southern California, 1971).

[71] Patrick J. McGowan (ed.), *Sage International Yearbook of Foreign Policy Studies* (Beverly Hills: Sage Publications, 1973, 1974 and 1975), Vols. I, II, and III.

[72] Robert L. Rothstein, *Alliances and Small Powers* (New York: Columbia University Press, 1968); V. V. Sveics, *Small Nation Survival: Political Defense in Unequal Conflicts* (Jericho, N.Y.: Exposition, 1970); and David Vital, *The Survival of Small States: Studies in Small/Great Power Conflict* (London: Oxford University Press, 1971) and *The Inequality of States: A Study of the Small Power in International Relations* (Oxford: Clarendon, 1967).

[73] Cf. Richard A. Butwell (ed.), *Foreign Policy and the Developing Nation* (Lexington: University of Kentucky Press, 1969); Charles F. Hermann and Maurice A. East, "Do Nation-Types Account for Foreign Policy Behavior?" in J. N. Rosenau (ed.), *Comparing Foreign Policies* (Beverly Hills: Sage Publications, 1974); Moore, *op. cit.*; James N. Rosenau and Gary D. Hoggard, "Foreign Policy Behavior in Dyadic

literature is beginning to emerge in which comparisons are organized around even more precise and narrower, but no less analytic foci. The degree to which a society has been penetrated by another,[74] the role played by personality variables in foreign policy making,[75] the interaction of racial stratification and foreign policy behavior,[76] the impact of regime structure and change on foreign policy behavior,[77] the role of common markets and other situational variables as sources of foreign policy;[78] the tendency to found present policies on previous ones [79]—these are but a few of the more creative analytic categories that have been employed to compare the external behavior of nations.[80] Furthermore, the comparative mode has even begun to affect single-nation studies, in which the behavior of a nation has been compared at different points in time and with respect to different dimensions of behavior in different parts of the world.[81] That these efforts amount to more than old wine in new bottles, that instead they reflect a basic reorganization of foreign policy analysis, can be demonstrated by noting that it has already proven possible to derive 118 propositions from 203 comparative studies in which foreign policy phenomena are com-

Relationships: Testing a Pre-theoretical Extension," in J. N. Rosenau (ed.), *Comparing Foreign Policies*; Salmore, *op. cit.*; and Singer, *op. cit.*

[74] Clair K. Blong, "Foreign Policy Behavior in Penetrated Political Systems," a paper presented at the Annual Meeting of the International Studies Association, New York, 1973.

[75] Margaret G. Hermann, "How Leaders Process Information and the Effects on Foreign Policy," a paper presented at the Annual Meeting of the American Political Science Association, Washington, D.C., 1972.

[76] Albert Eldridge, "Foreign Policy and Discrimination: the Politics of Indigenization," Duke University (mimeo, N.d.).

[77] Barbara Salmore and Steven Salmore, "Structure and Change in Regimes—Their Effect on Foreign Policy," a paper presented at the Annual Meeting of the American Political Association, Washington, D.C., 1972.

[78] W. Andrew Axline, "Common Markets, Free Trade Areas, and the Comparative Study of Foreign Policy," (mimeo, N.d.); and Linda P. Brady, "The Impact of Situational Variables on Foreign Policy," a paper presented at the Annual Meeting of the Midwest Political Science Association, Chicago, 1973.

[79] W. R. Phillips and R. C. Crain, "Dynamic Foreign Policy Interactions: Reciprocity and Uncertainty in Foreign Policy," paper presented at the Annual Meeting of the American Political Science Association, Washington, D.C., 1972.

[80] For abstracts of fifty-one empirical studies employing still other categories, see Susan D. Jones and J. David Singer, *Beyond Conjecture in International Politics* (Itasca, Ill.: Peacock, 1972).

[81] See, for example, Michael Brecher, *The Foreign Policy System of Israel* (New Haven: Yale University Press, 1972); John W. Eley, "Events Data and Foreign Policy Theory: an Analysis of American Foreign Policy Toward Internal Wars, 1945-1970," paper presented at the Annual Meeting of the International Studies Association, New York, 1973; Rudolph J. Rummel, "U.S. Foreign Relations: Conflict, Cooperation, and Attribute Distances," in B. M. Russett (ed.), *Peace, War, and Numbers* (Beverly Hills: Sage Publications, 1972), pp. 71-113; Franklin B. Weinstein, "The Uses of Foreign Policy in Indonesia: An Approach to the Analysis of Foreign Policy in the Less Developed Countries," *World Politics*, 24 (April 1972), pp. 356-81; and Gilbert R. Winham, "Developing Theories of Foreign Policymaking: a Case Study of Foreign Aid," *Journal of Politics*, 32 (February 1970), pp. 41-70.

pared across a number of nations.[82]

The comparative study of foreign policy, in short, is a serious enterprise, one that seems likely to be around for a long time and to entice an ever larger number of students to its ranks. And as the early faddishness has yielded to sustained inquiry, it has become clear that the idea of analyzing foreign policy phenomena in terms of independent, intervening, and dependent variables that are operational and manipulable is no mere fantasy. A field has emerged around a welter of variables that describe one or another aspect of the initiatory, implementive, and responsive stages identified seven years ago as necessary to delineate foreign policy phenomena as a separate and distinctive subject matter. The responsive stage has been relatively neglected, and much remains to be done in tracing the links among the variables encompassed by the three stages, but there can be no gainsaying that the collective efforts of many researchers have brought the study of foreign policy into existence as a rigorous, self-sustaining field of inquiry.

This conclusion is reinforced even further by another conception of what constitutes a field, namely, Kuhn's notion of a "normal science." [83] In my original article I asserted that for a field to exist it must have substantive discipline, that is, a specified subject matter and a theoretical perspective that structures the subject matter in a distinctive way. Kuhn, however, suggests that a field can be defined by looking at what researchers do in relation to one another, regardless of the content of the phenomena they investigate or the theory they follow. He sees the practitioners of a normal science as a community of like-minded investigators who share certain premises about how and when "truths" about the subject are established and who thus build on each other's work. They are commonly concerned, to use his phraseology, with solving certain "puzzles," and "no puzzle-solving enterprise can exist unless its practitioners share criteria which, for that group and for that time, determine when a puzzle has been solved." [84] Furthermore, in order to solve the puzzles and thereby extend understanding, the practitioners have a common interest in, and commitment to, building on each other's work and tying the loose ends of earlier solutions or unresolved puzzles:

---

[82] Patrick J. McGowan and Howard B. Shapiro, *The Comparative Study of Foreign Policy: A Survey of Scientific Findings* (Beverley Hills: Sage Publications, 1973).

[83] Thomas S. Kuhn, *The Structure of Scientific Revolutions* (Chicago: University of Chicago Press, 1970).

[84] Thomas S. Kuhn, "Logic of Discovery or Psychology of Research?" in I. Lakatos and A. Musgrave (eds.), *Criticism and the Growth of Knowledge* (Cambridge: University Press, 1970), p. 7.

Mopping-up operations are what engage most scientists through-out their careers. They constitute what I am here calling normal science. Closely examined, whether historically or in the contemporary laboratory, that enterprise seems to attempt to force nature into the preformed and relatively inflexible box that the paradigm (i.e., shared puzzle-solving orientations) supplies. No part of the aim of normal science to call forth new sorts of phenomena; indeed those that will not fit the box are often not seen at all. Nor do scientists normally aim to invent new theories, and they are often intolerant of those invented by others. Instead, normal-scientific research is directed to the articulation of those phenomena and theories that the paradigm already supplies.[85]

In short, Kuhn's formulation of a normal science allows for a field to be said to emerge when the degree of methodological and philosophical consensus among researchers is such that their contributions are merely elaborations and refinements of each other's work.[86] Viewed in this way, developments in the comparative study of foreign policy over the last seven years amply justify the conclusion that those engaged in the enterprise have nurtured a field into existence.

The vitality and persuasiveness of the events data movement is one indication of the emergent field. It has, in effect, provided a basis for consensus-building. Before large and wide-ranging data sets depicting the actions that foreign policy actors direct toward each other became available, researchers worked in isolation, confining themselves to case studies or imprecise observations of ambiguous phenomena that came under the general heading of "foreign policy." But the events data movement changed all this by making available a measure of repeated, concrete, and specifiable forms of behavior on the part of foreign policy actors which, in turn, made it possible for investigators to compare and cumulate their findings. The construction, perfection, application, and analysis of data sets that reflect what international actors are doing—act by act, day by day, and nation by nation—in contiguous, regional, and global situations has become a central preoccupation of researchers, involving them in a continual process of criticizing, revising, and extending each other's work. One need only peruse a number of compendia,[87] or scan the agendas of panels at the annual meetings of the International

---

[85] Kuhn, *The Structure of Scientific Revolutions*, p. 24.

[86] Kuhn gives the label *revolutionary science* to those rare instances when a researcher breaks with the prevailing puzzle-solving orientations and arrives at genuinely new theories that identify new puzzles.

[87] Such as Edward E. Azar, Richard A. Brody and Charles A. McClelland (eds.), *International Events Interaction Analysis: Some Research Considerations* (Beverly Hills: Sage Publications, 1972); Edward E. Azar and Joseph D. Ben-Dak (eds.), *Theory*

Studies Association or the American Political Science Association, to appreciate that mopping-up operations have begun and that what was once lip service to the virtues of behavioral research has now become a set of concrete premises and practices shared by a wide and ever-widening number of investigators.

Nor are these mopping-up operations confined to the realm of methodology. Events data present a host of methodological problems that continue to command the energy and attention of many researchers. But these do not constitute the only concern. Much energy and attention is also given to genuine substantive and theoretical problems, such as tests of hypotheses about the role of environmental factors;[88] formulations in which the sources of conflictual foreign policies in Africa,[89] Latin America,[90] and the Middle East[91] are subjected to intensive empirical scrutiny; evaluations of whether a cognitive balance model of the behavior of foreign policy officials better explains their actions than a role model;[92] assessments of the relative strength of internal and external factors as sources of foreign policy in one data set[93] and across data sets;[94] and — perhaps most indicative of all — replications of concrete substantive findings,[95] as well as findings pertaining to source coverage and category reliability.

and Practice of Events Research (New York: Gordon and Breach, 1974); Philip M. Burgess and Raymond W. Lawton, Indicators of International Behavior: An Assessment of Events Data Research (Beverly Hills: Sage Publications, 1972); Charles W. Kegley, Jr., Gregory A. Raymond, Robert M. Rood and Richard A. Skinner (eds.), International Events and the Comparative Analysis of Foreign Policy (Columbia: University of South Carolina Press, 1975); and John H. Sigler, John O. Field and Murray A. Adelman, Applications of Events Data Analysis: Cases, Issues, and Programs in International Interactions (Beverly Hills: Sage Publications, 1972).

[88] Dina A. Zinnes, "Some Evidence Relevant to the Man-Milieu Hypothesis," in J. N. Rosenau, V. Davis, and M. A. East (eds.), The Analysis of International Politics (New York: Free Press, 1972), pp. 209-52.

[89] John N. Collins, "Foreign Conflict Behavior and Domestic Disorder in Africa," pp. 251-93 in J. Wilkenfeld (ed.), Conflict Behavior and Linkage Politics (New York: David McKay, 1973); and Patrick J. McGowan, "Dimensions of African Foreign Policy Behavior: In Search of Dependence," a paper presented at the Annual Meeting of the Canadian Association of African Studies, Ottawa, 1973.

[90] John W. Eley and J. H. Peterson, "Societal Attributes and Foreign Policy Behavior in Latin America, 1963-1969," Western Kentucky University (mimeo, N.d.).

[91] Robert Burrowes and Bertram Spector, "The Strength and Direction of Relationships Between Domestic and External Conflict and Cooperation," in J. Wilkenfeld (ed.), Conflict and Behavior in Linkage Politics (New York, David McKay, 1973), pp. 294-321.

[92] Glen H. Stassen, "Individual Preference Versus Role-Constraint in Policy-Making: Senatorial Response to Secretaries Acheson and Dulles," World Politics, 25 (October 1972), pp. 96-119.

[93] Rosenau and Hoggard, op cit.

[94] James N. Rosenau and G. R. Ramsey, Jr., "External vs. Internal Sources of Foreign Policy Behavior: Testing the Stability of an Intriguing Set of Findings," a paper presented at the World Congress of the International Political Science Association, Montreal, 1973; reproduced in this volume as Chapter 8.

[95] Charles A. Powell, David Andrus, William Fowler and Kathleen Knight

All of this is not to say that comprehension of foreign policy phenomena lies immediately ahead. Normal science, as Kuhn notes, has limitations, an important one being that it tends to discourage theoretical venturesomeness. As a result, obstacles to understanding are sometimes swept under the rug instead of being mopped up. Two aspects of the field come to mind as obstacles that have not been adequately confronted. One is the possibility that the capacity of national governments to solve international problems is declining. The growing interdependence of societies and the resulting emergence of important international actors other than nation-states thus creates the possibility that foreign policy behavior may become increasingly less important as a factor in world affairs. If this is so, and if the field continues, as a normal science, to blind itself to theory and data that are not nation-state centered, then the progress of the last seven years may be short-lived. An exclusive focus on foreign policy behavior that fails to allow conceptually for other types of transnational interdependencies would surely negate not only the long-range aspiration for a deeper understanding of world politics, but in the short range it might also preclude adequate solutions to the puzzle of why nations act as they do in international affairs. To solve this puzzle, theoretical and empirical account must be taken of the differences between the kinds of issues to which foreign policy officials address themselves and those that they willingly or otherwise permit other international actors to process.

While there is reason to be concerned about the tendency of many, even most, investigators to be too nation-state centered in the hypotheses they frame and the data they gather to test them, happily the field is not without its gadflies who remind us that mopping-up operations can get out of hand.[96] In their enthusiasm for revolutionary science, some of these critics assert that nation-state-centered data and models of foreign policy behavior are becoming so obsolete that they should be replaced with a "world policy process" framework.[97] Such enthusiasm serves the field well, and one may hope that the response to it will be empirical investigation rather than outright rejection. My own view, elaborated elsewhere, is that the immediate problem is empirical rather than theoretical, that the world may be entering an asymmetrical era

"Determinants of Foreign Behavior: A Causal Modeling Approach," in J. N. Rosenau (ed.), *Comparing Foreign Policies* (Beverly Hills: Sage Publications, 1974); and Johnathan Wilkenfeld, "Domestic and Foreign Conflict," in J. Wilkenfeld (ed.), *Conflict Behavior and Linkage Politics*, pp. 107-23.

[96] See, for example, J. R. Handelman, J. A. Vasquez, Michael K. O'Leary and William D. Coplin, "Color it Morgenthau: a Data-Based Assessment of Quantitative International Relations Research," a paper presented at the Annual Meeting of the International Studies Association, New York, 1973; and Rober O. Keohane and Joseph S. Nye, Jr. (eds.), *Transnational Relations and World Politics* (Cambridge: Harvard University Press, 1972).

[97] Handelman et al., *op. cit.*

in which nation-states are the predominant actors in certain key issue-areas while subnational and supranational actors predominate in other areas, and that therefore we must develop data which will allow for the identification of the several types of issue-areas and the boundaries that divide them.[98]

A second obstacle to continued progress in the fields stems from the neglect of the responsive stage relative to the initiatory and implementive stages of foreign policy. As even this brief evaluation of the progress of the last eight years suggests, most of the effort has involved testing theories and cumulating findings about the sources of foreign policy behavior and the processes whereby policies come into being. The event rather than the undertaking has emerged as the basic unit of analysis, thus tending to preclude empirical inquiries into the responses to foreign policy behaviors evoked abroad and the feedback of these responses into subsequent behaviors. It is easy to see why the event is a more manageable unit of analysis than the undertaking. As noted in the original article, undertakings pose the enormous methodological problem of differentiating between responses to foreign policy acts and those that would have occurred anyway, and given all the work that was needed, researchers found valid reasons for not confronting it. The reasons for focusing on the responsive stage are no less compelling today, however, than they were seven years ago, especially in view of the insights yielded by the small amount of theoretical work that has included this stage.[99] Furthermore, perhaps the methodological obstacles to empirical inquiry into the responsive stage have been lessened by the advent of events data sets. Although events data are not necessarily constructed for the purpose of tracing feedback processes, it does seem possible to manipulate them in such a way as to allow for the creation of undertakings as analytic units by juxtaposing acts of different nations towards each other. Such a procedure is a poor substitute for the direct creation of undertakings data, but it may suffice to maintain forward movement until such time as more appropriate data sets become available.

In sum, there is still much to be done, but if progress in the next few years is anything like that which has marked the past eight, there is reason to believe that the dynamics of foreign policy will begin to yield rapidly to greater understanding. And in greater understanding there lies the greatest contribution that the field could offer: an enlarged

[98] James N. Rosenau, "Adaptive Policies in an Interdependent World," *Orbis*, 16 (Spring 1972), pp. 153-73.

[99] See Patrick J. McGowan, "A Formal Theory of Foreign Behavior as Adaptive Behavior," a paper presented at the Annual Meeting of the American Political Science

capacity to apply human intelligence to the alleviation and solution of real problems.

Association, Los Angeles, 1970; James N. Rosenau, *The Adaptation of National Societies: A Theory of Political System Behavior and Transformation* (New York: McCaleb-Seiler, 1970; reproduced in this volume as Chapter 18); and Stuart J. Thorson, "National Political Adaptation in a World Environment: Toward a Systems Theory of Dynamic Political Processes," in J. N. Rosenau (ed.), *Comparing Foreign Policies* (Beverly Hills: Sage Publications, 1974).

6 Pre-Theories and Theories of Foreign Policy *

To probe the "internal influences on external behavior"[1] is to be active on one of the frontiers where the fields of international and comparative politics meet. Initial thoughts about the subject, however, are bound to be ambivalent; it would seem to have been both exhausted and neglected as a focus of inquiry. Even as it seems clear that everything worth saying about the subject has already been said, so does it also seem obvious that the heart of the matter has yet to be explored and that

*Earlier versions of this chapter were presented to the Conference on Comparative and International Politics, sponsored by the Comparative Politics Program of the Northwestern Political Science Department in April, 1964, and published in R. Barry Farrell (ed.), *Approaches to Comparative and International Politics* (Evanston, Ill.: Northwestern University Press, 1966), pp. 27–92. Reprinted with the permission of the publisher.

[1] This is the original phrasing of the topic which I was asked to analyze for the conference that occasioned the earliest version of this chapter. Such influences are assumed to refer to the domestic sources of foreign policy, an assumption which is not the only one that could be made about the scope of the assigned topic. External behavior could also be defined as encompassing all the private ways in which the members of a society engage in activities beyond its boundaries. Tourists, students, soldiers, and traders are only a few of the individuals and groups whose private activities abroad can properly be viewed both as stemming from influences internal to a society and as constituting a crucial dimension of its external behavior. Notwithstanding their obvious relevance to the interrelationships of political systems, however, such activities have been excluded from the scope of this paper on the grounds that they are not in themselves political phenomena and that as political scientists we cannot afford to dissipate our energies on matters that fall outside our spheres of competence. For my conception of the nature of political phenomena, see Chapter 10.

American political science is on the verge of major breakthroughs which will make exploration possible.[2]

The exhaustion of the subject can be easily demonstrated. While it was not long ago that the external behavior of nations was considered to be exclusively a reaction to external stimuli, ever since World War II students of foreign policy have emphasized that the wellsprings of international action are also fed by events and tendencies within societies.[3] The literature of the field is now rich with "factors" that have been identified as internal sources of foreign policy. The role played by geographic and other nonhuman characteristics of a nation has received thorough treatment.[4] Capability analysts have uncovered a vast array of social, economic, cultural, and psychological processes which limit, enhance, or otherwise affect the external behavior of societies even as they sustain their internal life.[5] Other analysts have focused on political processes and delineated linkages between the foreign policy of a nation on the one hand and the shifting opinions of its citizenry,[6] the operations of its press and other media of mass communications,[7] and the character of its elites—their backgrounds,[8] attitudes,[9] and solidarity[10]—on the other.[11] Nor have violent internal pro-

[2] For a similar ambivalence, but one that was resolved very differently than my own, see Philip E. Mosely, "Research on Foreign Policy," in Brookings Dedication Lectures, *Research for Public Policy* (Washington, D.C.: Brookings, 1961), pp. 43–72.

[3] Perhaps the first to emphasize and elaborate the relevance of domestic variables was Richard C. Snyder. See his articles, "The Nature of Foreign Policy," *Social Science*, 27 (April 1952), pp. 61–69, and "Toward Greater Order in the Study of International Politics," *World Politics*, VII (April 1955), esp. pp. 473–474.

[4] Harold and Margaret Sprout, *Man-Milieu Relationship Hypotheses in the Context of International Politics* (Princeton: Center of International Studies, 1956), *passim*.

[5] See, for example, Klaus Knorr, *The War Potential of Nations* (Princeton: Princeton University Press, 1956), Parts I and II.

[6] Cf. Gabriel A. Almond, *The American People and Foreign Policy* (New York: Harcourt, 1950); Bernard C. Cohen, *The Political Process and Foreign Policy: The Making of the Japanese Peace Settlement* (Princeton: Princeton University Press, 1957); and Douglas H. Mendel, Jr., *The Japanese People and Foreign Policy: A Study of Public Opinion in Post-Treaty Japan* (Berkeley: University of California Press, 1961).

[7] For instance, see Bernard C. Cohen, *The Press and Foreign Policy* (Princeton: Princeton University Press, 1963).

[8] Donald R. Matthews, *The Social Background of Political Decision-Makers* (Garden City: Doubleday, 1954).

[9] See, for example, Hans Speier and W. Phillips Davison (eds.), *West German Leadership and Foreign Policy* (Evanston, Ill.: Row, Peterson, 1957).

[10] Cf. James N. Rosenau, *National Leadership and Foreign Policy: A Case Study in the Mobilization of Public Support* (Princeton: Princeton University Press, 1963).

[11] For an impressive case study that explores and synthesizes all these variables, see Karl W. Deutsch and Lewis J. Edinger, *Germany Rejoins the Powers: Mass Opinion, Interest Groups, and Elites in Contemporary German Foreign Policy* (Stanford, Cal.: Stanford University Press, 1959).

cesses been ignored as sources of external behavior.[12] Still another group of analysts, those who follow the decision-making approach, have called attention to a wide cluster of motivational, role, and organizational variables which operate within governments as determinants of foreign policy.[13] Inquiries into the contributions of particular types of decision-makers and decision-making institutions have also become abundantly available.[14] By focusing on the perceptions and choices of officials, moreover, students of decision-making have identified a host of additional nongovernmental variables which condition the behavior of policy-makers and thus become relevant to the quality and goals of international action.[15] The past experiences and present value orientations of a society, its educational institutions, its social structure and system of stratification—these are but a few of the many societal variables which have received attention as determinants of the identity, outlook, and capacities of those who occupy foreign policy decision-making roles.[16]

All this is in sharp contrast to previous tendencies either to ignore domestic variables or to deal with them through such broad and unmanageable concepts as nationalism or national character. The progress of the social sciences has rubbed off on students of foreign policy, and they are no longer content to use simple labels to explain complex behavior. Instead of explaining a policy in terms of, say, "rampant nationalism," now the inclination is to attempt to specify the components of the processes and attitudes which comprise the phenomena encompassed by such grandiose terminology. Thus have such concepts as image,[17] belief system,[18]

---

[12] Cf. James N. Rosenau (ed.), *International Aspects of Civil Strife* (Princeton: Princeton University Press, 1964).

[13] Richard C. Snyder, H. W. Bruck, and Burton Sapin, *Decision-Making as an Approach to the Study of International Politics* (Princeton: Organizational Behavior Section, Foreign Policy Analysis Series, No. 3, 1954), pp. 68–117.

[14] For example, see James A. Robinson, *Congress and Foreign Policy-Making: A Study in Legislative Influence and Initiative* (Homewood, Ill.: Dorsey Press, 1962); and Burton M. Sapin and Richard C. Snyder, *The Role of the Military in American Foreign Policy* (Garden City, N.Y.: Doubleday, 1954).

[15] Cf. Edgar S. Furniss, Jr., and Richard C. Snyder, *An Introduction to American Foreign Policy* (New York: Rinehart, 1955), Chap. 5.

[16] For much more thorough inventories of recent research in the foreign policy field, see Richard C. Snyder and James A. Robinson, *National and International Decision-Making: Towards a General Research Strategy Related to the Problem of War and Peace* (New York: Institute for International Order, 1961); and Richard C. Snyder, "Some Recent Trends in International Relations Theory and Research," in Austin Ranney (ed.), *Essays on the Behavioral Study of Politics* (Urbana: University of Illinois Press, 1962), pp. 103–71.

[17] Kenneth E. Boulding, "National Images and International Systems," *Journal of Conflict Resolution*, III (June 1959), pp. 120–131.

[18] Ole R. Holsti, "The Belief System and National Images: A Case Study," *Journal of Conflict Resolution*, VI (September 1962), pp. 244–252.

consensus,[19] and tension levels [20] come to be part of the storehouse of equipment used by those who probe the internal sources of external behavior.

Methodologically, too, the rate of progress has been encouraging. Not only have a number of creative techniques for developing and analyzing data been perfected,[21] but, equally important, students of foreign policy are no longer ignorant of the philosophy of science, its precepts, and its tools. They are now sensitive to the distinctions between description and explanation, correlation and causation, hypotheses and models, fact and value. They know that foreign policy behavior is a reaction to both external and internal stimuli and that one breaks into the chain of causation only for analytic purposes. Hence they no longer equate their inquiries with reality, recognizing instead that the operations they perform on data constitute distortions of reality that have to be undertaken for comprehension to occur. In short, the modern student of foreign policy is—or at least has the opportunity to become—a broad-gauged and sophisticated social scientist. He even has available for his undergraduate training a textbook which contains an introductory—and excellent—discussion of the nature of reliable knowledge, how it is acquired, and how different intellectual tools and perspectives can be used.[22]

I. THE NEED FOR THEORY

But it is also easy to exaggerate the rate of progress. Notwithstanding the varied and impressive accomplishments outlined above, the dynamics of the processes which culminate in the external behavior of societies remain obscure. To identify factors is not to trace their influence. To uncover processes that affect external behavior is not to explain how and why they are operative under certain circumstances and not under others. To recognize that foreign policy is shaped by internal as well as external factors is not to comprehend how the two intermix or to indicate the conditions under which one predominates over the other. And in these respects

[19] Roger Hilsman, "The Foreign-Policy Consensus: An Interim Research Report," *Journal of Conflict Resolution,* III (December 1959), pp. 361–382.

[20] K. J. Holsti, "The Use of Objective Criteria for the Measurement of International Tension Levels," *Background,* 7 (August 1963), pp. 77–95.

[21] For example, see Harold Guetzkow, et al., *Simulation in International Relations: Developments for Research and Teaching* (Englewood Cliffs, N.J.: Prentice-Hall, 1963); and Robert C. North, et al., *Content Analysis: A Handbook with Applications for the Study of International Crisis* (Evanston, Ill.: Northwestern University Press, 1963).

[22] Harold and Margaret Sprout, *Foundations of International Politics* (Princeton: Van Nostrand, 1962), Chap. 1.

progress has been very slow indeed. Rare is the article or book which goes beyond description of an internal factor and locates it in the ever changing interplay of variables—both external and internal—which combine to produce foreign policies. Even rarer is the work that contains explicit "if-then" hypotheses in which the "if" is a particular form of the internal factor and the "then" is a particular type of foreign policy. Rather, for all their philosophical and methodological sophistication, many analyses treat the internal factor under examination as the only variable in a world of constants. The different ways in which the factor can or does influence policy are described—thus making it a variable—but the situations at home and abroad through which the influence operates are taken for granted, thus giving rise to the false impression that qualities inherent in the factor itself are the only determinants of the particular way in which it is influential at any moment in time. Even worse, the factor is often treated as a constant in a world of variables. That is, irrespective of variations at home and abroad, its influence is seen to remain unchanged. A foreign policy may be aggressive or submissive, long range or short range, economic or diplomatic, but the internal factor is nonetheless considered to be present to the same degree.

The main reason for this situation is not difficult to discern: foreign policy analysis lacks comprehensive systems of testable generalizations that treat societies as actors subject to stimuli which produce external responses. Stated more succinctly, foreign policy analysis is devoid of general theory. Perhaps it has been exhausted as far as inventorying the determinants of external behavior is concerned, but it has not even begun to take shape as a theoretical enterprise. The field has an abundance of frameworks and approaches which cut across societies and conceptualize the ends, means, capabilities, or sources of foreign policy, but no schemes which link up these components of external behavior in causal sequences.[23] No framework has energized inquiry in foreign policy as Rostow's theory of the stages of economic growth did in the economic development field,[24] as Festinger's theory of cognitive dissonance did in social psychology,[25] or as Almond's functional model did in comparative politics.[26] As one observer puts it, "The study of foreign policy . . . is one applied social science that

---

[23] One possible exception is George Modelski, *A Theory of Foreign Policy* (New York: Praeger, 1962), but even this work is short on causal propositions and long on analysis of the points at which causation is operative.

[24] W. W. Rostow, *The Stages of Economic Growth* (New York: Cambridge University Press, 1960).

[25] Leon Festinger, *A Theory of Cognitive Dissonance* (Evanston, Ill.: Row, Peterson, 1957).

[26] Gabriel A. Almond and James S. Coleman (eds.), *The Politics of the Developing Areas* (Princeton: Princeton University Press, 1960), pp. 3–64.

largely lacks its counterpart in a pure science." [27] It is hardly surprising, therefore, that the influence of internal factors on external behavior has not been traced as sophisticatedly as recent progress in the field might lead one to expect. If students of foreign policy were inclined to structure their subject in such a way as to observe the differential interplay of variables under varying conditions, then obviously a multitude of if-then hypotheses bearing on the operation of internal factors would have long since been advanced.

Occasionally, to be sure, one comes upon materials which take note of causal relationships between external behavior and internal processes. The literature on economic and political development, for example, is full of references to the ways in which the foreign policies of modernizing societies are shaped by their internal needs—by the need of elites for identity and prestige, by the need of charismatic leaders to sustain their charisma, by the need of in-groups to divert attention away from domestic problems and thereby to placate their oppositions.[28] Propositions of this sort, however, amount to partial and not general theories. Usually they are articulated in terms of a particular country and cannot be applied to other modernizing societies. Sometimes they are even developed to explain the external behavior of a particular leader or elite and then lose their relevance when a *coup d'état* or some equivalent event alters the governance of the country. More important, such propositions are partial in the sense that they are exclusively confined to internal sources of external behavior and do not posit it as also a response to events occurring abroad. No doubt the foreign policies of some modernizing elites are especially designed to divert attention from domestic problems, but they are also intended to maximize control over the international environment and must thus be adjusted to shifts on the world scene.

Much the same can be said about the emerging theoretical literature that gives a central place to foreign policy in the processes of alliance building,[29] the dynamics of supranational integration,[30] and the competition among superpowers for influence in the nonaligned world.[31] While such

27 Mosely, *op. cit.*, pp. 44–45.

28 Cf. Robert C. Good, "State-Building as a Determinant of Foreign Policy in the New States," in Laurence W. Martin (ed.), *Neutralism and Nonalignment* (New York: Praeger, 1962), pp. 3–12.

29 See George Liska, *Nations in Alliance: The Limits of Interdependence* (Baltimore: Johns Hopkins Press, 1962); and William H. Riker, *The Theory of Political Coalitions* (New Haven: Yale University Press, 1962).

30 Cf. the following articles by Amitai Etzioni: "The Dialectics of Supranational Unification," *American Political Science Review*, LVI (December 1962), pp. 927–935; "The Epigenesis of Political Communities at the International Level," *American Journal of Sociology*, LXVIII (January 1963), pp. 407–421; and "European Unification: A Strategy of Change," *World Politics*, XVI (October 1963), pp. 32–51.

31 For example, see Morton A. Kaplan, "Bipolarity in a Revolutionary Age,"

efforts are theoretical in the sense that they posit external behaviors derived from specified stimuli, they are nonetheless partial and not general theories. They are founded on the premise that external events—individually or as structural characteristics of international systems—are the prime movers of foreign policy. Virtually none of them allow for the operation of internal causation. The external behavior called for in game-theoretical models, for example, presumes rational decision-makers who are impervious to the need to placate their domestic opponents or, indeed, to any influences other than the strategic requirements of responding to adversaries abroad.[32]

The lack of general theory is further indicated by the haphazard way in which many foreign policy analysts vary the external-internal mix from one set of explanatory propositions to the next. Sometimes policies are attributed to domestic factors and sometimes causation is ascribed to external sources, but the rationale for using one or the other explanation is never made explicit and is rarely systematic. Most foreign policy analysts, for example, are content to leave domestic causation out of their alliance theories even as their explanations of international activity in the foreign aid field contain a large mix of internal and external factors. Similarly, analysts are rarely troubled by the seeming inconsistency between their readiness to posit the behavior of individual decision-makers as cause in one instance and as effect in another. During the years between 1959 and 1964, for instance, it became commonplace to treat French foreign policy as a function of a free-wheeling and haughty De Gaulle and to view Soviet foreign policy not as a function of an unrestrained and ebullient Khrushchev, but as a consequence of stresses and strains within the U.S.S.R. and the Communist international system. Such discrepancies are not in themselves unreasonable. They may well be a reflection of empirical reality. Yet, to repeat, conspicuously absent is any body of theory which would account for the discrepancies. Under what conditions does the influence of individual leaders on foreign policy outweigh that of complex societal processes? Why are domestic factors more of a hindrance in the construction and maintenance of foreign aid programs than in the formation and conduct of military alliances? No answers to such questions are at present available.

Not being able to draw on general theories, work in the foreign policy field has been largely historical and single-country oriented. An overwhelming preponderance of the inquiries into foreign policy is confined either to analyzing the external behavior of a specific country at a specific

in Morton A. Kaplan (ed.), *The Revolution in World Politics* (New York: Wiley, 1962), pp. 251–266.

[32] For an elaboration of this point, see Bernard C. Cohen, "Military Policy Analysis and the Art of the Possible: A Review," *Journal of Conflict Resolution*, VI (June 1962), pp. 154–159.

moment in time or to identifying the patterns which mark its external behavior over a period of time. Indeed, so pronounced is this orientation that most, if not all, American universities offer courses which are exclusively devoted to depicting and analyzing the patterned external behavior of various countries. Courses in American foreign policy and in Soviet foreign policy abound, and those on the external behavior of India, England, Japan, France, and other leading nations are hardly less numerous. The evolution of such a curriculum has spurred the creation of a vast textbook literature, which in turn has reinforced the tendency to approach the field from a historical, single-country perspective. A measure of the spiraling process is provided by the fact that in 1958 a text containing a separate treatment of the foreign policies of ten different nations was published and that 1963 saw the publication of a similar book covering the external behavior of twenty-four different nations.[33]

It might be argued that this single-country orientation is the first step in a slow progression toward general theory, that analyses of the external behavior of many countries constitute bases for the construction of systems of testable generalizations about the foreign policies of general classes of countries, thus leading to the eventual development of if-then models accounting for the behavior of any country. Unfortunately, however, this line of reasoning is refuted by the unsystematic and uneven nature of the single-country research that has been and is being done. In the first place, the premises underlying the work on each country are so varied that comparative analysis is almost, if not entirely, impossible. It is difficult to find two analyses of two different countries that consider the same variables, ask the same questions, and gather comparable data. Even the aforementioned compilations of ten and twenty-four foreign policies do not make comparative analysis possible. In both instances the editors presented an introductory chapter suggesting certain common characteristics of the external behavior of all nations, but in neither case did the contributors adhere to the outline. In one case, moreover, the editor himself lost interest in developing his model and instead devoted the last half of his introduction to a discussion of "three obstacles that confound American policy-makers and that must at least be mitigated if the struggle is to be won." [34]

In addition to precluding comparison, the single-country analyses are themselves theoretically deficient. By placing a society's foreign policies in a historical and problem-solving context, analysts tend to treat each in-

---

[33] Roy C. Macridis (ed.), *Foreign Policy in World Politics* (Englewood Cliffs, N.J.: Prentice-Hall, 1958); and Joseph E. Black and Kenneth W. Thompson (eds.), *Foreign Policies in a World of Change* (New York: Harper and Row, 1963). For an analysis of the possibility that contrary trends in curricula and texts concerned with foreign policy are emerging, see Chapter 5.

[34] Macridis, *op. cit.*, p. 22.

ternational situation in which the society participates as unique and, consequently, to view its external behavior with respect to each situation as stemming from immediate and particular antecedents. This approach does not prevent the derivation of generalizations about the goals and character of the society's behavior in many situations, but it does inhibit the construction of if-then models which link the behavior patterns to a systematic set of stimuli. Rather the stimuli, being comprised of unique historical circumstances, are conceived to vary from one situation to the next, and rarely is a construct offered to account for the variations. Consider, for example, how numerous are the analyses of Soviet foreign policy which attribute causation to a Khrushchev in one situation, to a pent-up consumer demand in another, to a conflict within the leadership structure in a third, to a reality of Russian geography in a fourth, and to an aspect of the Sino-Soviet struggle in a fifth situation. Or reflect on the differential explanations of why the United States entered a war in Korea in 1950, avoided one in Indo-China in 1954, fomented one in Cuba in 1961, and enlarged one in Vietnam in 1965. Undoubtedly each of these actions was a response to a different combination of external and internal stimuli; and no doubt, too, there is considerable variability in the complex of factors which determine Soviet policies. But at the same time it is also true that the variability is patterned. The stimuli which produce external behavior must be processed by the value and decision-making systems of a society, so that it ought to be possible, as with rats in a maze, to link up varying types of responses with varying types of stimuli. To repeat, however, few foreign policy researchers structure their materials in such a way as to allow for this kind of analysis. Just as it is difficult to compare the external behavior of different countries in the same international situation, so it is often next to impossible to engage in comparative analysis of the actions of the same country in different situations. One is reminded of the state that the field of political theory was in not so long ago: We have many histories of American foreign policy but very few theories of American foreign policy, and much the same can be said about research on every country presently attracting the attention of foreign policy analysts.

II. A PRE-THEORY OF FOREIGN POLICY

The resolution of ambivalence is never easy. A residue of unease always seems to remain, especially if the resolution is in a negative direction. Having resolved initial ambivalence with the conclusion that the endless piling up of historical case materials is leading foreign policy research down to a dead end, one is inclined to pause and wonder whether extenuating circumstances have been overlooked or, indeed, whether one's focus is so narrow as to distort perception and exaggerate defect. There must be good reasons why the lack of theory has not aroused researchers to undertake corrective measures. Could it be that the author and not the field has gone astray?

The answer, of course, is that each has special needs—the field for solutions to urgent policy problems and the author for accretions to an ever-growing science of politics. The satisfaction of these needs leads down two different paths, neither better than the other.

But one wonders, too, whether the paths need be so divergent. Is a problem-solving orientation necessarily incompatible with the development of empirical materials that lend themselves to an if-then kind of analysis? Cannot historical investigation be carried out in such a way as to facilitate meaningful comparisons and generalizations that are not bound by time and place? An affirmative response to these questions is not unreasonable. Economic theory has been helped, not hindered, by work done in applied economics.[35] Sociological theory has been spurred, not stifled, by empirical inquiries into social processes.[36] Of late, political theory, as distinguished from the history of political thought, has been enriched and enlivened by research into the development of non-Western polities.[37] Surely there is nothing inherent in the nature of foreign policy phenomena which renders them more resistant to theortical treatment than the gross data that comprise these other applied fields.

The nontheoretical state of foreign policy research is all the more perplexing when it is contrasted with developments elsewhere in American political science. In recent years the discipline has been transformed from an intuitive to a scientific enterprise, and consequently the inclination to develop models and test theories has become second nature to most political scientists. Each day—or at least each new publication—brings into the field fresh concepts, propositions, and theories about local, national, and international political systems. New models of the processes of political development abound. And so do conceptualizations of how party, legislative, bureaucratic, and judicial systems function. In each of these areas, moreover, political scientists are beginning to build on one another's work (the surest sign of a maturing discipline), and thus innovative theorizing is being accompanied by a healthy convergence on similar models of the political process.

[35] Cf. Charles J. Hitch, *et al.,* "The Uses of Economics," in Brookings Dedication Lectures, *op. cit.,* pp. 91–126.

[36] Cf. Robert K. Merton, *Social Theory and Social Structure,* rev. ed. (Glencoe, Ill.: Free Press, 1957), Chap. III.

[37] See, for example, the studies sponsored by the Committee on Comparative Politics of the Social Scinece Research Council (cited in footnote 18 of Chap. 5).

In short, the lack of theory in foreign policy research cannot be readily justified or easily explained. Clearly it cannot be dismissed as a mere reflection of general tendencies in the discipline. Nor can it be attributed to the requirements of problem-solving and the precedents of history. Researchers in other areas of the discipline also engage in historical analysis and expend energy seeking solutions to immediate and practical problems, yet this does not inhibit their inclination to press ahead in the development of general theories. Nor, obviously, is it sufficient to speculate that in foreign policy research the "avoidance of the general in preference to the the individual, unique, and empirical may be a reflection of the very recent and chiefly American origins of this field of study."[38] Other more basic obstacles must be blocking the road to general theory, else long ago foreign policy researchers would have begun to move down it alongside economists, sociologists, and other political scientists.

Two basic shortcomings, one philosophical and the other conceptual, would appear to be holding back the development of foreign policy theory.[39]

---

[38] Mosely, *op. cit.*, p. 45. It is amusing, and perhaps even indicative of the impressionistic state of things, to note the enormous gap between this view of ourselves as nontheoretical and the view held by European analysts that "in the United States the theoretical study of foreign policy has become a thriving industry. Where Disraeli is said to have accosted aged Parliamentarians whose names escaped him with the question 'How's the gout?', American professors of international relations now reputedly ask of their younger colleagues 'How's the conceptual framework?'." F. S. Northedge, in a book review, *Political Quarterly*, 34 (July-September 1963), p. 310.

[39] A third shortcoming, so closely intertwined with the other two that its relevance is manifest throughout this volume and requires only brief identification here, is of an organizational nature: Namely, the discipline of political science is at present organized in such a way that the external behavior of national political systems does not fall within the purview of scholars who are interested in the construction of general theories. Neither of the two groups of model builders who might be expected to theorize about foreign policy—those in comparative politics and those in international politics—is drawn by conceptual necessity to find a theoretical home for the external behavior of societies. Students of comparative politics focus primarily on national political systems and the interaction processes that occur *within* them. Once a pattern of interaction moves outside a national system, therefore, the comparative politics specialist tends to lose interest in it. Of primary concern to students of international politics, on the other hand, are the processes of interaction that occur *among* national systems. Consequently, the international politics specialist tends to take internal influences on external behavior for granted and to become interested in the patterns generated by national systems only after they have crossed over into the international realm. Foreign policy phenomena, in short, are the unwanted stepchildren of political systems. They serve as outputs for one type of system and as inputs for another, but they do not constitute actions which both begin and culminate in any system that is of interest to present-day political theorists. Hence, notwithstanding their intense relevance to students of practical policy-making problems, foreign policy phenomena have been neglected by theoreticians and relegated to the residual category of systems theory known as "boundary problems."

The one exception to this pattern is, of course, those theoreticians for whom

Let us look first at the philosophical shortcoming. If theoretical development in a field is to flourish, empirical materials which have been similarly processed must be available. It is no more possible to construct models of human behavior out of raw data than it is to erect a building out of fallen trees and unbaked clay. The trees must be sawed and the clay must be baked, and the resulting lumber and bricks must be the same size, shape, and color if a sturdy and coherent building is to be erected. Note that the design and function of the structure are not determined by the fact that the materials comprising it have been similarly processed. The same bricks and lumber can be used to build houses or factories, large structures or small ones, modern buildings or traditional ones. So it is with the construction and use of social theories. There must be, as it were, pre-theory which renders the raw materials comparable and ready for theorizing. The materials may serve as the basis for all kinds of theories—abstract or empirical, single- or multi-country, pure or applied—but until they have been similarly processed, theorizing is not likely to occur, or, if it does, the results are not likely to be very useful.

Unlike economics, sociology, and other areas of political science, the field of foreign policy research has not subjected its materials to this preliminary processing. Instead, as noted above, each country and each international situation in which it participates is normally treated as unique and nonrecurrent, with the result that most available studies do not treat foreign policy phenomena in a comparable way. Thus it is that the same data pertaining to the external behavior of the Soviet Union are interpreted by one observer as illustrative of Khrushchev's flexibility, by another as reflective of pent-up consumer demands, and by still another as indicative of the Sino-Soviet conflict. To recur to the analogy of physical materials, it is as if one person cut up the fallen trees for firewood, another used them as the subject of a painting, and still another had them sawed for use in the building of a frame house.

It must be emphasized that the preliminary processing of foreign policy materials involves considerably more than methodological tidiness. We are not referring here to techniques of gathering and handling data, albeit there is much that could be said about the need for standardization in this respect. Nor do we have in mind the desirability of orienting foreign policy research toward the use of quantified materials and operationalized concepts, albeit again good arguments could be advanced on behalf of

the boundary between national and international systems is the core of their concern, i.e., those who specialize in the processes of supranational integration. It is perhaps significant that the most promising theory in this area is presently being developed by a sociologist, Amitai Etzioni, whose training and experience does not confine him to the traditional boundaries of the discipline of political science. See, for example, his three articles cited above in note 30.

such procedures. Rather, the preliminary processing to which foreign policy materials must be subjected is of a much more basic order. It involves the need to develop an explicit conception of where causation is located in international affairs. Should foreign policy researchers proceed on the assumption that identifiable human beings are the causative agents? Or should they treat political roles, governmental structures, societal processes, or international systems as the source of external behavior? And if they presume that causation is located in all these sources, to what extent and under what circumstances is each source more or less causal than the others? Few researchers in the field process their materials in terms of some kind of explicit answer to these questions. Most of them, in other words, are not aware of the philosophy of foreign policy analysis they employ, or, more broadly, they are unaware of their pre-theories of foreign policy.[40]

To be sure, foreign policy researchers are not so unsophisticated as to fail to recognize that causation can be attributed to a variety of actors and entities. For years now it has been commonplace to avoid single-cause deterministic explanations and to assert the legitimacy of explaining the same event in a variety of ways. Rather than serving to discipline research, however, this greater sophistication has in some ways supplied a license for undisciplined inquiry. Now it is equally commonplace to assume that one's obligations as a researcher are discharged by articulating the premise that external behavior results from a combination of many factors, both external and internal, *without* indicating how the various factors combine under different circumstances. Having rejected single-cause explanations, in other words, most foreign policy researchers seem to feel they are therefore free *not* to be consistent in their manner of ascribing causation. Deterministic theories have philosophical roots, much foreign policy research seems to say, so that in abandoning the theories it is also necessary to give up the practice of locating one's work in a pre-theoretical context. Thus, as previously indicated, rare is the observer who is troubled by the discrepancy between his attribution of causation to De Gaulle's personal qualities and not to Khrushchev's. On the contrary, many apparently believe that such discrepancies are the mark of flexibility in research and the surest sign of having avoided deterministic modes of thought.

Nothing could be further from the truth. The development and employment of a pre-theory of foreign policy does not, as noted below, neces-

---

[40] Briefly, by pre-theory is meant both an early step toward explanation of specific empirical events and a general orientation toward all events, a point of view or philosophy about the way the world is. Ideally pre-theories would be limited to the former meaning, but this requires that a field be in general agreement about the "proper" orientation toward its subject matter, a situation which the field of foreign policy research is far from even approximating.

sarily lead to determinism or even to greater rigidity. It merely provides a basis for comparison in the examination of the external behavior of various countries in various situations and, to repeat, there can be no real flourishing of theory until the materials of the field are processed—i.e., rendered comparable—through the use of pre-theories of foreign policy.

Perhaps the best way to indicate exactly what a pre-theory of foreign policy involves is by outlining the main ingredients of any pre-theory and then indicating how the author has integrated these ingredients into his own particular pre-theory. Although the statement is subject to modification and elaboration, it does not seem unreasonable to assert that all pre-theories of foreign policy are either five-dimensional or translatable into five dimensions. That is, all foreign policy analysts either explain the external behavior of societies in terms of five sets of variables, or they proceed in such a way that their explanations can be recast in terms of the five sets.[41] Listed in order of increasing temporal and spatial distance from the external behaviors for which they serve as sources, the five sets are what we shall call the individual,[42] role, governmental, societal, and systemic variables.

The first set encompasses the characteristics unique to the decision-makers who determine and implement the foreign policies of a nation. Individual variables include all those aspects of a decision-maker—his values, talents, and prior experiences—that distinguish his foreign policy choices or behavior from those of every other decision-maker. John Foster Dulles' religious values, De Gaulle's vision of a glorious France, and Khrushchev's political skills are frequently mentioned examples of individual variables. The second set of variables pertains to the external behavior of officials that is generated by the roles they occupy and that would be likely to occur irrespective of the individual characteristics of the role occupants. Regardless of who he is, for example, the U.S. ambassador to the United Nations is likely to defend American and Western positions in the Security Council and General Assembly. Governmental variables refer to those aspects of a government's structure that limit or enhance the foreign policy choices made by decision-makers. The impact of executive-legislative relations on American foreign policy exemplifies the operation of governmental variables. The fourth cluster of variables consists of those nongovernmental aspects of a society which influence

---

[41] For approaches which assert the utility of employing two and six sets of variables, see, respectively, J. David Singer, "The Levels-of-Analysis Problem in International Relations," *World Politics,* XIV (October 1961), pp. 77–92; and Robert C. North, *op. cit.,* pp. 5–7.

[42] In earlier versions of this chapter individual variables were referred to as "idiosyncratic" variables. Since the latter designation subsequently seemed misleading, the former appears in all the chapters that follow and thus it has been updated here to minimize confusion.

its external behavior. The major value orientations of a society, its degree of national unity, and the extent of its industrialization are but a few of the societal variables which can contribute to the contents of a nation's external aspirations and policies. As for systemic variables, these include any nonhuman aspects of a society's external environment or any actions occurring abroad that condition or otherwise influence the choices made by its officials. Geographical "realities" and ideological challenges from potential aggressors are obvious examples of systemic variables which can shape the decisions and actions of foreign policy officials.

But these are only the ingredients of a pre-theory of foreign policy. To formulate the pre-theory itself one has to assess their *relative potencies.* That is, one has to decide which set of variables contributes most to external behavior, which ranks next in influence, and so on through all the sets. There is no need to specify exactly how large a slice of the pie is accounted for by each set of variables. Such precise specifications are characteristics of theories and not of the general framework within which data are organized. At this pre-theoretical level it is sufficient merely to have an idea of the relative potencies of the main sources of external behavior.

Note that constructing a pre-theory of foreign policy is not a matter of choosing to employ only one set of variables. We are not talking about levels of analysis but, in effect, about philosophies of analysis with respect to one particular level,[43] that of national societies. We assume that at this level behavior is shaped by individual, role, governmental, societal, and systemic factors and that the task is thus one of choosing how to treat each set of variables relative to the others. Many choices are possible. One hundred and twenty pre-theories can be constructed out

---

[43] A level of analysis is distinguished by the units in terms of which behavior is explained, whereas a philosophy of analysis pertains to how the units are interrelated at a given level. The same behavior, therefore, can be analyzed both at several levels and in several ways at the same level. Consider the act of blushing. This can be explained both physiologically and psychologically, but S-R and Lewinian psychologists would offer different explanations of what caused the blush (as there might be, for all the author knows, be sharp differences among the physiologists). Likewise, a presidential speech at the United Nations can be explained both physiologically and politically, but some political scientists might see the behavior as the last act in a sequence fostered by a loose bipolar system and others would treat it as derived from the requirements of an oncoming election campaign. An even better example of different philosophies of analysis in the foreign policy field is provided by the role accorded to motivational variables by students of decision-making on the one hand and by "realists" on the other. Both groups attempt to explain the external behavior of societies, but the former give high priority to the motives of officials while the latter consider the examination of motives to be "both futile and deceptive" (confirm, respectively, Snyder, Bruck, and Sapin, *op. cit.,* pp. 92–117, and Hans J. Morgenthau, *Politics Among Nations,* 3d ed. [New York: Knopf, 1960], p. 6).

of the 120 possible ways in which the five sets of variables can be ranked. Some analysts may prefer to use one or another of the rankings to analyze the external behavior of all societies at all times. Others may work out more complex pre-theories in which various rankings are applied to different societies under different circumstances.[44] Whatever the degree of complexity, however, the analyst employs a pre-theory of foreign policy when he attaches relative potencies to the main sources of external behavior.

Attaching causal priorities to the various sets of variables is extremely difficult. Most of us would rather treat causation as idiographic than work out a consistent pre-theory to account for the relative strength of each variable under different types of conditions. One way to overcome this tendency and compel oneself to differentiate the variables is that of engaging in the exercise of mentally manipulating the variables in actual situations. Consider, for example, the U.S.-sponsored invasion of Cuba's Bay of Pigs in April 1961. To what extent was that external behavior a function of the individual characteristics of John F. Kennedy (to cite, for purposes of simplicity, only one of the actors who made the invasion decision)? Were his youth, his commitments to action, his affiliations with the Democratic party, his self-confidence, his close election victory—and so on through an endless list—relevant to the launching of the invasion and, if so, to what extent? Would any President have undertaken to oust the Castro regime upon assuming office in 1961? If so, how much potency should be attributed to such role-derived variables? Suppose everything else about the circumstances of April 1961 were unchanged except that Warren Harding or Richard Nixon occupied the White House; would the invasion have occurred? Or hold everything constant but the form of government. Stretch the imagination and conceive of the U.S. as having a cabinet system of government with Kennedy as prime minister; would the action toward Cuba have been any different? Did legislative pressure derived from a decentralized policy-making system

---

[44] Ultimately, of course, the number of pre-theories will dwindle. A large number seems plausible at present because of the undeveloped state of the field. So little systematic knowledge about the sources of external behavior is currently available that fault cannot be found with any pre-theory on the grounds that it is discrepant with observed phenomena. However, as pre-theories make theorizing possible, and as theories then facilitate more systematic observation and more incisive comprehension of how international behavior is generated, consensuses will develop about the nature of empirical reality. Accordingly, those pre-theories which prove to be most "unreal" will be abandoned. Whether the number will ever dwindle down to a single pre-theory espoused by all analysts seems doubtful. Or at least many decades will have to elapse before the mysteries of international life are fathomed to the point where widespread agreement exists on the dynamics of external behavior. More likely is a long-run future in which knowledge of empirical reality becomes sufficiently extensive to reduce the field to several major schools of thought.

generate an impulse to "do something" about Castro, and, if so, to what extent did these governmental variables contribute to the external behavior? Similarly, in order to pre-theorize about the potency of the societal variables, assume once more a presidential form of government. Place Kennedy in office a few months after a narrow election victory, and imagine the Cuban situation as arising in 1921, 1931, or 1951; would the America of the roaring twenties, the depression, or the McCarthy era have "permitted," "encouraged," or otherwise become involved in a refugee-mounted invasion? If the United States were a closed, authoritarian society rather than an open, democratic one, to what extent would the action toward Cuba have been different? Lastly, hold the individual, role, governmental, and societal variables constant in the imagination, and posit Cuba as 9,000 rather than 90 miles off the Florida coast; would the invasion have nevertheless been launched? If it is estimated that no effort would have been made to span such a distance, does this mean that systemic variables should always be treated as overriding, or is their potency diminished under certain conditions?

The formulation of a pre-theory of foreign policy can be further stimulated by expanding this mental exercise to include other countries and other situations. Instead of Kennedy, the presidency, and the U.S. of 1961 undertaking action toward Cuba, engage in a similar process of holding variables constant with respect to the actions taken by Khrushchev, the monolithic Russian decision-making structure, and the U.S.S.R. of 1956 toward the uprising in Hungary. Or apply the exercise to the actions directed at the Suez Canal by Eden, the cabinet system, and the England of 1956. Or take still another situation, that of the attack on Goa carried out by the charismatic Nehru and the modernizing India of 1961. In all four cases a more powerful nation initiated military action against a less powerful neighbor that had come to represent values antagonistic to the interests of the attacker. Are we therefore to conclude that the external behavior of the U.S., Russia, England, and India stemmed from the same combination of external and internal sources? Should the fact that the attacked society was geographically near the attacking society in all four instances be interpreted as indicating that systemic variables are always relatively more potent than any other type? Or is it reasonable to attribute greater causation to individual factors in one instance and to societal factors in another? If so, what is the rationale for subjecting these seemingly similar situations to different kinds of analysis?

Reflection about questions similar to those raised in the two previous paragraphs has led this observer to a crude pre-theory of foreign policy in which the relative potencies of the five sets of variables are assessed in terms of distinctions between large and small countries, between developed and underdeveloped economies, and between open and closed political systems. As can be seen in Table 6-1, these three continua give rise to eight types of countries and eight different rankings of relative potency. There is no need here to elaborate at length on the reasoning underlying each ranking.[45] The point is not to demonstrate the validity of the rankings but rather to indicate what the construction of a pre-theory of foreign policy involves and why it is a necessary prerequisite to the development of theory. Indeed, given the present undeveloped state of the field, the rankings can be neither proved nor disproved. They reflect the author's way of organizing materials for close inspection and not the inspections themselves. To be theoretical in nature, the rankings would have to specify *how much* more potent each set of variables is than those below it on each scale, and the variables themselves would have to be causally linked to specific forms of external behavior.

To be sure, as in all things, it is possible to have poor and unsound pre-theories of foreign policy as well as wise and insightful ones. The author's pre-theory may well exaggerate the potency of some variables and underrate others, in which case the theories which his pre-theory generates or supports will in the long run be less productive and enlightening than those based on pre-theories which more closely approximate empirical reality. Yet, to repeat, this pre-theory is not much more than an orientation and is not at present subject to verification.

One suspects that many foreign policy analysts would reject this pre-theory, not because they conceive of different rankings or even different sets of variables but rather because the very idea of explicating a pre-theory strikes them as premature or even impossible. Those committed to the single-country, historical approach to foreign affairs would no doubt object that developing a pre-theory is a fruitless endeavor, since every situation is different from every other and no pre-theory can possibly be so coherent as to account for the infinite variation that marks international life. Other analysts, including some who are more social-scientific in their orientation, reject the possibility of pre-theorizing on

[45] Suffice it to note that the potency of a systemic variable is considered to vary inversely with the size of a country (there being greater resources available to larger countries and thus lesser dependence on the international system than is the case with smaller countries); that the potency of an individual factor is assumed to be greater in less developed economies (there being fewer of the restraints which bureaucracy and large-scale organization impose in more developed economies), that for the same reason a role variable is accorded greater potency in more developed economies, that a societal variable is considered to be more potent in open polities than in closed ones (there being a lesser need for officials in the latter to heed nongovernmental demands than in the former), and that for the same reason governmental variables are more potent than societal variables in closed polities than in open ones.

Table 6 –1   An Abbreviated Presentation of the Author's Pre-Theory of Foreign Policy, in Which Five Sets of Variables Underlying the External Behavior of Societies Are Ranked According to Their Relative Potencies in Eight Types of Societies

Geography and physical resources	Large Country				Small Country			
State of the economy	Developed		Underdeveloped		Developed		Underdeveloped	
State of the polity	Open	Closed	Open	Closed	Open	Closed	Open	Closed
Rankings of the variables	Role Societal Governmental Systemic Individual	Role Individual Governmental Systemic Societal	Individual Role Societal Systemic Governmental	Individual Role Governmental Systemic Societal	Role Systemic Societal Governmental Individual	Role Systemic Individual Governmental Societal	Individual Systemic Role Societal Governmental	Individual Systemic Role Governmental Societal
Illustrative examples	U.S.	U.S.S.R.	India	Red China	Holland	Czecho-slovakia	Kenya	Ghana

the grounds that the same events can be explained in several ways and that therefore the problem of determining the relative potencies of different sets of variables can never be satisfactorily solved.[46]

The fact is, however, that one cannot avoid having a pre-theory of foreign policy whenever one takes on the task of tracing causation. Even the most historical-minded analyst makes the initial assumption that events derive from an underlying order, that every external behavior of every society stems from some source and is therefore, at least theoretically, explicable. To assume otherwise—to view the external behaviors of societies as random and impulsive, as occurring for no reason, and as therefore unknowable—is to render analysis useless and to condemn the analyst to perpetual failure. Since we cannot avoid the presumption of an underlying order, neither can we avoid having some conception of its nature. Yet causation is not self-revealing. The underlying order does not simply manifest itself for the diligent analyst who gathers every scrap of evidence and then takes a long, hard look at what he has accumulated. Inevitably he must organize the evidence in terms of some frame of reference, crude and premature as it may seem. There may be infinite variety in international life, but analysts are not so infinitely flexible. They cannot, and they do not, ignore their prior knowledge about foreign affairs and start over, so to speak, each time they undertake to analyze an external behavior. Furthermore, even if one were to assume that each international situation is different from every other situation, it is still necessary to have some basis for recognizing and explaining the differences. Similarly, even if one assumes that the same event is subject to a variety of interpretations, depending on the perspective of the observer, it is nevertheless necessary to adopt a particular perspective if any interpretation is to be made.

---

[46] A succinct illustration of this viewpoint is provided by the following: "All governments seek success in foreign policy. . . . But the determination or desperation with which they do so is due to their position in the balance of rising and declining energies and power that is a primary given, *not capable of satisfactory explanation*, of the politics of international systems. It is possible to explain particular expansionist drives as the result of a desire to escape from internal tensions; but it is also possible to impute the intensification of internal tensions and controls to the fact that a nation is committed to an expansionist policy in the first place. The *relative significance of internal and external determinants is as insoluble as is the question whether economic or political ones are more important*" (George Liska, "Continuity and Change in International Systems," *World Politics*, XVI [October 1963], p. 126, italics added). As indicated below, this line of reasoning assumes that there is only one "right" solution to every analytic problem, and it thus does not allow for the possibility that different observers, employing different perspectives (i.e., pre-theories), will arrive at different solutions to the same problem. In this sense the question of the relative importance of economic and political determinants is not as insoluble as Liska believes. The former determinants take on greater importance from the perspective of the economist, whereas greater significance attaches to the latter from the perspective of the political scientist.

While it is thus impossible to avoid possession of a pre-theory of foreign policy, it is quite easy to avoid awareness of one's pre-theory and to proceed as if one started over with each situation. Explicating one's conception of the order that underlies the external behavior of societies can be an excruciating process. As in psychoanalysis, bringing heretofore implicit and unexamined assumptions into focus may compel one to face considerations which one has long sought to ignore. Some of the assumptions may seem utterly ridiculous when exposed to explicit and careful perusal. Others may seem unworkable in the light of new knowledge. Still others may involve mutually exclusive premises, so that to recognize them would be to undermine one's previous work and to obscure one's present line of inquiry.

Nor are matters greatly simplified by emotional readiness to live with the results of explication. There still remains the intellectually taxing task of identifying the variables which one regards as major sources of external behavior and of then coming to some conclusion about their relative potencies under varying circumstances. Such a task can be very difficult indeed. Long-standing habits of thought are involved, and the analyst may have become so accustomed to them that for him the habits are part of ongoing reality and not of his way of perceiving reality. In addition, if these habits provide no experience in pre-theorizing about the processes of causation, it will not be easy to tease out variables and assess their potencies. For example, while it is relatively simple to observe that a De Gaulle is less restrained in foreign policy than a Khrushchev, many analysts—especially those who insist that every situation is unique and that therefore they do not possess a pre-theory of foreign policy—would have a hard time discerning that the observation stems from their pre-theoretical premise that individual variables have greater potency in France than in the Soviet Union.

Great as the obstacles to explication may be, however, they are not insurmountable. Patience and continual introspection can eventually bring implicit and unexamined premises to the surface. The first efforts may result in crude formulations, but the more one explicates, the more elaborate does one's pre-theory become.

But, it may be asked, if the purpose of all this soul-searching and anguish is that of facilitating the development of general theory, how will the self-conscious employment of pre-theories of foreign policy allow the field to move beyond its present position? As previously implied, the answer lies in the assumption that the widespread use of explicit pre-theories will result in the accumulation of materials that are sufficiently processed to provide a basis for comparing the external behavior of societies. If most researchers were to gather and present their data in the context of their views about the extent to which individuals, roles, governments, societies, and international systems serve as causal agents in foreign affairs, then even though these views might represent a variety of pre-theories, it should be possible to discern patterns and draw contrasts among diverse types of policies and situations. Theoretical development is not in any way dependent on the emergence of a consensus with respect to the most desirable pre-theory of foreign policy. Comparison and theorizing can ensue as long as each researcher makes clear what variables he considers central to causation and the relative potencies he ascribes to them. For even if one analyst ascribes the greatest potency to individual variables, while another views them as having relatively little potency and still another regards them as impotent, they will have all provided data justifying their respective assumptions, and in so doing they will have given the theoretician the materials he needs to fashion if-then propositions and to move to ever higher levels of generalization.

III. THE PENETRATED POLITICAL SYSTEM

But all will not be solved simply by the explication of pre-theories. This is a necessary condition of progress toward general theory, but it is not a sufficient one. Research in the foreign policy field would appear to be hindered by conceptual as well as philosophical shortcomings, and we will not be able to move forward until these more specific obstacles are also surmounted. Not only must similarly processed materials be available if general theory is to flourish, but researchers must also possess appropriate concepts for compiling them into meaningful patterns. Although rendered similar through the explication of pre-theories, the materials do not fall in place by themselves. Concepts are necessary to give them structure and thereby facilitate the formulation of if-then propositions.

The need to supplement processed materials with appropriate concepts is clarified by our earlier architectural analogy. One cannot erect a building merely by acquiring lumber and bricks. It is also necessary to be cognizant of engineering principles—that certain pieces of lumber should be placed upright, that others should be laid crosswise, and that the bricks should be laid on top of each other rather than interspersed among the lumber. Note again that the design and function of the building are not dependent upon these initial uses of the processed materials. To know which pieces of lumber are uprights and which are to be laid crosswise is not to determine how they are to be placed in relation to each other. So long as it is not done counter to the laws of gravity, the uprights and the cross pieces can be juxtaposed in all kinds of ways to form all kinds of buildings for all kinds of purposes. So it is with theories. An almost unlimited number can be fashioned out of similarly processed data so long as the initial organization of the data is consistent with the subject the theories are designed to elucidate. Regardless of the nature of a theory, however, if it is constructed out of inappropriate concepts, it is no more likely to endure than buildings erected in defiance of sound engineering principles or the laws of gravity.

Two interrelated conceptual problems seem to be holding back the development of general theories of external behavior. One concerns the tendency of researchers to maintain a rigid distinction between national and international political systems in the face of mounting evidence that the distinction is breaking down. The second difficulty involves an inclination to ignore the implications of equally clear-cut indications that the functioning of political systems can vary significantly from one type of issue to another. Let us anticipate much of the ensuing discussion by noting that the interrelationship of the two problems is such that a new kind of political system, the *penetrated system*, is needed to comprehend the fusion of national and international systems in certain kinds of *issue-areas*.

Myriad are the data that could be cited to illustrate the increasing obscuration of the boundaries between national political systems and their international environments. These boundaries may consist of the activities that result in "the authoritative allocation of values for a society,"[47] or of the interacting roles that sustain a society "by means of the employment, or threat of employment, of more or less legitimate physical compulsion,"[48] or of the processes in a society that "mobilize its resources in the interest of [positively sanctioned] goals,"[49] or "of the more inclusive structures in a society that have recognized responsibility for performing, at a minimum, the function of goal-attainment by means of legitimate decisions."[50] But however such boundaries may be drawn,

[47] David Easton, *The Political System: An Inquiry into the State of Political Science* (New York: Knopf, 1953), pp. 129–148.

[48] Almond and Coleman, *op. cit.*, p. 7.

[49] Talcott Parsons, " 'Voting' and the Equilibrium of the American Political System," in Eugene Burdick and Arthur J. Brodbeck (eds.), *American Voting Behavior* (Glencoe: Free Press, 1959), p. 81.

[50] Harry Eckstein, "The Concept 'Political System': A Review and Revision," a paper prepared for delivery at the 1963 annual meeting of the American Political Science Association, New York City, September 4–7, 1963, p. 4. Eckstein notes (p. 3) seven additional definitions of a political system that can be found in the literature. Rather than digress to explain the selection of one of these—or to defend the development of still another definition—in the ensuing discussion we shall henceforth use all of the above conceptions interchangeably and assume that more or less the same phenomena are involved whenever reference is made to the authoritative allocation of values, the quest to attain legitimately determined goals, and the mobilization of support on behalf of positively sanctioned goals.

ever since World War II they have been constantly transgressed by non-societal actors. The manner of transgression, moreover, has been quite varied. As these recent interaction sequences illustrate, even the last stronghold of sovereignty—the power to decide the personnel, practices, and policies of government—has become subject to internationalization:

When asked how he managed to continue in office despite a major shift in the control of the national government, the mayor of a city in Colombia replied, "The American Ambassador arranged it."[51]

"Ordinarily the [U.S.] aid missions have stayed aloof from local administrative differences, but there have been instances like that in Thailand where the mission served as a liaison unit among several departments of a ministry, enabling them to carry out important tasks that never would have been done otherwise."[52]

President Urho K. Kekkonen [of Finland] suggested tonight that opposition leaders who had incurred the hatred of the Soviet Union should withdraw into private life for the good of Finland.
Dr. Kekkonen made his suggestion in a radio and television report to the nation on his talks with Premier Khrushchev of the Soviet Union. The Finnish President spoke less than three hours after having returned from Novosibirsk in Siberia, where Mr. Khrushchev had agreed to postpone the joint defense negotiations demanded by Moscow on October 30.
If the politicians to whom the Soviet Union objects should retire, Dr. Kekkonen said, there would not be "the slightest doubt" that Finland could continue neutral in "all situations". . . .
The suggestion that anti-Soviet politicians retire is reported to have been foreshadowed in private conversations during the last two weeks between some of the President's close associates and members of Parliament.
These conversations indicated that demands would be forthcoming for the withdrawal into private life of at least four Social Democrats. . . . Others are a couple of members of the Swedish People's Party, at least one Conservative and . . . the only member of Parliament from the Small Farmer's Party.
All were prominent in the distintegrating five-party alliance that had pushed the Presidential candidacy of Olavi Honka. Mr. Honka announced his withdrawal from the race in "the national interest" while President Kekkonen was in Novosibirsk. [53]

And these are only illustrative of the obscuration of national boundaries that is observable to outsiders. Presumably similar processes are unfolding in governmental interactions that are conducted in private and

[51] This incident was reported to the author by a colleague who conducted interviews in Colombia in August 1963.
[52] John D. Montgomery, *The Politics of Foreign Aid* (New York: Praeger, 1962), p. 136.
[53] *The New York Times,* November 27, 1961.

not reported. Thus, to make our point even more emphatically, let us add a few hypothetical—but not unreasonable—examples to the empirical ones listed above. Imagine that the barriers to observation were lowered for a moment and revealed that:

President Johnson's note of January 6, 1964, to Sukarno, in which the former protested the latter's posture toward Malaysia, was drafted by a high official of the Indonesian Foreign Office who, concerned that his country was pursuing an undesirable course in the situation, sought out the American ambassador to Indonesia and persuaded him to urge upon the President the utility of issuing such a protest.

American State Department officials, concerned about the tendency of their Indian counterparts to accept uncritically the recommendations of India's military chiefs, work closely with the Indian Foreign Office to bring about administrative reorganization which interposes more Foreign Office personnel between the prime minister and the military chiefs.

The U.S. Secretary of State and his counterparts in the Alliance for Progress engage in joint planning on ways of circumventing legislative antagonisms and achieving Congress' acceptance of a wide-ranging foreign aid program. Let us further suppose that the Latin American foreign ministers agree to take, at just the right time, a public posture of having been outmaneuvered by Secretary Rusk, in order to convey the impression of a Secretary of State who is tough with "furriners", thereby solidifying congressional support for a wide-ranging foreign aid program.

But there is no need to pile example upon example. Whether historical or hypothetical, the foregoing are common occurrences, and not isolated incidents, in the postwar era. As one observer notes with respect to underdeveloped societies, "What happens in India or Iran is no longer intelligible in terms of parochial Indian or Iranian events and forces, but must be seen as part of a world transformation in which these particular pockets of semiautonomy are working out their distinctive yet somehow parallel destinies."[54] Nor are any developed nations so self-sufficient as to be immune from internationalization. The evidence is extensive that foreign elements have become central to certain aspects of the decision-making process of the large and industrial system called the United States.[55] Even our major political institution, the presidency, has been internationalized. According to the prevailing conceptualization of the office, the President is necessarily responsive to demands from five constituencies,

[54] Fred W. Riggs, "The Theory of Developing Polities," *World Politics*, XVI (October 1963), p. 171.

[55] Cf. U.S. Congress, Senate, *Activities of Nondiplomatic Representatives of Foreign Principals in the United States* (Washington, D.C.: Hearings before the Committee on Foreign Relations, 1963), Vols. 1–12, pp. 1–782.

"from Executive officialdom, from Congress, from his partisans, from citizens at large, and from abroad."[56]

In short, "the difference between 'national' and 'international' now exists only in the minds of those who use the words."[57] Unfortunately most political scientists are among those who still use the words. Notwithstanding widespread recognition that the postwar "revolution in expectations" in the nonindustrial parts of the world, the reliance of developing societies on foreign aid, the competition among industrial powers to provide aid, and the ever-quickening pace of technological change have greatly intensified the interdependence of nations and beclouded the line that divides them from their environments, most analysts have not made corresponding adjustments in their conceptual frameworks and have instead clung rigidly, and often awkwardly, to the national-international distinction. To be sure, there is widespread recognition that the boundaries separating national and international systems are becoming increasingly ambiguous,[58] but it is equally true that this recognition still awaits expression in conceptual and theoretical terms. The Sprouts, for example, concede that rigorous adherence "to the distinction between intranational (or domestic) and extranational (external) factors leaves certain highly important factors out of the picture," but they are nevertheless prepared to accept these omissions on the grounds that "the distinction has value for certain purposes."[59]

56 Richard E. Neustadt, *Presidential Power: The Politics of Leadership* (New York: Wiley, 1960), p. 7.

57 Mosely, *op. cit.*, p. 50.

58 See, for example, Chadwick F. Alger, "Comparison of Intranational and International Politics," *American Political Science Review*, LVII (June 1963), pp. 406–419; George F. Kennan, *American Diplomacy 1900–1950* (Chicago: University of Chicago Press, 1951), p. 99; and Otto Klineberg, "Intergroup Relations and International Relations," in Muzafer Sherif (ed.), *Intergroup Relations and Leadership: Approaches and Research in Industrial, Ethnic, Cultural, and Political Areas* (New York: Wiley, 1962), pp. 174–176.

59 *Foundations of International Politics*, p. 183. Another technique for preserving the distinction, while at the same time seeming to account for the many phenomena which the distinction obfuscates, is that of moving back and forth between different levels of analysis. By stressing a readiness to analyze international events at the international level and to examine national phenomena at the national level, one can deceive oneself into believing that no sequence of interaction can go unnoticed or unexplained. Wilbur Schramm, for example, recognizes that "the national system is made up of component systems and itself belongs to a partly developed world system," but he nevertheless avoids reconceptualization and preserves the national-international distinction by reasoning that "in order to deal effectively with a system of any magnitude it is sometimes necessary to shift the level of analysis from one level to another—up and down the scale—without losing trace of what units are interacting on the particular level which is being examined" ("Communication Development and the Development Process," in Lucian W. Pye [ed.], *Communications and Political Development* [Princeton: Princeton University Press, 1963], p. 31). This procedure, however, is not sufficient to account for the

Nor do students of international and comparative politics differ in this respect. The concern of the former with international systems and of the latter with national systems remains undiluted by the postwar fusion of the two types. While those who specialize in international systems acknowledge that such systems are largely subsystem dominant (i.e., their stability, goals, and processes are primarily the result of actions undertaken by the national systems of which they are comprised), one is hard pressed to cite any models of regional or global international systems that allow for differential subsystem impacts. Instead, the builders of international models tend to proceed on the assumption that the acknowledgment of subsystem dominance is the equivalent of explicit conceptualization. Likewise, students of national systems acknowledge that international events can significantly condition, even profoundly alter, the structure and dynamics of internal political processes, but they nevertheless treat the national system as a self-contained unit and no room is made in their models for the impact and operation of external variables. At most, such variables are handled by a notation that national systems have to develop and maintain foreign policies which facilitate adaptation to the international environment. The purpose of such a notation, however, is less that of attaining comprehension of how international systems penetrate national systems and more that of isolating those factors which would otherwise confound the conceptualization of national systems. In effect, by viewing foreign policy as taking care of events abroad, students of comparative politics free themselves of the responsibility of accounting for the penetration by international systems and enable themselves to focus on the internal processes that "normally" comprise national systems.

The recent work of Gabriel Almond is illustrative of this tendency. Nowhere in his pioneering efforts to conceptualize national systems did Almond build external variables into his model, with the result that his early writings contain "a tacit assumption . . . that the polities of developing countries can be treated as relatively autonomous or closed political systems."[60] Apparently sensitive about this drawback, Almond has recently attempted to come to grips conceptually with the pervasive presence of the international system by introducing the notion of "an international

---

breakdown of the national-international distinction. The readiness to shift back and forth between levels only serves to maintain the premise that a clear-cut differentiation can be made between them. Such a procedure is thus not likely to result in the uncovering, much less the probing, of the growing number of phenomena that occur at the unconceptualized level which fuses the national and international ones. For a general discussion of the problem of shifting the focus of analysis from one level to another, see Odd Ramsoy, *Social Groups as System and Subsystem* (New York: Free Press, 1963).

[60] Riggs, *op. cit.*, p. 171.

accommodative capability."[61] All national systems (with the possible exception of genuinely isolated oceanic island communities) are posited as possessing such a capability, and consequently "all political systems somehow cope" with the international environment.[62] In addition, Almond stresses that the accommodative capabilities of national systems also serve as internal variables in the sense that the extent of a system's capacity for accommodating to other systems contributes to the degree to which it achieves integration, mobilizes and distributes its resources, and allows for the participation of its citizenry in public affairs. Yet, despite the obvious merits of this innovation, Almond's model still contains a rigid national-international distinction. By clustering all international matters under the heading of accommodative capabilities, the model keeps national systems intact. Almond emphasizes that they may be greatly affected by the international environment and that they may even be destroyed by it [63] (presumably whenever their accommodative capabilities are insufficient), but his model does not allow for their transformation into something other than national systems. There are no "partial" national systems and no "mixed" national systems. A national system either exists or it does not, depending on whether its accommodative capabilities can absorb external threats.[64] In a profound sense, in other words, Almond avoids conceptual confrontation of the impact of external variables. His scheme takes no cognizance of the fact that events abroad are not only absorbed by a national system's accommodative capabilities but might also penetrate its processes of attaining integration, its methods of mobilizing and distributing resources, and its modes of conducting public affairs.

The rigidity of the national-international distinction is further illustrated by the wide gulf that separates students of comparative and international politics. It is the author's experience that each group is essentially uninterested in the work of the other. In one sense, of course, this is as it should be. We specialize in some fields because they arouse our interests, and we avoid others because they do not. But it is regrettable that when a specialist in comparative politics and a specialist in international politics get together, they tend to talk past each other. On two occasions of lengthy professional interaction between two such specialists, they were observed to have been first perplexed then dismayed, and finally wearied by each other's commentary.[65] The student of comparative politics is concerned

61 Gabriel A. Almond, "Political Systems and Political Change," *The American Behavioral Scientist*, VI (June 1963), p. 6.

62 *Ibid.*, p. 7.

63 *Ibid.*

64 Almond notes (*ibid.*) that national systems can also be destroyed by "internal disruptive development," but this point is not relevant to the discussion.

65 A noteworthy exception to this incompatibility is an undated collaborative

about the behavior of thousands and millions of actors, whereas only a few hundred serve as the focus of the student of international politics. The student of national systems is interested in what large groups of people (the citizenry) do either to each other or to the few (officialdom), whereas the student of international systems concentrates on what the few (nations) do either to each other or to the many (foreign publics). In addition, the actors who comprise national systems compete much more extensively for each other's clientele than do those in international systems. Given these differences in the number of actors and the goals of their interaction, students of international politics accord a much more prominent place to strategy and rationality in their thinking than do students of national politics, who are preoccupied with gross behavior that is often irrational.

As a consequence of these divergent interests, researchers in the one field tend not to be motivated to keep abreast of developments in the other. The student of international politics has little familiarity with the writings of, say, Almond or Parsons or Apter, and thus he is usually bewildered when his colleague in the comparative politics field talks about political functions, goal attainment, and political culture. Contrariwise, rare is the student of comparative politics who has read the works of, say, Schelling or Snyder or Kaplan, and thus equally rare is the comparative politics specialist who can locate himself in discussions of deterrence theory, foreign policy decision-making, and the balance of power. Even worse, each group relies on secondhand and digested accounts of the major works in the other's field; as a result each acquires undue biases and misconceptions about the literature which the other regards as basic. Few political scientists can be seized with apoplexy as quickly as the comparative politics specialist who is aroused to discuss Schelling's *The Strategy of Conflict* [66] or the international politics specialist who is moved to a discourse on Almond's first chapter in *The Politics of the Developing Areas*.[67]

Deeply entrenched habits of thought also sustain the rigidity of the national-international distinction. Most analysts are trained to emphasize the differences rather than the similarities between national and inter-

---

paper, "National Political Systems and International Politics: Notes on the Need for Research," written by Harry Eckstein and Harold Sprout for the Center of International Studies of Princeton University. Even this effort, however, failed to avoid the dilemmas of the national-international distinction. Not only is the latter explicitly cited as the basis of the paper, but, largely as the result of adhering to it, the paper is really two papers, and the reader can readily discern which parts were written by the comparative politics specialist (Eckstein) and which by the specialist in international politics (Sprout).

[66] Cambridge: Harvard University Press, 1960.
[67] Almond and Coleman, *op. cit.*

national politics.[68] Rare is the graduate program that provides systematic training in the comparison of national and international systems. Hardly less rare are the programs that equip students with a capacity to compare international systems. Rather, "comparison" has a very strict meaning in political science today; one learns only to compare practices and policies at subnational or national levels. It is not surprising, therefore, that every graduate program in the country lists comparative and international politics as two separate fields to be offered for the Ph.D. To offer a field of study in international politics is to be conversant with political activities undertaken in the absence of "a structure of authoritative decision-making," whereas to offer a field in comparative or national politics requires familiarity with the ways in which the presence of legitimacy and a legitimizing agency (government) enhance, limit, or otherwise condition the conduct of politics.[69] Indeed, students of comparative politics become so accustomed to casting their analyses in terms of the structure of authority that they even tend to lose interest in national systems when the structure breaks down and chaos and violence prevail.[70]

Of all the habits which reinforce the reluctance of political scientists to modify the national-international distinction in the light of changing empirical patterns, none is more damaging than the tendency to posit political systems as functioning "in a society" or in some other unit equivalent to a nation. This unnecessary and essentially arbitrary limitation of the scope of the processes defined as political will be found in every major conceptualization that has been advanced in recent years. As indicated above, Easton identifies the authoritative allocation of values as the core of political activity, but immediately restricts his conception by adding that the values must be authoritatively allocated "in a society." Such an addition seems more gratuitous than logical. Certainly it is not necessary to his formulation. What about the elders of a village who reapportion the land, the representatives on a city council who decide on slum clearance and provide for urban renewal, or the members of the Council of Ministers of the European Economic Community who increase the tariff on chicken imported from the United States? Surely such activities constitute the allocation of values. Surely, too, they are authoritative for persons residing in the units affected by each allocation. And surely, therefore, Easton would be inclined to investigate them, even though his focus would be a village, city, or region rather than a society.

[68] For an effort to celebrate the similarities, see Chapter 10.

[69] This distinction between the two fields is clearly set forth in Harold and Margaret Sprout, *op. cit.*, p. 75.

[70] For an illuminating discussion of this point, see Harry Eckstein, "Toward the Theoretical Study of Internal War," in Harry Eckstein (ed.), *Internal War: Basic Problems and Approaches* (New York: Free Press, 1964), pp. 1–7.

Similarly, Eckstein identifies political systems in terms of structures which facilitate the attainment of goals through legitimate decisions, but he then limits his conception by specifying that the structures must be "in a society" and that they must be the society's "most inclusive" structures (i.e., the structures of a national system). Again such a limitation seems unnecessary. Again the deliberations of the village elders, the city council, and the EEC are excluded, albeit in all three cases attention focuses on action designed to determine and realize the goals of large groups of people. Much the same could be said (to take one other example) about Deutsch's conclusion that the "essence of politics" involves "the dependable coordination of human efforts and expectations for the attainment of the goals of the society.[71] His formulation would hardly be weakened and its relevance would certainly be expanded if the last two words of the definition were changed to "an interaction unit."

Obviously the tendency to house polities in societies would not serve to reinforce the national-international distinction if it were accompanied by an inclination to apply the concept of society to any social unit with shared norms and interdependent institutions. However, although lip service is often paid to such an inclination, it does not in fact prevail. Most—and possibly all—analysts have in mind national units and not villages, cities, or supranational communities when they refer to societies.[72]

[71] Karl W. Deutsch, *The Nerves of Government: Models of Political Communication and Control* (New York: Free Press, 1963), p. 124.

[72] Despite disclaimers to the contrary, for example, Easton's exposition of what he means by a "society" is largely descriptive of a national system (*op. cit.*, p. 135). To be sure, in order to make the point that centralized governments are not prerequisites of societies, Easton cites international and nonliterate units as being societal in character (pp. 137–140). On the other hand, at no point does he specify that subnational units with centralized governments, such as villages or cities, constitute societies. Rather the impression is clearly conveyed that, except for an occasional international or nonliterate society, the world is made up only of national societies.

Similarly, in one of his efforts to delineate political systems, Gabriel Almond, borrowing from Max Weber, seeks to avoid equating societies and nations by positing "a given territory" as the home of polities ("Comparative Political Systems," *Journal of Politics*, 18 (August 1956), p. 394). His ensuing discussion, however, is plainly cast in terms of national societies, and in a later work, the first chapter of *The Politics of the Developing Areas,* Almond's central definition not only includes societies but, indeed, defines "independent societies" as the loci of political systems (p. 7).

Political scientists, however, are not the only, or even the worst, offenders in this respect. Sociologists pay extensive lip service to the notion that any patterned interaction can be considered a social system, but the author has yet to find a sociologist who is willing to treat, say, a friendship, a corporation, and a city as major foci of analysis in an introductory sociology course. Eventually—and invariably—it is conceded or otherwise becomes clear that by social systems are meant national societies and that all other interaction patterns are subsystemic in character.

The reasons for this convergence at the national level can be readily discerned. Analysts are interested in theorizing about greater and not lesser loyalties, about ultimate and not immediate authority, about the making and not the initiating of decisions; and for decades all these processes have tended to culminate at the national level. Conflicts between national societies and lesser units (such as villages or cities), for example, have traditionally been resolved in favor of the nation. So have clashes between national societies and supranational units. Legally, militarily, and politically, in other words, the actions of national officials have prevailed over those of village elders, city counselors, or supranational ministers. Faced with a choice, people have attached greater loyalty to national than to subnational or supranational units. As a result, the decision-making mechanisms of national societies have long enjoyed a legitimacy, an authoritativeness, and an inclusiveness that no other unit could match.

To restate our central point, however, major alterations in this pattern have occurred in the middle of the twentieth century. As has already been indicated, the national society is now so penetrated by the external world that it is no longer the only source of legitimacy or even of the employment of coercive techniques. The probability that most social processes will culminate at the national level has diminished, and instead the "most inclusive" structures through which groups strive to attain goals are increasingly becoming a composite of subnational, national, and supranational elements.

It must be emphasized that these changes involve considerably more than a significant increase in the influence wielded by nonmembers of national societies. We are not simply asserting the proposition that the external world impinges ever more pervasively on the life of national societies, albeit such a proposition can hardly be denied. Nor are we talking merely about the growing interdependence of national political systems. Our contention is rather that in certain respects[73] national political systems now permeate, as well as depend on, each other and that their functioning now embraces actors who are not formally members of the system. These nonmembers not only exert influence upon national systems but actually participate in the processes through which such systems allocate values, coordinate goal-directed efforts, and legitimately employ coercion. They not only engage in bargaining with the system, but they actually bargain within the system, taking positions on behalf of one or another of its components. Most important, the participation of nonmembers of the society in value-allocative and goal-attainment processes is accepted by both its officialdom and its citizenry, so that the decisions to which nonmembers contribute are no less authoritative and legitimate than are those

[73] That is, in certain issue-areas (see below).

in which they do not participate. Such external penetration may not always be gladly accepted by the officials and citizens of a society, but what renders decisions legitimate and authoritative is that they are felt to be binding, irrespective of whether they are accepted regretfully or willingly.[74] No doubt both the Finnish president and the people were less than delighted by the aforementioned participation of Soviet officials in their electoral processes, but the decisions that resulted from such participation do not appear to have been more widely challenged in Finland than are other decisions made exclusively by members of the society.

One could, of course, reject this line of reasoning on narrow legal grounds. From the perspective of the law, the participation of nonmembers in a society's deliberations can never be regarded as more than the exercise of external influence. Strictly speaking, Soviet officials have no "right" to participate directly in Finnish affairs. They cannot vote in Finnish elections, and they are not entitled to nominate candidates for office. They are *non*members, not members, of Finnish society, and thus their actions in Finland can never be viewed as legitimate or authoritative from a strict juridical standpoint. To repeat, however, the functioning of national political systems contrasts so sharply with this narrow legal construction that the latter is hardly adequate as a basis of political conceptualization. The boundaries of political systems are defined by activities and processes, not by legalities. Our interest is in political science and not in legal science, albeit the two need not be as discrepant as the situations discussed here.

The foregoing considerations not only lead to the conclusion that cogent political analysis requires a readiness to treat the functioning of national systems as increasingly dependent on external events and trends, but they also suggest the need to identify a new type of political system that will account for phenomena which not even a less rigid use of the national-international distinction renders comprehensible. Such a system might be called the *penetrated political system*,[75] and its essential characteristics might be defined in the following way: A *penetrated political system is one in which nonmembers of a national society participate directly and authoritatively, through actions taken jointly with the society's members, in either the allocation of its values or the mobilization of*

---

[74] Cf. David Easton, "The Perception of Authority and Political Change," in Carl J. Friedrich (ed.), *Authority* (Cambridge: Harvard University Press, 1958), pp. 179–181.

[75] This designation is nonevaluative. Although the word "penetrated" is sometimes used in connection with subversive activities, nothing invidious is intended by its use here. As will be seen, a penetrated system can be authoritarian or democratic, dynamic or static, modern or primitive. Indeed, in the ensuing discussion penetrative processes are conceived to be legitimate and authoritative for the society in which they unfold.

support on behalf of its goals.[76] The political processes of a penetrated system are conceived to be structurally different from both those of an international political system and those of a national political system. In the former, nonmembers indirectly and non-authoritatively influence the allocation of a society's values and the mobilization of support for its goals through autonomous rather than through joint action. In the latter, nonmembers of a society do not direct action toward it and thus do not contribute in any way to the allocation of its values or the attainment of its goals.

Obviously operationalization of these distinctions will prove difficult. When does an interaction between two actors consist of autonomous acts, and when does it amount to joint action? When are nonmembers of a society participants in its politics, and when are they just influential nonparticipants? Furthermore, how extensive must the participation by nonmembers be in order that a penetrated political system may come into existence?

In a sense, of course, operational answers to these questions must necessarily be arbitrary. What one observer treats as direct participation another may regard as indirect influence. Further clarification of the distinguishing features of penetrated systems, however, can be accomplished by citing some concrete examples of them. Vietnam and the Congo are two obvious ones. The U.S.'s role in the former and the U.N.'s role in the latter clearly involve thoroughgoing participation in the allocation of Vietnamese and Congolese values and in efforts to mobilize popular support for the selected values. No less thoroughgoing as penetrated systems were Japan and Germany from the end of World War II to the end of their occupation by the Allies.[77] The satellite arrangements between the Soviet Union and the countries of Eastern Europe since World War II or between the Soviet Union and Cuba since 1961 also illustrate thoroughgoing penetrated systems. So does mainland China during the period between the advent of the Sino-Soviet bloc in 1949 and the latter's deterioration after the withdrawal of Soviet technicians from China in 1960.

[76] For another even more elaborate systemic creation that was at least partly designed to compensate for the weaknesses of the national-international distinction, see Fred W. Riggs, "International Relations as a Prismatic System," *World Politics,* XIV (October 1961), pp. 144–181.

[77] While no other type of penetrated system can be more all-encompassing than a postwar occupation, it does not necessarily follow that all military occupations constitute penetrated systems. France during the German occupation of 1941–44, for example, would not be classified as a penetrated system, since the French did not accept German participation in their affairs as legitimate and therefore resisted being mobilized in support of values that the Germans had allocated for them. For other dimensions of the role played by military personnel in penetrated systems, see George Stambuck, *American Military Forces Abroad: Their Impact on the Western State System* (Columbus: Ohio State University Press, 1963).

Less thoroughgoing but nonetheless significant examples of penetration are the role of American citizens, companies, and officials in Cuba prior to 1958; the participation of U.S. officials in India's defense planning subsequent to the Chinese attack of 1962; the activities of the British armed forces in postindependence Kenya; the U.S.'s abandonment of Skybolt as a weapon for the British defense system; the aforementioned behavior of American aid officials in Thailand; and indeed the operation of any foreign aid program in which the aiding society maintains some control over the purposes and distribution of the aid in the recipient society. Equally indicative of the emergence of a penetrated system is the acceptance of a growing number of nondiplomatic foreign agents in the United States.[78]

As these examples indicate, penetrated systems, like international and national ones, are not static. They come into being, develop, or disappear as capabilities, attitudes, or circumstances change. Mainland China was a penetrated system during the 1950s, but emerged as a national system during the 1960s. Contrariwise, for centuries British defenses were national in character, but now they seem destined to be sustained through penetrative processes. Cuba represents the change, rather than the emergence or disappearance, of a penetrated system; for decades its politics was penetrated by the United States, but in recent years the latter has been replaced by the Soviet Union as the penetrator.

At the same time the examples suggest that it is false to assume that penetrated systems merely represent stages in the evolution or deterioration of national systems. As indicated by the Cuban example, and even more by that of East Germany, penetrated systems can be relatively permanent forms of political organization. Recognition of the relative permanence of certain types of penetrated systems will prove especially difficult for those who cling to the national-international distinction. Such an outlook fosters the view that the integrative or disintegrative processes prevalent in a region must inevitably culminate in its consolidation into a single national system or its fragmentation into two or more national systems. Yet there is no inherent reason why the processes which lead to the solidification of national systems should not also operate in penetrated systems. Given a cold war context, what has happened in East Germany may well be prototypical rather than exceptional in the case of newly established penetrated systems.

Another characteristic of penetrated systems suggested by the examples listed above is that national societies (as defined, say, by actual or pro-

[78] The number of these registered with the Department of Justice under provisions of the Foreign Agents Registration Act has risen from approximately 160 in 1944 to nearly 500 in 1963. See U.S. Congress, Senate, *op. cit.*, p. 10.

posed membership in the United Nations) always serve as the site for penetrated systems. Unlike an international system, which encompasses interaction patterns that occur between societies, the processes of a penetrated system unfold only in the penetrated society. In no way is such a system conceived to embrace the value allocations that occur in the societies to which the nonmembers belong and which account for their participation in the politics of the penetrated society. An inquiry into China as a penetrated system in the 1950s, for example, would not require investigation of value allocations that were made in Moscow, albeit a full analysis of the Sino-Soviet bloc during that decade would involve an examination of China as a penetrated system, the Soviet Union as a national system, and the two together as an international system.

Still another characteristic of a penetrated system is indicated by the examples of the Congo and Cuba—namely, that the nonmembers of such a system can belong either to an international organization or to another society and that in the latter case they can either hold official positions or be merely private citizens. The existence of a penetrated system is determined by the presence of nonmembers who participate directly in a society's politics and not by their affiliations and responsibilities.

More significantly, all but the last of the examples listed earlier indicate that penetrated systems are characterized by a shortage of capabilities on the part of the penetrated society and that an effort to compensate for, or take advantage of, this shortage underlies the participation of nonmembers in its politics. The shortage may be of an economic kind (as in the case of recipients of foreign aid); it may involve military weaknesses (as in Vietnam or Finland); it may stem from a lack of social cohesion (as in the Congo); or it may consist of an overall strategic vulnerability (as in Cuba). Whatever the nature of the shortage, however, it is sufficiently recognized and accepted by the members of a penetrated society to permit legitimacy to become attached to the direct participation of the nonmembers in the allocation of its values.[79] Hence it follows that penetrated systems are likely to be as permanent as the capability shortages which foster and sustain them.

But the last listed example, that of increasing numbers of nondiplo-

[79] This is not to imply, however, that the presence of nonmembers in a society marked by shortages necessarily renders a penetrated system authoritarian in structure or that their participation in its politics is necessarily based on superior-subordinate relationships. As illustrated by the Skybolt and foreign aid examples, penetrated systems can operate in open societies as well as in closed ones. Likewise, as the evolution of the Alliance for Progress demonstrates, many foreign aid programs are based on functional equality between the giving and the recipient societies. To be sure, some diffusion of the values of the nonmembers is bound to occur in the penetrated society, but such values can be as variable as their bearers and thus diffusion can lead to democratic structures as readily as to authoritarian ones.

matic foreign agents registered in the United States, cannot be dismissed merely as an exception. Capability shortages may underlie most penetrated systems, but obviously penetration of the United States did not occur for this reason. Yet because of the nature of the penetration the U.S. example is not as contradictory as it might seem at first glance. For again a capability imbalance would appear to have encouraged the growth of penetrative processes, the difference being that the United States possesses a relative abundance rather than a relative shortage of capabilities. Just as a society's shortages lead nonmembers to participate in its politics, so does the existence of plenitude serve to attract participation by nonmembers who wish to obtain either financial aid or political support.[80] Thus it is reasonable to speculate that as long as richly endowed societies maintain institutions that permit access to their resources, they are bound to become penetrated in certain respects.[81]

All the cited examples also reveal that for a penetrated system to function, there must be intensive face-to-face interaction between members and nonmembers of a society. Values cannot be authoritatively allocated, or goal-attaining activities authoritatively mobilized, from afar. Nonmembers of a society must come into contact with its officials and/or its citizenry in order to acquire sufficient information about the society's needs and wants to participate in its value-allocative processes in ways that are sufficiently acceptable to be authoritative. Moreover, even if the nonmembers could obtain appropriate information about the society without interacting with its members, their efforts to contribute to the allocation of its values would still be lacking in authority. While authority is often attached to mystical and distant entities, to be effectively sustained it requires some visible and human embodiment. The members of a society are not likely to regard the demands or suggestions of nonmembers as binding (that is, as authoritative) unless they have had some firsthand acquaintance with them.

This is not to say, of course, that intensive face-to-face interaction between members and nonmembers of a society occurs only in a penetrated system. Nor is it to imply that nonmembers of a society can contribute to the allocation of its values only through intensive face-to-face interaction with its members. It is quite commonplace for the political processes of international systems to underlie the reallocation of values

---

[80] For a lengthier analysis of the reasons why nonmembers are attracted to participation in the allocation of values in the United States, see U.S. Congress, Senate, *op. cit.*, p. 10.

[81] Nor is it unreasonable to contend that, for the same reasons, eventually even richly endowed closed societies are bound to experience penetrative processes. It was, after all, African students who gave Moscow its first recorded riots since the Russian Revolution of 1917.

in societies and to do so either with or without face-to-face interaction. Prolonged negotiations over a treaty which reallocates the values of all the signatories to it are illustrative of the former process, and an extreme example of the latter is provided by two societies that sever all contacts and then reallocate their values in response to the subsequent threats each makes toward the other. Although in both cases nonmembers contribute to the allocation of a society's values, both examples would nonetheless be regarded as reflecting international and not penetrative processes because in neither illustration do nonmembers participate directly in the allocation of a society's values. This is self-evident in the case of the two societies that sever relations, but it is no less true in the treaty example. For while the signatories to a treaty join together in face-to-face interaction in order to conclude it, each representative makes a commitment only with respect to his own society, and thus his actions at the negotiating table do not involve participation in the allocative processes of other societies.[82] In other words, treaties are best viewed as the sum of autonomous acts rather than as the result of joint action.

One final point with respect to penetrated systems needs to be made. As it stands at present, our formulation suffers from a lack of differentiation. While the analysis points to the conclusion that all national societies in the modern world are susceptible of swift transformation into penetrated systems, it treats all such systems as if they were similarly transformed and structured. Yet obviously there is a vast difference between the penetrated systems that have developed in Vietnam and the Congo and those that have evolved with respect to British or Indian defenses. In the former cases penetration is thoroughgoing, whereas in the latter it is limited to the allocation of a highly restricted set of values. Nonmembers may participate directly in the determination and attainment of Indian military goals, but clearly they are not a party to the processes whereby India's linguistic problems are handled. In Vietnam, on the other hand, nonmembers have been centrally involved in efforts to mobilize support for certain religious values as well as for a military campaign. Accordingly, so as to differentiate degrees of penetration as well as the structural differences to which they give rise, it seems appropriate to distinguish between multi-issue and single-issue penetrated systems, the distinction being based on whether nonmembers participate in the allocation of a variety of values or of only a selected set of values.

[82] One exception here would be a treaty in which one signatory agrees to allow another to participate subsequently in the allocation of its values and the mobilization of support for its goals. The treaty between France and Monaco is illustrative in this respect, as are many treaties that victors and vanquished sign after a war. Such exceptions can be regarded as the one type of penetrated system that has a formal constitution.

IV. THE ISSUE-AREA CONCEPT

The conclusion that national societies can be organized as penetrated political systems with respect to some types of issues—or issue-areas—and as national political systems with respect to others is consistent with mounting evidence that the functioning of any type of political system can vary significantly from one issue-area to another. Data descriptive of local, party, legislative, national, and international systems are converging around the finding that different types of issue-areas elicit different sets of motives on the part of different actors in a political system, that different system members are thus activated in different issue-areas, and that the different interaction patterns which result from these variations produce different degrees of stability and coherence for each of the issue-areas in which systemic processes are operative.

Perhaps the most impressive data along these lines are to be found in Dahl's inquiry into the politics of New Haven.[83] Using systematic survey techniques, Dahl examined the processes of governmental and non-governmental leadership activated by situations in three issue-areas—urban redevelopment, education, and nominations. His finding is stunning: The "overlap among leaders and subleaders" in the three areas involved only 3 percent of his sample, and only 1.5 percent were leaders in all three areas.[84] In effect, there are at least three New Haven political systems, and to know how values are allocated and how support is mobilized in any one area is not to be knowledgeable about the operation of these processes in the other areas.[85]

Similar findings on legislative and national systems are reported by Miller and Stokes, who employed survey data to correlate the attitudes of congressmen, the attitudes of their constituencies, and the congressmen's perceptions of their constituencies' attitudes in three major issue-areas—social welfare, foreign involvement, and civil rights.[86] Again the results compel reflection: The differences between the operation of the processes of representation in the civil rights area, on the one hand, and in the social welfare and foreign involvement areas, on the other, proved to be highly significant statistically, constituting "one of the most striking find-

[83] Robert A. Dahl, *Who Governs: Democracy and Power in an American City* (New Haven: Yale University Press, 1961).

[84] *Ibid.*, p. 175.

[85] For much additional evidence that "the pattern of decision-making" varies from issue-area to issue-area in local systems, see Nelson W. Polsby, *Community Power and Political Theory* (New Haven: Yale University Press, 1963), pp. 113–14, 124–28.

[86] Warren E. Miller and Donald E. Stokes, "Constituency Influence in Congress," *American Political Science Review*, LVII (March 1963), pp. 45–56.

ings of this analysis."[87] Given such variability at the center of the political process, again it seems reasonable to assert that there are at least two American national systems, and to comprehend the dynamics of one is not necessarily to understand the functioning of the other.

Still another indication of the importance of issue-areas has been uncovered in studies of the processes through which political parties mobilize support. For example, using interview data, Chalmers probed decision-making within the Social Democratic Party of West Germany and was led to conclude that, in effect, the party consists of two independent organizational mechanisms.[88] He found that different party leaders and different party followers engaged in different modes of deciding upon ideological matters on the one hand and campaign issues on the other, the differences again being such that knowledge of the party's functioning in one area did not insure comprehension of its dynamics in the other.

Nor do international systems appear to be different in this respect. Although here the data are more impressionistic than systematic, it does seem clear that the structure and functioning of international systems can vary significantly from one issue-area to another. The current scene provides a host of examples. Consider the Communist international system; plainly it operates differently in the admit-China-to-the-U.N. area than it does in the area bounded by disarmament questions. Or take NATO; obviously it has been a vastly different system with respect to Berlin than with respect to independence movements in Africa. Likewise, to cite an equally clear-cut dyadic example, the functioning of the U.S.-U.S.S.R. international system in the Berlin issue-area bears little resemblance to the processes through which it allocates values and mobilizes support for the attainment of its goals in the disarmament or wheat-production areas.

In the foreign policy field, too, there are numerous indications that the nature of the issue constitutes a crucial variable in the processes whereby the external behavior of national societies is generated. In the United States, for example, the complex of internal influences brought to bear in the ratification of treaties would seem to be entirely different from that which underlies the allocation of economic and military assistance to other countries.[89] One has the impression that much the same could be said about other societies that maintain foreign aid programs.

Whether they are impressionistic or systematic, in short, the data

[87] Ibid., p. 53.

[88] See Douglas A. Chalmers, The SPD: From Working Class Movement to Modern Political Party (New Haven: Yale University Press, 1964).

[89] Compare, for instance, the identity and number of the roles that were activated, the motives and attitudes that guided the behavior of the role occupants, and the character of the interaction that produced the external behavior in these two case studies: Bernard C. Cohen, The Political Process and Foreign Policy: The

on issue-areas are too impressive to ignore. Conceptual allowance must be made for them if theorizing in the foreign policy field is to flourish. Indeed, the emergence of issue-areas is as pronounced and significant as is the breakdown of the national-international distinction. Taken together, the two trends point to the radical conclusion that the boundaries of political systems ought to be drawn vertically in terms of issue-areas as well as horizontally in terms of geographic areas.[90] Stated in the context of the present world scene, the data compel us to cast our analyses as much in terms of, say, civil rights political systems, economic-development political systems, and health-and-welfare political systems as we do in terms of local, national, and international systems.

However, as in the case of the national-international distinction (and in part because of it), political scientists have not been inclined to make the conceptual adjustments which the data on issue-areas would seem to warrant. Certainly the more theoretically oriented analysts, with one notable exception, have not proceeded from the assumption that issues generate structurally and functionally significant differences.[91] Even Dahl himself ignores the relevance of issue-areas in a subsequent conceptualization of politics and polities.[92] Similarly, and again with one important exception, empirical-minded researchers have not followed up the implications of the findings cited above, and one is hard pressed to find empirical analyses of particular systems that explicitly explore the relevancy, strength, and boundaries of different kinds of issue-areas.[93] Instead most

Making of the Japanese Peace Settlement (Princeton: Princeton University Press, 1957); and H. Field Haviland, Jr., "Foreign Aid and the Policy Process: 1957," *American Political Science Review*, LII (September 1958), pp. 689–725.

[90] Accordingly, henceforth we shall distinguish between horizontal and vertical political systems. A horizontal system is conceived to be a set of interdependent procedures through which a geographic unit (e.g., a city, state, or nation) or a functional institution (e.g., a party, legislature, or bureaucracy) allocates values and mobilizes support in a broad range of issue-areas. A vertical system, on the other hand, is conceived to encompass a set of interdependent procedures whereby a cluster of values within an issue-area is allocated by either a single horizontal system or a fusion of horizontal systems. The number of vertical systems operative at any one time is conceived to be quite variable and dependent on the purposes of analysis. Just as it is useful to posit a variety of horizontal systems at every horizontal level (e.g., 130+ sovereign states at the national level), so is it likely to prove necessary to conceive of numerous vertical systems within every issue-area (e.g., the civil rights system of the 130+ sovereign states may be viewed as 130+ vertical systems within one major area).

[91] The exception is Herbert J. Spiro, "Comparative Politics: A Comprehensive Approach," *American Political Science Review*, LVI (September 1962), pp. 577–595.

[92] Robert A. Dahl, *Modern Political Analysis* (Englewood Cliffs, N.J.: Prentice-Hall, 1963).

[93] Here the exception is Aaron B. Wildavsky, "The Analysis of Issue-Contexts in the Study of Decision-Making," *Journal of Politics*, 24 (November 1962), pp. 717–732.

researchers continue to treat cities, parties, legislatures, and nations as if their processes of allocating values and mobilizing support for goals were constants rather than variables.[94] To be sure, fine distinctions *between* cities or parties or legislatures or nations are recognized and closely analyzed, but the same sensitivities are not trained on the variability *within* a given horizontal system.[95]

The neglect of issue-areas in systematic inquiry is all the more perplexing because there is one respect in which intuitively, and often unknowingly, political scientists do employ the concept: although reasons are rarely given for the distinction, one is usually made between foreign and domestic policy. Throughout the discipline it is assumed that national political systems function differently in formulating and administering foreign policies than they do in domestic areas. Most universities, for example, offer both undergraduate and graduate courses in "The Formulation of American Foreign Policy," a subject presumably sufficiently unlike "The Formulation of American Domestic Policy" to warrant separate presentation. However, since the reasoning underlying the distinction is never made explicit, its implications have not been recognized, and the idea of categorizing phenomena according to issue-areas has not been applied elsewhere in the discipline. Sociologists have developed subfields in industrial sociology, the sociology of law, the sociology of education, the sociology of religion, the sociology of art, the sociology of science, the sociology of medicine, the sociology of demographic behavior, the sociology of crime, and the sociology of mental illness, as well as in the sociology of the family, urban sociology, rural sociology, political sociology, and the sociology of particular societies.[96] Yet political scientists do not offer courses in, say, the politics of employment, the politics of transportation, the politics of conservation, the politics of foreign aid, the politics

94 In some cases it is more accurate to say that issue-areas are treated as unconceptualized variables in the political process. In their elaborate and impressive formulation of the legislative system and process, for example, Wahlke, Eulau, Buchanan, and Ferguson note the importance of issue-areas by including them among the "circumstantial variables" (p. 20), which are in turn made central to the diagrammatic presentation of their scheme (p. 18). In the diagram, however, they accompany the box that houses the circumstantial variables with the parenthetic phrase, "not conceptualized." John C. Wahlke, Heinz Eulau, William Buchanan, and Leroy C. Ferguson, *The Legislative System: Explorations in Legislative Behavior* (New York: Wiley, 1962).

95 Researchers who focus on the behavior of blocs in international organizations might be considered an exception here. Through analysis of bloc voting in the United Nations, they have turned increasingly to the question of how different issues affect the cohesiveness and functioning of blocs. See, for example, Thomas Hovet, Jr., *Africa in the United Nations* (Evanston: Northwestern University Press, 1963).

96 Cf. Robert K. Merton, Leonard Broom, and Leonard S. Cottrell, Jr. (eds.), *Sociology Today: Problems and Prospects* (New York: Basic Books, 1959).

of civil liberties, the politics of agriculture, the politics of defense strategy, the politics of health, the politics of commerce, the politics of education, and so on.[97]

The conceptual and empirical neglect of issue-areas would appear to stem from several sources. One is the sheer force of habit. Most analysts have become accustomed to perceiving and structuring political phenomena in terms of horizontal systems. Hence, confronted with findings like Dahl's, most researchers would be inclined to treat them merely as interesting characteristics of local communities rather than as pervasive phenomena that necessitate reconsideration of one's approach to the discipline.

The habit of horizontal analysis is reinforced by the tendency of some, and perhaps even many, researchers to view horizontal political systems as dominated by a "power elite" who perform the function of allocating all the system's values. A legislature has its "inner club," a party its "bosses," an executive his "kitchen cabinet," a community its "influentials," and an international organization its "powerful"—all of whom are believed to interact in the same way whenever they make decisions for, or mobilize support in, their respective systems. Such an approach is obviously incompatible with a recognition of issue-areas as a meaningful concept. Notwithstanding the findings uncovered by Dahl and others, however, power-elite theories still abound, and the strength of the habit of horizontal analysis remains undiminished.

Neglect of issue-areas would also seem to stem from a view that the issues which preoccupy horizontal systems are unique rather than recurrent and that therefore any model which posits them as variables encourages the writing of case histories rather than the testing of hypotheses and the construction of theories. Issues are temporary and situational, the reasoning seems to be, and to see horizontal systems functioning in terms of them is thus to reduce actors and action to a level of specificity that inhibits the discernment of patterns and regularities. Unlike the power theorists, in other words, some analysts appear to accept the validity of

---

[97] Exceptions, of course, can be cited. Some institutions, for example, are now offering courses in the politics of disarmament and the politics of civil liberties. As a general trend, however, political science is still organized in terms of units (local, national, and international) or institutions (party, legislative, administrative, and judicial) that process all types of issues, rather than in terms of issue-areas that activate all types of units and institutions. Even the exceptions do not usually extend beyond a particular unit. Courses in the politics of disarmament tend to focus on the Nuclear Club of a particular era, and those dealing with the politics of civil liberties are concerned primarily with the United States. The scope of the former is rarely extended to the problems of weapons management in other contexts, and the scope of the latter rarely encompasses civil rights problems in South Africa, Great Britain, or the Soviet Union.

the issue-area data even as they discount them on the grounds that such data reflect historical rather than political processes. The difficulty with this line of reasoning is that it is based on an excessively narrow conception of the nature of an issue-area. Both vertical systems and the issue-areas in which they function are best conceived in terms of broad types of values and the recurring need to allocate them. Hence, although issues may be temporary and situational, issue-areas are persistent and general. Each area must be conceptualized at a high enough level of abstraction to encompass a variety of vertical systems, and each of the latter must in turn be conceived as based on a continual processing of the values that its structure is designed to allocate. This is why Dahl, for example, constructed his three issue-areas out of data for fifty-seven, eight, and ten occasions when questions pertaining, respectively, to urban redevelopment, education, and political nominations were at issue during periods of nine, seven, and twenty years. Similarly if the "Berlin situation" were conceptualized as a vertical political system, the crises of 1948-49, 1958, 1961, and 1963 would all serve as data from which the boundaries, processes, and stability of the area would be inferred.

The boundaries of issue-areas and of the vertical systems within them would seem to be the focus of another more sophisticated line of reasoning that neglects both the concept and the evidence of its importance. The reasoning is that a system consists of "a boundary-maintaining set of interdependent particles"[98] and that while issue-areas and vertical systems certainly contain interdependent parts, their boundaries are not self-maintaining. Why? Because the processes of allocating values and mobilizing support within an issue-area are too vulnerable to continuous and significant external interference to justify treating their interdependent parts as political systems. And why should the boundaries of issue-areas be so vulnerable? Because bargaining among issue-areas is a major characteristic of geographic and other types of horizontal systems. Indeed, the stability of such systems is considered to be crucially dependent on their ability to resolve conflicts in one area by compromising in other areas. Hence, the argument concludes, the essential characteristic of boundary-maintenance—that the components of a system be so related as to divide the system from its environment—will at best be obscure and at worst non-existent in vertical systems.

There can hardly be any dissent from much of this reasoning. It is

---

[98] Schramm, *op. cit.*, p. 30. The author adds that "the key words are boundary and interdependent. By interdependence we mean a relationship of parts in which anything happening to one component of a system affects, no matter how slightly, the balance and relationship of the whole system. By boundary-maintaining we mean a state in which the components are so related that it is possible to tell where the system ends and its environment begins."

certainly true that the outcome of interaction patterns within an issue-area can be greatly influenced by external variables. The strong pull which national security considerations can exert in the area of civil liberties provides an obvious example. And surely it is also incontestable that bargaining among issue-areas can frequently occur in horizontal systems. Indeed, this is virtually a defining characteristic of legislatures, especially those in which logrolling processes are predominant.

The recognition of these points, however, does not diminish the potential relevance of the issue-area data. For the fact is that no political system has unmistakable and impermeable boundaries. Legislatures are penetrated by executives and parties; executives penetrate legislatures and parties; and parties in turn are penetrated by executives and legislatures. Local communities are penetrated by regional ones, and regional units are penetrated by national systems; and, as we have seen, it is increasingly difficult to distinguish national systems from their international environments. In short, the boundaries of horizontal systems are also far from invulnerable, perhaps no less so than those of vertical systems.[99] Certainly bargaining among horizontal systems can be just as consequential for the participating units as that which occurs among vertical systems. Executive-legislative relations and inter-nation relations provide obvious examples. Consider the former: Plainly the extent of the impact which executives and legislatures can have on each other is no less than the pull which issues can have on each other within even the most logrolling type of legislature.

In fact, one can think of some horizontal systems that are *less* boundary maintaining than some vertical systems. To take an extreme example, compare the horizontal system known as Vietnam and the vertical one known as disarmament, as they appear to be functioning at the present time. The boundaries of the former are so obscure that classifying it as a penetrated system is the only way in which its processes of allocating values and mobilizing support become comprehensible. On the other hand, it is not nearly so difficult to discern the line dividing the disarmament area from its environment. Governments take positions, seek support from other governments, send representatives to Geneva, and then attempt to allocate values with a minimum of penetration from other issue-areas. To

---

[99] Conversely, the structure of vertical systems can remain just as impervious to the effects of bargaining with other units as can the structure of horizontal systems. That is, the bargaining that occurs across issue-areas need not have any greater impact on the identity, motivations, and interaction patterns of the actors who conflict over the allocation of a particular set of values than, say, treaty negotiations would have on the identity, motives, and decision-making processes of the actors in the national systems that are signatories to the treaty. The resolution of the conflict in the vertical system, i.e., the way in which the values are allocated, may be affected by the intrusion of other issues, but the distinctive behavior which forms the boundaries of the system may well continue unaltered.

be sure, in the end values are rarely allocated and deadlock usually results, but this outcome is due less to the intrusion of other issues than it is to the rigidity of the positions which actors bring to disarmament negotiations. A good illustration of the relative ease with which the boundaries of the disarmament area can be discerned is provided by the last paragraph of these excerpts from a recent news story:

> Geneva, Feb. 12—Semyon K. Tsarapkin, leader of the Soviet delegation to the disarmament talks, accused Swiss authorities today of having shown a "clear lack of desire" to help find Yuri I. Nossenko, an "expert" who had defected from the delegation.
>
> Mr. Tsarapkin also accused the Swiss of permitting "provocative activity on their territory by foreign intelligence agents." He called on them to utilize "their sovereign rights" and to take "all necessary measures" to assure Mr. Nossenko's return "to his place of work, to his family and children." . . .
>
> Washington announced Monday that Mr. Nossenko was a staff officer in the Soviet security agency and had requested political asylum in the United States.
>
> At a suddenly called news conference, Mr. Tsarapkin said that "if Mr. Nossenko was in United States hands, it could mean only that the Swiss had not provided delegates to international conferences with elementary security." . . .
>
> Observers noted that Mr. Tsarapkin had not directed any accusations at the United States. His only reference to Washington was to acknowledge its announcement that Mr. Nossenko had applied for asylum. . . .
>
> Conference sources interpreted the avoidance of an attack on Washington as evidence that Moscow did not want to damage the arms talks or disrupt the current relaxed atmosphere in relations between the two capitals. . . .[100]

In other words, the argument that vertical systems are vulnerable because of the stability requirements of horizontal systems may not be as valid as it appears at first glance. Precisely opposite considerations may prevail in some instances. To maintain stability, horizontal systems may have to insulate certain issue-areas and prevent bargaining across their boundaries. Such a process of insulation may occur under two considerations: First, it may be precipitated whenever the actors of a horizontal system have common goals in one area but their lack of agreement on other matters results in the recognition that progress toward the attainment of the common goals can only be achieved through insulating the issue-area. The disarmament area within the U.S.-U.S.S.R. system would seem to be illustrative in this regard. Second, the process of insulation may be initiated whenever the actors of a horizontal system lack agreement in one area but their concurrence in other areas leads them to agree to contain the conflict in order to prevent it from destabilizing the other

[100] *The New York Times*, February 13, 1964, p. 1.

areas or the entire system. For many years the handling of civil rights issues in the United States corresponded to this pattern.

In short, further elaboration, rather than continued neglect, of the issue-area concept would seem to be in order. None of the arguments against the construction of vertical political systems out of identifiable issue-areas fully offset the compelling evidence that horizontal systems function differently in different areas. Let us turn, therefore, to the task of specifying more precisely the nature of issue-areas and the location of vertical systems within them.

Stated formally, an issue-area is conceived to consist of *(1) a cluster of values, the allocation or potential allocation of which (2) leads the affected or potentially affected actors to differ so greatly over (a) the way in which the values should be allocated or (b) the horizontal levels at which the allocations should be authorized that (3) they engage in distinctive behavior designed to mobilize support for the attainment of their particular values.* If a cluster of values does not lead to differences among those affected by it, then the issue-area is not considered to exist for that group of actors, and their relationships with respect to the values are not considered to form a vertical system. If a cluster of values does divide the actors affected by it, but if their differences are not so great as to induce support-building behavior, then the issue-area, and its vertical systems, is considered to be dormant until such time as one of the actors activates it by pressing for a reallocation of the value cluster. If a cluster of values induces support building on the part of the affected actors, but if their behavior is not distinctive from that induced by another cluster of values, then the issue-area is considered to encompass both clusters, and both are also regarded as being processed by the same vertical system.

It will be noted that the boundaries of vertical systems are delineated not by the common membership of the actors who sustain them (as horizontal systems are), but rather by the distinctiveness of the values and the behavior they encompass. The actors determine the state of a vertical system—whether it is active, dormant, or nonexistent—but the boundaries of the system are independent of the identity of the actors who are active within it. In fact, the horizontal affiliations of its actors may be quite varied. Some might be members of local systems. Others might belong to national systems. Still others might be participants in penetrated or international systems. The cluster of values associated with economic development provides an example of an issue-area that encompasses actors at every horizontal level.

This is not to imply, of course, that either the actors, the values, or the behavior that form the parameters of a vertical system are simple to identify. A number of operational problems will have to be resolved before empirical research on vertical phenomena yield worthwhile results. In particular, answers to three questions must be developed: How are the values over which men differ to be clustered together into issue-areas? At what level of abstraction should they be clustered? What characteristics render the behavior evoked by one cluster of values distinctive from that stimulated by other clusters?

The general line of response to the first two questions seems reasonably clear. A typology of issue-areas ought to be something more than a mere cataloguing of the matters over which men are divided at any moment in time. For vertical systems to be of analytic utility, they must persist beyond the life of particular actors. As has already been implied, not much would be accomplished if "issue-area" meant nothing more than the conventional usage, in which an "issue" is equated with any and every concrete historical conflict that ensues between identifiable individuals or groups. In brief, a typology of issue-areas must be cast in sufficiently abstract terms to encompass past and future clusters of values as well as present ones. Obviously, too, the level of abstraction must be high enough to allow for clusters of values that evoke behavior within all types of horizontal systems, from local communities to the global community. At the same time the typology cannot be so generalized as to erase the distinctiveness of the behavior which characterizes the vertical systems in each of its areas.

For the present, of course, any typology must be largely arbitrary. Until systematic and extensive data on the distinctive nature of certain issue-areas are accumulated, the lines dividing them cannot be drawn with much certainty. In order to suggest further dimensions of the concept, however, let us adopt a simple typology which seems to meet the above criteria. Let us conceive of all behavior designed to bring about the authoritative allocation of values as occurring in any one of four issue-areas: the *territorial, status, human resources,* and *nonhuman resources* areas, each of which encompasses the distinctive motives, actions, and interactions evoked by the clusters of values that are linked to, respectively, the allocation of territorial jurisdiction, the allocation of status within horizontal political systems or within nonpolitical systems, the development and allocation of human resources, and the development and allocation of nonhuman resources. Examples of vertical systems located in the territorial area are the persistent conflict over Berlin, the continuing Arizona-California controversy over rights to the Colorado River, and the recurring efforts to effect a merger of the Township and Borough of Princeton, New Jersey. Status-area systems are exemplified by the long-standing problem of whether Red China should be admitted to the United Nations, the unending racial conflict in South Africa, and the perennial question of higher pay for policemen faced by every American town. Enduring efforts to provide medical care for the aged, unceasing problems of population control, and periodic disputes over the training of teachers are illustrative of vertical systems that fall in the human resources area. Certain foreign aid programs, most housing and highway programs, and many agricultural policies illustrate the kinds of vertical systems that are classified in the nonhuman resources area.

In other words, each of the four issue-areas is conceived to embrace a number of vertical political systems, and the boundaries of each vertical system are in turn conceived to be determined by the scope of the interaction that occurs within it. Thus, as implied above, some vertical systems may function exclusively at local horizontal levels; others may be national in scope; still others may be confined to interaction at the international level. Given the interdependence of life in the nuclear age, however, empirical inquiry would probably find that an overwhelming preponderance of the world's vertical systems range upward and downward across several horizontal levels. The pervasiveness of penetrated systems is indicative in this respect. So is the large degree to which so-called local government in the United States is in reality a local-state or local-state-federal system in most issue-areas. Table 6–2, by using brief identifying labels for currently existing vertical systems in all four issue-areas, is designed to provide an even more concrete set of examples of the extent to which vertical systems extend across horizontal levels. Each system is entered in the table at the approximate horizontal level at which it came into existence, but crudely scaled arrows have been attached in order to suggest the subsequent extension of its scope. The scarcity of systems without arrows is intentional and designed to represent the small degree to which life in the nuclear age can be confined to a single horizontal level.

But how, it may well be asked, does this particular typology meet the criterion that the value clusters in each area must evoke distinctive motives, actions, and interactions on the part of the affected actors? Granted that the values themselves differ, why should it be presumed that these differences are sufficient to produce differentiation in the functioning of the systems that allocate the values in each issue-area? As previously indicated, the answers to these questions must of necessity be somewhat vague. Since the issue-area concept has not been the focus of systematic inquiry, data which would allow for comparisons of the functioning of vertical systems are not available, and any typology has perforce to be constructed out of crude impressions about the reasons for the findings uncovered by Dahl and others. In the case of the foregoing typology the four issue-areas were derived from an impression that the motives, actions, and interactions of political actors are crucially related to the

Table 6–2　Examples of Vertical Systems in Each of the Four Issue-Areas

Arrows suggest the degree to which the scope of each system was extended across horizontal levels subsequent to its activation

Horizontal Level	Territorial Area	Status Area	Human Resources Area	Nonhuman Resources Area
International	Berlin	Recognition of Communist China	The Population Explosion	East-West trade
National	Conflict between Greek and Turkish Cypriotes	Civil rights in the U.S.	Retraining of chronically unemployed in the U.S.	Economic development of India
Local	Statehood for Quebec	Civil rights in South Africa · Nominations in New Haven	Education in New Haven	Urban redevelopment in New Haven

degree of tangibility of both the values which have to be allocated and the means which have to be employed to effect allocation.[101] With respect to motives and actions, it was reasoned that the affected actors would be more strongly motivated and more persistently active the *greater* the tangibility of the *means* (since the rewards and costs to the actor of allocating a particular cluster of values are likely to be clearer the more easily comprehensible are the means necessary to realize the values); and that the more actors affected and active the *lesser* the tangibility of the *ends* (since tangibility involves specificity, and thus the aspirations of a greater number of actors are likely to be encompassed by issues in which intangible goals are at stake). With respect to interaction, the presumption was made that the greater the tangibility of both the *ends* and *means* involved in an allocative process, the more the tendency to bargain among the affected actors would increase. In short, among the distinctive characteristics of an issue-area are the number of affected actors, the intensity of their motivations to act, the frequency with which they act, and the extent of their readiness to bargain with each other.

That four main issue-areas derive from the foregoing is readily apparent. The processes of allocating tangible values through the use of tangible means will differ significantly from those in which intangible ends and means are involved; both of these will in turn be distinguished from the processes whereby tangible values are allocated through the utilization of intangible means; and still a fourth pattern of distinctive motives, actions, and interactions will occur whenever tangible means are employed to achieve intangible ends. In short, we have fashioned a 2 x 2 matrix, each cell of which corresponds more or less closely to one of the four kinds of values that are presumed to sustain political behavior:

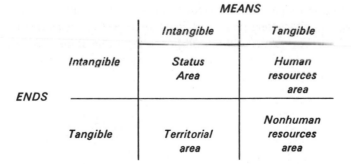

		MEANS	
		Intangible	Tangible
ENDS	Intangible	Status Area	Human resources area
	Tangible	Territorial area	Nonhuman resources area

[101] For traces of the idea that ends-means tangibility may be a central variable

Although crude and impressionistic, this derivation of the distinctiveness of the issue-areas does seem to hold up when one engages in the exercise of locating empirical findings in the matrix. Let us take Dahl's data as an example, and assume for purposes of illustration that the tangible-intangible scale of ends is operationalized in terms of whether the values involved can be photographed with a camera and that the tangibility of means is measured by the extent to which money must be expended in order to acquire the values. The values represented by education cannot be photographed, albeit money is necessary to build the schools and pay the teachers—prerequisites to the realization of educational values. Hence vertical systems designed to process educational issues fall in the human resources area of the matrix. Similarly, nominations in New Haven are not photographable, and, unlike the building and maintenance of a school system, money is not needed to have them allocated in a desired fashion. Thus they would be classified in the status area. Likewise, urban redevelopment in New Haven—or the need for it—is readily photographable, and great quantities of money must be committed to its realization, thereby locating it in the nonhuman resources area. Since Dahl offers no data for the territorial area, let us conclude this exercise with the example of Berlin as a vertical political system. In this case recent history —especially since the erection of the wall in August 1961—testifies poignantly to the photographability of the values involved. Yet diplomatic persuasion, rather than money and the military capabilities it buys, must obviously serve as the means through which a Berlin settlement will ultimately be accomplished.[102]

The impression that the fit between this formulation and empirical phenomena is sufficient to warrant further development of the typology is reinforced by one other consideration. The assumption that the tangibility of ends and means determines the number of affected actors and the extent of their readiness to bargain with each other permits specific conclusions about distinctive characteristics of at least two of the issue-areas. On the one hand, the status area, being composed of both intangible ends and means, is likely to evoke more uncompromising political behavior on the part of more actors than any of the other three; on the other hand, the

in the generation of issue-area differences, see Samuel P. Huntington, *The Common Defense: Strategic Programs in National Politics* (New York: Columbia University Press, 1961), pp. 242–48; and Raymond A. Bauer, Ithiel de Sola Pool, and Lewis Anthony Dexter, *American Business and Public Policy: The Politics of Foreign Trade* (New York: Atherton Press, 1963), pp. 124–126.

[102] It must be emphasized that these examples are provided only for the purpose of illustrating how an issue-area typology might be developed. The classification of data in terms of the tangibility of ends and means is clearly far more complex than this exercise implies. In each instance a case might be made for classifying these particular data in one or more of the other areas.

nonhuman resources area, being composed of both tangible ends and means, is likely to evoke more bargaining on the part of fewer actors than any of the other areas. That these two conclusions correspond to the differences between concrete vertical systems in each area can be readily demonstrated. Compare, for instance, the processes whereby values pertaining to civil rights are allocated with those that mark the allocation of values in the field of transportation (e.g., the development of rivers, harbors, and roads). Clearly more persons are aroused by the former cluster than by the latter, and plainly, too, uncompromising positions are as characteristic of civil rights issues as horse-trading is of rivers and harbors allocations.

Indeed, it is noteworthy that these characteristics of the status area would seem to be so powerful as to create still another distinctive characteristic of that area: The boundaries of vertical systems in the status area would appear to be more capable of expansion than are systems in any other area. Because they arouse a greater number of actors and a more uncompromising set of orientations, status issues can quickly move upward, downward, and sideward, once they are activated. The demand for civil rights in Angola, the attempt of James Meredith to enter the University of Mississippi, and the recognition of Communist China are illustrative of the vertical dynamism of status issues. Their horizontal dynamism— their capacity for intruding upon other issue-areas—is exemplified by recent civil rights debates in the United States. It was equally apparent in November 1963, when the arrest of Professor Frederick C. Barghoorn proved to be far more unsettling to the U.S.-U.S.S.R. system (as it was then being sustained in wheat and disarmament negotiations) than a concurrent flare-up of the Berlin crisis.

V. CONCLUSION

The implications of the foregoing conceptual adjustments for the construction of foreign policy theory are clear.[103] If the above formulation has any validity, the external behavior of horizontal systems at the national

---

[103] Of course, if the issue-area concept is at all valid, its implications are not confined to foreign policy research. As indicated above, for example, it would seem to provide a useful way of assessing the political stability of horizontal systems. From an issue-area perspective, a stable—though not necessarily desirable—polity is one in which the boundaries of its vertical systems are insulated from each other, whereas an unstable polity would consist of processes whereby one or more issues dominate political activity within the entire system. For other possible avenues of research opened up by the issue-area concept, see Chapter 17 and my "The Functioning of International Systems," *Background*, 7 (November 1963), pp. 116-117.

level is likely to vary so greatly in scope, intensity, and flexibility in each of the four issue-areas that any theory of foreign policy will have to include if-then propositions which reflect these variations. Similarly, theoretical account will have to be taken of the external behavior of penetrated systems. Their relations with the rest of the world will obviously be partly a function of differences in the degree and nature of the penetration they experience. Moreover, since the extent and manner of penetration are likely to vary from one issue-area to the next, any theory will have to encompass these additional differences.

Indeed, the penetrated and vertical systems concepts would seem to be sufficiently important to warrant revision at the pre-theoretical level. It seems reasonable to presume, for instance, that the relative potency of systemic variables would be greater in penetrated systems than in those which are strictly of a national kind. Thus the pre-theory summarized in Table 6–1 could fruitfully be doubled in scope by subdividing each of the eight columns into "penetrated" and "nonpenetrated" categories and introducing eight new rankings which elevate the systemic variables, say, one notch in each of the eight penetrated systems. Likewise, if the distinctive characteristics of the status and nonhuman resources areas have been correctly estimated, it is easy to envision still another expansion of the pre-theory—a twofold expansion in which societal variables are elevated one position in the rankings for status areas (because more members of the system are likely to be aroused to make more uncompromising demands) and lowered one rank in those for nonhuman resources areas (because fewer system members are likely to make less stringent demands). Table 6–3 presents these possible expansions of the pre-theory which the penetrated and vertical systems concepts facilitate.

While these concepts greatly complicate the task of theory building, they do not dictate or limit the kind of theory that can be constructed. As emphasized throughout, all we have done in this chapter is to identify and amplify the materials out of which any theory of foreign policy must be fashioned. A wide range of theories can be built out of these materials, and nothing inherent in the latter determines the design, elegance, and utility of the former. These qualities must be supplied by the analyst, which is what makes the task of theory building awesome and challenging.

Table 6–3 A Further Elaboration of the Author's Pre-Theory of Foreign Policy, in Which Five Sets of Variables Underlying the External Behavior of Societies Are Ranked According to Their Relative Potencies in Sixteen Types of Societies and Three Types of Issue-Areas

The table cross-classifies sixteen types of societies — **Large Country** and **Small Country**, each subdivided into **Developed Economy** and **Underdeveloped Economy**, each of these into **Open Polity** and **Closed Polity**, and each of these into **Penetrated** and **Non-penetrated** — against three types of issue-areas: **status area**, **nonhuman resource area**, and **other areas**. Each cell ranks the relative potency of five sets of variables using the codes below.

Legend:

- i = individual variables
- r = role variables
- g = governmental variables
- so = societal variables
- sy = systemic variables

7 Private Preferences and Political Responsibilities: The Relative Potency of Individual and Role Variables in the Behavior of U.S. Senators *

In order to develop a science of international politics and foreign policy, certain initial steps have to be taken. As in any science, an integrated body of tested or testable propositions about the dynamics of international life is necessarily an end product, a final stage in the lengthy processing of the materials of the field. Only after the relevant variables have been identified and their relative potency assessed through quantitative analysis is it possible to fashion a coherent body of empirical theory. If these initial steps are neglected and efforts to build integrated theory undertaken directly, there are likely to be as many theories as there are theorists, and the convergence around a common set of concepts and findings, which is necessary to the evolution of a unified science, is not likely to occur. To be sure, students of international phenomena need not have similar interests or work on similar problems. However, for all their diverse efforts to be cumulative—for them to permit the integration of the various

* An earlier version of this chapter was published in J. David Singer (ed.), *Quantitative International Politics: Insights and Evidence* (New York: The Free Press, 1968), pp. 17–50. Reprinted with the permission of the publisher. Copyright 1968 by The Free Press, a Division of the Macmillan Company.

pieces into a larger whole—the raw data of the field must undergo an initial processing which renders them sufficiently comparable to be fused and unified. Just as hides are processed into leather before shoes can be made, so must international phenomena be made ready for theory-building.

Although recent years have witnessed considerable progress in the specification of relevant international variables, the same cannot be said for the other initial task of assessing their relative potency. Stated differently, a variety of causal agents has been identified, but confusion and contradiction still prevail with respect to the degree to which, and the circumstances under which, each agent is causal. The literature on military relations and strategy is but one of many examples that can be cited. In it ambitious individuals, technological breakthroughs, particular ideologies, certain types of elites, spiraling mechanisms of the international system, and aggressive forms of government are varyingly posited as prime movers in the generation and sustenance of arms races. All of these variables may indeed be sources of an arms race, but analysts are far from a consensus on where to locate each one in the process. Even worse, the literature is totally lacking in any effort to determine which variables are likely to prove more potent when two or more of them come into conflict.

In large part, the field is in this condition because of insufficient quantitative analyses. To describe the causal potency of a variable is to make a probability statement about its effects, and such a statement can only be made if the operation of the variable is observed in a number of instances. A science of international politics, like any other science, seeks to explain and predict not particular events but general patterns; not single occurrences but the probable times out of, say, one hundred that a given stimulus will give rise to a given response.[1] Scientific analysis is thus more than merely systematic analysis. One can systematically analyze a single situation by carefully examining and interrelating its constituent parts, but such an inquiry does not become a scientific enterprise until the situation is treated as one of many that might occur under specified conditions. Hence a science of international politics must be founded on quantitative data analyzed in terms of the laws of probability (that is, statistically). Most research in the field, however, amounts to little more than analyses of single situations. Consequently, as illustrated by the litera-

[1] Perhaps it bears repeating that the same is true of the physical sciences. Contrary to a widely held belief, the physicist is unable to account for the behavior of every atom, nor intent upon doing so. Rather, his capacities and goals are limited to probability statements about how *most* atoms will respond to different kinds of stimuli.

ture on military policy, most attempts to contrast the causal strength of two variables are necessarily speculative, and often more confusing than clarifying.

It must be emphasized that the generation and analysis of quantitative data is not the end goal of scientific inquiry. The ultimate goal is—to repeat—general, unified, and empirical theory. Assessing the relative potency of key variables is an initial, and not the final, step toward this goal. It involves comparing the causal strength of variables prior to linking them up in causal sequences. It is to raise, for example, the question as to whether greater influence should be attributed to the functional require-ments of international stability or to the motivation of officials, but it is not to ask how systemic requirements and official motives *combine* to produce a series of events. To assess the relative potency of variables, in short, is to fashion the initial propositions upon which integrated theory is built and not to construct the theory itself.

QUANTITATIVE HISTORICAL COMPARISON

A variety of quantitative methods can be used to contrast the potency of two or more variables that might serve as causes of the same event. Controlled experiments, simulations of actual conditions, and survey tech-niques are perhaps the methods that have been most frequently used for this purpose. The method employed here, however, has not been explicitly developed elsewhere and thus we need to examine its utility and limitations in some detail. For want of a better label, we shall call it the method of "quantitative historical comparison." Four basic steps are involved in any application of the method. First, it is necessary to identify and observe a sequence of behavior that (a) was repeatedly undertaken by a number of actors in some past era; (b) occurred in such a way as to be measurable (i.e., each instance of it was recorded in the documents of the era); and (c) could reasonably be assumed to have been generated by at least the two (or more) variables which the analyst wishes to compare. Second, on the basis of the patterns discerned in the repeated occurrences of the behavior, the analyst develops an initial impression of the relative potency of the two variables and then translates these impressions into testable hypotheses which predict how the sequence of behavior would unfold if the order, operation, and/or presence of one or both of the variables in the sequence were altered. Third, the analyst finds and compiles the records of another era that is essentially comparable to the first in all respects except for the two variables being examined, these being essentially different in ways that are consistent with the hypotheses.[2] Finally, the assessment of the relative potency of the variables is made by examining whether the behavioral sequences of the second era are, to a statistically significant extent, patterned differently from those of the first era and in the directions predicted by the hypotheses. If, as may well be the case, the findings are not so clear as to confirm or negate the hypotheses unmistakably, then of course the analyst moves on to a third comparable period which is so structured as to allow for further confirmation or disconfirmation.

Any sequence of political behavior in which voting is a crucial step provides an obvious example of the phenomena to which the method of quantitative historical comparison can be readily and fruitfully applied. Whether the sequence occurs in an electorate, a legislature, or an international organization, voting involves a number of actors engaging in the same behavior; hence it is readily quantified. Usually the votes represent important choices for the people of an era, and key political variables are thus likely to be operative. Since important matters are at stake, moreover, the written records of the era will usually contain a tabulation of how each of the actors voted; therefore, the behavior is especially susceptible to accurate measurement even though it cannot be directly observed. Furthermore, whatever the site of the voting, it ordinarily occurs in the context of standardized procedures. Consequently, the number of factors that comprise the setting for behavior and that vary from one era to the next are likely to be fewer for voting sequences than for other types, and comparison between eras is made that much easier.

Although a number of students of international politics and foreign policy have already demonstrated that voting lends itself especially well to quantitative historical comparison,[3] it is not the *only* kind of activity that can be subjected to this method of analysis. Data on other aspects of international behavior are not so readily available as voting statistics, but they do exist and can be accumulated. As long as the behavior under

---

[2] This is not to say that everything else about the two eras must be equal or even virtually so. As will be indicated, exact equivalence can never be achieved, so that emphasis must be placed on the essentiality of the similarities and the differences.

[3] Cf. Hayward R. Alker, Jr. and Bruce M. Russett, *World Politics in the General Assembly* (New Haven: Yale University Press, 1965); Ernst B. Haas, "System and Process in the International Labor Organization: A Statistical Afterthought," *World Politics*, XIV (January 1962), pp. 322–352; Thomas Hovet, Jr., *Bloc Politics in the United States* (Cambridge: Harvard University Press, 1960); Thomas Hovet, Jr., *Africa in the United Nations* (Evanston: Northwestern University Press, 1963); Leroy N. Rieselbach, "Quantitative Techniques for Studying Voting Behavior in the U.N. General Assembly," *International Organization*, XIV (1960), pp. 291–306; and Marshall R. Singer and Barton Sensenig, III, "Elections within the United Nations: An Experimental Study Utilizing Statistical Analysis," *International Organization*, XVII (1963), pp. 901–925.

investigation is recurrent and recorded, quantitative comparison is possible. If the behavior is verbal, such as is found in legislative debates, state papers, and newspaper editorials, then the technique of counting recurrent phrases or themes—known as content analysis—can be used to sort out the relative potency of the variables giving rise to the behavior.[4] If the behavior is of a grosser kind, such as the maintenance of an international relationship or the occurrence of violence within and between societies, then mass media, census tracts, and a wide variety of other types of public records can be used for quantitative historical comparison.[5]

Notwithstanding the adaptability of various types of historical materials to quantitative comparison, this method of analysis is inflexible in certain important respects. Most notably, there is a rigid requirement that the hypotheses derived from inspection of the data of the first era be formulated before the data of the second era are examined. Indeed, ideally the data of the second era should not even be gathered until after the hypotheses have been formulated and made ready for testing. The researcher must be totally ignorant of how the data will be patterned in the second era. To be sure, he has to be sufficiently familiar with the general circumstances of the second era to know that it is comparable to the first in all major respects except for the variables he is contrasting. What quantitative patterns the data will reveal, however, must be a mystery to him. In this way the hypotheses can be fairly tested. The researcher will be neither consciously tempted nor subconsciously inclined to formulate his hypotheses on the basis of prior knowledge which will insure their confirmation. Like the experimenter in the laboratory, he must undergo the exquisite pleasure (or is it pain?) of waiting to see whether or not his predictions will be borne out by future events. For the laboratory researcher the "future" actually lies ahead in time, because he must conduct his experiment again in order to test his hypotheses. But, by clearly separating his research into two stages, the user of quantitative

---

[4] See Ole R. Holsti, "The Belief System and National Images: A Case Study," *Journal of Conflict Resolution,* VI (September 1962), pp. 244–252; Ithiel de Sola Pool, *The Prestige Papers: A Survey of Their Editorials* (Stanford, Cal.: Stanford University Press, 1952); J. David Singer, "Soviet and American Foreign Policy Attitudes: A Content Analysis of Elite Articulations," *Journal of Conflict Resolution,* VII (1964), pp. 424–485; and Dina A. Zinnes, Robert C. North and Howard E. Koch, Jr., "Capability, Threat and the Outbreak of War," in James N. Rosenau (ed.), *International Politics and Foreign Policy: A Reader in Research and Theory* (New York: Free Press, 1961), pp. 469–482.

[5] For example see Rudolph J. Rummel, "Dimensions of Conflict Behavior Within and Between Nations," *General Systems: Yearbook of the Society for General Systems Research,* VII (1963), pp. 1–50; Bruce M. Russett, *Community and Contention: Britain and America in the Twentieth Century* (Cambridge: MIT Press, 1963); and Raymond Tanter, *Dimensions of Conflict Behavior Within and Between Nations, 1958–1960* (Bloomington: Indiana University, Ph. D. Thesis, 1964).

historical comparison can also anticipate "future" events even though they actually transpired in the past.

But the case for this method of inquiry can be overstated. It is not a perfect instrument of research, free of defects and easily applied. Two drawbacks are particularly noteworthy. One concerns the possibility that crucial aspects of the variables which the analyst wishes to assess may not have found their way into the documented records of an era. This problem is particularly acute whenever foreign policy decision-making at the highest levels of officialdom is encompassed by the variables being assessed. State papers may be obtainable in archives, but modern techniques of telecommunications have diminished the extent to which high-level deliberations, either within or between national decision-making units, are recorded in writing.[6] Even if an adequate written record has been kept, moreover, there remains the additional problem that the archives may not be open to the researcher. Any effort to assess the relative potency of variables pertaining to the foreign policy behavior of officials in closed societies, for example, would prove to be an extremely arduous task for the user of quantitative historical comparison. It forces him to assess their potency in the context of more remote processes for which documentation *is* available. Indeed, whenever there is a scarcity of decision-making records, be it in relatively open or closed societies, comparison must move to the less reliable procedure of quantifying the events that both preceded and succeeded decision and then inferring the potency of decisional variables from variations in the stimulus-response patterns.

The second difficulty with this method of research is no less troublesome. It concerns the twofold question of whether the functioning of the variables being contrasted is sufficiently different in the two eras and whether these time periods are otherwise sufficiently similar to justify the assumption that quantitative comparison of the two sets of data constitutes measurement of the relative potency of the variables. From a certain perspective, it is obvious that no two eras of history can be regarded as identical, or even similar. Regardless of how brief the time which an era is defined as spanning, it is always possible to demonstrate that people differ, leaders change, technologies advance, norms evolve, and institutions alter from one era to the next if the analyst is inclined to view social processes idiographically. In the absolute sense, history does not repeat itself in *any* respect, much less in all respects but two. Yet no science, not even those that focus on physical matter, deals with absolutes. To

[6] For a useful enumeration and analysis of the many difficulties that are encountered when one attempts to develop data on high level decision-making, see Richard C. Snyder and Glenn Paige, "The United States Decision to Resist Aggression in Korea," *Administrative Science Quarterly*, III (1958), pp. 341–378.

repeat, science is concerned with the general and not the particular, which means, in effect, that it ignores small differences in order to discern large similarities. It is only in this sense, after all, that the experimental method has any meaning. In absolute terms, each run of an experiment involves different and uncontrolled conditions. One might control for the sex and size of the rats that are stimulated in one run of the experiment, but those stimulated in the next run are, like the people in two eras of history, not exactly the same rats, or, if they are, they are older, less agile, wiser, and otherwise different in a multitude of ways compared to what they were when the experiment was first conducted. Likewise, the planet whose path in space is charted is not the same object each time its location is recorded. From one day to the next it ages and is, to the extent of the differences that occur with the passage of time, as unlike the way it was as a society in two adjacent eras of history. Because their orientations are nomothetic, however, the rat psychologist and the astronomer ignore such differences and assume either that these differences are not central to the phenomena being measured or that they are distributed at random among the phenomena. So it is with quantitative historical comparison. The user of this method views history through nomothetic and not idiographic eyes. Thus in assessing the potency of variables pertaining to the English crown, to use an oversimplified example for purposes of emphasis, he would ignore the fact that it was worn by a man in one era and by a woman in the next, preferring instead to proceed on the assumption that he is measuring the operation of the monarchy when he contrasts the activities of the two individuals.

This is not to imply, however, that the problem of comparable eras can simply be wished away under the banner of scientific legitimacy. There still remains the need to demonstrate that the two *eras* are sufficiently *similar* and the assessed *variables* sufficiently *different* to warrant the conclusions derived from the quantitative comparison. There is no easy solution to this problem; it is a matter of consensus-building. Like the psychologist and the astronomer, the student of international politics must demonstrate to his colleagues that his assumptions and procedures were sound, and that therefore the conditions which he claims to have controlled and the variables which he claims to have measured were in fact subjected to his manipulations. The task of building a consensus in international politics is more difficult than in other sciences because so much still remains unknown. But it is possible. The researcher will know that he has succeeded when his case for the legitimacy of his quantitative historical comparison has been accepted and his findings are integrated into the subsequent work of his colleagues.

Of course, no method of empirical analysis is ideally suited to the scientific study of international politics and foreign policy. Each has special characteristics that make it appropriate to some kinds of problems and inappropriate to others. The researcher must thus remain flexible and let the method (or combination of methods) he employs be a consequence, and not a determinant, of the purposes of his research and the kinds of data available to him.

THE RELATIVE POTENCY OF INDIVIDUAL AND ROLE VARIABLES

The method of quantitative historical comparison is particularly suited to the main purpose of this inquiry—that of assessing the relative potency of role and individual variables in the behavior of top foreign policy officials. By analyzing the recurrent actions of *different* individuals who occupy the *same* roles during two *similar* historical eras, and by also focusing on the *same* individuals as they occupy *different* roles in the two eras, it should be possible to test hypotheses that predict the extent to which foreign policy behavior derives from (1) the requirements of high office on the one hand, and (2) from personal conviction and idiosyncratic experience on the other.

Comparison of individual and role variables is long overdue in the study of international politics and foreign policy.[7] The literature of the field is pervaded by inarticulate premises and contradictory assumptions about the contribution which such variables make to the behavior of nations and other international actors. Widespread, for example, is the tendency to depict one American President as bound by the limits of his office, while describing another's actions as stemming from an aggressive personality. In the same manner a De Gaulle might be posited as freewheeling and unencumbered by the limitations of role, while a Khrushchev is viewed as restricted by the need to maintain support at home.[8] On the other hand, exactly the opposite interpretations have been put forward to explain previous French and Soviet leaders. Similarly, even as Anthony Eden's personality is cited as the source of England's behavior in the Suez crisis of 1956, so it is also asserted that postwar British foreign policy is founded on both the need and the reluctance to reduce its over-

[7] For a recent analysis that should help to correct this situation, see Lewis J. Edinger, "Political Science and Political Biography," *Journal of Politics,* XXVI (May and August 1964), pp. 423–439 and 648–676.

[8] Contrast, for example, the accounts of the two leaders in William G. Carleton, *The Revolution in American Foreign Policy: Its Global Range* (New York: Random House, 1963), pp. 278–279 and 351–352.

seas commitments.[9] Endless examples of this kind of inconsistency could be cited. Most students in the field have not consciously made even a mental assessment, much less a quantitative historical comparison, of the relative strength of the two types of variables.

A primary consequence of this situation is the tendency of many researchers to attribute high potency to individual variables and either to ignore or to discount role variables. Lacking a clear-cut conception of relative potency, many observers find it easier to fall back on the notion that each moment of history is a function of the individuals— their talents, outlooks, and backgrounds—who made it, than to consider the possibility that the action of the moment arises out of considerations which *any* individual—or at least any within a wide range of talents, outlooks and backgrounds—would have found impelling. Research into international behavior thus tends to focus on the unique aspects and experiences of particular leaders, groups, or nations; on what attitudes and capabilities they bring to their roles rather than on the attitudinal and behavioral demands which the roles make of them.

Yet a strong case can be made for a contrary position that accords greater, or at least as much, potency to role as to individual variables. Human beings are not free-floating entities who respond compulsively and unpredictably to situations in terms of uncontrollable drives and needs. Rather, their drives and needs are tamed through socialization, and the counterargument thus asserts that throughout life most people learn and practice the habit of acceding to the major expectations of the roles they occupy. As has been persuasively argued,[10] there is adult as well as infant socialization, which means, in effect, that individual variables are constantly giving way to, and being reshaped by, role variables. Stated differently, people act out their roles as well as their impulses. Those whose impulses lead them to resist the requirements of a role usually are removed from it or, much less frequently, bring about changes in it with the tacit or explicit consent of the holders of the expectations that comprise the role. Thus do families endure, impersonal organizations persist, societies cohere. Role phenomena, in other words, are a major reason for the fact that human affairs are characterized by constancy as well as variety.

The application of this line of reasoning to the conduct of foreign policy is easily made. Policy makers occupy roles in the same sense that being a father or a child constitutes occupancy of a role. Such positions embrace certain responsibilities that have to be performed and expecta-

---

[9] A typical instance of this discrepancy can be found in Robert Murphy, *Diplomat Among Warriors* (New York: Doubleday, 1964), pp. 380 and 382.

[10] Orville G. Brim, "Socialization Through the Life Cycle," *Items*, XVIII (March 1964), pp. 1–5.

tions that have to be met if their occupants are to remain in them. Whatever prior experiences an official may have had, and regardless of the outlooks and talents he may have previously developed, he has to make some adjustments which render his attitudes and behavior compatible with the formal and informal requirements of his policy-making responsibilities. It is the process whereby these adjustments are made that comprises the socialization of foreign policy officials. Note that the process encompasses a much more precise and limited set of phenomena than is usually associated with the general concept of socialization. It is not a lifelong process, but rather its duration is confined to the term of office. It begins not when a person is born, but when he takes up his duties as a foreign policy official and undergoes the attitudinal and behavioral changes that they require. Just as a man is not socialized into the role of father until children enter the family, so the socialization of foreign policy officials begins only after they enter upon their jobs.[11]

The importance of this process can be readily indicated. Presumably it is a primary reason why the broad bases of a nation's foreign policy do not ordinarily undergo profound change from one generation of leaders to the next. It has even been argued that the shift from the Stalin to the post-Stalin era in Russia did not produce significant change in Soviet foreign policy.[12] Likewise, to cite but one more of many examples that could be listed, presumably role-induced attitudes underlie the fact that, despite differences in temperament, party, and social background, all postwar American Presidents have been champions of the foreign aid program.

To be sure, personalities do vary and these variations are not necessarily filtered out by the requirements of role, as the argument for attributing greater potency to role variables would concede. Presidents and presidencies do differ and, no doubt, so do the performances of any two occupants of the same role. Every role allows *some* leeway for individual interpretation and it is in this area of the role that personality and background variables are operative. Indeed, it seems reasonable to presume that the higher a role is located in a political system, the fewer the formal and informal demands it will make of its occupant (thus, for example, an American President can probably pursue his personal policy preferences

---

[11] This point is somewhat overstated in order to differentiate the socialization of foreign policy officials from that of people in general. Of course, some socialization occurs even before officials occupy their roles. Through observing their predecessors-to-be and anticipating their own occupancy, officials can begin to undergo some of the changes necessary to perform the role before they actually assume it. Similarly, anticipatory socialization occurs in the case of the father when the existence of a pregnancy is verified and the requirements of the new role thereby become imminent.

[12] Marshall D. Shulman, *Stalin's Foreign Policy Reappraised* (Cambridge, Mass.: Harvard University Press, 1963).

much further than can, say, a civil servant in the Department of State).
Nevertheless, concludes the argument, this leeway for individual interpretation is extremely small compared to the attitudinal and behavioral
requirements that high office imposes upon its occupants. Even the President must function within narrowly prescribed limits,[13] so much so that
it would be easier to predict the behavior of any President from prior
knowledge of the prevailing state of that role than from data pertaining to
his past accomplishments, orientations, and experiences.

One thing is clear from the juxtaposition of these two contradictory
lines of reasoning: the problem is essentially empirical and not philosophical.[14] It is not a matter of whether temperament and ideology lead
the analyst to attribute more potency to individual or role variables, but
rather a matter of what empirical data reveal to be the case. If they
reveal, as seems probable, that both individual and role variables contribute to the attitudes and behavior of foreign policy officials, the question
is still an empirical one. For then the problem becomes one of determining whether one set of variables is more potent than the other, and to
what degree.

Before turning to these empirical problems, let us briefly elaborate
the key distinctions between individual and role variables implicit in the
foregoing discussion. By an *individual* variable is meant any aspect of
an actor which characterized him prior to his assumption of policy-making
responsibilities and which did not necessarily characterize any other person
who might have occupied, through election, appointment, or other means,
the same position. Contrariwise, a *role* variable refers to any aspect of
the actor derived from his policy-making responsibilities and which is
expected to characterize any person who fills the same position. Thus
both an individual variable and a role variable can be a behavioral trait,
a possessed quality, or a mental orientation, depending on whether the
trait, quality, or orientation was unique to the person or required by his
position. An agile mind, a legal training, and an upper middle-class childhood are illustrative of the different types of individual variables that

[13] As one advocate of this line of reasoning puts it, "The President may be
the most powerful man in the country, but relatively speaking he has less control
over his cabinet than a lowly VA section chief has over his clerks or a corporal
over his squad." Samuel P. Huntington, *The Common Defense: Strategic Problems
in National Politics* (New York: Columbia University Press, 1961), p. 148.

[14] This point is a reversal of a position taken in the previous chapter, which
accords undue weight to the fact that there will always be some analysts who
would reject quantitative findings indicating a high potency for role variables, and
that they would do so by advancing a philosophy of history which ascribes primary
potency to individual variables. While any findings would no doubt meet resistance
of this sort, further reflection leads to the conclusion that differences in potency
are nevertheless subject to empirical verification and that therefore the problem is
not a philosophical one.

might characterize a high executive official of the United States, whereas a practice of consulting Congress, a lifelong record of accomplishment, and internationalist attitudes toward foreign policy exemplify role variables that might be inherent in his position. The key to the distinction is the word *necessary* in the foregoing formulation. An aspect of an official reflects individuality if there is no reason to presume that his predecessor or successor would have *necessarily* possessed a similar trait, quality, or orientation. Thus, even more concrete examples of individual variables would be the fact that Eisenhower was a Protestant Republican over sixty years of age who was educated at West Point, spent his earlier career in military service, and developed a deep commitment to a balanced federal budget, whereas Kennedy was a Catholic Democrat in his forties who was educated at Harvard, spent his adult life in elective politics, and developed a concern for the welfare of the underprivileged. That both men were whites over thirty-five, born in the continental United States, and committed to American participation in the North Atlantic community, on the other hand, is reflective of the state of the presidency at the time they occupied it in the mid-twentieth century.

It is worth emphasizing the notion that attitudes as well as behavior are conceived to be aspects of role. The idea that occupancy of a position requires a person to act in certain ways has long been accepted by social scientists, but the inclusion of the psychological processes which underlie behavior among the requirements of a role is less widespread. Since so much of politics involves the expression of attitudes, however, expansion of the concept to embrace this dimension serves as a valuable tool in explaining behavior that might otherwise seem inconsistent or hypocritical. When political actors move from being candidates to officeholders, from the opposition to the government, from minority to majority, from weakness to strength to mention but a few of the more obvious instances— their perceptions of the world and its problems undergo profound change and even complete reversal. The change in role increases or lessens their responsibilities and thus alters their perspective on relevant objects in their environment, making these appear more or less salient, desirable, and manageable. Responsibility, so to speak, breeds responsibility, with the result that both men and nations become more broad-minded and less aggressive the more responsibility they acquire for the course of events.[15] Few, for example, would accuse an American President of

---

[15] Presumably the diminution of responsibility precipitates a contrary process, albeit the process would appear to be slowed by the experience of having once held greater responsibility. The criticism which former American Presidents make of their successors of the opposite party, for example, is never so unrestrained as that voiced by colleagues in their party who have not occupied the White House.

hypocrisy if his inaugural address championed reduced tariffs even though earlier he had written his predecessor protesting tariff decreases on goods produced in his state. Such a reversal is extremely plausible in the context of role-induced attitude change, and it is in this sense that psychological processes are considered to be part and parcel of the requirements of office.

The inclusion of attitudes among role phenomena is often misinterpreted as indicating that a man is deprived of *all* freedom of choice and thought when he enters a new role. No such meaning is here intended. As previously suggested, a role is conceived to consist of three interrelated parts; its formal requirements, its informal requirements, and a range of choice within which the occupant can give expression to his talents, training, and convictions without either being removed from the role or bringing about significant changes in it. By *formal* role requirements is meant those aspects of a position which are constitutionally, statutorily, or in some other legal manner prescribed by the system in which the position is located. *Informal* requirements are conceived to be those behavioral and attitudinal prescriptions to which a role occupant must adhere, not because they have been recorded in the law books, but because they have evolved as unwritten norms which have, in political terms, the "force of law." It is true that, by definition, this conception makes the formal and informal aspects of a role deterministic. Its occupant *must* perform them, and if he is disinclined to do so, he *must* develop attitudes, which at the very least, do not prevent him from performing them. This is obvious in the case of the formal requirements, but it is no less the case for the informal requirements. There is nothing in the United States Constitution, for example, that says a Secretary of State must consult with allies abroad and members of Congress at home. Yet every Secretary of State since World War II has devoted considerable energy to both pursuits and there is every reason to expect that these informal requirements will continue to be inexorable parts of the office in the future.[16]

Notwithstanding the inexorable nature of the requirements, however,

[16] A recent instance of these requirements provides a good example of the extent to which a role can modify behavior and attitudes. Before he became Secretary of State, Dean Rusk delivered a series of lectures on the policy-making process and, in one of them, advocated an interpretation of the secretaryship in which its occupant should spend more time attending to matters at home and less to servicing alliances through travel abroad. By the time his secretaryship was several months old, however, Mr. Rusk logged a record number of miles of overseas travel. Subsequently he conceded this discrepancy between his advocated and actual behavior by observing that, "Fortunately, the lecture on the Secretary of State was not published" [United States Senate, Committee on Government Operations, *Organizing for National Security: Inquiry of the Subcommittee on National Policy Machinery* (Washington: Government Printing Office, 1961, Vol. I; Hearings), p. 1285.]

there does remain the third area of a role in which individual discretion is permissible. Here the occupant can not only express the capabilities and beliefs which are uniquely his own, but he can also exercise discretion with respect to the extent to which he wishes to press close to that outer limit of the role where he will either change the role or be removed from it. In addition, and no less important, the *range of choice* allows the individual some opportunity to decide which set of formal and informal requirements he will follow when those pertaining to two of the roles he occupies are in conflict. Only the Secretary of State, for example, can decide whether to favor allies or Congressmen whenever incompatibility develops between the formal or informal requirements of the two relationships. This area of individual discretion available to role occupants is perhaps even more clearly illustrated by the popular tendency to describe American Presidents as "strong" or "weak": such characterizations refer not to the physical prowess of those who reside in the White House, but to two alternative ways in which they interpret the requirements of, and resolve the conflicts among, the various roles they occupy as President.

In sum, it is only certain aspects of a role, and not the role itself, that deprives the occupant of choice. But, it must immediately be asked, how wide is this third area of policy-making positions? Is there greater room for individual discretion or are the opportunities for role occupants to express their talents and convictions few in number and narrow in scope? Posed diagrammatically, if the three aspects of a position are conceived as concentric circles, with the inner one representing the proportion of its scope covered by the formal requirements, the middle one the coverage of the informal requirements, and the outer one the range of free choice, will the position be more accurately portrayed by pattern A or B?

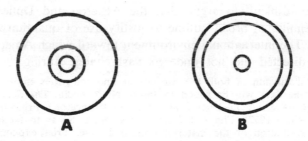

So we return to the empirical problem. These questions cannot be answered conceptually, but only through the accumulation and analysis of data on a variety of policy-making roles. Many different ones must be examined, because the relative potency of role and individual variables is not likely to be the same in different political systems. Just as the leeway for individual discretion is probably greater the higher a position is located in a system, so it may be that the range of choice is greater for a top policy-making position the more democratic the system in which it is located. Likewise, as indicated in the previous chapter, the relative potency of role and individual variables may differ for developed and underdeveloped systems, the former type of system being more bureaucratized than the latter and thus more likely to have explicit and elaborate role requirements to which its policy makers must conform. Before a general theory of foreign policy can be developed, in other words, separate theories of the international behavior of particular types of societies will have to be fashioned. The task of assessing relative potency is in reality a sequence of empirical problems, rather than a single problem.

Here, however, we have confined ourselves to an assessment of role and individual variables in one specific political system, that of the United States. Our method was that of quantitative historical comparison and our data were processed through the technique of content analysis.[17] The data themselves consist of the behavior of United States Senators in a particular foreign-policy-making role, that of friend or critic of the Secretary of State. Hypotheses were derived from their recurrent behavior in the years 1949–52, when Dean Acheson occupied the secretaryship, and these were then tested in the 1953–56 period, when the post was held by John Foster Dulles.[18] Henceforth we shall refer to the former as the "Acheson era" and to the latter as the "Dulles era," but it should be remembered throughout that our focus is on the behavior of Senators and not of Secretaries of State.

THE ACHESON AND DULLES ERAS COMPARED

It is not difficult to argue that the Acheson and Dulles eras were sufficiently similar in broad outline to justify use of quantitative historical comparison. The international environment toward which American foreign policy was directed did not undergo vast change during the eight-year

[17] A full discussion of both the procedures and categories employed to gather and organize the data will be found in James N. Rosenau, *The Senate and Dean Acheson: A Case Study in Legislative Attitudes* (Princeton: Princeton University Ph.D. Dissertation, 1957), Chaps. 1–2 and Appendix I. So as to facilitate comprehension and evaluation of the material presented here, brief explanations of the major categories and the rules governing their use are provided in footnote form where appropriate.

[18] In fact, Dulles held the post until early in 1959. But, in order to avoid the confounding effects of extraneous variables (such as those that are associated with a reelected administration), only the first four years of his secretaryship have been included in the comparison, thereby making the two periods equal in length and coterminous with one presidential term.

period. The bipolar organization of world politics which emerged from World War II had not yet been undermined by either the fragmentation of the two blocs or the emergence of a coherent group of neutral nations. Although Stalin passed from the scene in the second month of the Dulles era, it was not until the end of that era that the policies of the Soviet Union turned from minimal involvement with the non-Communist world to reliance on foreign aid programs, personal diplomacy, cultural exchange, and other nonmilitary techniques to gain influence abroad. Cold war rivalry during Acheson's secretaryship and the first four years of Dulles's was conducted in essentially military terms. To be sure, the Korean war began in the middle of the Acheson era and ended early in the Dulles era, but the situation in the Far East was far from peaceful during the latter period even though American troops were not actually involved in combat. In addition, throughout both eras the United States had a clear-cut superiority in atomic weapons and the capacity to use them at long range. The problems—and changes—fostered by nuclear stalemate had yet to become manifest when that part of the Dulles secretaryship which concerns us came to a close.

The essential constancy of the international environment evoked an essentially uniform response from the United States throughout the eight-year period. Continuity rather than change marked the transition from the Acheson to the Dulles era. Both Secretaries repeatedly warned against the aggressive policies of the Communist world. Both sponsored efforts to strengthen and unify the network of alliances in which the United States became inextricably involved after World War II. Just as Acheson nurtured NATO into being, for example, so did Dulles encourage the formation of SEATO and other treaty arrangements which, like NATO, committed the United States to the defense of its allies in the event of attack.

Admittedly the two eras were sharply differentiated in terms of the rhetoric with which American policy was articulated. The Dulles era was marked by catchy slogans designed, apparently for domestic political reasons, to suggest that major policy innovations were being introduced. Such phrases as "agonizing reappraisal," "massive retaliation," "brinkmanship," and "liberation in Eastern Europe" were used for this purpose and in fact did represent new ways of describing the ends and means of American action abroad. Leaving aside their descriptive labels, however, the actual contents of the policies pursued in the Dulles era were not significantly different from those followed in the 1949–52 period. As Hans Morgenthau put it,

Although Dulles consistently strove to make it appear that his foreign policies were different from, and superior to, the foreign policies of his predecessors, it is a historic fact that he essentially continued those very policies. Refusal to recognize the legitimacy of the *status quo* in [Eastern] Europe and defense of the *status quo* in [Western] Europe and elsewhere through containment, as well as foreign aid, were the cornerstones both of his and his predecessors' foreign policies.[19]

Similarly, another close student of the secretaryship observed that,

> Whatever may have been their abstract philosophies of international politics, both Acheson and Dulles met the pressing problems of their administrations with realism. With their Presidents, they gave more heed to the national security and to power politics than any secretary had since William Seward. Both spoke and acted from a conviction that the welfare of the nation can be served at this juncture in history only by power, ethically used, to prevent Soviet Russia from imposing on all a form of society in which ideals, ethics, and religion would be forever lost.[20]

Nor does the essential similarity between Acheson and Dulles end with the contents of the policies they sponsored. Both men were sons of ministers; both were born and brought up on the Eastern seaboard; both attended Ivy League colleges; both went through law school and eventually became partners in large firms specializing in corporation law. Perhaps even more important, both brought to the secretaryship extensive prior experience in the foreign affairs field at both the governmental and non-governmental levels. Indeed, Dulles's previous tour of duty in officialdom included nearly two years as a special adviser to Secretary Acheson. Together the two men successfully conducted the negotiations which culminated in the ratification of the Japanese Peace Treaty by forty-eight nations in September 1951, and its acceptance by the United States Senate in March 1952.[21]

The personal qualities of the two men, too, had much in common. Both were men of strong convictions. Both had agile minds and considerable forensic ability. Partly as a consequence of these qualities, the tenure of both men in the secretaryship was marked by stormy controversy. Neither, however, was abandoned by the President whom he served. They both consistently and unqualifiedly enjoyed the support and encouragement of their respective chiefs.

[19] Hans J. Morgenthau, "John Foster Dulles (1953–1959)," in Norman A. Graebner (ed.), *An Uncertain Tradition: American Secretaries of State in the Twentieth Century* (New York: McGraw-Hill, 1961), p. 306.

[20] Norman L. Hill, *Mr. Secretary of State* (New York: Random House, 1963), p. 162.

[21] Cf. Bernard C. Cohen, *The Political Process and Foreign Policy: The Making of the Japanese Peace Settlement* (Princeton: Princeton University Press, 1957); and Frederick S. Dunn, *Peace Making and the Settlement with Japan* (Princeton: Princeton University Press, 1963).

In short, a member of the Senate during the 1949–56 period would have found it difficult to distinguish between the problems, policies, and activities of the two Secretaries of State. To be sure, their personalities were different and their style of administering the State Department and selling policies to the public and Congress diverged in notable respects.[22] However, in terms of the more basic stimuli, namely, the efforts of the Secretary of State to cope with a relatively constant and hostile international environment, Senators were similarly exposed during the Acheson and Dulles eras.

What, then, was the major difference between the two eras that permits us to assess the relative potency of role and individual variables? If the international environment, American policies towards it, and the Secretaries responsible for the policies were essentially comparable over the eight-year period, what factor was so sharply altered halfway through the period as to justify dividing it into two separate eras and analyzing the recurring behavior of Senators through quantitative historical comparison? The answer is simple. From the perspective of a Senator perceiving the conduct of American foreign policy, the major difference lay in the party affiliations of the responsible officials: for the first four years policy was formulated and implemented by a Democratic Secretary of State under a Democratic President, whereas a Republican Secretary of State under a Republican President shouldered the burden during the last four years.

That this shift in party responsibility facilitates an assessment of the relative potency of role and individual variables becomes readily apparent as we turn now to specifying—and defining operationally—which of the many variables that underlie the behavior of Senators have been contrasted. In order to simplify the analysis, only two role and two individual variables have been subjected to empirical examination. One of the role variables, which we shall call the *party role*, is of a general nature, while the other is highly specialized and will be known as the *committee role*.[23]

---

[22] Acheson is deemed to have been much more concerned about and attentive to the adequacy of decision-making processes in the State Department than was Dulles, whereas the latter was more sensitive to congressional demands for tougher action against "security risks" than was the former. Indeed, most biographers of Dulles emphasize that his greater readiness to cater to congressional sensibilities in this respect stemmed from a conscious effort to avoid some of the legislative difficulties which Acheson had experienced after Senator Joseph R. McCarthy precipitated wholesale attacks on the loyalty of Department officials in February, 1950.

[23] This is not to imply that these are the only role variables that can shape Senatorial orientations toward the Secretary of State. It may well be that, say, the representational role—which requires Senators to be attentive to the needs of their constituencies and the values of their regions—is equally or more important as a source of their behavior. Unfortunately, however, space limitations do not permit additional breakdowns that would facilitate a refinement of the analysis along these

The essential components of the former (party role) are conceived to be all the norms, both formal and informal, that have long obliged Senators to support the officials of the executive branch when it is controlled by their party and to criticize them when the opposition is in control. The latter (committee role) refers to all the expectations which require—as a consequence of informal and continuous contact with the personnel and problems of the State Department—Senators on the Foreign Relations Committee to feel that they have a special responsibility for defending the Secretary of State or at least avoiding excessive criticism of him in public. The two individual variables are also of a general and a specific kind. The former, which we shall call *personal policy beliefs*, takes two forms, a positive form in which the private convictions of a Senator generally correspond to the aforementioned foreign policies pursued in the Acheson and Dulles eras, and a negative form in which a Senator's views are essentially contrary to the general policy line followed by the two Secretaries. The specific individual variable, consisting of what will be called *personalizing tendencies*, also takes a positive and a negative form. The former encompasses the inclinations of Senators to commend the Secretary's personal qualities as well as, or even apart from, his performances. The negative form of personalization refers to the practice whereby Senators find fault with the Secretary's personal qualities or condemn him as a symbol of evil forces at work, irrespective of whether or not they criticize him for his actions or his failures to act.

Plainly, both the general role and individual variables were operative for every Senator during the Acheson and Dulles eras.[24] Senators were

---

lines. Strictly speaking, therefore, it must be admitted that in measuring the potency of party and committee affiliations we may also be assessing the operation of other, unidentified role variables. On the other hand, the findings presented below are readily explicable within this framework and do not suggest the need to search for the influence of other variables. For an incisive discussion of the many other roles that legislators occupy, as well as of the applicability of the role concept to legislative behavior, see John C. Wahlke, Heinz Eulau, William Buchanan, and Leroy C. Ferguson, *The Legislative System: Explorations in Legislative Behavior* (New York: Wiley, 1962), pp. 7–28.

[24] I am indebted to Leroy N. Rieselbach for posing the question of whether this point is as self-evident as I have suggested. Noting that the importance of partisanship declined markedly when the "man-above-party" Eisenhower replaced the "hard-hitting" Truman in the White House, Rieselbach queries the propriety of presuming that the definition of the party role remained constant throughout the eight-year period. Without disputing the historical accuracy of this observation, its relevance to the formulation developed here seems doubtful. There can be no question that Eisenhower's presidency did introduce a nonpartisan tone into the conduct of party competition, but there is no evidence that this tone was so dominant as to drown out the basic expressions whereby Senators indicate their party loyalties. Certainly this was not the case with Eisenhower's Secretary of Agriculture, Ezra Taft Benson; see Sherman Adams, *Firsthand Report: The Story*

either Democrats or Republicans [25] and they generally either agreed with or dissented from the containment policies pursued by the Secretary of State. The simultaneous operation of two of these variables thus placed every Senator in a conflictive position in at least one of the eras: during the Acheson era a conflictive situation was experienced by Republicans with positive policy beliefs and Democrats with negative policy beliefs, whereas Democrats with positive policy beliefs and Republicans with negative policy beliefs underwent the same conflict during the Dulles era. Republicans on the Foreign Relations Committee and Democrats with negative personalizing tendencies were exposed to an additional dimension of conflict during the Acheson era, as were Democratic Committee members and Republican personalizers during the Dulles era.[26]

How Senators resolved these conflicts depended on whether role or individual variables were more potent. It will be recalled, however, that to assess their potencies we must first examine the data of the Acheson

---

of the Eisenhower Administration (New York: Harper & Row, 1961), Chap. 11. A period of nonpartisanship may allow a Senator to agree with the policies of the opposition, but surely it is not in itself sufficient to permit an obfuscation of party lines to the point where he is inclined either to praise his opponents for their behavior or to criticize the performances of the executive leaders of his own party. "We can do it better" is a time-honored theme of party competition that even the cordiality of the Eisenhower years did not diminish, and it is this theme that underlies the definition of the party role used here.

[25] There was one exception: Wayne Morse of Oregon, who was a Republican in the first four Congressional sessions examined, an Independent in the next two, and a Democrat in the last two. To simplify statistical analysis, however, here the middle phase has been ignored and Morse's standing as a Democrat is assumed to have spanned the entire Dulles era.

[26] It should be noted that under four specialized (and rare) conditions, a Senator could have either avoided or undergone these conflicts during both eras. If in late 1952 or early 1953 he changed party allegiances, received an assignment to the Foreign Relations Committee, reversed his personal policy beliefs, or acquired personalizing tendencies, then he would have avoided or undergone, depending on the direction of the shifts, simultaneous exposure to conflicting variables throughout the eight year period. Only the first two of these conditions, however, have been accounted for in the ensuing analysis. Although Senator Morse's change of party affiliation and the assignment of new members to the Foreign Relations Committee in 1953 is a matter of historical record, alterations in personal policy beliefs and personalizing tendencies are not so easily identified and are much less likely to occur. Perhaps a profound religious revelation or a traumatic psychological experience can produce sharp changes in certain kinds of personal convictions, but political beliefs are not usually the subject of such changes, at least not in the United States. To be sure, personal political beliefs can, as noted above, undergo permanent alteration as a result of adult role socialization, but alterations arising out of this source are of course merely an indication of the potency of role variables. Hence for the purposes of this inquiry it seems reasonable to presume that any differentiation in the patterns of criticism or approval which Senators exhibit in the two eras stem from role considerations rather than from sudden shifts in personalizing tendencies or personal beliefs.

era. To formulate hypotheses at this stage in the analysis would be to engage in little more than guesswork. Knowledge about how policy makers resolve conflicts between their jobs and their beliefs is too scant to permit such a procedure. But if the data of the Acheson era suggest hypotheses which can be tested in the Dulles era, then the method of quantitative historical comparison can be used to good advantage. Fortunately this is the case.

DERIVING THE HYPOTHESES: THE ACHESON ERA

The data of the Acheson era have been summarized elsewhere [27] and their major patterns need only be noted here. Of the 121 persons who served in the Senate during the 36 legislative months of the 1949–52 period, 92 Senators engaged in some behavior with respect to the Secretary of State [28] and, of these, 34 engaged in recurrent behavior.[29] This latter group, which we shall henceforth designate the Articulates, consisted of only 28 percent of the Senate membership, but it recorded 89 percent of the 3,502 references to Acheson made on the floor of the Senate during his secretaryship. Of the total references, 15 percent were

[27] James N. Rosenau, "Senate Attitudes Toward a Secretary of State," in John Wahlke and Heinz Eulau (eds.), *Legislative Behavior: A Reader in Theory and Research* (New York: Free Press, 1959), pp. 333–346.

[28] It is perhaps of interest that one of these was John Foster Dulles, who held a Senate seat for four months in 1949 and who made five references (defined below) to Acheson, of which two were classified as favorable and three as neutral.

[29] This behavior was "observed" in the *Congressional Record* and consisted of everything Senators said about the Secretary during recorded debate for the four-year period. The unit employed to measure the behavior was a "reference" and any Senator who served more than ten legislative months during the Acheson era and who averaged more than 0.07 references per month was considered to have engaged in recurrent behavior. The limits of a reference were determined by the limits of five mutually exclusive categories corresponding to the ways in which Senators identified Acheson as an object in their environment. That is, a reference is not equatable to every time Acheson's name was mentioned by a Senator. Rather *one* reference was defined as existing whenever a Senator mentioned *one* personal quality, or *one* performance, or *one* authority of Acheson's, or *one* symbol-collectivity performance or quality, or *one* of three complexes subsumed under a residual category. (Only the first, second, and fourth of these categories are relevant to the ensuing analysis and their nature is noted below in footnote 30.) Thus a reference might be a word, a phrase, a sentence, or several paragraphs in length (by procedural definition; however, it could not be longer than one column of the *Congressional Record*). In addition to being coded in substantive categories, each reference was also categorized in terms of whether the quality, performance, authority, and such, appeared to be cited by the Senator in favorable, unfavorable, or neutral terms. For the exact rules governing the coding of references in each substantive and directional category, see Rosenau, *The Senate and Dean Acheson*, pp. 26–43, 847–854.

Table 7 – 1 Distribution of References by Party in the Acheson Era (in percentages)

	(N)	Favorable	Unfavorable	Neutral	Total
Republicans	(2,665)	5	70	25	100
Democrats	(837)	48	6	46	100

classified as favorable, 55 percent as unfavorable, and 30 percent as neutral. The references to *personal* qualities were substantially fewer (18 percent) than those that were made to Acheson's *performances* (61 percent).[30]

That these raw data lend themselves to the formulation of hypotheses becomes immediately apparent when they are broken down in terms of party affiliation. Far from engaging in similar behavior, the Republicans and Democrats sharply diverged in both the quantity and quality of their reactions to Acheson. Stated succinctly, the Republicans were both more active and more hostile with respect to him than were the Democrats: while Republicans comprised only 45 percent of the Senators, they accounted for 76 percent of the total 3,502 references and 97 percent of the 1,921 unfavorable references. On the other hand, the Democrats were considerably more cordial toward Acheson, accounting for 74 percent of the 537 favorable references. These differences between the parties are depicted even more sharply in Table 7–1, which presents a directional breakdown of the references made by each group.

Hardly less distinctive are the patterns discernible in the data for the seventeen Senators of both parties who served on the Foreign Relations Committee during this 1949–52 period. Of their 526 references, 45 percent were classified as favorable, 9 percent as unfavorable, and 46 percent

---

30 The distinction between personal qualities and performances has been adapted from Talcott Parsons and Edward A. Shils (eds.), *Toward a General Theory of Action* (Cambridge: Harvard University Press, 1952), p. 57. References in which Senators identified Acheson in terms of what he *was, is,* or *should be* were classified in the personal qualities category, whereas those to what he *did, does,* or *should do* were treated as performance references. If Senators identified the Secretary neither as a complex of personal qualities nor as a complex of performances, but as a symbol of some phenomenon or collectivity (the "Acheson approach" or the "Dulles crowd") such identifications were treated as separate references. However, since the symbol-collectivity references were not too numerous and apparently stemmed from the same sources as did those to personal qualities, the presentation here has been simplified by combining them into the personal qualities category.

as neutral. This amounts to much greater cordiality toward Acheson than that exhibited by the 104 Senators who were not members of the committee, 10 percent of whose 2,976 references were recorded as favorable, 63 percent as unfavorable, and 27 percent as neutral.

Whiie the foregoing patterns suggest hypotheses that ascribe greater potency to role than to individual variables, further inspection of the data indicates that the patterns are not as one-sided as they may seem at first glance. Sufficient differentiation can be discerned within the ranks of each party to suggest that individual variables are not totally lacking in potency. These intraparty phenomena are especially manifest in the reference patterns of the twenty-four Republican and ten Democratic Senators who engaged in recurrent behavior, and thus it is to these Articulates that we now turn our attention.

As can be seen in Table 7–2, the Articulate Republicans engaged in three distinct forms of behavior. Four of them made more favorable than unfavorable references (a pattern that shall henceforth serve as our operational definition of *cordial* behavior and as the distinguishing characteristic of Cordial Senators). All the other Articulate Republicans engaged in hostile behavior (operationally defined as more unfavorable than favorable references and hereafter attributed to Hostile Senators), but differed considerably in the extent to which they confined their hostility to Acheson's performances. Thirteen did not distinguish Acheson the actor from Acheson the person and registered more than 10 percent of their unfavorable references in the latter category, behavior which shall henceforth be defined as *indiscriminate* hostility. On the other hand, seven Hostile Republicans directed their criticism largely at Acheson's actions and made only a minimum (less than 10 percent) of their unfavorable references to his person. Hereafter we shall refer to this pattern of criticism as *discriminate* hostility. Needless to say, it is highly relevant that *all* four of the Cordial Republicans and none of their twenty Hostile colleagues were members of the Foreign Relations Committee.

Although not nearly so pronounced, differentiation can also be discerned among the ten Articulate Democrats listed in Table 7–2. One of them (McCarran) diverged from the general cordiality of Democrats towards Acheson and recorded a pattern of discriminate hostility. Among the Cordial Democrats, moreover, a notable distinction can again be drawn between those who confined their reactions to Acheson's performances and those who engaged in the positive form of personalization. Using the same operational cutoff point employed in the case of Hostile Senators,[31] two

---

[31] It must be emphasized that the use of this cutoff point is not founded on the imputation of a magical quality to the quantity of 10 percent. Such a percentage is an arbitrary demarcation which was employed by way of permitting a more

of the Cordial Democrats engaged in what shall be called *discriminate* cordiality by directing a preponderant proportion of their praise at Acheson's performances and having less than 10 percent of their references coded in the personal qualities category. On the other hand, seven of the Cordial Democrats were not so selective in their approval and indicated support of Acheson as both an actor and a person. Indeed, not only did seven Democrats engage in *indiscriminate* cordiality (as we call the behavior of Cordial Senators who directed more than 10 percent of their favorable references at the Secretary's personal qualities), but five of them praised Acheson's person as much as or more than they did his performances. It is noteworthy that among these latter five were all three of the Articulate Democrats who held seats on the Foreign Relations Committee.

Eleven main hypotheses have been derived from these data for the Acheson era. The first seven arise out of the initial indication that, in general, role variables are more important than individual variables. Let us consider first the party role. It seems highly doubtful that the Republicans and Democrats would have engaged in such sharply different behavior, both quantitatively and qualitatively, if personal policy beliefs had been the predominant variable. Private convictions can arise out of a variety of sources and experiences, and although some differences in the social backgrounds of Republicans and Democrats have been uncovered,[32] these are not so great as to suggest a rationale that would systematically link the differences to the differential party behavior that was directed at Acheson. In the absence of such a rationale, it seems reasonable to presume that on chance grounds alone, the Hostile and Cordial Articulates would have been more equally divided among Senators from both parties if individual variables had been the prime source of behavior. To be sure, party affiliation and personal policy beliefs can often be mutually reinforcing, but to view such a process as operative in this case necessitates a presumption that Republican legislators personally rejected the postwar policy of containment, that Democratic Senators uniformly approved it, and that therefore the same patterns which prevailed in the Acheson era would also be manifest in the Dulles era. Such reasoning, however, violates common sense. As indicated by the continuity of American foreign policy through the Truman and Eisenhower administrations, the two parties were not so far apart in their general orientations for all Senators to have found

concrete analysis of what were regarded as significant, albeit relative, differences among the Hostile and Cordial Articulates. It was employed because it happened to fall approximately at the midway point in the widest gap near the center of the distribution of the two groups of Articulates, and thus it more nearly separated them than would have any other percentage.

[32] Donald R. Matthews, U.S. *Senators and Their Worlds* (Chapel Hill: University of North Carolina Press, 1960), Chap. 2.

Table 7 – 2   The Articulates in the Acheson Era (1949–1952)

Senator	Party	References per Month of 1949–52 Senate Tenure	Total References to the Secretary of State	PROPORTION OF REFERENCES RECORDED AS			PROPORTION OF FAVORABLE REFERENCES OF CORDIAL SENATORS, OR OF UNFAVORABLE REFERENCES OF HOSTILE SENATORS, TO			Form of Hostility or Cordiality
				Favorable	Unfavorable	Neutral	Personal Qualities	Performances	Other Aspects	
				THE HOSTILE ARTICULATES						
Welker	R	1.0	16	—	100.0	—	43.7	31.2	25.1	Ind.
Jenner	R	5.8	210	—	96.2	3.8	20.3	58.9	20.8	Ind.
McCarthy	R	9.0	324	—	95.4	4.6	38.9	53.7	7.4	Ind.
Malone	R	9.6	346	—	90.8	9.2	12.4	63.7	23.9	Ind.
Dirksen	R	2.6	26	—	84.6	15.4	22.7	63.6	13.7	Ind.
Taft	R	2.3	82	—	84.1	15.9	14.5	81.2	4.3	Ind.
Bridges	R	2.2	79	—	83.5	16.5	34.9	45.4	19.7	Ind.
Wherry	R	8.8	264	0.4	79.1	20.5	16.3	57.9	25.8	Ind.
Kem	R	4.1	149	†	78.5	21.5	23.1	57.3	19.6	Ind.
Capehart	R	1.6	58	—	77.6	22.4	20.0	66.7	13.3	Ind.
Bricker	R	0.8	28	—	75.0	25.0	23.8	71.4	4.8	Ind.
Brewster	R	2.4	88	9.1	69.3	21.6	8.2	82.0	9.8	Dis.
Mundt	R	1.6	58	1.7	69.0	29.3	17.5	72.5	10.0	Ind.
Langer	R	1.4	51	11.8	60.8	27.4	12.9	61.3	25.8	Ind.
Cain	R	3.5	127	5.5	58.3	36.2	8.1	82.4	9.5	Dis.
Knowland	R	3.6	130	7.7	54.6	37.7	4.2	80.3	15.5	Dis.
Ferguson	R	1.9	68	—	47.1	52.9	3.1	84.4	12.5	Dis.
Morse	R	2.8	99	10.1	45.5	44.4	2.2	71.1	26.7	Dis.
Watkins	R	2.2	80	1.3	43.7	55.0	2.9	97.1	—	Dis.
McCarran	D	1.0	35	2.9	37.1	60.0	7.7	92.3	—	Dis.
Donnell	R	2.4	47	—	34.0	66.0	—	100.0	—	Dis.

Table 7 – 2 (cont.) The Articulates in the Acheson Era (1949–1952)

Senator	Party	References per Month of 1949–52 Senate Tenure	Total References to the Secretary of State	PROPORTION OF REFERENCES RECORDED AS			PROPORTION OF FAVORABLE REFERENCES OF CORDIAL SENATORS, OR OF UNFAVORABLE REFERENCES OF HOSTILE SENATORS, TO			Form of Hostility or Cordiality
				Favorable	Unfavorable	Neutral	Personal Qualities	Performances	Other Aspects	
THE CORDIAL ARTICULATES										
Benton	D	3.8	98	75.5	2.1	22.4	21.6	43.2	35.2	Ind.
McMahon*	D	1.2	44	75.0	—	25.0	42.4	42.4	15.2	Ind.
Pepper	D	0.7	14	71.4	—	28.6	60.0	40.0	—	Ind.
Lehman	D	2.1	54	68.5	—	31.5	32.4	46.0	21.6	Ind
Vandenberg*	R	1.8	44	69.2	—	31.8	53.3	26.7	20.0	Ind.
Humphrey	D	1.7	62	66.1	—	33.9	46.3	24.4	29.3	Ind.
Connally*	D	4.1	146	54.1	—	45.9	43.0	39.2	17.8	Ind.
Wiley*	R	1.4	51	49.0	—	51.0	28.0	56.0	16.0	Ind.
Lucas	D	2.8	55	46.5	—	54.5	4.0	52.0	44.0	Dis.
Fulbright*	D	1.6	57	40.4	17.5	42.1	39.1	8.7	52.2	Ind.
Hickenlooper*	R	1.5	54	35.2	27.8	37.0	84.2	5.3	10.5	Ind.
Kefauver	D	0.9	32	25.0	18.8	56.2	—	62.5	37.5	Dis.
Smith (N.J.)*	R	1.3	48	20.8	14.6	64.6	30.0	50.0	20.0	Ind.

Key: *Member of the Committee on Foreign Relations. R = Republican; D = Democrat; Ind. = Indiscriminate (more than 10 per cent of directional references classified in the personal qualities category); Dis. = Discriminate (less than 10 per cent of the directional references classified in the personal qualities category).

reinforcement for their personal beliefs in the party alignment of the 1949–52 period. Rather it makes far greater sense to interpret the data as indicating that the potency of the party role was sufficient to lead Senators of both parties to subordinate those personal beliefs which were contrary to role requirements, with the result that Republicans voiced repeated criticism of the Secretary of State or avoided praising him while, to a lesser extent, Democrats either registered approval or avoided registering disapproval. Accordingly, keeping in mind the premise that American foreign policy was essentially the same in both eras, it is now possible to derive our first four predictions about the distribution of the data to be expected during the 1953–56, or Dulles, period. We shall call them the "party hypotheses," and they would seem to be self-evident if our comprehension of the Acheson era is sound and the attribution of greater potency to the party role thus proves accurate:

Hypothesis 1: Democrats were more active with respect to Dulles than were Republicans (they averaged significantly more[33] references per month of Senate tenure than did the Republicans and they also had a higher proportion of their group among the Articulates than did the Republicans).

Hypothesis 2: Republican Senators engaged in more cordial behavior with respect to Dulles than did their Democratic colleagues (the former averaged a significantly greater excess of favorable over unfavorable references than did the latter).

Hypothesis 3: Republican Senators engaged in cordial behavior with respect to Dulles (they averaged a significantly greater number of favorable than unfavorable references to him).

Hypothesis 4: Democratic Senators engaged in hostile behavior with respect to Dulles (they averaged a significantly greater number of unfavorable than favorable references to him).

But the potency of the party role is not absolute. The findings of the Acheson era plainly indicate that the requirements of *party* affiliation are susceptible to modification when they conflict with those of the *committee* role. The close association of the Secretary and Senators on the Foreign

---

[33] That is, "significantly more" in the statistical sense, by which is here meant the .05 level of probability ($P < .05$). Henceforth such words as *more, less, greater,* and *fewer* will be used only if the comparison will be or was tested in this way. Stated differently, an hypothesis will be viewed as confirmed only if the data are so clearly distributed in the predicted direction that the probabilities of such a distribution occurring by chance are less than 5 out of 100.

Relations Committee, along with the sense of responsibility committee members acquire as a result of participating in the State Department's deliberations, apparently give rise to a set of expectations that are strong enough to restrain committee members in the opposition party from fulfilling the demands of their party role. Indeed, the committee role would seem to be so potent that it also leads members who are in the Secretary's party to feel especially obliged to come to the defense of both his policies and his person. This interpretation brings us to the next set of predictions, which we shall call the "committee hypotheses" and which are not so obvious:

Hypothesis 5: Members of the Foreign Relations Committee were more cordial toward Dulles than were nonmembers (the former averaged a significantly greater excess of favorable over unfavorable references than did the latter).

Hypothesis 6: Democrats on the Foreign Relations Committee were less hostile toward Dulles than were Democrats not on the committee (the former averaged a significantly smaller excess of unfavorable over favorable references than did the latter).

Hypothesis 7: Republicans on the Foreign Relations Committee were more cordial towards Dulles than were Republicans not on the committee (the former averaged a significantly greater excess of favorable over unfavorable references than did the latter).

Hypothesis 8: Republicans on the Foreign Relations Committee were more indiscriminately cordial towards Dulles than were Republicans not on the committee (the former averaged a significantly greater number of favorable references in the personal qualities category than did the latter).

The task of deriving hypotheses pertaining to the operation of individual variables is not an easy one. That such variables are potent under certain conditions is clear from the presence of one Democrat (McCarran) among the Hostile Senators and from the fact that thirteen Republican Senators extended their criticism to embrace Acheson's personal qualities. The opposition party role encourages its occupants to voice criticism of the Secretary, but certainly it does not require Senators to engage in *indiscriminate* hostility. Presumably such behavior stems from individual factors which incline Senators to go beyond the opposition party role. What these factors are and how they operate, however, is far from clear. Negative personalization may have stemmed from unusually strong negative policy beliefs. Or it may have stemmed from a variety of background and personality variables that were in no way linked to personal policy beliefs. The difference between these two sources is extremely important because they lead to different and contradictory predictions about behavior in the Dulles era.

Let us first consider personal policy beliefs as a source of negative personalizing tendencies. To posit such a linkage is to make the not implausible assumption that when opposition to a set of policies is very intense, criticism becomes emotional and extends beyond the policies themselves to everything that is associated with them. Under circumstances of high attitudinal intensity, in other words, Senators are sufficiently agitated to fuse the contents and the makers of policy into an indistinguishable mass and, in so doing, to engage in behavior which goes well beyond the necessities of their role as members of the opposition party. Viewed in this way, the indiscriminate hostility toward Acheson can be interpreted as having been undertaken by a few remaining Republicans who still clung to the hope that prewar "normalcy" could be restored, and whose personal policy beliefs were therefore so strongly opposed to the postwar extension of American commitments that they could not contain their discontent within the requirements of their party role. If this was the source of their behavior, such Senators were not likely to be any more impressed with a Secretary from their own party than they were with Acheson. Certainly their strong policy beliefs would have prevented them from shifting to the ranks of the Cordial Articulates. Rather, at most, the requirements of their new party role would have had no greater effect than to induce them to remain passive [34] and, at least, it probably would have had the effect of removing the indiscriminate dimension from their hostility. Furthermore, if it is assumed that the residue of longing for prewar normalcy was limited to a handful of Republicans, whose party had once been identified with such a state of affairs, then it also follows that Democrats would not tend to hold personal policy beliefs strong enough to produce indiscriminate hostility toward Dulles. Additional support for this derivation is provided by the presence of only one Democrat among Hostile Senators in the Acheson era.

The foregoing line of reasoning gives rise to two "individual hypotheses" that the data for the Dulles era ought to confirm:

[34] Sustained hostility toward Acheson is one form such passivity could take. Checked by their new role as members of the new Secretary's party, these Republicans may have found an outlet for their strong negative policy beliefs by continuing to blame Acheson for everything that had happened, was happening, and would happen. A separate record of the references to Acheson during the Dulles era was kept and is noted in the analysis of the data.

Hypothesis 9: Republicans among the Hostile Articulates were discriminate rather than indiscriminate in their hostility toward Dulles (their average proportion of unfavorable references in the personal qualities category was not significantly greater than 10 percent).

Hypothesis 10: Democrats among the Hostile Articulates were discriminate rather than indiscriminate in their hostility toward Dulles (their average proportion of unfavorable references in the personal qualities category was not significantly greater than 10 percent).

Quite a different prediction, however, results if indiscriminate hostility is viewed as stemming from a variety of background and personality characteristics that are unrelated to policy beliefs and that are spurred by —or at least not inhibited by—the opposition party role to produce an especially aggressive mode of criticism. If this is the case, then Dulles' replacement of Acheson was bound to have a significant effect on those Republicans who possessed one or another of these characteristics. Such Senators were likely to find other outlets for their personalizing tendencies, because their new party role restrained them from expressing hostility and either encouraged them to engage in cordiality toward Dulles or permitted them to turn to other matters and remain passive with respect to him.[35] In addition, if this interpretation is correct, then it must be further assumed that the advent of the Dulles secretaryship relieved Democrats who possessed similar characteristics from the obligations of their opposition party role and allowed them to engage in indiscriminate hostility. While Democrats may not have held policy beliefs strong enough to result in negative personalization, there is no reason to assume that they differed from Republicans in their susceptibility to whatever nonpolicy variables might encourage such behavior. Accordingly, a third "individual hypothesis" was derived:

Hypothesis 11: The Hostile Articulates consisted only of Democratic Senators who were indiscriminate rather than discriminate in their hostility toward Dulles (the Hostile Articulates did not include any Republicans and the average proportion of unfavorable references recorded in the personal qualities category by its Democratic members was significantly greater than 10 percent).

Although hypotheses 9 and 10 on the one hand and hypothesis 11 on the other are mutually exclusive, neither of the rationales on which

[35] The additional possibility noted in the previous footnote is also relevant here. Republicans with personalizing tendencies may have found that Acheson continued to serve as a useful focus of their intense hostility.

they are based is so compelling as to warrant eliminating either the former or the latter. On the contrary, our comprehension of the sources of negative personalization is so scanty that they seem equally logical. In the absence of any basis for choosing between the two interpretations, therefore, it seems preferable to adopt the less rigorous procedure of letting all the hypotheses stand and seeing which are upheld by the data of the Dulles era.

It will be noted that in neither the derivation of hypotheses 9 and 10 nor in the interpretation leading to hypothesis 11 have we treated indiscriminate hostility as symmetrical with indiscriminate cordiality. The sources of negative personalization may be obscure in the data for the Acheson era, but at least some reasonable speculation as to its nature proved possible. This is not the case with respect to the positive form of personalization. Beyond the conclusion that the committee role conduces to indiscriminate cordiality (hypothesis 8), we are not able to discern any other factors that foster such behavior. Conceivably the same individual variables that underlie indiscriminate hostility are also operative for those at the cordial extreme, but there is nothing in the data that justifies hypothesizing such a symmetry. Hopefully, the dynamics of indiscriminate behavior will become more manifest as we turn now to the data for the Dulles era.[36]

TESTING THE HYPOTHESES: THE DULLES ERA

The data comprising Senatorial behavior toward Dulles are presented in Table 7–3 and analysis of them resulted in confirmation of seven of the hypotheses, while three were not confirmed and one was actually negated. Those that were confirmed included two party (2 and 4), three committee (5, 7 and 8), and two individual (9 and 10) hypotheses. Two party (1 and 3) and one individual (11) hypothesis comprised those that were not confirmed by the data. The fourth committee hypothesis (6) was not only not confirmed, but in fact the data were significantly arrayed in the opposite direction from the one that had been hypothesized. Before interpreting these findings, let us outline them in greater detail.

Although the pattern of activity in the Dulles era was sharply different from that which marked the Acheson era, the differences did not conform

[36] It must be emphasized that following the basic rule of quantitative historical comparison, the data for the Dulles era were not inspected by the researcher until after the analysis up to this point was written. Well-trained student assistants had previously gathered the data (using the same rules of procedure as were employed for the earlier study of the Acheson era), but all eleven of the hypotheses were derived before the data were examined.

Table 7-6   The Articulates in the Dulles Era (1953-1956)

Senator	Party	References per Month of 1949-52 Senate Tenure	Total References to the Secretary of State	PROPORTION OF REFERENCES RECORDED AS			PROPORTION OF FAVORABLE REFERENCES OF CORDIAL SENATORS, OR OF UNFAVORABLE REFERENCES OF HOSTILE SENATORS, TO			Form of Hostility or Cordiality
				Favorable	Unfavorable	Neutral	Personal Qualities	Performances	Other Aspects	
THE HOSTILE ARTICULATES										
Jenner	R	1.9	60	—	91.7	8.3	16.4	80.0	3.6	Ind.
Malone	R	3.3	106	6.5	82.1	11.3	9.2	73.6	17.2	Dis.
Fulbright*	D	2.3	72	9.7	76.4	13.9	12.7	81.8	5.5	Ind.
O'Mahoney	D	1.3	41	2.5	70.7	26.8	10.3	86.2	3.5	Ind.
Morse*	D	4.3	137	7.3	61.3	31.4	14.3	78.6	7.1	Ind.
Douglas	D	2.3	72	16.7	59.7	23.6	11.6	83.7	4.7	Ind.
McCarran	D	2.7	43	11.6	58.2	30.2	4.0	88.0	8.0	Dis.
Humphrey*	D	8.4	268	19.0	57.5	23.5	3.2	93.5	3.3	Dis.
Lehman	D	1.7	53	17.0	52.8	30.2	7.1	89.3	3.6	Dis.
McCarthy	R	2.3	74	17.5	51.4	31.1	—	100.0	—	Dis.
Gillette*	D	1.2	20	25.0	50.0	25.0	—	100.0	—	Dis.
Bricker	R	2.0	65	36.9	41.6	21.5	7.4	88.9	3.7	Dis.
Mansfield*	D	4.9	157	33.8	40.1	26.1	3.1	90.6	6.3	Dis.
Langer*	R	2.3	75	38.7	40.0	21.3	10.0	90.0	—	Dis.
THE CORDIAL ARTICULATES										
Thye	R	0.8	26	88.5	—	11.5	17.4	60.9	21.7	Ind.
Ferguson*	R	1.4	23	78.3	—	21.7	—	77.8	22.2	Dis.
Hickenlooper*	R	0.9	29	75.9	—	24.1	18.2	63.6	18.2	Ind.
Wiley*	R	5.3	168	75.6	—	24.4	22.8	70.9	6.3	Ind.
Knowland*	R	3.6	116	74.1	2.6	23.3	22.1	74.4	3.5	Ind.
Smith (N.J.)*	R	7.1	228	71.9	1.3	26.8	12.8	76.2	11.0	Ind.
Capehart*	R	1.0	31	71.0	—	29.0	9.1	72.7	18.2	Dis.
Neuberger	D	0.7	11	54.5	18.2	27.3	—	100.0	—	Ind.
Dirksen	R	1.1	34	53.0	2.9	44.1	50.0	38.9	11.1	Ind.
Cooper	R	1.2	21	47.6	19.1	33.3	20.0	70.0	10.0	Ind.
Sparkman*	D	1.1	34	47.0	11.8	41.2	12.5	75.0	12.5	Ind.
Kefauver	D	1.8	56	41.1	28.5	30.4	—	100.0	—	Dis.

Key: *Member of the Committee on Foreign Relations.   R = Republican; D = Democrat; Ind. = Indiscriminate (more than 10 per cent of directional references classified in the personal qualities category); Dis. = Discriminate (less than 10 per cent of directional references classified in the personal qualities category) to the expectation (contained in hypothesis 1) that Senators in the opposition party would be more active than those in the Secretary's party. Of 2,531 references to Dulles, 1,282 were made by Democrats and 1,249 by Republicans. In absolute terms, the former were more active than the latter, but this difference did not prove to be a statistically significant one ($t = .024$; $df = 119$).[37] Furthermore, of the 26 Senators who formed the Articulates in the Dulles era,[38] 14 were Republicans and 12 were Democrats, a difference which was neither significant ($x^2 = .159$; $df = 1$) nor in the predicted direction.

Table 7 – 4   Distribution of References by Party in the Dulles Era (in percentages)

	(N)	Favorable	Unfavorable	Neutral	Total
Republicans	(1,249)	52	22	26	100
Democrats	(1,282)	21	50	29	100

In terms of their evaluative content, on the other hand, the reference patterns did yield important distinctions between the two parties. The prediction (2) that the Republicans would be more cordial toward Dulles than would be the Democrats was amply confirmed by the data ($t = 2.70$; $df = 119$; $P < .01$); the former accounted for 71 percent of the 925 favorable references, whereas the latter tallied 70 percent of the 918 unfavorable references. Stated in comparative terms, the mean Republican excess of favorable over unfavorable references was 6.31, whereas the equivalent figure for the Democrats was -6.32. A further measure of the effects of the role shift occasioned by the Dulles era is provided by the contrast between the directional breakdown of the references made by each group (Table 7–4) and the equivalent data for the Acheson era (Table 7–1).

Yet, for reasons noted below, the anticipated performance of the party role was not confirmed as fully as the foregoing might suggest. The

[37] Except as indicated in the one case when a chi square (x^2) test was more appropriate to the question being asked (because proportions rather than means were being compared), a t-test was used throughout to assess statistical significance. Tables indicating when different values of t and x^2 are significant for various degrees of freedom (df) can be found in any textbook on statistics.

[38] These twenty-six Senators comprised 21 percent of the 121 persons (61 Republicans and 60 Democrats) who served in the Senate during the 32 months of the 1953–1956 period and they accounted for 80 percent of all the references to Dulles. It will be recalled that the equivalent figures for the Acheson era involved 34 Articulates who constituted 28 percent of the Senate and made 89 percent of the references.

expectation that the Republicans would engage in cordial behavior with respect to Dulles (hypothesis 3) was not upheld by the data. Although they averaged more favorable than unfavorable references, the difference did not prove to be significant ($t = 1.55$; $df = 61$). The Democrats, on the other hand, did conform to expectations (hypothesis 4) by engaging in hostile behavior toward Dulles. Their mean of 10.6 unfavorable references was significantly greater than their mean of 4.4 favorable ones ($t = 2.88$; $df = 60$; $P < .01$).

With one important exception, the data pertaining to the committee role were patterned along the lines that had been hypothesized. The expectation (hypothesis 5) that the 19 Senators who served on the Foreign Relations Committee during the 1953–56 period [39] would be more cordial toward Dulles than the 102 Senators who were not members of the committee was plainly upheld by the findings; the former averaged 14.3 more favorable than unfavorable references, whereas the equivalent mean for the latter was −2.5. This difference proved to be a significant one ($t = 2.69$; $df = 122$; $P < .01$). Stated in the same form as the findings for the Acheson era cited above (p. 172), the committee members had 47, 27, and 26 percent of their 1,329 references to Dulles classified as, respectively, favorable, unfavorable, and neutral, whereas the equivalent figures for the 1,202 references made by nonmembers were 25, 47, and 28 percent. Similarly, the predictions that Republican committee members would be both more cordial (hypothesis 7) and more indiscriminately cordial (hypothesis 8) than Republican nonmembers were confirmed by the data. While the former averaged 44.8 more favorable than unfavorable references, the mean difference for the latter was −1.2, and the difference between these means was indeed significant ($t = 5.12$; $df = 61$; $P < .001$). Likewise, the greater indiscriminate cordiality of Republican committee members is evident in the difference between the mean of 8.6 favorable references which they recorded in the personal qualities category and the equivalent figure for nonmembers of 0.6. This difference also proved to be significant ($t = 5.40$; $df = 61$; $P < .001$).

On the other hand, the behavior of the Democrats on the Foreign Relations Committee was strikingly contrary to what had been anticipated (hypothesis 6). They were not less hostile toward Dulles than their fellow Democrats, but, in fact, the mean difference between their favorable and unfavorable references indicated significantly greater hostility: the mean

---

[39] Two Republican Senators joined the committee in 1954 and one Democrat joined it in 1955. In the statistical calculations, the references for these Senators were broken down in terms of the years in which they were made and allocated to the committee and noncommittee totals accordingly.

for the nine committee members was -19.7, while that for the 52 non-members was -3.9 ($t = 2.73$; $df = 59$; $P < .01$).

As for the individual variables, the findings support the interpretation (hypotheses 9 and 10) that personal policy beliefs would lead both Republicans and Democrats to engage in hostile behavior, but that in neither case would the beliefs be so strong as to foster indiscriminate hostility. In the Dulles era the Articulates consisted of 14 Hostile Senators and 12 Cordial ones. The former group was composed of nine Democrats and five Republicans. While four of the Democrats and one of the Republicans compiled a record of indiscriminate hostility (Table 7–3), in each case the margin of unfavorable references in the personal qualities category was only slightly in excess of 10 percent, so that the over-all averages for both the Democrats and the Republicans conformed to the predictions set forth in hypotheses 9 and 10 and failed to uphold the expectation contained in hypothesis 11. That is, neither the Democrats nor the Republicans in the Hostile Articulate group averaged significantly more than 10 percent of their unfavorable references in the personal qualities category ($t = 1.53$; $df = 8$ for the former, and $t < 1$; $df = 4$ for the latter). On the contrary, the average for both groups was actually less than the cutoff point: the nine Democrats averaged 7.4 unfavorable references to Dulles' personal qualities and the equivalent figure for the five Republicans was 8.6.

Several other aspects of the data contained in Table 7–3 need to be pulled together and noted. Particularly relevant is the fact that all five of the Hostile Republicans in the Dulles era had engaged in indiscriminate hostility during the Acheson era. Likewise, we shall have occasion to comment on the fact that five of the nine Hostile Democrats were members of the Foreign Relations Committee.[40] Pertinent, too, is the finding that of the nine Republicans among the Cordial Articulates, six were members of the committee [41] and four of the six engaged in indiscriminate cordiality.

Although not covered by any hypotheses or included in Table 7–3, one other set of findings can usefully be summarized before we attempt to interpret the data. As previously indicated, a record of the references to Acheson during the Dulles era was kept and these reveal some interesting and highly relevant patterns. All told, 40 Senators made 284 references to Acheson during the 1953–56 period. Of these, 12 percent were classified as favorable, 73 percent as unfavorable, and 15 percent as neutral. Demo-

[40] Of the four other Democrats on the committee, one engaged in indiscriminate cordiality and the other three did not engage in sufficient behavior to be classified among the Articulates.

[41] One of the four other Republicans who served on the committee was indiscriminately hostile and the other three were insufficiently active to be grouped with the Articulates.

crats accounted for 19 percent of all the references, 85 percent of the favorable references, 5 percent of the unfavorable references, and 37 percent of the neutral references. Contrariwise, Republicans made 81 percent of all the references, 15 percent of the favorable references, 95 percent of the unfavorable references, and 63 percent of the neutral references. Most notably, 172 unfavorable references, or 83 percent of all the unfavorable references, were made by the eleven Republican Senators who continued to a hold a Senate seat in the Dulles era, after having engaged in indiscriminate hostility during the Acheson era.[42] Indeed, four of these eleven Senators actually made more unfavorable references to Acheson than to Dulles during the 1953–56 period.

INTERPRETING THE RESULTS

Interpretation of empirical findings is rarely easy. Only when every prediction is upheld by the data does interpretation become simple. Under such circumstances the researcher needs merely to restate the reasoning that led to the predictions and emphasize that the empirical data demonstrate its validity. Such complete validation, however, is usually confined to situations in which the various parts of a theory have been previously tested and refined. Otherwise it is an extraordinary, and perhaps even a suspicious, event when an entire series of hypotheses is confirmed. Knowledge of the behavior of public officials is far from the point where each hypothesis in a complex framework is proven accurate by the distribution of previously unexamined data.

Considered in this context, the fact that four of our hypotheses failed of confirmation is not as discouraging as it might otherwise seem. The fact that seven were confirmed indicates that the rationale for ascribing greater potency to role rather than individual variables has considerable merit. On the average, Senators from both parties did reverse themselves and behave differently toward Dulles than they had toward Acheson. The shift to the opposition role did lead the Democrats to engage in hostile behavior. The contrary shift did result in the Republicans being more cordial toward Dulles than were the Democrats, and it also appears to have curbed the personalizing tendencies of the most hostile Republicans. Members of the Foreign Relations Committee did engage in behavior which distinguished them from other Senators, albeit in the case of the Democratic committee members, the nature of their distinctive behavior was quite unexpected.

---

[42] Only Wherry and Kem of the thirteen Republicans who were indiscriminately hostile toward Acheson did not serve in the Senate during the 1953–1956 period. The former died in 1951 and the latter lost a bid for reelection in 1952.

Furthermore, the general reasoning which gave rise to the predictions is not undermined by the two party (1 and 3) and one individual (11) hypotheses that were not confirmed. These three findings can be readily explained without altering the ascription of greater potency to role than to individual variables. In the case of hypothesis 1, which was unlike all the others in that it dealt with the quantitative dimension of Senatorial behavior, it is now clear that we erred in presuming that role variables shape the extent of behavior in the same way that they affect its direction. No doubt there is some relationship between the quantitative and qualitative dimensions of policy-making roles, but there is no reason to assume that the relationship is a simple one in which high activity is associated with hostility and low activity with cordiality. More important, whatever the nature of the relationship, it is not of central concern here. Our attempt to assess the relative potency of role and individual variables would hardly have been hindered if hypothesis 1 had not been formulated in the first place.

Nor does the failure of hypotheses 3 and 11 present a serious problem. In both cases such a result was logically necessitated by the confirmation of other hypotheses. It will be recalled that hypothesis 11 was explicitly posited as contrary to 9 and 10, so the fact that it was not upheld is not so much a failure as a confirmation of an alternative line of reasoning. The confirmation of hypothesis 9, moreover, necessitated the failure of hypothesis 3. The latter predicted that the Republicans would be cordial toward Dulles, a prediction which could not have been supported if, as anticipated in hypothesis 9, strong policy beliefs led a segment of Republican ranks to continue the hostility toward the Secretary of State which had marked the Acheson era. If hypothesis 11, which reasoned that other than strong policy beliefs underlay the negative personalization, had proven valid, then such Republicans would not have sustained their hostility and hypothesis 3 would have been confirmed. As it was, these Senators siphoned off some of their antagonism by continuing to berate Acheson throughout the Dulles era. If they had not made 172 unfavorable references to Acheson during the four years *subsequent* to his secretaryship, probably their behavior toward Dulles would have been much more hostile than it was, and hypothesis 3 might then have been negated rather than simply not confirmed. In other words, the fact that hypothesis 3 was not confirmed serves as a measure of the extent to which the potency of role variables can be offset by the strength of individual variables, but at the same time the fact that the data for hypothesis 3 were arrayed in the predicted direction (though not significantly so) rather than reversed is an indication of how role considerations can mitigate and redirect individual tendencies.

Of course, there does remain the need to adjust our assessment of role and individual variables to the fact that hypothesis 6 was reversed. This is an important finding. No logical relationship between the hypotheses can be cited to explain the fact that Democrats on the Foreign Relations Committee actually compiled a record of substantial hostility toward Dulles. Clearly, our conception of role variables must be adjusted to account for this wholly unexpected result.

But this finding can also be viewed as an opportunity—as a chance to deepen our comprehension of the interplay between role and individual variables beyond what it would have been if all the hypotheses had been confirmed. For the lesson of hypothesis 6 is plain: we assumed too readily that the requirements of the committee role operate similarly upon all Senators who enter it. The data make it clear that in fact the requirements are subject to reinterpretation under special conditions. Note that we do not view the data as indicating that there are conditions which will make the requirements of committee membership subject to replacement by individual variables. Such an explanation might be justified if hypothesis 6 had merely fallen short of confirmation. In this event one might have concluded that no systematic differences prevailed between Democratic committee members and Democratic nonmembers, and that therefore the role requirements did not overcome the individual inclinations of Democratic Senators. However, and to repeat, hypothesis 6 was not only not confirmed, but it was negated. There was a significant difference between Democratic committee members and Democrats not on the committee, only the difference was one in which the latter were less hostile toward Dulles than were the former. Hence, even though different than those which prevailed in the Acheson era, role requirements, and not individual variations, can be presumed to have been operative. Unless individual variables functioned identically for all the Democrats on the committee during the Dulles era, a highly unlikely circumstance, the significance of the difference uncovered by the data could only mean that role variables were operative.

An examination of the content of the unfavorable references made by Democratic members of the Foreign Relations Committee provides at least a partial explanation of their unexpected behavior. Repeatedly, and vigorously, they complained about Dulles's manner of dealing with the committee. They contended that he either misinformed the committee or failed to keep it informed, and that he also used other channels of enunciating new departures or interpretations of American foreign policy. In effect, a recurring theme of their unfavorable references was that they were being used—rather than consulted—by the Secretary of State. The following excerpts from reactions to a single episode are typical of the way committee Democrats expressed their annoyance:

MR. MANSFIELD: Mr. President, the Secretary of State has set in motion a review and reappraisal of the foreign policy of the United States. I do not know whether that was his intention when he gave an interview to a reporter for *Life* magazine. It seems to me that if it were, he might have found a more appropriate method. If he wished to discuss the achievements of American foreign policy with the public, he had only to request an open hearing with the Committee on Foreign Relations.[43]

MR. HUMPHREY: If the *Life* magazine article is correct as to what Mr. Dulles's role was in the Indochina war, then the Secretary misinformed the Senate Committee on Foreign Relations. I was present during his testimony, and I say that Mr. Dulles had better say to this Congress that he told the truth to the Foreign Relations Committee or that he told the truth to the reporter for *Life* magazine, because he cannot have both stories. He cannot have *Life* magazine's report of his role in Indochina and, at the same time, his testimony before the Foreign Relations Committee, because they are diametrically opposite. I say regretfully that they are unalterably opposed.[44]

MR. FULBRIGHT: If there is anything to a bipartisan policy, it means co-operation between the administration and the legislative branch, so that the people of the country may be enlightened and their support enlisted. The Senator from Montana (Mansfield) and I do not get the same attention in the press as does the administration, and if we tell the people one story and the Secretary of State tells a different story, it creates an impossible situation for us.[45]

The recurrence of comments such as these suggest that hypothesis 6 was reversed, not because Democrats on the Foreign Relations Committee were resistant to the requirements of their role, but because they felt, rightly or wrongly, that Dulles's behavior altered their role requirements and relieved them of the responsibility to defend him in public. As previously indicated, the informal requirements of the committee role derive from special opportunities to participate in the making of foreign policy and the sense of responsibility that is fostered by the chance to work closely with the Secretary of State. Convinced that Dulles had not permitted these conditions for the performance of the role to come into being, the Democrats on the committee had even more reason to be critical of him than the nonmembers of their party, and they thus compiled a record of greater hostility than did other Democrats.

[43] United States Congress, *Congressional Record* (Washington: Government Printing Office, XCXII, 1956) p. 971.
[44] *Ibid*. p. 394.
[45] *Ibid*. p. 974.

Additional support for this explanation of the outcome of hypothesis 6 is provided by the fact that the Democrats on the committee evidenced a keen awareness of the requirements of the role and a deep regret that they could not abide by them. Time and again they referred to the excessive Congressional criticism of Dulles's predecessor and to the need to give the Secretary of State the benefit of any doubt. In the end, however, the restraints of the committee role gave way to the perception that Dulles had failed to provide justification for restraint. Both the conflict and its resolution is plainly manifest in this typical observation:

MR. FULBRIGHT: . . . I have no desire to vilify a Republican Secretary of State, as a recent Democratic Secretary of State was vilified because he did not reverse every world current that was adverse to America. Apart from the wrong to the person involved, we have seen all too clearly how this kind of partisanship makes the whole of America its victim. What we want and what we will support is the truth, however unpleasant. What we want and what we will support is a Secretary of State who will not treat us as children ready to clap in delight at every fairy story, however fanciful. What we want and what we will support is a Secretary of State who will come to us, not with packaged solutions to every ill that plagues the world, but who will come to us, instead, with a statement of facts about the nature of those ills. Such a Secretary of State would win our respect for his courage, and for the respect he himself showed the truth.[46]

Presumably the repeated expressions of this conflict would not have occurred if individual rather than role variables had underlain the reversal of hypothesis 6.

CONCLUSIONS

Since they involve an intricate series of assumptions and procedures, quantitative historical comparisons are bound to give rise to questions about the validity, relevance, and generalizability of the findings which they generate. What has been measured? How accurate are the measurements? What do they mean? Such questions always seem especially pertinent when a quantitative study comes to an end, and this inquiry is no exception: Do the findings demonstrate that role variables are more potent than individual variables for all kinds of foreign policy officials, or only for United States policy makers? Indeed, should our conclusions

[46] *Ibid.* p. 3369.

be limited only to Senators, or is it appropriate to presume that, say, officials of the executive branch are as circumscribed by role considerations as are their counterparts in the Congress? And what about the limited relevance of Senatorial behavior toward the Secretary of State? Is it not possible that the relative potency of role and individual variables would have been different, or even reversed, if reactions to more salient and central objects in the international environment, such as the Soviet Union or NATO, had been examined? [47]

It will be recalled that the answer to the first two of these questions had already been indicated. Yet it bears repeating that we have assessed the potency of role and individual variables only with respect to the foreign policy officials of one society in a limited historical period. One can think of other policy-making systems, particularly underdeveloped ones, that would not be likely to reveal, if analyzed in the same way, such potency accruing to role variables.

But does not this finding also emphasize that our assessment is limited to senatorial posts and inapplicable to the behavior of all American foreign policy officials? Here the answer is less clear. Strictly speaking, we have dealt only with legislative roles. The tasks Senators perform as makers of foreign policy are not the same as those undertaken by officials in the State Department and other executive agencies. By definition, both formally and informally, the legislative approach to foreign affairs is more partisan and less intellectual than the executive approach, and thus an assessment of executive positions might well yield a different balance of relative potency than the one uncovered here. On the other hand, it must also be noted that interpretations of the leeway for individual discretion in a role are, at least in part, culturally derived, and that, to the extent that this is the case, two officials in the same political culture will be similarly inclined to place role requirements ahead of individual preferences, even though the requirements be legislative in one instance and executive in the other. The formal and informal responsibilities of Senators and high State Department officials, in other words, differ in a variety of important ways, and for most analytic purposes these differences are crucial; but, in the absence of relevant data, it does not seem inappropriate to generalize

---

[47] A host of more specific questions also come to mind: Is the behavior of Senators on the Senate floor an adequate sample of their total behavior? Are not their activities outside the Senate chamber just as significant and, if so, what happens to the findings if, as is quite possible, such activities are different from and somewhat contrary to those that transpire on the floor of the Congress? In addition, by quantifying references in the way we did, have we not measured such irrelevant characteristics as loquaciousness, seniority, and illness rather than the potency of individual and role variables? Unfortunately, space limitations do not permit consideration of these more specific types of questions. However, a discussion of them can be found in Rosenau, *The Senate and Dean Acheson*, Chapter 1.

upon the findings of this study and to presume that the potency of role variables is equally great for foreign policy makers in both branches of the government.

As for the question of whether this conclusion would have to be altered if reactions to more salient objects in the international environment had been examined, here again the case can be argued along contradictory lines. Certainly it is true that Senatorial behavior toward the Secretary of State is of limited significance compared to most of the activities in which foreign policy officials engage. The daily press may make much of Congressional antagonism to the Secretary and his colleagues in the State Department, but in fact neither the content of policies nor the course of events are likely to be greatly affected by such matters. Furthermore, there are a multitude of choices which foreign policy officials have to make that do not involve their standing as Republicans or Democrats. If less partisan and more important forms of behavior had been investigated, therefore, the analysis might have revealed a different set of potencies accruing to role and individual variables.

On the other hand, it must also be observed that the conflicts between role and individual variables examined here are of a classic kind and in certain respects closely resemble many of the choices which foreign policy officials are called upon to make. At a higher level of generalization, we examined the question of how policy makers adjust to external changes which result in contradictions between objects in the environment that had been harmoniously linked prior to the changes. We found that policy makers do not accept the disharmony created by the changes and instead achieve balance by acquiescing to the requirements of role variables. In the absence of data on other types of behavior, it thus seems appropriate to presume that such a conclusion would hold up for a wide range of activities in addition to the reactions of Senators to the Secretary of State. Given the change occasioned by De Gaulle's divisive policies in NATO, for example, the findings of this inquiry point to the prediction that American policy makers would minimize their personal preferences with respect to De Gaulle or France and would instead engage in behavior that was consonant with the requirements of the role of a NATO member. Or take the change which occurred when two allies of the United States, Greece and Turkey, threatened each other over Cyprus. It would seem that American officials reacted not in terms of their personal beliefs as to where the blame should be placed, but rather in terms of the requirements of their role as allies of both parties to the dispute. Such a reaction is not inconsistent with the patterns revealed by the data analyzed here. Similarly, to take a third situation, when a duly elected regime is overthrown by a military junta in a country on which the United States relies for support against Communist advances in Asia or for contributions to the Alliance for Progress, the requirements of the role of military ally in Asia or of socio-economic ally in Latin America usually lead American policy makers to put aside their individual distaste for the downfall of democratic institutions. Again, such behavior is predictable on the basis of how Senators reacted to a Democratic and Republican Secretary of State.

Ideally, of course, these generalizations upon the findings of this inquiry should themselves be tested empirically. As previously indicated, the validity of an interpretation depends upon the degree to which a consensus prevails among other researchers, and doubtless these generalizations would be more widely accepted if additional data were available to support them. In the absence of such data, however, it is hoped that the findings of this study will incline more researchers to proceed on the basis of the general assumption that role variables are substantially more potent than individual variables insofar as the makers of American foreign policy are concerned. Or, if this is asking too much, then hopefully the findings might at least spur efforts to treat clashes between role and individual variables as an important source of international political behavior.[48]

---

[48] For an interesting re-analysis of the concepts and data set forth in this chapter that reaches somewhat different conclusions, see Glen H. Stassen, "Individual Preferences versus Role-Constraint in Policy-Making: Senatorial Response to Secretaries Acheson and Dulles," *World Politics*, XXV (October 1972), pp. 96-119.

8 External and Internal Typologies of Foreign Policy Behavior: Testing the Stability of an Intriguing Set of Findings * ---

At long last the field of international politics is beginning to experience the process of reciprocal enrichment between theory and research that other fields enjoy. Recent progress in the making of international data has made it increasingly possible for students in the field to seek to confirm and refine theory through quantified data and to then allow the findings to feed back as stimuli for fresh theorizing. The student of international politics can now be a creative theorist, and also plan ahead for theoretical extension and clarification through confrontations with empirical materials that are capable of depicting the recurring patterns of world politics. Exciting times thus lie ahead on the research frontiers of international studies. Many obstacles will be encountered and numerous frustrations experienced, but the opportunities for quantum leaps forward now exist. This paper seeks to seize one opportunity that may hold the promise of substantial forward movement.

THE EVENTS DATA MOVEMENT

A central element of the emerging opportunities is the recent creation of several data sets based on the actions and interactions of

* Written with George H. Ramsey, Jr.

† Reprinted from *Sage International Yearbook of Foreign Policy Studies*, Vol. *III*, Patrick J. McGowan, ed. © 1975, pp. 245-262, by permission of the publisher, Sage Publications, Inc. (Beverly Hills, London).

nation-states across extensive periods of time. Some of these data sets, such as the Correlates of War Project,[1] focus on selected forms of action and interaction; but an increasing number, such as the WEIS, COPDAB, and CREON projects,[2] cover virtually the entire range of international behavior. Furthermore, this "events data movement," as it has come to be called, has spawned a voluminous literature of its own which allows students to critically evaluate the problems and potentials of the data sets, individually and collectively, for their own theoretical concerns.[3]

The mounting pace of the events data movement is a necessary step in the progress toward a science of international politics. It follows a period of concern with interdisciplinary concepts and a preoccupation with model-building, and represents an effort to develop empirical measures of the dependent variables to which the concepts and models predict.[4] A number of researchers, led originally by Charles McClelland, saw the need to move beyond the prediction of such vague phenomena as "foreign policy" and "international tension" to the identification, reconstruction, and measurement of the basic units of behavior that constitute world politics. A consensus quickly developed that the "event" —generally defined as an occasion when one actor directs an action toward one or more others—is the basic core unit through which the patterns of international relations can be discerned, contrasted, and assessed. Through a day-by-day and country-by-country reconstruction of everything that happens (or at least that is reported) on the world stage, it seemed plausible that analysts would be in a position to test their hypotheses and determine the adequacy of their theories. And this is, of course, precisely the circumstance that has come into being: with each set consisting of thousands of events, for example, WEIS encompasses 130 nations for the 1966–1969 period, COPDAB 44 nations for the 1945–1969 period, and CREON 35 nations for three months of each year during the period 1959–1968.

Problems, of course, abound. One is that the several data sets vary somewhat in the operational definitions used to delineate an event.

[1] Compiled under the leadership of J. David Singer and Melvin Small. For both an account of the project and the data it yielded, see J. David Singer and Melvin Small, *The Wages of War 1816-1965: A Statistical Handbook* (New York: John Wiley, 1972).

[2] WEIS is the acronym for World Event Interaction Survey developed by Charles A. McClelland; COPDAB refers to the Conflict and Peace Data Bank headed by Edward Azar; and CREON is short for the Comparative Research on the Events of Nations project led by Charles F. Hermann, Stephen Salmore, and Maurice A. East.

[3] For a good summary and evaluation of the various data sets, and their respective strengths and weaknesses, see Philip M. Burgess and Robert Lawton, *Indicators of International Behavior: An Assessment of Events Data Research* (Beverly Hills: Sage Professional Paper in International Studies 02-010, 1972).

Another is that the various sets do not draw on the same sources for the information out of which events are reconstructed and the data sets compiled. The WEIS project relied exclusively on the New York *Times*, COPDAB used multiple sources (both global and regional), and CREON is based mainly on *Deadline Data*. Since global sources such as the New York *Times* and *Deadline Data* tend to report the hostile relations of nations, especially the more powerful ones, more extensively than friendly interactions, the data sets based on such sources may well constitute a biased picture of the world, one in which conflict is more pervasive than cooperation and large nations more active than small ones. Conversely, since regional sources tend to give disproportionate attention to the actions and interactions of the nations that fall within their boundaries, the resulting data sets may be biased in the direction of cooperation on the part of small nations.

One outcome of the discrepancies among the data sets has been a series of articles comparing their relative strengths and weaknesses. Azar, for example, reports that the overlap between the chronology of events in the Middle East reconstructed from the New York *Times* and the *Middle East Journal* was only 9.7%, primarily because the former did not report nearly as many events as the latter.[5] Similarly, Hoggard found that the New York *Times*, *Deadline Data*, and the *Asian Recorder* together reported only 26% of the diplomatic interactions culled from documents contained in the *Indian White Paper* for the same period.[6] In a like manner, Burrowes compared nine sources on four Middle Eastern nations, two of which were major regional sources (the *cahière de l'Orient Contemporain* and the *Middle East Journal*) and two of which were global prestige newspapers (the New York *Times* and the London *Times*), and found that "only one-third of the events in this universe appeared in more than one of the nine sources."[7]

It might be argued that such methodological inquiries and the discussions they precipitated about the proper way to generate events

---

[4] The place of the events data movement in the evaluation of the field can be clearly seen in the context of McClelland's cogent analysis of the various stages of emphasis in international relations research. See Charles A. McClelland, "On the Fourth Wave: Past and Future in the Study of International Systems," pp. 15-40 in J. N. Rosenau, V. Davis, and M. A. East (eds.), *The Analysis of International Politics: Essays in Honor of Harold and Margaret Sprout* (New York: Free Press, 1972).

[5] Cf. Edward E. Azar, "Analysis of International Events," *Peace Research Reviews*, 4 (November 1970), pp. 1-113.

[6] See Gary D. Hoggard, "Differential Source Coverage and the Analysis of International Interaction Data," in J. N. Rosenau (ed.), *Comparing Foreign Policies: Theories, Findings, and Methods* (Beverly Hills: Sage Publications, 1974), pp. 353-382.

[7] Robert Burrowes, "Mirror, Mirror, On the Wall . . . : A Comparison of Sources of External Events Data," in J. N. Rosenau (ed.), *Comparing Foreign Policies: Theories, Findings, and Methods* (Beverly Hills: Sage Publications, 1974), pp. 383-406.

data reveal the primitiveness of scientific inquiry into international politics. A critic might contend that the discrepancies among sources demonstrate the impossibility of reconstructing an accurate picture of the
course of world affairs from public sources and that the comparisons
illustrate a tendency on the part of scientifically oriented researchers
to become preoccupied with methodological trivia and to lose sight
of substantive problems.

Another reaction is possible, however. It is easy to understand the
frustrations generated by methodological preoccupations, but the results
of such inquiries can also be seen as a necessary stage in the perfection
of research instruments, one through which the field must pass before
theory can begin to be tested and revised through confrontations with
empirical data. As is likely to happen in any young science, discrepancies
in what their instruments measure have not deterred events analysts, who
have preferred to perfect these instruments rather than abandon them.
All concerned recognize that comprehension of substantive phenomena
can never be any better than the devices used to observe and measure
them, so that the energy invested in assessing the validity and reliability
of data sets reflects an aspiration to move on rather than a preoccupation with trivia. Such an aspiration seems well founded. Large as the
discrepancies are, there is no prima facie reason for assuming that a
systematic reconstruction of world political patterns accomplished
through events analysis is any less accurate than one founded on case
histories. The question of whether a particular historical episode is
sufficiently typical to warrant generalization is no different from that
of whether a particular data set is reliable enough to justify the derivation of substantive conclusions.

To be sure, it would be a much happier state of affairs if the
overlap among the various events data sets approached 90 or 100%. And,
obviously, analysis would be much easier if all the data sets were based
on a shared conception of what constitutes an event and if they were
comprehensive in their coverage of time and comparable in their coverage of actors. Because such conditions do not prevail, however, does
not mean that they never will. On the contrary, there is reason to believe
(if the history of science has any relevance) that events data analysts will
learn from each other that convergence will eventually occur around one
or another formulation and set of data-generating procedures,· all of
which will lead to increased confidence that the instruments for reconstructing world affairs are becoming more refined and an adequate
mirror of the phenomena they purport to measure.

In short, one can reasonably advance either a negative or a constructive posture toward the events data movement. Here we adhere
to the latter, not from naiveté or sheer optimism, but because it seems
that little can be gained by dismissing an avenue to understanding before

it has been fully tested. This attitude leads us to interpret discrepancies as a reflection of substantive phenomena as much as a reflection of methodological error.

THE ORIGINAL STUDY AND ITS INTRIGUING FINDINGS

The foregoing is relevant because the ensuing comparison of events data sources is motivated by substantive theoretical concerns and by an intriguing set of empirical findings as well as an interest in methodological clarification. In an earlier paper one of us developed a series of theoretical propositions that yielded rank order predictions about the amount of conflict and cooperation in which different types of nations are likely to engage abroad, both in general and in particular types of dyadic situations.[8] The theoretical thrust of that paper grew out of an interest in the relative utility of internal and external factors in promoting the construction of theoretically meaningful typologies. Three "national attributes" deemed to reflect internal factors and three "relational attributes" considered to reflect external factors were identified and predictions set forth as to how these would be ordered in terms of their relative success in predicting distributions of cooperative and conflictful behavior. The national attributes were demographic size, economic development, and political accountability, each of which was dichotomized, yielding eight types of nation-states (see the columns of Table 8–1a). The relational attributes of nation-state dyads were geographic distance (between the parties), sociocultural homogeneity, and military balance, each of which was also dichotomized, yielding eight types of dyadic relationships (see the columns of Table 8–1b).

The original paper presents the rationale for the relative strengths ascribed to each of the dichotomized attributes, and it need not be repeated here. The twenty hypotheses through which the rank order predictions were derived, however, can be summarized as follows: with respect to the national attributes, it was hypothesized that conflict would be mostly likely to involve (1) large rather than small nations, (2) developed rather than undeveloped nations, and (3) open rather than closed nations. Moreover, it was hypothesized that (4) size would be a greater contributor to conflict than development, and (5) development would be greater in this regard than accountability. These five propositions resulted in the predicted rank order for conflict listed in the second row of Table 8–1. The obverse of this reasoning (Hypotheses 6–10)

[8]James N. Rosenau and Gary D. Hoggard, "Foreign Policy Behavior in Dyadic Relationships: Testing a Pre-Theoretical Extension," in J. N. Rosenau (ed.), *Comparing Foreign Policies* (Beverly Hills: Sage Publications, 1974), pp. 117-150.

yielded the rank order prediction for cooperation presented in the first row of Table 8–1. In the case of the relational attributes, it was anticipated that more external conflict behavior would be initiated in (11) proximate than in remote dyads, (12) in dissimilar than in similar dyads, and (13) in unequal than in equal dyads. In addition, (14) distance was hypothesized to be a more potent determinant of external conflict than homogeneity, and (15) homogeneity a more potent source than balance. These five propositions gave rise to the rank-order prediction for conflict listed in the fourth row of Table 8–1 and the obverse of these derivations (Hypotheses 16–20) resulted in the rank-order prediction for cooperation in dyads presented in the third row of Table 8–1.

In the original paper, the WEIS data were used to test these four rank-order predictions. The 130 nations encompassed by these data were classified in terms of operational definitions of the three national attributes, and the 16,512 dyads that they form were classified in terms of operational measures of the three relational attributes. The 5,739 conflict acts and 7,781 cooperative acts identified in the WEIS data set for the 44-month period between January 1966 and August 1969 were then summed for all the nations embraced by each of the eight nation-types and for all the dyads embraced by each of the eight relational types. In order to offset the unequal distribution of nations and dyads in each type, each conflict and cooperation sum was divided by the number of nations and dyads in each type. The resulting ratios of acts-per-nation-type and initiated-acts-per-dyad-type were then used as the basis for the empirical ranking against which the predicted rankings were tested. Table 8–2 presents these paired sets of rankings.

It least three intriguing findings emerge from an inspection of Table 8–2. One is the large extent to which the four empirical rank orders are patterned. None of them is perfectly arrayed and the exceptions cannot be dismissed; indeed, the original paper attempted to account for them at least speculatively.[9] The salient impression, however, is one of orderliness, of systemic factors operating in accord with or in opposition to the predictions. A second and hardly less conspicuous feature of the data is that they negate the initial premise that the sources of international cooperation and conflict are the obverse of each other. For both the nation- and dyad-type the conflict and cooperation rank orders are very similar,[10] conforming more to the predicted orders for conflict than to those for cooperation. The third and perhaps most intriguing findings concerns the relative success in predicting amounts of cooperative and conflictful behavior in the rankings derived from the use of internal

[9] Rosenau and Hoggard, op. cit., pp. 135–136.
[10] Stated statistically, the Spearman rho value for the correlations between them is .8 for the nation-types and .6 for the dyad-types.

Table 8 – 1

a. Rank order predictions of the amount of conflictful and cooperative behavior that will be inititiated by eight types of national societies

	large				small			
	developed		underdeveloped		developed		underdeveloped	
	closed	open	closed	open	closed	open	closed	open
rank order of the societies in terms of the predicted amount of cooperative behavior that will be initiated	8	7	6	5	4	3	2	1
rank order of the societies in terms of the predicted amount of conflictful behavior that will be initiated	1	2	3	4	5	6	7	8

b. Rank order predictions of the amount of conflictful and cooperative behavior that will be initiated in eight types of dyads

	remote				proximate			
	similar		dissimilar		similar		dissimilar	
	equal		unequal		equal		unequal	
rank order of the dyads in terms of the predicted amount of cooperative behavior that will be initiated	1	2	3	4	5	6	7	8
rank order of the dyads in terms of the predicted amount of conflict behavior that will be initiated	8	7	6	5	4	3	2	1

1 = most amount of behavior; 8 = least amount of behavior.

factors, as compared with a marked lack of success when rankings were based on external factors. While the empirical rank orders of the eight nation-types do indeed approximate the hypothesized ranking based on national attributes, a comparison of the empirical and predicted rankings based on the relational characteristics of dyads reveals considerably less similarity.[11]

THE NEED FOR FURTHER INVESTIGATION

Rather than fostering the interpretation that the original hypotheses were confirmed, these findings provoked doubt on the part of both the researchers and those to whom the findings were communicated.[12] A question that could not be avoided was whether the results merely reflected the biases built into the WEIS data. Were the hypotheses that predicted higher ranks for large and developed nations confirmed because the New York *Times* reports more fully on the activity of these types? Does not the same bias also account for the greater potency of national than relational attributes? Were the conflict predictions more accurate than the cooperation ones because the New York *Times* is also biased in the direction of reporting more conflict behavior? Does the absence of differentiation between the conflict and cooperation rankings suggest that all that was measured was the extent of total behavior rather than two of its basic dimensions? Is it not a serious distortion to give the same weight to every conflictful or cooperative act? If, say, military actions or diplomatic concessions were given greater weight than mild protests or verbal assurances, would not the results have been considerably different?

How stable, in short, are these findings? Will they emerge from other data sets? Are the national and relational attributes conceptualized at a sufficiently fundamental level that the empirical patterns derived from the WEIS data may be discernible in other data sets that do not encompass the same nations or the same time period?

These questions are not simply methodological. They focus on the interface between theory and method and are, in this sense, profoundly substantive. At their core it the issue of whether we have identified

[11] As indicated by the Spearman rho correlations between the predicted and empirical rankings in each case: with cooperation not treated as the obverse of conflict (i.e., reversing the rank orders in the first and fifth rows of Table 2), the correlations for the two nation-type comparisons both exceed .92, whereas neither of those

for the dyadic pairings exceeds .36.

[12] For one systematic effort to reexamine the original findings, see Charles A. Powell, David Andrus, W. Fowler, and Kathleen Knight, "Determinants of Foreign Policy Behavior: A Causal Modeling Approach," in J. N. Rosenau (ed.), *Comparing Foreign Policies* (Beverly Hills: Sage Publications, 1974), pp. 151-170.

Table 8 – 2

a. Predicted and empirical rank orders of the amount of conflictful and cooperative behavior initiated by eight types of national societies

	large				small				Spearman's rho
	developed		underdeveloped		developed		underdeveloped		
	closed	open	closed	open	closed	open	closed	open	
predicted rank order for COOPERATIVE behavior	8	7	6	5	4	3	2	1	
empirical rank order for COOPERATIVE behavior	1	2	4	3	5	7	6	8	−.952
predicted rank order for CONFLICTFUL behavior	1	2	3	4	5	6	7	8	
empirical rank order for CONFLICTFUL behavior	1	2	3	6	4	5	7	8	.928

b. Predicted and empirical rank orders of the amount of conflictful and cooperative behavior initiated in eight types of dyads

	remote				proximate				Spearman's rho
	similar		dissimilar		similar		dissimilar		
	equal		unequal		equal		unequal		
predicted rank order for COOPERATIVE behavior	1	2	3	4	5	6	7	8	
empirical rank order for COOPERATIVE behavior	2	1	8	7	6	3	5	4	.214
predicted rank order for CONFLICTFUL behavior	8	7	6	5	4	3	2	1	
empirical rank order for CONFLICTFUL behavior	2	5	8	7	6	4	3	1	.357

1 = most amount of behavior; 8 = least amount of behavior.

dimensions of external conflict and cooperation so basic that they will be manifest irrespective of the instruments used to observe them.

To explore the foregoing questions we turned to the COPDAB and CREON data sets, in each case classifying nations in the same national and relational categories to which they had been assigned in the case of the WEIS data. The portion of the COPDAB data made available to us [13] consisted of 13,277 events initiated by 28 nations in 756 dyads for the same period covered by WEIS (1966–1969). The 7–13 points on the COPDAB weighting scale were considered to be conflictful acts and the 1–6 points were treated as cooperative acts.[14] This procedure resulted in a total of 5,512 conflictful and 7,765 cooperative acts. In the case of the CREON set, the 35 nations were also assigned to the same categories as previously and, all told, they initiated a total of 5,394 acts toward each other (i.e., in 1,190 dyads) during the randomly selected quarters of each of the years (1959–1968) encompassed by this data set. The CREON method of classifying events as conflictful and cooperative yielded 2,504 of the former and 2,890 of the latter.[15]

THE DISTINCTION BETWEEN COOPERATION AND CONFLICT

The initial research design proposed that both nation- and dyad-types exhibiting the *greatest* conflict behavior would exhibit the least amount of cooperative behavior. The empirical distributions in the WEIS data demonstrated exactly the opposite, suggesting that the relationship between the nation- or dyad-type's rankings on conflict and cooperation is in turn a function of the relationship between each dimension of behavior and the total volume of activity engaged in by that nation- or dyad-type. Thus, the question arises of whether the two forms of behavior would conform to the prediction of an inverse relationship in the COPDAB and CREON data sets, or whether the importance of the total volume of activity was so central as to result in a pattern similar to that uncovered in the WEIS data.

As can be seen in Table 8–3, which contrasts the rankings for each data set in terms of conflictful, cooperative, and total behavior by both

---

[13] Through extraordinary effort and kindness on the part of Professor Edward E. Azar, to whom we are deeply grateful.

[14] For an account of the components of the COPDAB scale and the methods for coding events in terms of it, see Edward A. Azar, *op. cit.*

[15] For an account of CREON's categories and coding procedures, see Charles F. Hermann, Maurice A. East, Margaret G. Hermann, Barbara G. Salmore and Steven A. Salmore, *CREON: A Foreign Events Data Set* (Beverly Hills: Sage Professional Paper in International Studies 02-024, 1974).

Table 8 – 3 Comparisons of the Rankings of Cooperative, Conflictful, and Total Behavior to Each Other Within Three Data Sets for Both National and Relational Attributes (using Spearman's rho)

	a. National Attributes *									b. Relational Attributes **								
	LDC	LDO	LUC	LUO	SDC	SDO	SUC	SUO	rho	RSE	RSU	RDE	RDU	PSE	PSU	PDE	PDU	rho
CREON																		
cooperation	2	5	3	4	7	6	8	8	.714	3	2	3	7	5	4	6	1	.905
total behavior	2	1	5	4	4	7	6	8		2	3	8	8	5	4	7	1	
cooperation	2	5	3	4	7	6	8	8	.714	3	3	8	7	5	4	6	1	.500
conflict	2	1	5	4	7	6	8	8		2	4	3	8	6	7	5	1	
conflict	2	1	5	4	6	7	8	8		2	4	3	8	6	5	5	1	
total behavior	2	1	5	4	7	6	8	8	1.000	2	3	6	8	5	4	7	1	.714
COPDAB																		
cooperation	1	3	4	6	7	5	8	8	.952	1	5	7	6	4	8	2	3	.857
total behavior	1	2	4	7	6	5	8	8		1	6	4	7	5	8	2	3	
cooperation	1	3	4	6	7	5	8	8	.643	1	5	7	6	4	8	2	3	.786
conflict	2	4	1	3	3	5	8	8		1	5	4	6	7	8	2	3	
conflict	2	1	1	6	3	5	8	8		1	5	4	6	7	8	2	3	
total cooperation	1	3	4	7	5	5	8	8	.810	1	6	4	7	5	8	2	3	.929
WEIS																		
cooperation	1	4	3	5	7	6	8	8	.976	2	1	8	7	6	3	5	4	.881
total behavior	1	3	4	5	7	6	8	8		1	3	8	7	6	4	5	2	
cooperation	1	4	3	5	7	6	8	8	.810	2	1	8	7	6	3	5	4	.616
conflict	2	3	6	4	5	7	8	8		2	5	8	7	6	6	3	3	
conflict	2	3	6	4	5	7	8	8		2	5	8	7	6	4	3	1	
total behavior	1	3	6	5	7	6	8	8	.881	1	3	8	7	6	4	5	2	.881

1 = most amount of behavior; 8 = least amount of behavior.
* For national attributes, L—large, S—small, U—undeveloped, C—closed, and O—open societies.
** For relational attributes R—remote, S—similar, D—dissimilar, E—equal, and U—unequal dyads.

nation- and dyad-type, the indications provided by the WEIS data are more reliable than the hypothesized inverse relationship set forth at the outset. In all three data sets, whether categorized in terms of national or relational attributes, the correlations between the cooperation and conflict rankings are all positive and reasonably strong, ranging from .500 to .810.[16] Even stronger positive correlations were uncovered for the relationships between the rankings of conflictful and total behavior on the one hand (.714 to 1.0) and cooperative and total behavior on the other (.714 to .976).

In short, the evidence on the lack of differentiation between cooperative and conflictful behavior is so uniform that it seems justified to abandon the original conception of them as the obverse of each other. Three different data sets, each differently compiled on the basis of different spatial and temporal dimensions, all tell essentially the same story, a story in which it is clear that increased international activity implies increased cooperation *as well as* increased conflict.

In view of the recurrence of this finding in two other data sets, our interpretation of it in the original analysis of the WEIS data is perhaps worth noting again. At that time we speculated that the direct relationship between conflict and cooperation was rooted in the necessity for a balance between the two types of behavior if any international relationship is to endure. Whatever the history of enmity or amity out of which such relationships emerge, they cannot be sustained by conflict or cooperation alone, else they will lead to either total war or total unification. In the case of conflict behavior, for example, it must be offset by cooperative acts if a situation is to be resolved or escalation to outright war avoided. Not every conflictful act may be followed by a conciliatory reaction, but the overall balance between the two must be such as to prevent a complete breakdown of the relationship. It is this overall balance that the similar patterns uncovered in all three data sets may be depicting.

THE STABILITY OF THE ORIGINAL FINDINGS

Let us turn to the finding that showed the original hypotheses to be mostly accurate with respect to national attributes and mostly erroneous with respect to relational attributes. Table 8–4 compares the conflict, cooperation, and total rankings for each data set along both the national and relational dimensions with those derived theoretically. Firstly, it should be clear that when nations are classified by national attributes

---

[16] These and the other correlations cited henceforth are all Spearman rho rank order coefficients.

[17] Edward A. Azar, *op. cit.*, pp. 19-22.

Table 8–4 Comparisons of the Rankings of Cooperative, Conflictful, and Total Behavior to those Derived Theoretically for Both National and Relational Attributes Across Three Data Sets (using Spearman's rho)

	a. National Attributes *									b. Relational Attributes **								
	LDC	LEO	LUC	LUO	SDC	SDO	SUC	SUO	rho	RSE	RSU	RDE	RDU	PSE	PSU	PDE	PDU	rho
Cooperation																		
WEIS-derived ranking	1	2	4	3	5	7	6	8	.952	2	1	8	7	6	3	5	4	−.214
hypothesized ranking	1	2	3	4	5	6	7	8		8	7	6	5	4	3	2	1	
COPDAB-derived ranking	1	2	3	4	6	7	5	8	.929	1	5	7	6	4	8	2	3	0.000
hypothesized ranking	1	2	4	3	5	6	7	8		8	7	6	5	4	3	2	1	
CREON-derived ranking	2	1	5	3	4	7	6	8	.881	3	2	8	7	5	4	6	1	.095
hypothesized ranking	1	2	3	4	5	6	7	8		8	7	6	5	4	3	2	1	
Conflict																		
WEIS-derived ranking	1	2	3	6	4	5	7	8	.928	2	5	8	7	6	4	3	1	.357
hypothesized ranking	1	2	3	5	6	7	8	8		8	7	6	5	4	3	2	1	
COPDAB-derived ranking	2	4	1	6	7	3	5	8	.643	1	5	4	6	7	8	2	3	−.143
hypothesized ranking	1	2	3	5	6	7	8	8		8	7	6	5	4	3	2	1	
CREON-derived ranking	2	3	1	5	4	7	6	8	.881	2	4	3	8	6	7	5	1	−.095
hypothesized ranking	1	2	3	4	5	6	7	8		8	7	6	5	4	3	2	1	
Total Behavior																		
WEIS-derived ranking	1	2	3	4	5	7	6	8	.976	1	3	8	7	6	4	5	2	−.048
hypothesized ranking	1	2	3	4	5	6	7	8		8	7	6	5	4	3	2	1	
COPDAB-derived ranking	1	3	2	4	7	6	5	8	.881	1	6	4	7	5	8	2	3	−.048
hypothesized ranking	1	2	3	4	5	6	7	8		8	7	6	5	4	3	2	1	
CREON-derived ranking	2	3	1	5	4	7	6	8	.881	2	3	6	8	5	4	7	1	−.048
hypothesized ranking	1	2	3	4	5	6	7	8		8	7	6	5	4	3	2	1	

1 = most amount of behavior; 8 = least amount of behavior.

* For national attributes, L—large, S—small, U—undeveloped, C—closed, and O—open societies.

** For relational attributes, R—remote, S—similar, D—dissimilar, E—equal, and U—unequal dyads.

(Table 8–4a) the correlations between the hypothesized rank order and each empirical rank order are positive and strong in all three data sets for conflict, cooperation, and total behavior (from .643 to .952). Secondly, and in sharp contrast, when dyadic classifications are used to differentiate the behavior of nations, Table 8–4b), all the correlations between the predicted and empirical rankings are consistently low. Indeed, the COPDAB and CREON correlations for the rational attributes are even lower than those uncovered earlier in the WEIS data (with none of the former exceeding .143).

In other words, the distributions found in the initial study, based on WEIS data, are similarly uncovered in the replication. The impression of an underlying order again arrests attention. Again the national-attributes typology yields empirical distributions for both conflictful and cooperative behavior that closely approximate those predicted theoretically. And again the dyadic-attribute typology fails to generate a relationship between the predicted and empirical rankings.

DIRECT COMPARISON OF THE THREE DATA SETS

The stability of these findings is further clarified by a contrast of the rankings of each of the data sets to those of each of the other two. Table 8–5a presents the national attribute rankings of the three sets paired with each other for conflictful, cooperative, and total behavior. Here a startlingly high correspondence among all three data sets is immediately evident, with four of the nine correlations exceeding .9. In all three data sets there was less correspondence for the conflict dimension than for cooperative and total behavior, but even in the former case the correlations all exceeded .6. Interestingly, the two lowest of the three conflict correlations involve the one data set (COPDAB) that was compiled out of regional as well as global sources. However, such a distinction between the pairings of the data sets cannot be drawn for cooperative and total behavior. In short, insofar as national attributes are concerned, it would appear that it does not matter what events data set one employs if one's theoretical concerns are cast at the general level employed here.

The correspondence across the three data sets is not nearly so great if nations are differentiated in terms of relational attributes. As can be seen in Table 8–5b, four of the nine correlations fell below .5 and only ᵗhree exceeded .7. Again some differences between the two data sets not founded on regional sources (WEIS and CREON) and the one that is (COPDAB) can be traced. The former were highly correlated in terms of cooperative and total behavior (over .8 in both instances), whereas the correlations between each of these and COPDAB along the same dimensions are the lowest presented in Table 8–5b. In the case of the

Table 8–5   Comparisons of the Empirical Rankings Derived from the WEIS, CREON, and COPDAB Data Sets for Both National and Relational Attributes and in Terms of Cooperative, Conflictful, and Total Behavior (using Spearman's rho)

	a. National Attributes*									b. Relational Attributes**								
	LDC	LDO	LUC	LUO	SDC	SDO	SUC	SUO	rho	RSE	RSU	RDE	RDU	PSE	PSU	PDE	PDU	rho
Cooperation																		
WEIS-derived ranking	2	4	3	5	7	6	1	8	.952	2	1	8	7	6	3	5	4	.833
CREON-derived ranking	1	5	3	4	7	6	2	8		3	2	8	7	5	6	4	1	
CREON-derived ranking	1	5	3	4	7	6	2	8	.857	3	2	8	7	5	6	4	1	.381
COPDAB-derived ranking	1	4	3	6	7	5	2	8		1	5	7	6	4	8	2	3	
WEIS-derived ranking	2	4	3	5	7	6	1	8	.952	2	1	8	7	6	3	5	4	.310
COPDAB-derived ranking	1	4	3	6	7	5	2	8		1	5	7	6	4	8	2	3	
Conflict																		
WEIS-derived ranking	2	3	6	4	5	7	1	8	.857	2	5	8	7	6	4	3	1	.524
CREON-derived ranking	3	1	5	4	7	6	2	8		2	4	3	8	6	7	5	1	
CREON-derived ranking	3	1	5	4	7	6	2	8	.667	2	4	3	8	6	7	5	1	.738
COPDAB-derived ranking	4	1	6	7	3	5	2	8		1	5	4	6	7	8	2	3	
WEIS-derived ranking	2	3	6	4	5	7	1	8	.691	2	5	8	7	6	4	3	1	.524
COPDAB-derived ranking	4	1	6	7	3	5	2	8		1	5	4	6	7	8	2	3	
Total Behavior																		
WEIS-derived ranking	2	3	4	5	7	6	1	8	.905	1	3	8	7	6	4	5	2	.857
CREON-derived ranking	3	1	5	4	7	6	2	8		2	3	6	8	5	4	7	1	
CREON-derived ranking	3	1	5	4	7	6	2	8	.833	2	3	6	8	5	4	7	1	.286
COPDAB-derived ranking	3	2	4	7	6	5	1	8		1	6	4	7	5	8	2	3	
WEIS-derived ranking	2	3	4	5	7	6	1	8	.905	1	3	8	7	6	4	5	2	.381
COPDAB-derived ranking	3	2	4	7	6	5	1	8		1	6	4	7	5	8	2	3	

1 = most amount of behavior; 8 = least amount of behavior.

* For national attributes, L—large, S—small, U—undeveloped, C—closed, and O—open societies.

** For relational attributes, R—remote, S—similar, D—dissimilar, E—equal, and U—unequal dyads.

conflict dimension, on the other hand, both correlations involving COPDAB were as great as or exceeded the WEIS-CREON correlation. While these findings, along with a similar one noted in the previous paragraph, are difficult to interpret, they do lend some credence to the conviction of many analysts in the events data movement that regional sources may yield a different picture of the flow of international affairs than global sources. Yet this conclusion can be exaggerated. The findings (Table 8–5a) that such a distinction cannot be drawn for cooperation and total behavior when a national attribute typology is employed suggests that regional and global sources are not entirely discrepant.

Summarizing all the data presented in Table 8–5, the rank order patterns are highly similar across all three data sets when a theoretical structure derived from national attributes is imposed on the empirical distributions of cooperative and conflictful behavior in the international system. However, when a theoretical structure derived from the relational characteristics of dyads is imposed, patterns that emerge in one data set are not as apparent in another.

DOES WEIGHTING MATTER?

Let us turn now to the question of whether the rankings are distorted by attaching the same weight to every conflictful or cooperative act. For technical reasons, a weighting scheme could not be introduced into the WEIS and CREON data sets, but as a part of the coding process each event in the COPDAB set was assigned a value derived from a 13-point scale. Since the measures of intercoder reliability involved in the application of this scheme proved to be high,[17] an assessment of the effects of weighting did prove feasible. Using both the national and relational typologies, Table 8–6 compares all the previously presented unweighted rankings based on the COPDAB data (i.e., each event coded between 1 and 6 on the scale was treated as equal to one cooperative act and those between 7 and 13 as equal to one conflictful act) with their weighted counterparts (i.e., allowing for the weight assigned to each event). The results of this analysis are clear-cut: weighting has almost no effect at all, either with respect to cooperation and conflict or with regard to national and relational attributes. All four of the correlations in Table 8–6 exceed .9. Whether the absence of any effect of weighting is due to an underlying similarity in the international activities of nations, or to the fact that we may have canceled out important distinctions by aggregating at such a high level of abstraction, cannot be deduced from the findings. But it does seem clear that the importance

17 Edward A. Azar, *op. cit.*, pp. 19-22.

Table 8–6 Comparison of Unweighted and Weighted Rangings Derived from the COPDAB Data Sets for Cooperative and Conflictful Behavior in Terms of Both National and Relational Attributes (using Spearman's rho)

	a. National Attributes*									b. Relational Attributes**								
	LDC	LDO	LUC	LUO	SDC	SDO	SUC	SUO	rho	RSE	RSU	RDE	RDU	PSE	PSU	PDE	PDU	rho
Cooperation																		
non-weighted ranking	1	2	3	4	6	7	5	8	.976	1	5	7	6	4	8	2	3	.929
non-weighted ranking	1	2	3	4	6	8	5	7		1	6	8	5	3	7	2	4	.976
Conflict																		
weighted ranking	2	4	1	6	7	3	5	8	.905	1	5	4	6	7	8	2	3	
weighted ranking	2	1	1	5	8	3	4	7		2	5	4	6	7	8	1	3	

1 = most amount of behavior; 8 = least amount of behavior.

* For national attributes, L—large, S—small, U—undeveloped, C—closed, and O—open societies.

** For relational attributes, R—remote, S—similar, D—dissimilar, E—equal, and U—unequal dyads.

of the weighting question can be exaggerated, perhaps because of a lack of clarity about whether conflictful and cooperative acts should be treated as dependent variables (as we have done) or as intervening variables that may give rise to desirable or deplorable international outcomes (as analysts do when they raise the question of weighting).

CONCLUSIONS

Let us be clear about what our analysis has and has not accomplished. We have not generated definitive findings with respect to the question of the relative potency of internal and external sources of foreign policy behavior. Our analysis has been cast at a very high level of abstraction and thus it would be misleading to claim that we are entitled to make probability inferences about the presence or absence of a causal association between a set of independent variables (i.e., the three national and relational attributes) and a dependent variable (i.e., the volume of cooperative and conflictful behavior). What we have done instead is to impose two different theoretical structures on the same empirical "reality" (i.e., distribution of events) in three different operational contexts and to then ask whether one of the structures produces order out of chaos better than the other. Viewed in this way, our findings point quite clearly to the beginnings of an answer to the question.

Stated differently, the basic implications of our investigations are twofold:

(1) When employing a theoretical typology derived from the attributes of nations, patterns in the empirical distribution of events across three different data sets (each utilizing different operational definitions, conceptual foundations, and journalistic sources) remained *consistent*. When utilizing a typology derived from the characteristics of dyads, the correspondence among data sets was considerably less. This difference indicates that the use of national attributes increases the comparability of events data sources.

(2) Empirical distributions of cooperative and conflictful behavior based on a *national* attribute typology closely approximated the hypothesized distributions. Those founded on a *relational* attribute typology, however, were consistently unrelated to the hypothesized distributions.

9 Puzzlement in Foreign Policy *

I

To appreciate the central idea of this paper, the reader must share the author's conviction that knowledge-building is essentially, though not exclusively, a social process. We add to, subtract from, or otherwise provoke each other. Our theories, data, findings and interpretations become coherent and significant only as they stimulate, inform and enlarge the work of colleagues. Knowledge cumulates, or it does not, only as its builders do, or do not, come to share, modify, refute or otherwise respond to each other's ideas, observations and conclusions. There cannot be a growing and enduring corpus of knowledge in a field without interaction and convergence among its practitioners. Viewed in this way, the content of our theories and findings may be less important than their capacity to stimulate and concentrate the intellectual talents and energies of our co-workers.

It appears that this social process may be grinding to a halt in the scientific study of foreign policy. While I do not retreat from the argument advanced elsewhere[1] that considerable progress has been made in the field over the last ten years, the long-term trend towards convergence seems to have slowed and, even worse, there are more than a few

[1] James N. Rosenau, "Restlessness, Change, and Foreign Policy Analysis," a paper presented at a meeting of the Inter-University Comparative Foreign Policy Project, Ojai, California, June 1973; and "Comparative Foreign Policy: One-Time Fad, Realized Fantasy, and Normal Field," in C. W. Kegley, Jr., A. G. Raymond, R. M. Rood, and R. A. Skinner (eds.), *International Events and the Comparative Analysis of Foreign Policy* (Columbia: University of South Carolina Press, 1975), pp. 3-38.

* An earlier version of this chapter was published in *The Jerusalem Journal of International Relations*, Vol. 1, No. 4 (Summer 1976), pp. 1-10. Reprinted with the permission of the publisher.

indications that we are going our separate ways, sustained individually by the momentum of the past but not by a never-ending process of mutual provocation.

We will not examine here the extent to which fragmentation has set in and knowledge-building has lessened. Hopefully, my fears are exaggerated and are excessively founded on my experience in the Inter-University Comparative Foreign Policy Project (ICFP), which creatively sustained the social processes of scientific convergence for years,[2] but which has lagged lately for want of any stimuli to interaction. Certainly there is a continuous and perhaps growing flow of scientific studies of foreign policy.[3] Whether the proliferation of studies is interactive and convergent, however, is less clear cut. One has the impression that diversity rather than continuity underlies the proliferation, that it is founded more on the dispersal than on the cumulation of effort. Instead of being provoked by each other's work, we seem to be preoccupied with the development of our own ideas, frameworks, hypotheses and models.

Thus there is some reason to wonder whether the processes of convergence have slowed. At the very least, whether my fears are accurate or exaggerated, there would seem to be utility in proceeding as if they are well founded and inquiring why this may be so.

Four explanations can readily be developed to explain the non-cumulative character of foreign-policy studies. The lack of an overall paradigm, the insufficiency of our theory, the limitations of our data, and the extraordinary rapidity of the change that currently marks world affairs can all be cited as compelling reasons for the slowing of our progress. Taken together, they appear to comprise an unassailable and full explanation of where we stand. Surely we are woefully lacking in a paradigm, not to mention competing paradigms, that would give coherence to our inquiries. Undoubtedly, our theories are weak [4] and not up to the task of sustaining interactive investigations. Certainly there are large gaps in our data base that prevent us from probing more deeply into a number of crucial problems. It is clear that the structure and dynamics of world politics are undergoing profound and rapid changes that may be fragmenting our efforts and constraining our inclinations to build on each other's work.

---

[2] Cf. James N. Rosenau, Philip M. Burgess and Charles F. Hermann, "The Adaptation of Foreign Policy Research: A Case Study of an Anti-Case Study Project," *International Studies Quarterly*, 17 (March 1973), pp. 119-44.

[3] See, for example, Patrick J. McGowan (ed.), *Sage International Yearbook of Foreign Policy Studies* (Beverly Hills: Sage Publications, 1973, 1974, and 1975), Vols. I, II, and III.

[4] Cf. Warren R. Phillips, "Where Have all the Theories Gone?" *World Politics*, Vol. XXVI (January 1974), pp. 155-88; and Oran B. Young, "Professor Russett: Industrious Tailor to a Naked Emperor," *World Politics*, XXI (April, 1969), pp. 486-511.

Yet, I doubt whether any or all of these explanations are sufficient. A paradigmatic context, better theory and extensive data would no doubt bring the dynamics of change into focus and thereby invigorate the pace and depth of our investigations. However, neither singly nor together would any of these factors necessarily enhance convergence. A motivational component seems to be missing, and it is this component that constitutes the central idea of this paper. Stated most simply, what is lacking is a feeling of puzzlement about both the continuities and the changes that mark world politics. We are confused as to why the continuities do not change and why the changes do not continue, but we are not genuinely puzzled by them.

Below I attach a precise meaning to the idea of a "genuine puzzle," but here it suffices to note that such a puzzle is founded more on awe than on confusion. Rather than our curiosities being aroused by the foreign-policy phenomena we observe, our defenses are heightened by them. Thus, rather than interactively and systematically probing the changes that confuse us, we are quick to offer interpretations that appear to account for them. I contend that our efforts are unlikely to converge around common problems, much less achieve the substantive clarity and methodological precision needed to trace and comprehend the changing world scene, until we allow ourselves to be puzzled—genuinely intrigued—as to why the underlying patterns and discontinuities we discern unfold as they do. In other words, notwithstanding all the questions we pose and probe, we lack genuine puzzles, puzzles comparable to Newton's bewilderment as to why apples fall. In elaborating on this point, I shall identify two puzzles that strike me as genuine and that, if solved, may go a long way towards reviving the social processes that are needed to sustain our knowledge-building efforts.

Let me state the case even more extremely. If puzzlement is the key motivational component, then we may not be able to develop a paradigmatic context, better theory and more extensive data *until* we become genuinely puzzled. Indeed, it can even be argued that genuine puzzles are a sufficient as well as a necessary condition of substantial paradigmatic, theoretical and empirical progress, that once we are overcome by puzzlement all else will fall into place.[5] Genuine puzzles

[5] I appreciate that this view that puzzles precede paradigms can be countered with the opposite argument. Puzzles can be viewed as emerging only when empirical anomalies persist and anomalies as persisting only in the context of a paradigm that identifies them, a line of reasoning which indicates that paradigms precede puzzles. Such an argument would interpret the Newton example as supportive by noting that he asked his question about apples in the context of a paradigm that had previously evolved in the field of physics. I resist this reasoning on the grounds, elaborated below, that genuine puzzles derive from highly patterned sequences and not from anomalies. Thus they do not necessarily arise from an explicit paradigmatic context and they may be just as puzzling in several paradigmatic contexts. After all, Aristotle also asked about falling objects (acorns), but he explained them much differently than did Newton. In effect, Newton had a different paradigm, but this did not prevent identification of the same puzzle.

may motivate us to evolve and sharpen shared paradigms, to frame and elaborate appropriate theories, to be ever more precise and relentless in gathering relevant empirical materials. They may do so because they may provide the psychic wherewithal to press on, compelling us to interact in determining where the pieces fit, to avoid dismay over those that do not fit, and to be unqualified in our curiosity about the pieces that are missing. Genuine puzzles, in short, may enable us to remain continuously in awe of the foreign-policy processes we investigate even as we reduce our confusion about them.

II

Genuine puzzles are not easily framed. They are not simply matters of bewilderment; nor do they come into existence merely by asking what is transpiring or why it transpires the way it does. Genuine puzzles derive from general "what" and "why" questions, but they are more focused. They identify processes with specified outcomes, as well as expressing curiosity about sources. It is not enough, for example, to ask what particular types of nations do or even why they do what they do. Such questions are so open-ended that they tend neither to sustain our curiosity nor to press us to refine our concepts and methods. They are so broad that they appear overwhelming, thereby encouraging us to go our separate ways and to give in to our immediate concerns and investigate whatever aspect of the problem intrigues us at the moment. Such open-ended quesions, in other words, tend not only to inhibit the process of convergence but, even worse, they can mislead us into believing that we are converging when, in fact, we are not. A number of analysts may think they are involved in a cumulative enterprise because they share interest in the initial question as to why nations do what they do. But, since nations engage in a variety of behaviors, the shared question accomplishes no more than to give each analyst the license to investigate whatever he or she finds interesting.

A question that asks about a sequence of activities that have particular consequences, on the other hand, narrows our analytic concern and imposes limits within which our inquiries must be contained. The specified consequences serve as boundaries beyond which those moved to investigate the question are disinclined to go, with the result that efforts undertaken to answer the question are likely to be disciplined and cumulative. Moreover, because such specific questions posit identifiable outcomes as part of the puzzle, our curiosity is not likely to lag for want of a focus. There is no need to feel overwhelmed and paralyzed by the question because it is phrased in such a way as to be potentially answerable—i.e., it will be answered when the specified outcomes are explained—rather than being open-ended and subject to a multiplicity of answers, none of which is sufficient.

Of course, the specific questions must be provocative and not trivial, which is to say they must spring from wonder that the specified outcomes occur so regularly, from an appreciation that the sources of the regularity are not simple and self-evident, and thus from a constant awe that the processes we observe give rise to the specified outcomes. If a question is provocative in this way and if it is precise in the outcomes it specifies, I call a "genuine puzzle." Newton's question as to why apples fall is a genuine puzzle, one that compelled him to press on to creative conclusions because he was asking about a phenomenon with a specified outcome. Had he asked, "Why do apples do what they do?" —a question that lacks a precise outcome—he and his disciples might well have gone off in a variety of unrelated directions ("Why do apples grow on trees?" "Why do they sometimes host worms?" "Why do they have yellow, red and green skins?") and may eventually have lost interest in the subject without contributing to such an important advance in our understanding of the world around us.

It is much easier to ask open-ended questions than to generate genuine puzzles. The open-ended question does not require much forethought. Since one does not have to be precise about outcomes, one can simply ask whatever comes to mind first, without pausing to consider how or why things culminate in the manner that they do. The open-ended question can thus be deceptive: it can lead us to think we are expressing curiosity when, in fact, asking the question may be a substitute for reflecting about the problem. A genuine puzzle, however, must stem from curiosity, since one has to be perplexed about an effect before one can raise questions about causation. Genuine puzzles are thus disciplining; they come out of repeated observations and they compel us to sort out from all the phenomena we observe those that are both patterned and intriguing. In other words, genuine puzzles are more difficult than open-ended questions because they force us to think, to understand our subject so well that we believe we perceive outcomes that occur regularly, or at least sufficiently so to be patterned.

III

This conception of genuine puzzles as necessary to the sustenance and disciplining of cumulative inquiry explains a good measure of the confusion and fragmentation that prevails in foreign-policy studies today. Neither the growing literature on comparative foreign policy nor the increasing concern over the implications of the underlying changes in global structure is conspicuously marked by genuine puzzles. None of the recurring questions that pervade the literature ("Has underlying change occurred?" "Do small nations behave differently than large ones?" "Is interdependence mounting?" "Are the foreign policies of nation-states as important as ever?" "Are foreign policies shaped more by bureaucracies than by external changes?" "Are there issue areas where actors other than nation-states are most influential?") meets both criteria of genuine puzzlement. These are not trivial questions, but each one is an open-ended query, leaving unspecified any outcomes that are perceived to flow regularly from the conduct and processes of foreign policy.

Nor are analysts of foreign policy alone in their lack of genuine puzzles. I have the impression that much the same condition obtains in other fields of international relations. Consider, for example, the emergent field of transnational relations and the questions posed at the outset of one of the leading works in the field, the highly regarded and widely cited symposium edited by Keohane and Nye.[6] These initial questions are treated by the editors as the five central concerns of their book:

(1) What seems to be the net effect of transnational relations on the abilities of governments to deal with their environments? To what extent and how have governments suffered from a "loss of control" as a result of transnational relations?

(2) What are the implications of transnational relations for the study of world politics? Is the state-centric view, which focuses on the interstate system, an adequate analytic framework for the investigation of contemporary reality?

(3) What are the effects of transnational relations on the allocation of value and specifically on asymmetries or inequalities between states? Who benefits from transnational relations, who loses, who controls transnational networks, and how is this accomplished?

(4) What are the implications of transnational relations for United States foreign policy? Insofar as the United States is indeed preponderant in transnational activity, what dangers as well as opportunities does this present to American policymakers?

(5) What challenges do transnational relations raise for international organizations as conventionally defined? To what extent may

6 Robert O. Keohane and Joseph S. Nye, Jr. (eds.), *Transnational Relations and World Politics* (Cambridge: Harvard University Press, 1972).

new international organizations be needed, and to what extent may older organizations have to change in order to adapt creatively to transnational phenomena? [p. xi]

Not one of these questions embraces a specified outcome. All of them can be answered in a multitude of ways, many of which are contradictory and none of which is likely to encourage confidence that confusion is giving way to comprehension. At first glance, they may seem to be challenging questions, but the challenge is likely to wane as it becomes clear that virtually any response is appropriate. Indeed, on second thought, they may not even seem challenging: not one begins with the word "why" and thus not one is even potentially puzzling.

Let me not convey a holier-than-thou attitude. My own work suffers as much from the lack of genuine puzzles as that of others. Indeed, I am especially culpable, since my 1966 pre-theory article [7] and the subsequent efforts to organize the ICFP around, and sustain it by, the questions posed by the pre-theory made a virtue of what is here treated as a sin. That is, for years I have championed the idea that we should be investigating why nations do what they do. I have described this question as constituting an exciting, dramatic, compelling and sobering challenge that can readily serve as a basis for constructive and convergent inquiry. Indeed, for several years convergence did ensue and important insights into the dynamics of foreign policy did emerge. Yet, as already indicated, the pace of progress appears to have slowed and may even have come to a halt. The prime reason for this deceleration, I am now convinced, is that neither the pre-theoretical formulation nor the ICFP wrestled with any genuine puzzles. The question why nations do what they do is totally open-ended. It invites researchers to investigate whatever they want, irrespective of what others are investigating. It provides justification for nonconvergence and it fails to permanently engage our curiosities because it is not inherently puzzling.

IV

We need to start afresh, to relax in our gardens, emulate Newton and ponder the scene around us, allowing ourselves to be puzzled by those recurring patterns that seem self-evident but that somehow have never been adequately explained. I make it sound easy. Obviously it is not, else we would long since have been genuinely puzzled. Indeed, the more I have tried to identify foreign-policy patterns that are genuinely puzzling, the more confused I have become. The confusion suggests

[7] Reproduced in this volume as Chapter 6.

either that I know less about the dynamics of nation-state behavior than I have ever admitted or that there are no noteworthy recurring patterns in foreign policy, and plainly I cannot presently accept either of these conclusions.

If only to preserve my self-image and my basic intellectual commitments, I therefore dare conclude by identifying some possible puzzles. These do not consist exclusively of foreign-policy patterns, but they are highly relevant to the way in which nations conduct their external affairs and they do strike me as awesome. The phenomena I find awesome may not seem so to others, or they may not seem to fully meet the criteria established for genuine puzzles, but I am persuaded that the best method for generating genuine puzzles lies in our wonderment over the symmetry and persistence of patterns. Thus I have to display my awe in the hope of highlighting a methodology that can lead us on from confusion to puzzlement. If enough of us articulate our awe over the dynamics of world politics, perhaps some among us will come upon inherently intriguing and substantially important outcomes that are patterned and that thus serve to focus and discipline our inquiries.

My wonderment has both micro and macro dimensions. At the micro level, I am in awe of the tourist and many other occupants of roles in authority structures who always seem to comply with the directives of national governments as they participate in transnational processes. Only terrorists are an exception and, while they might be regarded as forerunners of an emerging pattern, I tend (perhaps because I am still deeply enmeshed in the nation-state model of world politics) to dismiss terrorists as deviant cases best explained through psychological analysis. I am puzzled by the regulariy of the compliance at national borders by tourists, traders, financiers and others who engage in border-crossing activities. Given the tendency of citizens everywhere to feel increasingly alienated from their governments and the equally pervasive trend of ethnic and other subnational groups siphoning off the loyalties of their members, I am impressed with the uniformity of the compliance. Such behavior strikes me as the end product of complex processes of legitimacy formation that we do not adequately grasp and that might provide greater insight into the global system's capacity for underlying change if treated as a puzzle and then solved.

My awe at the macro level revolves around the presence of national governments as key actors in all the new issues to which the mounting interdependence, expanding technology and shrinking resources of the world have given rise. Why is that national governments always succeed in intruding themselves into the authority structures that form around the new issues, and therefore transform such issues into *their* problems? If the new issues of space, the oceans, pollution and the like span political boundaries and if national governments are undergoing a substantial diminution of their capacities to govern, I am puzzled that governments invariably manage to assimilate the new issues rather than turning elsewhere for their solutions cr being rebuffed by other actors in their efforts to cope with them.[8] Again, such behavior seems awesome in its constancy. Surely if we probed the complex processes that produce such constancy we might begin to bring the dynamics of underlying system change into clearer focus.[9]

I maintain that these micro and macro concerns are not naive, that it is by no means self-evident why border-crossing activities are marked by habitual compliance or why governments intrude upon all transnational activities that are controversial. But I recognise that they may appear naive and obvious to others. What is a genuine puzzle for one analyst may well be no more than a trite observation for another. However, the degree to which my concerns constitute genuine puzzles is not the issue. The point is that we need to stand back in wonderment, letting our imaginations have free reign, so that the recurrent and important outcomes of world politics can come to seem puzzling, thereby compelling us to interactively focus our talents in disciplined and creative ways. It matters not at all whether readers find my concerns trite; what does matter is that they allow themselves to be awed by their subject. What features of the world scene, I cannot resist concluding, genuinely puzzle you?

---

[8] By the assimilation of issues I mean a process wherein high-level officials of a nation-state wrestle with the new problems, both among themselves and through diplomacy with counterparts abroad, and then pass on to subordinates the task of routinely administering the policies they develop to cope with the issues. As Keohane and Nye put it, "Issues are unlikely, in general, to remain indefinitely at the top level of governmental attention. Politicization may facilitate the resolution of issues, or at least the establishment of new structures and new assumptions within which particular questions can be settled at lower levels of the governmental hierarchy." Robert O. Keohane and Joseph S. Nye, Jr., "Transgovernmental Relations and International Organizations," World Politics, XXVII (October 1974), p. 59.

[9] My theoretical impulses tell me that the solution to the puzzle of why governments invariably co-opt new issues lies in the adaptive orientations and capacities of nations. See James N. Rosenau, The Adaptation of National Societies: A Theory of Political Behavior and Its Transformations (Morristown, N.J.: General Learning Press, 1970), an abridged version of which is reproduced in this volume as Chapter 18.

Part Three:
Basic Concepts

The introduction of scientific methods into a field of inquiry is bound to have consequences for the identity and nature of its basic concepts. The insistence on precise and operational definitions that accompanies a commitment to science necessitates the abandonment of value-laden concepts and the reformulation of ambiguous ones. Just as the mystical qualities attributed to alchemy and phlogiston rendered them useless as analytic concepts when chemistry moved in a scientific direction, so have similar qualities in the concepts of power and national interest reduced their utility in the scientific study of foreign policy.

Perhaps the main consequence of this process of reconceptualization is a proliferation of analytic equipment. Where one concept was once sufficient to denote a broad range of phenomena, several are needed when differences among the phenomena have been identified. Where mutually exclusive behaviors were once embraced by the same ambiguous concept, new concepts are needed when different empirical referents can be specified. A close examination of power as a prescientific instrument of foreign policy analysis, for example, yields the realization that it embraces both the possessions of nations and their relations with other nations. Separate concepts are therefore needed for these two dimensions if the phenomena they encompass are to be subjected to scientific analysis.

Unlike the wide-ranging previous chapters, each of the four that follows is distinguished by its concern with a single concept. The last three chapters seek primarily to expose the inadequacy of the prescientific equipment used to study foreign policy rather than to construct new conceptual equipment designed for precise empirical inquiry. The chapters on the national interest, decision-making, and intervention thus do more debunking than creating. It seems fair to assert, however, that this was a necessary step in the development of a more precise and empirical set of conceptual tools. The more creative task of actually developing such tools is undertaken in the chapter on calculated control and in the other parts of the book where the concepts of a penetrated system (Chapter VI), an issue-area (Chapter XVIII), a linkage (Chapter XV), and an undertaking (Chapter IV) are presented.

10 Calculated Control as a Unifying Concept in the Study of International Politics and Foreign Policy *

INTRODUCTION

Ever since World War II, students of international politics and foreign policy have been engaged in a restless search for major concepts that would enable them to organize the diffuse phenomena of the field in a coherent and meaningful way. System and process, power and capability, national interest and security, idealism and realism, decision and action, image and field—these are but a few of the roads down which theoreticians have carried their searches. More often than not, they have done this with considerable benefit to those who follow. Many of the conceptual roads are now solidly paved and are lined with clear and useful guideposts. Work on the concepts of system and process, for example, has infused order into the analysis of the relations among nations and the equilibria that result from the recurring patterns of their interaction. Similarly, attention given to the components of national interest and national capabilities has enhanced the analysis of ends and means in foreign policy and has facilitated predictions about how clashes between

* An earlier version of this chapter was published as Research Monograph No. 15 of the Center of International Studies, Woodrow Wilson School of Public and International Affairs, Princeton University (Princeton, N.J., Februray 10, 1963). Reprinted with the permission of the publisher.

two or more nations pursuing different goals and possessing unequal resources will turn out. In like manner, the elaboration of the concepts of decision and decision-making has clarified and furthered analysis of national action and the reasons why policy-makers act and react as they do.

For each step toward clarification, however, a price has been paid. Those formulations that are centered on specific concepts facilitate the identification and organization of crucial dimensions of the field; but, in so doing, they also make it more difficult to establish conceptual links between the action and interaction levels of analysis. The highways are well paved and well built, but they are too straight and do not intersect, being connected, at best, by secondary roads on which it is easy to get lost. More precisely, the penalty for concentrating on decision-making is an inability to explain outcomes: that is, what happens after decisions have been made and action taken. Knowledge of the perceptions and motives of policy-makers can hardly serve as a predictor of outcomes if the officials are operating with erroneous estimates of either their own capabilities or the nature of the international environment. Conversely, the cost of concentrating on outcomes and treating them as the result of different nations achieving different balances between their interests and their capabilities is an inability to identify the sources of policy-making behavior. An understanding of what happens when weak nations attack strong ones is of little value in explaining why the former sometimes challenge the latter.

To a certain extent, of course, the differences between the two levels of analysis cannot be avoided.[1] Obviously a different perspective is required, one that asks different questions and seeks different answers, whenever attention shifts from the units of a system to the system itself. On the other hand, comprehension of both national action and international interaction would presumably be advanced if an analytic framework were developed that served to link the two levels of analysis. Different questions may be posed at each level, and thus different data may have to be gathered; but the organizing concepts for both levels need not be separate or unique. Is it not possible to add well-paved interchanges to the highway system— to develop conceptual links between outcomes and decisions, between dynamic processes and static capabilities, between, in effect, international politics and foreign policy? This essay contends that such links can be developed and that the highway system is incomplete without them.

In order to construct a unified framework, however, we must avoid the widespread tendency to assume rather than to conceptualize the nature

---

[1] For a full and illuminating discussion of this point, see J. David Singer, "The Level-of-Analysis Problem in International Relations," *World Politics*, XIV (October 1961), pp. 77–92.

of the politics which occur at the international level. One reason for the lack of conceptual links is that most students in the international field have not treated their subject as local politics writ large. Instead, like advocates of bipartisanship in foreign policy, most students tend to view politics as "stopping at the water's edge" and consider that something different, international politics and foreign policy, takes place beyond national boundaries. Consequently, so much emphasis has been placed on the dissimilarities between international and other types of politics that the similarities have been overlooked and the achievement of conceptual unity has been made much more difficult. For example, because of their stress upon the fact that international political systems are lacking in authoritative decision-making structures, many analysts have largely overlooked unifying concepts developed in areas where the focus is upon sovereign actors. Lasswell and Kaplan's *Power and Society*[2] and Dahl and Lindblom's *Politics, Economics, and Welfare*[3] are only two of the major works which conceptualizations of international phenomena rarely cite, albeit some of their concepts might prove both relevant and useful.

In other words, just as atoms will be found in all types of matter, so will common elements be found in all types of politics. Political actors at all levels must engage in behavior that is uniform in certain respects. Whether authority is exercised legitimately, nonlegitimately, or illegitimately, there are, presumably, some types of action that occur in any political situation; and it is here, in the behavioral uniformities, that we must look for conceptual links. We must, in short, place international politics and foreign policy in a larger context. Such a context is outlined below, and a derivative of it—the concept of calculated control—is subsequently offered as a basis for constructing a unified framework.[4]

INTERNATIONAL POLITICIANS AND THEIR POLITICS

The tendency of researchers to assume rather than to conceptualize the politics of international life can be readily demonstrated. Even our language is illustrative. Terminologically, the world is peopled by all kinds

[2] Harold D. Lasswell and Abraham Kaplan, *Power and Society: A Framework for Political Inquiry* (New Haven: Yale University Press, 1950).
[3] Robert A. Dahl and Charles E. Lindblom, *Politics, Economics, and Welfare* (New York: Harper, 1953).
[4] The concept of calculated control has been elaborately developed in Neil A. McDonald, *Politics: A Study of Control Behavior* (New Brunswick, N.J.: Rutgers University Press, 1965). For other cogent treatments of control as an analytic concept, see Dahl and Lindblom, *op. cit.*, Chap. 4; and Felix E. Oppenheim, *Dimensions of Freedom* (New York: St. Martin's Press, 1961), Chaps. 2 and 3.

of politicians except international ones and is full of all kinds of politics except foreign ones. Office politicians sustain corporation politics; labor politicians perpetuate union politics; and academic and church politicians maintain the politics of educational and religious institutions. Indeed, the list is virtually endless, for wherever the endeavors of men are formally organized, some persons will engage in activities that others will view as "playing politics." In government and public affairs, of course, such activities amount less to a game that is played and more to a profession that is practiced—to a full-time occupation that is pursued in a host of functional areas and at a variety of systemic levels. Divide public affairs vertically by issue areas, and each area will be the subject of a specialized politics and will be the domain of specialized politicians. It is no strain on our common-sense use of words, for example, to speak of farm politics, of defense politics, or of the politics of the budget. Nor is our vocabulary taxed when we introduce horizontal subdivisions by cutting across all the issues and grouping them systemically. Such issue composites are readily designated as local, state, regional, or national politics and are viewed as the concern of local, state, regional, or national politicians.

Neither ordinary language nor the terminology of political analysis, however, maintains this consistency when inquiry moves to the international level. At least two inconsistencies stand out. The international equivalent of the action we normally call "domestic politics" is not foreign politics but foreign policy.[5] Similarly, logic requires that a practitioner of international politics be called an "international politician"; but, in fact, this term is rarely employed. Instead, he is called a "statesman," a "diplomat," a "world leader," or a "foreign policy official"—to mention but a few of the conventional designations. Even the late Dag Hammarskjöld, who devoted his full energies to practicing politics on an international scale, was never characterized as an "international politician." He may have been an "able diplomat," a "distinguished statesman," and a "gifted administrator"; but no one ever described him as a "skilled politician."

In view of the pejorative connotations often associated with politics, it is easy to understand why the mass media never refer to "international politicians" and their "foreign politics." More puzzling, however, is the presence of these inconsistencies in scholarly discourse. Why did not political scientists long ago iron out these simple and illogical quirks in their analytic language? Does their persistence reflect conceptual insufficiency rather than simply tolerance for imprecise terms? While our purpose is not that of advocating terminological tidiness or change, we would suggest

---

[5] Interestingly, in a number of other languages this inconsistency does not occur, because "policy" and "politics" are represented by the same word—which is usually translated as "politics."

that an affirmative answer must be given to the latter question. If a precise and accepted formulation of the political content of international phenomena were available, quirks in the language of political analysis would have probably disappeared long ago.

Even more persuasive evidence of the tendency to take the nature of international politics for granted is provided by the textbooks on the subject. Most text writers inadvertently avoid such conceptualization by mistaking the boundaries of the field for its contents. Instead of inquiring into the nature of political phenomena, these writers usually start by emphasizing that the field is a subcategory of a larger subject, international relations. All types of interaction—from the tourism of individuals to the trade of large companies—comprise the relations of nations, so the student is told, and thus to study international politics is to investigate only one of the many kinds of relations that occur among nations. Which kind? Why, obviously, the *political* relations of nations. Unfortunately, most text writers do not then proceed to conceptualize the distinctive features of political relations, apparently believing that they did so when they narrowed their focus down to only one of the possible types of international relations that might be studied.

Much the same kind of logic is employed by authors who analyze the notion that the international system lacks an environment because it encompasses all worldly phenomena. Such a conception is properly criticized on the grounds that we can hardly expect to be interested in everything that marks human affairs and that our focus must therefore be narrowed to a limited type of international system. Accordingly, it is cogently argued, the myriad phenomena which fall outside this limited system constitute its environment. At this point, however, the analysis usually loses its force. For again, text writers tend to fall back on an undefined concept when they are faced with the problem of characterizing the limited type of system that concerns them. Which type? Why, obviously, an international *political* system—the boundaries of which are said to be clearly delineated by virtue of the fact that it exists in an environment of nonpolitical phenomena.

Occasionally, text writers will attempt to break out of this circular chain of reasoning, stressing that international political relations involve relations between governments and that the boundaries of international political systems are delimited by the interactions of governments. Such a refinement, however, is also insufficient, since it merely substitutes "government" for "politics" and leaves unresolved the question of what distinguishes an international political act from all those international acts that are nonpolitical. Are governments the only actors that engage in international political relations and that comprise international political systems? Is every act of government a political act? Is the purchase of raw materials abroad by a government an international political act, and is the same behavior by a private corporation only an economic act? Or, if the government purchase is both a political and an economic act, which of its aspects are of the former type and which are of the latter? The text writers shed little light on such questions because they presume that the essential elements of politics are self-evident.

Harold and Margaret Sprout's *Foundations of International Politics* [6] is a noteworthy exception to the tendency of text writers to assume rather than to conceptualize the central phenomena of the field. The Sprouts are sensitive to the need to differentiate political transactions that cross national boundaries from those that are nonpolitical. Thus they develop the notion that "some conflict of purpose or interest" is the distinguishing feature of political transactions. They are aware that an element of opposition or resistance may be present in any transaction, and they therefore emphasize that their formulation obtains only under certain circumstances: "When the conflict of purpose or interest is significant—that is, when it is the essence of the situation—the transaction is called political."[7] The Sprouts recognize that this qualification can also lead to difficulties and that there are some situations (for example, a hard-fought soccer game between two international teams) in which conflict is the essential purpose, but which nevertheless can hardly be regarded as international politics. Hence they further refine their conceptualization by noting that only conflicts involving "the interaction and relations of organized political communities" constitute international politics, and by "organized political communities" they essentially mean national governments.[8]

Although the Sprouts' formulation is a vast improvement over those texts that take the nature of politics for granted, it is also insufficient. By restricting international politics to conflicts in which governments are involved, they never probe the nature of conflict in order to identify what renders it political. Their scheme does not differentiate political conflicts from other types, and thus it does not identify the characteristics that are present wherever politics is practiced—be it in a neighborhood, in a nation, or in an international organization. In effect, they define an international political act in terms of a particular actor—the organized political community—rather than in terms of certain qualities of the act

[6] Princeton: Van Nostrand, 1962.

[7] *Ibid.*, p. 76.

[8] *Ibid.*, p. 75. Apparently the Sprouts prefer to subsume national governments under the broader term "organized political communities" in order to cope with the problem that "in all states—but especially in Communist and other totalitarian systems—it is always difficult, and sometimes impossible," to distinguish between international political acts "that are official and those that are unofficial" (p. 142).

itself. Yet, if international politics is to be seen as simply one form of politics, then the behavior that constitutes it must be conceived and elaborated independently of the actor who engages in it.

Recent changes in the character of international actors further emphasize the need for a conception of international politics that is founded on the "what" and not on the "who" of behavior. The traditional actors, national governments, are no longer exclusive occupants of the world's political stage, and thus an analysis confined to their actions and interactions might overlook many crucial phenomena. Most notably, it might underrate the role played by increasing numbers of nongovernmental units which engage in behavior that in every respect but one—the legitimacy of sovereign authority—appears to have all the characteristics of international politics. More precisely, because of distintegrative tendencies in underdeveloped societies and because of integrative tendencies in regional international systems, a significant number of subnational and supranational units have emerged as actors who participate in diplomatic negotiations and in other transactions with national governments. Should not, for example, the U.N. Secretary-General's efforts to persuade members to meet their financial obligations be considered as international political acts? Cannot the same be said about many decisions reached by the Council of Ministers of the European Economic Community? Should not the activities of the Union Minière du Haute-Katanga in the Congo crisis (including its alleged attempt to buy Costa Rica's diplomatic recognition of Katanga Province for $850,000) be considered as international political behavior? Do not Angolese rebels engage in international politics whenever they seek arms and bases from foreign sources? Do not the broadcasts of Radio Free Europe, a nongovernmental organization, constitute international politics? Was not Bertrand Russell's public exchange of messages with Khrushchev at the height of the Cuban crisis, in October 1962, an international political act? Was it not such an act when, in May 1960, the Seafarers' International Union protested the United Arab Republic's practice of blacklisting ships that put in at Israeli ports by picketing U.A.R. ships that docked in New York? Although it seems logical to answer all these questions in the affirmative, this response cannot be given if international politics is considered to be sustained only by national actors. Nevertheless, most observers cling to such a conception. They do not deny the increasing importance of blocs, rebels, secessionists, and other nongovernmental groups; but, for a variety of reasons, few are willing to adjust their analytic equipment accordingly.[9] Instead,

[9] For a notable exception, as well as a compelling solution of the problem of delineating international actors, see Fred W. Riggs, "International Relations as a Prismatic System," *World Politics*, XIV (October 1961), pp. 144–150.

the tendency is to emphasize that the decline of the nation-state has not yet removed it from the center of the stage. Ultimate authority, it is stressed, still accrues primarily to national actors and therefore it is "unrealistic" or "premature" to give equal analytic status to subnational or supranational units. Consequently, nongovernmental actors are usually treated as secondary elements—"as components of the environment in which organized national political communities interact"[10]—even though it is conceded that their behavior can strongly influence the course of events and that, accordingly, their actions are both political and international.

But what renders a particular kind of behavior political? What are the common elements that will be found in all types of politics, irrespective of the identity of the actors? They have been variously identified in the literature. For Lasswell and Kaplan, the distinguishing feature of political phenomena is "the shaping, distribution, and exercise of power."[11] For Dahl, the key variables in political analysis are the base, means, amount, and scope of the power which actors exercise.[12] For Parsons, the process of mobilizing support has come to be the essential element of a political act.[13] For Banfield, "the patterns of influence by which action is concerted in public matters" constitute the core materials for students of politics.[14] Although such formulations underlie much that follows, we prefer not to employ any of them or even a composite of several of them explicitly. When extended to international phenomena, concepts such as power have tended to confound rather than to clarify matters. As noted below, these concepts also incline researchers to focus on peripheral rather than on central questions. Hence, although no scheme is free of methodological problems, it seems worthwhile to develop our own formulation by searching anew for the behavior that is common to all kinds of politics.

Such a search can be profitably launched by reducing to the simplest possible terms the phenomena that attract our attention when we regard political elements as being present in any situation. Whatever the identity of the actors involved—be they persons, roles, organizations, nations, or blocs of nations—our interest is awakened whenever one actor engages in an action that is designed to affect the behavior of another. If the behavior of the second actor is different from that which would have been

---

10 Harold and Margaret Sprout, *op. cit.*, p. 75.

11 *Op. cit.*, p. 75.

12 Robert A. Dahl, "The Concept of Power," *Behavioral Science*, II (July 1957), pp. 201–215.

13 Talcott Parsons, " 'Voting' and the Equilibrium of the American Political System," in Eugene Burdick and Arthur J. Brodbeck (eds.), *American Voting Behavior* (Glencoe: Free Press, 1959), pp. 80–120.

14 Edward C. Banfield, *Political Influence* (New York: Free Press, 1961), p. 4.

expected in the absence of action by the first, our interest is then fully aroused. For it is at this point, when the behavior of one actor has been modified in response to intervening acts by another, that we are inclined to wonder whether the situation has become a political one. And, upon further reflection, it becomes clear that these intended behavioral modifications and the processes whereby they occur—what we shall call control acts and relationships—constitute the elements that are present in any situation to which the label of politics might be attached. Attempts to modify behavior pervade smoke-filled rooms, legislative chambers, and diplomatic conferences. They constitute the orientations both of candidates toward electorates and of electorates toward candidates. They are present when chief executives seek legislative approval, when dictators subjugate masses, when factions search for support, when nations build alliances and contest enemies, when parties resign from cabinets, when agencies ask for larger budgets, when economic aid is allocated to foreign societies, and when interest groups contact mayors, governors, and presidents. It is possible, in short, to treat any political situation as an interaction pattern in which some actors (the controllers) are either producing or attempting to produce behavioral modifications on the part of other actors (the controllees).

Such a formulation, however, is much too general. Although it identifies the elements that are present in any political situation, these elements, under certain circumstances, will also be found in relationships that are not ordinarily considered to be political. Attempts to modify behavior also occur in families, classrooms, and factories. They are among the orientations of parents to children and children to parents. They are present when sellers offer their wares to buyers, when ministers exhort parishioners, when unions bargain for higher wages, when friends advise friends, when generals command troops, and when husbands and wives make requests of one another. Virtually every social role, in other words, requires that its occupant attempt to modify the behavior of others in certain ways and at certain times. Yet, obviously, we are only interested in particular kinds of roles, those that contribute to public affairs, and any scheme that obscures this focus is clearly in need of further development. More precisely, we need to identify criteria for distinguishing those behavioral modifications that are attempted or produced in situations with a high political content from those that are sought or induced in situations with a low political content (henceforth to be designated as nonpolitical relationships).

The essential difference between these two types of situations lies in what we shall call the "functional distance" that separates the controller from the controllee on those central matters that serve to initiate or to sustain the interaction between them. In any relationship, interaction ensues on the basis of the expectations that each actor has of himself and of the other actor, and functional distance is a measure of the clarity and the perceived coincidence of these expectations. Two actors are considered to be functionally close when their responses to one another are founded on expectations that are clearly defined and are perceived to be very similar, if not identical. Conversely, they are regarded as functionally far apart when their interaction expectations are ambiguous and are perceived to be actually or potentially discrepant. Role clarity is measured neither by the variety of occasions in which interaction is expected to occur nor by the number of role expectations that link controllers and controllees. Rather, it is measured by the preciseness and the perceived mutuality of the expectations—by the extent to which the actors have a shared knowledge of how they are supposed to respond to one another on those critical matters that form the basis of their relationship.

A comparison of political and nonpolitical situations suggests that the functional distance that prevails in the former type tends to be greater than the distance that is usually characteristic of the latter type. The difference, of course, is not an absolute one. As we have already noted, activity labeled "politics" can be present in the family, the corporation, the church, or any organized situation. It is certainly true, moreover, that on occasion the effort of a controller to make the controllee's expectations of their interaction coincide with his own—an effort that might be regarded as the essence of a political act—can be as great in, say, a family as in an international relationship. Relatively speaking, however, the presence of role clarity and perceived mutuality of expectations is less noticeable in those matters that initiate and sustain political situations than in those that comprise the central aspects of nonpolitical relationships.

Let us first look more closely at nonpolitical situations. Virtually any example that comes to mind is distinguished by the functional proximity of its interacting roles. Whatever behavioral modification is attempted or produced in nonpolitical relationships, ordinarily the actors will have been guided by relatively clear and coincident expectations of how they are supposed to interact. These expectations can range from the very general to the highly specific; but, whatever the degree of generality, both the controller and the controllee share the same conception of the basis for their interaction. Contrast the milkman and his customer with the boss and his employee. In the first case, the mutual expectations are quite specific. Both know that the milkman will deliver four bottles of skimmed milk and one of buttermilk every two days and that the customer will pay the going price for them. They also know that if the customer wishes to change his order to two bottles of buttermilk, the milkman will modify his behavior to comply with the request. The boss and the employee, on the other hand, may not know precisely what each will do in every situation in which they interact, but both are clearly aware that if the boss insists, the employee will comply with his wishes. Nonpolitical relationships can also vary from those in which the interaction expectations are derived from a concentration of authority in one of the actors to those in which the expectations are based on an equal division of authority between them. But again, whatever the degree of hierarchy, both parties accept it and guide their responses accordingly. A comparison of parent-child and husband-wife relationships illustrates this variability. Both the parent and the child know that their roles are hierarchically linked and that authority is concentrated in the parent. Hence, on a variety of occasions, their interaction is determined by what they commonly understand to be behavior appropriate to such a hierarchical arrangement. Just as parents are likely to modify their child's behavior when they tell him to go to bed, so will the child probably modify parental behavior when he asks to be taken to the movies. In the husband-wife case, however, there may be no hierarchical dimension whatsoever. Yet, the two actors remain functionally close because, on most matters, they both understand when it is appropriate to comply with one another's requests. Thus, the husband is likely to modify the wife's behavior when he asks for a sandwich, and the reverse is likely to happen when she asks him to mow the lawn.

In political situations, however, the functional distance that separates controllers and controllees is usually much greater. Behavioral modification is attempted or produced through interaction in which both actors' expectations of how they are supposed to respond to one another are neither clear-cut nor perceived to be coincident. Expectations may, in fact, coincide in political relationships, but normally one of the actors (or both) is uncertain as to whether coincidence prevails. Consequently, he acts to achieve clarity and mutuality of expectations. Once role clarity is achieved and expectations are shared—that is, when all concerned know how they are supposed to interact—the situation is transformed from a political to an administrative one. An executive agency or an army, for example, is not ordinarily regarded as a political organization precisely because the bases of interaction within it have been plainly explicated. Consequently, because they consist of roles that are less plainly specified and expectations that are less widely shared, political relationships are not characterized by a high degree of hierarchy. Rather, authority is usually dispersed more or less equally among the actors. Consider the case of the elected official and the citizen—perhaps the most obvious example of a political relationship. Neither role is subordinate to the other, and thus both must bargain in order to modify one another's behavior. But how they should do so—when demands are appropriate, when acquiescence is desirable, or when compromise is in order—is not a specified and explicit dimension of their roles. The latter do not even require them to be personally acquainted or to engage in direct interaction except on the infrequent occasions when elections are held. Indeed, the citizen and the official are functionally so far apart that the citizen may not be aware that he is interacting with the official or even that his acceptance or rejection of a proposed policy may be a consequence of that interaction.

This does not mean that political relationships are totally lacking in role clarity and shared expectations. Certain kinds of political situations may be highly formalized and may be founded on a number of clearly defined patterns of interaction. Diplomatic situations are an obvious example. Negotiations are usually conducted within an elaborate framework of formal role requirements that are widely accepted and that condition the manner in which even the most antagonistic diplomats respond to one another. Similarly, executive-legislative relations are, to a large extent, routinized in all governments and, consequently, both the executive and the legislator share many expectations of how they should interact. The President of the United States knows he should answer legislative mail promptly and the member of Congress knows that he should defer to presidential wishes on ambassadorial appointments. In spite of the numerous expectations that may be unambiguous and widely shared in political relationships, however, their central dimensions tend to lack clear and mutual role definitions. On the substantive matters that initiate and sustain political relations—on those matters that we ordinarily call "policy questions"—role clarity is at a minimum and the outcome of interaction is far from predetermined. In these critical areas of the relationship, none of the parties to it can be sure of how the others will react or of the type of action that will produce behavioral modifications. Neither the diplomatic situation nor the executive-legislative relationship encompasses role expectations that clearly indicate how the interaction should unfold when one of the actors presses for approval of a new policy.[15]

15 To be sure, and as previously noted, the President and the Congressman may have compatible expectations with respect to their interaction on the proposed policy, but the compatibility is not part of the relationship and, therefore, neither actor is likely to be certain of the extent to which their views coincide. Indeed, the fact that a minimum of role clarity on substantive matters is inherent in political relationships becomes especially evident if we posit one or both of the actors as recognizing that compatible expectations prevail in a particular instance. Under these circumstances the compatibility is likely to be intentionally obscured by the actors who recognize it in order to enhance their bargaining position on those matters which are not characterized by shared expectations. Refusal to admit coincident expectations is, in short, the politician's way of creating or maintaining leverage in a situation.

The functional distance that distinguishes political situations from nonpolitical ones may be discerned in the rhetoric of the appeals on which controllers base their efforts to modify the behavior of controllees. The less the actors are functionally interdependent—that is, the greater the distance between them—the higher will be the level of abstraction at which their interests converge and thus the more abstract must be the appeals of the controller. In nonpolitical situations, the interacting roles tend to be so close that concrete appeals can serve to bring about the intended modifications. The parent is able to exert control by appealing to the specific interests of his child ("The picnic begins early tomorrow, so go to bed"), as is the boss with respect to his employee ("Improve this sales campaign, or you will be fired") or the wife with respect to her husband ("Our lawn is a mess, so please mow it"). Controllers in political situations, on the other hand, must rely on more abstract appeals in order to bridge the greater distance that separates them from controllees. The elected official, for example, is not able to appeal to the immediate interests of every citizen. Rather, if he is to succeed in modifying the behavior of a large number of citizens, he must invoke precise and abstract goals ("Vote for me and you will contribute to the nation's security!"). Similarly, if the President is to succeed in modifying the behavior of a majority of the members of Congress, he must appeal to a generalized set of widely shared values. He could, to be sure, cast his appeal to a particular Congressman in a very concrete mold ("Support my program and your district will receive government contracts"), but this may not be very compelling to other legislators whose constituencies have different needs and make different demands. Besides, such concrete appeals can backfire in a number of ways. The Congressman may feel he is being blackmailed and immediately reject the appeal. He may go even further and publicize the President's methods, thereby arousing the antagonism of other legislators as well as the hostility of the public. Indeed, precisely because they are so concrete, such appeals are widely regarded as "dirty politics." Thus, the President is likely to make concrete appeals only as a last resort in a highly critical situation. Normally he will appeal to the Congressman's sense of fair play, party loyalty, or patriotism before he cites the immediate benefits that may accrue to the legislator's constituency. Because they are functionally remote, in short, controllers in political situations have to persuade, cajole, or otherwise convince the controllees, whereas their counterparts in nonpolitical situations need merely to direct, command, or request in order to evoke the desired responses.

Let us summarize by emphasizing again that the distinction between political and nonpolitical situations is relative and not absolute. Functional distance can be of varying magnitudes and all we are saying is that the more distant two actors are from one another, the more likely we are to regard as political acts their attempts to modify one another's behavior. To state the point in McDonald's terms, when politics is the dominant feature of a situation, and not just an element of it, the objects of the controller's attempts to modify behavior are located in his "more remote" rather than his "close at hand" environment.[16] Exactly where the line is drawn between the two types of environment depends, of course, on the purposes and the criteria used. What is "close at hand" from one perspective may be quite remote from another.[17]

Both the similarities and the dissimilarities between international and other types of politics follow logically from the foregoing considerations. On the one hand, international politics is similar to local or national politics through the fact that, in each case, the actors seek to modify behavior in their remote environments. Whether the actors are engaged in local, national, or international politics, their task is to mobilize support —to engage in control relationships—which will facilitate the preservation of those aspects of the environment that are desirable and the altera-

---

[16] *Op. cit.*, Introduction and Chap. 1.

[17] Consider, for example, the hypothetical case of two concerts given by the New York Philharmonic, one in New York and the other in Moscow, both for devotees of music. If these events are analyzed exclusively in musical terms, the orchestra and its audiences will be treated as proximate to each other and attention will focus on differences in the quality of the two performances. But if the Moscow audience is recognized to be functionally more remote than the New York audience, the Moscow concert acquires political overtones and, accordingly, it immediately becomes apparent that performance quality is not the only difference between the two occasions. In the first place, the Moscow concert is likely to have been arranged by an international actor. Secondly, its program probably will have included two opening numbers—the American and the Russian national anthems—not played in New York and included as abstract appeals that would span the greater functional distance prevailing in the Moscow auditorium.

The notion that relationships become increasingly political (and thereby require more diffuse and abstract appeals) as the functional distance between controllers and controllees increases can also be seen in situations that are normally considered to be nonpolitical. Let us examine the case of a department chairman in an academic institution who is seeking to win both administrative acceptance of a new research center and approval of an appointee to a vacant post in his department. In making the latter request, he is functionally close to university officials in the sense that they are supposed to interact on such matters. Consequently, in trying to modify their behavior to the extent of having them approve the new appointment, he is likely to contend that such an addition to the staff would be "good for the department" or "good for the students." His appeal, in other words, would be a specific one and his action would be called administrative rather than political. In seeking acceptance of the research center, however, precedents are fewer, and the university officials would therefore be functionally more distant from him. Hence, his appeal is likely to be based on the argument that the center would be "good for the university and the society" or "good for science and knowledge." Upon hearing such an appeal, many observers would be inclined to regard it as an indication of the presence of politics in the situation.

tion of those that are not. Just as participants in local politics seek to reduce opposition to fluoridation of water, so do their counterparts at the national level seek to win acceptance of a program of medical care for the aged. And, in essentially the same manner, so do international actors seek to build support for a different arrangement in Berlin, for a new arms control plan, or for an altered hemispheric policy toward Cuba.

On the other hand, international politics is differentiated from other types of politics by the much greater functional distance that separates its actors. Stated succinctly, local or national politics consists of the acts and processes whereby control over more remote environments *within* societies is either attempted or exercised, whereas international politics involves control relationships that *transcend* national boundaries. Viewed in this way, and given the strength of the loyalties and traditions encompassed by national boundaries, it might be said that international politics is the "purest" type of politics. Unlike most politicians, who are at least linked to controllees through common citizenship, international actors are not members of the society to which the objects of their control belong. Thus the functional distance that they must span is especially wide. Indeed, international politicians are so remote from controllees that their control acts must ordinarily involve appeals at the highest possible levels of abstraction. Whereas local politicians seek to modify the behavior of controllees by pledging to remove the snow from their streets, and whereas national politicians attempt to mobilize the support of controllees by promising them greater security from attack, international politicians can offer little more than ambiguous conditions, such as "world peace" or "lessened tensions," in exchange for alterations in their behavior. Little wonder that foreign policy officials the world over are criticized by their domestic publics for not accomplishing more in the international arena. The international politician has so little to offer in exchange for modified behavior on the far side of national boundaries that his is an almost impossible task. He is doing well if he can keep existing situations abroad from getting any worse. The international politician who promotes new and desired changes in the external environment is a rare figure indeed!

The preceding formulation also offers a means for identifying the international politician. Any actor who undertakes to control the behavior of others not belonging to his own society and not otherwise functionally related to him is, for all practical purposes, an international politician. Thus, all chief executives, secretaries of state, defense ministers, and other top officials are international politicians. So are bureaucrats who plan foreign aid programs or who develop propaganda strategies.[18] So too are

18 Such persons may adhere to a strict neutrality on domestic issues and thereby exemplify the ideal civil servant. But if they engage in calculations about the

executives and bureaucrats of international organizations who seek to preserve or to re-establish peace in, between, or among nations. And, no less significantly, so were the Union Minière, the Angolese rebels, Radio Free Europe, Bertrand Russell, and the Seafarers' International Union in the aforementioned situations. In all of these cases, the actors made an effort to bring about changes on the part of persons or groups abroad with whom they had no functional relationship. Of course, and to repeat, whenever a controller is functionally close to the foreign actor whose behavior he seeks to modify (for example, when an importer bargains with an exporter abroad or when a new defense minister nurtures the loyalties of his commanders in the field), then his actions would not ordinarily be regarded as international politics, albeit they might constitute international relations.

It should be noted that some international politicians—those who hold high offices in national subsystems—occupy a dual role and are burdened with the additional responsibilities of domestic politics. They must, as it were, live in two worlds and attempt to maintain control over two different environments. Usually the two worlds are inextricably linked, thereby forcing dual politicians to work to achieve some balance between them. Reconciliation is not, however, always possible. The requirements of the two kinds of politics frequently conflict, and dual politicians find that they necessarily lose support in one environment as a consequence of mobilizing it in the other. Compromises made in diplomatic negotiations, for example, may bring about desirable modifications abroad while arousing opposition at home. In other instances, dual politicians can achieve a balance only through the circuitous process of mobilizing support in one environment as a means of exercising control in the other. In order to win acceptance of their domestic policies, they may have to achieve "successes" abroad or, contrariwise, the outcome of their efforts to modify behavior in the international environment may depend on their ability to marshal support at home. In short, the tasks of dual politicians are probably more complex, more delicate, and more difficult than those performed by any other type of political actor.

This line of reasoning also helps to clarify the role played by sovereignty and legitimacy in international politics. Thus far we have ignored these central phenomena in order to discern the behavioral uniformities that link international with other types of politics. On the basis of the foregoing, however, it seems plain that the absence of an authori-

---

ways in which other societies will be affected by one type of foreign aid rather than by another, then they are making the kinds of control estimates that politicians have made since time immemorial, and it is in this sense that they must be regarded as international politicians as well as national civil servants.

tative decision-making structure introduces more than mere legal distinctions between international and other types of politics. If politics is viewed as the exercise of control across wide functional distances, then sovereign and legitimate authority emerge as environmental conditions that tend to enhance the tasks of local or national politicians and to inhibit the efforts of international politicians. People are predisposed to regard as binding the decisions and directives issuing from legitimate governmental authority. No less importantly, at both the local and national levels the legitimacy of governments renders them units to which people attach strong loyalties. Man's predispositions to abide by the law and to attach loyalties to governments dominate the environment of any politician. These predispositions facilitate the work of local and national politicians because, obviously, it is easier to modify the behavior of controllees who are inclined to regard the control acts as emanating from legitimate sources. Furthermore, local or national politicians are able to identify themselves with symbols to which the objects of their control are loyal. They can, as it were, take advantage of the legitimacy inherent in their positions. International politicians, on the other hand, must *overcome* these environmental conditions. They cannot invoke a widely shared set of symbols in order to command the obedience of the objects of their control. Nor can they rely on the law-abiding inclinations of the controllees. Rather, they have to modify behavior in spite of such factors. The objects of their control attach loyalty to different sovereign units and abide by different conceptions of legitimacy. International politicians must somehow bypass these obstacles if their control acts are to be successful. Our formulation does not, in short, downgrade the relevance of sovereignty to international politics. Clearly sovereignty is no less important when it is conceived in a control context than when it is viewed in a legal context.

Finally, the concept of modifying behavior across wide functional distances helps to clarify the nature of international political systems and to delineate the boundaries between them and their nonpolitical environments. Such systems consist of the interaction patterns through which the actors who comprise them exert control over one another. Thus, to analyze the balance and stability of international systems is to investigate recurring control acts in juxtaposition to the responses they invoke. When viewed in this context, a perfectly balanced international system is one in which the acts of the controllers are exactly offset by the counteracts of the controllees. Conversely, international systems experience lessened stability whenever one of their actors is able to modify the behavior of another system member to either a greater or a lesser extent than in the past. Systemic processes do not operate, however, if the interaction among the actors is based on something other than efforts to modify behavior. Consider the extreme example of musicales held by chiefs of state for the diplomatic corps. Such events would not ordinarily be regarded as part of an international political system as long as the actors involved were responsive to the music rather than to one another's control acts. The boundaries of international systems, in other words, are determined by the actions and resources that contribute to the initiation or maintenance of control relations between functionally distant international actors. All other phenomena form the environment within which international systems function and to which they adapt. Some environmental phenomena may be highly relevant to the functioning and stability of an international system, but they would not be regarded as systemic properties unless they served control purposes. The pattern of foreign trade, for instance, can be extremely important as either a stabilizing or an unsettling factor in the international political system. Whatever its effects, however, such a pattern is normally sustained by efforts to maximize profits rather than control, and thus it is best viewed as an international economic system prominently located in the environment of the international political system.[19]

THE CALCULATED CONTROL FRAMEWORK

Having said that international politics and foreign policy consist of the calculated acts and the processes of interaction whereby behavior is modified across national boundaries, we must now look more closely at the component parts of these core phenomena. In order to emphasize that the concept of calculated control can serve to unify the diverse aspects of the field, and in order to proceed on the basis of explicit definitions, we will analyze the core phenomena in the following terms:

Attempts to modify behavior are defined as *control acts*. These are undertaken by *controllers* who seek to induce modifications on the part of *controllees*. The modifications envisioned by controllers are designated as *control objectives* and the characteristics of controllees toward which acts are directed are regarded as *control targets*. Objectives, targets, and acts are derived from calculations that controllers make in the form of

[19] Much the same can be said in reply to the aforementioned question of how governmental purchases of raw materials abroad differ from those made by private corporations. If the purpose of the purchase is, for example, to shore up the economy of the selling society and thereby to make it more resistant to Communist penetration, it matters little which actor acquires the materials. Under such circumstances, the purchases constitute international political acts that either perpetuate or alter an international political system. If, on the other hand, the purchases were made in order to supply the needs of domestic consumers, then, irrespective of the identity of the purchaser, they would be international economic acts that either maintain or change an international economic system.

control decisions. Those factors that controllers can or cannot mobilize in support of their acts are conceived to be *control capacities* and the translation of capacities into acts is seen as the use of *control techniques.* Modifications of otherwise expected behavior are considered to be *control changes* undertaken or experienced by controllees, while the factors that can or do enable controllees to offset acts and to minimize changes are viewed as *control limits.* The interaction between controllers and controllees is defined as a *control process.* Actors that participate in the same process are regarded as having a *control relationship* or as being in a *control relation.* Finally, the new condition of a relationship that results from process and change is considered to be a *control outcome.*

Several general features of this scheme must be noted at the outset. First, it should be emphasized that the classification of an actor in a relationship as either a controller or a controllee depends on the observer's perspective. An actor (politician, nation, or bloc of nations) is a controller to the extent that it attempts to modify the behavior of other actors and a controllee to the extent that it experiences changes induced by others. This means that the designation of controller and controllee can apply to both actors in a relationship. If each engages in calculations leading to acts that posit the other actor as the target, then both will be the initiators and the objects of control. Indeed, this is the "normal" situation in international politics. Concessions made by both sides in diplomatic negotiations illustrate the large extent to which international actors occupy the twin role of controller-controllee. Occasionally, even a small nation that cowers before the military strength of a large one is able, through the threat of noncompliance, to modify the latter's oppressive behavior. In short, we do not equate controllers with the most powerful actors and controllees with the weakest. The key to classification lies in an actor's location in a sequence of behavioral modification and not in its relative capabilities.

The possibility that weak actors can be classified as controllers suggests a second general characteristic of the control framework: namely, that the concept of control is used in an analytic rather than an evaluative way. The control framework contains neither implicit nor explicit judgments as to the desirability of using or avoiding control techniques. Controllers are neither "bad" nor "good"; rather, they are simply actors who attempt to modify behavior. To be controlled is neither desirable nor undesirable; rather, it is only a condition in which actors are observed to be. To control is to coerce or to persuade, to use emotional appeals or scientific proof, to promote tyranny or freedom. Control is operative as long as behavioral modification is intended or induced, irrespective of the direction and nature of the changes that might or do result. This value-free use of the concept requires emphasis because, more often than not, social scientists either attach value connotations to it or eschew its use in order to minimize value judgment. It is probably not much of an overstatement to assert that, for many observers, the word "control," and perhaps especially the words "calculated control," stir up images of *1984* and of onslaughts on human dignity in which secretive and devious men trick unsuspecting people into acting contrary to their own self-interest. Such connotations, however, are not inherent in the word and tend only to hinder the development of a concept that, as will be shown, has many advantages over allied and more "acceptable" concepts such as power and influence.

The reasons for limiting our framework to control that is calculated, as distinguished from control that occurs unintentionally, also require comment. Certainly, much of the modification of behavior that occurs in human relations is not planned by those whose actions intervene to alter the expected behavior of others. Commonplace are the situations in which the attempts of an international actor to control one situation lead to unforeseen changes—modifications of behavior—in the target or in other actors. Indeed, a foremost task of foreign policy officials is that of anticipating unintended consequences of control decisions and determining whether these will be more damaging than the changes that the calculated acts are expected to yield.[20] Because control is sometimes used to describe unplanned behavioral modifications, the adjective "calculated" has been introduced into the framework. Furthermore, since unexpected behavior can occur in response to nonhuman events, the restriction of our focus to calculated control emphasizes that we are chiefly interested in action that stems from human thoughts, perceptions, and evaluations.

But why confine the framework only to control that is calculated? We do this because, upon reflection, it is clear that the attention of students of international politics and foreign policy is usually drawn to those acts, decisions, relationships, events, or situations that are the result of intentionality. International crises, for example, interest us precisely because they involve two or more actors who have developed contrary and conflicting calculations as to how the same target should be controlled. To be sure, unexpected events, such as the crash of an airplane carrying the Secretary-General of the United Nations, can precipitate crisis situations. For such situations to be sustained, however, a clash must ensue between the calculated acts of different actors who aim to prevent the newly created

[20] Strictly speaking, if the potentially damaging and unintended consequences are anticipated and are nevertheless accepted as necessary to the achievement of other objectives, they become, in effect, calculated changes that officials regretfully foster.

conditions from adversely affecting their interests. In like manner, foreign policies occupy our attention precisely because they involve purpose and calculation. Indeed, a foreign policy might be roughly defined as a set of planned guidelines for exercising as much control as possible over existing, anticipated, or unforeseen circumstances in the international environment. Although unexpected incidents or unplanned consequences may be among the most dramatic moments in world affairs, we invariably find ourselves interpreting and evaluating both exciting and mundane events in the context of encounters between purposeful acts that are derived from explicit estimates and based on conscious motives. In short, wherever we begin, our interests always return us to control that is calculated. Using the concept of calculated control explicitly as the organizing principle of our framework thus enables us to identify and examine those aspects of diverse phenomena that are of primary rather than of secondary interest.

This does not mean that the calculations of international actors are necessarily rational or elaborate. The concept of calculation assumes only that acts are undertaken deliberately rather than at random. It may well be that rational action in international affairs is ordinarily impossible. It may well be that most actors usually proceed on the basis of only the dimmest perceptions of the international environment, that their ability to relate means to ends is highly circumscribed, that they are far from clear as to whether their acts will produce the intended effects, and that, in fact, their efforts are frequently destined to fail and perhaps even to be counterproductive.[21] It is no doubt true, moreover, that actors often see themselves as "probing" rather than "controlling," as "taking a chance" rather than "attempting to control," as merely "coping" with situations rather than "controlling" them. However, in spite of their self-perceptions, and notwithstanding their imperfect pictures of the world and of the processes by which behavior is modified, actors do proceed consciously rather than capriciously. They do act on the basis of some kind of estimate of what needs to be done rather than for no reason at all. At least they think they know why they are doing what they are doing. The 1962 blockade of Cuba is a case in point. "No one can foresee precisely what course it will take," President Kennedy conceded in explaining the action. But this lack of clarity did not prevent an assessment that more would be gained and less would be lost by imposing a blockade than by

---

[21] For an excellent analysis of the reasons why policy-making ordinarily falls far short of being fully rational, see Charles E. Lindblom, "The Science of 'Muddling Through,'" *Public Administration Review*, XIX (Spring 1959), pp. 79–88. Another valuable source is Sidney Verba, "Assumptions of Rationality and Non-Rationality in Models of the International System," *World Politics*, XIV (October 1961), pp. 93–117.

launching an air strike or an invasion. International action, in short, does not occur by chance. It stems from at least a minimal set of expectations about changes that may be achieved or prevented abroad, and it is in this sense that control acts are considered to be calculated.[22]

Nor is our restriction of the framework to calculated control meant to imply that we are dismissing as irrelevant the unintended consequences of control. Clearly, these can be of considerable importance in world politics. They can substantially affect the balance between the controller's capacities and the limits imposed by the controllee, and an alteration of this sort might thereby change their relationship and alter the potentialities for future control. The unintended consequences of a given act may even prove to be more significant than the planned changes which it initiates. Furthermore, the very acts by which controllers change controlees may result in consequences for a third actor (or even for the interaction between the third and still a fourth actor), and these consequences may, in turn, feed back as determinants of the controller-controllee relationship. The solid backing given by the Organization of American States to the United States' decision to blockade Cuba, for example, was not anticipated by the Soviet Union when the latter introduced offensive weapons into the Caribbean, and this hemispheric solidarity appears to have had a marked effect on subsequent relations between East and West. Yet, while the unintended consequences of control acts are obviously too numerous and too important to ignore, it seems preferable not to give them a formal place in our framework and, instead, to treat them as part of the ever-changing environment to which actors must adapt. In this way, we recognize their importance without attentuating our primary concern with behavioral modifications that are calculated.

One other general characteristic of the framework needs to be emphasized: namely, that it does not encompass all the behavioral modifications

---

[22] Admittedly, there may still be some international actors whose decisions are not based on even a minimum degree of calculation. It has been reported, for example, that the Dalai Lama of Tibet relied on the "will of the gods" in deciding not to flee when the Chinese Communists occupied his country in October 1950: instead of estimating whether he could best serve Tibet by going abroad or by remaining at home, the Dalai Lama is alleged to have written "stay" on one slip of paper and "leave" on another, to have then wrapped each slip in a wax ball affixed to the spokes of a giant wheel, and, finally, to have whirled the wheel around until one ball came off and thereby conveyed to him the course of action that the gods wanted him to take. Such a decision-making process, however, attracts our attention precisely because calculation is conspicuously absent. For this reason, occasions of this sort are perhaps better characterized as exceptions that prove the rule than as refutations of the presumption that international action emanates from conscious calculations. Indeed, when mass demonstrations led the Chinese to tighten their control over Tibet in March 1959, the Dalai Lama apparently used different decision-making procedures and managed to go safely into exile.

that international actors experience. Only the modifications that would not otherwise be expected signify the presence of control acts and alert the observer to the operation of control processes. Alterations in the foreign policies of democratic societies that result from elections are illustrative of behavioral modifications not falling within the control framework. The policy revisions could have been expected since they are fully explicable in terms of domestic political variables. They are, of course, highly relevant to future control acts and relations; but, in themselves, the revised policies cannot be traced to acts by other international actors and thus they do not reflect control.

PRESERVATIVE VERSUS PROMOTIVE CONTROL

As the foregoing paragraphs suggest, a useful distinction can be made between control acts that are designed to prevent modifications on the part of controllees and those acts that are intended to foster new behavioral patterns. The former type will be designated as "preservative control" and the latter type as "promotive control." This distinction is important for at least two reasons. First, the preservation of .prevailing behavior may involve entirely different techniques, capacities, limits, and relationships than are required for the promotion of new behavior. It is likely, for example, that the direction and the intensity of change are easier to control—that is, fewer and less elaborately mobilized capacities are needed to offset fewer limits—when acts are designed to prevent the deterioration of old patterns than when they attempt to encourage the growth of new ones. Second, the requirements of preservative control are often opposed to those of promotive control, thereby confronting controllers with perhaps the most difficult kind of decision they have to make—the choice between desirable preservative changes that have undesirable promotive consequences or, alternatively, undesirable preservative consequences that accompany desirable promotive changes. In many respects, this choice has been a central dilemma of American foreign policy since the end of World War II: should emphasis be placed on the preservation of NATO at the expense of antagonistic consequences in the underdeveloped countries, or should new ties with the latter countries be promoted at the cost of setbacks to the strength of the Western alliance?

The two types of control are also distinguished by the fact that preservative control is more difficult to research than is promotive control. Empirical investigation of the former is hindered because, paradoxically, it equates modified behavior with unaltered action. Preservative control involves efforts to prevent the disruption of behavioral patterns that, in the absence of intervening acts, would be expected to change. Under these circumstances the unexpected, and thus the modified, behavior is that which remains unaltered when viewed from the perspective of passing time. Again we can use the example of a democratic nation that has just had an election that is expected to alter its foreign policies. Let us assume that the alterations are expected to be directed at a nondemocratic neighbor. If the latter country has intervened with a threat to counter the proposed policy revisions by cutting off trade relations and if, subsequently, the revisions fail to occur, then the undemocratic actor may be regarded as having controlled the democratic actor even though no net change in the behavior of the latter has taken place.

THE TARGETS OF CONTROL

Thus far we have said that calculated control is operative when controllees undergo unexpected behavioral modifications. Elaboration of our framework, however, requires us to specify the various types and characteristics of controllees that can experience modification. It seems necessary to identify nine concrete types of controllees toward which acts can be directed.[23] In addition, there are three analytic [24] aspects of controllees, at least one of which must serve as a target for these acts. More precisely, acts can be directed either at the *structure of* international organizations, of alliances or blocs, of bilateral or multilateral relationships, of issues or situations, of national societies, and of subnational groups; or at the *behavior* or *attitudes* of officials, elites, and mass publics. Thus, as Table 10-1 indicates, our framework comprises a total of twelve primary control targets.

The basis for separating the structural, behavioral, and attitudinal aspects of controllees is that each of these can change independently of the other two, and each can do so at a different rate and in a different direction. Neither social nor individual changes necessarily occur in simple, linear sequences. If attitudes are defined as predispositions to respond in particular ways and if behaviors are defined as the responses that actually take place, it becomes clear that behavioral modifications can occur without corresponding attitudinal changes. When the Communists erected

---

[23] This total could, in turn, be doubled if the distinction between preservative and promotive control were introduced; and it could then be nearly tripled if an "ally-neutral-enemy" subcategorization were employed (see the columns of Table 10-1).

[24] For a discussion of the distinction between analytic and concrete units of analysis, see Marion J. Levy, Jr., *The Structure of Society* (Princeton: Princeton University Press, 1952), pp. 88–89.

Table 10 - 1   The Targets of Control and the Changes They Can Undergo

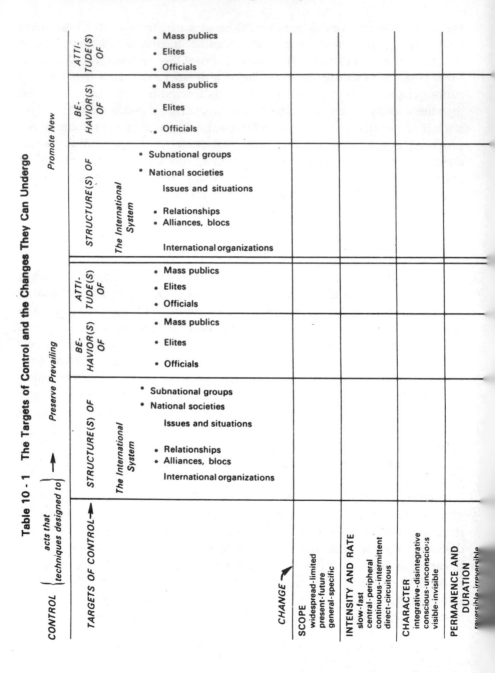

a wall in Berlin, for example, they controlled the behavior of East Germans by preventing their escape across the border, but apparently they did not alter the hostile attitudes that East Germans hold toward their rulers. Likewise, attitudinal modification can take place without corresponding alterations in behavior. The circumstances surrounding Russia's decision to resume nuclear testing on September 1, 1961—the very day when the leaders of neutralist countries were convening in Belgrade—are illustrative. Apparently, the resumption decision was based on a calculation that, although such an act might have attitudinal consequences in Belgrade, it would not produce immediate behavioral change. This gamble paid off nicely for the Soviet Union: the neutralist leaders were reported to have grumbled and to have expressed regrets in private, but they did not publicly assert their opposition to the Soviet act. Similarly, if structure is defined as recurring patterns of interaction, it becomes readily apparent that the social, economic, and political structures of a society can be changing even as its foreign policy officials continue to cling to unaltered attitudes and to engage in unmodified behavior. Indeed, this is a precise description of the major purpose of the United States foreign aid program as it emerged during the 1960s: namely, to bring about structural change through economic development in the recipient society while preserving attitudinal and behavioral independence from the Communist bloc on the part of its officials.

One way of differentiating more clearly among attitudinal, behavioral, and structural changes is by conceiving of them as being operative at different stages in interaction sequences. Attitudinal changes occur at, so to speak, pre-action points in a sequence. They can serve as antecedents to immediate and specific actions, or they can be more long-range in scope and can involve alterations in outlook that may eventually result in action. For example, propaganda programs constitute control acts usually designed to foster new opinions on the part of officials, elites, or mass publics that will pave the way for vaguely defined behavioral modifications at some unspecified time in the future. Behavioral changes, on the other hand, are conceived to occur at any specific action point in an interaction sequence. A vote in the U.N., a withdrawal of troops, an agreement to negotiate, a resumption of diplomatic relations—all of these exemplify modifications in behavior that can be induced by control acts. As for structural changes, these are conceived to occur in the action-reaction patterns that make up interaction sequences. Structural change, in other words, refers to the sequential rather than to the discrete occurrences of behavior. Specific actions cannot be a measure of structural change, since only those actions that recur with sufficient frequency to be patterned can be viewed as reflections of structure. Stated differently, behavioral change refers to the *actions* of a single controllee, whereas structural change involves the *interactions* of two or more controllees. Structural change occurs, for example, when subversion is used as a control technique and succeeds in reducing the respect and obedience that a citizenry renders its officials. Behavioral change occurs when the populace rises up and ousts its officials, but the alterations in the society that predisposed the citizens to act in this way constitute structural change.[25]

Having noted that controllees experience attitudinal and structural changes as well as behavioral modifications, we need to pause briefly to make adjustments in our terminology. No longer is it appropriate to speak generally of "behavior" as that which is modified when control occurs, for we have now established that any one of three aspects of controllees may be affected by control processes. Furthermore, one of these aspects—attitudes—cannot be regarded as behavior, but must instead be viewed as unobservable predispositions to act that can only be inferred from behavior. Thus, in order to maintain terminological clarity and to reserve the concept of behavior for phenomena that are directly observable, we shall henceforth refer to the *responses* of controllees whenever we generalize about the modifications that they experience in control relationships.

Let us turn now to the nine concrete targets of control (see Table 10–1). The distinctions among them are more or less self-evident, once the differentiation is drawn between *action* targets that can experience attitudinal or behavioral changes and *interaction* targets that can undergo only structural change. Obviously the patterns of interaction between two national actors, or between two subgroups within a society, are not subject to attitudinal or behavioral change. Only single actors can experience altered reactions or perceptions, whereas changes in an alliance, in a bilateral relationship, or in an "issue" must be confined to the direction, scope, and intensity of the interaction of its constituent parts—that is, to its structure. Great Britain's decision to press for membership in the

[25] The fact that behavioral changes are frequently the culmination of structural changes rather than of isolated events is relevant to a major difference between American and Soviet foreign policies toward the underdeveloped world. The United States has tended to concentrate on behavioral change and to treat it in isolation. The USSR, on the other hand, places greater emphasis on structural change. Consequently, for example, the United States often becomes preoccupied with the commitments contained in a speech by a neutralist leader, while the USSR does not usually become agitated over single events, apparently preferring to expend its energies on controlling the processes that culminate in commitments and speeches. If we assume that structural change is more permanent and widespread than behavioral change, this difference between American and Soviet policies may be an important reason why some neutralist countries tend to be more receptive to positions taken in Moscow than to those asserted in Washington.

Common Market, for instance, involved behavioral change on the part of British officials and attitudinal change on the part of that nation's elite groups and its mass public. In turn these changes will, if Britain is eventually admitted to membership, result in alterations in the patterns of interaction between Britain and the other members of the Common Market. In addition, its membership will cause alterations in the patterns of interaction among various groups within British society. Consequently, as Table 10–1 indicates, it is possible to treat both national societies and international relationships as subjects of structural change and, at the same time, to view national societies as capable of attitudinal and behavioral change whenever they are treated as actors rather than as systems of patterned interaction.

It follows that considerable overlap can occur when the processes of control encompass both action and interaction targets. A control act that produces attitudinal or behavioral change in an elite group can also be part of a sequence of acts designed to foster alterations in the society of which the group is a part. Conceivably, for example, the entrance of the Peace Corps into an underdeveloped country might dramatically alter the attitudes of intellectuals toward the United States even as it introduces change into the society's social structure by providing training to a much wider segment of the population. Similarly, behavioral and structural overlap could result from acts that evoke responses on the part of officials of one nation and, in so doing, lead to changes in its relationship with another country.

Despite the possibility of overlap, however, the distinctions among the various concrete targets are useful. Indeed, to the extent that control acts are directed at only one specific target, such differentiations are essential. American economic assistance to Poland, for instance, can best be understood not as an act designed to evoke responses on the part of Polish officials or the Polish people (although they do have this effect), but rather as an attempt to affect the structure of the Soviet-Polish relationship. In the same way, Russia's acts in the Berlin situation are better viewed as efforts to alter the structure of relations among the Western allies and between NATO and the Soviet world than as attempts to bring about structural change in the city itself (although such change has occurred, as the hastily erected wall so poignantly indicates). Similarly, the initiatives involved in launching NATO and the Marshall Plan are most fruitfully treated as acts in which the United States sought, respectively, to produce structural change between and within societies (although NATO also involved responses by officials in the member countries and although the Marshall Plan also involved inter-societal modifications). With respect to a particular society, moreover, control acts need not be directed at its overall structure or even at its substructures; they may instead be directed at the attitudes or behavior of specific segments—at its officials (say, in the form of diplomatic overtures), at its elites (say, through educational exchanges), or at its masses (say, by means of radio broadcasts).

THE OBJECTIVES OF CONTROL

An important advantage of the control framework is that empirically —and, to a certain extent, conceptually—it bypasses the problem of whether particular actions constitute ends or means of foreign policy. It does this by treating both the goals and the steps necessary to achieve them as control objectives. The purpose of control acts is the modification of one or more aspects of one or more concrete targets. These modifications may be viewed as the end products of or as parts of a change sequence; but, in either case, analysis proceeds by asking which changes occurred, how they occurred, and in what directions.

There are, of course, almost an unlimited number of kinds and degrees of change that controllers can posit as objectives and that controllees can experience. From either viewpoint, or from the perspective of an outside observer, this diversity of modified responses can be analyzed in terms of a fourfold conception of change—its scope, its intensity, its character, and its duration. In turn, as the rows in Table 10–1 indicate, each of these four dimensions can be subcategorized into several continua.[26]

Looking first at *scope*, it seems useful to differentiate the modifications experienced by the target according to whether most of its component parts or only a few of them were affected. This might be designated as the *widespread-limited* continuum, and it is exemplified at the former extreme by a propaganda technique designed to induce attitudinal change on the part of millions and, at the latter extreme, by a diplomatic maneuver intended to alter the thinking or premises of a dictator who dominates the decision-making apparatus of his society. The scope of change also includes a time dimension—what we might call the *present-future* continuum—that differentiates changes according to when they are expected to occur. This range can be exemplified, at one extreme, by an immediate diplomatic concession and, at the other, by an economic aid program that contributes to the eventual redistribution of a society's wealth. A third continuum related to the scope of change might be given a *specific-general* label and be used to distinguish between those acts that are under-

---

[26] These continua should not be regarded as definitive. They are merely meant to suggest the lines that subcategorization might follow.

taken with the intention of bringing about precisely specified modifications and those that are based on less exact and less detailed expectations. The range of variation in this instance can be illustrated by the difference between the dispatch of an ultimatum specifying conditions that must be met and the sending of a symphony orchestra abroad to create an unspecified set of attitudes called "good will."

With respect to the *intensity* of change that controllers initiate and controllees experience, several continua also suggest themselves. An obvious one is a *slow-fast* continuum identifying the rate of change that is anticipated or experienced. Military action, for example, is designed to produce a rapid change in the authority structure of controllees, whereas technical assistance programs are intended to induce gradual modifications in the socioeconomic structure of recipient societies. Closely related to this measure of the rate of change is a *central-peripheral* continuum. This distinguishes between acts that have a profound impact upon the target (such as a complete reversal from a cordial to a hostile relationship) and those acts that have marginal effects (such as a minor revision of one clause of a treaty). Intensity can also be measured in terms of a *continuous-intermittent* scale differentiating changes that unfold without interruption from those that occur only sporadically. Acts of sabotage are illustrative of how intermittent change is induced, while long-term economic aid programs usually foster a process of continuous modification. A *direct-circuitous* continuum is still another dimension that might be employed to measure intensity. Here the distinction is between a series of changes that follow cumulatively from one another and those that do not unfold interdependently. The fostering of cordial attitudes in a country so as to facilitate a subsequent alliance with it exemplifies the induction of direct change, whereas trade with a hostile country in order to affect its relations with a third nation might be considered the initiation of circuitous change.

If we turn to the *character* of the modifications that targets undergo, changes at this level can also be portrayed and analyzed in a number of ways. Perhaps the most important characterological changes are subsumed in an *integrative-disintegrative* continuum that permits assessments of how control acts affect the stability and coherence of the target. At one extreme is the type of control that brings the components of the target into greater harmony with one another, and at the other extreme is the type that introduces greater dissonance among the components. The effects of the Marshall Plan in Europe provide an example of the results of integrative control, whereas subversive tactics (such as political strikes or guerrilla warfare) illustrate attempts at disintegrative control. The character of change can also be located on a *conscious-unconscious* continuum. This scale ranges from modifications that controllees know they are experiencing to those of which they are completely unaware. Bargaining between two international actors normally reflects conscious control, since usually each party to the negotiations deliberately modifies its position in response to concessions made by the other. On the other hand, a subtle propaganda campaign aimed at mass publics can produce attitudinal changes that are not recognized until they have taken place. The effort of the Soviet Union to portray communism as the wave of the future can probably be classified as an attempt to precipitate unconscious attitudinal change on the part of publics abroad, if not of foreign elites and officials. Quite similar is a *visible-invisible* continuum that differentiates between changes that are manifest to controllers or to outside observers and those that cannot be discerned while they are occurring. Acquiescence to diplomatic demands is an illustration of visible change, whereas the changes in morale that accompany the acquiescence may long remain invisible, even to the astute analyst. Invisible and unconscious modifications are not necessarily identical, since controllees can be unconscious of changes that are far from hidden to the controller or to the outside observer.

Finally, the *duration* dimension of controlled change can be usefully broken down for further analysis. Obviously a *long-run-short-run* continuum is needed to distinguish envisioned or actual modifications that are enduring from those that are only momentary or temporary. Short-run change is exemplified by a situation in which a public declaration of policy temporarily deters a controllee from a course of action, whereas long-run change is exemplified by the modifications wrought by a technical assistance program. A somewhat more complex continuum pertaining to the duration of change might be called the *irreversible-reversible* scale. This differentiates between acts initiating changes that tend to be permanent and acts fostering changes that can be undone by subsequent counteracts. A technical assistance program and a diplomatic overture are also illustrative of the two extremes of this scale: technical assistance can lead to an alteration of the skills of a society, thereby permanently changing its capabilities, while diplomatic overtures can lead to new attitudes or behavior, both of which may be reversed as soon as a contrary diplomatic position on the same issue is asserted. Closely linked to this distinction is one expressed in terms of a *guided-unguided* continuum. This scale distinguishes between acts precipitating changes that the controller is unable to direct once he has initiated them and those acts that remain subject to his control after he has brought them into being. The attachment of "strings" to foreign economic assistance programs can be viewed as a use of guided control, whereas the act of severing diplomatic relations would normally be an example of unguided control.

The purpose of enumerating the various kinds of targets and changes that can be controlled is not to show the complexity of international politics—although, certainly, this breakdown indicates that the formulation and conduct of foreign policy are extraordinarily complicated. Rather, the point here is that different control techniques, calculations, capacities, and processes may be necessary to precipitate changes at *each* point on *each* of the continua that have been noted. Some techniques are best suited to the achievement of limited, present, specific, fast, intermittent, circuitous, integrative, conscious, visible, reversible, guided, and short-run change, whereas other techniques lead to different types of changes. Indeed, every possible combination of points taken from all the continua constitute a unique type of change that may require a particular technique or set of techniques for its achievement. It probably would not be too difficult to construct a "profile" for each technique by locating on each continuum the range within which it can be effective.

THE TECHNIQUES OF CONTROL

The changes that actually take place—the outcomes of control acts—are determined by the interplay of the techniques employed, the capacities mobilized, and the limits encountered. Some techniques, of course, require greater capacities than others if their effectiveness is to be maximized, just as some are designed primarily to overcome behavioral limitations and as still others are directed mainly at attitudinal limitations. Military techniques, for example, are more costly than propaganda techniques since their implementation requires greater capacities. The two are also distinguished by the fact that military techniques are more likely to effect behavioral changes than are propaganda techniques.

Having noted the close connection among techniques, capacities, and limitations, let us, for the moment, hold the last two constant and examine more closely the range of techniques available to controllers. This range can be subcategorized in a variety of ways. Most classification schemes are organized around standard forms of international action, such as diplomacy, economic aid, foreign trade, propaganda, subversion, and military action. Harold Sprout, for instance, has developed an elaborate eightfold scheme along these lines:

Diplomatic intercourse; negotiation, etc.

Public declarations of policy

Other public relations activities

Economic and technical assistance

Nonviolent psychological warfare

Nonviolent economic warfare

Limited violence: sabotage and military action

Unlimited violence: total war [27]

Although models such as this are obviously valuable for a variety of purposes, the notion that techniques produce either behavioral, attitudinal, or structural modifications suggests that it may prove fruitful to develop new inventories of the techniques employed by actors. The standard categories are somehow too broad and too all-encompassing when considered in the context of controlled change. Within this framework, certain kinds of acts that are crucially important do not fall neatly under the conventional headings, and consequently they tend to be neglected by students in the field. Consider, for example, the self-fulfilling prophecy as a technique of foreign policy. It seems clear that the Soviet Union often employs this technique in its international actions. Indeed, as illustrated by the events that have attended Khrushchev's repeated assertions that West Berlin will be made a free city without a third world war resulting, the practice of continuously reiterating in public speeches and *aide-mémoires* what will and what will not happen in the future can be of enormous strategic value in fostering the realization of the prophecy. Yet, virtually no work of either a conceptual or an empirical nature has been done on the use and potentialities of this phenomenon in international politics.

One possible way of reclassifying the kinds of techniques available to controllers is to assign to each of them a position on a scale according to the degree of coercion that the technique requires. Presumably the scale would range from techniques involving the use of unqualified force to those involving the assertion of scientific proof. At the latter extreme are situations in which coercion is at a minimum: controllees change as a result of having been convinced by rational explanation, and perhaps even by demonstrations of the validity of the controller's contentions. In the fall of 1961, for example, the United States controlled Nationalist China by getting it not to cast an otherwise expected veto against the admission of Outer Mongolia into the United Nations. This control was apparently achieved by outlining carefully and systematically to the Formosan leadership the consequences of a veto: namely, that the Soviet Union would then veto the admission of Mauretania and there would

[27] Harold Sprout, "International Politics and the Scholar," *Princeton Alumni Weekly*, LIX (January 23, 1959), p. 14.

thus be created a greater likelihood of African support for the admission of Communist China. Similarly, the efforts to negotiate a treaty banning nuclear tests proceeded on the basis of arguments citing the potential danger to human life that is inherent in radioactive fallout. The fact that such a treaty has yet to be promulgated insofar as above-ground tests are concerned does not negate the use of the technique; rather it indicates the insufficiency of the technique under certain conditions. Indeed, the typical situation is one in which controllers have to use persuasion, manipulation, intimidation, and other types of appeals to nonlogical or irrational motives and values. More characteristic, for instance, are the efforts of the major powers to secure the support of African nations on the grounds that anti-colonialism will thereby be served. Similarly, if Nationalist China's decision not to cast the veto had been brought about by a threat to cut off economic assistance, this would have represented the use of neither scientific proof nor unqualified force, but rather of a technique located somewhere in the middle of the coercion scale. On occasion, of course, techniques at the force end of the scale are employed. Sometimes, but probably less often than is realized, targets confront controllers with limits that can be overcome only by brute strength. The armed escort of American officials through the wall into East Berlin is illustrative of situations in which control can be maintained only by force. The quelling of the Hungarian uprising of 1956 by invasion serves as another example: no other technique could have enabled the Russians to control the situation in a manner consistent with their objectives.

A major virtue of inventorying control techniques in terms of a coercion scale, or along some similar dimension, is that categories are thereby generated which link controllers and controllees more closely than is the case in conventional classifications. The use of persuasion not only suggests something about what the controller is doing, but also indicates something about what the controllee will have to experience or resist. To speak of the use of diplomatic or economic techniques, on the other hand, is to refer mainly to the actions of the controller and thus to convey little information about the processes of change that the controllee will have to undergo or avoid. Furthermore, different forms and degrees of coercion can be and are associated with the standard techniques. Both scientific proof and intimidation, for example, enter into many diplomatic negotiations, just as both manipulation and force are often used to carry out subversive activities among controllees.

CONTROL CAPACITIES AND LIMITATIONS

The ultimate test of whether a control technique is sufficient lies, of course, in the response of the controllee. If the latter undergoes the intended change, then control has occurred, and the techniques employed can be deemed appropriate. In large part, the success or appropriateness of a technique is determined by whether the capacities that the controller mobilizes in support of his acts impress, deceive, encourage, or otherwise affect the controllees in such a way as to evoke the proper response. This suggests the crucial point that capacities cannot be analyzed or evaluated in a vacuum. They must be assessed in terms of the impact they are likely to make upon controllees. An international actor may be richly endowed with all sorts of capacities, both human skills and nonhuman resources, but these will be of little value if poorly endowed neighbors defiantly resist attempts to modify their behavior. Stated differently, it is not possible simply to enumerate the capacities of two actors and then to anticipate the structure of their relationship by comparing their respective abilities. Analysis of this sort is static and does not take into account the dynamics of whether the controllee will make the same calculations and will rationally base his responses on the comparative tabulations.[28] Given the world's angry response in 1962 to the explosion of 50-megaton bombs by the Soviet Union, for example, there is a real question as to whether Russia's capacities were increased or decreased by the addition of a new and tested weapon to its stockpile. Its destructive capacity was increased, but was its capacity to control?

This does not mean that students of foreign policy and international politics should not engage in elaborate and systematic analyses of national capacities. Clearly, a technical assistance program cannot be conducted unless an actor has skilled technicians to send abroad. Propaganda programs require facilities, supplies, and personnel in order to be initiated and sustained. Manpower and military equipment must be available if force is to be used as a technique. In short, there can be no control without capacities, and these capacities must thus be a major focal point of analysis. Nevertheless, and to repeat, capacities are operative only in the context of a control relationship, and it is in this context that elaborate and systematic assessments of national strengths and weaknesses need to be made.

The close link between the controller's capacities and the controllee's

[28] For empirical evidence that rational calculations of comparative capabilities are not the only or even the major source of behavior, see Dina A. Zinnes, Robert C. North, and Howard E. Koch, Jr., "Capability, Threat, and the Outbreak of War," in James N. Rosenau (ed.), *International Politics and Foreign Policy: A Reader in Research and Theory* (New York: Free Press, 1961), pp. 469–482.

responses suggests the additional point that capacities can also serve as techniques. If they are to be utilized in some future situation, they are capacities; at the time of their usage, however, they take on the characteristics of control techniques. Sending troops abroad during a period of international tension is a good illustration of this functional duality. If publicity is given to the overseas reinforcement, the sending of troops serves both as a technique designed to alter the intentions of a potential aggressor and as an increment in capacities in the event that a new control relationship (war) replaces the old one (peaceful tension).

The effect of the controller on the controllee is not only dependent upon the former's capacities, but is also determined by the limitations that the latter brings to the relationship. To a certain extent, of course, limitations and capacities may be treated as similar phenomena, since both are characteristics of actors. A controllee mobilizes his human and nonhuman resources in the same way as a controller does, except that his purpose involves the offsetting of control acts rather than their implementation. In a sense, then, comparative analysis of capacities and limitations is relatively simple: each capacity can be contrasted with a corresponding limitation, and this procedure can then be projected across a broad range of factors, thereby culminating in comparable national estimates. Two considerations, however, complicate comparisons of this sort. First, as noted above, because such comparisons exclude motivational factors, they are static and have limited value in predicting outcomes. Second, although capacities are those human and nonhuman resources that can be mobilized—that is, developed and utilized to support particular purposes—this is not the case with all limitations. Some obstacles to change cannot also be agents of change. For example, certain cultural values (such as those pertaining to birth control) may be barriers to attitudinal and behavioral modification even though they are hardly subject to mobilization as capacities which can be used for control purposes.

Breaking down the resources of nations into both the capacities they can muster as controllers and the limitations they can impose as controllees not only facilitates comparative analysis, but also emphasizes the constant elements of international politics and foreign policy. These elements are frequently overlooked by observers, who naturally try to keep their analyses abreast of the dynamic and changing features of world affairs. The concept of limitations, however, calls attention to the narrow margin within which one nation can alter the prevailing patterns of another. The ability of international actors to control one another is easily and often exaggerated. Many Americans, for instance, believe that all kinds of desirable benefits will result from the appointment of United States ambassadors who speak the language of the country to which they are assigned. Similarly widespread is the view that the recognition of an unfriendly actor, such as China in the present era or the USSR in 1933, will lead to a host of unfortunate consequences. These would seem to be naive conceptions. Beneficial or regrettable consequences may flow from such acts, but this is not necessarily the case. An ambassador who must implement unpopular policies is not likely to be much more successful if he speaks the native tongue than if he does not. In fact, there are parts of the world where such an ability can do more harm than good. According to Harold Nicolson, "the more educated people" in Southeast Asia take pride in their ability to speak English or French and thus "would be hurt if addressed in their native language by foreign diplomatists." [29] Likewise, the impact of an aggressive nation is not likely to be much different under the circumstances of nonrecognition than under those of recognition.

In short, human behavior and attitudes are not easily or swiftly changed. Internally fostered societal change can ordinarily be accomplished only in small increments at the margins. Even in revolutionary situations, when the center of societal life may be especially susceptible to major alteration, the initiators of change cannot readily maintain control over the direction and scope of the change. If this is so within nations, the same can be said with even greater conviction about the possibilities of initiating modification from outside the geographic and cultural boundaries of a society. Because of the limitations of controllees, in other words, the foreign policies of nations tend to offset each other. Consequently, transformations in the state of the international system tend to occur very slowly and can usually be recognized only from the perspective of several decades or more.

CONTROL RELATIONSHIPS

It is important to note that the control framework allows for a variety of types of relationships between actors. In the first place a useful distinction can be made between symmetrical and asymmetrical relationships.[30] In the former the response of the controllee is directed at the controller, whereas in the latter a third actor is the recipient of the modifications that the controllee undergoes in response to the controller. Diplomatic ·negotiations between two countries are an obvious example of a symmetrical relationship. The actions of East German officials in

[29] Harold Nicolson, "Diplomacy, Then and Now," *Foreign Affairs*, XL (October 1961), p. 41.

[30] This distinction has been adapted from Richard C. Snyder, H. W. Bruck, and Burton Sapin, *Decision-making as an Approach to the Study of International Politics* (Princeton University: Foreign Policy Analysis Project, 1954), pp. 32–33.

Berlin provide a good illustration of an asymmetrical relationship: they are a response to Soviet control acts even though they are directed toward Western officials. Similarly, Castro's attempts to generate anti-United States feelings in Latin America reflect an asymmetrical relationship between Cuba and the United States. This example further suggests the important point that two actors can have a relationship even though the severance of diplomatic ties has eliminated direct interaction between them.

Secondly, a differentiation must be made among what we might call official, semi-official, and unofficial relationships. The distinction involves the identity of the parties to the relationships. In official relationships both the controllers and the controllees are government policy-makers, whereas in semi-official relationships government officials constitute one of the actors and elite groups and/or mass publics constitute the other. Unofficial relationships are those in which neither of the actors consists of officials. Since diplomatic negotiations always involve interaction between policy-makers, they exemplify official relationships. Propaganda messages directed at mass publics would be illustrative of a semi-official relationship because policy-makers are only one of the parties to the interaction. The impact of an economic assistance program upon the economy of the recipient nation is another example of this type of relationship. Indeed, with the emergence of mass publics as a primary factor in twentieth-century international politics, most relationships today are probably of the semi-official kind. On the other hand, because of the central role of governments, unofficial relationships are probably the least numerous type. They can be exemplified by pacifist groups who appeal for support from similar groups in other countries.

The frequency of interaction is still another central variable in control relationships. While contact between the controller and the controllee need not be continuous for their relationship to be sustained, the frequency of their interaction is usually high. In general, controllers have to re-enact their control often in order either to cope with each new response to their previous act or to insure that the behavior of controllees remains modified. Diplomatic negotiations exemplify the former kind of high interaction relationship, and foreign aid programs illustrate the latter kind. Certain kinds of relationships, on the other hand, can be sustained even if the parties to them are not in contact for a long period of time. Even a single control act, for example, can evoke a series of responses that spans several years and that is sufficiently acceptable to the controller to relieve him of the need to re-enact or reinforce his control. Russia's intervention in the domestic politics of Finland in November 1961 is a case in point. It seems reasonable to presume that, for the foreseeable future, the Finns will refrain from pursuing certain policies because the 1961 action served to indicate the limits beyond which their responses would not be acceptable to the Soviet Union. Similarly, it will probably be a long time before the Russians again decide to introduce offensive weaponry into Cuba. Each time they decide not to do this, or not to engage in some similar venture in the Western Hemisphere, they are, in effect, still responding to the naval blockade through which the United States exerted control in October 1962. In each case, the relationship is maintained even though the controller no longer actively participates in it. There is, of course, a limit to the extent to which an initial control act may prove effective. Every so often—whenever time elapses to the point where the controllee becomes uncertain of the state of the relationship and is tempted to move outside the range of acceptable responses—the controller either has to re-enact his control, or he has to become the controllee and thereby acquiesce to an altered relationship. At some time in the future, the Russians will no doubt have to reinforce their 1961 act by reminding the Finns of how the good relations existing between their countries can be maintained. Periodic American reminders to the Russians about the viability of the Monroe Doctrine can also be expected in the future, as memories of the 1962 Cuban crisis fade.

The fact that not every modification experienced by the controllee is in response to a previous act by the controller might be regarded as undermining the central place that we have accorded to control which is calculated. If Finland refrains from a course of action out of fear of Russian retaliation, it could then be argued that the Soviet Union has exerted control without calculation. If the decision to refrain from acting is viewed strictly in terms of a single interaction, such an argument would, of course, be valid, and we would have to speak in terms of noncalculated control. Yet, such a narrow perspective is misleading. In the first place, controllers often calculate that their initial act will evoke a series of repeated responses. To consider one of these responses as evidence of noncalculated control is thus to overlook the dynamic nature of control relationships. Secondly, on those occasions when the controller does not consciously calculate the responses subsequent to the first one, we tend to consider the controllee as the controller and to concentrate on his efforts either to avoid repetition of the initial control act or to prevent an even less desirable retaliation. In short, one of the parties to a control relationship is always engaging in calculation. This is the essential reason why we have treated control relationships not as single interaction sequences, but rather as recurring sequences in which the two actors shift back and forth in the roles of both controller and controllee as they attempt to modify one another's behavior. The phenomenon of control thus assumes much greater complexity, but the concept of calculation nevertheless remains central to the scheme.

The number of parties to control relationships is another variable that requires elaboration. In order to simplify the presentation, the discussion has thus far tended to posit relationships as being comprised of two actors, the controller and the controllee. In fact, of course, this is only the simplest type of relationship. Depending upon how many actors interact over a particular matter, the parties to a relationship can vary greatly in number. In multi-actor relationships, some of the parties, at any given stage of the interaction sequence, are acting as controllers while others are in the role of controllee. Indeed, some may occupy both roles by attempting to modify the behavior of other parties to the relationship even as they experience modifications initiated by still others. Regional blocs and international organizations exemplify this larger and more complex type of relationship. Assuming that the exercise of control becomes increasingly difficult as the number of parties to a relationship grows, the size variable would seem to be a logical starting point for any inquiry into the conditions that foster stable and effective international relationships. Other things being equal, for example, are there certain relationship sizes in which a maximum degree of stability is likely to be maintained? Do other sizes conduce to a quicker and a more effective realization of the goals of a relationship?

Finally, important differentiations among control relations can be made in terms of the duration and the scope of the interaction. These two variables are closely related to one another and are functions of the compatibility of the objectives that international actors bring to a relationship. The more the objectives of the controller and the controllee are in conflict, the more enduring will be their interaction and the greater will be the number of issues with respect to which they seek to modify one another's behavior. The distinctions between temporary and enduring interactions and between single-issue and multi-issue relationships should also be helpful in analyzing the stability and the effectiveness of control relations.

POSTSCRIPT

Let us conclude by noting that the control framework is a conceptual and not a theoretical scheme. It identifies new and reorganizes old phenomena, but it does not explain why international affairs unfold as they do. We have attempted to establish links between the different levels of analysis and across seemingly unbridgeable gaps, but we cannot claim to have dealt with questions of cause and effect or even with the sources of these links. Hopefully, however, the concept of calculated control will prove to be among the useful and solid building blocks out of which explanatory theories can be fashioned.

11 The National Interest *

The concept of the national interest is used in both political analysis and political action. As an analytic tool, it is employed to describe, explain, or evaluate the sources or the adequacy of a nation's foreign policy. As an instrument of political action, it serves as a means of justifying, denouncing, or proposing policies. Both usages, in other words, refer to what is best for a national society. They also share a tendency to confine the intended meaning to what is best for a nation in foreign affairs.

Beyond these general considerations, however, the two uses of the concept have little in common. In its action usage the concept lacks structure and content but, nevertheless, serves its users, political actors, well. As an analytic tool the concept is more precise and elaborate but, nevertheless, confounds the efforts of its users, political analysts. These differences arise out of the fact that the national interest is rooted in values ("what is best"). While analysts have discovered that the value-laden character of the concept makes it difficult to employ as a tool of rigorous investigation, actors have found that this very same characteristic renders the concept useful both as a way of thinking about their goals and as a means of mobilizing support for them. That is, not only do political actors tend to perceive and discuss their goals in terms of the national interest, but they are also inclined to claim that their goals *are* the national interest, a claim that often arouses the support necessary to move toward a realization of the goals. Consequently, even though it has lost some of its early appeal as an analytic tool, the national interest enjoys considerable favor

* An earlier version of this chapter was published in the *International Encyclopedia of the Social Sciences* (New York: The Macmillan Company and The Free Press, 1968), Vol. 11, pp. 34–40. Reprinted with the permission of the publisher. Copyright 1968 by Crowell-Collier and Macmillan, Inc.

as a basis for action and has won a prominent place in the dialogue of public affairs.

HISTORY OF THE CONCEPT

The national interest has a much longer history as an instrument of action than as a tool of analysis. According to a historian who traced past uses of the term, political actors made claims on behalf of the national interest as early as the sixteenth century in Italy and the seventeenth century in England.[1] At that time claims made in the name of "the will of the prince," "dynastic interests," *raison d'état,* and other older catchwords began to lose their effectiveness as a new form of political organization, the nation-state, came into being and served as the political unit to which men owed their allegiance. Thus, the old terms were gradually replaced by new ones that reflected the new loyalties. The national interest was one of these, as was "national honor," "the public interest," and "the general will." Beard also found that "the term, national interest, has been extensively employed by American statesmen since the establishment of the Constitution."[2]

Many decades elapsed, however, before the national interest attracted attention as a tool of analysis. Not until the twentieth century, when two world wars made it clear that mass publics had both a vital stake in foreign affairs and played a vital role in them, did analysts focus on the national interest as a concept which could be used to describe, explain, and assess the foreign policies of nations. Beard was himself one of the first to develop the concept for this purpose and to distinguish it from the "public interest," which through convention has come to be used in reference to the domestic policies of nations.

Initially, the national interest appealed to analysts whose main concern was to evaluate the foreign policies which led to World War II. Impressed with the thought that the global conflict might have been avoided if the British and the French had not acquiesced to Hitler at Munich in 1938 and if the United States had not adopted isolationist policies throughout the 1930s, a number of analysts turned to the national interest as a way of determining the adequacy and effectiveness of past, present, or future policies. They reasoned in retrospect that the advent of World War II made it clear that the prewar policies of the three nations were ill-advised and that the policies proved to be contrary to the best interests of England,

[1] Charles A. Beard, *The Idea of National Interest: An Analytical Study in American Foreign Policy* (New York: Macmillan, 1934), pp. 22–24.
[2] *Ibid.,* p. 26.

France, and the United States. To these analysts it thus seemed obvious that the best interest of a nation is a matter of objective reality and that by describing this reality one is able to use the concept of the national interest as a basis for evaluating the appropriateness of the policies which a nation pursues. Because of their underlying assumption that the national interest can be objectively determined, we shall call these analysts "objectivists."

It should be noted that most objectivists do not have an explicit and elaborate rationale for their approach to the national interest. Interested primarily in analyzing the contents of foreign policy, the objectivists are not particularly concerned about the methodological and philosophical foundations of their inquiries. They make no special effort to explain how and why their descriptions of the national interest are in accord with reality because, for them, the correspondence between their descriptions and the objective situation is self-evident. Objectivists thus leave to their readers the task of inferring their conceptualization of the national interest from substantive observations which are as variable as the situations which they describe.

It is possible, however, to derive some insight into the underlying rationale of the objectivists from the writings of one analyst who did undertake to develop an explicit framework for explaining why his substantive interpretations of the national interest reflect objective reality. The analyst is Hans Morgenthau, whose works advance "a realist theory of international politics" founded on the concept of national interest. "Interest is the perennial standard by which political action must be judged and directed," Morgenthau wrote,[3] emphasizing that, therefore, the "objectives of a foreign policy must be defined in terms of the national interest."[4] And exactly what constitutes the interest of a nation? Morgenthau recognized that "the kind of interest determining political action in a particular period of history depends upon the political and cultural context within which foreign policy is formulated,"[5] but he envisioned accounting for these contextual factors by defining interest in terms of power.[6] For Morgenthau the power at a nation's command relative to that of other nations is, at any moment in time, an objective reality for that nation and thus serves to determine what its true interest is and should be. As will be seen, however, the difficulty with Morgenthau's formulation is the lack of a method for determining what a nation's relative power is. That

---

[3] Hans J. Morgenthau, *Politics Among Nations: The Struggle for Power and Peace* (New York: Knopf, 2d. ed., 1954), p. 9.

[4] *Ibid.*, p. 528.

[5] *Ibid.*, p. 8.

[6] *Ibid.*, p. 5.

is, he does not indicate how use of the criterion of power will enable nations to "follow . . . but one guiding star, one standard for thought, one rule for action: *the national interest.*"[7]

As the discipline of political science gave increasing emphasis to scientific explanation, another group of analysts joined the objectivists in converging upon the national interest as an analytic concept. Concerned less with evaluating the worth of foreign policies and more with explaining why nations do what they do when they engage in international action, this group found the national interest attractive as a possible means of probing the sources of foreign policy. They reasoned that nations do what they do in order to satisfy their best interests and that by describing these needs and wants the analyst would be in a position to use the concept of the national interest as a tool for explanation. These analysts, in other words, deny the existence of an objective reality which is discoverable through systematic inquiry. For them the national interest is not a singular objective truth that prevails whether or not it is perceived by the members of a nation, but it is, rather, a pluralistic set of subjective preferences that change whenever the requirements and aspirations of the nation's members change. For want of a better term, hereafter we shall call those who approach the national interest in this way the "subjectivists."

The advent of the decision-making approach to international politics [8] provided the subjectivists with an additional rationale for their approach to the national interest. Partly as a reaction to the objectivists and partly out of a concern to render concepts usable by linking them to observable behavior, students of decision-making contend that the national interest, being composed of values (what people want), is not susceptible of objective measurement even if defined in terms of power and that, accordingly, the only way to uncover what people need and want is to assume that their requirements and aspirations are reflected in the actions of a nation's policy makers. For these analysts, in other words, the national interest is whatever the officials of a nation seek to preserve and enhance. As two leading spokesmen for this approach put it, "The national interest is what the nation, i.e., the decision-maker, decides it is." [9]

It is worthy of emphasis that although the objectivists and subjectivists differed profoundly in their premises and conclusions, both came to accept the appropriateness of analyzing foreign policy and international politics

[7] Hans J. Morgenthau, *In Defense of the National Interest: A Critical Examination of American Foreign Policy* (New York: Knopf, 1951), p. 242.

[8] Richard D. Snyder, H. W. Bruck, and Burton Sapin, *Decision-Making as an Approach to the Study of International Politics* (Princeton: Princeton University, Organizational Behavior Section, 1954).

[9] Edgar S. Furniss and Richard C. Snyder, *An Introduction to American Foreign Policy* (New York: Rinehart, 1955), p. 17.

in terms of the national interest. To be sure, the two groups focused on different phenomena when they investigated the national interest, but they both emphasized that its relevance to the external actions of nations was considerable.

LIMITATIONS OF THE CONCEPT

Despite the claims made for the concept and notwithstanding its apparent utility, the national interest has never fulfilled its early promise as an analytic tool. Attempts by both objectivists and subjectivists to use and apply it have proven fruitless or misleading, with the result that, while textbooks on international politics continue to assert that nations act to protect and realize their national interests, the research literature of the field has not been increased and enriched by monographs which give central prominence to the concept.

The reasons for this failure of the concept as an analytic tool are numerous. One is the ambiguous nature of the nation and the difficulty of specifying whose interests it encompasses. A second is the elusiveness of criteria for determining the existence of interests and for tracing their presence in substantive policies. Still another confounding factor is the absence of procedures for cumulating the interests once they have been identified. This is in turn complicated by uncertainty as to whether the national interest has been fully identified once all the specific interests have been cumulated or whether there are not other, more generalized, values which render the national interest greater than the sum of its parts.

These limitations are readily discernible in the premises and writings of the objectivists. What is best for a nation in foreign affairs is never self-evident. More important, it is not even potentially knowable as a singular objective truth. Men are bound to differ on what constitute the most appropriate goals for a nation. For, to repeat, goals and interests are value-laden. They involve subjective preferences, and thus the cumulation of national interests into a single complex of values is bound to be as variable as the number of observers who use different value frameworks. Yet the objectivists proceed on the assumption that some values are preferable to others (for example, that it is better for the nation to survive than not to survive) and that therefore it is possible to discover, cumulate, and objectify a single national interest. Consequently, the objectivists find it possible to characterize every foreign policy as either reflecting or opposing the national interest. Indeed, it was precisely this line of reasoning that enabled them to posit an objective reality about the conditions of prewar Europe and to conclude that Great Britain and France did not follow their national interests when they ignored this reality and acquiesced to Hitler at Munich.

However, such reasoning breaks down as soon as it is recalled that the national interest is rooted in values. If every member of a nation wishes to have it go out of existence by joining a larger world federation, who is to say that the goal or act of federation is contrary to that nation's interest? If the British and the French believed they were satisfying their wants and needs when they compromised at Munich, who is to say they were wrong and acted in violation of their national interests? The analyst who does make such an observation is merely enjoying the benefits of hindsight to justify the superiority of his own values over those of the British and French policy makers who decided to acquiesce to Hitler (obviously, the policy makers would have acted differently if they could have foreseen the consequences of acquiescence). Since values are not susceptible of scientific proof, the objectivists have never been able to demonstrate the validity of their assessments of the extent to which foreign-policy actions reflect a nation's interest. To explain that a certain policy is in the national interest, or to criticize it for being contrary to the national interest, is to give an imposing label to one's own conception of what is a desirable or undesirable course of action.

The objectivists do not consider that their own values serve as criteria for determining the substantive content of the national interest. Rather, as has been noted, they conceive of a nation's power as the source of what is best for it and as the basis for ranking some values as preferable to others. From their point of view, a nation's power has an objective existence and thus values need not enter into a determination of its national interest. The objectivists concede that the national interest may be defended, criticized, or explained in value, rather than power, terms. Such formulations, however, are regarded as merely ideological justifications and rationalizations which conceal the true nature of the policy under consideration. Policy makers may claim that moral principles serve as the basis for their actions, but the objectivists assume that in fact "statesmen think and act in terms of interest defined as power."[10]

This reasoning of the objectivists is essentially erroneous. The dictates of power are never clearly manifest. Power is as elusive and ambiguous a concept as is interest. Its components are a matter of dispute. Furthermore, many power components consist of intangibles, such as morale, which are difficult to measure. Even more difficult, if not impossible, is the task of cumulating the tangible and intangible components into a single entity called "the power of a nation." For not only does the cumulation of unlike factors constitute a difficult problem in itself, but it also

10 H. Morgenthau, *Politics Among Nations*, p. 5.

necessitates the introduction of values. To cumulate the components of power one must assess the relative importance of each component, and such an assessment can only be made by referring to the goals which the power is designed to serve. Hence, whether he wishes to or not, the analyst must inevitably fall back on a value framework—the one from which goals are derived—if he is to define the national interest in terms of power. It follows that there is no reason to assume that different analysts will necessarily arrive at similar, much less identical, interpretations of what a nation's power dictates its national interest to be.

In short, there may be an "objective reality" about the situations in which nations find themselves at various periods of history, but neither predictively nor retrospectively can its contents be clearly demonstrated. A description of the national interest can never be more than a set of conclusions derived from the analytic and evaluative framework of the describer. The objectivists unknowingly concede this point whenever they criticize foreign policies for not being in a nation's interest. For such a criticism contradicts their view that the national interest determines the contents of what nations do abroad. For example, Morgenthau goes to great lengths in his writings to show how "a foreign policy guided by moral abstractions, without consideration of the national interest, is bound to fail," [11] an observation which undermines his assumption that policy makers always think and act in terms of interest defined as power.

Nor have the various subjectivist approaches to the national interest been conspicuously successful. Although subjectivists carefully and explicitly avoid the premise that the national interest can be objectified, their formulations and uses of the concept are far from free of its inherent limitations. The recognition that many groups in a nation have different and often conflicting concepts of what external actions and policies are best for it—and that consequently the national interest is a reflection of these preferences rather than of objective circumstances—gives rise to as many conceptual and methodological difficulties as it avoids. First there is the problem of which groups constitute a nation. Should the boundaries of a nation be equated with those of national societies or does a nation consist of persons with a common background who speak the same language? If the latter, more traditional formulation is used, then analysis is complicated by the fact that some nations exist within or extend beyond the boundaries of national societies. Such nations may have neither governments nor foreign policies, so that inquiries into their interests would be far removed from the concerns which attract attention to the concept of national interest. For this reason most subjectivists equate nations

11 H. Morgenthau, *In Defense of the National Interest*, pp. 33–34.

with national societies and employ the terms interchangeably. In other words, the national interest usually means the societal interest.

Defining the nation in this way, however, is a relatively minor problem and only proves troublesome for the terminological purist. Much more difficult is the problem which follows immediately from the assumption that nations are heterogeneous units encompassing a multitude of ethnic, cultural, social, and other types of groups: namely, the problem of identifying and classifying all the diverse and conflicting interests which clamor for satisfaction in a national society. Stated simply, how does the observer determine which groups have an interest in a particular foreign policy and how does he specify what the substantive contents of the interests of each group are? The subjectivist's obvious reply is that interests are equivalent to the demands and recommendations which group spokesmen in the society articulate and press. But this answer is of little help to the researcher. The groups with specialized interests in modern industrial societies are so numerous, and the types of policies in which they have a stake are so varied, that the quantitative dimensions of such a procedure render it virtually unusable. Furthermore, even if this quantitative problem could be overcome, there would remain the qualitative task of accounting for the groups whose interests lack a spokesman (for example, future generations, consumers, and repressed minorities). Presumably this can only be accomplished through estimates of what is best for such groups, a procedure which brings the subjectivist perilously close to the objectivist's practice of ascribing his own values to others.

Nor does the subjectivist's dilemma end here. Assuming that he is somehow able to identify all the expressed and unexpressed interests of a society, he must then combine the multiplicity of values into a meaningful whole. Not to do so would be to treat the national interest as a mass of contradictory needs and wants, a procedure which is hardly suitable to the description, explanation, and evaluation of foreign-policy goals. But in order to aggregate many contradictory values into an over-all formulation of the national interest, one must face the probability that some of the specific interests carry greater weight than others, and it is this probability that perpetuates the dilemma. For it raises the question of how the relative weight of the conflicting interests is to be determined. The most tempting solution is to attach weights on the basis of one's own assessments, but this procedure would again lead the subjectivist down the misleading path followed by the objectivist.

Most subjectivists avoid these complex, seemingly insurmountable problems by relying on a procedural rather than a substantive definition of the national interest. Rather than attempt to sum the values that prevail in a society, they rely on the society's political processes to do it for them. That is, they fall back on a decision-making conception in which the foreign-policy goals that a society sets for itself are considered to result from bargaining among the various groups claiming satisfaction of their needs and wants. If some interests carry greater weight than others, it is assumed that the differences will be recognized and accounted for in the policy-making process. In other words, regardless of whether democratic or authoritarian procedures are employed, the needs and wants of groups within national societies are assumed to constitute demands that policy makers must sort out and obey, an assumption which relieves the observer from having to resort to his own values to determine which interests are weightier. Operationally, the substantive content of the national interest thus becomes whatever a society's officials decide it to be, and the main determinant of content is the procedure by which such decisions are made.

This approach also allows for the operation of generalized values which render the national interest greater than the sum of its parts. If the over-all perspective of their high offices leads policy makers to conclude that the demands made upon them are, taken together, insufficient to serve the welfare of the nation, and if they therefore superimpose their own values on the decision-making process, then clearly the analyst can treat the national interest as more than the cumulated total of subnational interests without falling back on his own view of what is best for the society he is examining.

Yet the decision-making approach to the national interest also suffers from limitations. The main weakness is that it is not always possible to ascertain when a policy has been officially decided upon, since most policies undergo a continuous process of evolution and revision as external conditions change and internal demands shift. This difficulty cannot be circumvented by focusing on the values which officials espouse at any point in the decision-making process. For the various officials of a society often hold and assert different conceptions of what the goals of foreign policy ought to be. Under these circumstances, which usually prevail in open democratic societies, the analyst gets little guidance from the formulation that the national interest of a society is what its duly constituted policy makers claim it to be. The United States offers a good example of this dilemma. Not infrequently does it happen that the president, members of his cabinet, other executive-branch officials, and the leaders, committees, and individual members of Congress pursue values and policy goals which are in direct conflict and which they all contend are best for the nation. Who is correct? Operationally, they all are, as they all have some official responsibility for formulating and executing foreign policy. What, then, is the national interest? The question seems unanswerable unless the analyst is willing to fall back on his own values to decide which officials express the soundest and most representative views.

A second difficulty with the decision-making approach concerns closed authoritarian societies. Many groups in such societies have no opportunity to articulate their needs and wants, thereby undermining the assumption that the various interests of a society are sorted and summed in its political processes. It hardly seems plausible, for example, to equate the national interest of Germany during the Nazi period with the actions, pronouncements, and aspirations of Hitler. Such a formulation runs counter to the concerns which make the national interest attractive as an analytic concept. Yet, under the decision-making approach the analyst has no choice but to view Hitler's purging of the Jews and his launching of World War II as in the German national interest. To do otherwise is either to fall back on an objectivist view that there is a "true" national interest of Germany which Hitler violated or to be confronted with the insuperable problem of identifying and aggregating the unarticulated interests of the various groups then existent in Germany.

FUTURE OF THE CONCEPT

There can be little wonder, then, that the national interest has not sparked research or otherwise lived up to its early promise as an analytic tool. All the approaches to it suffer from difficulties which defy resolution and which confound rather than clarify analysis. As political inquiry becomes more systematic and explicit, the concept is therefore likely to be used less and less. Serious doubts about its analytic utility have already been expressed,[12] and it seems probable that objectivists and subjectivists alike will find that they can evaluate and explain foreign-policy phenomena adequately without having to resort to the national interest as an over-all explanation or characterization.

The trend toward more systematic inquiry is not the only reason why the abandonment of the concept is likely to be hastened in the future. The ever greater interdependence of nations and the emergence of increasing numbers of supranational actors is also bound to diminish reliance on the concept. Increasingly, decision makers act on behalf of clusters of nations as well as their own. They identify their own interests as inextricably tied to the welfare of their region, their continent, or their way of life. Many U.S. officials, for example, now argue that the public must make sacrifices for Latin America because a higher standard of living

12 George A. Modelski, *A Theory of Foreign Policy* (New York: Praeger, 1962), pp. 70–72.

throughout the Western Hemisphere is in the best interests of the United States. Similarly, other statesmen make decisions with a view to enhancing unformalized supranational communities, such as "the West," "the Arab world," and "the communist bloc," or formalized economic and political unions, such as the Common Market, Malaysia, and the West Indies Federation. Clearly such global tendencies further reduce the utility of an attempt to explain international behavior in terms of the national interest.

Yet, the national interest cannot be entirely abandoned. Even though the nation is declining in its importance as a political unit to which allegiances are attached, the process of decline is many decades—perhaps even centuries—away from an end. Political actors will no doubt continue to make extensive use of the national interest in their thinking about foreign-policy goals and in their efforts to mobilize support for them. And, to the extent that they do, political observers must take cognizance of the national interest. In other words, while the national interest has little future as an analytic concept, its use in politics will long continue to be a datum requiring analysis.

12   The Premises and Promises of Decision-Making Analysis *

 Like countries in the twentieth century, the sciences of human behavior seem to pass through several stages as they move toward modernization. During the *traditional* stage the practitioners in a field of inquiry rely on ambiguous concepts and untested theories to guide their impressions of the dynamics of their subject matter. Unrestrained by standards of reliability and unconcerned about the relationship of data to theory, the practitioners do not hesitate to attribute human characteristics to abstract entities and then to equate their insights into the behavior of these entities with human behavior itself. At this stage, consequently, knowledge is not cumulative. Being free to pursue their own interests in their own way, the various researchers do not build on each other's work. Case studies proliferate, but do not converge. New concepts and theories are advanced, only to go unheeded. What stands out are practitioners with a capacity for impressive insights, rather than insights with an impressive capacity for explaining an ever-widening range of phenomena.

 At a certain point, however, a few practitioners become dissatisfied with the procedures and assumptions of the traditional stage and develop the aspiration to modernize. The absence of progress toward unified knowl-

* An earlier version of this chapter was published in James C. Charlesworth (ed.), *Contemporary Political Analysis* (New York: The Free Press, 1967), pp. 189–211. Reprinted with the permission of the publisher. Copyright © 1967 by The Free Press, a Division of The Macmillan Company.

edge provokes them into protesting the reliance on ambiguous formulations, reified entities, and undisciplined modes of inquiry. Human behavior is not, the modernizing practitioners contend, abstract, mystical, or capricious, but is undertaken by concrete and identifiable actors whose behavior can be observed. Rather than being capricious, this behavior is the result of causal processes and thus exhibits regularities and patterns. Hence it is capable of being measured and quantified. Measurement and quantification, however, require explicit theory and operationalized concepts. Data do not fall into place on their own, but must be rendered meaningful by models and constructs that clearly identify how the components of behavior are structured and how they relate to each other. What is needed, the protest concludes, is greater attention to the accumulation of quantified data, to the formulation of empirical theories to explain the data, and to the utilization of scientific procedures which make both the data and the theories independent of those who use them.

Although the traditionalists in the field tend to feel threatened by the modernizing practitioners and to dismiss their protests as impracticable and misleading, the appeal of a more empirically based science cannot be denied and as the ranks of the protesters grow, the field moves into the *take-off* stage of development. Hence, as in the countries that move into this stage, the air becomes charged with excitement and commitment. A self-generating sense of change emerges and, with it, a headlong rush into uncharted areas of inquiry. No phenomenon is too minute to be considered; no fact is too established to be questioned; no abstraction is too sacrosanct to be challenged. Previously unrecognized sources of behavior are recognized and explored, giving rise to the identification of previously unidentified actors and the discernment of previously undiscerned relationships. New concepts, theories, models, frameworks, approaches, formulations, and hypotheses are proposed and modified. Schools of thought abound and factions within them emerge. Propositional inventories are compiled and philosophical underpinnings are contested. Sister disciplines are ransacked for relevant materials. Articles and arguments on methodology multiply. Untapped sources of data are discovered and exploited. Seemingly ungainly words are coined to designate the phenomena revealed by the new data or indicated by the new formulations. Diagrammatic presentations, replete with linking arrows and proliferating categories, are introduced to accommodate the new materials and depict their interrelationships.

Like the leaders of protest movements in traditional societies, however, the modernizing practitioners are not able to contain their revolutionary fervor once they overcome the forces of tradition and shoulder the responsibilities of leadership. The surge of innovative activity is too exciting and the vision of its ultimate potential is too exhilarating to temper enthusiasm with perspective, involvement with restraint, and creative formulations with scientific procedures. In the name of greater discipline the field comes to be marked by undisciplined inquiry. Freed of the traditional rules and as yet unconcerned about the need for modern ones, its newly ascendant practitioners are receptive to almost any innovative framework, irrespective of whether it is capable of yielding reliable empirical findings. Despite the welter of activity, therefore, knowledge is no more cumulative in the take-off stage than in the preceding one. Rather than building on each other's work and converging around accepted concepts and standardized procedures, the practitioners support each other's innovativeness even as they pursue their own. What stand out are insights that encompass an ever-widening range of phenomena, rather than an ever-widening range of phenomena that have been reliably explained.

The take-off stage lasts perhaps a decade or two—long enough for it to become apparent that the initial burst of activity has not resulted in a solid and expanding body of reliable knowledge. To be explicit and innovative about observable phenomena is not to engage in the painstaking task of actually observing them and then making the theoretical revisions that the observations require. Nor does the avoidance of impressionistic and reified analysis lead automatically to the formulation of viable frameworks and researchable propositions. As the modernizing practitioners slowly become aware that a science of human behavior cannot be built overnight and that instead slow, patient, and disciplined inquiry is required, the field moves into the third or *mature* stage of development. The innovative frameworks are scaled down to manageable proportions, the new concepts are rendered operational, and the resulting hypotheses are tested, revised, and tested again. As a result, the school of thought gives way to the empirical finding, the grandiose theory to the rigorous study, the propositional inventory to the research design, the philosophical challenge to quantitative analysis, and the all-encompassing insight to the precise formulation. Equally important, as the field becomes a mature science the criteria of relevance are toughened and the standards for processing data are raised. Where theories proposed during the take-off stage were accepted or rejected on the basis of speculation about their utility, those offered in the mature stage are broken down into their component parts and subjected to the test of empirical validation. Where journals were once filled with diagrammatic presentations, now they are characterized by tabular data tested for statistical significance. And with this greater discipline, the practitioners begin to take cognizance of each other's hypotheses, to use each other's methods, to carry each other's work one step further, to replicate each other's findings—in short, to build on each other's research. Consequently, knowledge cumulates, even explodes, and the practitioners settle into a sustained period of growth that is satisfying even if not exhilarating.

Since it is crucial to the central theme of the ensuing discussion, stress must be laid on the necessity for the take-off stage to intervene between the traditional and mature stages. It cannot be by-passed. There is no shortcut. The creativity must precede the discipline, the seminal thinker must precede the patient researcher, and the compelling scheme must precede the refined theory. Ofttimes the premises, concepts, and procedures that permitted the take-off are so thoroughly reworked as to be unrecognizable in the later stage, but without them maturity could not ensue.

THE PARADOX OF THE DECISION-MAKING APPROACH

The foregoing considerations have not only helped me to resolve my personal ambivalence (noted below) toward the concept of decision-making, but, more importantly, they also serve to summarize the paradox and controversy that have marked the concept since its introduction into American political science after World War II. Stated most succinctly, the paradox is that as a wide consensus formed over the utility of the concept, so did a deep dissensus develop over its contents, boundaries, and premises. Unlike, say, the extensive efforts at empirical validation that followed the initial enthusiasm which the introduction of the theory of cognitive dissonance aroused in social psychology,[1] the advent of the decision-making approach in political science evoked immediate attention and provoked considerable excitement that were not accompanied by endeavors to clarify its contents, eliminate its ambiguities, and trace the limits of its relevance. Rather than perfecting the concept of decision-making and narrowing its empirical meaning through subsequent inquiry, political scientists found it to be relevant in a variety of contexts. As a result, the concept has come to stand for an inconsistent set of diverse individual and group processes. For some, especially those attracted to game-theoretical formulations, decision-making phenomena connote rational calculations undertaken by hypothetical political actors. For those who find psychoanalytical notions persuasive, such phenomena pertain to the irrational drives that underlie the choices of real political actors. For still others, including both the probers of historical documents and the users

---

[1] The theory was introduced in Leon Festinger, *A Theory of Cognitive Dissonance* (New York: Harper, 1957). For a summary of the extensive efforts at empirical validation that followed, see Jack W. Brehm and Arthur R. Cohen, *Explorations in Cognitive Dissonance* (New York: Wiley, 1962).

of simulation techniques, the concept embraces all the factors, both rational and irrational, that enter into the process whereby empirical political actors select one course of action from among several possible alternatives.

For me both the history and the contents of the concept have always had a special meaning. In the early 1950s I had the good fortune of closely observing, as a graduate student at Princeton, Richard C. Snyder's attempts to develop what subsequently became the first systematic treatment of decision-making phenomena in the study of foreign policy and international politics.[2] Those were exciting days. Over and beyond the usual enthusiasm of a graduate student for a stimulating teacher, one was keenly aware of being in the presence of a modernizing practitioner at the very moment when his protest against traditional modes was being launched. Snyder went out of his way to be tactful and to avoid offense to the traditionalists. The emphasis was on the worth and potential of new concepts, not on the ambiguous and misleading nature of old ones. Yet there was no mistaking that a major skirmish in the battle for modernization was being joined. This was not to be merely a reformulation of a few marginal concepts. Rather the new concepts were conceived to be inextricably interrelated and, as such, to constitute nothing less than a full-fledged "approach" to the study of international political phenomena. The inexperienced graduate student may have been perplexed by the virulence of the controversy that the approach occasionally aroused in the Princeton community even before its publication, but he could hardly fail to recognize that Snyder's assumptions were a departure from the past and that acceptance of them necessitated a rejection of certain long-standing ways of thinking about international actors and processes.

[2] After initially formulating an approach to decision-making processes in foreign policy and international politics, Snyder outlined ways in which it might be broadened to encompass virtually any political process. However, I have confined my attention here mainly to the initial formulation, since it is the more elaborate of the two versions and has occasioned much more discussion than the broadened outline. In addition, since Snyder was the main creator of the approach, I have not included in the analysis references to the two junior colleagues who assisted him in developing the initial formulation and who are also listed as its authors. For the initial formulation, see Richard C. Snyder, H. W. Bruck, and Burton Sapin, *Decision-Making as an Approach to the Study of International Politics* (Princeton: Foreign Policy Analysis Project, Organizational Behavior Section, Princeton University, 1954), later reprinted in Richard C. Snyder, H. W. Bruck, and Burton Sapin, (eds.), *Foreign Policy Decision-Making: An Approach to the Study of International Politics* (New York: Free Press, 1962), pp. 14–185. For the broadened version of the formulation, see Richard C. Snyder, "A Decision-Making Approach to the Study of Political Phenomena," in Roland Young (ed.), *Approaches to the Study of Politics* (Evanston, Ill.: Northwestern University Press, 1958), pp. 3–38. Still another version, simplified for comprehension by undergraduate students, can be found in Richard C. Snyder and Edgar S. Furniss, Jr., *American Foreign Policy: Formulation, Principles, and Programs* (New York: Holt, 1954), Chap. 3.

Having had the introduction of the concept of foreign policy decision-making into American political science conjoined with the start of my own professional career, I have followed the evolution of the concept subsequent to its publication with particular care, rejoicing when a consensus formed and lamenting when dissensus also developed. Even more personally, the history of the concept since its publication has been the cause of considerable ambivalence. On the one hand, Snyder's framework so brilliantly clarified for me the nature of certain key aspects of international politics that I feel an enormous indebtedness to it and still fall back on it for stimulation. On the other hand, only one empirical application of the framework has ever found its way into the literature of the field,[3] and with each passing year I have increasingly come to doubt the merits of a framework that fails to spark empirical inquiry and thereby to meet the ultimate test by which any analytic scheme must be assessed. Only lately, and with the help of the analogy between the modernization of nations and intellectual disciplines, have I been able to resolve this ambivalence and evaluate the history and utility of the concept in a coherent way. What follows are the essential elements of this evaluation. The format is somewhat autobiographical and the tone is occasionally aggressive, but the commitment is to accuracy and balance. To anticipate the main thrust of the analysis, the decision-making approach is conceived as having been a crucial front in the behavioral revolution in political science and, like its parent movement, to have become the victim of its own achievements. In effect the ensuing pages etch another epitaph onto another monument to the same successful protest.[4]

DECISION-MAKING VARIABLES

At the heart of Snyder's original decision-making framework is the simple notion that political action is undertaken by concrete human beings and that comprehension of the dynamics of this action requires viewing the world from the perspective of these identifiable actors. The observer may regard the action as unwise and it may in fact prove disastrous, but neither the judgment nor the outcome serves to explain why the

---

[3] Richard C. Snyder and Glenn D. Paige, "The United States Decision to Resist Aggression in Korea: The Application of an Analytic Scheme," *Administrative Science Quarterly*, 3 (December 1958), pp. 342–378, amplified in Glenn D. Paige, *The Korean Decision* (New York: The Free Press, 1968).

[4] For a history and analysis of the behavioral revolution, see Robert A. Dahl, "The Behavioral Approach to Political Science: Epitaph for a Monument to a Successful Protest," *American Political Science Review*, LV (December 1961), pp. 763–772.

actors proceeded as they did. Only by transcending his own judgments and adopting the perspective of the actors can the observer engage in explanatory analysis. To facilitate reconstruction of the world of the actors, Snyder suggested that all their activities can be examined in terms of one main form of behavior, the decision to pursue one course of action rather than many others that might be pursued. Whatever the actors do, and however sound their actions may be, they proceed on the basis of prior choices, and the presence of this decision-making activity at the core of all political action provides a common focus for the analysis of otherwise disparate political actors, situations, and processes. Decision-making sustains bureaucracies, dominates legislatures, preoccupies chief executives, and characterizes judicial bodies. Decisions lead to policy, produce conflict, and foster cooperation. They differentiate political parties and underlie foreign policies, activate local governments and maintain federal authorities, guide armies and stir international organizations. To explain any sequence of political actions, therefore, the analyst must ascertain who made the key decisions that gave rise to the action and then assess the intellectual and interactive processes whereby the decision-makers reached their conclusions.

To facilitate further the reconstruction of the world of decision-makers, Snyder outlined and categorized the main factors that operate on them and give structure and content to their choices. In the case of foreign-policy choices, he subdivided the world of officials into three main sets of stimuli—those that emanate from the society for whom officials make decisions; those that arise out of circumstances or actions abroad, and those that are generated within the governmental organizations of which they are a part. Labeled, respectively, the "internal setting," the "external setting," and the "decision-making process," these categories were further subdivided in terms of certain major types of factors—nonhuman as well as human, attitudinal as well as behavioral—that each encompassed.[5] The internal setting was conceived to subsume not only such standard political phenomena as public opinion, but also "much more fundamental categories: major common-value orientations, major characteristics of social organization, group structures and function, major institutional patterns, basic social processes (adult socialization and opinion formation), and social differentiation and specialization."[6] The external setting was posited as comprising such phenomena as "the actions and reactions of other

---

[5] When he recast the framework to account for decision-making at any governmental level, Snyder understandably abandoned the external-internal distinction and referred instead to the "social" and "political institutional" settings (cf., Young, op. cit., p. 22). Here I have chosen to confine myself to the framework for the analysis of foreign-policy decisions because it has been more fully elaborated.

[6] Ibid.

states (their decision-makers), the societies for which they act, and the physical world."[7] The decision-making process was envisioned to consist of three main subcategories: spheres of competence, communication and information, and motivation. Taken together, these decision-making sub-categories include the roles, norms, goals, and functions within both the government in general and the particular unit making the decisions being subjected to analysis. In a diagrammatic presentation of the main categories and subcategories, and using a series of two-way arrows to link them together, Snyder demonstrated that the framework embraces a complex and interdependent set of social, political, and psychological processes. Most notably, he drew on a vast array of concepts developed in sociology, social psychology and psychology to show how the internal, external, and organizational worlds acquire structure and content—as well as how the links among them are fashioned—through the perceptions, motives, experiences, and interactions of the decision-makers.

Many years later all of this may seem so obvious as to be trite. But when photo-offset copies of the original formulation of the decision-making approach were distributed to a selected list of political scientists in the field of international politics in June, 1954, its basic premises were neither obvious nor trite. At that time, for example, precision about the identity of international actors and the sources of their behavior was not a domi-nant characteristic of research. Instead, the prevalent tendency was to regard the state as the prime actor and to look for the sources of its behavior in what were regarded as the objective realities of its position in the world. But who or what was the state? And how could the analyst, who inevitably had to rely on some degree of subjective interpretation, ever know what constituted the objective reality of its position? These troublesome questions had long been ignored. Many analysts were still content to treat the abstract state as if it were a concrete person and, in so doing, to impute to it the entire range of aspirations and traits normally associated with individual human actors. The fears of France and the hopes of India were treated as no less real and empirical than the quirks of a Charles De Gaulle and the idealism of a Jawaharlal Nehru.

Similarly, not being inclined to examine the attitudes and actions of concrete human beings, researchers still tended to search for the goals and sources of a state's behavior in geographic, historical, political, and technological circumstances, and these circumstances always seemed so unmistakable that the state was conceived to be subservient to them. Geography, history, politics, and technology were not conditions to be subjectively evaluated by officials, but rather were objective realities to which they had to pay heed. To know the goals of a state and identify

[7] Snyder, Bruck, and Sapin (eds.), *op. cit.*, p. 67.

its national interest, therefore, the analyst had only to discover the objective circumstances in which it was situated at any moment in time. That the "discovered" circumstances might be nothing more than the analyst's own subjective interpretation never gave much pause: in the absence of procedures for rendering findings independent of those who uncovered them, the inclination to equate reality with one's perceptions of it exerted a powerful and understandable hold on even the most dispassionate observers.[8]

With the publication of the decision-making approach, however, these long-standing habits of analysis could no longer be practiced with blissful unconcern. Whatever one may have thought of Snyder's scheme, there was no denying that it constituted a serious challenge to the prevailing assumptions. In a decision-making context, reification of the state and objectification of its circumstances are neither necessary nor desirable. By definition, the state becomes its decision-makers, those officials of a society who have the authority and responsibility for preserving its integrity and enhancing its values through the selection of appropriate courses of action. To be sure, officials speak in the name of abstract entities and many may even act as if such entities do have a concrete existence, but whatever the content of the speeches and actions, they constitute empirical phenomena that allow the analyst to come down from the rarefied atmosphere of abstractions to the observable world of interacting human beings.

In searching for the goals and interests of a state, moreover, analysts no longer had to run the risk of equating their subjective interpretations with objective realities. As indicated in the previous chapter, the decision-making approach offered a clear-cut operational solution to the problem: national interests and aspirations are neither more nor less than what the duly constituted decision-makers conceive them to be, and while ascertaining the aims and values of officials can be extremely difficult, at least it is possible. Stated differently, the reality of any situation is what the decision-makers, as aware (or unaware) of geographic, historical, political, and technological considerations as they may be, perceive it to be, and while the actions resulting from their perceptions may prove to be disastrous, such an outcome is due to the observable miscalculations of fallible men and not to the unknowable impact of inexorable forces.

Does this mean that the decision-making approach compels the analyst to ignore all the needs and wants of the members of the society and thus to posit a national interest that bears no relation to the hopes and fears of either the public in general or the particular segments of which it is

[8] For an elaboration of this reasoning, see Hans J. Morgenthau, *Politics Among Nations: The Struggle for Power and Peace*, 2nd ed. (New York: Knopf, 1954), Chap. 1.

comprised? Not at all, as no group of decision-makers that in fact has the authority to bind the society to a course of action can ever be totally cut off from its demands and aspirations (or else it will lose the authority). Indeed, one of the innovative virtues of the decision-making approach was that it provided a way of empirically tracing the role of domestic variables as sources of foreign-policy behavior. Traditionally, students of the subject tended to assume that international actors were moved primarily by each other and, as a result, they dealt only superficially, if at all, with the processes whereby the history, composition, structure, and dynamics of a society condition its international behavior. Viewed in a decision-making context, however, domestic factors are, along with those located in the external setting and the decision-making organization, a major source of foreign policy and cannot be ignored. Just as the analyst is led to ask how perceptions of events abroad condition the choices that decision-makers make, so is he inclined to probe how developments at home enter into the formulation and selection of policy alternatives.

The fact that the decision-making process is itself treated as a major source of the policies adopted constituted still another clarifying innovation fostered by Snyder's framework. Previously analysts had been inclined to assume a simple one-to-one relationship between the stimuli to which officials are exposed and the decisions whereby they respond. But, Snyder contended, what the contents of a decision are, depends partly—and sometimes crucially—on how it is formulated as well as on the circumstances to which it is a response. At least in large industrial societies, which necessarily have evolved complex bureaucratic structures for making decisions, external events and internal demands must be processed as well as perceived by officialdom if decisions are to be made, and in this processing—in the rivalries of agencies, the procedures for convening and conducting committees, the techniques for collecting and distributing intelligence, the role requirements of particular policy-makers, the general structure of authority, the accepted style of framing and winnowing alternatives, the precedents for resolving conflicts, the modal backgrounds and career motivations of top officials—factors are introduced that shape the contents, direction, and adequacy of the resulting decisions. Most of Snyder's framework is devoted to an elaboration of these organizational variables and the many ways in which they can affect the choices that emerge from a decision-making organization.

REASONING AND MOTIVATION
IN DECISION-MAKING ANALYSIS

That the decision-making approach constituted a radical departure from traditional practices at the time of its publication is perhaps best demonstrated by the nature of the criticisms it evoked. While some critics properly noted that the framework suffered from an absence of theory,[9] others were so provoked that they misunderstood its basic premises and criticized the scheme for proposing research strategies that in fact it explicitly rejected. As noted below, the approach is not lacking in severe limitations, but to criticize it for the assumptions it makes about the rationality or irrationality of officials and the policy-making process is to fail, in the most profound way, to grasp the central thrust of the analysis. Indeed, it is a measure of the extent of this failure that some of Snyder's least sympathetic critics rejected his approach on the grounds that it posited the decision-making process as too rational and that some condemned it for exaggerating the irrationality of the process. The former, apparently appalled by the proliferation of categories and subcategories in the discussion of the decision-making process, somehow concluded that the scheme viewed decision-makers as carefully weighing the pros and cons subsumed in each subcategory before framing alternative courses of action and of then giving serious consideration to every possible alternative before finally choosing one of them. Such a process, the critics rightly noted, involves a degree of rationality that bears little relationship to the world in which officials conduct their deliberations. Neither the time nor the resources are available to identify and relate all the ends and means that might be relevant when a situation requiring a decision arises.[10] As I read it, however, Snyder's formulation does not suggest that foreign-policy decision-making necessarily unfolds in a rational and conscious fashion. It merely asserts that officials have some notion, conscious or unconscious, of a priority of values; that they possess some conceptions, elegant or crude, of the means available and their potential effectiveness; that they engage in some effort, extensive or brief, to relate means to ends; and that, therefore, at some point they select some alternative,

[9] Cf. Herbert McClosky, "Concerning Strategies for a Science of International Politics," *World Politics,* VIII (January 1956), pp. 281–95; and Vernon Van Dyke, *Political Science: A Philosophical Analysis* (Stanford, Cal.: Stanford University Press, 1960), p. 153.

[10] For a specific criticism of Snyder for positing "highly conscious moves and choices which can be analyzed in terms of neat categories," see Stanley H. Hoffmann, "International Relations: The Long Road to Theory," *World Politics,* XI (April 1959), p. 364. For a general critique of the decision-making literature that elaborates this theme, see Charles E. Lindblom, "The Science of 'Muddling Through,'" *Public Administration Review,* 29 (Spring 1959), pp. 79–88.

clear-cut or confused, as the course of action that seems most likely to cope with the immediate situation. Game theory may posit rational actors, but the decision-making approach does not, In effect, Snyder left the question open. In his approach it is an empirical question: intellectual and interactive processes necessarily precede decision, but whether they do so rationally or irrationally is a matter to be determined through the gathering and analysis of data.

Much the same can be said about the proliferation of categories. While the decision-making approach assumes that the antecedents of decision do occur in terms of a wide variety of role requirements, communication processes, and motivational determinants, the relevance of these variables to the choices that are made is not assumed in advance. If empirical investigation indicates that some of the subcategories will not yield particularly significant findings, then they are passed over and more fruitful matters are considered. For example, if in certain situations stimuli in the external setting prove more central to the responses of officials than those arising within the decision-making organization or internal setting, then in those situations the latter are not examined as thoroughly as the former. By calculating the relative strength of the different sets of variables, however, the analyst has at least made sure that he searches for the sources of behavior in the only place where they can be found, namely, in the responses of officials to the external setting and not in the external setting itself. To proliferate categories is not to make a commitment to divide attention equally among them. Rather it is to ensure that no relevant considerations are overlooked.

While some analysts discerned an assumption of rationality in the fact that stimuli inherent in the decision-making process received considerably more attention than those located in the internal or external settings, others responded to this perceived imbalance by objecting to Snyder's framework for exactly opposite reasons. These critics concluded that the decision-making approach required the researcher to proceed as an amateur psychoanalyst in search of personality traits, private prejudices, and uncontrolled drives that might underlie the behavior of officials.[11] This line of criticism seems even more unwarranted than the one which posits the decision-making approach as overly preoccupied with rational actors. For not only did Snyder avoid an assumption of irrationality, he explicitly and emphatically rejected it, In what is unques-

[11] For an example of a critic who concluded that "those who hold to the decision-making approach . . . consider it necessary to probe into the personal events that take place within the psyches of men," see Arnold Wolfers, "The Actors in International Politics," in William T. R. Fox (ed.), *Theoretical Aspects of International Relations* (Notre Dame, Ind.: University of Notre Dame Press, 1959), esp. p. 92.

tionably one of the most incisive and thorough translations of the psychological literature on motivation into a political context,[12] Snyder stresses that while students of foreign policy cannot afford to ignore motivational factors if they are to explain the behavior of concrete international actors, they need not be concerned with the entire range of motives that might be operative. Motives are conceived to be of two kinds, those that an official acquires through membership and participation in the decision-making organization and those he develops as an individual in a vast array of prior experiences during childhood and adulthood. The former are what Snyder calls *in order to* motives, since they impel officials to act in order to achieve or maintain a future state of affairs in the decision-making organization, in the internal setting, or in the external setting. The latter are labeled *because of* motives, since the behavior to which they lead can be said to occur because of idiosyncratic predispositions acquired in the course of past experience. Political scientists, Snyder emphasized, may not have to devote equal attention to both types of motives. Students of foreign policy are not interested in the official as a whole human being, but only in that part of him that gives rise to his behavior as an official. Hence, while psychologists and historians might have reason to examine the idiosyncratic aspects of his personality and past experience, political scientists may be able to develop sufficient explanations of his behavior without ever investigating the "because of" motives that gave rise to it. Indeed, in what comes closest to an explicit theoretical proposition in the entire formulation, Snyder contends that usually the behavior of officials can be satisfactorily explained through an exploration of the motives derived from their decision-making organization, from their interpretations of the society's goals, and from their reactions to demands of situations in the internal and external settings—and that therefore it is usually not necessary to investigate their "because of" motives. Ordinarily, for example, one does not need to know the details of a chief executive's upbringing or the profession in which he was trained after completing his formal education in order to explain his decision to arm allies and otherwise contest the aggressive behavior of a potential enemy. The decision is entirely comprehensible in terms of the perceptions and values which any occupant of the role is likely to have.

Yet this is not a rigid proposition. Even as he asserts it, Snyder acknowledges that the analysis of "in order to" motives may not always yield a satisfactory explanation, that there may be circumstances in which the individual variables are so strong that "because of" motives must be investigated if an adequate assessment is to be made. If this should be the case, the decision-making approach does not preclude such an

[12] Snyder, Bruck, and Sapin (eds.), *op. cit.*, pp. 137–173.

investigation. Snyder argues only that since "because of" motives are likely to be least relevant, considerable time and energy can be saved by examining the "in order to" motives *first*. Individual variables, in other words, are treated as a residual category which the researcher considers only if there is a residue of behavior that is unaccounted for. Proceeding in this way the researcher not only avoids in most instances the difficult task of searching for personality data, but he also isolates, in the remaining cases, "what area of behavior must be accounted for in terms of idiosyncratic factors, that is, self-oriented needs not prompted by the system."[13]

Plainly this reasoning is not the equivalent of assuming that comprehension of the decision-making process requires exploration of the psyches and irrational impulses of officials. Again the question is left open. Motives are operative and they must be examined, but whether they are rational or irrational is a matter to be determined by the accumulation and inspection of empirical data.[14]

THE IMPACT OF THE
DECISION-MAKING APPROACH

Despite the critical preoccupation with the rationality problem, Snyder's emphasis upon decisional phenomena stirred widespread thought among political scientists, especially those in the fields of international politics and foreign policy. Of course, it would be patently false to argue that he was alone responsible for the shift away from the analysis of reified abstractions and toward the investigation of empirical choices. Intellectual ferment never stems from only one source, and there was no lack of protest against the traditional modes of analyzing international actors prior to 1954. Not until the decision-making approach was published in that year, however, did a shift in analytic practice become manifest.

---

13 *Ibid.*, p. 161.

14 Furthermore, there is nothing in the decision-making approach which suggests that "in order to" motives are rational and "because of" motives irrational. It was the critics of the approach that introduced the criterion of rationality. Snyder himself never distinguished between the two types of motives in terms of this criterion nor even implied that one type is likely to be more rational than the other. On the contrary, the dynamics of organizational decision-making are conceived to be just as capable of fostering inappropriate behavior as are the psychological processes of individuals. One can readily imagine circumstances under which the idiosyncratic experiences of an official will give rise to choices that are more consistent with the analyst's criterion of rationality than are the choices provided the official by his organization. For a cogent discussion of these matters, see Sidney Verba, "Assumptions of Rationality and Non-Rationality in Models of the International System," *World Politics*, XIV (October 1961), pp. 93–117.

Perhaps the shift and the publication of the approach were mere coincidence, but I have always felt that the coherence and thoughtfulness of Snyder's formulation served to crystallize the ferment and to provide guidance—or at least legitimacy—for those who had become disenchanted with a world composed of abstract states and with a mythical quest for single-cause explanations of objective reality.

In any event, whatever the historical relation between the publication of the decision-making approach in 1954 and subsequent practice, in the ensuing years decisional phenomena did become a central concern of students of politics. Signs of this shift were everywhere—in the language analysts employed, in the phenomena that they studied, in the concepts they developed, and in the methods they used to generate data. The most obvious of these signs, of course, was the acceptance of the terminology of decision-making. The phrase itself began to appear in the titles of books and articles as well as in their contents,[15] and soon became a permanent fixture in the vocabulary of political analysis. Indeed, the phrase even overcame the layman's tendency to dismiss the scholar's terminology as unnecessary jargon and found its way into the vocabulary of politics. It is one of the few technical terms of political science that occasionally appears in the speeches of presidents, the appeals of candidates, the debates of Congressmen, and the editorials and headlines of newspapers. It seems more than a mere accident of style that led a recent President of the United States to refer to "the dark and tangled stretches in the decision-making process."[16] Like political scientists—and, I believe, because of them—many top officials have been attracted by the substance as well as the terminology of decision-making analysis.[17]

The impact of the decision-making approach could even be discerned in the work of scholars who continue to use some of the traditional terminology. For several years subsequent to 1954 it became quite commonplace for analysts to preface their use of abstract terms with qualifying footnotes that took note of the dangers of reification and that recast the

---

[15] For example, see Donald R. Matthews, *The Social Background of Political Decision-Makers* (Garden City: Doubleday, 1954); Dwaine Marvick (ed.), *Political Decision-Makers* (New York: Free Press, 1961); and Karl W. Deutsch, "Mass Communications and the Loss of Freedom in National Decision-Making: A Possible Research Approach to Interstate Conflicts," *Journal of Conflict Resolution,* I (June 1957), pp. 200–211.

[16] John F. Kennedy, "Foreword," in Theodore C. Sorenson, *Decision-Making in the White House: The Olive Branch or the Arrows* (New York: Columbia University Press, 1963), p. xiii.

[17] For a multitude of evidence along this line, see U.S. Senate, Committee on Government Operations, Subcommittee on National Policy Machinery, *Organizing for National Security* (Washington, D.C.: Government Printing Office, 1961), Vols. I–III; and Charles J. Hitch, *Decision-Making for Defense* (Berkeley: University of California Press, 1965), *passim.*

traditional language into a decision-making context. The following is a typical expression of this qualification:

Although there are frequent references in this study to such collective nouns as the "nation," "country," "state," and "government," it is to be clearly understood throughout that these terms are used merely for the sake of convenient exposition. Only individuals have motives, expectations, and interests, and only they act or behave. Strictly speaking, it is not the "state," in the above reference, which substitutes its schedule for that of private persons, but certain officials who, with the acquiescence of other persons, shift resources to new goals and away from others valued highly in peacetime.[18]

More significantly, the terminological shifts were accompanied by changes in the way political scientists structured their subject matter and the concepts they used to probe it. The substantive shifts were subtle and gradual, but in retrospect they are clearly discernible. Students of foreign policy, for example, were not only less disposed to posit abstract actors, but they also spoke less of compelling realities and more of conflicting alternatives, less of the formalities of diplomacy and more of the dilemmas of diplomats, less of the demands of situations and more of their limits and opportunities, less of the primacy of international affairs and more of the competition between domestic and foreign policy goals. To be more specific, during the decade subsequent to 1954 the literature of the field was swollen by a veritable flood of new inquiries that, coincidentally or otherwise, reflected the premises of the decision-making approach: the origins of World War I were probed in terms of the perceptions which key officials in the various countries had of their capabilities and their adversaries;[19] the production of information for the makers of foreign policy was examined in terms of a conflict between the perspectives of the gatherers and users of intelligence;[20] the capabilities available to policy-makers were conceived in terms of a distinction between those perceived by officials (the "psychological environment") and those that existed irrespective of whether they were perceived (the "operational environment");[21] the evolution and choice of policy alternatives were analyzed in terms of the requirements and processes of consensus-building

[18] Klaus Knorr, *The War Potential of Nations* (Princeton: Princeton University Press, 1956), p. 64.

[19] Dina A. Zinnes, Robert C. North, and Howard E. Koch, Jr., "Capability, Threat, and the Outbreak of War," in James N. Rosenau (ed.), *International Politics and Foreign Policy* (New York: Free Press, 1961), pp. 469–482.

[20] Cf. Roger Hilsman, *Strategic Intelligence and National Decisions* (New York: Free Press, 1956).

[21] Harold and Margaret Sprout, "Environmental Factors in the Study of International Politics," *Journal of Conflict Resolution*, I (December 1957), pp. 309–328.

among executive agencies,[22] military services,[23] and nongovernmental leaders;[24] the development and change of policy goals were assessed in terms of shifting motivational patterns among participating officials;[25] the relationship between executive and legislative policy-makers and agencies was posited and probed as a communications process,[26] as were the relations between policy-makers and their publics,[27] between officials and the press,[28] and between legislators and interest groups;[29] psychological warfare was seen in terms of the intellectual and organizational context of those who conduct it as well as those toward whom it is directed;[30] the role of delegate to the United Nations was conceived in terms of the stimuli experienced by its occupants;[31] the role of legislator was conceptualized in terms of the conflicts between internal and external variables [32] and between role and individual variables;[33] the relevance of personal experience and professional training for the foreign policy outlooks of academics,[34] scientists,[35] military officers,[36] Southerners, [37] and other

[22] Roger Hilsman, "The Foreign-Policy Consensus: An Interim Research Report," *Journal of Conflict Resolution*, III (December 1959), pp. 361–382.

[23] Samuel P. Huntington, *The Common Defense: Strategic Programs in National Politics* (New York: Columbia University Press, 1961).

[24] James N. Rosenau, *National Leadership and Foreign Policy: A Case Study in the Mobilization of Public Support* (Princeton: Princeton University Press, 1963).

[25] Vernon Van Dyke, *Pride and Power: The Rationale of the Space Program* (Urbana: University of Illinois Press, 1964).

[26] James A. Robinson, *Congress and Foreign-Policy Making: A Study in Legislative Influence and Initiative* (Homewood, Ill.: Dorsey, 1962).

[27] Bernard C. Cohen, *The Political Process and Foreign Policy: The Making of the Japanese Peace Settlement* (Princeton: Princeton University Press, 1957); also see Karl W. Deutsch and Lewis J. Edinger, *Germany Rejoins the Powers: Mass Opinion Interest Groups, and Elites in Contemporary German Foreign Policy* (Stanford, Cal.: Stanford University Press, 1959).

[28] Bernard C. Cohen, *The Press and Foreign Policy* (Princeton: Princeton University Press, 1963).

[29] Raymond A. Bauer, Ithiel de Sola Pool, and Lewis Anthony Dexter, *American Business and Public Policy: The Politics of Foreign Trade* (New York: Atherton, 1963).

[30] Robert T. Holt and Robert W. van de Velde, *Strategic Psychological Operations and American Foreign Policy* (Chicago: University of Chicago Press, 1960).

[31] Chadwick F. Alger, "United Nations Participation as a Learning Experience," *Public Opinion Quarterly*, XXVII (Fall 1963), pp. 411–426.

[32] Roland Young, *The American Congress* (New York: Harper, 1958).

[33] See Chapter VI.

[34] Gene M. Lyons and Louis Morton, *Schools for Strategy: Education and Research in International Security Affairs* (New York: Praeger, 1965).

[35] Robert Gilpin, *American Scientists and Nuclear Weapons Policy* (Princeton: Princeton University Press, 1962). See also Robert Gilpin and Christopher Wright (eds.), *Scientists and National Policy-Making* (New York: Columbia University Press, 1964).

[36] Morris Janowitz, *The Professional Soldier: A Social and Political Portrait* (Glencoe: Free Press, 1960), and John W. Masland and Laurence I. Radway,

role occupants[38] was subjected to searching inquiry, as was the socialization of legislators,[39] foreign service officers,[40] and secretaries of state[41] into their roles; and the relevance of goals in different issue-areas as a source of differential behavior on the part of the same actors was explored.[42]

As even this small sample of illustrations indicates, however, the post-1954 concern with decisional phenomena was scattered over a vast range of diverse and unrelated problems. Decisional phenomena served as a common concern, but they did not serve to foster coherence in research. Few analysts probed different aspects of the same problem and even fewer built upon the findings of others. Comparison of the foreign policy process of different nations became a widespread preoccupation,[43] but the comparisons generally lacked uniformity and, in effect, were little more than single-nation analyses juxtaposed with each other. Spurred by the application of game theory to the problems of deterrence in a world of nuclear superpowers, efforts to develop formal models of the utility-probability calculations made by foreign-policy actors also attracted a number of practitioners,[44] but these too failed to achieve uniformity as many of the analysts became restless in face of the difficulty of estimating

Soldiers and Scholars: Military Education and National Policy (Princeton: Princeton University Press, 1957).

[37] Alfred O. Hero, Jr., *The Southerner and World Affairs* (Baton Rouge: Louisiana State University Press, 1965).

[38] R. Joseph Monson, Jr., and Mark W. Cannon, *The Makers of Public Policy: American Power Groups and Their Ideologies* (New York: McGraw-Hill, 1965); and Hans Speier and W. Phillips Davison (eds.), *West German Leadership and Foreign Policy* (New York: Harper, 1957).

[39] James David Barber, *The Lawmakers: Recruitment and Adaptation to Legislative Life* (New Haven: Yale University Press, 1965).

[40] James L. McCamy, *Conduct of the New Diplomacy* (New York: Harper, 1964), Part III.

[41] W. Lloyd Warner, Norman H. Martin, Paul P. Van Riper, and Orvis F. Collins, *The American Federal Executive: A Study of the Social and Personal Characteristics of the Civilian and Military Leaders of the United States Federal Government* (New Haven: Yale University Press, 1963), and Dean E. Mann, with Jameson W. Doig, *The Assistant Secretaries: Problems and Processes of Appointment* (Washington, D.C.: Brookings, 1965).

[42] Theodore J. Lowi, "American Business, Public Policy, Case Studies, and Political Theory," *World Politics*, XVI (July 1964), pp. 677–715. See also James N. Rosenau (ed.), *Domestic Sources of Foreign Policy* (New York: Free Press, 1967), *passim*.

[43] For example, see Joseph E. Black and Kenneth W. Thompson (eds.), *Foreign Policies in a World of Change* (New York: Harper, 1963); Roy C. Macridis (ed.), *Foreign Policy in World Politics*, 2nd. ed. (Englewood Cliffs: Prentice-Hall, 1962); and Kurt London, *The Making of Foreign Policy: East and West* (Philadelphia: Lippincott, 1965).

[44] For example, see Bruce M. Russett, "The Calculus of Deterrence," *Journal of Conflict Resolution*, VII (June 1963), pp. 97–109; and J. David Singer, "Inter-Nation Influence: A Formal Model," *American Political Science Review*, LVII (June 1965), pp. 420–430.

the subconscious and subjective factors that underlie the calculations of utilities and probabilities in a particular situation.[45] Anxious to account for these subjective factors under various circumstances, other analysts turned to simulating international phenomena in a laboratory,[46] but the wide use of the technique of simulation has yet to yield a coherent body of findings.

Least of all did the post-1954 lines of inquiry yield any extension of the original decision-making approach itself. Stimulating as Snyder's scheme was, as of this writing it has yet to arouse widespread attempts at conceptual modification or empirical validation. Thought was provoked and decisional phenomena came to be emphasized, but the approach itself remains unamplified. There has been no rush of graduate students to expand its propositions in Ph.D. dissertations and no accumulation of case studies utilizing its categories. As previously noted, only one direct effort to apply the approach has been undertaken and even this failed to yield amplification or clarification of the foreign policy decision-making process in other than the single situation to which it was applied. To be sure, the approach has been widely excerpted in anthologies[47] and students in undergraduate and graduate programs still receive an introduction to its premises. Otherwise, however, the approach as such has tended to disappear from sight. The original formulation no longer recurs in the footnotes of professional articles or in discussions at professional conferences.

THE NEED FOR THEORY

How can we explain the decision-making approach's apparent lack

[45] Cf. Martin Patchen, "Decision Theory in the Study of National Action: Problems and a Proposal," *Journal of Conflict Resolution,* IX (June 1965), pp. 164–176; and Bruce M. Russett, "Pearl Harbor: Deterrence Theory and Decision Theory," *Journal of Peace Research,* 2 (1967), pp. 89–106.

[46] Among the many who moved in this direction was the main author of the decision-making approach himself: see Richard C. Snyder, "Experimental Techniques and Political Analysis: Some Reflections in the Context of Concern Over Behavioral Approaches," in James C. Charlesworth (ed.), *The Limits of Behavioralism in Political Science* (Philadelphia: American Academy of Political and Social Science, 1962), pp. 94–123; and Harold Guetzkow, Chadwick F. Alger, Richard A. Brody, Robert C. Noel and Richard C. Snyder, *Simulation in International Relations* (Englewood Cliffs: Prentice-Hall, 1963).

[47] For example, see Heinz Eulau, Samuel J. Eldersveld, and Morris Janowitz (eds.), *Political Behavior: A Reader in Theory and Research* (New York: Free Press, 1956), pp. 352–359; Stanley H. Hoffmann (ed.), *Contemporary Theory in International Relations* (Englewood Cliffs: Prentice-Hall, 1960), pp. 150–165; and James N. Rosenau (ed.), *International Politics and Foreign Policy: A Reader in Research and Theory* (New York: Free Press, 1961), pp. 186–192, 247–253.

of durability? How do we resolve the contradiction between the claim that its impact was pervasive and the conclusion that it failed to generate theoretical elaboration or even empirical case studies? If the impact was so extensive, why are traces of the original formulation vanishing from present-day literature and research? Is it that Snyder was so far ahead of the field that it is still catching up and that the *next* decade will witness attempts to apply and expand his formulation? Or, more personally, is it that I have engaged in wishful thinking and allowed my assessment of the merits and impact of the decision-making approach to be distorted by the way it enriched my own graduate training? Could it be that the approach never was capable of elaboration and that I have been blinded by attachments to a favored teacher?

The answer to these questions has two dimensions which, taken together, serve both to explain the discrepancies in the previous analysis and to justify indebtedness to Snyder and his approach. One dimension concerns the lack of theory in the original formulation and the other posits a justification for this lack. While many of the criticisms of the approach were ill-founded, it is certainly true that Snyder identified the existence of a number of relationships without attempting to theorize about their components and structure. Notwithstanding the vast array of categories and subcategories, the links among them remain unspecified. As previously indicated, only the place of individual variables—"because of" motives—are the subject of predictive assessment and even here the prediction is cast in such broad terms as to have little relevance for specific situations. To posit decision-making as a central activity and the internal, external, and organizational settings as prime sources of this activity is not to suggest the relative strength of these sources under varying conditions or the interaction between them. To indicate that the strengths of the relevant variables have to be assessed and compared is not to outline a method for assessing them or a basis for comparing them. Yet, self-admittedly, Snyder did not carry his analysis to these lengths. He identified unexplored phenomena, but did not indicate how they might unfold. He called attention to new premises and concepts, but did not specify when, where, and how they might be used. He suggested problems that could be fruitfully researched, but did not provide substantive guidance as to how the researcher should proceed.[48]

---

[48] Some years later Snyder, with another colleague, somewhat offset this deficiency by outlining fifty-six research projects that could usefully be undertaken. However, again there was a shortage of theoretical propositions and the guidance provided for carrying out each project was mainly in the form of questions that might be considered and bibliographical sources that might be consulted. Cf. Richard C. Snyder and James A. Robinson, *National and International Decision-Making:*

Conspicuously missing from the decision-making approach, in other words, are any "if-then" hypotheses—propositions which indicate that *if* certain circumstances are operative, *then* certain decisions and actions are likely to ensue. The difficulty with all the categories and subcategories subsumed by the approach is not that they have been proliferated, but rather that they have been isolated from each other. Our computer technology is fully capable of coping with the proliferation problem. But the computer has to be programmed. It cannot in itself handle the problem of cross-tabulating and analyzing the subcategorized data. For this, theory —or, if theory is too stringent a requirement, simple if-then propositions— is needed that instructs the computer how to process the data in terms of the interaction that is presumed to take place within and among the categories.

The main reason for the lack of theory is clear. While the organization variables are elaborated at length, those in the internal and external settings are merely identified. Anxious to demonstrate the relevance of the decision-making process to the contents of foreign-policy decisions, Snyder explicitly passed quickly over the domestic and foreign sources of motivation, pausing only long enough to note their existence and the necessity of viewing them from the perspective of officials in an organizational context. But to theorize about the decisions that officials are likely to make, one must have some notion of the nature of the stimuli to which they are exposed. Variables within the decision-making organization may be crucial, but they are variables, and events or trends outside the organization are key determinants of the way in which they vary. Domestic demands and national aspirations may be increasingly important sources of foreign policy, but the conditions under which they are salient for officials can fluctuate markedly. External demands are perhaps subject to even wider and more erratic fluctuation. Since Snyder did not enumerate any of the factors in the internal and external settings to which decision-makers might respond, naturally he was not led to hypothesize about the choices that they might make in different types of situations.

Theories of political decision-making, in other words, can never be exclusively comprised of propositions about the officials who make choices. Processes located in the environment toward which officials direct their decisions are no less relevant than those which occur in their minds and interactions. To reconstruct the world from the perspective of the decision-maker, the researcher must examine the world itself in order to comprehend the dynamics and limits of the decision-maker's perspective. To predict the direction, timing and nature of political decisions, one must

A Report to the Committee on Research for Peace (New York: Institute for International Order, 1961).

include and interrelate variables pertaining to the targets of the decisions, the actors making them, and the relationship between the targets and the actions. To expect decisional phenomena to provide the sole basis for if-then propositions about politics is thus to establish an unattainable goal. There can be no theory of political decision-making that is divorced from the political environment with respect to which decisions are made. The decision-maker may serve as the organizing focus, but propositions about his behavior are bound to be as diverse and discontinuous as the targets of his behavior and the circumstances under which he makes his choices. A unified theory of political decision-making would be nothing less than a theory of the entire political process.

Little wonder, then, that students of foreign policy did not converge upon the decision-making approach in an effort to apply and extend it. Lacking theoretical propositions and all the materials out of which such propositions must be fashioned, it contained no encouragement to application and extension. The premises were clarifying and the concepts new and useful, but there were no loose ends to tie, no intriguing hypotheses to challenge or empirical observations to test. One could only adapt the premises and concepts to whatever substantive problems and phenomena one might be interested in—say, to the origins of World War I, to the conflicts between gatherers and users of intelligence, to the analysis of capabilities, to the role of U.N. delegate.

But hindsight is easy. Reconstructing the world of political science from the perspective of the mid-1950s, another, more justifiable reason emerges as an explanation of why Snyder settled for the decision-making approach rather than attempting a theory of international politics and foreign policy. Comprehension of international phenomena at the time he developed his scheme was rudimentary. Since international action had previously been conceived to be undertaken by abstract actors, data on interaction among decision-makers, their organizations, and their internal and external settings had not been systematically developed. For Snyder to have enumerated, assessed, and compared the strength of the relevant variables in 1954 would thus have been to engage in sheer guesswork. He could not turn to a body of reliable findings as a basis for articulating theoretical propositions. For such findings to come into existence a break with traditional modes of analysis had to be made. Reification had to be undermined. The quest for insight into reality had to be redirected. The nature of decisional phenomena had to be brought into focus. The existence of organizational and domestic variables had to be established. The case for inquiring into motivation had to be made and the legitimacy of importing concepts from other social sciences had to be demonstrated. In short, the field had to pass into and through the take-off stage before its practitioners would be in a situation to evolve theoretical propositions that would assess and compare the relevant organizational, internal, and external variables.

The study of foreign policy has since advanced well into the take-off stage and is rapidly approaching the transition to maturity. Almost every day—or at least every issue of the professional journals—brings fresh evidence that practitioners are beginning to assess the relative strength of internal and external variables as sources of international behavior undertaken by officials whose deliberations occur in different types of governments and societies. In so doing they take for granted that action is sustained by concrete and identifiable persons, that the goals of this action arise out of a need to balance internal and external demands, that the way in which officials experience these demands is a consequence of organizational as well as intellectual processes, and that therefore the researcher must investigate both the nature and processing of the demands if he is to comprehend, explain, and predict the quality and direction of the action.

The decision-making approach, in other words, has been absorbed into the practice of foreign policy analysis. The habits it challenged have been largely abandoned and the new ones it proposed have become so fully incorporated into the working assumptions of practitioners that they no longer need to be explicated or the original formulation from which they came cited. Unencumbered by mystical concepts, unconcerned about reified abstractions, disinclined to search for objective reality, and willing to settle for replicable findings, practitioners are now free to devote themselves to the painstaking tasks of constructing and testing hypotheses about the behavior of international actors. Now they can utilize the technique of simulation and pursue the logic of game theory in meaningful and productive ways. Now they are free to enjoy the prime pleasure of empirical research: that endless sequence whereby new theoretical propositions exert pressure to gather new data which, in turn, initiate pressure for still newer theory. None of these opportunities or pleasures would have been available if an earlier generation had not cleared the way by calling attention to the centrality of decision-making phenomena.

13 The External Environment as a Variable in Foreign Policy Analysis *

The behavior of any human system, whether it be a single person or a complex society, results in part from the cumulative weight of past experience and in part from the impact of current stimuli. Anyone who has ever enjoyed the task of raising a small child can provide ample testimony on the interplay of the historical and the environmental—the habits and characteristics that have been shaped by previous conditions and the impulses and responses that are evoked by new circumstances. Indeed, child development becomes most intriguing when prevailing demands and established habits come into conflict. For these are the times when unexpected behavior occurs as the child achieves a new synthesis between the past and the present.

The characteristics and behavior of social systems can also be seen, at any moment in time, as products of both their cultural tradition and their changing environments. Consider societies undergoing rapid economic and political development. The dynamics of development alter the objective circumstances of a society and, in the process, they also equip individuals with new skills that give rise to new attitudes which, in turn, foster new institutions. These new circumstances, skills, attitudes, and institutions, however, do not necessarily replace the old patterns that prevailed prior to the onset of the developmental process. The cultural norms and the historical traditions passed down from earlier generations may continue to operate upon the members of the society. An American

* An earlier version of this chapter was published in James N. Rosenau, Vincent Davis, Maurice A. East (eds.), *The Analysis of International Politics* (New York: The Free Press, 1972), pp. 145-165. Reprinted with the permission of the publisher. Copyright © 1972 by The Free Press, a Division of The Macmillan Company.

engineer is a U.S. citizen as well as a skilled technician. An African physicist has tribal ancestors as well as complex knowledge. An Asian economist may be as familiar with the teachings of Buddha as he is with those of Keynes. But which are the dominant forces, those derived from national culture or those inherent in industrialization? Do new circumstances, skills, attitudes, and institutions compete with and ultimately replace the old ones? Or do they coexist and eventually yield a new synthesis that is a blend of the historical and the environmental? Are the educated African and the educated American more like each other in their attitude toward, say, political involvement and public issues than the former is like uneducated Africans and the latter like uneducated Americans? Even more specifically, if a sample of 2,000 persons consisting of 500 Africans with a Ph.D. in political science, 500 Africans with no more than a sixth-grade education, 500 Americans with a Ph.D. in political science, and 500 Americans with no more than a sixth-grade education were asked to respond to questions that probed their sense of competence as a citizen, would their responses be distributed as follows?

	high competence	low competence
African Ph.D.'s	500	0
6th-grade Africans	0	500
American Ph.D.'s	500	0
6th-grade Americans	0	500

Or would the American democratic heritage and the lack of one in Africa result in a distribution that looked more like this?

	high competence	low competence
African Ph.D.'s	200	300
6th-grade Africans	0	500
American Ph.D.'s	500	0
6th-grade Americans	400	100

At the foreign policy level, too, the forces of the past and those of the present can conflict, coexist, or synthesize. The choices and activities of foreign policy decision-makers can be guided by the cultural norms and historical precedents that governed the behavior of their predecessors; or the choices and activities can be guided by the changing demands that emanate from the international system or from the decision-makers' own society. Consider severe international crises. These can generate demands that uncover previously unrecognized values which, in turn, can channel behavior in new directions. Yet these new behavior patterns do not necessarily supplant the historical ways of conducting foreign policy. A Russian decision-maker is a Russian as well as a skilled diplomat. His United States counterpart is an American as well as an adroit politician. But which of these factors are the dominant ones? Do past precedents operate in situations? Or do crises evoke a momentum of their own, a momentum in which the historical norms and characteristic forms of behavior give way? Or does some combination of these factors shape the undertakings through which decision-makers relate their societies to their external environments? Even more specifically, if a sample were compiled of 200 well documented foreign policy actions, 100 undertaken by the Soviet Union and 100 by the United States, with half of each group being a response to intense crises and half being a response to routine situations, would their distribution in terms of the amount of ideological rhetoric that accompanied the behavior be as follows?

sources foreign policy stimuli	nature of foreign policy stimuli	
	SPECIFIC	GENERAL
HISTORICAL EXPERIENCE	1 policy commitments	2 value orientations
PRESENT ENVIRONMENT	3 situations	4 contexts

Or would the formal character of Soviet ideology and the unstructured nature of American ideology result in a distribution that looks like this?

	high rhetorical content	low rhetorical content
USSR in crisis	0	50
USSR in noncrisis	50	0
US in crises	0	50
US in noncrisis	50	0

I. HORIZONTAL, VERTICAL, AND DIAGONAL ANALYSIS

Although some empirical evidence bearing on the interaction of historical and environmental stimuli is available insofar as behavior in national political systems is concerned,[1] no systematic data have been developed on their respective roles in foreign policy. Indeed, except for the Sprouts' effort to delineate five basic approaches to the causal relationship between foreign policy officials and their environments,[2] the conceptual problem has not been confronted by students in the field. One is hard pressed to hazard even a reasonable guess as to which of the two distributions of the 200 foreign policy actions in our example is likely to prove most valid, much less to offer a rationale for a third distribution that may reflect even more accurately the dynamics of foreign policy. To be sure, attention has long been paid to the role of historical precedent and style—or, in the terminology of an earlier era, of national character—and lately foreign policy behavior in crises has increasingly been the subject of conceptual and empirical investigation.[3] Other than the studies bearing on crisis behavior, however, foreign policy analysts have not made environmental variables the focus of theoretical inquiry. As a consequence, their literature contains neither propositions nor data bearing on the interaction and relative strength of the demands that arise out of past experiences on the one hand and out of present circumstances on the other.[4] This is not the occasion to generate data that would clarify the problem, but an exploratory discussion of some of its conceptual dimensions would seem to be in order. Such is the purpose of this paper.

Doubtless there are a number of reasons why aspects of the prevailing environment have not served as an analytic focus. In the first place, there is a compelling simplicity about the task of uncovering the precedents and style born of past experience—what we shall call "vertical" analysis since it involves tracing trends down through history. The external actions undertaken by societies can always be seen as the extension of some previous pattern. The citizens of every society share a history that is not experienced by any other peoples; and embedded in this history are cultural norms that are refined and passed on from one generation to the next, culminating in the predispositions shared

[1] See, for example, Gabriel A. Almond and Sidney Verba, *The Civic Culture: Political Attitudes and Democracy in Five Nations* (Princeton: Princeton University Press, 1963).

[2] Harold and Margaret Sprout, *The Ecological Perspective on Human Affairs— With Special Reference to International Politics* (Princeton: Princeton University Press, 1965), esp. Chapters 3-7.

[3] For example, see Charles F. Hermann, *Crises in Foreign Policy: Simulation Analysis* (Indianapolis: Bobbs-Merrill, 1969), and Charles F. Hermann, "International Crisis as a Situational Variable," in James N. Rosenau (ed.), *International Politics and Foreign Policy: A Reader in Research and Theory* (New York: Free Press, rev. ed., 1969), pp. 409-21.

[4] For a discussion of what foci are contained in the literature on foreign policy, see Chapters 4-6.

by the present generation. The residue of the past can thus be seen as differentiating the behavior patterns and attitudinal tendencies of any society from those of every other society. Moreover, since the norms that sustain a nation's culture are not entirely consistent with each other, contradictions among the external policies that a society may pursue can be easily explained as reflecting the diversity inherent in the society's culture. If, for example, a society avoids involvement in one situation abroad and becomes deeply involved in another, a perusal of its past would probably yield enough evidence of flexible orientations to permit one to posit the contradictory behavior as expressive of a pragmatic style.[5]

Secondly, while vertical analysis is not simple, it certainly appears more manageable than the task of coherently organizing all the diverse stimuli that may emanate from the many situations extant at any moment in time—what we shall call "horizontal" analysis, since it involves tracing trends across a range of concurrent behaviors. The identity of the situations that comprise the external environment of any society toward the end of the 20th century may continuously change, but their number will always be high; and since each situation has unique antecedents and dynamics, the foreign policy behavior required to cope with all of them would appear to be so variable as to render hopeless any attempt to analyze it in terms of properties that may be common to some situations and not to others. And the variability of the behavior is broadened further by virtue of the fact that certain situations may also embrace developments within the society and that, in any event, internal conditions may shape the response to some external ones and not to others. Hence, with the possible exception of characteristics that follow from the distinction between crisis and non-crisis situations, the challenges posed by the environment would seem to be too disparate in terms of the responses they evoke to justify the use of horizontal analysis. Instead of the compelling simplicity of vertical analysis, environmental variables present a seemingly incredible complexity—or at least enough complexity to reinforce the analytic inclination to emphasize historical commitments and experiences as the basis of present choices and behavioral styles.

If horizontal analysis thus appears unmanageable, the task of combining it with vertical analysis—what we shall call "diagonal" analysis, since it involves discerning trends across situations in terms of predispositions acquired down through history—seems even more hopeless. For in order to assess the extent to which historical precedents are

---

[5] For an analysis of American foreign policy that follows this procedure, see Herbert J. Spiro, "Foreign Policy and Political Style," *The Annals*, Vol. 366 (July 1966), pp. 139-48.

offset by environmental demands, the foreign policy behaviors of at least two societies confronted with similar external problems need to be compared. Such a procedure seems to defy mastery because the circumstances that confront different societies are never exactly the same, thus making it difficult for the researcher ever to be certain that the environment stimuli he has compared are sufficiently similar to justify his assessments of the relative strength of vertical and horizontal factors. It is little wonder, in short, that diagonal analysis has not become common practice among foreign policy researchers and that the vertical mode of inquiry remains the dominant approach to the subject.

II. CONCEPTUALIZING THE ENVIRONMENT

Notwithstanding the accuracy of the foregoing explanations of why vertical analysis dominates the study of foreign policy, they hardly amount to a sufficient set of reasons for the lack of horizontal and diagonal analysis. Assuming that horizontal variables are no less important empirically than vertical ones, and that therefore diagonal analysis ought to characterize researchers in the field, it seems highly unlikely that students of foreign policy avoid this form of analysis simply because they are fearful of its complexity. Foreign policy researchers are no less venturesome than those in other fields. On the contrary, they are often quick to point to the complexity of their subject and to avoid simplistic approaches to it.

So there must be more to the neglect of horizontal and diagonal analysis than the compelling simplicity of vertical inquiry. Reflection about other possible reasons for the neglect leads to the realization that little work has been done on the concept of the environment, that for the most part it is treated as merely the source of stimuli rather than as an organized set of processes, and that consequently analysts have found it more clarifying to explain the conduct of foreign relations in terms of the policy commitments and value orientations acquired from the past. As noted, these commitments and orientations are the product of organized processes. Their shape and contents can be traced from one generation to the next and any foreign policy behavior can thus be seen as the most recent expression of a coherent, overall, and self-sustaining pattern. For the most part, however, an equivalent conception of the environment at any moment in time has not developed. At worst the environment is conceived to consist of an unspecified variety of objects, actors, and situations with which the environed society copes by drawing upon its past experience and utilizing its present resources. At best the environment is conceived to consist of specific objects, actors, and situations, each of which has distinct characteristics that can serve as stimuli to action on the part of the environed society. Yet there is more to the environment than the specific situations to which a society is linked. It also consists of self-sustaining processes that arise out of the interdependencies of the various objects, actors, and situations, quite apart from any connections these may have with the environed society. That is, the environment constitutes a generalized context besides comprising specific situations, just as history consists of a cumulative experience as well as of particular episodes. And it is with respect to the environment as a generalized context that conceptualization is lacking, thereby holding back the development of horizontal analysis. Rare indeed are conceptualizations of the external environment that posit and trace patterns of interaction which, in the process of unfolding, become independent variables in relation to the behavior of the environed society's foreign policy officials.

In other words, it is not enough to categorize various environmental phenomena and to analyze them separately as sources of foreign policy. To proceed in this manner is not to specify the interdependencies among the phenomena that sustain and give coherence to the environment and that, in so doing, also serve as sources of foreign policy. The interdependencies also operate as policy determinants because they form a generalized context that conditions both the content and style of the responses to specific situations. Consequently, the categorization and analysis of specific situations must be supplemented by concepts which delineate types of environmental contexts that can result from different degrees and forms of interdependencies among the actors, objects, and situations in the environment. Once various types of environmental contexts are identified, propositions about the relationship between each environmental type and the behavior of foreign policy decision-makers can be developed.

It must be stressed that both the generalized contexts and the specific situations of the environment shape the conduct of foreign policy and that they do so independently of each other. An environmental context consists of attributes of the interdependencies of foreign objects, actors, and situations and not of the attributes of particular objects, actors, or situations. At any moment in time, therefore, a society's total environment has structural and behavioral characteristics of its own and these, being the cumulative result of all the extant objects, actors, and situations, are different from any of them.

Although it follows that both the specific situations and generalized dimensions of the environment contribute to the external behavior of societies, this is of course not to imply that they are equally potent as independent variables. This may or may not be the case, and under some circumstances specific situations may be more potent while under other circumstances greater potency may accrue to certain generalized dimensions. Determining their relative potencies is an empirical problem that cannot be addressed until after conceptualization of the structural and behavioral characteristics of the environmental context is undertaken. Thus here it is only asserted that both the specific and generalized dimensions operate as independent variables.

It is also important to emphasize that while the environed society is directly connected to specific situations of the environment that shape its foreign policy style, such is not the case with respect to the interdependencies of the environment that operate as independent variables. The interdependencies unfold irrespective of the nature and behavior of the environed society. They serve to condition the society's behavior, to be sure, but their status as independent variables is in no way dependent on a connection to the society. Obviously, on the other hand, the operation of a specific situation as an independent variable is entirely dependent on a connection between it and the society. The earlier analogy to a child serves to clarify this point. The behavioral characteristics of a first-grader are in part a result of the specific teacher assigned to teach his class. The connection is direct in the sense that the teacher's treatment of the child is to some degree a consequence of how the child behaves even as it also contributes to the nature of the child's responses. At the same time developments in the community that shape the goals and structure of the school system contribute substantially to the behavioral characteristics of the child even, though, being a first-grader, he has no direct connection to the general affairs of the community. Thus both specific and generalized dimensions of the child's environment at age six contribute to who he is and how he behaves. Furthermore, the analogy highlights the relevance of vertical as well as horizontal factors: obviously the child's behavior is also a consequence of his experience over the previous six years.

An illustration of these distinctions drawn from the foreign policy field is provided by the recent conduct of United States policy toward Cuba. While U.S. policy is in large part a consequence of the advent of a Cuban Communist regime that, being different from its predecessor, provoked direct U.S. responses, the Cuba-oriented activities of the United States are also a result of the interdependencies of Latin American countries and of a number of other developments in the international system to which the United States did not contribute. In addition, of course, United States' behavior with respect to Cuba arises out of a long history of relations with that country.

Interestingly, the relevance for foreign policy style of the distinction between the specific and generalized dimensions of a society's environment can also be illustrated by noting that a similar distinction operates with respect to the consequences of past experience. History yields both specific and generalized guides to present behavior. The conduct of American foreign policy in Latin America, for example, is in part a consequence of the reiteration of the Monroe Doctrine throughout the 19th and 20th centuries. The Doctrine and its frequent reiteration set specific precedents that continue to guide the behavior of American officials. At the same time the cumulated experience of the American past has resulted in characteristic ways of approaching problems and this pragmatic style—if that is what it is—also underlies the behavior of officials toward Latin American situations.

III. THE SEARCH FOR CONCEPTUAL EQUIPMENT

In sum, diagonal analysis of foreign policy behavior requires that conceptual equipment be available for the analysis of the relationship between such behavior and each of the types of phenomena embraced by the cells of the following matrix:

	high rhetorical content	low rhetorical content
USSR in crisis	45	5
USSR in noncrisis	50	0
US in crisis	5	45
US in noncrisis	50	0

It does not take much reflection to recognize that extensive conceptual equipment is available for the analysis of the phenomena embraced by Cells 1, 2, and 3. Foreign policy analysts have long focused on such phenomena and have developed a number of concepts and methods for examining them. For example, the concept of the national interest, the decision-making approach, and game or strategic theory are but a few of the tools that are used to probe the interaction of past policy commitments and present situational dynamics in the determination of the external behavior of a national society. Similarly, analysis of the contribution that the major value orientations of a society make to the conduct of its foreign policy has been facilitated by the concepts of role, national style or character, and political culture—to mention but a few of the available tools.

But what about Cell 4 of the matrix? Have environmental contexts also been subjected to close scrutiny? Have any conceptual tools been developed for linking them to the conduct of foreign policy? Have practitioners in other areas of inquiry perfected tools for contextual analysis that can be refashioned for application to foreign policy phenomena? Anticipating our answers to these questions, the search for relevant concepts was only minimally rewarding. Some conceptual equipment has been developed, but it is still crude and limited in scope. Certainly environmental contexts have not been explored as fully as the other phenomena in the foregoing matrix and there is even some evidence of a tendency to avoid focusing on the interdependencies that sustain the environment. At the same time the possibility of adapting concepts should not be discounted. In particular, the concept of change appears promising as a connecting link between environmental interdependencies and foreign policy behavior.

That the conceptual equipment available for environmental analysis is not extensive—and, indeed, that the main tendency is to avoid conceptualization of the interdependencies that sustain the external environments of societies—can be readily illustrated. Consider the work of David Easton. Although his efforts to delineate the nature of political systems and the boundaries between them and their environments are probably more extensive than those undertaken by any other student of politics, Easton devotes more attention to the processes of the system than to those of its environment. To be sure, he does not deny that the political processes of a society are responsive to developments that unfold in the world beyond its borders. Yet he does not indicate any systematic ways in which the developments abroad may be interdependent and thereby generate environmental patterns which may in turn condition societal processes. Rather he distinguishes between the intra- and extra-societal environments of a political system and notes that the latter consists of international political systems, international ecological systems, and international social systems. International political systems are conceived to consist of such entities as other political systems and international organizations like NATO, SEATO, and the United Nations. Similarly, the international cultural system, the international social structure, the international economic system, and the international demographic system are offered as examples of international social systems.[6] One can hardly quarrel with the utility of categorizing the environment of any society along these lines. Such entities do exist and their functioning does have consequences for the society. Yet in a basic sense they are little more than categories and subcategories. Nowhere in Easton's discussion are the phenomena embraced by his categories posited as interdependent. Nowhere are they conceived as self-sustaining

---

[6] David Easton, *A Framework for Political Analysis* (Englewood Cliffs, N.J.: Prentice-Hall, 1965), Chapter V. For more elaboration of Easton's formulation, see his *A Systems Analysis of Political Life* (New York: John Wiley, 1965).

processes which, like the cumulative impact of historical experience, lead to predictable forms of behavior. To know that the external environment of a society consists of other political, economic, and social systems is not to know anything about how that society may respond to them. To assert that specified categories of phenomena are the source of inputs into a system is not to suggest the way in which behavior might be a function of the particular attributes of the interdependencies encompassed by the environmental categories. Categorization, in short, is not conceptualization, and thus Easton offers no help to the researcher interested in horizontal forms of analysis.

Another example of the problem is provided by the decision-making approach to foreign policy. Again the external environment is posited as a major source of stimuli to action on the part of those responsible for the conduct of foreign policy. And again aspects of the environment that can lead to activity on the part of decision-makers are differentiated. One formulation, for example, elaborates the "external setting of decision-making" in terms of the nonhuman environment, other cultures, other societies, and other governments.[7] Here again, however, the view is essentially one in which the environment consists exclusively of specific objects, actors, and situations. Notwithstanding the assertion that "the external setting is constantly changing,"[8] the differentiated aspects of the environment are not posited as interdependent. No suggestion is made as to the generalized dimensions of the prevailing environment that might condition the behavior of decision-making. Indeed, the only cumulative phenomena stressed by the authors of the decision-making approach are the societal norms and values passed on by one generation to the next that serve to guide the behavior of foreign policy officials.[9]

A seemingly more promising lead in the search for concepts that allow for a causal treatment of environmental contexts is provided by recent attempts to view the environment as a complex of issue-areas. An issue-area is conceived to consist of a variety of conflict situations that may differ in numerous ways, but that are similar in the sense that the same values serve as the focus of conflict. One formulation, for example, posits the external environment of any society as consisting of four basic issue-areas—status, territorial, human resources, and nonhuman resources—that are differentiated by the fact that the different values they encompass will trigger different responses on the part of its foreign

---

[7] Richard C. Snyder, H. W. Bruck, Burton Sapin (eds.), *Foreign Policy Decision-making: An Approach to the Study of International Politics* (New York: Free Press, 1962), pp. 67-72.

[8] *Ibid.*, p. 67.

[9] *Ibid.*, pp. 156-60.

policy officials.[10] Theoretically, therefore, this approach allows for an environment with both specific and generalized dimensions. In each issue-area it posits the existence of environmental interdependencies and, in so doing, it suggests how the external behavior of a society may be linked to the processes that are sustained by different types of conflicts. Once the researcher identifies the core values at stake in a situation and classifies it in the appropriate issue-area, he should theoretically be in a position to compare how historical precedent in different societies is modified by the common issue-area values involved in the situation. That is, it should be possible for him to engage in horizontal and diagonal analysis. Unfortunately, however, the clusters of values that generate similar behavior have yet to be worked out conceptually and the causal processes that differentiate the areas have yet to be traced empirically.[11] As of now, the issue-area approach is only a hunch that situations sustained by common values generate common responses. Unless and until this hunch can be given theoretical coherence and supported by empirical evidence, therefore, it remains little more than another collection of categories.

Conceptual equipment that more closely approximates the kind that is needed to facilitate environmental analysis is to be found in the work of Morton A. Kaplan.[12] Concerned about stability and change in the international system, Kaplan posits six "states" of the system—balance of power, loose bipolar, tight bipolar, universal, hierarchial, and unit veto—each of which has certain "essential" rules that must be followed by the national actors comprising the system for the state to persist through time. Among the essential rules for each system state, for example, are stipulations that specify the conditions under which its national actors should negotiate, mobilize resources, fight, stop fighting, join alliances, contest some changes, and accommodate to other changes. Although Kaplan's rules for each system state are highly abstract, he does not make their existence dependent on the behavior of any national actor. A single actor might alter the system state by breaking one or more of its rules, but the rules themselves derive from the over-all patterns of interaction among the actors. From the perspective of a single national actor, therefore, the essential rules are a part of its environment. Irrespective of the policy commitments and value orientations that the decision-makers of a society acquire from the cumulative experience

10 See Chapters 6 and 17.

11 However, for one successful effort to empirically trace issue-area differences in foreign policy, see Ole R. Holsti and John D. Sullivan, "France and China as Nonconforming Alliance Members," in James N. Rosenau (ed.), *Linkage Politics: Essays on the Convergence of National and International Systems* (New York: Free Press 1969), pp. 147-98.

12 See, in particular, his *System and Process in International Politics* (New York: John Wiley & Sons, 1957), Chapter 2.

of their predecessors, and irrespective of the specific situations with which they must cope, their actions must conform to the systemic requirements if the prevailing state of the system is to endure.

This is not to imply that Kaplan's formulation is free of defects. The *if* clause that ends the previous paragraph is of course a large one. The state of the international system is not permanent. Its interdependencies can undergo transformation, and while Kaplan acknowledges this point, his formulation does not deal with the processes whereby the system is transformed from one state to another. Even in Kaplan's terms, therefore, during periods of transformation decision-makers will presumably have difficulty adjusting their behavior to the systemic requirements. Furthermore, there are many areas of foreign policy behavior for which the essential rules of Kaplan's model are irrelevant. His formulation of environmental interdependencies is essentially addressed to the issue-area bounded by questions of military and national security which, while extremely important, are far from a predominant majority of the external problems with which societies must contend.

Notwithstanding the limitations in the scope of his model. Kaplan does highlight the relevance of environmental contexts and suggests ways in which horizontal analysis might be undertaken. Indeed, by distinguishing between democratic and authoritarian regimes (what he calls "nondirective" and "directive" actors),[13] at one point Kaplan even suggests a way in which this horizontal approach can be extended into a diagonal form of analysis. The presumption here is that the historical commitments and value orientations of the two types of regimes are likely to lead to different interpretations of how adherence to the essential rules of a particular system should be achieved. Kaplan's analysis here is abstract and sketchy, to be sure; but at least it allows for the interaction of environmental and historical factors as stimuli to foreign policy behavior.

As previously indicated, still another set of conceptual tools that might facilitate horizontal analysis can be found in the efforts to probe whether crisis situations give rise to distinctive forms of behavior.[14] Hermann's work is particularly illustrative in this regard. He posits three characteristics as distinguishing crisis from noncrisis situations—high threat to national goals, short decision time, and lack of anticipation. The joint presence or absence of these three characteristics is hypothesized to have a variety of consequences for the way in which foreign policy is conducted. Among the behavioral consequences that Hermann hypothesizes to be linked to crises, for example, are the tendencies of decision-makers to increase the rapidity of responses to stimuli, to reduce

[13] *Ibid.*, Chapter 3.
[14] Mermann, *op. cit.*

the number of cooperative responses, to increase the number of exploratory responses, to reduce the search for alternative solutions, to increase the search for support of their position, to reduce the number of participants in the decision-making process. Quite apart from the empirical question of whether this line of reasoning is affirmed by the available evidence,[15] the conceptual utility of the crisis/noncrisis distinction is that tendencies such as the foregoing are posited as operating irrespective of historical circumstances. Whatever the policy commitments made by their predecessors, and whatever the value orientations that normally guide their policy-making conduct, decision-makers in crisis share a readiness to respond to stimuli in similar ways. That is, their behavior is seen to be primarily a consequence of concurrent rather than past events in their external environments.

While the crisis concept can thus serve as a valuable tool in the horizontal analysis of foreign policy behavior, it is not free of difficulties. Like Kaplan's formulation, it tends to be confined to phenomena in one issue-area, namely, to situations in which military considerations predominate. The three characteristics associated with crisis do not preclude the possibility that economic or social situations may develop into crisis proportions, but the combination of high-threat, short-decision time, and lack of anticipation is certainly most likely to occur when political situations reach the point where actors are ready to resort to the use of force. Secondly, the crisis formulation is weakened by its dichotomization of the environment and the fact that the dichotomy is not conceived in variable terms. Crises are conceived to have certain characteristics, but these are treated as attributes of situations that always induce the same form of behavior rather than as variables that can generate several types of responses. Unlike Kaplan's formulation, in other words, the crisis concept as developed so far does not take formal account of the processes and interdependencies of the environment, thus limiting its utility as a tool to analyze the contents of the external undertakings of society.

IV. THE CONCEPT OF TURBULENCE

The search for conceptualizations of the environment yielded one other formulation, developed by students of organizational theory, that is sufficiently different from those outlined above to warrant notation. Although organizational theory is much more advanced than foreign

---

[15] Although Hermann has found considerable support for most of his hypotheses (*ibid.*), his data were derived from situations simulated in the laboratory and thus further tests of the hypotheses need to be made.

policy theory,[16] it too is lacking in formulations that treat the environment as a dynamic pattern. Organizational theorists recognize that organizations must, like societies, adapt to their external environments. Yet only recently have they developed an appreciation of the need to conceive of organizational behavior as a response to self-sustaining interdependencies within the environment as well as to interdependencies within the organization and to exchanges between it and its environment.[17] Thus, for example, drawing upon general systems theory as a means of clarifying the role of environmental interdependencies, two organizational theorists have suggested four "ideal types" of environments in which organizations can be located.[18] Their basis for differentiating between the four types is the degree of *system connectedness* that prevails among the components of the environment. The environment with the least connectedness they have called the *placid, randomized environment*, in which the value attached to the objects that constitute the environment are relatively unchanging and are randomly distributed. Amoebas, human foetuses, and nomadic tribes are posited as existing in such an environmental context, but it is difficult to conceive of a modern nation-state being located in a placid, randomized environment. However, the foreign policy behavior appropriate to such an environment can be theoretically deduced. In such a context a society would not distinguish "between strategy and tactics," but would instead come to regard "the optimal strategy . . . [as] the simple tactic of attempting to do one's best on a purely local basis." [19]

Moving up the scale of system connectedness, the next context to be differentiated is the *placid, clustered environment*. This is a more complex environment in the sense that some of its objects "hang together in certain ways," [20] but it is nevertheless placid in the sense that the values attached to the objects are relatively unchanging. The environments of human infants or of plants that are subjected to seasonal cycles are offered as illustrative of this type. Again it is hard to imagine a modern society in such a context, though perhaps it prevailed in earlier eras when classical diplomacy sustained international relations. Should such a context exist for a society, however, its foreign policy would distinguish between strategy and tactics, since the clustering of the objects in the environment means that short- and long-range calculations have to be made if the society is to achieve its goals.

[16] For a thorough review of the substantial progress that has occurred in organizational theory, see J. G. March (ed.), *Handbook of Organizations* (Chicago: Rand McNally, 1965).

[17] Cf. Shirley Terreberry, "The Evolution of Organizational Environments," *Administrative Science Quarterly*, Vol. 12 (March 1968), pp. 590-613.

[18] F. E. Emery and E. L. Trist, "The Causal Texture of Organizational Environments," *Human Relations*, Vol. 18 (1965), pp. 21-32.

[19] Emery and Trist, *op. cit.*, p. 24.

[20] *Ibid.*, p. 25.

The third ideal type, called the *disturbed-reactive environment*, involves a significant qualitative change over the previous two. It is characterized by the existence of at least one—and usually many—other systems similar to the one that is environed. While the two placid environments do not contain any other objects comparable to the environed one, the disturbed-reactive environment does, and this difference is of considerable import. It means that there are other objects in the environment that may have the same goals with respect to the environment as the environed object, thus compelling the latter to act on the knowledge that what it knows can also be known by the others. Such knowledge can lead all the objects in the environment to seek to thwart the others, and every object, knowing such is the case, will have to foster and react to disturbing events in their environments. That is, it will have to launch undertakings that combine strategy and tactics in such a way that the behavior of other objects is anticipated and countered, thus facilitating the procurement of goals in the environment. Examples of systems that exist in this type of environmental context can readily be cited. Certainly the disturbed-reactive environment is descriptive of the context in which the human being that survives infancy and the interest group or business organization that persists through time must operate. And frequently it would also appear to be characteristic of the context in which modern societies find themselves. Their environments consist of other societies also seeking to realize external goals. Since the goals sought by societies are often mutually exclusive, their environments are bound to be pervaded by disturbances with which they become strategically and otherwise interdependent.

Further reflection on the structure and functioning of organizations, however, led the authors of the foregoing distinctions to a fourth ideal type of environment, one that they call a *turbulent field environment*, and that they claim "is new, at least to us, and is the one that for some time we have been trying to identify." [21] A turbulent field environment is conceived to consist of even more system connectedness and complexity than the disturbed-reactive type. This greater complexity is seen to stem from dynamic processes that arise not only from the interactions of the component organizations in the environment, but "also from the field itself." That is, the actions of the environment components and linked sets of them "are both persistent and strong enough to induce autochthonous processes in the environment. An analogous effect would be that of a company of soldiers marching in step over a bridge." [22] In other words, in contrast to the other types of environments, the accelerating rate and complexity of change in the turbulent environment "exceeds the component systems' capacities for prediction and, hence, control of

[21] *Ibid.*
[22] *Ibid.*, p. 26.

the compounding consequences of their actions." [23] Uncertainty thus becomes the dominant characteristic of the turbulent environment and, the organizational theorists contend, such a characteristic is increasingly the condition in which modern organizations find themselves. The behavioral response to the conditions imposed by turbulent environments, they imply further, is the convergence, either formally through legal mergers or informally through the emergence of shared values, of the environed unit with comparable units in its environment. The individual organization recognizes that it cannot rely exclusively on its own strategy and tactics to cope with the turbulence of the environment and thus it joins, as it were, with parts of its environment. The recent trend toward mergers of business corporations, colleges, and interest groups are illustrative in this regard.

It hardly needs documenting that much the same can be said about the environments of modern societies. These also appear to be turbulent as well as disturbed-reactive. Treating the Soviet Union as the environed unit, recent trends in Eastern Europe exemplify the point, albeit at this writing it could be argued that the Russians are coping with the turbulence by contesting rather than joining with other societies in Eastern Europe.[24] Indeed, it is not unreasonable to view the existence of "mergers" in the international system—such as the European Common Market and regional arrangements like the OAS, SEATO, and the OAU —as expressive of the predicted responses to a turbulent field, namely, the postwar environments of national societies.

Suggestive as this typology of organizational environments is, its application to foreign policy behavior is necessarily limited. While it serves to identify one important way in which societies react to the interdependencies of the international system, cooperative efforts to build supranational institutions are not the only bases of foreign policy. Unlike the crisis approach, the concept of the turbulent field does posit environmental interdependencies and links them to a specific form of foreign policy behavior, but, like Kaplan's formulation, it does so only with respect to behavior in a narrow range.

V. CHANGE AS AN ORGANIZING CONCEPT [25]

The search for conceptualizations of environmental interdependen-

[23] Terreberry, *op. cit.*, p. 593.

[24] On the other hand, if one equates the Soviet Union with the leadership of its Communist Party, its recent behavior becomes quite consistent with that predicted by the presence of a turbulent environment. For the tides of upheaval in Eastern Europe have connected the Soviet party leaders even more firmly to their counterparts in control of several other East European societies (particularly East Germany and Poland).

[25] The ensuing formulation draws heavily on James N. Rosenau, "Foreign Policy as Adaptive Behavior: Some Preliminary Notes for a Theoretical Model," *Comparative Politics*, Vol. 2 (April 1970), pp. 355-74.

cies has not been fruitless, but neither has it turned up a formulation which delineates: (1) types of foreign policy behavior that may be a response to (2) varying forms of environmental interdependencies across (3) a wide range of issue-areas. All three of these dimensions emerge as desirable features of any attempt to explore the role of environmental contexts, but even the most promising of the formulations examined above include only two of these dimensions. Moreover, none of the formulations allows for the operation of interdependencies that are external to their society. Easton and the authors of the decision-making approach do posit an internal as well as an external environment, but they merely categorize the two environments rather than treating them as a series of self-sustaining processes. Thus there would appear to be plenty of room for additional efforts to conceptualize the environment in which foreign policy behavior occurs and it is not a rejection of the foregoing formulations to suggest still another. While the one developed below must be viewed as sketchy and tentative, it seeks to incorporate the three desired conceptual dimensions and, in addition, to allow for the distinction between internal and external interdependencies.

The central concept in the ensuing formulation is that of change. Change is measured by alterations in the occupants and requirements of the governmental and nongovernmental leadership statuses and roles in the environed society and in its environment. When the passage of time results only in deaths and retirements that alter the occupants of the leadership statuses and roles, then the degree of change that occurs during this period is considered to be low. Under these conditions the identity of leaders will be different, but their behavior will be responsive to the same requirements and thus will be essentially undifferentiated from that of their predecessors. When the passage of time is accompanied by the emergence of new social, political, economic, and technological conditions that alter the requirements as well as the occupants of the leadership roles and statuses to which new requirements are attached, the behavior of leaders in and out of government, at home and abroad, will tend to vary from that of their predecessors. If these variations are extensive, the degree of change is considered to be high, amounting, in effect, to a turbulent environment.

If for analytic purposes the innumerable degrees of change that societies experience are dichotomized into low and high, and if allowance is made for the possibility that both degrees of change can occur either at home or abroad, then four basic types of environmental contexts in which foreign policy is conducted can be distinguished (see the matrix below). More significantly, it seems reasonable to hypothesize that these four types of contexts will foster four very different modes of foreign policy behavior—what we shall call, respectively, the habitual, spirited, deliberative, and convulsive modes.

The *habitual* mode refers to the condition in which the degree of both internal and external change are low; and it is so designated because, with not much changing either at home or abroad, the routinized decision-making processes of governments will suffice to cope with the course of public and world affairs. There is no need for top level officials to deliberate over the most appropriate responses to internal demands and external pressures. Change is so minimal that the lower levels of a society's bureaucracy can—and are authorized to—handle any demand or pressure that may arise by resorting to established policies and applying established procedures. The international behavior of Switzerland during the 1920s might be expected to exhibit this mode if data depicting it were to be gathered.

```
                        EXERNAL CHANGE

                     High          Low
 ─────────────────────────────────────────────
                      C
                      O            S
                      N            P
             H        V            I
             i        U            R
             g        L            I
 N C         h        S            T
 T H                  I            E
 E A                  V   D
                      E
 ───────────────────────────────────────────
             D
 R N         E
             L            H
 N G         I            A
             B            B
 A E   L     E            I
       o     R            T
 L     w     A            U
             T            A
             I            L
             V
             E
 ─────────────────────────────────────────────
```

The *deliberative* mode is a response to the condition in which internal change is low and environmental change is high; it is so designated because the absence of new internal demands on government allows officials to weigh carefully the appropriate course of action to follow in meeting the rapidly changing scene abroad, but at the same time the high degree of environmental change involves too much responsibility for the bureaucracy to handle alone and the top level of officialdom must thus participate in the decision-making process. Their participation and the presence of high uncertainty and change abroad means that recourse to established policies and procedures will not be sufficient and that therefore top officialdom must informally deliberate over the choices to be made as well as formally ratify them. The behavior of the United States during the first years immediately following World War II is perhaps illustrative of the deliberative mode. Between 1945 and, say, the school desegregation decision of the early 1950s, developments at home were slow to unfold, but considerable change was occurring abroad, with the result that top leaders of the State Department and the Congress joined with the President in prolonged and wide-ranging calculations of how to cope with such developments as a blockade of Berlin, a collapse of Europe's economy, a military threat to Western Europe, an attack in Korea, and a reemergent Japan. Accounts of these episodes reveal a highly reasoned and innovative quality in American foreign policy behavior,[26] with perhaps the epitome of the deliberative mode being achieved during the fifteen weeks in 1947 when extended assessments and discussions of the decaying European economy culminated in the Marshall Plan.[27]

The *spirited* mode is conceived to characterize foreign policy behavior in the condition in which internal change is high and external change is low; it is so designated because the high degree of change at home leads to demands that officials act quickly and energetically to alter the unchanging environment in such a way as to render it more compatible with the unfolding variations in the society's essential structures. Officials are not free to handle these domestic demands as deliberatively as they can when the pressures of change arise in the environment. For these demands require them to promote, rather than to cope with, new situations abroad; and whether the changes are such as to lead to demands that involve aggressive military conquest of parts of the environment or whether they give rise to a peace movement that demands efforts to disarm the environment, they require officials to act precipitously abroad and to do so in a much more spirited way than is the case when the internal scene is relatively unchanging. The foreign policy behavior of Germany during the 1930s exemplifies this spirited

[26] See, for example, W. Phillips Davison, *The Berlin Blockade: A Study in Cold War Politics* (Princeton: Princeton University Press, 1958); Glenn D. Paige, *The Korean Decision: June 24-30, 1950* (New York: Free Press, 1968); and Bernard C. Cohen, *The Political Process and Foreign Policy: The Making of the Japanese Peace Settlement* (Princeton: Princeton University Press, 1957).

[27] See Joseph M. Jones, *The Fifteen Weeks* (New York: Viking Press, 1955).

mode. Arising out of the economic and political dislocation of Germany, it was characterized by persistent diplomatic claims and insistent military threats that were justified in moralistic and vigorous terms.

Finally, the *convulsive* mode is hypothesized to arise out of the condition in which both internal and environmental change are high; it is so designated because, with a great deal transpiring at home and abroad, the top leadership of governments must respond quickly to societal demands and external pressures that are often contradictory and that thus necessitate erratic, unpredictable, and agitated efforts to keep the interdependencies of the external environment in balance with the shifting structures of their societies. The combination of high change at home and abroad tends to make established policies and procedures unreliable and compels policy-makers to fall back on hasty and makeshift judgments that give rise to sudden shifts in external behavior which may, in turn, heighten internal tensions that foster the need for further shifts in policy. The convulsive mode is thus marked by more of a self-sustaining quality than the other modes. It is also a primary source of tension in the international system. Mainland China's external behavior in the 1960s is perhaps the most recent and clearcut example of the convulsive mode and some would say that the United States also exhibited this mode during the latter half of the 1960s. Certainly it is true that both societies underwent considerable change during this period and that constancy did not mark the foreign policy behavior of either.

VI. CONCLUSION

All of this does not imply that the concept of change resolves the problem of how horizontal and vertical factors combine to shape the external behavior of societies. The tasks of diagonal analysis, however, are essentially empirical ones. They involve comparisons of the external behavior of societies with different historical experiences located in similar environmental situations and contexts; or, conversely, societies with common pasts coping with different stimuli in the present. The concept of change does seem to provide a needed supplement to the conceptual equipment available for horizontal analysis. With it, it becomes possible to probe the contexts as well as the situations that comprise the external environments to which societies are responsive. Notwithstanding the many difficulties that will be encountered in the measurement of change, the concept does seem to create equipment with which to analyze, in a wide range of issue-areas, the links between interdependencies that sustain the environment and different forms of behavior that constitute the conduct of foreign policy. As developed here, the concept is still crude and unwieldly, but it would appear to offer a

new means for engaging in the kind of horizontal analysis that must
precede the empirical task of ascertaining the specific manner in which
a society's external behavior is a result of yesterday's experiences and
today's circumstances.

14 Intervention as a Scientific Concept *

The deeper one delves into the literature on intervention, the more incredulous one becomes. The discrepancy between the importance attached to the problem of intervention and the bases on which solutions to it are founded is so striking that at first one wonders whether an adequate sample of the literature has been examined. Enlargement of the sample, however, only makes the discrepancy more glaring, and after pursuing every footnote that suggests a different approach and ruminating in a wide variety of documents, one is compelled to conclude that the literature is indeed incredible. The spirit of scientific explanation appears to have had no impact on it whatsoever. In an age when it is second nature to assume that the solution of problems requires comprehension of their sources, scholarly writings on the problem of intervention are singularly devoid of efforts to develop systematic knowledge on the conditions under which interventionary behavior is initiated, sustained, and abandoned. Rather than treating intervention as a challenge to empirical explanation as well as to moral principles, legal precedents, and strategic doctrines, the literature consists wholly of inquiries into these three dimensions of the problem. The empirical bases are either taken for granted or varied to suit the normative, juridical, or policy-oriented thrust of the analysis.

This is not to imply that a moral, legal, or strategic concern with

* Earlier versions of this chapter were presented to the Conference on Intervention and the Developing States, sponsored jointly by the Princeton International Law Society and the Woodrow Wilson School of Public and International Affairs in November, 1967, and published in *The Journal of Conflict Resolution*, Vol. XIII (June 1969), pp. 149–71. Reprinted with the permission of the publisher. Copyright 1969 by the University of Michigan.

intervention is misguided. Intervention is the international form of the most pressing moral issues to be found in any community. It involves the human spirit, the liberty of individuals, the structure of groups, the existence of order. It can undermine or enhance the dignity of people and it can facilitate or inhibit their capacity to realize their aspirations and work out their own destinies. Thus one needs only a modicum of humanity to be concerned about the question of when and how it is appropriate for one international actor to intervene in the affairs of another. And, given a moral concern about intervention, it is only logical that attention should turn to the legal question of when it is legitimate for one actor to intervene in another's affairs and the strategic question of how to intervene successfully when the legitimacy of such behavior is either accepted or ignored. Far from being misguided, in short, the predominance of moral, legal, and strategic emphases in the literature is both understandable and desirable. The incredulity pertains rather to the absence of a fourth emphasis upon scientific explanation.

This is not to say that the literature is lacking in empirical data and propositions about the sources of interventionary behavior. Meaningful analysis of the legality and strategy of intervention cannot proceed without some consideration of the conditions under which legitimacy attaches to its use and success to its results. Indeed, since interventionary behavior is of such crucial importance to the course of international affairs and the prospects for world order, inquiries into the subject are especially rich in descriptions and interpretations of actual situations. Many of the legal studies, for example, focus on the question of how a more widespread acceptance of the norm of nonintervention can be achieved and most of their authors are thus led to examine historical cases for clues as to the limits to which international behavior may be governed by such a norm. Likewise, those who approach the subject from a strategic viewpoint are usually concerned with the question of how foreign policy goals can be efficiently and effectively realized through intervention and this focus leads them to investigate the attitudes, institutions, and other conditions abroad that must be altered for intervention to succeed. Hence there is no dearth of empiricism in the literature. Data and insights in themselves, however, do not necessarily lead to an ever-accumulating body of reliable knowledge about the conditions under which intervention does and does not occur. This requires a process in which interrelated propositions are constantly being formulated, tested, and revised, and such scientific procedures seem totally absent. All the data to be found in the literature were gathered and analyzed for the instrumental purpose of either establishing the legitimacy of interventionary norms or improving the quality of interventionary behavior and, consequently, they lack the empirical comparability and theoretical explicitness that is necessary for a scientific explanation of the dynamics of intervention.[1]

For all the vast literature on the subject, in other words, not much is known about intervention. There is an abundance of specific detail, but no general knowledge; a profusion of elaborate impressions, but no verified findings. The role of intervention in the Spanish civil war of 1936–39, in the Hungarian uprisings of 1956, in the Middle Eastern crises of 1956, 1958, and 1967, and in a host of other historical situations has been amply documented, but no attempt has been made to use the case materials as data with which to frame or test hypotheses that might apply to any intervention or even to specific types of interventionary behavior. The factors that foster, precipitate, sustain, channel, constrain, and/or curb intervention simply have not been scientifically explored, with the result that the literature is barren of any established generalizations. All that exists is an enormous amount of conventional and legal wisdom in which conclusions are asserted on the basis of a jumble of ringing affirmations, impressive insights, clear-cut preferences, and supportive historical examples. It is as if the literature on lung cancer consisted of treatises written by either thoughtful smokers or their concerned spouses.

Nor need the characterization of the literature be so mild. After all, conventional and legal wisdom has its place, and in any realm of inquiry there is always room for creative insights and clear-cut values. Indeed, if all the literature was of this order, it would not be difficult to interject scientific procedures and move quickly to the accumulation of a reliable body of knowledge about intervention. Unfortunately, however, a large preponderance of the conventional and legal wisdom does not lend itself to scientific processing; it is more obtuse than insightful and more confounding than clarifying. Quite apart from a persistent naïveté in which moral aspirations are allowed to shape and guide empirical assessments, the normative, legal, and strategic studies all seem to be plagued by analytic problems that inhibit wisdom and leave major questions unanswered. Stated more specifically, the moral dimension of the literature is plagued by a double standard problem, the legal dimension suffers from a definitional problem, and the strategic dimension is beset by the problem of operationalizing the national interest. To the extent that the three dimensions are interdependent, moreover, so are the problems, thus further compound-

[1] The comparability and theoretical explicitness necessary for scientific explanation need not involve quantitative data, complex formulas, and involved statistical analyses. To call for the scientific study of intervention is not to ask students of the subject to retrain themselves in new methods of research. Rather, it involves processing their case materials in such a way that findings derived from one case can be applied to and tested by other cases. For an elaboration of this point, see Chapter 4.

ing the confusion. In addition, to the extent that the three dimensions are concerned with empirical phenomena, they are all harassed by the problem of measuring influence.

I. THE DOUBLE STANDARD

Like many problems of morality, those that involve the use of intervention as a technique of international action are not simple and clear-cut. However it may be defined, intervention is not in and of itself either good or bad. A double standard prevails: most interventions may be undesirable for a variety of reasons, but some are eminently desirable for equally compelling reasons. Most interventions probably invade the privacy of people and undermine the stability of the international system, but some interventions uphold human rights and preserve international order. Intervention, in other words, is normally an instrument of action, a means and not an end, and the morality or immorality of interventionary behavior thus depends on the end toward which it is directed. To intervene in the affairs of a peaceful Latin American country may be unwarranted, but to intervene in the stormy and horrendous activities of a Hitler's Germany seems entirely justifiable, even mandatory. The moral problem, then, is that of developing a view of intervention in which it is generally condemned but which also allows for specifiable types of exceptions. This problem plagues the literature and doubtless it is also disturbing to those in high policy-making positions. For while acceptance of a double standard is not in itself morally difficult, consistency with respect to the legitimate exceptions is anything but easy. While consistency may be the mark of small minds, men everywhere like to think that their occasional tolerance or advocacy of intervention stems not from sheer whim or capricious interpretations of prevailing circumstances, but from some larger principle that is applicable across a variety of situations. And, once one admits that one's own morality must be the ultimate arbiter of when exceptions are to be tolerated as legitimate, one must acknowledge that the morality of others is entitled to the same discretion, an admission that opens up the possibility, even the probability, that interventionary behavior will come to enjoy a greater legitimacy than it deserves. If every actor makes his own determination of what violations of the doctrine of nonintervention are acceptable and legitimate, the system becomes one of men, not laws, and what is despicable intervention for one actor is welcome liberation for another.

Further complications set in, moreover, when it is recognized that even if the problem of specifiable exceptions is solved, intervention may still not be warranted. An exceptional situation in which intervention is a moral imperative may nevertheless require a noninterventionary stance. If, for example, intervention greatly heightens the probability of global war even as it also serves humanitarian values—a choice that faced the West with respect to the Hungarian uprising of 1956—then presumably the rule pertaining to exceptional cases would not obtain. In other words, intervention is only a means to an end, but sometimes there are more highly valued ends than the one for which it is a means. Clearly, as one astute observer put it, "There is no obvious synthesis between morality and intervention."[2]

Essentially the moral problem seems to stem from the fact that whereas an actor must—to use a colleague's favored phrase—often "rise above his principles," in the area of intervention this necessity has yet to be acknowledged. Most observers and actors prefer to seek justifications for rising above their principles that are just as compelling as the principles themselves, an effort which results in a never-ending "clarification" of the moral issues involved.

A number of solutions to the moral problem are available, most of them in the international law literature. Perhaps the best is to treat the doctrine of nonintervention as an absolute insofar as national actors are concerned and to allow for exceptions to it only on the part of international actors whose interventionary behavior stems from a collective rather than an individual morality.[3] Such a procedure amounts, in effect, to a government of laws and not of men, but it suffers from the fact that social and political factors or changes may produce an international morality from which the individual actor dissents, thus facing him again with a double standard.

Which resolution of the double standard is adopted—and there are many approaches to the problem besides the one noted in the previous paragraph—depends on the priorities one attaches to man's needs and wants. A scientific analysis of intervention would thus not solve the moral problem. Science can explain empirical phenomena, but it can never provide the basis for choosing among value alternatives. Yet it seems reasonable to assert that the moral problem would not be confounded by the availability of a scientific literature on intervention; on the contrary, it might be greatly clarified if the sources, processes, and consequences of

[2] Manfred Halpern, "The Morality and Politics of Intervention," in James N. Rosenau (ed.), *International Aspects of Civil Strife* (Princeton: Princeton University Press, 1964), p. 255.

[3] For a persuasive case along these lines, see Richard A. Falk, "The Legitimacy of Legislative Intervention by the United Nations," in Roland J. Stanger (ed.), *Essays on Intervention* (Columbus: Ohio State University Press, 1964), pp. 31–61.

interventionary behavior were more fully comprehended. If, for example, more reliable knowledge was available on the conditions under which international actors would be likely to undertake interventions, the utility of the collective solution to the moral problem noted above would be clearer and thus possibly its selection or rejection among a variety of alternatives would be more easily determined.

II. THE PROBLEM OF DEFINITION

Notwithstanding the voluminous literature on intervention, there appears to be no agreement whatsoever on the phenomena designated by the term. Even in international law, where the definitional problem is an especially recurrent preoccupation, uniformity of usage has yet to develop.[4] On the contrary, both in law and in general "intervention has a perplexing vagueness of meaning."[5] Some observers posit it as certain forms of behavior; others conceive it to involve certain intentions underlying behavior; still others think of it in terms of certain consequences stemming from behavior; and a fourth approach is to equate it with certain standards to which behavior ought to conform.[6] A major result of so many definitional options is that a number of observers merge two or more of them and, in effect, end up by defining intervention as any action whereby one state has an impact upon the affairs of another. Thus the literature is pervaded with discussions of military interventions,[7]

[4] Indeed, the absence of definitional uniformity has recently been the source of heated controversy among students of international law. See Eberhard P. Deutsch, "The Legality of the United States Position in Vietnam," *American Bar Association Journal*, 52 (May, 1966), pp. 436–442, and William L. Standard, "United States Intervention in Vietnam is Not Legal," *American Bar Association Journal*, 52 (July, 1966), pp. 627–634. See also John Norton Moore, "International Law and the United States Role in Viet Nam: A Reply," and Richard A. Falk, "International Law and the United States Role in Viet Nam: A Response to Professor Moore," *Yale Law Journal*, 76 (May, 1967), pp. 1051–1158.

[5] Percy H. Winfield, "Intervention," *Encyclopedia of the Social Sciences*, 8 (New York: Macmillan, 1932), p. 236.

[6] For a more detailed discussion of some of the definitional problems encountered in the field of international law, see William T. Burke, "The Legal Regulation of Minor International Coercion: A Framework of Inquiry," in Stanger, *op. cit.*, pp. 88–90; Ann Van Wynen Thomas and A. J. Thomas, Jr., *Non-Intervention: The Law and Its Import in the Americas* (Dallas: Southern Methodist University Press, 1956), pp. 66–74; and Martin Wight, "Western Values in International Relations," in Herbert Butterfield and Martin Wight (eds.), *Diplomatic Investigations: Essays in the Theory of International Politics* (Cambridge: Harvard University Press, 1966), pp. 111–120.

[7] Cf. Quincy Wright, "Intervention, 1956," *American Journal of International Law*, 51 (April 1957), pp. 257–276.

propaganda interventions,[8] economic interventions,[9] diplomatic interventions,[10] and ideological interventions,[11] not to mention customs interventions and other highly specific actions through which one state experiences the impact of another.[12] Indeed, often intervention is defined in such a general way that it appears to be synonymous with imperialism, aggression, colonialism, neocolonialism, war, and other such gross terms that are used to designate the noncooperative interactions of nations. One observer, for example, finds it useful to define imperialism in terms of "actions that . . . are intrusions into the affairs of another people,"[13] a definition which is hardly differentiable from the view that " 'intervention' refers to conduct with an external animus that intends to achieve a fundamental alteration of the state of affairs in the target nation."[14] Nor is noncooperative animus necessarily considered to be a characteristic of interventionary behavior. Foreign aid programs have been classified as intervention,[15] and, to the distress of some international law specialists,[16] so have collective security measures taken by several nations to protect their common interests. Finally, the height of definitional vagueness is occasionally reached when inaction is regarded as intervention: Having defined intervention as the impact that one state has on the affairs of another, logic leads some observers to classify inaction as intervention whenever consequences follow within a state from the failure of another to intrude upon its affairs.[17] Such a conception, for example, leads to the absurd conclusion that the United States avoidance of the conflict in

[8] Cf. C. G. Fenwick, "Intervention by Way of Propaganda," *American Journal of International Law*, 35 (October 1941), pp. 626–631.

[9] See, for example, W. B. Dickinson, Jr., "Challenged Monroe Doctrine," *Editorial Research Reports*, II (August 10, 1960), pp. 585–602.

[10] Cf. Quincy Wright, "The Munich Settlement and International Law," *American Journal of International Law*, 33 (January 1939), pp. 12–32.

[11] See Hans J. Morgenthau, "To Intervene or Not to Intervene," *Foreign Affairs*, 45 (April 1967), pp. 425–436.

[12] Cf. L. Morley, "Invasion and Intervention in the Caribbean Area," *Editorial Research Reports*, II (July 22, 1959), pp. 535–552.

[13] Paul A. Varg, "Imperialism and the American Orientation Toward World Affairs," *Antioch Review*, 26 (Spring 1966), p. 45. For a similar conception with a different label, see Kenneth J. Twitchett, "Colonialism: An Attempt at Understanding Imperial, Colonial and Neo-Colonial Relationships," *Political Studies*, 13 (October 1965), pp. 300–323.

[14] Falk, in Stanger, *op. cit.*, p. 42.

[15] For example, see Michael H. Cardozo, "Intervention: Benefaction as Justification," in Stanger, *op. cit.*, pp. 63–85; and Doris A. Graber, "The Truman and Eisenhower Doctrines in the Light of the Doctrine of Non-Intervention," *Political Science Quarterly*, LXXIII (September 1958), pp. 321–334.

[16] James Oliver Murdock, "Collective Security Distinguished From Intervention," *American Journal of International Law*, 56 (April 1962), pp. 500–503.

[17] For a summary of the literature that adheres to this logic, see Thomas and Thomas, *op. cit.*, pp. 67-68.

Indochina in 1954 and its extensive involvement in that part of the world a decade later both constitute intervention.

Concerned about the problem of vagueness inherent in general definitions, some analysts have sought to conceptualize intervention in more precise terms. Most notably, precision is sought through a formulation in which interventionary behavior is limited to dictatorial interference by one state in the affairs of another. That is, intervention occurs when the affairs of one state are altered against its will by the actions of another. So conceived, intervention is associated with the use or threat of force. Coercion must be the indicator of intervention, the reasoning seems to be, because states are sovereign and thus would not undergo unwanted alteration if force were not threatened or applied.[18] Most students of international law, however, reject such a precise formulation because it omits so much behavior that seems relevant to the subject. Even worse, the military or coercive definition

. . . excuses various types of interference that have often occurred, particularly in modern times. The totalitarian nations have reduced intervention to a science, and to them it has become a duty and a legitimate method of political warfare. Economic pressures on other states; diplomatic demands backed up with political threats to force a state to curb freedom of speech, press, and radio; fifth column activities; the inciting of another state's people to rise against its government; and a multitude of other refined techniques of interference must in many instances come under the heading of intervention.[19]

Accordingly, it is argued that compulsion or constraint, which may or may not be based on the coercive use of force, is the key to both a precise and useful definition of intervention; that whether an act of interference is undertaken through physical force, economic pressure, or some other form of compulsion, it is the compulsion and not its form that constitutes intervention.[20] More accurately, "the essence of intervention is the attempt to compel."[21] The trouble with this broader formulation, of course, is that it reintroduces a vagueness about the line that divides interventionary behavior from other types of international action. How are acts of compulsion or constraint to be differentiated from those that allow for voluntary compliance or outright rejection? Is not the nature of international transactions such that a price is attached to every offer (i.e., attempt to compel) and therefore cannot acceptance of the offer be interpreted as an unwillingness to suffer the penalty attached to its rejec-

18 For a further discussion of this reasoning, see *ibid.*, pp. 68–69.
19 *Ibid.*, p. 69.
20 *Ibid.*, p. 72.
21 *Ibid.*

tion (i.e., as an acquiescence to constraint)? It would seem, in other words, that once definitions move beyond observable behavior to the motivation or intent underlying it, precision suffers and ambiguity prevails.

However loosely or precisely intervention may be defined, its use as an analytic concept is further complicated by a variety of distinctions that are sometimes drawn in terms of the identity of the intervening actor or the nature of the affairs into which the intervening actor intrudes. Falk, for example, distinguishes five types of intervention—unilateral, counter-, collective, regional, and universal—and argues that the differences among them are sufficient to generate different normative and legal structures for evaluating their application.[22] Other writers make a similar argument with respect to the distinction between "internal" and "external" intervention, the former involving "interference by one state between disputant sections of the community in another state" and the latter pertaining to "interference by one state in the relations . . . of other states without the consent of the latter."[23]

But there is no need to pile distinction upon distinction. Plainly the concept of intervention suffers from a lack of definitional clarity. Notwithstanding all the ways in which it has been defined—and many more could be cited—the line that differentiates the presence of intervention from its absence remains elusive. So many diverse activities, motives, and consequences are considered to constitute intervention that the key terms of most definitions are ambiguous and fail to discriminate empirical phenomena. Animus, intrusion, interference, impact, compulsion, and other such terms convey meaning, but they do not enable one to recognize an interventionary act when it occurs. The meaning they convey is thus of little use when the concept of intervention is applied to a specific moral, legal, or strategic situation. What is animus for one observer is responsibility for another. What some call compulsion, others regard as acquiescence. Little wonder, then, that uniformity in usage does not characterize the concept of intervention.

The vagueness and inapplicability of the concept is further compounded by a tendency to presume that intervention has an objective existence apart from those who define it. The literature is full of efforts to determine what constitutes the "essence" of intervention. The belief seems to be that if the proper definition is formulated, and if the evidence to which it points is carefully examined, intervention will unmistakably reveal itself. Of course, since different observers prefer different definitions and interpret their evidence differently, the essence of intervention reveals

---

[22] In Stanger, *op. cit.*, pp. 40–41.
[23] Winfield, *op. cit.*, pp. 236–237.

itself to be highly variable, with what is essential for one observer being peripheral for another.

A scientific approach to intervention would go a long way toward resolving these definitional problems. In contrast to its marginal usefulness in solving the moral problems posed by intervention, scientific analysis does offer a means for precisely discriminating among empirical phenomena and avoiding a fruitless search for their essence. Science deals exclusively with observables—with phenomena that can be measured, either presently or theoretically—and thus those who engage in scientific inquiry must operationalize their definitions before they proceed to make empirical observations. Scientists may construct models with conventional concepts, but ultimately—i.e., when they move to test their models—they must either employ operational definitions or abandon the models. To operationalize a concept is to specify the operations that one performs in order to observe the phenomena that it encompasses. Bridgman's original formulation of operationalism still makes this point most succinctly: "In general, we mean by any concept nothing more than a set of operations: *the concept is synonymous with the corresponding set of operations.*" [24] Intervention, then, becomes the operations that one uses in order to identify its existence. If "conduct with an external animus that intends to achieve a fundamental alteration of the state of affairs in the target nation" is operationalized in terms of certain types of hostile and motivational statements made by the leaders of the intervening nation, then intervention exists when these statements are observed and not otherwise. If intervention is equated with interference and interference is operationalized in terms of protests voiced by specific segments of the target nation, then intervention is neither more nor less than the observed occurrence of these protests. Operational definitions, in short, avoid ambiguity. The resulting concepts may or may not be incisive and relevant, but they will not be vague. Operational definitions cannot be either right or wrong, but only more or less useful. If they are not useful—if they involve operations that do not adequately identify all the phenomena in which one is interested—then they will not be widely employed. Agreement eventually forms around those operational definitions that prove most incisive for most observers. The scientific literature on a subject, therefore, perpetuates precision rather than vagueness.

Such precision may not be concentrated in a single operational formulation. Several definitions of the same concept may be widely accepted,

24 P. W. Bridgman, *The Logic of Modern Physics* (New York: Macmillan, 1928), excerpted in Herbert Feigl and May Brodbeck (eds.), *Readings in the Philosophy of Science* (New York: Appleton-Century-Crofts, 1953), p. 36. Italics in the original.

either because different schools of thought take different approaches to the phenomena to which it refers, or because the purposes for which it is used are variable. One does not operationalize the concept of an inch with a ten-cent store ruler if one is building a space vehicle. Contrariwise, one does not go to a precision-instrument store for an instrument to measure whether a grand piano can be moved through one's front door. Similarly, agreement may form around several operational definitions of intervention that variously reflect the different uses to which the concept may be put. If one is interested in military intervention, operationalization may be accomplished in terms of the movement of a specified number of troops into or near the target society. Such a definition does not encompass other forms of intervention, but the omission of these does not mean that other forms do not occur. It simply means that the user of this definition has a particular interest in the military dimension of interventionary phenomena, and the question to be asked about the definition is not whether it encompasses all interventionary phenomena, but whether counting the movement of troops is an appropriate operation to perform for the purposes that the concept is designed to serve.

All of this is not to say that intervention is an easy concept to operationalize or that agreement will quickly form around a few useful definitions. As noted below, intervention presents difficulties hardly less formidable than those that attach to the concept of influence. It *is* to say, however, that an inclination to operationalize the concept of intervention would surely reduce the vagueness and confusion that presently marks its use.

III. STRATEGIC ANALYSIS AND THE PROBLEM OF THE NATIONAL INTEREST

The lack of a scientific approach to interventionary phenomena is also conspicuous with respect to their strategic dimension. For here the central concerns are empirical rather than evaluative. Under what conditions can intervention successfully achieve its goals? What risks have to be run and what unintended consequences have to be endured if success is to be realized? What will be the consequences of nonintervention? When is intervention likely to result in outright failure? Such questions, of course, cannot be answered by moral principles and juridical standards. They are queries about behavior—about how individuals, small groups, and large aggregates are likely to react to new stimuli. Normative and juridical evaluations may be made of the uses that are subsequently made of these strategic estimates, but the estimates themselves are neutral predictions of behavior and, as such, can be developed accurately only through theoretical and empirical inquiry. Indeed, it is not an exaggeration to note that strategic estimates of this kind probe the very core of political behavior and are thus concerned with central problems of empirical political inquiry. As seen in Chapter VII, politics is about the way in which actors seek to modify each other's behavior across wide functional distances and, in this sense, given the extent of the modification attempted and the functional distances spanned through intervention, no situation is more purely political than the attempt of one nation to intervene in the affairs of another.

The vast literature on the strategic dimension of intervention is not lacking in sensitivity to the empirical character of the queries to which it is addressed. On the contrary, there is a pervasive recognition, sharpened by the significance of such postwar interventions as have occurred in Hungary, the Suez Canal, Cuba, the Dominican Republic, and Vietnam, that the strategic problems of intervention as an instrument of foreign policy must be approached through assessments of behavioral probabilities rather than through adherence to moral or legal imperatives. In the words of one distinguished observer, "It is futile to search for an abstract principle which would allow us to distinguish in a concrete case between legitimate and illegitimate intervention."[25] The strategic literature is thus pervaded with both empirical propositions and data pertaining to the conditions under which success or failure can be expected to follow intervention. Citing, for example, the postwar failures of the United States, China, the Soviet Union, and Cuba to achieve interventionary goals in (respectively) Vietnam, Africa, Europe, and Latin America, many authors stress the obstacles to successful intervention and conclude with the general proposition that normally the prevailing conditions do not conduce to success. "Intervention is a better-late-than-never proposition at best," observes Tarr.[26] "When in doubt, don't intervene," echoes Yarmolinsky.[27] On the other hand, it is also recognized that some interventions do achieve their goals; that, say, the Soviet Union did achieve success in Hungary in 1956[28] and the United States "did intervene to good advantage in Lebanon in 1958;"[29] and, therefore, that the risks of failure are sometimes less than the gains of success. In other words, "the nature of the oppor-

[25] Morgenthau, *op. cit.*, p. 430.

[26] David W. Tarr, "The American Military Presence Abroad," *Orbis*, 9 (Fall 1965), p. 649.

[27] Adam Yarmolinsky, *United States Military Power and Foreign Policy* (Chicago: University of Chicago Center for Policy Study, 1967), p. 17.

[28] Morgenthau, *op. cit.*, p. 431.

[29] Leonard Binder, *The Middle East Crisis: Background and Issues* (Chicago: University of Chicago Center for Policy Study, 1967), p. 16.

tunity [for successful intervention] differs from country to country,"[30] with the result that

> Intervention, like surgery, is not an evil in itself, but it must be applied sparingly and with consummate skill. Just as intervention cannot be a guiding principle of diplomacy, so nonintervention cannot be observed irrespective of time or place. All situations are not equally important.[31]

However, notwithstanding its empirical orientation and its clear-cut recognition that different conditions conduce to different interventionary results, the strategically-oriented literature is conspicuously lacking in a scientific approach. For instead of formulating and testing empirical hypotheses in order to comprehend the range of situations in which interventionary behavior is likely to occur and the conditions under which it is likely to succeed or fail, students of intervention strategy invariably fall back on a standard that is just as misleading and unempirical a means of explanation as any moral principle or legal precept, namely, the national interest. To examine a sample of interventions and conclude that such behavior occurs because nations are "guided in their decisions to intervene and their choice of the means of intervention by what they regard as their respective national interests"[32] is not to offer a meaningful explanation. The national interest is merely a label that may denote the entire spectrum of human wants and needs and thus it in no way differentiates the circumstances that are likely to lead a nation to define its wants and needs as requiring interventionary behavior.[33] To advise policy-makers that they ought to base their strategy on the national interest rather than on abstract principles and then intervene only when situations are "vital" to their "own security,"[34] when "vital interests are unmistakably and imminently threatened,"[35] is to give unusable advice. The criteria for *vital, unmistakable,* and *imminent* remain unexplicated. All situations— or none—can be viewed as inescapable and posing threats to security, depending on how the world is viewed and what is meant by security. These are not self-evident phenomena. What is vital for one observer is peripheral for another and what is unmistakable for the former may be obscure to the latter.

[30] John P. Plank, "The Caribbean: Intervention, When and How," *Foreign Affairs,* 44 (October 1965), p. 42.

[31] Ronald Steel, *Pax Americana* (New York: Viking, 1967), p. 334.

[32] Morgenthau, *op. cit.,* p. 430.

[33] For a lengthy discussion of the limitations of the national interest, see Chapter 11.

[34] Steel, *op. cit.,* p. 331.

[35] Herbert S. Dinerstein, *Intervention Against Communism* (Baltimore: Johns Hopkins Press, 1967), p. 53.

In other words, the concepts of interest and security are infinitely variable. They can be used to interpret the advent and avoidance of intervention, to recommend both the necessity of intervention and the wisdom of nonintervention, to justify both rejection of abstract principles and adherence to legal norms. A good example of this infinite variability can be found in the contrast between Morgenthau's unqualified warning [36] against making interventionary decisions on the basis of national interests derived from abstract conceptions of legitimacy (such as the tenets of international law) and Falk's vigorous argument [37] that in such decisions "real interests" are best served by "a fair-minded attention to the restraints and procedures of the international legal order." In effect, the national interest becomes a substitute for understanding. Since any behavior can be classified as serving or undermining national interests, the concept cannot provide comprehension of when, how, and why interventionary behavior unfolds as it does; instead it can only offer the comfort that an attempt at explanation has been made.

It is not difficult to discern some of the reasons why discussions of the strategy of intervention are so dependent on the national interest concept rather than on scientific explanation. One reason, perhaps the most important one, is that values and value conflicts—conflicts over what are moral or immoral goals and legitimate or illegitimate means—are so central to the phenomena of intervention that the utility of building upon scientific answers to strategic questions is neglected in the search for clarity on the value questions. Scientific procedure seems too slow and value questions too urgent to postpone finding solutions to the latter until the time when they can be considered in the context of empirical probabilities. The national interest, on the other hand, appears to offer a means of solving the normative and juridical problems while at the same time taking advantage of the lessons that can be learned from an examination of a sample of past interventions. To have an explicit interest, be it personal or national, is to have a guide to moral choice. Why, then, devote energy to the development of scientific theory and findings? These have to be assessed in the light of value preferences anyway. So is it not wiser to rely on the dictates of the national interest, which does not ignore realities but which also builds in the necessary evaluative considerations? The question appears to compel an affirmative response, with the result that for all its empirical propositions and data, the strategic literature is devoid of any systematic theory and tested findings.

The second reason for the reliance on national interest follows. In the absence of any empirical theory and systematic data that differentiate

36 *Op. cit.*, pp. 430–436.
37 *Yale Law Journal, op. cit.*, p. 1153.

the sources and outcomes of intervention under varying conditions, the very variability of the national interest as an analytic concept gives the impression of advancing understanding to the point of distinguishing between those interventions that succeed and those that fail. This is especially so for the preponderant majority of analysts who interpret postwar American interventions as based exclusively on the general principle of contesting and containing Communism. Since it ignores situational differences and treats all Communist threats as uniform in their nature and degree, this principle is seen to underlie many occasions when an intervention policy has not proved successful. Hence a more adequate concept, one that allows for the empirical fact that the Communist world has split into several camps and that thus takes account of situational differences, seems needed, and it is at this point that further support for the idea of founding interventionary strategy on considerations of the national interest arises. Given the variability of the concept, it seems logical to assert that intervention succeeds when it is consistent with the national interest and fails when it is not. Why? Because consistency with national interests means that the attempt to intervene is pursued unqualifiedly and without vacillation, whereas in situations of failure other interests intrude to reduce the commitment to—and thus the effectiveness of—the intervention. Morgenthau, for example, explains that this is why the 1956 Soviet intervention in Hungary succeeded, whereas the opposite outcome followed the 1961 U.S. intervention in Cuba. The Soviet Union, heeding its national interest, "put the success of the intervention above all other considerations, and succeeded." Soviet prestige subsequently suffered, to be sure, but only temporarily. Within a few years its prestige was restored even as Hungary remained in the Communist world. The United States, on the other hand, did not approach "the problem of intervening in Cuba in a rational fashion." It allowed its national interest to become obfuscated by trying to topple the Castro government without a temporary loss of prestige. Consequently, Castro remained in power even as U.S. prestige suffered a serious setback.[38]

To repeat, however, such an explanation is profoundly deceptive. It cannot be wrong. If an intervention succeeds, it is rational and consistent with the national interest. If it fails, it is irrational and inconsistent. To apply national interest criteria, therefore, is not to identify either the conditions under which an unqualified commitment to interventionary policy will be made or the situations in which such a commitment can bring about modifications in the target nation. Systematic knowledge about these crucial matters can be obtained only through the procedure of formulating and testing empirical theory.

[38] *Op. cit.*, p. 431.

IV. THE PROBLEM OF MEASURING INFLUENCE

Perhaps another reason why strategic analyses have been guided by the concept of the national interest rather than by scientific explanation is that the central process of intervention—influence—is so difficult to measure. However it may be defined, intervention involves modifications of the behavior of persons and groups in the target nation that would not have occurred if the intervening nation had not engaged in interventionary activities. Intervention succeeds when the intended modifications occur and it fails when they do not. The production of intended effects—i.e., influence—is thus both the central purpose and the key process of intervention. As has been amply documented elsewhere, however, observing and measuring the unfolding of influence processes presents enormous analytical and methodological problems.[39] Indeed, the measurement of influence is easily the most troublesome problem of political analysis. For it not only involves the tracing of changes in political behavior, but it also requires linking the changes to a specific set of actors who sought to evoke them, and this is an awesome task because there is always the possibility that the behavior deemed to represent intended effects would have occurred even in the absence of efforts to produce it. A multiplicity of factors underlies any modification of behavior, and identifying the particular factors that result from influence attempts is thus a task that staggers the imagination and taxes the patience of even the most sophisticated political analyst. Since intervention subsumes influence processes that span national boundaries and that weave their way through extraordinarily complex social networks, it is little wonder that analysts of the subject have shied away from scientific procedures. For these procedures require the formulation of theory in which influence processes are key variables and the perfection of techniques for observing and measuring their operation.

V. A BASIS FOR AN OPERATIONAL DEFINITION

It could well be argued that if a concept is as laden with normative dimensions, legal precedents, and strategic orientations as is intervention, it ought not be the subject of scientific inquiry. Overtones of morality, vague definitional habits, and reliance on ambiguous terms seem bound to intrude and render the development of empirical theory and systematic data on interventionary phenomena virtually impossible. It would be better

[39] For example, see James G. March, "An Introduction to the Theory and Measurement of Influence," *American Political Science Review*, XLIX (June 1955), pp. 431–451.

to formulate new concepts or break intervention down into its component parts, the argument might conclude, than to try to work with the concept at the emotionally charged level at which it has been customarily used.

Although similar reasoning has led this author to urge abandonment of the national interest as an analytic concept,[40] such a conclusion cannot be accepted in the case of intervention.[41] For interventions have an empirical existence as well as an evaluative one. They embrace moral questions and legal standards, but they also find expression in the activities of identifiable human beings. Policy-makers plan interventions, nations sustain them, international organizations debate them, citizens ponder them. The Soviets have a doctrine of intervention; so do the Chinese; so do the Cubans; and the three argue vigorously over the behavior through which their doctrines are implemented.[42] Nor are Americans incapable of wrangling over interventionary doctrines and governing their behavior accordingly. Not only are recent activities in the Dominican Republic and Vietnam widely considered to be interventions in the affairs of nations, but the policy reflected in these activities is now the central issue of American foreign policy.[43] In short, intervention may be differently and vaguely conceptualized, but it does refer to empirical phenomena and these do constitute a central problem of world politics. Indeed, as technology shrinks the world and makes nations ever more dependent, interventionary phenomena may grow increasingly important behaviorally as well as morally. Hence the scientifically oriented analyst cannot turn aside. If he dismisses interventionary phenomena as too illusory or too difficult for the procedures he employs, he prevents himself from confronting the theoretical challenge of explaining primary international processes. For analytical purposes he may find it useful to break intervention down into its component parts, but in the end he will have to piece them together again—not only because the resulting knowledge can serve moral, legal, and strategic purposes, but also because it will significantly advance comprehension of world politics.

This is not the occasion to develop a scientific theory of intervention. Time and space limitations permit only a brief identification of the basic

[40] See Chapter 11.

[41] It should be noted, however, that others seem to have found so little analytic utility in the concept as to justify its abandonment. Such, at least, would be a logical inference from the fact that the recently published *International Encyclopedia of the Social Sciences* does not follow the lead of its illustrious predecessor published in 1932 and include an article on intervention among its seventeen volumes.

[42] For an interesting and succinct discussion of these arguments and the behavior to which they refer, see Georgie Anne Geyer, "The Threat of 'Vietnams' in Latin America," *The Progressive*, 31 (August 1967), pp. 22–25.

[43] See, for example, Don Oberdorfer, "Noninterventionism, 1967 Style," *The New York Times Magazine*, September 17, 1967, pp. 28–31, 102–112.

elements that would enter into such a theory. More specifically, the ensuing analysis suggests the basis for an operational definition of interventionary phenomena and then indicates how theoretical propositions about them might be constructed.

The first of these tasks is the easiest. The criteria for an operational definition seem plain. It must be broad enough to identify those phenomena that are generally associated with the term, and yet not so broad that it fails to discriminate them from other aspects of international politics. As previously implied, a scientific approach to intervention requires a formulation that is more precise than the common-sense usage of the term which, in effect, allows for any action directed toward another nation to be regarded as intervention. As it is commonly used, the word "intervene" suggests an event that occurs between two other events. Viewed in this way, the term becomes applicable to any international action: for example, a request for negotiations or an offer of aid to earthquake victims is an intervention in the sense that the request or the offer comes between the condition that preceded it and the response to it. Indeed, as noted, this common-sense usage permits even the absence of action to be regarded as intervention, since the choice of inaction in a situation necessarily intervenes between the conditions that prevailed before and after the choice. Clearly, intervention would lose its utility as an analytic concept if its operationalization allowed for such broad interpretations. Lest interventionary phenomena be equated with all of international politics, therefore, a more restricted definition must be developed.

However intervention may be defined in the literature, and irrespective of whether it is approached from a moral, legal, or strategic perspective, two characteristics are usually associated with behavior classified as interventionary. Indeed, although the association is often left implicit, it is so pervasive in the literature that the two characteristics would appear to be necessary attributes of interventionary phenomena and, as such, to provide a basis for an operational definition. One is what might be called the *convention-breaking* character of interventions. The other is their *authority-oriented* nature. Stated briefly, all kinds of observers from a wide variety of perspectives seem inclined to describe the behavior of one international actor toward another as interventionary whenever the form of the behavior constitutes a sharp break with then-existing forms *and* whenever it is directed at changing or preserving the structure of political authority in the target society.

The first of these characteristics highlights widespread agreement on the finite and transitory nature of interventions. Virtually all the historical cases cited in the literature are conceived to have a beginning (when conventional modes of conduct are abandoned) and an end (when the conventional modes are restored or the convention-breaking mode becomes conventional through persistent use). Their consequences for the target society may be profound and enduring, but once the consequences become accepted and established, the behavior is no longer regarded as interventionary even if the presence of the intervening actor in the target society remains undiminished.

Throughout the period between 1945 and 1956, for example, the Soviet Union expended considerable energies and resources through diplomatic, economic, propaganda, and other channels to preserve the prevailing authority structure of Hungary, but at no point during these eleven years did actors or observers characterize these activities as interventionary. They were the accepted mode of behavior even though they had significant preservative consequences for the Hungarian authority structure (i.e., even though the Russians had, in the common-sense use of the term, long been intervening in Hungarian affairs). But when, in October 1956, Russian behavior with respect to this structure was drastically altered, the changed behavior was widely regarded as an intervention. The preservative goal remained the same, but the adoption of a fundamentally new means of achieving it altered the conventional pattern of behavior so sharply as to evoke interventionary norms and perceptions on the part of both actors in and observers of the international system. Once the new means achieved the preservative goal and the conventional pattern was restored with the withdrawal of Soviet troops from Hungary, the intervention was considered to have come to an end. Not since 1956 has Russian behavior with respect to Hungary been viewed as interventionary even though it has continued to be directed toward the authority structure of that country.

Much the same can be said about the U.S. intervention in Vietnam. Such a characterization was not widely used prior to February 7, 1965, although American efforts to affect the authority structure of South Vietnam had been conducted through conventional diplomatic, economic, and military channels for several years previously. When the United States resorted to bombing on that date, however, the conventional pattern was abruptly changed and the world came to view it as interventionary and to assess it accordingly.

Persistent patterns of behavior, in other words, have a way of establishing their own legitimacy, irrespective of their illegitimacy when they originate. Although it does not involve behavior directed at authority structures, an especially clearcut example of this point is provided by the argument during the Cuban missile crisis that U.S. missile sites in Turkey were no different from Soviet sites in Cuba. Such an argument may be compelling in terms of moral logic, but it did not prove to be compelling in terms of the logic of politics because during the previous fifteen years the sites in Turkey had come to be accepted as part of the conventional mode. Acceptance of U.S. bombing in Vietnam would take much longer because different norms and attitudes are evoked by the use of devastating weapons than by their mere emplacement; but if their use persists for, say, a decade, the inclination to view it as interventionary will probably dissipate slowly and at some point the "American intervention" will have ceased and have been replaced by the "Vietnam situation."

In short, the study of intervention is the study of the unconventional in international politics and, since unconventionality becomes conventional the longer it persists, it is also the study of finite and temporary phenomena. For this reason, interventions may be more easily operationalized and measured than is the case with other types of influence. Inasmuch as they occur only when sharp breaks with prevailing patterns also occur, interventions are readily recognizable and thus do not seem to present such great obstacles to observation as those that, as noted above, usually obtain in the analysis of influence processes.

It must be emphasized that the convention-breaking characteristic of interventionary phenomena need not take the form of a sudden shift to armed force. Although all the examples used above to illustrate this characteristic are of a military nature, obviously there are a variety of other ways in which the prevailing mode of conduct can be abruptly altered. Military interventions are perhaps the most dramatic and clearcut departures from existing patterns and, for reasons having to do with the resistance of authority structures to external manipulation, they may also be the most frequent form of intervention.[44] Yet, as illustrated recently when General De Gaulle spoke about self-determination and federalism in Canada during a tour of that country, other kinds of intervention do occur. The definitional stress, in other words, is on the sharpness of the break with existing patterns and not on the type of pattern that is broken. De Gaulle's comments about Quebec constituted an intervention because such a theme had not previously marked French diplomatic behavior toward Canada. Similarly, a propaganda program that abruptly gave up a stress on cultural themes and turned to emphasizing desired changes in the authority structure of the target society would be widely regarded

---

[44] The closeness of the link between military action and interventionary phenomena that is suggested by the examples used here can also be seen in the fact that some analysts are inclined to use the word "intervention" to describe certain kinds of situations in domestic politics, namely, those in which military officers seek to capture the governance of their own society. Cf. Robert D. Putnam, "Toward Explaining Military Intervention in Latin American Politics," *World Politics*, XX (October 1967), pp. 83–110; and Martin C. Needler, "Political Development and Military Intervention in Latin America," *American Political Science Review*, LX (September 1966), pp. 616–626.

as interventionary. The introduction of political "strings" into a previously unpolitical foreign aid program is another obvious example of a nonmilitary type of intervention.

Not all sharp breaks with conventional patterns, however, are considered to be interventions. The second characteristic of such phenomena is no less important than the first. A close reading of the literature reveals that the inclination to classify international or foreign policy behavior as interventionary does not arise when the goal of the behavior is other than political. A nation might suddenly decide on a trade program designed to obtain a larger portion of a particular market in the target society, and its officials might pursue the program aggressively, but such behavior would not be deemed as interventionary. Likewise, to cite a more concrete example, the newly adopted American program to get more foreign tourists to vacation in the United States rather than elsewhere was not condemned as an intervention by actors in the international system nor classified as such by students of the subject. Reactions of this sort by actors and scholars occur only when the convention-breaking behavior is addressed to the authority structure of the target society—that is, to the identity of those who make the decisions that are binding for the entire society and/or to the processes through which such decisions are made. New foreign policy initiatives designed to modify the behavior of voters abroad are thus likely to be regarded as interventionary even though equally extensive efforts to modify the behavior of tourists in the same country are not. In a like manner a convention-breaking attempt to get more representation for large groups of disenfranchised people (such as the blacks in Angola) would be viewed as an intervention, but a new program aimed at encouraging large groups to look more favorably upon the motives and achievements of the propagandizing society would not.

In short, neither of the two characteristics of intervention that seem appropriate as a basis for an operational definition is in itself sufficient to allow for the delineation of empirical materials. Both must be present. Either alone may sustain important types of foreign policy behavior, but both are necessary to sustain interventionary behavior. Moreover, as implied above, the two are often interdependent. The dearness of an authority structure to those encompassed by it makes the structure extraordinarily difficult to change or preserve from abroad even if its nature is the subject of controversy at home. Hence the inclination to resort to convention-breaking behavior is often reinforced whenever a desire to affect a foreign authority structure arises.

The advantages of using these two prime characteristics of interventions as a basis for operationalizing the concept are numerous. In the first place, such a formulation narrows the subject to manageable proportions and prevents all foreign policy actions (or inactions) from being treated as interventionary. By restricting intervention to convention-breaking behavior, the danger of analysis being confounded by the common-sense usage of "intervene" is greatly reduced and perhaps even eliminated. Secondly, the fact that the convention-breaking behavior must be directed at external authority structures serves as a further preventive against equating the study of intervention with the analysis of foreign policy. A large proportion of the foreign policy undertakings that interest the student are convention-breaking (or they would not catch his eye), but relatively few are directed at the structure of authority in other nations. A severance of diplomatic relations, a Marshall Plan, an alliance, or a Cuban missile crisis, for example, involves behavior that breaks sharply with the past and is central to foreign policy analysis, but such actions are directed at the policies or capabilities of other nations and not at their authority structures. Hence they would not fall within the analytic scope of the study of intervention. To be sure, authority structures might be indirectly affected by such actions, but by the time long-run consequences of this sort became manifest the original policies that brought them about would no longer be convention-breaking. Thirdly, the foregoing approach also narrows the concept of intervention in such a way that it is not equivalent to colonialism or imperialism. These latter phenomena involve the continued presence of the intervening actor in the target society, whereas interventions are considered to come to an end as time elapses and the presence of the intervening actor becomes conventional.

Another important advantage of the basis for operationalizing intervention outlined above is that it obviates the enormously difficult task of tracing motivation. In this formulation, neither the underlying goals of the intervening actor nor the attitudes of those in the target society need to be probed in order to determine the existence of interventionary phenomena. Under the best of circumstances, goals and attitudes can be inferred from observed behavior only crudely, and interventions hardly constitute the best conditions for deriving motivational inferences. To be faced—as many students of international law consider they are—with the task of inferring whether the intervening actor really meant to behave coercively and whether the targets of the action actually felt coerced is to take on a staggering, if not impossible, assignment. As developed above, however, such problems do not arise at the definitional level. Whatever the purposes of the intervening state and whatever the feelings of the target state, an intervention exists when the former makes a sharp break with the prevailing manner of relating to the latter and directs behavior at the latter's structure of authority. The analyst may want to probe the motives and attitudes of the parties to an intervention in order to evaluate its success, but the foregoing formulation does not require him to do so merely in order to identify the phenomena of interest.

This is not to say, of course, that operationalizing this formulation will be easy. It is not always clear when a conventional mode of behavior has been broken, or when the unconventional behavior has persisted long enough to have established a new convention. Nor is it always plain whether authority structures are the target of the unconventional behavior. Difficulties will thus doubtless arise when the analyst turns to specifying the operations that will be performed to differentiate between conventional and unconventional behavior on the part of the intervening actor and between the authority structure and other aspects of the target society. However, generally speaking—or at least in comparison to most definitions of an intervention—these difficulties do not appear insurmountable, and the definition suggested here does seem to be particularly conducive to operationalization.

VI. TOWARD A THEORY OF INTERVENTION

Assuming that it can be used operationally, moreover, this formulation facilitates theory-building. It does so by clarifying the key questions around which scientific inquiry can usefully be organized. In turn these questions provoke a line of reasoning that can be transformed into hypotheses subject to empirical testing. Hence let us conclude by outlining some of the theoretical implications of the foregoing formulation.

More specifically, let us pursue the questions suggested by the conception of intervention as convention-breaking behavior directed at foreign authority structures. Under what conditions is a nation or an international organization likely to be ready to break with the prevailing mode of conduct and attempt to alter or preserve the structure of authority in another society? To what extent are developments within nations or international organizations likely to heighten their propensities to engage in such behavior? To what extent are differences among individual leaders, role-generated perceptions of bureaucracies, and the nature of constitutional restraints likely to contribute to interventionary propensities? To what extent are developments within the authority structure of a nation likely to attract convention-breaking behavior on the part of actors external to it? To what extent are the dynamics of intervention to be found, not in the actor that undertakes such behavior nor the one toward which it is directed, but elsewhere in the international system? In short, what is the relative potency of individual, role, governmental, societal, and systemic variables with regard to intervention as a form of foreign or international policy?

Several lines of reasoning are precipitated by casting the task of theory-building in this form. The clearest concerns the potency of the societal variable. Insofar as this involves the demands made upon officials by individuals and groups in the society, the likelihood of societal variables heightening interventionary propensities seems extremely small. Public opinion can constrain the behavior of foreign policy officials,[45] but rarely is it so aroused and organized as to press for new initiatives that break with conventional modes. Passivity tends to be the dominant posture of publics towards foreign affairs. Moreover, on the few occasions when developments abroad do arouse major segments of the public to clamor for convention-breaking behavior, the focus is usually the actions of foreign governments and not their authority structures. Publics do get preoccupied with enemies or potential enemies, for example, and they may thus press for severance of diplomatic relations, for retaliatory economic measures, for reversals of votes in U.N. debates, or for new departures in alliance policy. Such preoccupations, however, are rooted in a desire for protection against the threats posed by the enemy and, perhaps for a variety of reasons, the threats never seem so great as to generate public pressure for efforts to alter the personnel or procedures by which the enemy governs itself. The principles of sovereignty and self-determination relieve publics of worrying about how and by whom others are governed and, in any event, foreign authority structures are too far removed from the daily concerns of citizens to warrant their sustained advocacy of convention-breaking behavior.[46]

In addition, given the nature of its target, an intervention normally relies on an element of surprise and is launched suddenly; the processes of opinion formation and submission do not ordinarily get precipitated in the predecisional stage. Subsequently they may well be provoked by officials anxious to insure the success of the intervention by demonstrating the depth and breadth of public support for it, but we are concerned at this point with the variables that give rise to interventions and not those that account for their success or failure.

The relatively low potency that thus seems to attach to societal variables serves to emphasize the high potency of individual and bureaucratic role variables as sources of intervention. In the absence of public

---

[45] For an analysis of this relationship, see my *Public Opinion and Foreign Policy: An Operational Formulation* (New York: Random House, 1961), esp. Chap. 3.

[46] The reasoning underlying this conclusion is spelled out in greater detail in Chapter 17. For an empirical exception to this reasoning, India's 1961 intervention in Goa might be cited.

pressure for or against convention-breaking behavior of this kind, and in view of the advantages that stem from surprise and secrecy, interventions are very much the product of the perceptions, calculations, and decisions that occur within decision-making organizations and their leaderships. Indeed, since conventions in international politics are not easily broken even if support for such behavior is sought from other governments prior to its initiation, the planning of interventions also tends to be cut off from the international system and the flow of encouraging and restraining messages from it that any proposed policy normally evokes. Hence it could well be argued that interventions are more exclusively a consequence of decision-making activity than any other type of foreign policy, that assessments of the need for and probable outcome of interventionary behavior are more subject to the whims of individual leaders and the dynamics of bureaucratic structures than the diplomatic, economic, military, and political policies through which nations conventionally relate themselves to the international system. It is not mere coincidence, therefore, that—unlike other innovations in foreign policy—interventions are normally followed by intense debates over the responsibility of individual leaders for their initiation and conduct. Eden's role in the Suez intervention of 1956; Eisenhower's in the Lebanon intervention of 1958; Kennedy's in the Bay of Pigs intervention of 1961; and Johnson's in the Dominican Republic intervention of 1965 were controversial highlights of their respective careers not only because of the moral issues that attach to interventions, but also and perhaps primarily because their authority in these instances—and thus their range of choice —was greater than at most other points during their tenures in office.[47]

Further evidence of the strength of individual and bureaucratic role variables is provided by the apparent irrelevance of basic governmental structure as a source of interventions. If the more outstanding postwar interventions are any indication, the hierarchical arrangements among the various branches of government and the degree to which they are accessible to each other and to nongovernmental organs of public sentiment would seem to bear little relationship to the level of a nation's interventionary propensities. A strong cabinet system with two highly disciplined parties, a weak cabinet system with many parties, a presidential government with two loosely knit parties, and a totalitarian system with only a single party have all spawned interventions within the same six-

---

[47] The autobiographies of top leaders offer ample support for this point. Or at least chapters recounting interventionary decisions always seem to cite fewer external restraints and greater personal anguish over the decisional alternatives than do any other chapters. See, for example, Dwight D. Eisenhower, *Waging Peace 1956–1961* (Garden City, N.Y.: Doubleday, 1965), esp. pp. 266–282.

year period,[48] and the only feature common to all of them is that the authority of the top leadership in all four cases could be challenged only after the convention-breaking undertaking had been launched.

Yet top policy-makers and their staffs do not act in a vacuum. Whatever their unique attitudes and characteristics, they do operate in an international context and they do have some view of what is a desirable state of affairs abroad and what events foster or inhibit its realization. Consequently, irrespective of whether they are rational or irrational, paranoic or confident, rigid or flexible, arrogant or accommodative, strong or weak —to mention but a few of the many individual variables to which high potency can attach—leaders and bureaucracies accord salience to some aspects of the international environment and ignore others. Pressure for or against interventions may not arise in the domestic environment, but developments in the foreign environment can be perceived to alter (or threaten to alter) the structure and/or functioning of the international system to such a degree that decision-makers and their organizations feel compelled to consider whether interventionary behavior is in order. In sum, as filtered through the screen of individual variables, systemic variables can be highly potent as sources of the perceptions, calculations, and decisions that result in interventionary behavior.

While the potency of individual variables is such that different leaders and bureaucracies will respond differently to the same developments in the international system, certain systemic variables seem likely to be especially potent as sources of interventions for those leaders and bureaucracies which, perhaps for a variety of individual reasons, are predisposed to undertake such behavior. In particular, three systemic variables appear likely to have a high potency in this regard: the basic structure of the international system, the degree to which ideological rivalry sustains the structure, and the stability of the nations that comprise the system.

By the basic structure of the international system is meant the degree to which the capability for affecting the conduct of international life is dispersed or concentrated within the system. A balance-of-power structure, for example, involves a greater dispersion of capabilities than a bipolar structure. The more dispersed the structure of the international system, of course, the less the likelihood that it can be rapidly and radically altered by a single development. Hence decision-makers are less likely to succumb to the temptation to engage in convention-breaking behavior toward an unfolding situation in the international system the less capabilities are concentrated in the system. Contrariwise, interventionary behavior

---

[48] The reference is, respectively, to England's 1956 Suez intervention, India's 1961 Goa intervention, the U.S.'s 1961 Cuba intervention, and the U.S.S.R.'s 1956 Hungarian intervention.

seems more likely to occur the more tightly the system is structured.[49] In a tight system a potential shift in the allegiances and ties of a nation will seem more threatening to other nations (those which stand to suffer if the shift occurs) than would be the case in a loosely structured era of world politics.

The potency of these variables is closely related to the second type of systemic variable noted above. The kind and degree of ideological conflict that marks the international system both shapes its structure and is in turn channeled by the distribution of capabilities. When ideological rivalry is intense, decision-makers are more likely to attach greater import to possible governmental changes abroad than is the case when blueprints of the future are less salient features of international life. For the more such blueprints are seen to be at stake in international politics, the more are top officials and their staffs likely to allow their personal inclinations to become involved in their perceptions and calculations, and thus the more will they be ready to undertake convention-breaking behavior. Indeed, when politics is highly ideological, the desirability of governmental changes abroad may generate interventionary behavior even if the possibility of such changes is extremely remote. United Nations interventions in South Africa and externally sponsored guerrilla movements in Latin America are illustrative in this regard.

The third type of systemic variable is the stability of nations in the system. The more precarious are the authority structures of foreign nations, the more likely it is that convention-breaking attempts to preserve or alter them will be launched. This is perhaps the most potent of all the systemic variables. While publics may be unconcerned about authority structures abroad, those responsible for the maintenance of a favorable international environment will be constantly alert to any sudden changes that may alter the personnel and orientations of foreign governments. Aside from the consequences of war, the major turning points in world politics occur when old regimes collapse and are replaced by new ones with substantially different policies.[50] A nationalist regime in China succumbs to a Communist one, a Sukarno is ousted, a military revolt in France brings a De Gaulle to power, a Stalin dies—changes in authority structures such as these lie at the root of radical transformations in the

---

[49] These hypotheses were stimulated by Morton A. Kaplan, "Intervention in Internal War: Some Systemic Sources," in James N. Rosenau (ed.), *International Aspects of Civil Strife*, pp. 92–121. Indeed, this is one of the few works in the literature on intervention that is rooted in a scientific mode of analysis. Kaplan's conclusions about intervention are derived not from moral, legal, or strategic considerations, but from a theoretical model of the international system.

[50] Cf. Richard N. Rosecrance, *Action and Reaction in World Politics* (Boston: Little, Brown, 1963), pp. 280–285.

international system. Whatever their individual differences, top officials everywhere are likely to be particularly sensitive to the stability of foreign governments. The less the stability the greater their readiness to break with tradition and undertake unconventional efforts to avert the dangers of—or to. seize advantages in—the unstable situations.

VII. CONCLUSION

The foregoing is, of course, only the beginning of a theoretical inquiry into intervention. It suggests some lines of reasoning that might be pursued and leaves undone the task of deriving operational hypotheses through which the relative potency of the key variables can be assessed. Certain implications for the problem of intervention in the developing states, however, can be discerned even in this highly general formulation. Most notably, it follows directly from these tentative assessments that interventionary behavior in the coming decades is likely to be a recurrent feature of the world scene. The developing nations are by definition— that is, by virtue of the fact that they are undergoing rapid economic, social, and political change—burdened with unstable and delicate authority structures. The legitimacy of the developmental process is in itself a political issue; so, too, is the authority structure committed to its continuance and the identity of the persons and groups who at any moment in time occupy the key positions in the structure. Hence the international system appears likely to be characterized by a preponderance of unstable subsystems in the foreseeable future.

Since this condition will doubtless be accompanied by a continuance of the pattern whereby the distribution of capabilities in the system is concentrated in but a few of the subsystems, and inasmuch as the Soviet-Chinese split has heightened the ideological content of world politics, incidences of intervention seem likely to occur at a greater rather than a lesser rate in the years ahead, and the developing nations appear destined to be the primary focus of this form of international behavior. The one factor that seems capable of negating this hypothesis is that the nature and potency of individual and role variables will change as leaders and bureaucracies are exposed to and learn from a succession of interventionary experiences.

Here, it might be added, is where scientific inquiry can serve moral, legal, and strategic concerns. The very fact that individual variables appear to be so potent as sources of interventions gives a basis for action to those who aspire to the creation of new moral, legal, and strategic norms. By developing a more profound comprehension of the dynamics of inter-

Basic Concepts 367

ventionary behavior, the lessons of experience can be fed back into the roles occupied by top leaders and their staffs. Such a process could alter the individual variables that determine the inclination to break with convention and intervene in authority structures abroad.

Part Four: International and Domestic Contexts

Foreign policy does not occur in a vacuum. Nor does it arise exclusively out of the demands that originate within societies. The more encompassing international systems of which societies are subsystems also serve as stimuli to external behavior. As suggested throughout the previous chapters, students of foreign policy must also be students of international politics. They cannot study the external behavior of nation-states independently of the larger international context in which it occurs and toward which it is directed. Stated more formally, they must proceed on the basis of some estimate of the relative potency of systemic variables. And, in order to develop balanced estimates of the comparative strength of domestic and international factors, they must perforce focus on the processes of world politics.

There is a risk here, however. The necessity of focusing on world politics creates the danger that analysts may lose sight of why they were led to such a focus. They may come to view international system variables as so potent that the interaction rather than the action of nation-states become their central concern, with the result that the domestic sources of foreign policy are minimized or ignored. If they wish to remain students of foreign policy, therefore, analysts must be sure that they approach the processes of international politics not as a subject in itself, but as one of the contexts for the behavior that interests them. The question of whether it is a more important context than the domestic one must thus be kept in mind at all times and efforts to compare the two sets of variables must be a continuous preoccupation of foreign policy analysis.

A conscious effort to sustain this preoccupation and stress the need for comparative analysis underlies the organization of this last part of the volume. All five of its chapters focus on both the international and domestic contexts of foreign policy and, equally important, on the interaction between them.

15 Toward the Study of National-International Linkages *

.Strange things seem to be happening on the political landscape. An American President declares he is a Berliner.[1] A Soviet Premier sees himself as supplying the crucial 200,000 votes that elected the same American President.[2] The Parliament of New Zealand engages in a heated debate over the characteristics and aspirations of United States citizens.[3] While the British Labor Party is fractionated by differences over the policies of the United States as well as those of the United Kingdom, Yugoslavia's only political party, the Communist led Socialist Alliance of Working People, is torn by the role of the CIA in Yugoslavian life.[4] Soviet authors believe that their freedom to write is highly dependent on the prevailing degree of international tension.[5] The United States Secretary of State appoints a Special Assistant for Liaison with the Governors

* Earlier versions of this chapter were presented at the 1966 Annual Meeting of the American Political Science Association in September, 1966, and published in James N. Rosenau (ed.), *Linkage Politics: Essays on the Convergence of National and International Systems* (New York: The Free Press, 1969), pp. 1–11 and 44–63. Reprinted with the permission of the publisher. Copyright 1969 by The Free Press, a Division of The Macmillan Company.

[1] The declaration was made by John F. Kennedy during his visit to Berlin on June 26, 1963.

[2] In a television interview presented by the National Broadcasting Company on July 12, 1967, former Soviet Premier Nikita Khrushchev reported having told President Kennedy at their Vienna meeting about the strategy the Kremlin followed in order to supply the margin of victory over Richard Nixon in the 1960 election.

[3] *The New York Times,* October 8, 1967.

[4] *The New York Times,* October 5 and November 1, 1967.

[5] *The New York Times,* July 9, 1967.

and gives him responsibility for "presenting their (the Governors') views in connection with . . . the many problems they have in their states as related to other nations."[6] A group of Dutch citizens organize thousands of their. countrymen to "vote" (by sending "opinion cards" to *The New York Times*) in the 1968 American presidential election, arguing that "it is unacceptable that one and one-half per cent of the world population decides who shall be the most powerful man in the world, who decides for us in matters of war and peace, racial relations and the fight against poverty."[7]

Events such as these may seem unusual in a world of sovereign states, but their frequency seems to be mounting. Almost every day incidents are reported that defy the principles of sovereignty. Politics everywhere, it would seem, are related to politics everywhere else. Where the functioning of any political unit was once sustained by structures within its boundaries, now the roots of its political life can be traced to remote corners of the globe. Modern science and technology have collapsed space and time in the physical world and thereby heightened interdependence in the political world.

Political science, however, has yet to accommodate itself to this shrinking world. Even at the level where the changes appear most pronounced—the functioning of national units—events abroad are still regarded as 'external to, rather than part of, a nation's politics. To be sure, it has long been recognized that national political systems, like all organized human groups, exist in, are conditioned by, and respond to a larger environment. Nor is it denied that international political systems, like all interdependent groups, are shaped by and are responsive to developments that occur within the units of which they are comprised. Yet these national-international linkages have never been subjected to systematic, sustained, and comparative inquiry. The traditional subdivisions of political science are such that most analysts treat linkages as parameters rather than as data. Students of comparative politics tend to take the international environment for granted, as if national systems were immune to external influences and had full control over their own destinies. Similarly, students of international politics tend to make a series of simplifying assumptions about the international behavior of national systems, as if all such systems reacted in the same way to the same stimuli.

Although it may once have been possible to tolerate these gaps in political analysis, today the division of labor that created them no longer seems sufficient. As technology shrinks the world and heightens the interdependence of nations, linkage phenomena are too plentiful and too

[6] *Department of State Newsletter*, No. 74 (June, 1967), p. 3.
[7] *The New York Times*, October 15, 1968.

influential to be ignored. No society is immune from the stresses and strains of the cold war, from the demands of neighbors and the cross-pressures of hemispheric tendencies, from the shifts · of trade and the emergence of supranational organizations, from the surge toward development of the new states and the restructuring of their historic relationships. One can no more comprehend the internal political processes of a Latin American country without accounting for the United States presence (or, more accurately, the multiple United States presences) than one can explain the dynamics of political life in Pakistan or India without reference to the Kashmir issue. Recent events in the Congo, Cyprus, Vietnam, and the Dominican Republic are but extreme examples of a worldwide blurring of the boundaries between national and international systems.

THE NEED FOR LINKAGE THEORY

This is not to say, of course, that national-international linkages have never been probed by researchers. Political scientists do not deny or ignore the existence of complex linkages between national and international systems. Their numerous inquiries into the sources and wisdom of the foreign policies of national systems reflect a widespread sensitivity to such phenomena, as does the vast literature on colonialism and most of the work on political movements and revolution. Inquiries into the politics of foreign trade and much of the research into the functioning of international organizations are similarly rich with findings and insights bearing on linkage phenomena.

Despite their abundance, however, the relevant data have never been organized and examined *systematically*. To acknowledge the interdependence of national and international systems is not necessarily to make conceptual allowance for it. To probe linkage phenomena intensively is not necessarily to recognize their theoretical implications. It may no longer be possible to ignore such phenomena, but their abundance does not necessarily stimulate intensive investigation of them. On the contrary, virtually all of the findings and insights bearing on linkage phenomena are derivatives of other concerns, and thus their common content has never been probed and compared.[8] Moreover, being only secondarily

---

[8] A possible exception is the set of inquiries stemming from Hartz's interest in and elaborate conceptualization of the "fragment." Concerned with the residues of European civilization "spawned by Europe throughout the world," the fragment could be regarded as a special form of linkage. Cf. Louis Hartz et al., *The Founding of New Societies: Studies in the History of the United States, Latin America, South Africa, Canada and Australia* (New York: Harcourt, 1964). Other exceptions can be found scattered throughout the essays of three recent symposia:

interested in the linkages they uncover, most researchers tend to see them as results rather than as bases of the functioning of national and international systems. Such phenomena are treated as outcomes of foreign policy, not as sources of it; as necessary consequences of life in a shrinking world, not as mechanisms for absorbing and coping with complexity. In other words, to the extent that they are dealt with at all, national-international linkages are treated as dependent variables, not as independent ones.[9]

Stated in another way, political science as an intellectual discipline has yet to develop theoretical constructs for explaining the relations between the units it investigates and their environments. Students of national and comparative politics have no equivalent of the theory of the firm in economics or the plant in ecology, theories which consist exclusively of propositions about the external relationships of, respectively, basic human and biological organisms. Nor is there a subfield of political science with a history comparable to that of social psychology, which emerged precisely because neither psychology nor sociology was equipped to explain the interaction between their respective units of analysis.[10] Rather the political unit is simply assumed to have an environment to which it responds and with which it interacts. Students of foreign policy examine the responses and students of international relations investigate the interactions, but neither group considers how the functioning of the unit itself is conditioned and affected by these responses and interactions. In short, the problem with which we are concerned stems from a shortage of theory, not of empirical materials. What may be needed is the advent of an Einstein who, recognizing the underlying order that national boundaries obscure, will break through them and bring about a restructuring of the study of political processes.[11]

R. Barry Farrell (ed.), *Approaches to Comparative and International Politics* (Evanston: Northwestern University Press, 1966); Herbert C. Kelman (ed.), *International Behavior: A Socio-Psychological Analysis* (New York: Holt, 1965); and James N. Rosenau (ed.), *International Aspects of Civil Strife* (Princeton: Princeton University Press, 1964). Still other commendable efforts to deal with linkage phenomena systematically can be found in Henry A. Kissinger, "Domestic Structure and Foreign Policy," *Daedalus* (Spring, 1966), pp. 503–529, and Kenneth N. Waltz, *Foreign Policy and Democratic Politics: The American and British Experience* (Boston: Little, Brown, 1967).

[9] For a recent study in which an especially wide variety of linkages are uncovered, quantitatively analyzed, and then treated as dependent variables, see Ernst B. Haas, *Beyond the Nation-State: Functionalism and International Organization* (Stanford: Stanford University Press, 1964).

[10] For an elaboration of this analogy to social psychology, see my "Compatibility, Consensus, and an Emerging Political Science of Adaptation," *American Political Science Review*, LXI (December, 1967), pp. 983–988.

[11] For useful discussions, though not resolutions, of the unit-environment problem, see David Easton, *A Framework for Political Analysis* (Englewood Cliffs,

Some concrete examples may help to demonstrate the need for unit-environment theory. Consider the processes whereby the top political leadership of a society acquires and maintains its position of authority. To what extent are these processes dependent on events that unfold abroad? Under what conditions will the stability of cabinets and the tenure of presidents be reduced or otherwise affected by trends in the external environment? Are certain leadership structures more vulnerable to developments in the international system than others? Political theory presently offers no guidance as to how questions such as these might be researched and answered. One is hard pressed to uncover even a tentative hypothesis, much less a coherent set of propositions, that links the authority of national leadership to external variables. When the contribution of such variables to the rise or fall of a particular leader is unmistakable, political scientists are forced to fall back on detailed historical accounts to explain what happened.[12] Within a recent six-month period, for instance, international circumstances plainly contributed to the fall of two national regimes, Ben Bella's in Algeria and Kwame Nkrumah's in Ghana. Yet students of comparative politics and government have nothing better to resort to than explanations based on the clash of personalities and other factors unique to Algeria and Ghana at those particular moments in their histories.

The conflict in Vietnam poses equally unanswerable challenges to presently available conceptual equipment. The situation in that distant land is manifestly a part of the American electoral process. Unlike other foreign policy questions of recent memory, during 1966 and 1967 events in Southeast Asia became central to the nomination of candidates for *local* offices and to their campaigns for victory on election day. Why should this be so? To say that Vietnam is an important foreign policy issue begs the question. Such an answer tells us nothing about the dynamics of the electoral process whereby external situations are in effect transformed into issues of domestic policy.[13] Yet again one is hard pressed

---

N.J.: Prentice-Hall, 1965), Chap. V, and Harold and Margaret Sprout, *The Ecological Perspective on Human Affairs: With Special Reference to International Politics* (Princeton: Princeton University Press, 1965).

[12] For an explicit attempt to trace how the internal political processes of a society paralleled developments in the international system over a century-long period, see J. C. Hurewitz, "Lebanese Democracy in Its International Setting," in Leonard Binder (ed.), *Politics in Lebanon* (New York: Wiley, 1966), and especially the table entitled, "The Growth of Lebanese Democracy and Its Interaction with Changing Regional and International Systems," on pp. 236–237. However, even this highly self-conscious analysis of linkage phenomena did not yield any theoretical propositions that might be applied to other societies.

[13] For an attempt to identify those types of foreign policy issues that are indistinguishable from domestic issues insofar as the general operation of political systems is concerned, see Chapter 17.

to discover any theoretical propositions that systematically link the course of events abroad to electoral processes and outcomes at home, for either a specific polity or a general class of polities. No dissertations have been written on "elections and foreign policy."[14] Nor do any of the voting behavior models offer guidance in this respect, and the multitudinous writings on political parties and their organization are even more conspicuously inattentive to linkage phenomena. For all practical purposes the political scientist is no better equipped than the journalist to assess when and how international circumstances become woven into the fabric of electoral life.

Another example of the need for linkage theory is provided by the absence of anything but the crudest tools to explain the rash of *coups d'état* that have occurred in various African countries. The similarity of these events, as well as their proximity to each other in time and place, suggests that linkage processes were at work in each instance. But how to account for them? The most that we seem to be able to say is that "a wave of violence presupposes a degree of transnational political community," that one *coup* triggers another through "the power of example," that insurgents in one country are moved to emulate their counterparts in another when these successfully take over the reins of power.[15] Such lines of reasoning, however, can hardly be regarded as theoretical. They do not tell us when the power of example can be expected to operate and when intervening political processes are likely to prevent the establishment of linkages. They say nothing about the range of institutions in a polity that are susceptible to emulation or the conditions under which susceptibility is maximized.[16]

But waves of *coups* and local electoral processes are only among the more obvious instances of linkage phenomena. Viable theory and sustained investigation would undoubtedly yield equally numerous examples of linkages that are no less critical but much less visible. The reversal in American policy toward Communist China between the 1950s and the 1960s is a case in point. It is difficult to explain the shift from intense avoidance to purposeful involvement in terms of conventional theories

14 However, although from the somewhat different perspective of "foreign policy and elections," an initial recognition and exploration of some of these linkages can be found in Theodore Paul Wright, Jr., *American Support of Free Elections Abroad* (Washington, D.C.: Public Affairs Press, 1964).

15 Samuel P. Huntington, "Patterns of Violence in World Politics," in Samuel P. Huntington (ed.), *Changing Patterns of Military Politics* (New York: Free Press, 1962), pp. 44–47.

16 For an elaborate study of an earlier wave of upheavals in which myriad linkages are explained (p. 7 of Vol. 1) simply "as one big revolutionary agitation," see R. R. Palmer, *The Age of the Democratic Revolution: A Political History of Europe and America, 1760–1800* (Princeton: Princeton University Press, 1959, 1964).

of national and international politics. To accept the explanation that the reversal was merely a response to a changing international scene is to overlook the subtle operation of latent linkage processes involving interaction between transformations in the legitimacy attached to certain goals and forms of domestic political action on the one hand and realignments in the structure and functioning of certain international systems on the other.

Nor is our capacity to explain manifest and latent linkages that originate in national and culminate in international systems any greater than our ability to identify and account for those which flow in the opposite direction. Again examples abound. Consider again the fall of Ben Bella. The very conditions in the international system that precipitated it— a pending summit conference of non-Western nations to be held in Algeria —were in turn profoundly affected by his political demise. Not only was the conference never convened, but the stability and decision-making capacities of the emergent non-Western international system was substantially reduced by the fall of the ill-fated sponsor and chief organizer of the ill-fated occasion. Yet international systems theory provides no basis for anticipating such an outcome. No models are available which attempt to assess the dependence of various types of international systems upon various types of leadership structures within the national systems of which they are comprised. Indeed, since models of foreign policy behavior that estimate the relative potency of the variables underlying purposeful international behavior have yet to be developed,[17] it is hardly surprising that theories which systematically link national processes to their unintended international consequences are also scarce.

In short, the need for linkage theory is multidimensional. The examples suggest that political analysis would be greatly facilitated if propositions that link the stability, functioning, institutions, and goals of national political systems to variables in their external environments could be systematically developed. They also indicate that much would be gained if hypotheses linking the stability, functioning, and organizations of international systems to variables within their national subsystems were available. In addition, the Ben Bella example points up the need to trace linkages in which national and international systems function in such a way as to continuously reinforce each other (what are referred to below as "fused" linkages).

OBSTACLES TO LINKAGE THEORY

Before turning to the question of what research strategy might best facilitate the generation of systematic propositions pertaining to the structure and operation of linkage phenomena, it is instructive to examine briefly some of the reasons for the present shortage of theory. Perhaps the most basic reason is the lack of communication between those who specialize in comparative and national politics on the one hand and those who focus on international politics on the other. Since the discipline of political science has not developed a unit-environment subfield comprised of linkage specialists, linkage theory will obviously have to be generated by a sharing and integration of perspectives on the part of those in the traditional subfields. Yet the record of communication along these lines is not encouraging. A multitude of barriers, most of them conceptual and few of them historical, appear to intervene. There are no long-standing disputes keeping national and international specialists apart, no record of jurisdictional jealousy and righteous bickering over the proper road to political wisdom. Rather the barriers to effective communication and theory building are to be found in the way each group structures political data. Not only do the boundaries that each draws around the phenomena it regards as relevant tend to be mutually exclusive, but each set of boundaries also tends to encompass different kinds of actors who employ different kinds of methods in order to engage in different kinds of behavior. Consequently, far from being jealous of one another, students of national and international politics are essentially disinterested in each other's research and tend to talk past each other when they get together. They are kept apart not by mutual antagonism, but by reciprocal boredom.[18] Each group is trapped, as it were, in its own conceptual jail and, like all prisoners, its members rarely get a glimpse at the life of those incarcerated elsewhere.

While it may be easier to escape from a conceptual jail than to ameliorate an historical antagonism, the obstacles to communication are formidable and the incentives to avoid them considerable. In the first place, there are good reasons why the jails have been built. Some kind of framework is necessary for analysis and research to proceed, and since national and international politics do differ in crucial respects, it is only logical

[18] This lack of communication can be readily discerned in the proceedings of an occasion designed to bring specialists in comparative and international politics together. Cf. James N. Rosenau, *Of Boundaries and Bridges: A Report on a Conference on the Interdependencies of National and International Political Systems* (Princeton: Center of International Studies, Research Monograph No. 27, 1967), pp. 11–62.

that the practitioners in each field have developed specialized models and concepts suitable to their particular concerns.

Second, there are equally compelling reasons to remain confined within the boundaries of either field. Each field contains more of its own distinctive problems than can be studied in a lifetime of research, and there is thus plenty to do without also worrying about the problems that lie in the area of overlap between the fields. The student of foreign policy has enough difficulty estimating the external impact of a nation's foreign policy without also focusing on the internal functions which it serves. Similarly, the student of comparative politics is amply challenged by the dynamics of political change within a society without also having to account for the role external stimuli play as a source of internal changes.

Third, understandable, though not commendable, resistances to a jailbreak arise out of the possibility that the attribution of conceptual relevance to variables from the other field may diminish the elegance of existing models and require substantial revision in their central concepts. One's own jail is comforting as well as confining. For the student of national politics to concede that domestic processes may be significantly conditioned by foreign affairs is to run the risk of introducing a number of seemingly unpredictable factors into matters that he has become accustomed to taking for granted. Likewise, for the student of international politics to treat national phenomena as variables rather than constants is to invite a seemingly endless confounding of that which has otherwise proven manageable.

Fourth, in view of these considerations it is hardly surprising that both the national and international jails are solid structures indeed. The one housing the students of international politics and foreign policy is founded on the bedrock of the national interest. This concept facilitates the boredom of such students with the functioning of national systems by allowing them to view all foreign policies as being similarly motivated. By regarding every national system as acting to enhance or preserve its basic interests, however these may be defined and from wherever they may come, the foreign policy analyst can focus on the international actions themselves and is relieved of having to treat them as responses to variable internal sources as well as to external stimuli. No less sturdy and protective is the conceptual jail that students of comparative and national politics have built for themselves. Its foundations are solidly encased in the prerogatives of sovereign authority. By viewing national systems as ultimate masters of all that transpires within their borders, students of such systems need not be concerned about variations in the international environment and instead can treat it as an undifferentiated condition that operates equally upon the domestic processes and institutions that interest them.

Last, but most important, even if one should overcome boredom with the other field and conclude that the overlap of the fields can no longer be avoided, there remain the tasks of communication and theory building, of learning to use unfamiliar conceptions of what constitute the units, sources, purposes, consequences, and settings of political activity. Such a task is not easily performed: Where students of comparative politics are accustomed to analyzing the behavior of thousands and millions of actors (voters, party officials, interest groups, elites), their counterparts in the international field are used to only a few hundred or so (nations, foreign secretaries, diplomatic representatives, decision-makers); where specialists in national systems are interested in what large groups of people (the citizenry) do either to each other or to the few (officialdom), international specialists concentrate on what the few (nations) do either to each other or to the many (foreign publics); where those who analyze domestic policy actors get used to behavior that is designed to affect wholesale changes, those who focus on foreign policy actors become adjusted to action that is intended to produce slow and relatively marginal alterations; where students of comparative politics tend to perceive grand policies emanating from the clash of actors, foreign policy analysts are inclined to see the emergence of specific decisions; where researchers into national systems can usually afford to lose interest when policies are formally adopted (since compliance by those thereby affected can normally be assumed), their international colleagues cannot take policy outcomes for granted and must instead engage in calculations as to whether the strategy underlying a proposed course of action is likely to produce desirable responses on the part of those toward whom it is directed; where comparative specialists are thus inclined to analyze causes (why parties succeed or why cabinets fall), international specialists tend to focus on effects (what foreign aid accomplished or what the United Nations can do); where students of domestic policy tend to examine the motives of actors, foreign policy analysts concentrate on their capabilities; where those who investigate national systems become used to presuming that action will unfold in an institutionalized context (legislatures, courts, bureaucracies), those who analyze international systems become attuned to dealing with unfamiliar or unexpected settings for behavior (situations, crises, informal contacts); where specialists in national politics are accustomed to looking for stability in the prevailing attitudes toward authority and political activity, international specialists tend to search for it in the prevailing patterns of interaction; and so on through all the many variables that conventionally distinguish the national and international fields from each other.

In sum, the obstacles to theory building require a radical revision of the standard conception of politics that posits a world of national and international actors whose interrelationships look like this:

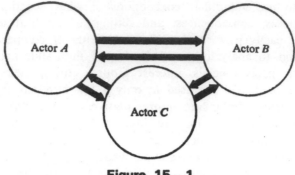

Figure 15 – 1

Linkage theory requires supplementing this conventional conception with one that looks like this:

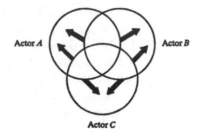

Figure 15 – 2

or even this:

Figure 15 – 3

Clearly, given their range and depth, the obstacles to linkage theory cannot be easily or quickly surmounted. The development of new conceptual models and a reorientation of long-standing habits of analysis are bound to take a lot of time. Such a lengthy process, moreover, seems unlikely to evolve on its own. It needs to be initiated. The conceptual jails are too solidly built for an unplanned emergence of linkage theory to occur. The problem must be confronted directly and self-consciously. The difficulties inherent in identifying and tracing linkage phenomena need to be experienced and the task of accounting for them theoretically needs to be attempted if new analytic habits are to form and flourish.

Hence, the purpose of the framework presented here is a modest one. It does not pretend to be an analytic model or even to provide a set of initial propositions about the interdependence of national and international systems. Rather its purpose is simply that of identifying points at which the two types of systems overlap and of precipitating thought about the nature and scope of the phenomena that fall within the area of overlap. What follows, in other words, is intended as an agenda and not as a design for research. It is hoped that the agenda will seem sufficiently compelling to stimulate the formulation and implementation of manageable research designs.

THE CONCEPT OF A LINKAGE

Our approach to the phenomena bounded by the overlap of national and international systems is strictly an empirical one. We wish to identify and analyze those recurrent sequences of behavior that originate on one side of the boundary between the two types of systems and that become linked to phenomena on the other side in the process of unfolding. Since the boundaries can be crossed by processes of perception and emulation as well as by direct interaction, allowance must be made for both continuous and intermittent sequences. Hence we will use a *linkage* as our basic unit of analysis, defining it as any recurrent sequence of behavior that originates in one system and is reacted to in another.

In order to distinguish between the initial and the terminal stages of a linkage, we shall refer to the former as an *output* and to the latter as an *input*. Each of these in turn will be classified in terms of whether they occur in a polity[19] or its external environment (i.e., the international system).[20] That is, *polity outputs* are defined as those sequences of behavior

[19] In order to distinguish national political systems from the societies of which they are a part, we shall henceforth refer to the former as polities.

[20] Although the term "environment" has special meanings for students of international politics (cf. Harold and Margaret Sprout, *The Ecological Perspective on Human Affairs*), in this discussion it is employed in the more general, systems theory sense with which students of comparative politics are familiar. It is conceived as an analytic entity consisting of all the human and nonhuman phenomena that exist external to a polity, irrespective of whether their existence is perceived by the actors of the polity. Our use also posits the environment as having external and internal dimensions, with the "external environment" referring to the human and nonhuman phenomena located external to the geographic space of the society of which the polity is a part and the "internal environment" referring to those phenomena that are external to the polity but exist within the geographic space of the society. Since we shall be mainly concerned with the external environment,

that originate within a polity and that either culminate in or are sustained by its environment, whereas *environmental inputs* are considered to be those behavioral sequences in the external environment to which the polity outputs give rise. Similarly, *environmental outputs* are those sequences of behavior that start in the external environment of a polity and that are either sustained or terminated within the polity, whereas *polity inputs* are those behavioral sequences within a polity to which environmental outputs give rise.

Conceptual clarity also requires distinguishing outputs and inputs in terms of their purposefulness. Some outputs, conventionally called foreign policy, are designed to bring about responses in other systems. These we shall call either *direct polity outputs* or *direct environmental outputs*, depending on whether the intentional behavior was designated by a polity for its environment or vice versa. Yet there are a host of other patterns of behavior within a polity or its environment that are not designed to evoke boundary-crossing responses but that nevertheless do so through perceptual or emulative processes. Elections and *coups d'état* that provoke reactions abroad exemplify outputs of this latter kind, which we shall call either *indirect polity outputs* or *indirect environmental outputs* depending on the locus of their origin. A similar line of reasoning results in four types of inputs and the corresponding labels of *direct polity inputs*, *indirect polity inputs*, *direct environmental inputs*, and *indirect environmental inputs*.

A final dimension of our formulation concerns the way in which outputs and inputs get linked together. Three basic types of linkage processes are identified, the penetrative, the reactive, and the emulative. A *penetrative* process occurs when members of one polity serve as participants in the political processes of another. That is, they share with those in the penetrated polity the authority to allocate its values. The activities of an occupying army are perhaps the most clearcut example of a penetrative process, but the postwar world has also seen foreign aid missions, subversive cadres, the staffs of international organizations, the representatives of private corporations, the workers of certain transnational political parties, and a variety of other actors establish linkages through such a

---

however, we shall simplify matters by referring to it as the "environment," while always using the proper designation when we have occasion to mention the internal environment. Furthermore, as a result of this formulation the external environment of a polity is conceived to be equivalent to the same phenomena as comprise any international system of which the polity is a component part. Thus we shall be using the notions of environment and international system interchangeably, depending on whether we wish to refer to the phenomena in the context, respectively, of a single polity or of the interaction of two or more polities.

process.[21] Virtually by definition, penetrative processes link direct outputs and inputs.

A *reactive process* is the contrary of a penetrative one: It is brought into being by recurrent and similar boundary-crossing reactions rather than by the sharing of authority. The actors who initiate the output do not participate in the allocative activities of those who experience the input, but the behavior of the latter is nevertheless a response to behavior undertaken by the former. Such reactive processes are probably the most frequent form of linkage, since they arise out of the joining of both direct and indirect outputs to their corresponding inputs. Recurrent reactions to a foreign aid program illustrate a reactive process involving direct outputs and inputs, whereas instances of local election campaigns in the United States being responsive to trends in Vietnam exemplify a reactive process stemming from indirect outputs and inputs.

The third type of linkage process is a special form of the reactive type. An *emulative process* is established when the input is not only a response to the output but takes essentially the same form as the output. It corresponds to the so-called "diffusion" or "demonstration" effect whereby political activities in one country are perceived and emulated in another. The postwar spread of violence, nationalism, and aspirations to rapid industrialization and political modernization are but the more striking instances of linkages established through emulative processes. Since the emulated behavior is ordinarily undertaken independently of those who emulate it, emulative processes usually link only indirect outputs and inputs.

Several aspects of this formulation require emphasis and elaboration. In the first place, it should be noted that our terminology has been deliberately chosen. In order to stay out of the conceptual jails built by national and international specialists, we have purposely employed definitions and terminology that are not identified exclusively with either group. The concept of linkages formed out of outputs and inputs appears neutral in this regard and is at the same time easily grasped. Furthermore, the concept is neutral with respect to the question of whether the growing overlap of national and international systems represents a subtle process of integration and the emergence of a world political community. Polities are increasingly dependent on their environments and interdependent with each other in the sense that, increasingly, what transpires at home would unfold differently if trends abroad were different. However, this interdependence may or may not involve greater integration among the polities. Some linkages may in fact be founded on enmity and be highly disinte-

---

[21] For a more elaborate formulation and analysis of penetrative processes and linkages, see Chapter 6.

grative for polities, international systems, or both.[22] Communist China's linkages to its environment are a case in point. Hence, so as to avoid the positive evaluation that often is implicit in the notion of interdependency, we have opted for the less elegant but more neutral terminology of linkages.

Another advantage of this terminology is that it neither denies nor exaggerates the relevance of national boundaries. While it is tempting to conclude that because a shrinking world is linking polities ever more firmly to their environments it is also making them increasingly indistinguishable from their environments, such is not necessarily the case. Many political continuities still occur solely within the boundaries of a single polity and cannot be understood without reference to the existence and character of the boundaries. Transnational politics are a long way from supplanting national politics and, if anything, the world may well be passing through a paradoxical stage in which *both* the linkages and the boundaries among polities are becoming more central to their daily lives. In affirming the existence of national boundaries, however, it is easy to obscure the sequential nature of many behavioral patterns that cross over them. Such sequences often go unrecognized because the existence of the boundaries leads the analyst to treat their initial phase as a foreign policy action that comes to a halt once it crosses into the environment of the initiating polity. Consequently, the responses to foreign policy action in other polities are viewed as new and separate sequences of behavior rather than as the next phase of the same sequence. Although the concept of national-international linkages may not prevent such a practice, it should inhibit undue segmentation of behavioral sequences. It should provide a context for the analysis of foreign policy in which the importance of polity boundaries is acknowledged but not accentuated.

Another aspect of this formulation that requires emphasis is the concept of recurrent behavior. Outputs, inputs, and the linkages that they form are not conceived to be single events. Theory building would hardly be possible if individual actions or discrete occasions served as analytic units. Rather in order to move beyond the case method to productive theorizing, outputs, inputs, and linkages are conceptualized to be events which recur with sufficient frequency to form a pattern. To be sure, any

[22] One observer has estimated the prospect of distintegrative linkages as follows: "Since there is small chance that international politics will diminish in importance and salience in the next half century, and since judgments of alternative policies and proposals will necessarily rest on highly controversial assessments of very great risks, gains, and costs, a variety of foreign policies, military affairs, treaties, regional and international organizations and alliances all promise a steady flow of internal conflict." Robert A. Dahl, "Epilogue," in R. A. Dahl (ed.), *Political Oppositions in Western Democracies* (New Haven: Yale University Press, 1966), p. 398.

discrete event can, at some level of generalization, be regarded as an instance of a more encompassing pattern and we do not preclude examining any event with a view to determining whether it is a case of what we have classified as a national-international linkage. If such a determination cannot be made, however, the event itself will not hold our attention for long. If, for example, an official of a stable polity is assassinated or an official of the United Nations killed in an airplane crash, such events will not be treated as outputs or inputs. They might well have boundary-crossing repercussions, but, being unexpected and nonrecurrent, their repercussions are likely to be short-lived and more habitual modes of behavior are likely to be quickly reestablished.

In other words, it is the recurrence and not the occurrence of events that serves as our focus. We are interested, to use a more commonplace example, in how the elections of a polity affect and are affected by its external environment, not in the international consequences of a specific election. The immediate consequences of a particular election might be extensive, but they would be treated as reflections of linkages rather than as linkages themselves. Similarly, given a recurrent behavior within a polity, external reactions to it are not considered to form linkages with it unless they too are recurrent. In polities where elections are held regularly, for example, these would not be treated as indirect polity outputs unless they fostered a recurrent pattern of responses in the environment. National elections in Norway and the United States are illustrative of this distinction. They recur with equal regularity in both polities but only in the case of the latter do NATO deliberations and East-West relations consistently come to a halt during the preceding campaign period. American presidential elections, in short, are integral parts of environmental patterns, whereas the equivalent events in Norway are not. The former would thus be viewed as indirect polity outputs, while the latter would not.[23]

---

[23] The example of American electoral consequences also serves to highlight another aspect of our formulation, namely, that the same behavior pattern can be part of more than one linkage. If it recurrently fosters similar consequences in two or more polities or international relationships, as the quadrennial contests for the White House apparently do, then obviously it must be treated as a different output in a number of different linkages. Likewise, if a behavior pattern is conditioned by a variety of international developments, it would be treated as a different input in each case. It follows that the same behavior pattern can also serve as *both* an output and an input. We are concerned about a wide range of linkages and do not lose interest in a particular pattern just because its role in one type of linkage has been identified. The practice of giving CIA briefings to American presidential nominees, for example, has become recurrent in response to seemingly permanent aspects of the cold war. So have certain campaign themes and possibly even certain voting patterns. Thus, just as American presidential elections can serve as outputs in one set of linkages, so can they simultaneously

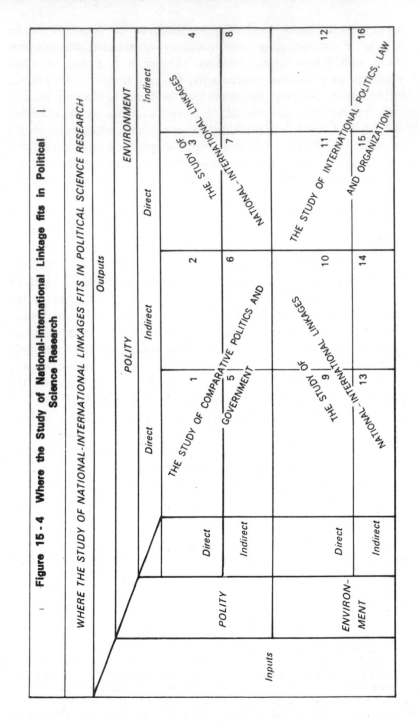

Figure 15 - 4   Where the Study of National-International Linkage fits in Political Science Research

WHERE THE STUDY OF NATIONAL-INTERNATIONAL LINKAGES FITS IN POLITICAL SCIENCE RESEARCH

Summing up our formulation thus far, we seem to have uncovered an almost unlimited number of possible national-international linkages that can, without undue simplification, be clustered into a manageable set of nine basic types of linkages. Eight of these stem from the convergence of the four types of outputs and inputs (see Cells 3, 4, 7, 8, 9, 10, 13, 14 in Figure 15–4). The ninth, which we shall call the *fused* linkage, arises out of the possibility that certain outputs and inputs continuously reinforce each other and are thus best viewed as forming a reciprocal relationship. In other words, a fused linkage is one in which the patterned sequence of behavior does not terminate with the input. Stated in positive terms, a fused linkage is conceived to be a sequence in which an output fosters an input that in turn fosters an output in such a way that they cannot meaningfully be analyzed separately.[24]

THE COMPONENTS OF A LINKAGE FRAMEWORK

In order to facilitate the development of linkage theory, we now expand the foregoing into a larger framework in which twenty-four aspects of polities that might serve as or give rise to outputs and inputs have been identified along with six aspects or (from a polity perspective) sub-environments of the international system that might generate or receive outputs and inputs. The prevalence of linkage phenomena becomes immediately apparent when the two sets of variables are combined into a matrix that yields 144 areas in which national-international linkages can be formed. This matrix is presented in Figure 15–5. The number of possible linkages is actually much greater than 144, since in many cells of the matrix all three types of linkage processes can occur and all of the aforementioned nine basic types of linkages can be established. To convey the full array of possible linkages, in other words, the matrix should be reproduced three times to account for the varying linkage processes and then each of these should in turn be reproduced nine times, eight of them covering all the possible combinations of the direct-indirect and output-input distinctions and the ninth allowing for the identification of fused linkages. While an inquiry into each of the 27 forms of linkage that can occur

---

operate as inputs in another. Similarly, to the extent that elections in Norway are significantly conditioned by regional or cold war issues, they would be treated as inputs in some linkages even though they do not seem to be outputs in any.

[24] An obvious example of a fused linkage is the foreign policy of a polity that serves the function of unifying its citizenry and provoking reactions abroad that further solidify the unity and thus reinforce the impetus to maintain the policies. The reciprocity between American public opinion and the conflict in Vietnam is an even more specific illustration of this fusion.

Figure 15 - 5   A Proposed Linkage Framework

POLITY Outputs and Inputs	ENVIRONMENTAL → The Contiguous Environment	The Regional Environment	The Cold War Environment	The Racial Environment	The Resource Environment	The Organizational Environment
Actors						
1. Executive Officials						
2. Legislative Officials						
3. Civilian Bureaucrats						
4. Military Bureaucrats						
5. Political Parties						
6. Interest Groups						
7. Elite Groups						
Attitudes						
8. Ideology						
9. Political Culture						
10. Public Opinion						
Institutions						
11. Executive						
12. Legislatures						
13. Bureaucracies						
14. Military Establishments						
15. Elections						
16. Party Systems						
17. Communications Systems						
18. Social Institutions						
Processes						
19. Socialization and Recruitment						
20. Interest Articulation						
21. Interest Aggregation						
22. Policy-Making						
23. Policy-Administration						
24. Integrative-Disintegrative						

in each of the 144 different cells of the matrix is feasible in an age of high-speed computers, and while all of them might well be investigated —at least to the point where it is established that their empirical existence is insufficient to make them theoretically relevant—this is not the place to undertake such a full analysis. Here we can only indicate some of the more fruitful lines of linkage theory that are suggested by such a framework. Before doing so, however, the limitations and tentative character of the framework represented by the matrix must be briefly acknowledged, lest the reader be so put off by its proliferation of categories that he overlooks its advantages and the many interesting theoretical questions to which it points. Most notably, it must be admitted that the various categories are imprecise, incomplete, impressionistic, and overlapping. Our purpose at this stage is to be suggestive, not exhaustive, and thus we have made no effort to formulate precise definitions or to delineate mutually exclusive boundaries between categories. Further refinement would no doubt result in the merging of some categories and the replacement of others. In the case of the twenty-four polity subcategories, we have merely listed some of the more obvious determinants of outputs and inputs, trusting that their general characteristics are self-evident.[25] The listing includes phenomena that sustain behavior at different levels (actors, attitudes, institutions, and processes[26]) and that unfold in different settings (the government, the polity, and the society). Likewise, in the case of the environmental categories, we have proceeded on an equally simple and impressionistic basis. The only rationale for the categorization is the impression that both actors and observers tend, often unknowingly, to think about international phenomena in terms of the units represented by the six subenvironments.[27] Again no claim is made that these six are

[25]*All but the last six subcategories listed in Figure 15-5 are quite commonplace in the study of Western and non-Western politics and the abbreviated labels for them should convey a general sense of the phenomena they encompass. Those listed as Rows 19-23 are taken from the formulation in Gabriel A. Almond and James S. Coleman (eds.), *The Politics of the Developing Areas* (Princeton: Princeton University Press, 1960), pp. 16–58, while the last subcategory is intended to facilitate analysis of how such phenomena as social change, group cleavage, societal stability, and so on, shape the direction and quality of direct polity outputs.

[26] By an actor is meant any concrete persons or collectivities who engage in the specified set of activities. Attitudinal determinants are conceived to be those mental-emotional states (e.g., moods, preferences, cultural norms, intellectual habits) which guide the behavior of actors. Institutions are regarded as stylized patterns or structures of inter-personal relationships through which the specified set of activities can be performed. Process refers to interactive relationships that exhibit describable patterns through time.

[27] That is, the tendency to attach relevance to location, distance, and space, as perceived and reacted to in the perspective of historical experience, would seem to be a widespread one and underlies establishment of the "contiguous environment" and the "regional environment." Equally common is the inclination to attach

exhaustive or mutually exclusive. Further inquiry may well reveal that other output or input phenomena, such as those of a legal, technological, and military kind, are so important as to justify the establishment of additional categories. We do contend, however, that these six environments are operative in the minds of actors and that they are thus at least a meaningful sample for our purposes here. (Indeed, this contention is, in effect, a basic hypothesis about national-international linkages that can and should be subjected to empirical verification.)

Despite the crudeness of the categories, the framework outlined in **Figure 15–5** offers a number of advantages. In the first place, it prevents perpetuation of the analytic gap between comparative and international politics and compels thought about the way in which they are linked. By juxtaposing aspects of systems, we identify a number of points at which they can overlap and make it easier to break the habit of separately examining political systems from an exclusively national or international perspective.

Second, the framework prevents us from focusing on only manifest linkages. By subdividing polities and their environments into many components, we call attention to a number of unfamiliar and latent linkages that might go unrecognized or be quickly dismissed as being of no importance if a less explicit framework were employed. Although many of the linkages derived from the framework may not prove to be worthy of extended analysis, at least they will have to be considered and their relevance assessed.

Third, the polity side of the framework should greatly inhibit the tendency to treat national governments as having undifferentiated internal environments and thus to rely on the national interest as an explanation of international behavior. By breaking down polities into aspects that are not ordinarily considered in an international context, we have encouraged inquiry into the processes by which the needs and wants of a polity are determined and discouraged the assumption that its outputs merely serve interests. Moreover, by identifying nongovernmental actors, attitudes, institutions, and processes, as well as those connected with formal decision-making, we have made it possible to examine fused linkages and

relevance to the particular pattern of Great Power relationships that prevail at any moment in history; hence the selection of the "Cold War environment." Similarly, associating relevance to certain types of trans- and subnational group or individual relationships is widely practiced and the "racial environment" and the "resource environment" have been chosen to reflect this manner of categorizing phenomena. Still another practice is that of ascribing relevance to the existence and activities of international organizations and thus we have separated out the "organizational environment." For an elaboration of the boundaries and nature of these subenvironments, see Appendix A of this chapter.

to pose functional questions about the ways in which external behavior serves the internal workings of polities.

Similarly, and fourth, the environmental side of the framework should substantially curb the tendency to regard polities as having undifferentiated external environments. By identifying several international systems of which polities are a part, we have made it difficult to presume that events abroad operate as constants rather than as variables in the functioning of polities. Such a procedure also permits comparisons of the stability of different international systems in terms of the varying ways in which polities may be linked to them. If, for example, the consequences of the historic differences between India and Pakistan, France and Germany, Korea and Japan, Greece and Turkey, and Israel and Egypt are any indication, it would seem that the close-at-hand environment of a polity can dominate its foreign policy and internal life far more extensively than other, more remote, environmental ties.[28] These differential environmental ties have never been subjected to the systematic and comparative analysis that is inherent in the linkage framework.

Fifth, all of these advantages are further served by the distinction between direct and indirect linkage phenomena. By emphasizing that behavior sequences can be either intentional or unintentional, we allow for the analysis of two basic sets of linkages that tend to be ignored. One involves those initiated by the direct outputs of polities. Obviously a preponderance of the actions purposefully directed at the environment are undertaken by the governments of polities, so that the primary category of direct outputs consists of all those activities, both decisional and implementive, that are usually described as the foreign policies of a nation. In the context of nation-international linkages, foreign policies are recurring forms of action—or inaction—that the duly constituted authorities of a polity initiate toward one or more objects in their external environment, with a view to either preventing the object from hindering the satisfaction of polity needs and wants or obtaining resources from it that will facilitate satisfaction of polity needs. But foreign policy activities are not the only direct outputs of polities. A major advantage of the linkage framework is that it calls attention to another major category of purposeful behavior that is often overlooked and that ought to be subjected to extensive inquiry, namely, those recurrent activities that private persons or groups undertake with the intent of preserving or altering one or more aspects of the polity's external environment. Corporations, religious bodies, professional organizations, labor unions, some political parties, special interest groups, distinguished citizens, and a variety of other private actors sometimes

[28] For some evidence along these lines, see Leonard Binder, *The Ideological Revolution in the Middle East* (New York: Wiley, 1964), pp. 261–262.

pursue, in many polities, goals designed to establish desired patterns of behavior abroad. An obvious example of the importance of these non-governmental direct outputs is provided by the overseas activities of U.S. corporations. As Samuel P. Huntington puts it,

> There is the whole question—which is far from just a Marxist myth—of the impact which private economic groups have on the politics of underdeveloped countries where they have investments and on their developed home countries. This is a subject which political scientists have avoided, but my own very limited studies on Latin America convince me that it is of fundamental importance. . . . The international corporation which owns property in a dozen or more countries today escapes control by government and has much the same relationship to weak developing governments that the American railroad corporation had to our state governments in the 1870s. A comparative study of the politics of the supranational corporation, of how ITT, Shell, Standard Oil, General Motors, General Electric, etc., respond to and influence the politics of the countries in which they function seems like a high-priority item for any study of national-international linkages. Another interesting issue would be the more general problem of why economic bodies (like corporations and, to some extent, unions) can function effectively across international lines, while purely political bodies, e.g., parties, cannot. To the best of my knowledge, every attempt to maintain an international political party has foundered on the rocks of nationalism. The RDA and the Baath are only the latest examples in a list strewn with the wreckage of the second and third internationals. If this is true internationally, why is this the case, and what implications does it have for the probable success of the efforts by parties and other groups to integrate countries like Burma, Malaysia, Nigeria, or the Congo?[29]

Likewise, on the input side the direct-indirect distinction has the advantage of emphasizing that the life of a polity is conditioned by far more than the purposeful actions that other polities direct at it. This point is often ignored in research. Many analysts rely heavily on the concept of intervention as a means of analyzing the international situation of polities and focus on the ways in which actors in a polity's environment intervene in its affairs. In doing this, they tend not to question whether a number of its activities have been unintentionally affected by events and trends abroad. Intervention implies resistance, or at least the conscious interposition of foreign elements that must be brought under control and managed. Subversion must be contested, economic penetration offset, military threats countered, diplomatic demands bargained with, propaganda charges answered. Yet, obviously, there is more to life in a world of other polities. While we do not minimize the importance of the behavioral patterns that are precipitated by purposeful interventions,

[29] In a personal communication, dated July 7, 1965.

we would argue that there are also myriad ways in which polities adjust to circumstances in their external environments that were not designed to affect them. Hopefully the concept of indirect inputs will encourage more extensive inquiry into these adjustment patterns.[30]

Finally, but no less importantly, the linkages framework responds to the need for more genuine comparisons in the study of foreign policy. As we have implied here and elaborated elsewhere,[31] the great preponderance of foreign policy analyses focus on the international behavior of a single polity and most of them do so by moving back and forth indiscriminately between explanations that posit the polity's foreign policies as stemming from, say, geocultural factors in one situation, from the personality of leaders in another, and from resource and other capability variables in still another. Rare indeed are attempts to identify and assess the causal potency of key variables through a comparison of their operation in two or more polities. By bringing both the internal and external variables together in a framework that can be applied to any polity, hopefully we have provided a way of overcoming this deficiency and a basis for assessing and comparing the relative potency of the variables underlying the international behavior of any two polities.

AN AGENDA FOR RESEARCH

Of course, the test of such a framework lies not in the advantages that are claimed for it, but in the theoretical questions that it generates. One innovative line of inquiry suggested by the matrix in Figure 15–5 involves a focus on linkages per se, so as to compare their origins, duration, flexibility, stability, and functions irrespective of the kind of polity that sustains them. The impact of the contiguous environment on party

[30] Recognition of indirect inputs, it might be added, is facilitated by investigation of those political roles in a polity that either have undergone recent changes or are newly established. Such a procedure often turns up clues as to where and how the impact of the external environment is being experienced. Consider, for example, electoral politics in the United States. Where White House aspirants were once predominantly state governors because of a norm that presidents ought to have prior executive experience, today the informal requirements of the candidate role have changed to emphasis on a "foreign affairs" background, with the result that presidential nominations have increasingly gone to members of Congress in recent years. Similar indirect inputs can even be discerned at lower levels of American politics as, for example, candidates for state and local offices increasingly cite their previous international experiences as grounds for their election. Likewise, the tendency of church, labor, business, and educational organizations to create high-ranking positions that are specifically charged with responsibility for handling the organization's international contacts and interests is another reflection of the occurrence of indirect inputs.

[31] Chapters 4 and 6.

systems, for example, could be contrasted with the way in which the cold war environment affects the competition, number, organization, and solidarity of the parties within different systems. Questions such as the following might be researched: Do dimensions of the contiguous environment create more or less divisiveness within and among parties than do aspects of the cold war environment? Does the former tend to foster penetrative or emulative processes that divide parties and the latter reactive processes that unite them? Indeed, is one environment more likely than another to create issues that encourage the emergence of new parties whose existence and strength is in turn a function of the duration and intensity of the issues posed by the environment? How do party system-contiguous environment linkages differ from party system-cold war environment ones in terms of their impact upon the capacity of parties to raise funds, recruit members, select leaders, and resolve conflicts? In contrast, what is the likelihood of one-, two-, or multi-party systems being differentially linked to the two types of environments and thus differentially affecting their structure and stability? Are fused linkages more likely to occur with respect to the cold war than to the contiguous environment? That is, is it reasonable to hypothesize that the former is more likely than the latter to foster issues that divide parties and that in turn serve as outputs?

While these questions suggest the potentialities of comparing linkages within each row of the matrix, others indicate the utility of comparing them within each column and, more broadly, of comparisons among rows and among columns. It is interesting to ask, for example, whether the cold war environment is more securely linked to, say, the structure of mass public opinion and the functioning of the system of mass communications than to the various processes of governmental policy-making? Indeed, is it not conceivable that public opinion-cold war linkages are more predictable and enduring than those in which this environment is tied to the activities of parties or to the patterns of voting behavior? These questions lead to the broader one of whether such cold war linkages are likely to be stronger, more extensive, and less flexible than those linking the resource or organizational environment to various polity institutions? Are some external environments likely to be linked to only a few selected aspects of polities, whereas with others linkage occurs across the entire range of polity activities? Are some environments more likely to foster penetrative or emulative processes than others? Or does the nature of the linkage process stem less from environmental characteristics and more from the structure of polities? Posed in systemic terms, how do the linkages that support or disrupt contiguous systems compare with those that sustain regional ones? Is it not reasonable to hypothesize that the former, consisting of especially proximate ties between polities and their environments, are more fragile and subject to greater fluctuation in intensity and direction than the latter?

A second major line of inquiry, one that will appeal particularly to students of comparative politics, would be to contrast linkages from the perspective of a single polity. A host of questions come to mind: How widespread are the linkages to which the polity contributes outputs? Are these exclusively of a direct (foreign policy) kind or also of the indirect variety? To what extent are its ties to the external world characterized by direct or indirect inputs? Are some polity actors, attitudes, institutions, and processes more subject to penetration or emulation than others? Do linkages occur primarily with one type of environment? Or is the pattern of linkages not a clear-cut one? Are, say, the polity's policy-making processes linked more extensively to the cold war environment, whereas its processes of interest articulation and aggregation are tied more closely to the regional environment? Does the organizational environment create issues for interest groups? Or are the latter tied more closely to the resource environment, whereas bureaucracies and elite groups sustain most of the links to the organizational environment? What function does each linkage serve in terms of the polity's capacity to define its domestic goals, mobilize its resources, and implement its decisions? How is the polity's ability to identify and pursue goals in the foreign policy area enhanced or restricted by the nature of its linkages? Are some linkages more functional than others? Are some that are functional offset by others that are dysfunctional?

Questions such as these lead naturally to a third line of inquiry in which the linkage patterns of particular types of polities are traced and compared: Are democracies similarly linked to the outside world and are their linkage patterns in turn different from those of authoritarian polities? Do different types of environments press more closely upon unintegrated polities than upon integrated ones? Do superpolities have similar linkage patterns that are distinguishable from those of small polities? Is the former type of polity more subject to emulative processes than the latter type, whereas small polities are more vulnerable to penetrative processes than super ones? Are polities in, say, Latin America more closely linked to the regional environment than European ones? Are wealthy polities more successful in managing their direct linkages than poor ones?

Equally intriguing questions arise out of an approach which classifies and compares polities entirely in terms of their linkage patterns, instead of using more conventional categories. For example, four basic types of polities could be identified by classifying them in terms of the number of linkages to which they contribute outputs, by doing the same in terms of the linkages for which they are the input recipients, by dividing the two scales into low and high, and by then combining them in a fourfold table. The four types of polities created by such a scheme would be (1) those that are high on both scales; (2) those that have many linkages to which they contribute outputs and few in which they receive inputs; (3) those that have the pattern opposite to (2); and (4) those that are low on both scales. If the world's polities were to be classified in terms of these four types, such a procedure would pose the tantalizing question of whether there are other ways in which those similarly classified resemble each other. Might one find, as seems reasonable at first glance, that many outputs are fostered by superpolities and by those medium-sized polities for whose allegiance superpolities compete; that few outputs are generated by disunited new polities and by traditionally neutral ones; that many inputs are experienced by new polities and by those for which superpolities compete; and that both superpolities and traditionally neutral ones are likely to be the recipients of few inputs? In short, might research yield clusters of polities such as in Figure 15–6?

Figure 15 – 6

OUTPUTS

		High	Low
INPUTS	High	Egypt	Congo
		Nigeria	Cyprus
	Low	U.S.	Sweden
		U.S.S.R.	Switzerland

Another line of inquiry, one that will be especially appealing to students of foreign policy, would concentrate on those linkages in which the outputs are direct and result from governmental activities. Unlike the more conventional types of foreign policy analysis, such a focus insures that comparison will not be confined to policy content, but will also be extended to its sources and its effectiveness. By treating foreign policies as only one aspect of recurring patterns, the analyst would be compelled to assess them in terms of the factors that led to their adoption and of the behavior to which they became linked abroad. Again a variety of interesting questions seem worth pursuing. Are direct governmental outputs likely to be linked more profoundly and less transitorily to the contiguous environment than to the regional or racial environments? Are governmental linkages with the contiguous environment likely to be formed mainly through diplomatic and economic activities, whereas those with the latter are more likely to be based on propaganda or military behavior patterns? Do governments tend to be imaginative in linking themselves to the familiar dimensions of the contiguous environment, but cumbersome in coping with the obscure and uncharted terrain of the cold war environment? For similar reasons, is public opinion more likely to underlie governmental outputs that are part of linkages to the crisis ridden cold war environment than governmental outputs that are tied to the routinized behavior patterns of the regional environment? Are cabinet governments likely to initiate more enduring linkages than presidential governments?

Fused linkages provide still another intriguing realm for comparative inquiry. Such research would focus on the interdependence of polities and their environments, and would thus be of special interest to students of international institutions and to those concerned with the prospects of supranational integration. The kinds of questions that might be investigated seem almost endless: Are fused linkages more likely to occur with respect to contiguous, regional, resource, or more highly structured environments than to cold war, racial, or other more volatile environments? Are certain types of polities likely to have a predominance of fused linkages, while others have virtually none? Do such linkages tend to involve elections and public opinion more than other aspects of polities? Is fusion between interest groups and the resource environment likely to be more stable than comparable linkages involving government actors? Is the stability of a fused linkage primarily a function of its environmental or of its polity components? Do fused linkages tend to be more or less enduring than those in which fusion does not occur? Does a rapid expansion in the number of an environment's fused linkages signify that it constitutes an international system that is becoming increasingly integrated?

POSTSCRIPT

One further line of questions comes to mind: Is it irresponsible to raise questions that one neither answers nor provides the basis for answering? Is it self-defeating to propose research based on impressionistic and overlapping categories that have not been derived from a theoretical model and that may thus prove more misleading than helpful? In a discipline that is seeking to find itself as an empirical science, is it counterproductive to argue for theory building without also specifying how appropriate data might be gathered and processed? Furthermore, if the need for linkage theory is so great, why have efforts not been made to develop it? Could it be that in fact there is no such need, that present modes of analysis are more than adequate to handle the convergence of national and international systems?

The answer to these questions can be found in one's reaction to the substantive ones suggested by the framework and to the empirical attempts undertaken to explore them.[32] If our efforts seem mundane, then the call for greater attention to linkage phenomena may well be misleading and unnecessary. On the other hand, if our agenda for research evokes curiosity and reflection, then further work would seem to be in order. And, if use of the framework does appear to have resulted in the identification of important phenomena, then the task of moving on to the construction of research designs should prove both possible and exhilarating.

APPENDIX A: ELABORATION OF THE SIX SUBENVIRONMENTS

In considering the contiguous, regional, cold war, racial, resource, and organizational subenvironments (see Figure 15–5), it must be remembered that these are a breakdown of the external world from the perspective of any polity. Looked at from an international systems perspective, these categories comprise patterns of interaction that recur, respectively, among contiguous polities; among polities in the same general geographic area (such as a continent, region, or hemisphere); among superpolities and their alliance systems (such as the United States, the USSR, the West, and the East); among those in different polities who prevent, enhance, or otherwise affect relations between races; polities who develop, distribute, and consume human or nonhuman resources; and among and within international organizations.

Before elaborating on these categories, it is also useful to locate more precisely the origins of the outputs of these subenvironments. In each of the six cases an output can be the product of behavior patterns that unfold either within or between one or more of the units comprising the subenvironment. In other words, from the perspective of a polity that receives environmental outputs as inputs, the outputs can originate either in other polities or in the interaction among them. If the outputs are purposefully designed by one of the polities in the environment, or if they result from

---

[32] For a listing and discussion of many of these attempts, see James N. Rosenau, "Theorizing Across Systems: Linkage Politics Revisited," in Jonathan Wilkenfeld (ed.), *Conflict Behavior and Linkage Politics* (New York: David McKay Company, 1973), pp. 25–56. A reproduction of this essay can also be found in James N. Rosenau, *The Study of Global Interdependence: Essays on the Transnationalization of World Affairs* (London: Frances Pinter Publishers, 1980).

the planned coordination of two or more of them, then they are classified as direct environmental outputs. If, for example, both the United States and NATO regularly seek to obtain, say, Sweden's support for certain arms control proposals, both patterns would be viewed as direct outputs from Sweden's cold war environment. On the other hand, if aspects of Swedish political life were to become unintentionally linked to sequences resulting from unilateral tariff decisions taken by the United States and to others that consisted, say, of United States-British trade agreements, both would be regarded as indirect outputs of Sweden's resource environment.

Much the same can be said about environmental inputs. These can be part of behavioral patterns that unfold both within and among the polities that comprise the subenvironments of any polity. Patterned reactions to American presidential elections in England and NATO, for example, would both be treated as the environmental input components in linkages in which the outputs were contributed by the United States.

The Contiguous Environment—This category refers to any cluster of polities that border geographically upon a given polity. Hence the contiguous environment allows for the consideration of such phenomena as boundary disputes, historic rivalries, traditional friendships, and the many other distinctive features of relations among immediate neighbors.

The Regional Environment—This category is based on considerations similar to those underlying the previous one. In this case, however, the scope is extended to include the entire region in which a given polity is located. The concept of region is a flexible one, its referent depending on whether geographic, cultural, religious, or historical variables are used as the basis of delineation. Thus the size of a region can range from small areas (such as Central America or the Outer Seven) to partial continents (e.g., Subsaharan Africa, Southeast Asia, or the Arab world) to entire continents (e.g., North America or Europe). Even combined continents, such as the Western Hemisphere, can be treated as a regional environment if it is "natural" for polities to segment the external world along such lines. In other words, the regional environment falls between the close-at-hand and the remote environments to which polities must relate. As such, it would seem to play an important role in the life of many polities, or at least this impression is readily derived from the widespread postwar tendencies toward the institutionalization of regional relationships in a variety of federations, confederations, and common markets. Such integrative tendencies, as well as those of a distintegrative sort, will be among the phenomena identified by this category.

The Cold War Environment—Although perhaps less so than many aspects of the contiguous and regional environments, the competition that marks relations among the world's superpolities and their blocs is obviously a highly salient element of the external world of any polity. Particular polities may be geographically removed from the question of whether there will be war or peace in Berlin, Vietnam or the Congo, but they can hardly remain unaffected by the ways in which East and West relate on such matters. Nor is the problem of war and peace the only dimension of the great power or (as we have called it here) cold war environment. It also encompasses any pattern that is predominantly a consequence of the state of East-West relations. Questions of disarmament, foreign aid, space exploration, and cultural exchange are thus also part of the cold war environment, as are socioeconomic policies pertaining to the economic role of government, the rights of groups, and the welfare of individuals.

The Racial Environment—This is a frankly experimental category that encompasses phenomena that might perhaps be subsumed under any of the others. It is designed to include all those expectations, trends, and conflicts external to a polity that pertain to relations between racial or ethnic groups. Our purpose is to determine whether categorization at the level of a major issue area is likely to yield significant insights that might not otherwise be developed into the nature of national-international linkages. If inquiry along these lines does prove fruitful, then an attempt to establish other categories of this sort could be undertaken.

The Resource Environment—Encompassed here are all the activities through which goods and services in the external world of any polity are created, processed, and utilized. By "goods" is meant nonhuman resources of all kinds, from unmined ore to foodstuffs to advanced machinery. By "services" is meant human resources, including such diverse phenomena as the training of technicians, the education of youth, and the skills of armies. But it is *the activities that result in the utilization of goods and services,* and not the goods and services themselves, which comprise the resource environment. While nonhuman goods are crucial to the satisfaction of a polity's needs and wants, satisfaction results from the use and not the existence of resources. Hence it is the activities in the environment which permit, foster, limit, or prevent usage by the polity of given resources that can become linked to activities within it and which thus constitute this subenvironment.

National-international linkages, in other words, are conceived to occur exclusively among humans. In one sense, to be sure, men are "linked" to their physical surroundings, but these are not linkages as we conceive them here because they can be sustained or altered by the action of only some, but not all, of their components. Physical surroundings impose limits or provide opportunities, but in themselves they cannot act as causal agents in a relationship. What varies is the use (or disuse) of the physical world—the decisions men make about the resources they possess, the resources they desire to possess, and the means they will employ to narrow the discrepancy between their possessions and their desires. Conceived in this way, the resource environment consists of such regularized activities as trade and fiscal relations, economic development programs, attempts to acquire nuclear weapons or, indeed, attempts to acquire any capabilities that will facilitate the conduct of foreign policy.

The Organizational Environment—The proliferation and growth of international organizations has required polities to devote increased attention to institutionalized patterns of activity that transpire in their environment. This category is designed to facilitate analysis of the linkages that have thereby been created. It encompasses all those organizations that have structure and personnel apart from the polities belonging to them, such as the United Nations, the Organization of American States, and the International Court of Justice. It does not include, however, the many alliances and agreements in which elaborate specifications for interaction and cooperation are not accompanied by the establishment of implementing machinery that has an identity of its own. Such agreements might be part of the contiguous, regional, cold war, or resource environments, but here we are interested only in separate organizations, which by virtue of being separate, introduce an additional set of actors into the environment of all polities.

16 Race in International Politics: A Dialogue in Five Parts *

I. PROLOGUE

The Author: The more one ponders the task of assessing the role of race in world politics, the more staggering does it become. Where does one begin? What is the problem? Is the problem an empirical one of measuring the extent to which race operates as an independent variable, or is it a theoretical problem of determining the circumstances under which race may operate as a relevant variable in world politics?

The Author's Moral Conscience: Others have not been staggered by the vastness of the problem.[1] Why should you? The problem is simple: the world is troubled by racial tensions and one thus begins by demonstrating their pervasiveness, showing how the relations between nations are shaped by the existence of racial conflicts within them.

The Author's Analytic Conscience: I wonder. Just because an issue arises within societies does not mean that it necessarily agitates relations between them. Race is intimate and proximate. It is pervaded, the psychologists say, with sexual connotations and other deeply felt personal needs.

* An earlier version of this chapter was presented at the Symposium on Conceptual Approaches to International Racial Factors, sponsored by the Graduate School of International Studies, University of Denver, February 1969. The chapter also appeared in the Graduate School's Monograph Series (Vol. 7, No. 2, 1969–70). Reprinted with permission.

[1] For example, see Robert S. Browne, *Race Relations in International Affairs* (Washington, D.C.: Public Affairs Press, 1961); Robert K. A. Gardiner, "Race and Color in International Relations," *Daedalus*, 96 (Spring 1967), pp. 296–311; Harold R. Isaacs, "Color in World Affairs," *Foreign Affairs*, 47 (January 1969), pp. 235–250; and Ronald Segal, *The Race War* (New York: Viking, 1967).

How, then, can it possibly operate as a variable that shapes the relations of such large aggregates as nation-states? Conceivably a host of other considerations enter in as the issue escalates from the level of interpersonal relations to the local community, and then to the national community and beyond. Indeed, it could be argued that by the time racial tension reaches the level of international conflict it has been transformed into a contest for economic and political advantage.

Author: In other words, the task is a theoretical one of developing a set of mutually consistent hypotheses that allow for clarification of the various roles that race may play in international politics.

Author's Moral Conscience: Why do you always shy away from confronting a problem directly? There is nothing theoretical about the problem of race. Racial conflict is a daily problem everywhere—a real problem for which solutions are needed today, not later after you have over-intellectualized the obvious.

Author: But there are some impressive data that raise serious doubts about the potency of race as a source of human conflicts. One analyst, for example, found that, if a person has information about others' beliefs, he is more likely to respond to them in terms of these beliefs rather than in terms of their skin color.[2] If this is so at the level of interpersonal relations, it becomes difficult to imagine how physical characteristics could be dominant at the level of international relations.

Author's Moral Conscience: How incredible can you be! Recently a chief of state broke down in tears while delivering a public speech at a United Nations conference on the treatment of blacks in Rhodesia.[3] Now surely that is concrete evidence that race operates as a variable in behavior at the international level!

Author: One example does not prove anything. Certainly it does not justify the assumption that race *is* an important variable. Such an assumption may salve one's moral conscience, but it does not make for systematic inquiry. Race is so loaded with value connotations that the analyst has an obligation not to rush headlong into the subject. Someone has to be dispassionate, to pause and develop a theoretical perspective, if the affronts to human dignity that mark life today are ever to be eliminated.

Author's Moral Conscience: You are inclined to be dispassionate because your skin is white. If it were black, you wouldn't be arguing

---

[2] Milton Rokeach, *Beliefs, Attitudes and Values: A Theory of Organization and Change* (San Francisco: Jossey-Bass, 1968), Chap. 3.

[3] President Kenneth D. Kaunda of Zambia "was unable to continue his speech for almost a minute after he spoke of the 'duplicity and contradiction in the policy of those who profess to be the foremost advocates of freedom, liberty and rule of law.'" *The New York Times,* September 17, 1968, p. 8.

for theoretical perspective. Could it be that your championship of a social scientific approach to the problem is a form of racism?

Author's Analytic Conscience: I don't see how that follows.

Author's Moral Conscience: By arguing for scientific detachment you in effect defend the postponement of an effort to solve the urgent problems that can reduce chiefs of state to tears. Such an approach even leads you to raise the possibility that the problems are not racial in character! Have you considered the possibility that your approach serves unrecognized racial prejudices while it preserves your self-image as an open-minded liberal?

Author's Analytic Conscience: Yes, I have, and I must reject that possibility, at least for the present. It seems to me that the requirements of scientific analysis are such that no assumption is beyond reconsideration. Social science is color free. One either accepts its procedures or one does not; and while one's acceptance or rejection may be partly a consequence of one's status in life, prejudice is by no means the most likely basis for a commitment to social science. Quite the opposite is the case, I believe, insofar as my own commitment is concerned. I believe that human problems can best be solved through the application of human intelligence, which means that a problem must be understood before successful attempts can be made to solve it. If we are to make progress in ameliorating racial conflicts, we need to comprehend their dynamics, and for that we need a theoretical perspective. If racial tensions in the local community are transformed into contests for political and economic advantage when they reach the international arena, then clearly it makes little sense to approach these contests as if race were still the dominant variable.

Author's Moral Conscience: But why seek abstract theory for phenomena that are self-evident! It hardly takes any knowledge of public affairs to recognize that race is a central factor on the world scene. Look at the Congo, or Biafra, or the U.N.'s condemnations of apartheid in South Africa. Or consider the British efforts to obtain new policies towards blacks in Rhodesia. Skin color is even an issue in the Communist world, with the Chinese citing it as the basis for excluding the Russians from conferences in which the plight of non-Western peoples is to be considered. And these are but a few of the most obvious issues of world politics that presently turn on questions of race. Many others could be cited—including the international consequences of race relations in the United States—and thus it seems absurd to pose the problem in abstract terms. What is needed is comprehension of how racial factors affect world politics. The fact that these factors are significant can be taken for granted.

Author's Analytic Conscience: Nevertheless, such an assumption makes me uneasy. If one looks at virtually any textbook published in the field of international relations in recent years, one will find virtually no discussion of racial factors. Indeed, of eleven texts published since 1960, the entry "race"—or some equivalent—could be found in only five of their indexes and in three of these five the index referred the reader to less than three paragraphs of actual text.[4] Surely this suggests that it is presumptuous to treat the importance of racial factors as given!

Author's Moral Conscience: You're straining. You know as well as I that most texts posit a "billiard ball model" of world politics in which international actors are not differentiated in terms of their domestic political structures (much less their ethnic and racial composition). Even less do the text-writers cast international relations in terms of the operation of independent and dependent variables, so that it is hardly surprising that race does not emerge as a focus of extended attention on their part. Moreover, if you want to pose the issue in terms of its recognition by experts, it should also be noted that no less an authority than Arnold Toynbee has stressed that the future of world politics may be organized along racial lines.[5]

Author's Analytic Conscience: You are right. It would not be hard to find experts on both sides of the question. But that is all the more reason to start from scratch and to delineate clearly the problem we are trying to solve. If equally competent observers differ on the importance of racial factors, dare we take their significance for granted? To do so is to prejudge our conclusions as to whether and how race affects world politics. One's moral conscience may say that it has a crucial effect, but careful inquiry may fail to yield proof for such an assertion. Compelling moral issues often prove to be a composite of lesser processes and values when they are subjected to close theoretical and empirical scrutiny. Just because international actors cite race as a basis for their behavior is no reason to assume that their behavior does in fact spring from racial sources. Why

[4] The only two texts to list a substantial number of entries under race in the index were W. W. Kulski, *International Politics in a Revolutionary Age* (Philadelphia: Lippincott, 2nd. ed., 1968), and Norman J. Padelford and George A. Lincoln, *The Dynamics of International Politics* (New York: Macmillan, 2nd ed., 1962). A few paragraphs on the subject were found in Hans J. Morgenthau, *Politics Among Nations* (New York: Knopf, 4th ed., 1967), Harold and Margaret Sprout, *Foundations of International Politics* (Princeton: Van Nostrand, 1962), and John G. Stoessinger, *The Might of Nations* (New York, Random House, Rev. ed., 1965). The indexes of the following five texts listed no entry whatsoever equivalent to race: Ivo D. Duchacek, *Conflict and Cooperation Among Nations* (New York: Holt, 1960). K. J. Holsti, *International Politics: A Framework for Analysis* (Englewood Cliffs, N.J.: Prentice-Hall, 1967), A. F. K. Organski, *World Politics* (New York, Knopf, 2nd ed., 1968), Charles P. Schleicher, *International Relations* (Englewood Cliffs, N.J.: Prentice-Hall, 1962), and Vernon Van Dyke, *International Politics* (New York: Appleton-Century-Crofts, 2nd ed., 1966).

should the Chinese Communists be taken at face value in this regard when everything else they do is picked apart for underlying motives? Why should the current impulse of American Negroes to search their African past for identity necessarily be a key link in the causal chain whereby U.S. foreign policy toward events in Africa is formed? Not all domestic conflicts have international repercussions. Why should it be presumed that racial conflict is of the kind that always spreads beyond national boundaries? Indeed, exactly what do we mean by racial conflict? Is it not possible that experts differ on the importance of racial factors either because they fail to define what they mean by race or because they use different definitions?

Author's Moral Conscience: There you go again, avoiding the problem by casting it in a methodological context. One can always sidestep the need to reach substantive conclusions by dwelling on definitional nuances and noting that different observers use different definitions. To insist on drawing exact boundaries is to paralyze inquiry. There is no lack of definitions of race and racial conflict. On the contrary, it is an overworked subject with an abundant literature filled with precise and neatly italicized definitions.[6] So let us not get bogged down in a sterile discussion of whether a particular attribute or event is or is not essentially racial in character. We know what we mean by race—it pertains to inherited physical characteristics. So why can't we bypass questions of definitional nuance by agreeing on this formulation? Can't we simply agree that to the extent that inherited physical characteristics create issues among individuals and groups, then to that extent there is racial conflict?

Author: It would make things much easier. No definition is completely satisfactory anyway, so perhaps a broad definition such as that is best suited to a wide-ranging assessment of the role of race in world politics.

Author's Analytic Conscience: I'll accept that. But a definition is not a theoretical perspective, and our agreement on this broad definition of race does not relieve us of the responsibility for specifying the main dimensions of our problem. Neither empirical observations nor moral solutions can be obtained outside of a theoretical context. The observer can never grasp reality in its entirety, but must select some of its aspects as important and dismiss others as trivial and, in order to do so, he must have some idea of how its component parts interact with each other. His hypotheses about how these components interact are his theory, whereas

[6] A useful point of departure with respect to this literature is the new *International Encyclopedia of the Social Sciences* (New York: Macmillan and the Free Press, 1968). In particular see the bibliographies in Vol. 13, pp. 267–268, 276–277, and 282.

it is not the purpose of a definition to account for the interactional dynamics of the defined object. For this a theoretical perspective is needed from which hypotheses can be derived that specify how, why, and under what circumstances physical appearance and its inheritance can enter into the external behavior of nations and thus serve as the basis of international conflict. Unfortunately such a perspective is not to be found in the literature on international politics and we must start from scratch.

At the risk of further offending an impatient morality, therefore, we must insist that the task is theoretical. We need to develop some tentative hypotheses about the ways in which race can enter foreign policy and international politics before we can reach meaningful conclusions about the role it actually plays. Data gathered in the absence of hypotheses can provide conclusions about particular historical situations, but only through the derivation and testing of explicit and interrelated propositions can enduring knowledge about the potency of race variables be developed. As indicated elsewhere, the alternative to theory-building is an endless series of case analyses that are neither cumulative nor comparable,[7] and there is no dearth of these analyses insofar as the role of race in international conflicts is concerned. Hundreds upon hundreds could be listed.[8] But they are not cumulative. Those that focus on South Africa offer little guidance for the analysis of the Congo, and those that explore the Congo are of little help in comprehending the situation in Nigeria, much less situations in the future that have yet to emerge. The need to develop testable hypotheses would seem to be inescapable!

Author's Moral Conscience: Your capacity for avoiding the real problems is apparently unlimited. How can you say that the available literature lacks perspectives appropriate to the analysis of race? The field of international politics has a surfeit of models and approaches that can be as easily applied to racial conflict as to any other kind that mars the relations of nations. You yourself have outlined a scheme in which the "racial environment" is one of six international environments to which the institutions and functioning of nation-states may be linked.[9] And you have also suggested that political behavior can be differentiated in terms of four basic issue-areas and that racial conflicts fall naturally into the status area.[10] Why, then, develop still another formulation? Why not apply an existing framework? If your own conceptual schemes are still too crude, then one of the more developed approaches can be used. The

[7] See Chapter 4.

[8] In *Foreign Affairs* alone, for example, the reader will find in virtually every issue a couple of articles that probe specific situations in which racial factors are considered to be important.

[9] See Chapter 15.

[10] See Chapter 6.

trouble with you general-theory types is that your first impulse is always to move up rather than down the ladder of abstraction. Mankind is suffering too much to allow for abstract theorizing on the part of social scientists, especially since there is no shortage of frameworks that can be adapted to the analysis of racial factors in international politics.

Author's Analytic Conscience: Name one—leaving aside my own, which are still so crude that they cannot be regarded as theoretical. At present the linkage and issue-area frameworks are a collection of analytic categories and not a set of testable hypotheses. It is not even clear that they can be rendered theoretical through further refinement. And the same can be said about the other frameworks. Name one that is either theoretical or readily adaptable to the derivation of relevant hypotheses.

Author's Moral Conscience: I can name many. North's "mediated S-R" model,[11] Kaplan's systemic formulation,[12] Snyder's decision-making approach,[13] Deutsch's linkage group scheme[14]—these are but a few of the available models that lend themselves to the analysis of racial conflict at the international level. In the case of North's model, one need merely treat a racial conflict as an environmental stimulus (S) that is perceived by officials (r) in such a way as first to trigger the expression of their attitudes towards race (s) and then to lead them to engage in behavior directed at the conflict (R). Similarly, each of Kaplan's several "states" of the international system specifies the circumstances under which nations engage in such basic kinds of action as mobilizing for war, forming alliances, and going to war. Hence, all the analyst needs to do is to ascertain which state of the international system prevails at the time a racial conflict breaks out and then trace the systemic consequences that it predicts. In like manner racial phenomena are readily incorporated into Snyder's decision-making approach. Indeed, the approach allows for their occurrence within a society or external to it. In either case the analyst can probe how awareness of the phenomena is fed into and then processed by the society's decision-making organization, culminating in action abroad designed to cope with the foreign policy implications of the phenomena.

---

[11] For a succinct summary of this model, see Robert C. North, "Research Pluralism and the International Elephant," *International Studies Quarterly*, Vol. 11 (December 1967), pp. 394–416.

[12] Morton A. Kaplan, *System and Process in International Politics* (New York: Wiley, 1957).

[13] Richard C. Snyder, H. W. Bruck, Burton Sapin, *Foreign Policy Decision Making: An Approach to the Study of International Politics* (New York: Free Press, 1962), pp. 14–185.

[14] Karl W. Deutsch, "External Influences on the Internal Behavior of States," in R. Barry Farrell (ed.), *Approaches to Comparative and International Politics* (Evanston, Ill.: Northwestern University Press, 1966), pp. 5–26.

As for Deutsch's linkage group scheme, it seems especially suited to the analysis of racial conflicts that transgress national boundaries. Racial groups are prototypical of Deutsch's conception of a linkage group and the international repercussions of racial conflict can thus be clearly traced through his scheme.

I'm not saying that all the available models are equally applicable to the analysis of racial conflict. Some may well be more appropriate than others and I'll bow to your judgment in this respect. But I do insist that it is irresponsible to start from scratch in the search for theoretical perspective. The necessary conceptual equipment is abundantly available and all you have to do is select those concepts and models that seem most suitable.

Author's Analytic Conscience: If only the tasks of analysis were that simple. It is true that racial conflicts are not precluded by any of the existing frameworks, but neither are they explicitly conceptualized as part of the frameworks. With one possible exception,[15] none of the analysts even hint at, much less hypothesize about, the potency of race as an independent variable. North's model, for example, certainly does allow the analyst to treat racial factors as stimuli that are mediated by perceptions before resulting in behavioral responses; but it in no way indicates the kinds of perceptions and responses to which such stimuli might give rise. As far as the model is concerned, a racial conflict is no different from a nuclear explosion, a peace overture, a quadrennial olympics, or a tariff conference as an independent variable. Each is a stimulus and each fosters perceptions that mediate the resulting responses, but the model does not differentiate among types of stimuli. And much the same can be said about the Kaplan and Snyder approaches. Neither identifies race as an independent variable. Indeed, neither even specifies a general type of independent variable of which race can be presumed to be one case. To derive from Kaplan how a balance of power system processes a conflict in one of its member societies differently from a loose bipolar system is not to facilitate very useful conclusions as to the differential impact of, say, racial and economic conflicts on each type of system. Similarly, Snyder's framework does not differentiate how various types of situations affect the processes of foreign policy decision-making, so that a racial conflict is the analytic equivalent of a patriotic motive, a diplomatic offer, or a bureaucratic ploy. As for Deutsch's scheme, it is true that racial minorities can readily be treated as linkage groups, but so

---

[15] Louis Hartz, *The Founding of New Societies* (New York: Harcourt, 1964). But this exception is cast so fully in historical terms that its application beyond the phenomena investigated is extremely limited.

can a number of other minorities and Deutsch does not delineate how racial ones might function differently from other types.

So it is not evasive to conclude that a model appropriate to the analysis of race is not available. The existing frameworks offer a number of concepts that can usefully be employed once it is determined how inherited physical appearance operates as a variable. If it is found to be similar to other sources of behavior, then the existing frameworks can be adapted. If, on the other hand, race is found to have unique characteristics as an independent variable, then the adaptation of the existing models is likely to be difficult and an attempt to generate a new set of integrated hypotheses may prove to be the wisest course.

Author: I am lost again. You speak of determining the operation of a variable and of generating hypotheses in the same breath. The former is an empirical task and the latter is a theoretical task. Which comes first? What can we accomplish in this chapter? Should we take an inventory of empirical findings relevant to the potency of the race variable? Or should we try to conceptualize the points at which the variable can operate in international political processes, whatever its potency? Or should we go beyond either of these to the development of a set of integrated hypotheses that specify the variations in international political processes that are caused by the variable potency of racial factors? You have said so many things fending off my moral conscience that I need clarification. I am still not clear on the nature of the problem to be confronted in this chapter.

Author's Analytic Conscience: The problem is threefold. It is empirical. It is conceptual, And it is also theoretical. The three tasks are interdependent and thus we need to undertake all of them. This is not the occasion to compile an exhaustive inventory of the relevant findings, but plainly we cannot proceed without making at least a preliminary assessment of the potency of inherited physical appearance as a source of individual and group behavior. Likewise, while we do not have time to engage in an elaborate conceptualization, we can hardly proceed to derive hypotheses unless we have at least a broad notion of the main gates through which race can enter the international arena. And, as has already been stressed, we cannot avoid the task of theorizing. This third step must be taken even though time and space permits the derivation of only a crude set of hypotheses which may eventually be proven false. Unless we can derive some hypotheses, further research is not likely to be generated by our empirical survey and our conceptualization. Bad theory is better than no theory, since, as long as they are reasonable and internally consistent, hypotheses at least stimulate subsequent investigation.

In short, let us start with a discussion of the potency of race as an independent variable, proceeding thereafter to a conceptual outline of the ways in which racial factors can be brought into the international arena and, lastly, to the derivation of some hypotheses that link the racial factors to various degrees or forms of international behavior. You are the author, so go ahead. I'll keep your moral conscience at bay until you have completed all three tasks.

II. EMPIRICAL CONSIDERATIONS

Author: At least three main conclusions are likely to emerge from any inventory of the welter of available empirical materials that bear on the relevance of race to international politics. One is that a person's physical attributes have personal and social significance, and since major dimensions of a person's physical appearance are linked to race, racial identity acquires emotional and social importance. Hence, despite persuasive scientific evidence that intelligence, skills, and orientations are not race-linked, people continue to be sensitive to what their lineage signifies for their capacities and impulses. As such, race can come to mean all kinds of things for an individual, becoming part of his fondest hopes and his deepest fears. In like manner, racial groups can come to have their own histories and identities that, being rooted in the intimacy of personal experience, can generate and sustain conflict within and among groups. Insofar as public affairs are concerned, therefore, race consists as much, if not more, of subjective as of objective fact. Its role is best understood not in terms of scientific definitions and findings, but in terms of perceptual definitions that are held by different people at different times.

Secondly, it is clear that consciousness of racial identity is a pervasive and worldwide phenomenon. Blacks and whites are not alone in their sensitivity to the psychological dynamics of racial identity. Perhaps their colonial heritages render them especially vulnerable in this regard, but it does not require a long history to heighten racial feelings. The evidence is overwhelming that awareness of inherited physical characteristics can acquire a symbolic meaning and serve as a source of conflict elsewhere than in those areas of the world where black and white are proximate to each other. Black and yellow are also conscious of the differences in their appearance,[16] as are those with various shades of black, or with various shades of yellow, or, indeed, as are virtually every cluster of people whose visible characteristics vary. More specifically, sensitivity

[16] For a poignant set of data in this regard, see E. John Hevi, *An African Student in China* (London: Pall Mall Press, 1965).

to physical differences can be found to mark the relations between tribes in Africa, between Africans north and south of the Sahara, between Chinese and Malays—to mention but some of the more salient instances of racial tension that are not of a black-white hue. Among Filipinos, to illustrate even more specifically, "there is an almost obsessive preoccupation with color and physical characteristics. It appears in almost every aspect of everyday family life, in dating and mating, in the raising of children, and at every point of contact between people of varying groups and kinds in the population." [17] In short, the decline of white colonialism in most of Africa and Asia has not been accompanied by a corresponding diminution of race as a source of conflict. Africans and Asians have won their political freedom, but insofar as race relations are concerned the newly-won independence "has often meant . . . displacement of European white racism by a non-European non-white racism." [18]

Despite its intensity and pervasiveness, however, the potency of race as a variable can be exaggerated. This is the third conclusion to emerge from an inventory of the materials on the relevance of race to public and international affairs. The color of a man's skin and his other physical characteristics may be a visible badge that has deep psychological meaning for him, but his clothes, speech, and style of life are also readily apparent and, equally important, these evidences of class and ethnicity reflect his economic circumstances and social standing, not to mention his education, religion, and politics. Race is just one of the many variables that can underlie individual and group behavior. Although analysts vary on the relative potency they attach to racial variables, there is wide agreement that these variables do not operate alone and that other variables may be just as important, if not more so, as sources of behavior in particular situations. As already noted, for example, racial identity has been found to be less important under certain circumstances than beliefs.[19] Data comparing the strength of race and class identifications suggest similar patterns, as is illustrated by the attitudes and behavior of middle-class American Negroes.[20]

Teasing out the effects of race as an independent variable thus presents a formidable empirical problem. Normally the several identities to which a person is responsive are not contradictory but mutually reinforcing. Ethnic groups are usually predominantly of the same race. Ordinarily racial minorities are poor and located predominantly in the lower class. And, in turn, class differences reinforce and are reinforced by religious

[17] Harold R. Isaacs, "Group Identity and Political Change: The Role of Color and Physical Characteristics," *Daedalus,* Spring, 1967, p. 363.

[18] *Ibid.,* p. 364.

[19] See footnote 2.

[20] See E. Franklin Frazier, *Black Bourgeoisie* (Glencoe, Ill.: Free Press, 1957).

practices, educational attainments, occupational skills, and a host of other factors, each of which contributes to the behavior the analyst is seeking to explain. Only rarely do two or more of the variables come into conflict in such a way as to make their relative potency self-evident. Some American Negroes do get professional training and move into the middle class. Some Negroes adhere to the Jewish religion. Some holders of a Ph.D. earn little money and are classified as lower-class. Such exceptions, however, are few in number and, indeed, often require the analyst to resort to experimental techniques of inquiry in order to contrast the potency of various factors.[21]

Nor is the problem any less complex at the international level. Nonwhite nations also tend to be poor nations. The former tend to be located south, the latter north, of the equator, and this geographic and climatic distinction is accompanied by differences in resources, technology, and social organization. How, then, can the potency of racial factors be assessed? How much of the conflict between, say, African and North Atlantic nations is attributable to race variables and how much of it to other sources? The answer is not self-evident but, given the temper of the times, it is easy to exaggerate the potency of racial factors. The immediate visibility of physical characteristics, and the ideological meaning that has come to be attached to them in recent years, makes it all too tempting to ignore the complexity of international behavior and to assume that, in the words of one analyst, "The gap is primarily a gap between races."[22] Race may be the primary variable in certain situations, but the sources of international behavior are so complex that it seems preferable to proceed on the basis of a different assumption, namely, that race is among the more important variables. Situations vary and so does the potency of the variables that sustain them. Hence, rather than attach primacy to race or presume that its potency is equal to or greater than that of such factors as technology and resources, it would seem both sufficient and advisable to start with the presumption that skin color and other physical characteristics are not irrelevant to international situations and that they may be the key factors in many situations.

Author's Analytic Conscience: Excuse the intrusion, but haven't you, perhaps inadvertently, just engaged in exaggeration? You caution against overstatement, but then conclude that racial factors are neither irrelevant nor even secondary. You have offered no evidence for this conclusion. Is it not conceivable, as I suggested at the outset, that they are irrelevant?

Author: Admittedly the foregoing offers a summary rather than

[21] This is how Rokeach uncovered the findings cited in footnote 2.
[22] Peter F. Drucker, "A Warning to the Rich, White World," *Harper's,* December 1968, p. 67.

a documentation of the empirical evidence, but the main point that emerges is that the operation of race is not constant. To conclude that the evidence is sufficient to start with the assumption that physical characteristics are not irrelevant is hardly to assume that they are relevant. We assume only that race varies in its potency, which means that primacy may be a proper description of its influence under certain circumstances and irrelevance an appropriate characterization in other circumstances. Although many of the empirical investigations on the subject are confined to noncomparable case analyses, it is clear that the role played by racial factors is not the same in every situation. In some, such as the United Nations' involvement in Rhodesian and South African affairs, its role is paramount. In others, such as the United States' involvement in the Nigeria-Biafra conflict, its role is not paramount, but neither is it negligible. In still other situations, such as the United States' policies in Vietnam, its role seems virtually irrelevant in comparison to the strategic and political variables that are operative.

Stated in more general terms, human behavior seldom springs from a single source and the social scientist is fortunate indeed when the variance in the situations of interest to him can be accounted for by one or two variables. Usually a number of variables contribute to the total variance and the task of analysis becomes that of determining which variables account for, say, ten or more percent of the total variance. Most analysts are content if they can perform this task and are willing to accept the presence of unspecified variables that account for the variance that remains after those that account for more than ten percent have been identified and contrasted. Following this line of reasoning, exaggeration of the potency of racial factors can be avoided by posing the conceptual problem to be faced here as that of identifying the processes through which race can operate as an independent variable in such a way as to account for at least an arbitrary ten percent of the variance among international situations. Once these processes have been identified we can turn to the theoretical problem of hypothesizing about the conditions under which the potency of the race variable is likely to increase or decrease.

III. CONCEPTUAL CONSIDERATIONS

Any conceptual framework that can be used to theorize about the role of racial factors in international politics must identify the units of action, the independent variables that underlie their actions, and the dependent variables that represent their actions. That is, the framework must clearly specify three main elements: (1) the persons or groups whose behavior brings consciousness of physical characteristics into the international arena; (2) those sources of their behavior that can infuse it with racial consciousness; and (3) the types of behavior in which they can engage that reflect racial factors. Having enumerated these components, the analyst can move on to the construction of hypotheses that link changes in the sources of behavior to its nature and extent.

In order to develop such a framework, the analyst must limit the scope of his interests. The number and variety of persons and groups who can engage in the relevant behavior are so great, and the sources of their behavior and the forms it can take are so multitudinous, that he cannot possibly undertake to account for all the international processes and repercussions to which race may be related. Perforce he must narrow his attention to those actors and types of behavior that seem most central to his concerns. Since our aspiration here is to develop hypotheses that permit inquiry into the impact of racial factors upon international politics, we shall organize the framework in terms of the external conflict behavior engaged in by those who act on behalf of national societies. This is not to deny that the external cooperative behavior of foreign policy officials can be pervaded with racial consciousness.[23] Nor is it to ignore the capacity of private persons and groups to engage in external conflict behavior that derives from a preoccupation with physical characteristics. However, international politics is sustained essentially through the interaction of national governments and its contents are shaped mainly by situations in which the goals and actions of governments conflict. Hence, foreign policy officials are the actors around whom the ensuing framework is organized, its dependent variables are conceived in terms of the conflict behavior in which they can engage, and its independent variables are conceptualized in terms of five kinds of sources from which racial considerations can arise as a basis for conflict behavior. Lest this be regarded as too narrow a framework, let it be added that the activities of private citizens and groups constitute a key variable in one of the five clusters of independent variables (see the discussion of societal variables below).

Author's Analytic Conscience: This is too important a point to postpone until the discussion of societal variables. Is it not unrealistic to construct a framework in which minority groups and mass publics are not treated as actors? The attitudes of publics in Africa and Asia toward race relations in the United States are an important dimension of current international affairs. And certainly there is considerable international relevance in the demand of the Black Panthers for a U.N.-sponsored plebiscite that would pave the way for a separate state in the Ameri-

---

[23] A good example in this regard is provided by the recent U.S. efforts to get food and medical supplies into wartorn Biafra.

can South. Yet phenomena such as these would not be subsumed by the foregoing framework.

Author: Yes, they would be, as independent variables that contribute to the behavior of foreign policy officials. The presumption is that if the attitudes of foreign publics toward U.S. race relations are in fact important, then they will operate as societal variables underlying the behavior of foreign officials and as systemic variables shaping the behavior of U.S. officials. Likewise, if in fact the demands of the Black Panthers are as relevant as they appear, then they are bound to constitute conditions to which officials are responsive and, accordingly, to which the analyst is sensitive. Our framework is designed to render the subject manageable, to provide a perspective from which any relevant phenomena can be analyzed. The fact that the behavior of government officials serves to organize our perspective does not mean that nongovernmental actors and processes are excluded from it.

Author's Analytic Conscience: One other question before you go on: by organizing the framework in terms of a foreign policy rather than an international politics focus, have you not precluded the direct analysis of racial conflicts in the international system? Since the external actions of national societies are your prime concern, your model cannot possibly also trace and explain the outcome of their actions. To account for outcomes one must focus on what happens when two or more actors react to each other, that is, the interactions of national societies rather than the actions of their foreign policy officials must organize the analysis.[24] Moreover, the interactions that sustain world politics have a dynamic of their own that cannot be explained through only the behavior of the actors that constitute the interaction. Racial conflicts, for example, can spiral and be self-sustaining because the parties to them have mutually reinforcing hostile perceptions of each other, and any attempt to explain such conflicts that does not allow for a direct focus upon the spiraling process would appear to be insufficient. It is as if one sought to explain the Detroit riots by examining the behavior of Negroes independently of the behavior of the police. Plainly the behavior of all the actors in a situation, be they individuals or nations, must be seen in juxtaposition to each other if the dynamics of their conflict are to be revealed. So it would seem that the basic premises of your model are faulty.

Author: The point is well taken, but I question its relevance at this stage. A focus on interaction phenomena makes eminent sense when the system under consideration is system rather than subsystem dominant —that is, when no actor in the system is capable of altering the struc-

---

[24] Cf. J. David Singer, "The Level-of-Analysis Problem in International Relations," *World Politics,* XIV (October 1961), pp. 77–92.

ture of the system through his own actions.[25] Under these circumstances the analyst need not dwell at length on the behavior of the actors that constitute the system. He knows none of them individually can alter its structure. Thus he need only know the shared attitudes guiding their participation in the system and can concentrate on the spiraling and other interaction processes to which these shared attitudes give rise. Rioting Detroit is a case in point. It approaches a system-dominant situation in the sense that no individual black or white person can alter its tension-ridden structure. Hence the analyst can proceed quickly to an interaction focus. He knows what the main actors bring to the interaction—a shared distrust of white society and, particularly, its policemen on the part of most Detroit Negroes and a contrary set of attitudes on the part of most Detroit whites—and consequently he can investigate outcomes (i.e., riots) per se.

International systems, on the other hand, are not system dominant. They are dominated by their national subsystems, any one of which is capable of altering their structures, if only by virtue of its sovereign capacity to alter its manner of relating to the system. Hence, while international systems do have their own dynamics, including those that make conflicts spiral, a great deal more needs to be known about the behavior of their national subsystems before these dynamics can be meaningfully analyzed independently of the actors who sustain them. The comparative study of foreign policy is only in its infancy,[26] so that students of international systems have been compelled to construct models that are so abstract as to be almost inapplicable to concrete issue-areas such as those that encompass racial phenomena. Stated differently, national societies are far more varied in their composition and orientations than are the components of system-dominant systems, with the result that the student of international politics cannot proceed on the basis of an assumption that certain common dimensions underlie the behavior of most of the actors that concern him. The tendency to form alliances when threatened or to fight when attacked may constitute a shared predisposition that allows for the construction of convincing abstract models,[27] but it is hardly the basis for insight into the ways in which racial considerations enter into and sustain international conflicts.

Furthermore, since the actors who sustain international conflicts are significantly more complex than the individuals or groups who contribute to conflicts in local communities, the number of interacting variables at

[25] The useful distinction between system- and subsystem-dominant systems is developed at greater length in Kaplan, *op. cit.*, pp. 16–17.

[26] See Chapter 5.

[27] For an example of a convincing model at this level of abstraction, see Kaplan, *op. cit.*, Chap. 2.

the international level is proportionately greater and, accordingly, the potency of racial factors is presumably more intricately woven into the fabric of conflict than is the case in less comprehensive systems. Teasing out the role of race in Detroit's riots would thus appear to be considerably easier than delineating its operation in international situations. Until more is known about how racial considerations are introduced into the processes of world politics, it seems imprudent to organize our hypotheses around the functioning of international systems. Only a foreign policy focus seems capable of identifying the processes through which racial variables enter international politics. If the price of such a focus is an inability to account for outcomes, then it seems a small one to pay in exchange for greater knowledge of the conditions that make race one of the values over which conflicts in international systems may be waged. Besides, as will be seen, key aspects of international systems are not excluded from the ensuing model. They constitute one of the five main clusters of independent variables and we have no intention of minimizing their importance as stimuli to external behavior on the part of national societies.

Author's Analytic Conscience: But if the 130-plus national societies of the international system are varied in their composition and orientations, how can you expect to develop useful theory? Does not a foreign policy focus lead the analyst toward an endless series of case studies and away from hypotheses that can be used and tested for theory-building purposes?

Author: Let me get on with the analysis. You may be holding my moral conscience at bay, but you keep asking questions that prevent me from outlining the model. The questions may be important, but they have been dealt with elsewhere[28] and by asking them again here you only confirm the charge that theorizing is used to avoid confrontation of the substantive issues. Obviously the 130-plus societies of the world are varied in their composition and orientations, and the danger exists that one will employ a model that leads only to case histories of these differences. But we have no intention of facilitating additions to the existing welter of case studies. The ensuing hypotheses are cast at a middle level of abstraction, one that allows both for the discernment of similarities among national actors and for the identification of those points where the differences among them are crucial. The actors do differ in their structure and behavior, but in one form or another the same variables are operative in all cases and it is comparisons among these variables that our hypotheses seek to make possible. From such comparisons the variations among the 130-plus phenotypical actors can be reduced to a few meaningful genotypical actors. If, for example, the racial composition of a society is

[28] See Chapter 4.

treated as a dichotomous independent variable, such that one can compare the external behavior of racially homogeneous and racially heterogeneous actors, then presumably useful hypotheses that are neither too abstract nor too bound to time and place can be developed.

Author's Analytic Conscience: But given the variability among societies, their distribution across a racial composition scale would be so scattered that dichotomization of the variable would constitute gross distortion of its effects on foreign policy.

The Author: That is a minor question that can be readily resolved when the time comes to process empirical data in terms of the hypotheses. Let's get on with the task of identifying the variables out of which the hypotheses have been fashioned. Let us start with the dependent variables through which race may operate in the international arena and then turn to the independent variables from which its operation may derive.

Since national societies can engage in innumerable forms of foreign conflict behavior, it is neither possible nor necessary to elaborate an exhaustive list of dependent variables. Rather it is sufficient for our purposes to specify six major types of foreign conflict behaviors that constitute a continuum ranging from a minimum to a maximum degree of violence and that can be treated either as separate variables or as a single variable in the ensuing analysis. For the most part we have not been able to derive hypotheses that predict specific forms of conflict behavior and have had to settle for predicting whether the conflict behavior, whatever its form, will be more or less extensive or more or less violent. Listed in order of increasing violence, the six forms of conflict behavior are as follows: verbally supporting or denouncing one side in disputes between two other societies or between two factions within another society (as distinguished from not taking sides and adopting a neutral or accommodating stance); recalling or expelling diplomatic personnel; imposing negative sanctions that restrict or prevent the exchange of goods, people, or ideas; severing diplomatic relations; issuing military threats; and undertaking military actions.[29]

Author's Analytic Conscience: Something seems to be missing here. What is the relevance of race to these various forms of conflict behavior? Societies engage in these forms of behavior for all kinds of reasons besides those derived from considerations of race. How do you plan to differentiate

---

[29] For listings of other forms of conflict behavior, see Rudolph J. Rummel, "The Relationship Between National Attributes and Foreign Conflict Behavior," in J. David Singer (ed.), *Quantitative International Politics: Insights and Evidence* (New York: Free Press, 1968), pp. 187–214, and Charles A. McClelland and Gary D. Hoggard, "Conflict Patterns in the Interactions Among Nations," in James N. Rosenau (ed.), *International Politics and Foreign Policy* (New York: Free Press, 1969, rev. ed.), pp. 711–724.

those conflict behaviors that are based on racial factors from those that are not?

Author: The presumption is that concern over inherited physical characteristics can lead to verbal denunciations, the recall of ambassadors, and every other form of conflict behavior. However, in deriving the hypotheses no attempt has been made to differentiate between race-pervaded and race-free conflict behaviors. It is highly probable that the conflict behavior the analyst observes in order to measure the operation of the dependent variables will have stemmed from a variety of sources. A decision to employ economic sanctions or sever diplomatic relations, for example, is rarely a response to a single stimulus. Racial sensitivities may underlie such a decision, but in all likelihood so will economic and political calculations as to the consequences and risks of such behavior. Yet this is not a serious problem. Our concern is with racial factors and the likelihood that other factors may also be operative is irrelevant as long as we can be confident that we have identified the presence of racial ones. Thus if data reveal a significant association between the racial factors that are treated as the independent variables in the hypotheses and the degrees or forms of conflict behavior that are treated as dependent variables, then it seems reasonable to assume that the operation of racial factors has been identified and measured.

It follows that in selecting the independent variables we must differentiate precisely between those that involve racial considerations and those that do not. If we do not clearly delineate the racial factors that can give rise to conflict behavior, then we can never be confident that the observed behavior reflects their presence. The selection of independent variables, however, is not a simple matter. There are so many ways in which race may contribute to foreign conflict behavior that we obviously face a sampling problem. Not only do we need to select independent variables that are likely to account for at least ten percent of the variance in the dependent variables, but we must also select a sample that is representative of the various types of sources from which a concern for race can arise.

In order to achieve representativeness we have fallen back on an earlier analytic scheme that posits five basic clusters of independent variables as sources of foreign policy.[30] In effect, the five clusters encompass variables from five basic types of systems in which the foreign policy official is located. Listed in order of increasing complexity, these systems are those unique to the individual official; the top policy-making system of which his official role is a part; the larger governmental system from which his position derives; the societal system whose policies he formulates and

[30] See Chapter 6.

conducts; and the international system in which his society is located. That is, it is presumed that the behavior of foreign policy officials is a response to the requirements and demands of five types of systems, each of which contains some variables that reinforce those of the other systems and some that oppose them. The interaction of the individual (I), role (R), governmental (G), societal (SO), and systemic (SY) variables—as we shall respectively label (and abbreviate) each cluster—determines the external behavior of officials at any moment in time, and thus a prime task of the comparative study of foreign policy is to uncover the key variables in each cluster and to delineate the ways in which they contribute to the behavior under investigation. In terms of the more specific assignment of analyzing the dynamics whereby physical characteristics and racial consciousness become a part of international politics, it follows that our task at this point is that of selecting variables in each cluster that can range from a high to a low degree of susceptibility to racial factors. Once these *race-susceptible* variables—as we shall call them—in each cluster have been identified, we can turn to an assessment of their potency by constructing hypotheses that link them to foreign conflict behavior. However, in order to put the operation of racial factors to a stiff test, the hypotheses must not only compare the behavioral consequences of high and low degrees of the race-susceptible variables. They must also contrast the behavioral consequences of the high extreme with powerful *nonracial* variables from each cluster, that is, variables whose variance is judged not to be reflective of racial factors at any point. For example, in addition to hypothesizing about the differences between societies that have a high and a low degree of racial tension, our analysis has also been structured to yield a hypothesis that contrasts the foreign conflict behavior of societies that are marked by a high degree of racial tension but that are differentiated in terms of being either developed or underdeveloped economically. In other words, the ensuing discussion singles out both race-susceptible and nonracial variables in each cluster for comparison in the next section. Furthermore, since the variables in each cluster are, given the complexity of the systems involved, too numerous even to be listed, we shall confine our discussion only to those that seem likely to account for significant degrees of variation in foreign policy behavior. Indeed, in order to avoid the development of an unmanageable framework, the hypotheses we derive from this analysis will be confined to only one or two race-susceptible and nonracial variables in each cluster.

Individual Variables—Since racial consciousness is profoundly intimate and personal, it is perhaps appropriate to begin the analysis with the cluster of individual variables. These refer to those aspects of an official that cannot be expected to characterize his predecessor or successor. They are unique to him, arising out of his experience in other nongovernmental systems (such as the family, the church, and the professional association) in which he currently occupies or previously occupied a role. No two persons have the same prior experiences or present affiliations, so that some of the talents, values, training, orientations, loyalties, and personality traits that a person brings to his official policy-making role are bound to be different from those of other occupants of his office. It should be noted, however, that not all of the personal characteristics of an official are necessarily unique to him. Some are so central to the policy-making role he occupies that his predecessors and successors can also be expected to have them. The skin color of foreign secretaries, for example, is not likely to vary from one occupant of the office to the next. Rather, it is likely to reflect the color of the dominant group in the society and thus must be viewed as a societal rather than an individual variable.

It is easy to exaggerate the potency of individual variables. There are so many variations in the attitudes, training, skills, and traits of officials that it is tempting to explain the differences in their behavior in terms of these individual characteristics. To a considerable degree, however, such individual characteristics operate within limits set by role, governmental, societal, and systemic variables. The private aspirations and political convictions of an official, for example, must be tempered by the dictates of his superiors, by the requirements of diplomatic protocol, by the constraints of interagency bargaining, by the demands of pressure groups, by the challenges of other nations—to mention but a few of the variables that limit the range within which officials can give expression to their unique characteristics. Indeed, the requirements derived from role, governmental, societal, and systemic variables have been found to be attitudinal as well as behavioral. Officials not only tend to act in patterned ways, but their responsibilities also conduce to common patterns of thought. Whatever their prior orientations, for instance, defense officials tend to favor increased military preparedness once they enter their offices, whereas those who assume positions in foreign offices become inclined to stress diplomatic rather than military flexibility.[31]

Notwithstanding the political constraints within which an official must operate, presumably his consciousness of race may be greater or lesser than that of his predecessors or successors. Not every African chief of state is led to tears in public by his acute torment over the plight of black people. Not every Governor of Georgia is as assertive of white superiority as Lester Maddox. Not every German leader is anti-

[31] For a more elaborate discussion of how individual tendencies are altered by the requirements of office, see Chapter 7.

Semitic. Different past experiences and personality needs create differences in the extent to which officials are sensitive to the fact and symbolism of skin color. To be sure, some part of an official's racial consciousness stems from the system in which his governmental position is located. Given the history of Africa and the struggles for national autonomy presently being waged there, all African chiefs of state are likely to regard physical characteristics as politically relevant phenomena, just as postwar racial tensions in the United States are likely to heighten racial consciousness on the part of American foreign policy officials. The degree of such consciousness, however, is likely to vary within these historical and societal constraints, and thus it would appear to be a race-susceptible individual variable of sufficient importance to justify inclusion in the ensuing analysis. So as to facilitate assessment of the potency of this *consciousness* variable, the degree to which officials had prior experience in foreign affairs—the *experience* variable—has been selected as the nonracial variable from the individual cluster. Presumably officials with extensive experience of this kind are more appreciative of the limits of foreign policy—and thus more inclined to avoid extreme policies—than are those with no previous experience in foreign affairs. Hence, by constructing hypotheses that predict different behavioral consequences depending on the degree of racial consciousness and the extent of prior foreign affairs experience of the relevant officials, an estimate of the way in which individual variables may bring race into the international arena can be developed.

An equally important means of estimating the potency of race-susceptible individual variables is through hypotheses that probe what is likely to happen to an official's degree of racial consciousness when it is subjected to the requirements of role, governmental, societal, and systemic variables. Do racially prejudiced representatives at the United Nations allow their private orientations to affect how they perceive—and what they report to their governments about—the deliberations of the world organization? Does a white person mostly free of racial sensitivities espouse and enforce anti-nonwhite immigration policies when he becomes foreign secretary of, say, Australia? Does a black person who was educated in London and who has not been dominated by hatred for whites vote to ignore the rule of law when he becomes foreign secretary of, say, Mali and the question of South African rights in international organizations becomes an issue? Questions such as these suggest how race-susceptible individual variables might interact with other types and they also suggest the complexity of the problems that we attempt to clarify below as a means of developing hypotheses that assess the relative potency of the independent variables.

Role Variables—As the foregoing implies, existing policy goals are among the prime variables in the cluster that stems from the requirements of top policy-making roles. Whatever the private attitudes and unique talents of officials, and whatever the systems in which they have had previous experience, the responsibility they acquire when they enter their offices includes commitments to the practices and orientations of their predecessors. The goals that comprise their policy-making roles may be changed if individual, governmental, societal, or systemic variables prove to be more powerful; but until such changes occur, the policy requirements of the roles impinge upon their occupants. More accurately, the requirements are operative to the extent that they neither change nor allow for individual discretion. Some policy goals are couched in such general terms that different role occupants can interpret them in different ways, depending on the strength of their individual convictions or the societal or systemic pressures upon them. For example, chiefs of state in the North Atlantic area are at present required to support efforts to maintain defensive arrangements that inhibit military attacks on Western Europe. Such an attitude and the behavior to which it leads are built into their roles and, barring a return to isolationism in the United States or a substantial moderation of the Cold War (i.e., barring a shift in basic societal or systemic variables), it is therefore reasonable to expect that all future top officials in the region will adhere to this role requirement. On the other hand, the requirement is not so stringent as to have prevented some of the individual (and societal?) variables from making France alter the nature of its commitment to NATO. De Gaulle did not abandon his European allies nor totally reject the necessity of achieving defense arrangements in Europe, but the interaction between his unique qualities and this role requirement resulted in changes in the nature of the French contribution to and involvement in NATO.

Although the cluster of role variables is not confined to those that involve policy goals,[32] it follows that it is within this type that race-susceptible variables are to be found. With the decline of European colonialism and the emergence of many nonwhite nation-states after World War II, every national society has been compelled, irrespective of the nature of its racial composition, to adopt general policies that govern when skin color and other physical characteristics are considered to be relevant to a situation in the international system. In some societies, especially those with a history of racial conflict and oppression, persons entering top policy-making roles are required to accept the pre-existing policy

[32] Other examples of the requirements built into top policy-making roles can be found in the attitudes and behavior of the role occupants with respect to other top policy-makers, the bureaucracy, domestic groups, and the general public.

standard that attaches a high degree of racial relevance to most of the major issues that sustain world politics at any moment in time. In other societies, particularly those that have not had a racially troubled past, such a standard does not exist and in these cases other standards lead officials to attach a minimum of racial relevance to most international situations. The presence or absence of such a standard—what we shall henceforth refer to as the *relevance* variable—thus appears to be appropriate as the race-susceptible role variable to be subjected to further treatment. In order to assess its potency relative to nonracial role variables, the requirement whereby occupants of top policy-making positions must be concerned about the economic welfare of their societies has also been singled out for additional analysis. Built into most top policy-making roles is the necessity of being sensitive to the need for a continual flow of goods and services—what we shall hereafter call the *trade-and-aid* variable —and as illustrated by recent events in Rhodesia, this nonracial role variable can come into conflict with the requirement that a high degree of racial relevance be attached to the unfolding situation, thus affording an opportunity to assess the relative strength of role requirements that do and do not introduce racial factors into the international arena.

Equally important, of course, is the interaction between the race-susceptible role variables and individual, governmental, societal, and systemic variables. If a racially conscious individual enters a role that does not require the attachment of racial relevance to issues, or if there is a buildup of pressures within the national or international system for the attachment of racial relevance to such a role, are the requirements of the role likely to be altered? More precisely, under what conditions will the degree to which officials are required to attach racial relevance to policy goals vary? Answers to questions such as these are crucial to an understanding of the dynamics of racial conflict in world politics and, as indicated below, there is good reason to hypothesize that the relative strength of role variables is greater than might be supposed.

Governmental Variables—The governmental cluster of independent variables refers to those aspects of the larger political system in which the top policy-making positions are located that determine the nature and extent of the information and demands that reach top officials and condition their behavior. The structural features of a government and the party system that sustains it thus comprise the main variables in this cluster. The distinction between a presidential and cabinet form of government, or between a two-party or multiparty system, are examples of structural aspects of government that can shape the behavior of officials. Government variables, being structural in nature, do not contribute directly to the content of foreign policy, but rather affect it by serving as a filter through which the values that underlie individual, role, societal, and systemic variables must pass. For example, the same values introduced into a presidential system and a cabinet system are likely, for a variety of reasons related to the differences between the two types, to result in policies that differ somewhat in their scope, decisiveness, and clarity.[33]

In other words, although it is not a distinction that will be stressed here, strictly speaking governmental variables are intervening and not independent variables. They shape the direction and quality of the external behavior that officials undertake, but they do not in themselves consist of values that give content to the behavior. Consequently, the distinction between race-susceptible and nonracial variables does not apply to the governmental cluster. Being intervening variables, they are all nonracial and our task here is thus one of selecting powerful governmental variables that can be used to test the strength of the race-susceptible variables in the other clusters. Two such variables seem especially appropriate in this regard. One, the *executive form* variable, involves the aforementioned distinction between presidential and cabinet systems of government. The other, the *authority structure* variable, involves the degree to which a government is responsive to the demands and tensions of the society. Here the distinction is between open, multiparty authority structures that allow racial groups in the society to assert their needs and closed, single-party structures that do not provide nongovernmental groups with ready access to officials. It is a distinction that facilitates, for example, investigation of whether the substantial difference between the Middle Eastern policies of the Soviet Union and the United States is crucially related to their respective authority structures. At first glance the potency of this variable would seem to be considerable, since the aspirations of Jewish groups in the United States are heard because of its relatively open structure, whereas the relatively closed structure of the U.S.S.R. prevents similar aspirations from getting articulated and advanced. An additional advantage of the authority structure variable is that the degree to which a government is responsive to societal pressures can also affect the extent to which racial groups go outside of established channels and conduct, in effect, their own private foreign policy by seeking support in the international system.

Societal Variables—The fourth cluster of independent variables, those derived from the society on whose behalf the individuals occupying top policy-making roles undertake foreign policy behavior, is conceived to encompass both human and nonhuman factors. Any

---

[33] For an incisive discussion of the impact that different governmental structures can have on policy content, see Kenneth N. Waltz, *Foreign Policy and Democratic Politics: The American and British Experience* (Boston: Little, Brown, 1967).

aspect of societies that is related to their functioning and that may vary from one society to another is treated as a societal variable, irrespective of whether it consists of material resources or human efforts. Thus the daily production of oil, the average rainfall, and the complexity of overland transportation routes are as much a part of the societal cluster as are the degree of social cohesion, the values shared by the population, and the educational structure through which human talent is perfected. Some societal variables combine human and nonhuman dimensions, and one of these, the degree of economic development, has been found to be sufficiently powerful as a source of political behavior [34] to justify singling it out as the nonracial variable with which to compare the race-susceptible societal variable in the ensuing analysis. Internal racial conflicts may contribute to the pace and extent of a society's development, but these are so relatively minor as determinants of its gross national product that the hypotheses that contrast the two types of societal variables will not be significantly contaminated. To simplify the analysis the *developmental* variable will be used dichotomously, a distinction being drawn between societies that are developed and those that are underdeveloped.

An extensive list could be compiled of race-susceptible societal variables from which to select one for further examination. The degree to which societies are racially homogeneous or heterogeneous, the extent to which the leadership of their racial minorities is trained and articulate, and the stratification system whereby the racial minorities have access to wealth and status are but a few of the societal variables that are regarded as race-susceptible and that can introduce racial factors into the international arena. One race-susceptible societal variable, however, seems so powerful in this respect as to warrant its use in the hypotheses developed below—namely, the degree of tension among the racial groups in a society. Since tension gives rise to value conflicts and demands for their resolution, officials and publics are sensitive, either empathically or fearfully, to tensions rather than harmonies among groups. Accordingly, it seems reasonable to presume, without prejudging the relative potency of race-susceptible societal variables, that the greater the degree of racial tension in a society, the more likely it is to attract foreign conflict behavior on the part of officials and groups abroad and the more are its own officials and groups likely to engage in external activities that reflect sensitivity to racial factors. This cannot necessarily be said, however, about the other race-susceptible societal variables. Different degrees of racial

---

[34] Cf. Jack Sawyer, "Dimensions of Nations: Size, Wealth, and Politics," *The American Journal of Sociology*, 73 (September 1967), pp. 145–172, and R. J. Rummel, "Some Dimensions in the Foreign Behavior of Nations," *Journal of Peace Research*, 3 (1966), pp. 201–224.

heterogeneity may or may not be accompanied by tensions among groups with different physical characteristics; and if tension does not exist, the racial composition of a society is likely to be irrelevant to its foreign conflict behavior. Similarly, if racial minorities and their articulate leaderships are accepting of a stratification system that denies them wealth and status, then racial tensions will not characterize the society and any assessment of the potency of such variables under these conditions would give a misleading picture of the extent to which race-susceptible societal variables can affect world politics. The United States is a good example in this respect. Its racial composition and its stratification system have remained essentially unchanged for decades, but it is only recently that traces of racial sensitivity have been discernible in its external behavior, a tendency that coincides with heightened internal tensions stemming from the intensified demands for wealth and status by American Negroes in the 1950s. Thus the *racial tension* variable would seem to be the most overriding of the many that might be included in the ensuing analysis. Furthermore, it has the advantage of being equally applicable to a society in which the racial minority is dominant (e.g., South Africa) and one in which it is dominated (e.g., the United States), thus relieving the analyst of the need to include this important distinction as an additional variable in the analysis.

Systemic Variables—Like societal variables, those comprising the systemic cluster include both human and nonhuman aspects of the international system. Any human event that occurs in, or nonhuman characteristic that distinguishes, the world external to a society can be viewed as a systemic variable. It is true that many nonhuman dimensions of the international system, such as a society's geographical location and the resources of its nearest neighbors, do not vary and can be treated as constants from the perspective of a particular society. But from the perspective of the researcher committed to comparative analysis, these nonhuman aspects of the international system vary from one society to another and must thus be treated as variables. For example, one geographic variable in the systemic cluster is the number of contiguous societies with which a society shares its border, a number that normally does not change but that is different for different societies.

It will readily be recognized that the systemic cluster encompasses an almost infinite number of variables. Developments within all the other societies external to the environed society, not to mention among them, are alone so numerous as to be virtually incalculable. Thus here we can take note of only a few of the more general types of variables that are likely to have a high potency and that, conceptualized at a high level of abstraction, operate for all societies. The overall political structure of the

global system, consisting of the relationships between the superpowers and
the formal and informal arrangements whereby other societies relate to
each other and to the superpowers, is the most obvious, and perhaps the
most important, systemic variable. The readiness of any society to engage
in external conflict behavior is bound to be at least partly conditioned
by whether a bipolarity, a balance of power, or some other structure
characterizes the global system. If only because the overall structure
provides an indication of whether a superpower is likely to contest its
conflict behavior, every society must consider the possible systemic consequences before it undertakes the behavior. Accordingly, *global structure*
would appear to be a systemic variable of sufficient generality and importance to be included in the ensuing analysis. Since it refers to alliances
and the norms governing their formation and dissolution, and since such
norms derive primarily from considerations of military security and only
secondarily—if at all—from a concern for skin color or other physical
characteristics, global structure can reasonably be treated as a nonracial
systemic variable. Furthermore, in order to simplify matters, we shall
treat it as a dichotomous variable, differentiating between a tight bipolar
structure in which the superpowers exact a heavy price from other societies
for nonadherence to their demands and a loose balance of power structure
in which deviance on the part of other societies is tolerated by the more
powerful societies.

However, the overall structure of the global system is not so much
a direct stimulus to external action on the part of societies as it is a
screen through which their reactions to more specific events and trends
are filtered. Hence it would seem desirable to include a second nonracial
systemic variable in the hypotheses that follow, one that is sufficiently
general to apply to all societies and yet specific enough to constitute
direct stimuli to external conflict behavior on their part. Sustained conflicts
between and within other societies—what we shall refer to as the *situational* variable—meet these criteria. Both types of situations constitute
concrete developments that no society can ignore. Its interests may be
at stake in any conflict, if only because one or more of the warring
factions may seek its support and threaten possible reprisals if the support
is not forthcoming. Every conflict situation abroad is thus a stimulus to
some kind of action on the part of every society, and while many may
choose to respond through inaction, none can avoid adopting a stance
toward each situation. Crucial to a society's stance, however, is whether
the external conflict situation occurs within or between other societies.
Societies act in terms of the values they perceive to be at stake in a
situation, but these values can seem very different if they are at stake

in *intersocietal* or *intrasocietal* situations—as the two aspects of the situational variable shall henceforth be called.

Another reason to include the *situational* variable in the ensuing analysis is that it provides a way of identifying a race-susceptible systemic variable. Some situations between or within other societies are pervaded with racial tension, whereas such tensions are essentially peripheral to or absent from other situations. This distinction, which we shall call the *race-dominant* variable, is presumably central to the way in which the international system itself contributes to the role racial factors play in world politics. That is, by comparing how societies respond to *race-free* and *race-pervaded* external situations—the two extremes of the race-dominant variable—an assessment can be made of the extent to which race is a source of escalating, or at least self-sustaining, conflict in the international system. This is especially so if the situational and race-dominant variables are combined and comparisons are made between race-free and race-pervaded conflicts that occur within other societies on the one hand and between them on the other. For if race-pervaded intrasocietal situations can be shown to evoke different forms and degrees of conflict behavior on the part of other societies than race-free intrasocietal situations, it should be possible to develop considerable clarification of the processes whereby racial factors become internationalized.

Although it makes the ensuing analysis more cumbersome, combining the situational and race-dominant variables has the advantage of facilitating comparisons between systemic variables and those in the other four clusters. Are officials occupying positions that require them to attach a high degree of racial relevance to issues likely to respond to a class war in a white society abroad in the same way as they react to a race war in a racially heterogeneous society? Are race-pervaded intrasocietal conflicts abroad likely to evoke similar or different behavior on the part of societies in which such tension is nonexistent? Do the diplomatic restraints built into foreign policy roles, particularly those that pertain to the principle of nonintervention in the affairs of other societies, tend to limit the intensity of reactions to race-pervaded intrasocietal situations while not limiting responses to intersocietal situations where the issue of nonintervention is irrelevant? Are underdeveloped societies more or less likely than developed ones to engage in conflict behavior toward intrasocietal situations? Questions such as these suggest some of the possibilities for probing comparison that are opened up by these additional systemic variables included in the analysis.

These variables selected from the systemic cluster have the additional advantage that they can be used as the occasion for the various behaviors that are conceived to constitute the dependent variables. Of course, external conflict behavior does not require a foreign situation to occasion it. In fact, such behavior operates frequently as a creator of situations rather than as a response to them. Yet, if assessments of the relative potency of the various independent variables with respect to the several types of external conflict situations can be developed, it should not be difficult to generalize about their potency as a source of external conflict behavior under all conditions. In effect, by including the situational and race-dominant variables, we have narrowed the theoretical task to that of constructing hypotheses about the forms and degrees of conflict behavior toward four types of international situations that individuals with different backgrounds in different governmental roles are likely to undertake on behalf of different kinds of societies.

Author's Analytic Conscience: That is hardly a narrow task. You have made frequent references to the need to limit the number of variables, but what you have fashioned seems more like an analytic monster than a manageable inquiry. Table 16–1 summarizes all the independent variables that have been singled out for inclusion in the hypotheses. There are eleven in all, drawn from five basic clusters and consisting of four

Table 16 – 1 Independent Variables Selected for Analysis

Variable Clusters	Nonracial Variables	Race-susceptible Variables
Individual	experience	racial consciousness
Role	trade-and-aid	racial relevance
Governmental	executive form authority structure	
Societal	developmental	racial tension
Systemic	global structure situational	race dominant

that are race-susceptible and seven that are essentially nonracial in character. You seem to have committed yourself not only to developing hypotheses in which each of the former is contrasted with its counterpart from the same cluster among the latter, but also to comparing across the clusters in such a way that each race-susceptible variable is contrasted with every possible combination of the other variables. That amounts to no less than 508 hypotheses! And that figure allows for only one dependent variable, but you have suggested the possibility of predicting to six forms of foreign conflict behavior. Surely you are not going to put the reader through the exercise of deriving hypotheses for all these combinations. You have space and time for only a few derivations and, in being forced to cut back, you have played straight into the hands of your moral conscience.

Author's Moral Conscience: You sure have! Science is supposed to be parsimonious, but the foregoing demonstrates the extraordinary complexity of human affairs and thus the impossibility of subjecting them to scientific analysis!

Author: It certainly highlights the complexity of the problem and, admittedly, our efforts to limit the scope of our inquiry have been less than successful. However, while we are thus forced to cut back and confine ourselves to only a few derivations, this does not prove that scientific analysis is bound to fall short of its goal. Parsimony is the ultimate goal of science, not its guiding procedure. One moves toward parsimony as comprehension is acquired, and comprehension requires a recognition of complexity and a readiness to deal with small segments of it at a time. Only after the parts of the problem are understood can the whole be pieced together and parsimonious statements made about its underlying dynamics. The real reason we must cut back is because comprehension, rather than time and space, is limited. Our grasp of the role that race can play in world politics is not such that useful multivariate hypotheses can be derived. It would be difficult, for example, to offer convincing reasons for a hypothesis that predicted the differences between the reaction of experienced, nonracially conscious officials of an open, developed society to a race-free situation in another society and the reaction of inexperienced, racially conscious officials of a closed, underdeveloped society to the same conflict—much less to a race-pervaded situation between several other societies. On the other hand, plausible underpinnings for one- and two-variable hypotheses do seem possible. If other things are assumed to be equal, then it seems possible to develop rationales for hypotheses that predict the behavior that results from the operation of one or two independent variables. Thus we shall cut back to the task of first deriving univariate hypotheses that assess the operation of the race-susceptible variables in each cluster and then deriving bivariate hypotheses in which each race-susceptible variable is compared with the nonracial variable in both its own cluster and in every other cluster— a total of thirty-two hypotheses.[35] In so doing we shall at least put each of the ways in which racial factors can enter the international arena to a stiff and thorough, though still incomplete, test.

To be sure, other things never are equal, as our ignoring of innumerable multivariate hypotheses demonstrates. To reiterate *ceteris paribus*, however, is not to offer a substitute for parsimony. Rather it is a necessary step toward the construction of parsimonious theory.

IV. SOME HYPOTHESES

Individual Variables—Let us start again at the level of the individuals who occupy high posts in the foreign policy organizations of their governments. Other things being equal, will the degree to which they are conscious of physical characteristics affect the extent of the foreign conflict behavior they undertake or recommend with respect to conflict situations abroad? This is the question to which our initial reasoning must be addressed; and since it requires the derivation of a univariate hypothesis with all other variables held constant, the answer may seem fairly obvious. Action flows from motivation and perception, and if racial consciousness is part of a person's motivational and perceptual equipment, it would seem bound to shape the action he takes or recommends unless it is offset by other motives and perceptions. Such an answer, however, is not sufficient. It leaves untouched the relationship between the degree of racial consciousness and the extent of foreign conflict behavior. To presume that an individual is likely to take or recommend more stringent foreign policy measures the more racially conscious he is, is not to say that the stringency of the measures will increase in direct proportion to the degree of his racial consciousness. For such a relationship to prevail it must be assumed that racial consciousness is unrelenting in its intensity and global in its scope, thus fostering more stringent behavior as it deepens. Such an assumption hardly seems warranted. By its very nature, racial consciousness is likely to be most intense with respect to close-at-hand situations involving the family, community, and possibly the national society. One may be aware of and

[35] Actually the ensuing analysis deviates slightly from this format. In several instances it seemed appropriate either to encompass more than one comparison in a single hypothesis or to hypothesize about the interaction between a race-susceptible variable and the nonracial extreme of a race-susceptible variable in another cluster—with the result that thirty-four formal hypotheses are presented.

care about racial arrangements in more distant parts of the world, but a sense of intimacy about them declines the more distant they are. Presumably this is part of the reason why severances of diplomatic relations, economic blockades, and armed attacks are not daily features of the international scene. The world is full of top officials who are highly conscious of race, yet they do not constantly employ extreme forms of foreign conflict behavior when conflict situations arise abroad. To be sure, other variables attenuate the operation of their racial consciousness, but presumably the restraint stems in part from their lesser concern about race relations in remote parts of the world than within their own country or region. In sum, it does not seem reasonable to derive a hypothesis that posits the dependent variable in scalar rather than dichotomous terms. Rather than referring to more or less conflict behavior, we must confine ourselves to anticipating its presence or absence:

Hypothesis I$_1$: Other things being equal, the greater the racial consciousness of an individual who occupies a top policy-making position, the more likely he is to undertake or recommend some form of foreign conflict behavior.

If we now relax the assumption that other things are equal and allow for nonracial motives and perceptions that might offset the potency of this race-susceptible individual variable, the potency of the latter is greatly reduced. In the case of the nonracial individual variable (the extent of an official's prior experience in foreign affairs), it seems reasonable to presume that the more contact the individual has had with the procedures and proprieties whereby governments interact, the more inclined he will be to perceive the narrow limits within which foreign policy can be effective. The capacity of societies to organize their external environments so that their own values are better served is miniscule at best. Even in small communities the task of altering attitudes, mobilizing support, and restructuring institutions is extraordinarily difficult, but the difficulties are greatly magnified when the attitudes, support, and institutions are located in other cultures and separated by national boundaries. Appreciation of these difficulties, however, is not automatic. The inexperienced person might well underestimate the obstacles that must be overcome in the conduct of foreign policy and, imbued with strong convictions about how conflicts abroad should be resolved, act precipitously, perhaps even resorting to forms of behavior consistent with the intensity of his convictions. In other words, not only does it appear that racial consciousness is subordinate to other individual variables, but it would also seem possible to treat the dependent variable as continuous when allowance is made for the influence of an official's previous contact with world politics:

Hypothesis I_2: Other things being equal, the more foreign affairs experience a racially conscious individual has had before he enters a top policy-making position, the less foreign conflict behavior will he be likely to undertake or recommend.

The potency of race-susceptible individual variables appears to diminish even further when they are contrasted with nonracial variables from the other clusters. As previously implied, this is especially so with respect to role variables. If an official's position requires adherence to policies that give high priority to the maintenance of overseas markets and trade patterns, and does not have a built-in predisposition toward the attachment of racial relevance to the external environment, then even the most racially conscious official is likely to keep his personal sensitivities in check and stress economic considerations when a foreign conflict situation arises. The probabilities of such behavior doubtless become even greater if there is a prohibition against the attachment of racial relevance, rather than just the absence of such a requirement. Those officials that reverse this order of priority will not long remain in their jobs. To be sure, officials of many countries are presently forfeiting markets in Rhodesia and South Africa because of the apartheid practices of these societies. Such exceptions, however, actually uphold the rule. Priorities are reversed with respect to Rhodesia and South Africa, not because somehow the situations in those societies are such that racially conscious officials are unlikely to contain their private feelings and are willing to risk removal from office, but because the roles of officials who maintain an economic boycott of Rhodesia and South Africa include a requirement that racial relevance be attached to such situations. In other words, with role and individual variables reinforcing each other, other things are not equal in these cases. Where they are, however, race-susceptible individual variables appear likely to be subordinated to nonracial role requirements, a relationship which is perhaps even more clearly discernible in the propriety that marks the interaction of top officials from different societies. Undoubtedly there are many diplomats who are personally prejudiced and conscious of skin color. Yet they receive, call upon, toast, hail, and otherwise honor officials of other races on almost a day-to-day basis. The discrepancy between their public behavior and their private orientations is not mysterious. It can be explained by the courtesies and rituals that comprise the requirements of diplomatic roles. In sum, there are good reasons to be confident that empirical data would uphold the following proposition:

Hypothesis I_3: Other things being equal, the more a top policy-making role requires a racially conscious individual to minimize the attachment of racial relevance to situations and to maximize the flow of trade and aid, the less likely he is to undertake or recommend foreign conflict behavior.

Taken by itself, the interaction between race-susceptible individual variables and those relating to government structure does not seem worthy of prolonged discussion. Some interaction can reasonably be hypothesized, but it is so much influenced by role, societal, and systemic variables that treating it in bivariate terms is misleading. Nevertheless, if the other variables are held constant, the fact that authority is more concentrated in a cabinet form of government than in a presidential form would seem to have some consequence for the degree to which officials can pursue personal convictions that deviate from the policies of the chief executive. Top executive and legislative posts in a cabinet system derive from the same authority and the resulting collective responsibility limits the individual discretion of those who occupy the positions. Since the top officials in a presidential system have different responsibilities and bases of power, they are somewhat freer to give expression to their idiosyncratic tendencies. In the United States, for example, an Allen Ellender can return from a tour of Africa and publish racist views of that continent without damage to his career as a Senator.[36] On the other hand, in England an Enoch Powell is quickly dismissed from his post in the shadow cabinet when he gives public expression to similar views.[37] Of course, this difference is most pronounced with respect to two-party cabinet systems. A multi-party system may well include minority parties with deviant views on race and the political balance may be such as to give some of their leaders seats in the cabinet. In sum, while the foregoing differences should not be exaggerated, and while much depends on the role, societal, and systemic variables that are operative, it does seem plausible to derive the following proposition:

Hypothesis I_4: Other things being equal, racially conscious individuals who occupy top policy-making roles in cabinet systems of government are less likely to undertake or recommend foreign conflict behavior than their counterparts in presidential systems.

[36] *The New York Times*, March 8, 1963.
[37] *The New York Times*, April 22, 1968.

Nor need we dwell long on the interaction between racial consciousness at the individual level and nonracial variables at the societal level,
since it does not appear to be a very important interaction in comparison
to most of those analyzed in subsequent hypotheses. The factors that
operate between the racial consciousness of an official and the economic
development of his society are so numerous that the interaction between
the two variables would seem to be weak at best. Yet, if all else is held
constant, presumably the fact that economic development requires an
increasing reliance on achievement, rather than ascription, of status is of
sufficient importance to interpose progressively greater restraints on the
racial consciousness of officials as their society develops. That is, while
it may not warrant extensive investigation, the following proposition can
be logically deduced:

Hypothesis I_5: Other things being equal, a racially conscious individual
who occupies a top policy-making position in an underdeveloped
society is more likely to undertake or recommend foreign conflict
behavior than is a similarly conscious official of a developed society.

If the interaction between individual and societal variables is so weak
as to render the derivation of hypotheses hazardous, the connection between
individual and systemic variables seems virtually impossible to trace. So
many factors can intervene to affect the relationship that it seems doubtful
whether individual differences can be specifically linked to differences in
either the global structures of the international system or the specific
situation to which officials must respond. All else being equal, a racially
conscious individual would probably perceive physical characteristics as
determinants of behavior regardless of the type of conflict involved, and
in all likelihood this lack of differentiation would obtain whether the
relationship that prevailed between the superpowers was polarized or not.
Hence, for the sake of thoroughness, these hypotheses need to be formulated:

Hypothesis I_6: Other things being equal, a racially conscious individual
in a top policy-making position is likely to undertake or recommend
as much foreign conflict behavior toward situations within other societies as toward situations between other societies.

Hypothesis I_7: Other things being equal, a racially conscious individual
occupying a top policy-making position is as likely to undertake
or recommend foreign conflict behavior in a tight bipolar system
as in a loose bipolar one.

Role Variables—While individual variables do not emerge as particularly relevant to the introduction of racial factors into the international arena, the opposite conclusion emerges from an assessment of the relative potency of role variables. It will be recalled that the race-susceptible variable selected for analysis is the degree of racial relevance policy-makers are required to attach to external developments. Although the high extreme of this relevance continuum is subject to the moderating influence of societal and systemic variables (see Hypotheses SO_3 and SY_3 below), its potency does not appear ever to be erased by the operation of other variables and, indeed, in several instances it would seem to be the more powerful variable. The basis for such an estimate becomes apparent in a comparison of the relevance variable and its nonracial counterpart, the trade-and-aid variable. Notwithstanding the strength of the requirement that officials give high priority to economic considerations, there is considerable evidence that they are willing to sacrifice the flow of goods and services when their positions also require them to be sensitive to the skin color or racial policies of potential partners in a trade or aid relationship. Most noteworthy in this respect is the willingness of officials in a number of nations to participate in a boycott of Rhodesia and South Africa; and the unwillingness of Rhodesian and South African officials to recover their markets by altering their apartheid policies is certainly no less indicative of the strength of race-susceptible role variables. Indeed, the recent effort to suspend South Africa from the United Nations Conference on Trade and Development, undertaken and pressed by African and Asian nations despite a stern rebuke in the form of a legal opinion that characterized the proposed suspension as unconstitutional and as threatening to the entire structure of the United Nations, offers a good measure of the extensity as well as the intensity of this variable. Repeatedly quoted as believing that "whether it is legal or not, we will do what we think is right," forty-nine members voted for the suspension in the U.N.'s Economic Committee, while twenty-two voted against it and twenty-three abstained.[38] In other words, the relevance variable can even be so powerful as to overwhelm the requirement of all other roles, including those that sustain systemic structures and legal procedures.

To be sure, it was concluded above that a racially conscious official would keep his personal sensitivities in check in the face of requirements arising out of the economic and diplomatic requirements of his role (Hypotheses I_3). To now posit the trade-and-aid variable as subordinate

---

[38] *The New York Times*, December 8, 1968, p. 2. Subsequently, in the General Assembly, the proposal was defeated, falling eleven short of the necessary two-thirds majority for adoption. See *The New York Times*, December 14, 1968, p. 11.

is not to be contradictory. Here we are assessing the potency of a role variable, whereas earlier we sought to trace the operation of racial consciousness as an individual variable, unreinforced by the presence of the requirement that racial relevance be attached to situations.

In view of the extremes within which the relevance variable would appear to operate, a direct correlation between it and the behavior of officials can reasonably be predicted—both when it is the only variable being examined and when account is taken of its interaction with nonracial role variables. In short, the following hypotheses can be derived with considerable confidence:

Hypothesis R_1: Other things being equal, the more the top policy-making positions of a society require their occupants to attach racial relevance to external situations, the more foreign conflict behavior are they likely to undertake or recommend.

Hypothesis R_2: Other things being equal, the more the top policy-making positions of a society require their occupants to attach racial relevance to external situations, the less will they be inclined to take account of economic considerations and thus the greater will be the foreign conflict behavior they undertake or recommend.

But is the existence of a role requirement that racial relevance be attached to situations sufficient to offset the effects of such individual characteristics as lack of racial consciousness or foreign affairs experience? Although perhaps more psychologically than politically interesting, this is the essential question to which the comparison of the relevance and individual variables is addressed. All the evidence suggests that individual variations are likely to prove less potent than role variables. If the policy-making system in which a position and its occupant is located is to persist, any mismatch between the role and the individual cannot be so great as to permit the latter to alter the former. If the individual is not capable of altering his attitudes and behavior to conform to the minimum requirements of the role, then either he will not be recruited to the role or he will not long remain in it. This process of role socialization would seem to operate for roles both which do and do not involve positing one race as superior to another as part of the relevance requirement. Black officials of Malawi, for example, seem just as unlikely to advocate a racial reconciliation on their continent as are white officials of South Africa. Similarly, just as socialization into the presidency shifted Lyndon Johnson's behavior from speeches espousing the values of the American South to one that echoed "We shall overcome," so may the role requirements of the Rhodesian prime ministership have compelled Ian Smith to cling to positions in negotiating with the British over race relations that, allegedly, were less moderate and more anti-black than he was personally inclined to favor.[39] It will be noted, moreover, that at least the first of these examples does not involve a novice in politics and that it depicts role socialization occurring despite long experience in policy-making. If it is assumed that these examples are typical of the interaction of role and individual variables during periods when the role requirements are reasonably stable, an assumption that seems warranted by the logic of how policy-making systems persist as well as by available data,[40] then the derivation of this proposition follows:

Hypothesis R_3: Other things being equal, the more the top policy-making roles of a society require their occupants to attach racial relevance to external situations, the less inclined they will be to base their actions on predilections derived from their own past personal and political experience and the greater will be the foreign conflict behavior they undertake or recommend.

Much the same line of reasoning results from a comparison of the role and government variables. Given the existence of the role requirement that racial relevance be attached to external situations, it seems unlikely that the strength or direction of the requirement will be greatly affected by structural aspects of the governmental process. The executive form variable may, as indicated above, account for whether an official is able to act on the basis of his own racial consciousness, but the requirements of his role are presumably operative irrespective of whether he is responsive to cabinet or presidential authority. To be sure, governmental structure may be crucial to whether officials are required to attach racial relevance to external situations (see Hypotheses G_2, G_3 and G_4 below). Yet, once such requirements become part of top policy-making roles, it would seem that their continued existence is independent of governmental form. Thus it seems reasonable to derive the following:

Hypothesis R_4: Other things being equal, top policy-making officials in a cabinet system of government and in a presidential system, both of whose roles require attachment of racial relevance to external situations, are likely to undertake or recommend similar amounts of foreign conflict behavior.

Since the role requirements of top policy-making positions will reflect

[39] *The New York Times*, October 14, 1968, p. 15.
[40] See Chapter 7.

the basic aspirations of the societies in which they are located, some moderation of the strength of race-susceptible role variables can be anticipated when their interaction with societal variables is analyzed. In a society that is free of racial tension, or which is experiencing a lessening of such tensions, demands that its officials be sensitive to the physical characteristics of the parties to situations abroad will either be non-existent or increasingly muted. Under these circumstances other variables will operate more effectively and will lessen the extent to which top policy-makers must attach racial relevance to external events. Racially conscious officials may still be able to follow their personal predilections under such circumstances, but these will not be supported by the requirements of their roles and may even be offset by contrary requirements, for example, by societal demands that officials curb their personal predilections and treat external situations as nonracial in character.[41] To be sure, one can readily think of exceptions to the foregoing reasoning. The attachment of racial relevance to external situations is very much a requirement of top policy-making roles in black African societies, for example, even though most of these societies, being racially homogeneous, are mostly free of racial tensions. Such exceptions, however, do not hold other variables constant. Black African officials are required to attach a high degree of racial relevance to developments abroad because another societal variable, recent history and the colonial memories of which it is comprised, operates to sustain the requirement even in the absence of internal tensions over physical characteristics. Indeed, whenever this historical variable is operative, the above analysis must be modified. But multivariate analysis that would pick up exceptions of this kind lies beyond our present scope. Here we are interested in the central tendencies that can be uncovered through bivariate inquiry, and thus the following hypothesis can reasonably be derived from the foregoing:

Hypothesis R_b: Other things being equal, the less a society is marked by racial tensions, the less inclined its officials will be to attach racial relevance to external situations and thus the less likely they will be to undertake or recommend foreign conflict behavior.

Similarly, the potency of the relevance variable seems likely to be diminished when it interacts with the nonracial societal variable. Irrespective of the degree of racial tension in a society, as it undergoes economic development the responsibilities of its officials will widen and so will their

---

[41] The reaction to Senator Ellender's aforementioned venture into African politics, for example, was of this order, albeit there is no evidence as to whether the outcry subsequently curbed similar predispositions on the part of like-minded Senators.

sensitivities to issues other than those that are racial in character. Hence, the more of such development there has been, the greater will be the division of labor in the society and thus the greater the number of cross-cutting relationships that moderate the demands that racial relevance be attached to external situations. Stated differently, the variety of societal demands to which officials are exposed is likely to be much greater in developed societies than in underdeveloped societies. Hence the potency of the relevance variable seems likely to decline as the developmental process unfolds, a conclusion that leads to the following derivation:

Hypothesis R_6: Other things being equal, as a society passes through successive stages of economic development, the requirement that its top policy-making officials attach racial relevance to external situations is likely to weaken, making them less likely to undertake or recommend foreign conflict behavior.

Reflection about the interaction of race-susceptible role variables and nonracial systemic variables leads to hypotheses that both reaffirm the strength of the former and show them to be subject to some moderation of the latter. Their strength is revealed by an analysis of what happens to the relevance requirement when race-free situations develop abroad. Are officials whose roles require them to attach a high degree of relevance to external situations likely to do so even with respect to conflicts within or between other societies in which the contesting parties are of the same race and thus in conflict over nonracial matters? The answer here is not as obvious as it may seem. While it might seem that the relevance requirement is applicable only to external situations where racial factors are operative, such a conclusion assumes that role requirements are rational, or at least that they are not so irrational as to require their occupants to read relevance into situations that are manifestly nonracial in content. Yet, roles are the products of human expectations and are thus as susceptible to distortion as the perceptions of those who create them. In many societies the relevance requirement does not extend to nonracial situations, but under certain circumstances the relevance variable can become so potent that officials are required to attribute racial significance to virtually any situation, including those in which all the participants have the same physical characteristics. These special circumstances include a sense of racial identification with or antagonism to one or more of the parties to the conflict that is of sufficient strength to produce seemingly unwarranted attributions of racial relevance. The reactions of nonwhite countries to the Suez and Hungarian crises of 1956 are a case in point. The two situations had a great deal in common. They occurred at the same time.

They both involved intervention by a great power in the domestic affairs of a lesser power. And both interventions were undertaken for political reasons (i.e., the ouster of a hostile regime) rather than racial ones. Notwithstanding the similarity of the situations, however, many nonwhite nations were quick to condemn the aggressor in the Suez incident while remaining silent with respect to the Hungarian affair. Although the reasons for this are doubtless complex and numerous, the relevance variable seems to have played an important role. One observer elucidated the operation of the relevance variable in this way, referring to a November 1956 editorial in a Ceylonese newspaper:

> . . . The author of the editorial questioned why it was that Ceylon and other so-called Afro-Asian members of the United Nations responded to the Suez incident within a matter of hours, condemning the United Kingdom, France and Israel for their "aggression" against a weaker state, while even a few weeks after the Hungarian incident, these same Afro-Asian United Nations members still "needed more time to get all the facts" before taking a stand. He answered his own question by pointing out that all of the African and Asian countries had experienced colonialism at the hands of a white colonial power and, thus, anything that even vaguely smacked of white colonialism was met with a very visceral and immediate reaction. On the other hand, he argued, while it was conceptually possible to have white colonialism perpetrated upon a weaker white country, it was simply outside the Afro-Asian range of perpetual reality. Somehow, it was simply not colonialism if it was white against white.[42]

Verbal condemnation of the United States role in the Vietnam war offers perhaps another example of this line. Despite the lack of clear evidence that racial feelings about the nonwhite population of Vietnam are in any way a source of the U.S. role, officials of a number of nonwhite societies have cited differences in skin color as part of their reason for denouncing U.S. actions in the situation.

While it can thus be seen that race-susceptible role variables can be sufficiently potent to override some systemic differences, an analysis of their strength in relation to intrasocietal as compared to intersocietal external conflicts reveals that other systemic variables do affect the extent to which racial relevance is attached to situations. Stated succinctly, the practices of diplomacy and the norms of international law circumscribe involvement in intrasocietal situations, whereas there are few, if any, restraints on conflict behavior toward intersocietal situations. The principles of sovereignty have long prohibited involvement in the domestic life of other societies and only as recently as December 21, 1965, the

[42] Marshall R. Singer, *Weak States in a Power-Full World* (mimeo.), Chapter Four, p. 39.

General Assembly of the United Nations reaffirmed, by a near unanimous vote, these principles through a resolution on intervention which declared that no state had a right to intervene in the "internal or external" affairs of another state by *any* form of interference or coercive measure.[43] Given this norm, and the reality that to violate it by intervening in the domestic affairs of another society is to legitimate or even invite interference in one's own affairs, officials are less likely to allow the relevance variable full potency when the external stimulus is intrasocietal rather than intersocietal. Indeed, the power of sovereignty is such that this difference even seems likely to obtain in the case of intrasocietal situations that are unmistakably of a race-pervaded kind. To be sure, the Rhodesian and South African situations are exceptions and even international law seems to be undergoing change that allows for treating them as such flagrant offenses to "basic principles of justice" as to warrant violation of the sovereignty principle.[44] However, while the exceptions demonstrate again that the potency of the relevance variable is such that it can never be eliminated, the central tendency is one of dominance by the systemic variable.

The potency of the requirement that officials attach racial relevance to developments abroad would appear to be also responsive to variations in the global structure of the international system. Irrespective of whether an external situation unfolds within or between other societies, the predisposition to attach racial relevance to it is likely to be curbed to the extent that the resulting conflict behavior seems capable of evoking a counter-response on the part of one or more great powers. Enhancing and preserving national security is a basic responsibility of top policymakers in all societies and the effects of this responsibility are thus likely to interact with those of the global structure variable. That is, while no structure of the international system may ever entirely negate a built-in predisposition to respond to a situation in terms of its perceived racial relevance, those structures which facilitate interventionary behavior on the part of the great powers seem likely to limit the predisposition and reduce the amount of conflict behavior officials of lesser powers might otherwise undertake or recommend. As Kaplan has persuasively argued, the tendency for great powers to intervene in the affairs of other societies is maximized when the global structure is tightly organized in terms of

---

[43]For an analysis of the vote on this resolution, see *The New York Times*, December 21, 1966.

[44]Cf. Howard J. Taubenfeld, *Race, Peace, Law, and Southern Africa* (New York: Association of the Bar of the City of New York, 1966), pp. 36–79, and Vernon Van Dyke, "Violations of Human Rights as Threats to the Peace" (mimeo, 1968).

two major blocs.[45] Such a structure is based on a commitment of the great powers to the status quo and thus it heightens the incentives for them to resort to drastic measures whenever other societies engage in foreign conflict behavior that might loosen the existing ties within and between the blocs. Accordingly, the sensitivity of officials of lesser powers to the relevance requirements of their roles will depend on the degree of emphasis which the prevailing global structure places on the prerequisites of national security.

In sum, the above analysis yields three propositions relevant to the interaction of role and systemic variables:

Hypothesis R_7: Other things being equal, and irrespective of whether racial factors are operative in external situations, the more a top policy-making position requires its occupant to attach racial relevance to external situations, the more likely he is to do so and to undertake or recommend foreign conflict behavior toward them.

Hypothesis R_8: Other things being equal, top policy-making positions are more likely to require their occupants to attach racial relevance to external situations involving conflicts between other societies than to those involving conflicts within other societies. As a result, the undertakings or recommendations of officials with respect to intrasocietal situations are likely to be confined to verbal participation, whereas more severe forms of foreign conflict behavior are likely to be directed at intersocietal situations.

Hypothesis R_9: Other things being equal, the more tightly structured a bipolar international system is, the less likely are the occupants of top policy-making positions to attach racial relevance to external situations and to undertake or recommend foreign conflict behavior toward them.

Governmental Variables—An assessment of the potency of governmental variables need not be very elaborate. It will be recalled that, being structural rather than substantive in nature, these are essentially intervening variables and that the distinction between race-susceptible and nonracial variables cannot be applied to them. In effect, their only utility is that of testing the strength of the race-susceptible variables from the other clusters. This is not to say, however, that governmental variables are necessarily weak. On the contrary, there is consider-

[45] Morton A. Kaplan, "Intervention in Internal War: Some Systemic Sources," in James N. Rosenau (ed.), *International Aspects of Civil Strife* (Princeton: Princeton University Press, 1964), pp. 92–121.

able evidence that the distinction between open and closed authority structures, while not in-itself founded on racial considerations, is crucial to the racial policies that a society pursues at home and abroad. The differences between Russian and American policies toward Israel and the Middle East have already been cited as an example of the importance of the authority structure variable, and this illustration could be supplemented with innumerable others. For the degree of openness determines the extent to which information about, debates over, and demands with respect to racial matters are introduced into the deliberations of officials. And, of course, the more they are exposed to the information, debates, and demands of the society, the more likely are the personal values and role requirements of the officials to be adjusted to societal needs and wants. To be sure, officials in closed societies cannot entirely ignore the racial aspirations and tensions of their publics, but their authority is such as to permit them to minimize or even suppress organization and agitation for new racial policies. If the authority structure should open up, however, domestic groups will begin to organize and foreign groups will begin to feed information into their counterparts within the society, with the result that demands involving race will get expressed if the society has aspirations or tensions in which physical characteristics are central factors. It is not a coincidence, for example, that when illness forced the replacement of Salazar as Portuguese chief executive in 1968, opening up what heretofore had been a highly dictatorial regime, there followed protest demonstrations against Portugal's racist policies in Angola, Mozambique, and Portuguese Guinea.[46] Indeed, the future course of Portuguese foreign policy offers a good test of the potency of the authority structure variable: if our estimate is sound, it is reasonable to anticipate a moderation of Portugal's policies in Portuguese Africa if the post-Salazar regime that eventually emerges is more open than its predecessor.

In short, it would seem that societal and systemic variables on the one hand and individual and role variables on the other are related to the authority structure variable in opposite ways. Whereas societal and systemic variables are strengthened as a government becomes more open and weakened as it becomes more closed, individual and role variables are, respectively, weakened and strengthened by such trends. Four hypotheses thus suggest themselves:

Hypothesis G_1: Other things being equal, the more open a governmental system is, the less likely will its officials be to undertake or recommend foreign conflict behavior that reflects their personal values.

---

[46]For an account of one such protest in Lisbon, see *The New York Times*, January 2, 1969, p. 1.

Hypothesis G_2: Other things being equal, the more open a governmental system is, the less likely will the occupants of its top policy-making roles be to undertake or recommend forms of foreign conflict behavior that are consistent with historical precedents.

Hypothesis G_3: Other things being equal, the more open a governmental system is, the more likely will the occupants of its top policy-making roles be to undertake or recommend foreign conflict behavior that is consistent with existing societal pressures about racial values.

Hypothesis G_4: Other things being equal, the more open a governmental system is, the less likely will the occupants of its top policy-making roles be to ignore race-pervaded external situations and, accordingly, the more likely they will be to undertake or recommend foreign conflict behavior.

Societal Variables—As has been indicated in connection with Hypotheses R_5, R_6 and G_3, societal variables tend to be highly potent. Their strength can be discerned in virtually all of the interactions thus far examined and the ensuing analysis of the interactions involving the race-susceptible societal variable reveals their strength even more clearly. Indeed, being powerful, the racial tension variable yields some of the most interesting and controversial hypotheses.

Perhaps no hypothesis is more controversial than the one that assesses the potency of the societal tension variable by comparing its two extremes with each other. Should we anticipate that the foreign conflict behavior of a society with no racial tensions will be essentially the same as or different from that of a society continuously racked by such tensions? Our hypothesized answer to this question is controversial because it runs counter to some impressive empirical evidence. Several analysts, using sophisticated quantitative techniques, have converged around the finding that the external conflict behavior of societies is not correlated with their internal conflict behavior.[47] These studies compare more than eighty national societies in terms of thirteen forms of foreign conflict behavior and nine domestic forms, but the central tendency resulting from all these comparisons is the absence of any relationship between the two types of conflict. Yet our reasoning leads us in a contrary direction. As racial tensions mount in a society, all of its members, citizens as well as officials, seem likely to be affected. Assuming such tensions stem on the one hand

[47] Most notably, see Rudolph J. Rummel, "Dimensions of Conflict Behavior Within and Between Nations," *General Systems: Yearbook of the Society for General Systems Research*, Vol. VIII (1963), pp. 1–50; and Raymond Tanter, *Dimensions of Conflict Behavior Within and Between Nations* (Bloomington, Ind.: Indiana University, Ph.D. Thesis, 1964).

from efforts by one or more racial minorities to acquire more status in and greater benefits from the society, and from resistance on the part of the groups presently deriving status and wealth from the society on the other, once the tensions begin to increase they seem bound to spiral and to eventually encompass the entire society. Unwilling to fully meet the demands of the minorities, the dominant groups either offer them concessions or resort to repressive measures to maintain their control and, as a consequence, the minorities are led to assert their demands ever more stridently and perhaps even to enlarge them, thus encouraging still greater resistance on the part of the dominant groups. This familiar pattern is self-sustaining and self-intensifying. Unless the dominant groups make basic concessions that reverse the trend, no aspect of life in the society remains untouched by it. Accordingly, irrespective of whether spiraling tension results in widespread violence, it is only a matter of time before its effects spread beyond the society's borders. The minorities turn to comparable groups abroad for support and the latter in turn press their governments and international organizations for remedial action. Once the tension becomes internationalized, of course, the officials responsible for the conduct of the society's foreign policy get caught up in the spiral and are compelled either to address their external behavior to a defense of the society's racial balance or to insure that their external behavior reflects responsiveness to the internal tensions.

It could be argued that most of foreign policy is a luxury enjoyed only by tension-free societies because those pervaded with racial problems must turn inward as their tensions mount. To the extent that this is so, there would be no necessary relationship, as Rummel and others have found, between internal and external conflict behavior. Such an argument has much to commend it. If tension rises, resources not previously devoted to the domestic scene must be allocated to the task of alleviating or otherwise coping with them. The recent history of the United States is illustrative in this regard, and a comparison of the domestic budgets of a number of countries racked by racial tension would undoubtedly show increases and decreases corresponding to periods of heightened and lessened tension. Yet greater preoccupation with internal problems need not be at the expense of external activities. On the contrary, we would contend that precisely because of the racial tensions, those responsible for foreign policy must be ever more active. They must deal with the consequences of the minorities' appeals for support abroad. The growing criticism in the foreign press must be answered.[48] The good intentions, or at least the

---

[48] For evidence that foreign criticism mounts as racial tensions increase see William Parente, "A Comparative Analysis of American Racial Conflict in the Communist Press" (Washington: American Political Science Association, mimeo., 1968).

sovereign rights, of the society must be asserted. Its prevailing practices must be explained. Its attempts to ameliorate tension must be proclaimed. And, equally important, notwithstanding the society's greater preoccupation with its domestic situation, the processes of world politics continue to unfold and to yield foreign situations to which it must respond. Indeed, where once the society may have been able to take a neutral or an accommodating stance toward most or all external situations, the dynamics of its mounting racial tensions seem likely to require it to publicly favor one or another of the contending parties in many of the situations. That is, as groups within the society become more sensitive to status, privilege, and justice, they will apply their refined criteria to external situations, if only as a means of giving greater force to the arguments they advance on the domestic scene. So it is, for example, that racial minorities around the world have been increasingly inclined to take stands on the race situation in the United States, just as American Negro leaders have become increasingly concerned about U.S. policy toward various conflict situations in Africa and Asia. Indeed, it was the Negro leaders who, perhaps more than any other group, compared the skin colors of the combatants in Vietnam.

For a variety of reasons, therefore, it seems plausible to anticipate that the foreign conflict behavior of societies will increase as their racial tensions mount. However, since the changing domestic scene is likely to require the allocation of new resources, it seems doubtful that the more costly forms of foreign conflict behavior will be employed. It is likely that they will be eschewed in favor of the less economically expensive techniques of adopting verbal stances toward or recalling diplomatic personnel from the external situations. In sum, our reasoning leads us to the following proposition:

Hypothesis SO$_1$: The more intense the racial tension in a society, the more likely its officials are to undertake or recommend the recall of diplomatic personnel from some parties to external conflicts and to express verbally support of other parties.

Author's Analytic Conscience: But what about Rummel and his colleagues? Are you simply going to ignore their findings? Are you going to put your impressionistic reasoning ahead of quantitative empirical data? Do you not have an obligation to offer some data of your own to justify your expectation that, as tension mounts in a society, foreign policy officials will engage in external behavior that reflects it?

Author: This is not the place to analyze Rummel's work. I respect it and delight in the fact that at long last quantitative inquiries have resulted in convergent findings in the study of international politics. However, I do not see the foregoing reasoning as a rejection of these findings. We are concerned here with a particular form of tension, whereas Rummel's research includes many forms. For reasons bearing on the intimacy of racial feelings, I would argue that the spiral precipitated by racial tensions is likely to be more intense and with more ramifications than those precipitated by other kinds of conflicts and that, accordingly, it is also more specific than the relationships reflected in Rummel's data. In addition, Rummel himself offers some reasons for believing that certain revisions in his assumptions and procedures would yield findings showing a stronger relationship between internal and external conflict behavior.[49]

As for data to support my own reasoning, I have been able to collect only a few and they are extremely rudimentary, certainly far from what is needed for a thorough test of Hypotheses SO_1. The data come from a comparison of the frequencies with which references with racial content (i.e., references to skin color or physical characteristics) occur in three weekly or bi-weekly publications distributed in the United States by three governments, that of Pakistan, West Germany, and South Africa.[50] Cast in the format of a newsletter, these publications are essentially public relations documents, designed to present the American reader with an up-to-date and favorable picture of life in the country distributing the newsletter. If a basic premise underlying Hypothesis SO_1 is valid—namely, that racial tensions cannot be confined within a society's boundaries and that its foreign policy officials are bound to be sensitive to its international implications—it ought to follow that these three countries, being so different in their racial compositions and histories of racial tension, should reveal strikingly different patterns when compared in this way. More specifically, assuming that racial tensions in South Africa are much more intense than in the two other countries and that they are least intense in Pakistan (which is racially homogeneous, whereas West Germany has the problem of anti-Semitism), it can be expected that the South African publication would yield the most references to race and the Pakistani one least, the West German publication falling in between. Such an expectation was fully confirmed. As can be seen in Table 16–2, except for one year the figures for South Africa are more than thirty times larger than those for Pakistan, and in all cases the figure for West Germany falls between the other two.

To be sure, these data are skimpy and they do not necessarily reflect

---

[49] In J. D. Singer (ed.), *Quantitative International Politics*, pp. 213–214.

[50] *Pakistan Affairs* (issued by the Embassy of Pakistan, Washington, D.C.); *The Bulletin* (issued by the Press and Information Office of the German Federal Government); and *News from South Africa* (issued by the Information Service of South Africa, New York).

Table 16 – 2   The Racial Content of Weekly Newsletters Distributed in The United States by Three Governments

	1963	1964	1965	1966	1967	1968	All years
Pakistan	.4	3.0	1.2	.8	.2	.4	.9
South Africa	27.8	31.4	33.8	32.6	38.8	36.3	33.6
West Germany	27.0	*	*	16.5	6.3	7.9	7.9

*publications not available

the kind of behavior referred to in Hypothesis SO_1. Yet, although they certainly are not proof of anything, they are relevant to the foregoing reasoning and they do not negate it. Thus while Rummel's data cannot be ignored and are the kind that need to be gathered for hypothesis-testing purposes, it seems legitimate to retain Hypothesis SO_1, although it is derived mainly from theoretical rather than empirical sources. Indeed, the foregoing analysis suggests that the potency of the tension variable is sufficient to justify similar propositions with respect to its interaction with nonracial individual, role, and societal variables. Although in Hypothesis R_6 considerable potency was attached to the nonracial societal variables on the grounds that the processes of differentiation inherent in economic development were likely to diminish the role requirement that officials attach racial relevance to external situations, such an estimate was based on the assumption that other variables remained constant and did not account for the presence of mounting racial tensions. Once tensions begin to mount, however, it seems unlikely that the extent to which a society has passed through the various stages of economic development would have any consequence for the spiraling processes that accompany racial crises. Similarly, in view of the reasoning developed above, it is hard to imagine how officials who are not racially conscious, or who have had extensive foreign affairs experience, or whose role requires them to attach greater importance to the economic content of external situations than to their racial relevance, can long remain unaffected by increasing racial tensions within their societies. Their experience may lead them to avoid resorting to the recall of diplomatic personnel, but it seems unlikely that they will be able to maintain a posture of neutrality toward external situations. Some long-time American officials, for example, may feel privately that the situations in Biafra and elsewhere in Africa are peripheral problems relative to the main thrust of world politics, but that has not been the basis of their public stance toward such issues since race has become such a tension-ridden aspect of American life in the 1960s. In short, our analysis leads us to three additional propositions that run counter to Rummel's findings:

Hypothesis SO₂: Other things being equal, the more a society is marked by racial tension, the more likely are its officials, irrespective of the extent of their experience in foreign affairs or their degree of racial consciousness, to undertake or recommend the expression of verbal support for parties to external conflicts.

Hypothesis SO₃: Other things being equal, the more a society is marked by racial tension, the more likely are its officials, irrespective of role requirements that minimize the racial relevance of external situations and maximize the importance of trade and aid, to attach racial relevance to external situations and to undertake or recommend the recall of diplomatic personnel from some parties to them and the expression of verbal support for others.

Hypothesis SO₄: Other things being equal, the more a society is marked by racial tension, and irrespective of its degree of economic development, the more likely are its officials to undertake or recommend the recall of diplomatic personnel from some parties to external conflicts and the expression of verbal support of other parties.

But the potency of race-susceptible societal variables is not unlimited. As has already been indicated in the derivation of Hypothesis G_3, some moderation of their strength can be anticipated in their interaction with at least one governmental variable, the authority structure variable. It seems clear that the spiraling processes that accompany mounting racial tensions are likely to unfold more rapidly and fully in open societies than in closed ones. The governments of the latter are not only much more capable of suppressing civil disorder than are those of the former, but their very structure also makes them more inclined to use repressive measures against minorities. The spiraling process may never be entirely subject to governmental control, but its pace and continuity are likely to be responsive to the degree to which officialdom is accessible and amenable to demands for new statuses on the part of racial minorities. Accordingly, the following proposition can be derived:

Hypothesis SO₅: Other things being equal, the officials of an open society marked by a high degree of racial tension are more likely than those of a closed society with similar degrees of tension to undertake or recommend the recall of diplomatic personnel from some parties to external situations and the expression of verbal support for other parties.

The relationship between racial tensions and the executive form variable, on the other hand, is less clear. Both a presidential and cabinet system with more than one political party are open authority structures. Thus they will both be sensitive to rising tension and receptive to its inherent demands. Whether the differences in the degree to which responsibility is concentrated in their respective executives will make a presidential system more sensitive and receptive than a cabinet system seems doubtful. The one case in which this difference might be sufficient to account for a large difference in external behavior is a cabinet system in a fragmented society with many political parties. In such a multiparty system, as compared to a two- or three-party cabinet system, racial minorities might have sufficient organizational strength to place their party representatives among the top policy-making officials. Under these conditions, of course, there would be an especially strong inclination for officials to attach racial relevance to conflict situations abroad and to take a stance toward them. Most cabinet systems, however, are not multiracial in composition, so that a general proposition that predicts an interaction between the executive form variable and the race-susceptible societal variable seems unwarranted. By a process of elimination, therefore, the following has been derived:

Hypothesis SO₆: Other things being equal, the more an open society is marked by racial tension, the more likely are its top policy-making officials, irrespective of whether they hold office in presidential or cabinet forms of government, to undertake or recommend the recall of diplomatic personnel from some parties to external situations and the expression of verbal support for other parties.

An analysis of the interaction between the race-susceptible societal variable and the nonracial systemic variables also suggests that the potency of the former is not unlimited. This is particularly so in the case of the global structure variable. At least one key aspect of the spiraling process that accompanies racial tension, the tendencies for minorities to seek support abroad, seems likely to be affected by the degree of looseness in the polarity of the global system. The looser the system, the more success are the minorities likely to have in their search for support. Virtually by definition, there is more flexibility in a loosely structured system than in a tightly structured one for new arrangements to develop in the relationships among its members. Hence the evolution of both moral and substantive ties between the minorities and external groups or governments would be tolerated, if not accepted, by the great powers in a loosely structured system. The interaction of the two variables is such that it might even be argued that the external support-seeking efforts of racial minorities contributes to the loosening of the system once it has begun to move away from an extremely tight form of bipolarity. Or at least it would not be difficult to find historical connections between the loosening of the global system and the rising racial consciousness of black groups in Africa during the 1950s. In a tightly structured system, on the other hand, the improbability of obtaining external support would lessen the pressures that the minorities put on officials and, accordingly, their readiness to engage in external conflict behavior. In the light of this reasoning, the following proposition about the interaction between the global structure and racial tension variables can be derived:

Hypothesis SO_7: Other things being equal, the officials of a society marked by racial tensions are more likely to undertake or recommend foreign conflict behavior in a loose bipolar system than in a tightly structured one.

Reflection on the interaction of the situation and tension variables makes it difficult to maintain the assumption that other things are equal. If all the restraints of diplomacy are ignored, an unlikely circumstance (see Hypothesis R_8), a racially tense society could be expected to press officials to take a greater interest in intrasocietal situations abroad than intersocietal ones. The various parties to the spiraling tension are more likely to perceive counterparts similarly embattled within other societies and to regard intersocietal situations as incomparable, if not as largely irrelevant. The problems of NATO, for example, do not arouse the American Negro, whereas the problems of South Africa do. Furthermore, from the perspective of minorities seeking support abroad, the unfolding circumstances within other societies will seem to be a much more important determinant of the support they can procure than will intersocietal situations. Support comes mainly from other countries, not from their interactions. To be sure, international organizations can provide support, but their decisions in regard to intervention are highly political and the result of how their members vote, which depends largely on the unfolding circumstances within other societies. For a variety of reasons, therefore, racially tense societies will tend to press their officials to be especially active with respect to intrasocietal situations. This tendency, however, is unlikely to prevail, given the strength of the previously noted pressures not to violate the principle of national sovereignty. Nevertheless, for the sake of completeness, the following can be logically derived:

Hypothesis SO_8: Other things being equal, the officials of societies marked by racial tension are more likely to undertake or recommend foreign conflict behavior toward intrasocietal than toward intersocietal situations.

                        Systemic Variables — Do race-pervaded external situations evoke more foreign conflict behavior than race-free ones? Is the strength of the nonracial variables from the several clusters moderated in the former type? These are the essential questions to be probed in an analysis of the race-susceptible systemic variable and the ensuing hypotheses suggest that considerable potency accrues to the combination of racial and systemic factors. This is perhaps less apparent in a consideration of the univariate hypothesis addressed to the first question than it is in the remainder of the analysis. For while it seems clear that race-pervaded situations are likely to arouse the concern of more nations than are race-free ones, it seems equally clear that the former are likely to evoke more violent forms of conflict behavior. Racial factors can lead to the use of military threats and action (see Hypothesis n_1 below), but it does not take much reflection to realize that most wars are fought over territory, legitimacy, and a host of considerations that have little to do with physical characteristics. Indeed, reasons for anticipating that racial factors frequently will lead to verbal rather than military forms of conflict behavior have already been noted (see the derivation of Hypothesis SO_1). Hence, it seems unrealistic to posit race-pervaded situations as evoking more intense conflict behavior than race-free ones. On the other hand, a contrary conclusion suggests itself if stress is placed on the extensity of conflict behavior. For a variety of reasons, race-pervaded situations seem likely to evoke verbal stances on the part of many more societies than race-free situations. Partly because a sense of justice and of basic human rights are so central to racial issues, but perhaps more because race-pervaded situations abroad can serve as a mirror to race relations at home, external developments that are pervaded with racial relevance are not likely to seem so remote as those that are sustained by other types of values. Except for superpowers and nations in the same region, for example, most societies have no reason to get involved in a nationality war in Cyprus, a territorial dispute over Kashmir, or a *coup d'état* in Brazil. Why offend the Turks or the Greeks, or the Indians or the Pakistani, or some Brazilians by taking a stand on these situations since their repercussions are likely to be local rather than global in scope? The question is rhetorical and thus most societies choose to remain silent with respect to most situations outside their regions. Racially explosive situations abroad, however, will not seem so distant nor so narrow in scope. The demonstration effect is not geographically bound and thus a South African can seem very proximate, or at least not so distant as to justify silence. Accordingly, it seems reasonable to derive the following prediction:

Hypothesis SY$_1$: Other things being equal, the top policy-makers of a society are more likely to undertake or recommend a verbal stance toward race-pervaded external situations than toward race-free ones.

Comparisons between the race-susceptible systemic variable and those from the individual and role clusters are not difficult to make. There would seem to be little question, essentially for the same reasons as those set forth above, that the former is capable of erasing the differences among the latter. It is difficult to imagine that officials who are personally not conscious of physical characteristics, or whose long experience in international affairs makes them keenly aware of the limits of foreign policy, could ignore external situations that are pervaded by racial connotations. On the contrary, once such situations come into being, even the least racially conscious and most experienced official seems likely to become sensitive to them and to the external behavior they may necessitate. External situations do not transform personalities, but they can transform personal orientations. Those that turn on the status ascribed to skin color are so laden with uncertainty and so infused with values as to be among those that are capable of transforming individual predispositions. Given their potential for precipitating chainlike reactions elsewhere in the world, much the same can be said about the impact of race-pervaded situations on top policy-making roles. Even the requirement that officials not attach racial relevance to external situations would seem subject to modification when overtones of racial conflict become manifest in developments abroad. Role variables may be powerful enough to lead to the attachment of relevance to nonracial situations (see Hypothesis R$_7$), but they do not appear so powerful as to prevent the attachment of relevance to racial ones. This asymmetry can be explained in terms of the role requirement that impels officials to maximize their information about the factors at work in the international system, whatever significance they may then be required to attach to these factors. The rationality inherent in this role requirement may not lead immediately to the transformation of the low extreme of the relevance variable, since race-pervaded situations can be slow to emerge; but the more manifest their racial content becomes, the less will officials be able to treat them as nonracial or to consider only their implications for foreign trade and aid programs. The postwar American experience is illustrative in relation to both the individual and role variables. Starting in the late 1950s, as racial situations on the African continent became progressively explosive, the priorities whereby U.S. officials were preoccupied with the defense of Europe and unconcerned about race relations abroad were gradually changed, if not reversed. And, eventually, so was the value that policy be conducted irrespective of race, creed, and color. Today Negro ambassadors are assigned to African posts partly because race is relevant to the situations they will have to face, an assessment which an earlier generation of policy-makers were required to avoid. In short, there is reason to have confidence in the validity of the following derivations:

Hypothesis SY_2: Other things being equal, top policy-making officials, irrespective of their prior personal and professional experience, are more likely to undertake or recommend a verbal stance toward race-pervaded situations than toward race-free ones.

Hypothesis SY_3: Other things being equal, top policy-making officials, irrespective of any other requirements built into their positions, are more likely to undertake or recommend verbal stances toward race-pervaded than toward race-free situations.

Nor does the potency of the race-susceptible systemic variable seem likely to be offset by the nonracial governmental and societal variables. Whether a governmental system is opened or closed, or whether it is structured along presidential or cabinet lines, the implications of race-pervaded situations will doubtless be appreciated by those responsible for the conduct of foreign policy. The fact that closed systems can maintain control over the internal repercussions of external racial conflicts is not a reason for the officials of such systems to minimize their existence. On the contrary, these controls may seem especially vulnerable to the demonstration effects that foreign racial conflicts can precipitate, making the top policy-makers of such societies just as sensitive to race-pervaded situations as those who preside over open societies. Similarly, these sensitivities seem unlikely to be differentially affected by the degree to which the policy-maker's society is economically developed. Development may introduce cross-cutting relationships that highlight an ever-wider range of issues and reduce the relative potency of the relevance variable (see Hypothesis R_6), but this is not to say that sensitivity will be reduced to situations abroad that are unmistakably race-pervaded. Only when the racial content of situations is unclear does the potency of the development variable seem likely to prevail. For a number of previously cited reasons, therefore, the following propositions can also be derived:

Hypothesis SY_4: Other things being equal, top policy-making officials, irrespective of the authority structure and executive form of their government, are more likely to undertake or recommend a verbal stance toward race-pervaded than toward race-free situations.

Hypothesis SY_5: Other things being equal, top policy-making officials, irrespective of the extent to which their society is economically developed, are more likely to undertake or recommend a verbal stance toward race-pervaded than race-free situations.

Like all the variables considered here, however, the race-susceptible systemic variable is not so powerful as not to be modified by any other. An analysis of its interaction with nonracial systemic variables leads to the identification of ways in which its potency can be expected to vary. For reasons that have already been outlined, variations in the global structure and situational variables seem likely to offset the extent to which race-pervaded situations are the focus of foreign conflict behavior. That is, it is difficult to conceive of reasons why the potency of such situations should be impervious to the increased likelihood of great power intervention when the structure of the international system moves toward lesser tightness or to the greater restraint of diplomacy which the norms of diplomatic practice impose when the locale of racial conflict moves from an intersocietal to an intrasocietal setting. To be sure, the norms may be undergoing transformation in the Rhodesian and South African situations, but these are exceptional cases that are unlikely to set a precedent insofar as most intrasocietal situations are concerned. Even in these cases, moreover, the operation of diplomatic norms is evident. It is hard to imagine that the foreign conflict behavior directed toward them would be confined to verbal stances and economic sanctions if their scope was intersocietal. Accordingly, the following propositions suggest themselves:

Hypothesis SY_6: Other things being equal, the looser the structure of the international system, the more likely are top policy-making officials to undertake or recommend a verbal stance toward race-pervaded situations.

Hypothesis SY$_7$: Other things being equal, top policy-makers are likely
to undertake or recommend less foreign conflict behavior toward
race-pervaded situations within other societies than toward comparable situations among other societies.

V. EPILOGUE

Author's Analytic Conscience: I have two questions.
Author's Moral Conscience: I have one.
Author: Keep them brief.
Author's Analytic Conscience: Your use of the dependent variable
is puzzling. At the outset you indicated that the hypotheses would predict
six forms of foreign conflict behavior, but in fact they are confined to
anticipating either unspecified types of behavior or to predicting that
the least violent forms will be employed. At no point do your derivations
include the use of violent techniques of statecraft. Why, then, did you
conceptualize the dependent variables to include the threat or use of
military action?

Author: The expectation that the analysis would yield hypotheses
that embraced the full range of dependent variables proved to be unwarranted. In retrospect it is clear that resort to the more violent forms of
conflict behavior is never due to one or two factors and that it was
unrealistic to expect that univariate or bivariate hypotheses could be
derived that embraced all the dependent variables. If the prohibition
against multivariate analysis is relaxed, however, it becomes possible to
specify one set of conditions that is likely to result in some form of
military operations, namely, when the high extremes of all the race-susceptible variables are operating simultaneously. Under these circumstances
it seems doubtful whether any of the usual restraints on foreign conflict
behavior will be sufficient to curb the impulse to go to war, a conclusion
which is presently being tested by events in Rhodesia and South Africa.
Thus, by altering our procedures with respect to the independent variables,
the other dependent variables can reasonably be included in the following
derivation:

Hypothesis n_1: Other things being equal, if racially conscious persons
hold the top policy-making positions of a society, if these positions
require them to attach a high degree of racial relevance to external
situations, and if racial tensions in the society are extensive when
a race-pervaded situation abroad becomes critical, then the officials
of the society are likely to undertake or recommend military action
with respect to the situation.

Author's Analytic Conscience: My other question concerns the task of putting any or all of your hypotheses to an empirical test. I wonder if some of your variables can be satisfactorily operationalized. How does one get at the consciousness of individuals, delineate the requirements of roles, or measure the degree to which external situations are race-pervaded? These complex phenomena do not readily lend themselves to observation.

Author: They certainly do not, but I have always felt that the most serious obstacles to research are theoretical and that, if meaningful hypotheses can be derived, all else will gradually fall into place. Operational definitions can always be developed, if necessary through the use of panels of judges who are asked to classify particular phenomena in terms of the researcher's categories. Useful theory, on the other hand, is much more difficult to generate. As indicated earlier, most inquiries into world politics are nontheoretical and, even worse, few of them aspire to the construction of middle- or high-level theory. Perhaps one reason for this situation is that the empirical complexities always seem too great to justify formulation of generalized propositions. Here we have sought to avoid this constraint by emphasizing the derivation of hypotheses and leaving the task of testing them for later. Doubtless some hypotheses will prove to be ill-founded and unwieldy, if not untestable. But, to repeat, bad theory is preferable to no theory. Of course, good theory is preferable to bad theory, but the extent of our success in this respect cannot be judged until the empirical task is undertaken.

Author's Moral Conscience: One final question. You indicated at the outset some doubt about the importance of the role of racial factors in world politics. Yet, your hypotheses and their underlying reasoning attribute considerable potency to race-susceptible variables. It is as if the more you thought about them, the more you recognized how crucial they could be. How do you reconcile your initial doubts and your conclusions?

Author: I told you that moral ends are not forsaken, and may even be served, by scientific inquiry.

17 Foreign Policy as an Issue Area *

The concept of an issue plays an inconsistent and deleterious role in political analysis. On the one hand, many analysts ignore it and presume that the political process unfolds similarly with respect to any issue. On the other hand, numerous analysts accord such a prominent place to the concept that the political process is assumed to be as infinitely variable as the issues that sustain it.

"You cannot make such a statement," the latter say to the former, "it all depends on the issue."

"Sure we can," respond the former, "political systems have general characteristics that are operative irrespective of the issue being processed at any moment in time."

It is a major contention of this chapter that both approaches are insufficient but that an empirically accurate and theoretically viable approach lies between them. Stated succinctly, the approach suggested here rests on the premise that it all depends on the issue-area.

I. THE PROBLEM OF ISSUE PHENOMENA

Before examining the issue-area concept, however, it is useful to look

*Earlier versions of this chapter were presented at the Conference on Public Opinion and Foreign Policy, sponsored by the Foreign Policy Association and the Center of International Studies, Princeton University in March, 1965, and published in James N. Rosenau (ed.), *Domestic Sources of Foreign Policy* (New York: Free Press, 1967), pp. 11–50. Reprinted with the permission of the publisher. Copyright 1967 by The Free Press, a division of The Macmillan Company.

briefly at the ways in which the two prevailing approaches hold back political inquiry. Perhaps the greatest damage is done by those who emphasize the infinite variability of issues and their effects. The notion that the outcome of an interaction sequence is dependent on the issue that precipitated it rests on the premise that each issue either encompasses different actors whose motives vary in intensity and direction or evokes different motives on the part of the same actors. Regardless of the identity of the actors, therefore, the interaction patterns that unfold with respect to each issue are presumed to be too distinctive to permit generalizing about the operation of political systems.

Such reasoning thus serves as one of the great bulwarks against inquiry. It provides a simple and effective means of cutting off any discussion of the political process. By observing that "it all depends on the issue," one can quickly halt any effort at generalization. The strength of a political party becomes unassessable because on some issues the party is unified and on others it is fragmented. The stability of an international relationship becomes incalculable because the parties to it agree on some issues and differ on others. The influence of a leader becomes inestimable because the public is responsive on some issues and not responsive on others. The effectiveness of an interest group becomes unmeasurable because on some issues it commands respect and on others it does not. Indeed, there is hardly a political phenomenon that has not been assumed to be so subject to issue fluctuation as to render futile any attempts to trace general patterns.

Perhaps in reaction to the paralyzing implications of this approach, general theorists have tended either to ignore the relevance of issue fluctuation or to assume that its impact on the political process is not sufficient to warrant theoretical attention. Models of the legislative process depict structures and functions, but these are usually posited as unvarying in the way in which they handle different types of issues. Formulations of the processes by which equilibrium is maintained in party, national, and international systems do not conceive of various equilibria constantly replacing each other as the focus of systemic activity moves from one type of issue to another. Most models of executive and bureaucratic decision-making also tend to presume an underlying uniformity and to delineate a process that is undifferentiated by the matters that are the subject of decision. Similarly, those who focus on the linkage between public opinion and foreign policy tend to ignore the differential impact of issues. Virtually every model presently available posits foreign policy as a constant, as a set of values and activities that are taken for granted and assumed to be unvarying in the motives, interests, and processes they activate. Indeed, there is hardly a major type of political process which has not been denuded of issue fluctuation by the theory-builders.

To be sure, theorists allow for variability in the functioning of political systems. Considerable attention is devoted to both the potentialities for and the processes of change in the operation of legislatures, party systems, international organizations, bureaucracies, and all the other units that serve as theoretical foci. But the variability and the change always seem to be attributed to structural or capability components of systems and not to their functional or dynamic elements. Variability is seen to exist in the functioning of legislatures when, say, the size of the majority alters, but it is not also seen when the focus of activity shifts from one type of consideration to another. Variability in the operation of international systems is conceived to exist when the capabilities of one or another bloc increase or diminish, but variation is not also ascribed to changes in the matters that occupy the attention of diplomats.

Whatever the reason for this neglect of issue fluctuation—and many possible sources could be cited[1]—it clearly seems to be unwarranted. There is abundant evidence that motives, actors, and interaction sequences do not remain constant for all issues and that therefore the functioning of political systems can be differentiated in terms of the values that are being contested. Election campaigns in open systems are a good case in point. Most candidates or parties scour the contemporary scene in search of the one or two issues that will appeal to the electorate and bring about victory at the polls. Presumably such behavior is based on the premise that voters distinguish between issues, that they are aroused by some and bored by others, and that consequently the task of a campaign is to identify the combination of issues which is most likely to activate support.

Nor does one have to look far to find empirical support for the politician's wisdom. For years his presumption that success depends on the achievement of consonance with the changing concerns of the electorate has been amply demonstrated by nationwide poll data showing variations

---

[1] One important source is the conception that a major function of political systems is that of aggregating issues, of canceling out conflicts between issues so that systems can endure without being dominated by a single issue or a single cluster of issues. In this sense, political systems are treated as being, so to speak, above issues. They are viewed as impartial arbiters of the many conflicts which are outstanding at any moment in time and which might bring about chaos if the system did not exercise supervision. In fact, of course, many political systems are single-issue dominant and they can collapse when the dominant issue is either resolved or otherwise removed. The loss of integrative potential suffered by many newly established Asian and African systems is an obvious example: when independence has removed the anticolonial issue, fragmentation has often followed.

in attitudinal structure and intensity from one issue to another.[2] Equally clear-cut are the interview data that describe the large degree to which people, in face-to-face situations, are influenced by different opinion leaders on different issues.[3]

But issue fluctuation is not confined to the intellectual-emotional processes of the individual and the resulting patterns of mass opinion. Systematic analyses of the functioning of all types of political systems— from local to national to international on the geographic scale and from party to legislative to executive at the functional level—are also converging on the finding that different types of issues elicit different sets of motives on the part of different actors in a political system, that different system members are thus activated by different issues, and that the different inter-action patterns that result from these variations produce different degrees of systemic stability for each type of issue. Data along these lines have already been indicated for local and national systems,[4] and it is not difficult to cite comparable findings that are descriptive of issue differences at the international level. Hovet's inquiry into the patterns of bloc voting in the United Nations is illustrative in this regard. Leaving aside the Soviet bloc, the degree of coherence within the other nine blocs examined was found to vary substantially when broken down in terms of some seven types of recurrent issues in the General Assembly.[5] Consequently, just as it seems necessary to posit the existence of at least three New Haven political systems and at least two American national systems,[6] so does it appear reasonable to conclude that, insofar as the functioning of international organizations is concerned, there are at least several inter-national systems and that to comprehend the processes of any one of them is not necessarily to grasp how the others function.

II. THE NEED FOR AN ISSUE-AREA TYPOLOGY

In short, there is ample evidence for presuming that the functioning of a political system depends on the nature of the issues that it is proc-essing at any moment in time. Such a presumption poses an important conceptual challenge: how to accommodate issue-generated differences

[2] V. O. Key, Jr., *Public Opinion and American Democracy* (New York: Knopf, 1961), Chap. 9.
[3] Elihu Katz and Paul F. Lazarsfeld, *Personal Influence: The Part Played by People in the Flow of Communications* (New York: Free Press, 1955).
[4] See Chapter 6.
[5] Thomas Hovet, Jr., *Bloc Politics in the United Nations* (Cambridge: Harvard University Press, 1960), *passim*.
[6] See pp. 133–34.

without permitting their multitude to overwhelm analysis and reduce it to a fragmented and idiographic enterprise. The response is as obvious as it is difficult to implement. What is needed is a typology of issue-areas—of categories of issues that affect the political process in sufficiently similar ways to justify being clustered together. If the entire range of issues that are processed by political systems could be classified into a manageable number of mutually exclusive areas, with each area distinguished by the political dynamics it generates, then it should be possible to probe the political process without being paralyzed by idiographic description.

The construction of such an issue-area typology, however, is not a simple task. An imposing set of theoretical and operational problems must be overcome: On what bases are the many values and interests over which men differ to be clustered together into distinctive issue-areas? At what level of abstraction should they be clustered? Are the boundaries of each area to be defined in terms of the nature of the issues they encompass, the nature of the processes through which the issues are resolved, or the kinds of units in which they are activated? How many areas would be both empirically manageable and theoretically viable? How similar must issues be to justify treating them as falling within the same area? What aspects of the political process are affected by the nature of issues and how do these issue-generated differences vary from one area to another?

While a full response to these questions cannot be undertaken here, some general guidelines can be noted. Plainly, a typology of issue-areas ought to be something more than a mere catalogue of the matters over which men are divided at any moment in time. As has already been implied, not much would be accomplished if "issue-area" came to mean nothing more than that which is conventionally designated as an "issue," namely, any conflict over values or interests among identifiable individuals or groups. Rather, a typology of issue-areas must be cast in sufficiently abstract terms to encompass past and future conflicts as well as present ones. To posit issue-areas as persisting beyond the lives of particular actors, it is necessary to conceive of them as structures of roles that derive their patterned relationship to each other from the nature of the values or interests they encompass. That is, each issue-area must be seen as comprised of certain kinds of actors whose values and interests are such that they can be expected to engage in certain kinds of behavior when issues are activated in the area. If, for example, a civil rights area were included in the typology, its structure would include minority group leaders, journalists and other civic leaders in ethnically heterogeneous urban communities, law-enforcement officers, certain governmental officials, and a variety of others likely to be sympathetic or opposed to civil rights.

It follows that several aspects of the political process can be traced to the nature of issues. The intensity and extensity of the motivation that leads citizens and officials to participate in a controversy seems to be clearly a function of the values and interests that are being contraverted. Similarly, the number and identity of the roles, both in and out of government, that are politically active at any moment in time are manifestly a consequence of the nature of the issues that the system is processing at that moment. In addition to motivational intensity and role activation, and partly as a consequence of these variables, the direction and degree of the interaction through which issues are processed would also appear to be shaped by the values and interests at stake.

General guidelines are much more difficult to establish with respect to the questions of how the boundaries of issue-areas should be delineated and of how issues should be classified within them. Both the possibilities and the difficulties can be indicated through a brief examination of some of the crude categories that are generally used, often unknowingly, to denote broad classes of issues. Three kinds of issue-area typologies frequently seem to be embedded in discussions of the political process. One might be called a *value* typology, wherein issues are clustered together on the basis of the kinds of values or interests over which controversy ensues. The widespread tendency to distinguish among, say, agriculture, labor, education, and finance issues exemplifies the employment of a value typology. Such typologies rest on the assumption that significantly different goals underlie the major activities comprising the life of a community, and thus value typologies consist of as many issue-areas as seem appropriate to account for the diverse pursuits of the community. In a second kind of typology, issues are clustered together on the basis of the kinds of processes through which they are conducted and settled. This can be designated a *process* typology and it is illustrated by the inclination to differentiate between, say, legal and administrative issues or crisis and routine issues. Underlying the use of process typologies is the premise that issues which are resolved in the same way also tap similar motives and activate similar roles. The third technique of classifying issues is what we shall label the *unit* typology. In this widely used approach, issues are clustered together on the basis of the kinds of units in or for which they are contested. The local-national and domestic-foreign dichotomizations of issues are illustrative of unit typologies and of the premise that issues processed in one (local-national) or for one (domestic-foreign) type of unit evoke significantly different motives and roles than do those processed in or for other kinds of units.

That such typologies pose complex problems for those who would use them can be readily discerned in the few systematic efforts to employ the issue-area concept as an analytic tool. Perhaps most revealing in this regard is Dahl's inquiry into the politics of New Haven.[7] Although not intended as an elaboration of the concept, this work is illustrative of a value typology. His three issue-areas represent different aspects of life in New Haven and each consists of more than a single issue in the sense that his investigations in each area focused on more than a single conflict of values and the interaction sequence through which it was processed and resolved. In all, thirty-four major interaction sequences (or, as Dahl calls them, "decisions") that spanned different segments of an eighteen-year period were examined, and eight of these were considered to be, on the one hand, distinct from the other twenty-four and, on the other hand, sufficiently alike to cluster together into the "urban redevelopment" area. A similar process led to the clustering of another eight into the "education" area and the remaining eighteen into the "nominations" area.

While the derivation of the last of these areas presents no serious difficulty—since the motives, roles, and processes involved in contesting a mayoralty nomination arise out of clear and long established sources that presumably were operative in all eighteen of the issues classified in the area—the first two are not so narrowly bounded and, in their greater diversity, pose troublesome conceptual and empirical problems. Consider first the eight major decisional sequences that Dahl identifies as falling within the redevelopment area:

1. Creating the Redevelopment Agency.
2. Building and extending the Oak Street Connector.
3. Redeveloping the Oak Street area.
4. Creating the Citizens Action Commission.
5. Redeveloping the Church Street area.
6. Redeveloping the Wooster Square area.
7. The Long Wharf project.
8. Negotiations between Savitt, a jeweler, and the city over the proper price for his property.[8]

Some of these issues, to be sure, are as much alike as any two mayoralty nominations are to each other. Presumably, for example, the goals, roles, and interaction patterns involved in the third, fifth, and sixth issues are virtually identical, differing only to the extent that the configuration and residents of Oak Street, Church Street, and Wooster Square differed. Likewise, it is not difficult to presume similarity between the sequences whereby the Redevelopment Agency and the Citizens Action

[7] Robert A. Dahl, *Who Governs: Democracy and Power in an American City* (New Haven: Yale University Press, 1961).
[8] *Ibid.*, p. 333.

Commission came into being. On the other hand, assumptions become more tenuous and data more elusive when, say, the clustering together of the first and last of the issues is considered. The immediate values at stake in the creation of the Redevelopment Agency and the acquisition of Savitt's property were obviously disparate. Due to the legal measures that Savitt took in order to get a higher price for his property, some of the roles and interaction patterns activated by the two issues were no less disparate. Clearly, therefore, Dahl was compelled to presume that the more general goals of a modernized New Haven gave sufficient commonality to these seemingly diverse interaction sequences to justify clustering them together. Upon investigation, some support for this presumption was found. Creation of the Redevelopment Agency initiated a shorter and much less complex interaction sequence than did the acquisition of Savitt's property, but many of the same leadership roles participated in essentially the same ways in both situations. Nonetheless, to classify these two issues in the same area is plainly to make a delicate set of assumptions for which the empirical evidence is not abundant.

Much the same can be said about the eight major "decisions on public schools" which Dahl grouped into the "education" area:

1. Selling the high schools to Yale and building two new ones.
2. Accepting or rejecting a proposal to change procedures on promotions.
3. Major appointments, particularly an assistant superintendent for secondary education.
4. An eye-testing program.
5. A proposed ratio plan on salaries.
6. Budgets.
7. A proposal to deal with delinquency.
8. Proposals to increase appropriations for school libraries.[9]

Again it seems clear that several of the issues are highly comparable but that in a couple of instances the clustering would appear to rest more on analytic presumptions than on empirical data. In drawing boundaries around such seemingly diverse considerations as, say, how to test the sight of pupils, whom to appoint as an assistant superintendent, and whether to accept the new ratio plan on salaries, Dahl again had to rely on the unverified premise that at a higher level of generalization—namely, the one delineated by the goal of perfecting the educational system of New Haven—the motives, roles, and interaction patterns involved in these issues converged sufficiently to warrant classifying them in the same area.[10]

[9] *Ibid.*

[10] It should be re-emphasized that in raising these questions about the clustering of issues within the same area we are not doubting the distinctions among the

If Dahl's inquiry suggests some of the problems inherent in the construction of issue-area typologies, the work of Theodore J. Lowi provides an exciting glimpse into their potential utility.[11] Where Dahl lacks explicitness about the motives, roles, and interaction sequences common to the issues in each area. Lowi's typology is exceedingly self-conscious in this respect. Its main focus is the national system of the United States, but it is at the same time a process typology that contains an explicit rationale for attributing similar underpinnings to seemingly different issues. Indeed, Lowi explicitly asserts that each area (his term is "arena") of the typology "tends to develop its own characteristic political structure, political process, elites, and group relations." [12]

Instead of subdividing the community in terms of the many activities that sustain it, Lowi starts from the premise that in politics governmental policies determine the conflicting expectations of people and that political issues therefore arise out of "the impact or expected impact on the society" of governmental policies.[13] This approach enables him to construct his typology at a more general level than Dahl's and to classify all domestic issues within three areas. One encompasses issues that arise around the *distribution* of resources; another embraces conflicts over the *regulation* of the use of resources; and the third subsumes disputes over the *redistribution* of resources. For reasons that are too complex to elaborate here, Lowi's derivations allow him to equate the interaction sequences in each of the three areas with, respectively, the coalition, pluralist, and elitist models of the political process. Indeed, so convincing is the logic of his scheme that it seems entirely justifiable for him to delineate each area in terms of the "primary political unit," the "relation among units," the "power structure," the "stability of structure," the "primary decisional locus," and the process of "implementation" that it encompasses.[14]

What Lowi's formulation lacks is the kind of quantified data that Dahl gathered as a basis for discerning the presence of different political structures within each issue-area. At best, Lowi shows how the findings

---

areas. As has already been indicated, ample evidence confirming existence of boundaries separating the areas was uncovered by Dahl when he found a startling lack of overlap between the leadership roles activated in each area.

11 The most thoroughgoing formulation of his typology, along with the promise of subsequent elaboration at book length, is presented in "American Business, Public Policy, Case-Studies, and Political Theory," *World Politics*, XVI (July, 1964), pp. 677–715. For an earlier, more restricted, and less developed version of the typology, as well as some supporting empirical data, see Theodore J. Lowi, *At the Pleasure of the Mayor* (New York: Free Press, 1964), Chaps. 6 and 7.

12 "American Business, Public Policy, Case-Studies, and Political Theory," pp. 689–690.

13 *Ibid.*, p. 689.

14 See his "diagrammatic summary," *ibid.*, p. 713.

of another recent study[15] take on added meaning when reinterpreted in the light of his scheme. But this weakness may be short-lived. Lowi makes a persuasive case for expecting that the findings of empirical inquiry will uphold his distinctions among the three areas. Clearly a major break-through in political theory will have occurred if, as seems likely, it proves possible to accommodate issue-generated differences at this level of analysis.[16]

III. THE FOREIGN-DOMESTIC DISTINCTION

For present purposes, Lowi's typology is more a source of encourage-ment than an instrument of analysis. It suggests that theorizing about issue-areas is likely to pay off, but it offers no help with respect to the main concern of this chapter. Here we want to assess the validity and utility of one particular unit typology, namely, the one in which domestic policy issues are presumed to be different from foreign policy issues. The latter are not included in Lowi's scheme. He regards them as "not part of the same universe" and puts them aside as "obviously a fourth category" of issues in addition to the three domestic types.[17] Hence we must make a fresh start in our effort to determine whether foreign policy is indeed a different universe of issues and, if it is, whether it is a unified world or one divisible into several logical areas.

The task is not an easy one. Perhaps because the question straddles the fields of national and international politics, it has not been systemati-cally explored and discussion of it consists largely of either unrefined impressions or gross contradictions. Numerous observers compare, briefly and on the basis of unstated assumptions, the foreign and domestic realms in the course of launching an analysis of world affairs. Gunnar Myrdal, for example, recently noted: "After two decades of continuous study, I have come to the conclusion that foreign-policy decisions are usually

[15] Raymond A. Bauer, Ithiel de Sola Pool, and Lewis A. Dexter, *American Business and Public Policy: The Politics of Foreign Trade* (New York: Atherton, 1963), a review of which served as the immediate occasion for Lowi's article.

[16] For three other efforts to cope with issue-generated phenomena, see the even more abstract typologies in Herbert J. Spiro, "Comparative Politics: A Compre-hensive Approach," *American Political Science Review*, LVI (September 1962), pp. 577–595; Ernest A. T. Barth and Stuart D. Johnson, "Community Power and a Typology of Social Issues," *Social Forces*, 38 (Oct., 1959), pp. 29–32; and Chapter 6 above.

[17] Lowi *op. cit.*, p. 689. In the light of the analysis that follows here, it is noteworthy that Lowi accompanies the isolation of this fourth category with the confounding observation that, "Of course, those aspects of foreign and military policy that have direct domestic implications are included in my scheme."

less well-founded on the available facts and alternatives than domestic-policy decisions; that they are, in general, much more influenced by irrational motives."[18] Why this should be the case is, typically, not elaborated. One can readily think of circumstances that seem to contradict Myrdal's impression. Indeed, in the absence of systematic efforts to delineate how the foreign and domestic areas might differ, contradictory assertions abound. Even as issues of foreign and domestic policy are assumed to be distinct from one another, so is there also a tendency to stress that in a shrinking world, foreign and domestic matters have become inextricably linked and that only for analytic purposes can distinctions between them be drawn. Stated more concretely, not only do political scientists presume that the processes of making foreign policy are sufficiently unlike those of domestic policy to justify writing special texts and giving special courses, they are also inclined to call the attention of their students to the wisdom of the practitioner who observed that "if ever the line between domestic and foreign affairs could be drawn, it is now wholly erased."[19]

More importantly, regardless of whether the distinctions between the two areas are concrete or analytic, they are seldom identified, and even more rarely are their sources specified. One is hard pressed to find even a mere listing of the differences between the motives, roles, and interaction sequences that foreign and domestic issues are, respectively, likely to activate. There is no consideration of the possibility that certain kinds of foreign and domestic issues may precipitate political processes more akin to each other than to the other foreign and domestic questions with which they are usually clustered. In short, foreign policy issues may or may not constitute an area with clear-cut boundaries and distinguishable characteristics, but, whichever the case, the reasons therefor have yet to be expounded.

What follows is thus an initial effort to consider the foreign-domestic distinction in a detailed and organized fashion. Our observations are no less impressionistic than those of others. In the absence of empirical inquiries designed to contrast foreign and domestic issues, we have been forced to rely on speculation rather than data. Throughout, our assertions about the motives and behavior of individuals, groups, and governments must thus be viewed as hypotheses rather than findings. We did not start with any preconceptions as to whether foreign and domestic issues are different or similar, but the fact that we reached conclusions on the question should not be interpreted as meaning that we tested it. Our analysis,

[18] Gunnar Myrdal, "With What Little Wisdom the World is Ruled," *The New York Times Magazine*, July 18, 1965, p. 20.

[19] Senator J. W. Fulbright, "What Makes United States Foreign Policy?" *The Reporter*, 20 (May 14, 1959), p. 19.

in other words, is distinguished not by its validity, but by its effort to be systematic. While no special claim is made for the accuracy of our hypotheses, we would contend that by systematizing thought on the foreign-domestic distinction we have taken a necessary first step toward empirical investigation of it.[20]

Let us specify the scope of our concern more precisely. By "foreign policy as an issue-area" we mean all the controversies within a society that, at any moment in time, are being waged over the way in which the society is attempting to maintain or alter its external environment. The attempts to exercise control over the environment constitute "foreign policy," whereas the controversies engendered by the attempts (or lack of them) comprise the "issue-area." Once an attempt is no longer controversial, either because it comes to be accepted or because changes in the external environment allow it to be modified or abandoned, then the issue-area is diminished accordingly. Contrariwise, new issues are considered to enter the area whenever developments in the environment occasion controversy within the society over how it should react. Foreign policies are regarded as issues within the area only if the controversy over them persists and extends to major segments of the society's governmental organization or to segments of its public. A brief argument over how to respond to an environmental event between, say, a prime minister and his foreign minister would not be treated as an issue in the foreign policy area. Such a sequence is part of the routinized procedures whereby all societies conduct the day-to-day aspects of their foreign relations. On the other hand, a prolonged disagreement over a proposed military strategy between, say, a foreign office and a defense establishment involves major elements of the government and would thus be considered a foreign policy issue.

In other words, our focus is on national political systems and not on international systems. We are interested in the processes through which national systems undertake to cope with their external environment and not in the processes which transpire in the environment.[21] Within this framework, we wish to consider whether the controversies over what courses of action to pursue abroad involve different motives (on the part of both citizens and officials), roles (within both the public and the government), and interaction sequences (both within the government and between it and the public) than do those controversies that are occasioned by

[20] Indeed, quantitative data designed to test some of the main hypotheses developed here have already been gathered and are presently being analyzed.

[21] Throughout, our discussion will employ examples drawn mainly from American experience, but this is only because of greater familiarity with the United States policy-making process. Presumably many of the conclusions can be applied to any national system.

the question of what courses ought to be pursued at home. Even more specifically, we are interested in analyzing whether foreign or domestic issues differ in the degree of involvement they arouse (motivational intensity), whether the two areas can be differentiated in terms of the number of high-arousal issues they contain (motivational extensity), whether the ranks of the citizens and officials activated by each type of issue are likely to differ in size (role number) and in social and occupational character (role identity), and whether the areas vary in the extent to which those activated must confront each other (degrees of interaction) in either equal or superior-subordinate situations (direction of interaction). Stated diagrammatically, if the cells of Table 17–1 represent the scope of our concern, to what extent do foreign policy issues call for different entries in the cells than do domestic policy issues?

Table 17 - 1   The Components of an Issue-Area

	MOTIVES		ROLES		INTERACTION SEQUENCES	
	Intensity	Extensity	Number	Identity	Direction	Degree
Private citizens and groups						
Government officials and organizations						

IV. FOREIGN POLICY AS AN ISSUE-AREA

Let us begin our analysis by making two simplifying assumptions: that the political processes of the foreign and domestic areas operate independently, and that in each area all the issues are processed in the same manner. Later we shall have occasion to relax these assumptions, and to emphasize the existence of a third area that lies between the foreign and domestic areas and that embraces issues which are a composite of the foreign and domestic policy processes. In order to trace and clarify the boundaries separating the three areas, however, it is useful to proceed at the outset as if there were only two.

Motivational Differences [22]—It does not require much thought to discern at least one major distinction between the motives aroused by foreign policy issues and those that are operative with respect

[22] So as to avoid undue complexity, no effort has been made here to draw sharp distinctions among the various stages in the mental-emotional process whereby actors initiate behavior and react to stimuli. For our purposes it is sufficient to subsume such psychological dimensions of behavior as intentions, drives, habits, attitudes, and perceptions under the general heading of "motives" and to use these terms more or less interchangeably.

to domestic affairs. For the citizenry, the former area is likely to generate motivation that is less complex and ambivalent, and therefore more clear-cut and intense, than is the domestic area. Foreign policy deals with events and circumstances outside the system and, being in the environment, these events and circumstances can appear potentially threatening to the members of the system. Whatever the differences among the members, they would seem minimal compared to the distinctions that set them all apart from the members of the other systems that comprise the environment. Fellow system members thus come to be viewed as a "we" who are constantly endangered by a "them." Hence, proposals designed to ward off and manage "them" tap motives that are relatively unfettered by cross-cutting interests and therefore remain undiluted in intensity.

Domestic issues, on the other hand, cast members of the system in opposition to each other and their common system membership is, except under revolutionary conditions, usually irrelevant as a motivational source. Instead, individuals bring a multiplicity of affiliations and loyalties to domestic issues. Goals thus become confounded by cross-cutting interests, and the maintenance of a clear-cut priority of values with respect to one's fellow citizens becomes a delicate and complicated task. Things are never so clear-cut as they are with respect to non-citizens. Motives offset each other; perhaps they even cancel each other out; and presumably the resulting complexity curbs the intensity of the feeling that is invested in domestic controversies.

Treason and war suggest the extent to which the simplicity and intensity of motives differ in the foreign and domestic areas. In the sense that they involve a system's relations with its environment, both phenomena can be classified as foreign policy issues. Historically both treason and war have aroused the members of national systems to heights of involvement that are rarely, if ever, matched in the domestic area.[23] Indeed, treason, the act of enriching the environment at the expense of the system, evokes such intense motives that the framers of the American Constitution went to much greater lengths in protecting the rights of those accused

---

[23] At first glance this assertion might seem dubious on the grounds that intense nationwide involvement frequently focuses on kidnappings, lost children, and other forms of tragedy. Upon reflection, however, such events seem irrelevant to the comparison. Without denying that crime and catastrophe arouse high degrees of involvement, particular instances of tragedy do not ordinarily become public issues. They are not normally the focus of subsequent controversy and thus it seems inappropriate to classify them within the domestic policy issue-area. Here we are concerned with motivation and behavior toward public issues and not toward all the events that come to the attention of the public. To be sure, the prevalence of crime can become a public issue, but there is no evidence that as a generalized concern it evokes the intense and sustained feelings that accompany war and treason.

of it than they did in the case of any other situation they envisioned as controversial.[24]

The simpler and more solidary motives that sustain foreign policy issues are also illustrated by the large degree to which the concept of "bipartisanship" is reserved for such issues in most national systems. Even if the norm is expressed more through lip service than actual practice, its prevalence signifies a recognition of the distinctive quality of foreign policy issues. Certainly its emphasis on the thought that dealing with "them" requires greater solidarity and less ambiguity than dealing with "ourselves" is consistent with the foregoing interpretation.

Still another example along these lines is provided by the leaders in underdeveloped countries who often seem to be better able to overcome domestic strife and inertia by citing the hostility of the external environment than by stressing the need for hard work and patience at home. In effect, they attempt to solve domestic issues by redefining them as falling in the foreign policy area.[25]

Intensity, however, is not the only motivational dimension along which foreign and domestic issues seem to be differentiated. An important distinction obtains with respect to their extensity. Paradoxically, while the foreign policy area may tap simpler and more intense motives, for the ordinary citizen these do not extend across as wide a range of phenomena as do those operative in the domestic area. Foreign policy deals with remote and obscure matters that, if they are kept under control, seem too distant from the daily needs and wants of most citizens to arouse concern. "There are enough things to worry about in one's immediate surroundings," many say, "without fretting over the arrangements whereby people abroad conduct their lives." For most citizens the external environment is simply an "out there," an undifferentiated mass that can be threatening but rarely is. It is only when rapid changes occur in the environment that this mass acquires structure for most citizens and thereby appears to be linked to their own welfare in potentially damaging ways. As long as the environment persists unaltered and inchoate, or at least as long as the changes in it are slow and localized, few persons are likely to perceive it as having a structure and thus to feel that it might threaten their interests. In short, for most citizens the intense feelings that can be directed toward the external environment usually lie dormant. Usually

[24] In the case of treason the Constitution states (Art. III, Sec. III) that there must be two eye-witnesses to "the same overt act," a criterion of evidence that surely exceeds in its stringency that required for proof of any other offense.

[25] This is not to say that the leaders of developed systems are immune to the temptation to rest the case for internal changes on the ground of external necessity. The tendency of many American leaders to cite negative world opinion as a reason to accord civil rights to Negroes is also illustrative of this point.

they are inclined to leave its management to officialdom, an inclination which is not nearly so widespread with respect to those seemingly close-at-hand, highly structured phenomena that constitute domestic affairs.

What we are trying to stress is that one's interests are linked to a variety of interaction sequences that recur among individuals and groups, but that most of these sequences are perceived to unfold within the boundaries of one's own system. Thus, for example, it becomes possible for many Americans to be concerned about racial strife in Mississippi even as they ignore similar strife in South Africa. Events in Jackson are part of their lives, but those in Johannesburg are not. The former become intimate in the sense that they are perceived to unleash a chain of events into which every American may eventually be drawn, whereas the latter remain remote because their repercussions seem far away. For the same reasons, to use a more mundane and thus even more pertinent example, Americans can become concerned about the contents and outcomes of proposals to provide medical assistance to aged Americans even as they remain totally uninvolved in the question of whether the British system of socialized medicine should be extended. The arrangements of the former potentially encompass them, whereas those of the latter do not. It follows that the ordinary citizen has few convictions about how things should be arranged abroad and many about the arrangements at home. The arrangements abroad are the business of others, but those at home are his—unless, of course, those abroad should suddenly shift and appear capable of moving across his doorstep, in which case, to repeat, they are likely to seem especially ominous.

A good measure of the concern about close-at-hand events is provided by the response of a nationwide sample of Americans to the question, "Of all the things you could hope for, what one thing, if you had to choose, do you look forward to most in your life?" As can be seen in Table 17–2, an overwhelming proportion of the reported aspirations are highly specific, material, and immediate, whereas only 5 percent related themselves to a chain of events ("peace") of which at least some necessarily occurred in the external environment.

It must be emphasized that the perception of oneself as affected by the chains of events within the system and unrelated to those in the environment is not merely the result of the socio-psychological process whereby people develop a sense of community and acquire loyalties to the system. Feelings of nationalism, to be sure, can contribute to the perceived distinction and they may even lead to an exaggeration of its sharpness. It is also true, however, that the distinction has a reality of its own and that perceptions of it are in many respects accurate. One's health, house, and job, along with the health, education, and proximity of one's children,

Table 17 – 2

Main Goals in Life	Total Public (percent)
Good health for self and family	23
Get ahead on job, new job	15
Live more comfortably	14
Give children good education (college)	10
Own a house	8
Get a raise	5
Peace in the world, no war	5
Want children near me	5
Want to travel	4
Go back to school	3
Raise children well	2
Retire from work	2
Move to different area	2
Get married and have children	2
	100

*Reported by Louis Harris in *The Daily Home News*, New Brunswick, N.J., December 14, 1964.

are in fact crucially dependent on what happens in the neighborhood or community. A host of legal, political, economic, and social aspects of a national system do in fact make all its members subject to events that originate within it. The simple fact that all the members of a system are subject to its laws means that whenever events in one part of the system precipitate a legal response, repercussions are bound to be felt elsewhere in the system. On the other hand, such chain reactions do not follow when events in other systems evoke legal responses. Indeed, in many instances the boundaries of a system are explicitly designed to cut off sequences that start in other systems.

Tariffs and trade barriers constitute an obvious example of the foregoing. They allow people to ignore a steel price rise abroad even though the same people correctly expect to be caught up in the repercussions of a similar event within their own system. Likewise, an American is justified in perceiving himself as a part of the interaction sequences initiated by racial strife in Mississippi and as essentially separate from those in South Africa. The former give rise to new political forces, new legislation, and new judicial interpretations that are bound to affect all Americans, whereas comparable events in South Africa initiate sequences that are largely confined to the politics of that country. Much the same can obviously be said about the Medicare illustration. By definition, Americans residing in the United States are not eligible for benefits under Britain's socialized medicine program and thus they are not likely to experience the political, economic, and social consequences of changes in it. Alterations in the U.S. social security program, however, are eventually felt by all Americans, through either the taxes they pay or the benefits they receive.

There is still another reason why the distinction between the foreign and domestic areas fosters different degrees of political involvement on the part of the citizenry. The very fact that citizens are subject to the laws of their system also entitles them—at least theoretically—to help shape or change its legal arrangements and political balances. On the other hand, events or situations in the environment—that is, in somebody else's system—clearly lie beyond their control and jurisdiction. Consequently, it seems reasonable to presume that most citizens bring to domestic issues a much greater sense of what Almond and Verba call "subjective competence" [26] than they bring to foreign issues. That is, they feel more capable of influencing the outcome of disputes in the former area than in the latter. In turn this difference in subjective competence is likely to lead most citizens to participate more extensively in domestic political processes than in those through which foreign policy is developed. Support for this conclusion is provided by this comment of one observer who had ample opportunity to assess its validity in the American system:

In domestic affairs, a presidential decision is usually the beginning of public debate. In foreign affairs, the issues are frequently so complex, the facts so obscure, and the period for decision so short, that the American people have from the beginning—and even more so in this century—delegated to the President more discretion in this vital area and they are usually willing to support any reasonable decision he makes.[27]

Quantitative support for presuming that the two areas differ in this respect is also available through an extension of Almond and Verba's finding that, in all five countries they surveyed, "the sense of subjective competence occurs more frequently vis-á-vis the local government than the national government."[28] Stated more analytically, just as Almond and Verba concluded that "one reason why individuals differ in the frequency with which they adhere to participatory norms is that the structure of government and community organization changes from one nation to another," [29] so might we say that the citizens of one nation vary in the

[26] Gabriel A. Almond and Sidney Verba, *The Civic Culture: Political Attitudes and Democracy in Five Nations* (Princeton: Princeton University Press, 1963), esp. Chaps. 7–9.

[27] Theodore C. Sorenson, *Decision-Making in the White House* (New York: Columbia University Press, 1963), p. 48.

[28] *Op. cit.*, pp. 184–185.

[29] *Ibid.*, p. 168.

extent of their adherence to such norms because the structure of policy-making changes from one issue-area to another.[30]

In sum, it is not just parochialism that leads most people to have a greater interest in domestic than in foreign affairs. Good reasons for such a distinction are rooted in the structures of the two areas. But, it might be argued, the independence of national systems can be exaggerated. It is self-deception to see oneself as unrelated to environmental events or incapable of affecting them. Legal barriers do not necessarily contain all the chains of events that are forged in the life of polities, economies, and societies. On the contrary, some legal arrangements either necessitate or facilitate interaction sequences that start in one system and culminate in others. Commercial and financial treaties, for example, enable goods and currency to be exchanged across system boundaries and in so doing they also render a nation's economy vulnerable to economic trends in its environment. Security treaties go even further in this respect. They not only facilitate the linkage of systems to their environments; they also necessitate such arrangements and require the signatories to come to each other's defense in the event of external attack. Surely, for instance, a Russian attack on Turkey would initiate, both legally (through NATO) and politically (through the prevailing structure of world politics), a chain of events that would quickly extend into the lives of many Americans.

Furthermore, the argument might continue, even the legal barriers to international interdependence can be surmounted. There is the "demonstration effect" whereby events in one system leap across the boundaries of other systems merely by being perceived and then either emulated or countered. Price rises in one system can affect the economy of another if members of the latter anticipate repercussions and act to offset them. News of race riots in Johannesburg can so impress groups in Jackson as to lead them to act in ways that sustain the causal chain despite the geographic and other barriers. It can even be argued that Medicare programs are subject to the demonstration effect. The vigor and frequency with which the American Medical Association calls attention to the defects of Britain's socialized medicine program is illustrative in this regard.

There is, of course, considerable validity to this argument that the structures of the foreign and domestic areas are not as distinct as they might seem and that more interaction sequences cross national boundaries than most people realize.[31] To assert this argument, however, is to relax

---

[30] Almond and Verba are not unaware of the possibility of extending their conclusions to account for variability within as well as between nations: see *ibid.*, pp. 483–484 (footnote 12).

[31] For an interesting empirical effort to identify all the ways in which the life of a community is linked to chains of events in the international environment,

our simplifying assumptions prematurely and to move on from the analysis of how citizens are differentially motivated in the two areas. As will be seen, some citizens do, under certain conditions, recognize the interdependence of environmental and system events. Likewise, as noted in the next paragraphs, officialdom is dedicated to an awareness that situations need not be confined to the system in which they originate. Nevertheless, this mode of analysis would not appear to be appreciated by the citizenry in general. Except for those who directly experience the demonstration effect and the other more intricate boundary crossings, recognition of such processes requires a capacity and an inclination to perceive the subtleties of causation that most members of most systems do not seem to possess. The subtleties, moreover, are obscured by the aforementioned reality that many interaction sequences unfold only in the environment and that still others are kept there by the protective barriers with which systems surround themselves.

In short, however extensive the interdependence of systems and their environments, it usually does not become a part of the ordinary citizen's awareness. And, since motives are aroused only by events that seem to impinge on one's interests, activities, or aspirations, there would seem to be no reason to modify the conclusion that foreign and domestic areas evoke different motivational patterns on the part of most people and that, relatively speaking, high intensity-low extensity characterizes the pattern in the former area and low intensity-high extensity distinguishes the pattern in the latter area.

But "most people" are not "all people." Our hypothesis is clearly inappropriate insofar as officialdom is concerned. The notion that motivational intensity and extensity are functions of the real and perceived structure into which daily life fits leads to quite different conclusions when applied to those whom systems endow with responsibility for scrutinizing and managing the interaction sequences that unfold in the environment. From the perspective of policy-makers at the national level, every event in the environment is approached as if it potentially might be linked to the daily life of the system. Be he elected or appointed, the official is required to be sensitive to the possibility that causal chains forged abroad may acquire links at home. His job is to take care of the system's needs and to protect the integrity of its boundaries. His interests, activities, and aspirations all converge on the question of whether the environment is enhancing or endangering the system's welfare. Thus the extensity of his motives toward foreign policy issues is likely to be as high as that which he brings to bear on domestic issues.

see Gerard J. Mangone, *Foreign Policy and Onondaga County* (Syracuse: The Maxwell Graduate School of Citizenship and Public Affairs, 1964).

This conclusion must be qualified somewhat by the fact that most national systems divide the labor of caring for their internal and external affairs between different segments of officialdom. Specialization among career civil servants is perhaps so narrow that those assigned to cope with issues in the foreign area rarely need to pay attention to domestic considerations, just as the reverse situation obtains for bureaucrats who work in the domestic area. Country desk officers in the Department of State, for example, are not likely to be alert to controversies over collective bargaining in the railroad industry; nor are their counterparts in the Department of Labor who respond to industrial issues likely to be aroused by border disputes in Asia or Africa. Similarly, low motivational extensity would presumably distinguish the professional staffs of congressional committees that process issues pertaining, respectively, to foreign and labor relations.

On the other hand, the political superiors of executive and legislative specialists cannot so easily ignore issues that fall outside their immediate jurisdiction, and thus our general point still holds with respect to top officials who hold elective or appointive posts. Their legal and political responsibilities are too extensive for them not to be sensitive to the whole range of foreign and domestic issues that can suddenly be activated. Indeed, chiefs of state and chief executives are constitutionally required by national systems to be alert to both internal and external needs. Nor is such a broad perspective any less relevant at the next level of officialdom. Although some division of the labor of caring for a system's needs usually prevails at this second level, the specialization is not so great that those with primary tasks in one area can take the management of events in the other area for granted. The specialization does not diminish their overall responsibility. The member of Congress who becomes chairman of his chamber's Committee on Labor does not thereby lessen his foreign policy responsibilities. Contrariwise, the Secretary of State cannot proceed to cope with the external environment without being cognizant of the possible domestic consequences of his actions. One can readily think of circumstances in which he must even apprise himself of the labor-management situation at home as he enters into diplomatic negotiations or makes a foreign policy address.

If the extensity of officialdom's motivation toward developments abroad is thus much greater than the citizenry's, quite the opposite would seem to be the case with respect to motivational intensity. Whereas citizens are capable of investing extremely intense feelings into the few foreign policy issues that arouse them, officials are not likely to direct an equivalent intensity toward the many issues in the foreign area that engage their concern. Being aware of the interrelatedness of issues and of the subtle and circuitous routes whereby causal chains forged abroad may acquire links at home, the top official tends to exercise restraint and to avoid positing any single issue as a life-or-death problem. He recognizes that system survival would be jeopardized if he reacted so intensely to an issue that he lost perspective and did not pause to consider how its solution would affect the outcome of other issues. In addition, he knows— or learns soon after entering his official role—that the habits of people are hard to change and that, consequently, issues cannot usually be solved by one dramatic action. He becomes accustomed to partial solutions and slow progress. Unlike citizens, he rarely allows himself the luxury of unqualified involvement in a foreign policy issue. The extreme intensity with which American officials are reported to have participated in the 1962 Cuban missile crisis stands out as an exception in this regard. At least history does not record any other instance when an American President gave his aides a special souvenir in gratitude for their help in resolving a single issue that lasted less than two weeks.

In fairness to the reader, it should be noted that this interpretation of the approach of officials to foreign policy questions is in sharp conflict with the widespread view, previously implied in the quoted observation of Myrdal, that greater "irrationality" is operative in foreign affairs than in domestic. One observer, for example, recently claimed that "In all countries foreign affairs are likely to become the object of more emotionalism and irrationality than domestic questions," [32] while another confined his assertion of this thesis to the United States:

If, then, we recognize that in regard to foreign policy the Johnson administration is under far less popular constraint than in regard to domestic policy, and if we also bear in mind that our constitutional system allows the President very large powers in conducting external affairs, we must conclude somewhat unhappily that on problems like Vietnam and the Dominican Republic Johnson has a relatively free hand. Confronting a Medicare bill he must calculate and measure; considering a proposal to send marines to Latin America he can act upon what he takes to be the national interest, or what at the moment comes to little more than his, or his advisers', panic or pique.[33]

From our perspective, however, such an analysis overlooks the enormous constraints that the international system imposes on officials. While their own systems do permit them much greater leeway in foreign affairs, as we shall also have occasion to emphasize below, this is more than

[32] Grayson Kirk, "World Perspectives, 1964," *Foreign Affairs,* 43 (October, 1964), p. 1.
[33] Irving Howe, "I'd Rather Be Wrong," *The New York Review of Books,* IV (June 17, 1965), p. 3.

offset by the international constraints. We would contend that the opportunities for them to express "panic or pique" are much more varied and numerous in the domestic than the foreign area.

In positing officials as cautious in their approach to the foreign area, we do not mean to imply that they will be particularly vague or vacillating. On the contrary, clarity of official behavior appears to be one of the distinguishing characteristics of foreign policy issues. The price of being misunderstood in this area is much greater than it is in the domestic area. The former involves issues in which "we" are pitted against "them," and while restraint must be exercised to avoid provoking "them" unnecessarily, it can never be carried to the point where the line between "we" and "them" is confounded. So that the "we" can continue to provide support and the "them" can continue to avoid ruinous miscalculations, the officials must always let each know exactly where he stands—at least he must do so to a much greater extent than is the case on domestic issues.[34] In the latter area, in fact, there are a number of incentives that might lead him to adopt somewhat vague positions. Clearly distinguishing the "good" citizen from the "bad" can weaken the system and hinder the solution of issues, whereas, to repeat, plainly drawing the line between citizens and noncitizens can only facilitate the work of officialdom. Hence the view that in underdeveloped countries "leaders are encouraged to adopt more clearly defined positions on international issues than on domestic issues"[35] would seem to be applicable to any system.

It follows from the preceding analysis that the foreign policy area is marked by a motivational gap between the citizen and the policy-maker that is not nearly so pronounced in the domestic area. Domestic issues arouse the public and the government alike, but only rarely is the public activated by questions of foreign policy. The implications of this gap are manifold. It means that on most foreign policy issues officials are likely to be far ahead of citizens in terms of their perception, comprehension, and concern. No less importantly, the motivational gap normally has the consequence of freeing officialdom from the restraints that the citizenry imposes in the domestic area. At the same time, to anticipate our discussion of the interaction differences between the two areas, the gap also means that in the foreign policy area officials are confronted with a herculean consensus-building task whenever they need domestic support for their endeavors abroad. The task is no less than that of demonstrating for an

[34] For an elaboration of the difficulties that confront officials who try to maintain the support of both foreign and domestic publics, see the discussion of the "dual politician" in Chapter 10.

[35] Lucian W. Pye, *Politics, Personality, and Nation Building: Burma's Search for Identity* (New Haven: Yale University Press, 1962), p. 28.

uninterested public how it is linked to the events in the environment. A succinct portrayal of the breadth of the motivational gap and the enormity of the task required to bridge it is provided by the contrast between the reactions of Algerian officials and citizens to the 1964 Belgian-American expedition to rescue white missionaries held captive by Congolese rebels in Stanleyville. That those responsible for managing the environment tend to perceive the system's boundaries as vulnerable to processes initiated abroad is plainly evident in the comment of Ben Bella, then the Algerian President: "If the Congo falls [as a result of the rescue expedition], it will be next the turn of Brazzaville, then Burundi, Tanzania, Uganda, Cairo and why not Algeria? We have lost Stanleyville but Africa remains." That citizens regard the environment as remote and causality as rooted within the system is equally clear in the reaction of a middle-aged hotel employee: "I don't want to be an Arab, a Berber, an African or anything else. I just want to be an Algerian." Similarly, after listening to Mr. Ben Bella's speech, a housewife said: "Why doesn't he talk about our problems here at home. My brother can't find work and the cost of living keeps going up." [36]

There is one respect, however, in which citizen and official orientations toward the two areas are quite similar. Like the citizenry, officialdom can be expected to have a greater sense of subjective competence toward domestic affairs than they do toward foreign policy issues. Although their freedom of action is not nearly so limited by the demands and restraints which the citizenry imposes in the domestic area, officials are nevertheless likely to feel especially constricted in their ability to cope effectively with foreign policy issues. For success in this area is crucially dependent on persons and groups who belong to other national systems and whose actions are guided by other goals, rules, and precedents. In attempting to resolve domestic issues officials can at least rely on those affected by their actions to respond in terms of the rules of the game whereby the system is organized. They can at least count on compliance with decisions that have emerged from the policy-making process.[37] In dealing with foreign policy issues, on the other hand, officialdom cannot take such factors for

---

[36] *The New York Times,* December 6, 1964. For an inquiry into the elaborate efforts needed to bridge this motivational gap in the foreign policy area, see James N. Rosenau, *National Leadership and Foreign Policy: A Case Study in the Mobilization of Public Support* (Princeton: Princeton University Press, 1963).

[37] This is especially the case in large industrial societies where people are likely to develop what has been appropriately called "a *role readiness,* a predisposition to accept behavioral requirements that are legitimately sanctioned." See Daniel Katz, Herbert Kelman, and Richard Flacks, "The National Role: Some Hypotheses about the Relation of Individuals to Nation in America Today," in Walter Isard and Julian Wolpert (eds.), Peace Research Society (International): *Papers, Volume I, 1964: Chicago Conference, 1963* (Tokyo, 1964), p. 119.

granted. Many of the participants play a different game and often respond
half-heartedly or defiantly to the products of the policy-making process.
In other words, mobilizing domestic support for foreign policy proposals
may be a huge task, but it is simple in comparison to mobilizing the
foreign support necessary to implement such proposals. Thus, like the
citizenry, and for similar reasons, officialdom is also bound to feel more
frustrated and less competent toward issues in the foreign area than they
do toward those in the domestic area. This distinction is poignantly illustrated in the following response of John F. Kennedy to a reporter who
asked, "As you look back upon your first two years in office, sir, has
your experience in the office matched your expectations?" Without even
mentioning domestic issues, the President focused immediately upon his
competence in the foreign area:

Well, in the first place, I think the problems are more difficult than I had
imagined they were. Secondly, there's a limitation upon the ability of the
United States to solve these problems. We are involved now in the Congo
in a very difficult situation. We've been unable to secure the implementation
of the policy which we've supported. . . . There is a limitation, in other words,
on the power of the United States to bring about solutions. . . . So that I
would say the problems are more difficult than I imagined them to be. The
responsibilities placed on the United States are greater than I imagined them
to be, and there are greater limitations upon our ability to bring about a
favorable result than I had imagined it to be.[38]

But this is not to imply that the motivational gap between the citizen
and the policy-maker that prevails in the foreign policy area is bridged
by their shared lack of subjective competence toward it. On the contrary,
it seems doubtful whether the citizen is aware that he shares this feeling
with those in policy-making positions. Having accepted the division of
labor that casts him in the role of citizen, he tends to assume that
officialdom is able to maintain control over the external environment and
therefore tends to ascribe a much higher degree of subjective competence
to policy-makers than they actually possess.

While the breadth of the motivational gap cannot thus be minimized,
note must be taken of two bridges that do span it. One is a temporary
and fragile structure, namely, the aforementioned capacity of citizens to
become intensely concerned about the occasional situation abroad that
does appear likely to initiate a chain of events which will upend or otherwise intrude upon their daily lives. Under these circumstances the gap
is not only narrowed, but often is actually reversed as an aroused public

becomes anxious to move quicker and further toward resolution of the issue than does a cautious officialdom. The second bridge is a more solid and enduring structure. It consists of those persons in the society whose interests do lead them to perceive themselves as linked to the interaction sequences that transpire in the external environment. This small stratum of the public is comprised of two main elements: nongovernmental leaders whose occupational responsibilities, like those of officialdom, require them to be attentive to the international scene, and those few citizens—such as intellectuals—whose interests are not directly linked to the environment but who are nonetheless indirectly led to an involvement in foreign affairs by a need to protect their self-images. An American, for example, who defines himself as a civil libertarian is likely to feel obliged to be as attentive to incidents of racial strife in South Africa as to those in Missis-sippi. In the ensuing discussion of role differences between the foreign and domestic areas we shall have occasion to elaborate on the roles that form this permanent bridge between the citizenry and officialdom. Here it suffices to note that, having a longer gap to span, the bridge is much narrower in the foreign than the domestic area.

Role Differences—Our conception of the structure of a public issue calls to mind the giant wall maps that corporation execu-tives and military commanders use to depict the distribution and utilization of their resources. Where the twinkling lights on such maps indicate the points at which resources are either located or being employed, in our image of an issue being processed by a national system the flashing lights correspond to those roles in the system that have been aroused to partici-pate in the controversy over the issue. We conceive of the map as com-posed of many more lights than flash at any one time because the system is regarded as consisting of innumerable roles that do not require con-tinuous activity on the part of their occupants. Hence the pattern of lights on our map is considered to vary from one issue-area to another, depend-ing upon the number and identity of the roles that are activated.

Stated less metaphorically, we see the inclination and capacity to participate in the discussion of public issues as aspects of roles rather than as characteristics of people. National political systems consist of roles, both public and private, that are filled by different persons in each generation but that nevertheless require or stimulate similar activity (or inactivity) on the part of their occupants, whoever they may be at any moment in time. In the United States, for example, labor leader, person of Polish descent, editor, intellectual, and bureaucrat are but a few of the roles out of which activity on certain issues can be expected to emanate, irrespective of the particular persons involved. In other words, behavior on an issue theoretically can be anticipated in advance of its activation.

If one had sufficient knowledge of the system, for each area one could plot the set of roles that are likely to be active and that thereby form its structure.[39]

In developing this conception of issue-areas as role structures we are not ignoring our earlier discussion of motives. Obviously it is people, and not roles, who experience motivation. And clearly the inclination and capacity to participate in public debate is conditioned by personality and other individual variables as well as by those arising out of role expectations and requirements. Yet, there would seem to be two good reasons to use the analytic device of attaching motives to roles rather than to people. One is that to a large extent role variables precede individual variables as motivational sources and, consequently, limit and channel the ways in which individuality gets expressed. The expectations of others always serve as the backdrop for action and it is these expectations that constitute the foundations of a social role. Expectations, however, do not dictate every aspect of behavior and roles do allow for and even necessitate the exercise of individuality. Nevertheless, some adherence to the expectations inherent in the roll must occur if occupancy of it is to continue. Thus it is that one's behavior changes after entering a new role and that in important ways so do one's motives and attitudes.[40]

Secondly, and no less important, the concept of role would also appear to underlie the crucial motivational dimension whereby the degree of a person's participation in the processing of a public issue depends upon whether he does or does not perceive himself as a potential link in the chain of events. What in fact he perceives is the presence or absence in the chain of one of the roles he occupies. He does not know the individuals who may act in such a way as to precipitate events that lead to his doorstep. Hence, to link himself to events he must perceive a process whereby the unknown occupants of certain roles are led to impinge on other unknown role occupants who in turn affect still others —and so on until a role he occupies is affected. From a perceptual standpoint, in other words, issues and the chain of events they initiate are structures of overlapping roles. Let us illustrate. If an American is of Polish descent and a proposed foreign aid program for Poland becomes an issue, then his ethnic ties to the homeland and other aspects of his ethnic role may foster the view that his interests constitute a link in the sequence whereby aid is or is not distributed in Poland. If, on the other hand, the issue focuses around aid for India, he will probably not have such a perception

[39] For an elaboration of this formulation, see my *National Leadership and Foreign Policy*, pp. 9–16.
[40] The interrelationship of individual and role variables is amplified at greater length in Chapter 7.

nor be aroused to participate in the issue unless he perceives some other role he occupies as potentially linked to the chain of events that aid to India might initiate. Persons of Polish descent who also occupy the role of intellectual, for example, may perceive events in India as linked to them through the expectation that intellectuals should be attentive to crises anywhere in the world. Individual variables—or conflicting roles—may inhibit some intellectuals from participating in the issue, but nevertheless activity can be expected to emanate from many occupants of this role. In sum, our formulation of issue-areas as role structures can be viewed less as a contradiction than as an elaboration of the foregoing discussion of motivational intensity and extensity.

Turning now to the differences between the role structures that mark issues in the foreign and domestic areas, we must begin with one that exists virtually by definition. Stated in terms of the earlier analogy, our map is not big enough to encompass the entire pattern of lights activated by issues in the foreign policy area. Unlike their domestic counterparts, foreign policy issues necessarily include the occupants of roles that are not part of the system. Foreigners are participants in such issues because, by definition, the objects or values that are the subject of controversy exist in the system's external environment and thus the rearrangement of the objects or the restructuring of the values cannot be accomplished without the consent of those in the environment who are thereby affected. The consent may result from voluntary acquiescence, hard bargaining, or forced compliance. Whatever the basis of the consent, however, the foreigners who provide it inevitably become parties to the interaction whereby the issue is resolved. To be sure, national systems reserve the right to decide their own foreign policies and their members may resent the intrusion of outsiders who seek to influence the policies. Yet, even if a system manages to resolve differences among its members by ignoring foreign demands and deciding independently on a course of action, such an exercise of sovereignty may not bring an end to the issue. To achieve consensus within a system over a foreign policy is not to guarantee the cessation of controversy, as it is with domestic issues. If the foreigners toward whom the policy is directed resist, then the external environment will not be altered to conform to the internal consensus and the differences will probably reappear, reopening the issue. Obviously, for example, there would never have been a Korean issue in the United States during the early 1950s if the North Koreans had accepted the American decision to intervene and immediately had withdrawn their troops to the pre-invasion boundary.

Another evident distinction between the role structures of the domestic and foreign areas is the much greater number of roles from which activity is likely to emanate in the former. The presence of foreign roles in the latter area does not nearly offset the numerous citizens and officials who can be expected to participate only in domestic controversies. Domestic issues, involving as they do the distribution of resources and the arrangement of relationships at home, impinge upon highly generalized social roles and large categories of occupational roles. The healthy and the sick, the aged and the young, the rich and the poor—these are but a few of the broad social roles that can be directly linked to one or another of the main issues in the domestic area, whereas businessmen, workers, teachers, housewives, doctors, and mayors illustrate the all-encompassing occupational roles that such issues can activate. On the other hand, issues of foreign policy, being concerned with resources and relationships that are primarily distributed and rearranged in the environment, do not normally draw their participants from such large classes of people. Rather the occupants of much more specialized kinds of roles are likely to perceive a potential linkage between themselves and events abroad. Whereas domestic issues may activate a wide variety of, say, businessmen and teachers, foreign ones are likely to energize only exporters and professors of international relations. While the role of worker or housewife may easily be coupled to domestic issues, an equivalent linkage to foreign issues cannot be experienced unless, say, the former has relatives abroad or the latter has a son in military service.

At the leadership level, too, domestic issues are likely to evoke behavior on the part of a greater number of individuals than are foreign ones. This becomes readily apparent if a distinction is drawn between multi-issue and single-issue leadership roles. The former afford their occupants an opportunity to circulate opinions and exert influence on a variety of issues, whereas the latter limit the leadership of their occupants to the specialized set of concerns that brought the roles into being. Editors of daily newspapers are an obvious example of multi-issue leadership roles. Indeed, not only are they expected to express themselves on all issues of the day, but they are even permitted to create a few new ones. Editors of technical publications, on the other hand, illustrate single-issue roles. They can exercise leadership only with respect to matters that are covered by the specialized foci of their journals. If they attempt to use their roles as the basis for leadership on other issues, they will either be ignored by their readers (who have turned to their publications precisely because of the specialization they offer) or, eventually, they will be removed from their roles.[41]

[41] Additional discussion of the distinction between multi- and single-issue leaders will be found in my *Public Opinion and Foreign Policy: An Operational Formulation* (New York: Random House, 1961), Chap. 5.

If we now superimpose the foreign-domestic dichotomy upon this distinction between multi- and single-issue leaders, it becomes clear that the foreign area contains substantially fewer single-issue roles than does the domestic area.[42] Foreign policy issues are no less technical than domestic ones, but since they deal with resources and arrangements abroad they do not fall within the spheres of competence of nearly as many technicians as do domestic issues. Contrast, for example, the nuclear test-ban treaty and water pollution, two issues that have in common the question of the extent to which natural resources shall be poisoned. Both issues would no doubt precipitate equivalent behavior on the part of multi-issue leaders (e.g., editors, politicians, and religious figures); but the single-issue leadership evoked by the nuclear question would not be likely to include more than a handful of lawyers specializing in international law, a few geneticists, a group of engineers acquainted with the problems of detection, and perhaps some political scientists who specialize in East-West relations, whereas the water pollution issue would probably necessitate opinion-making activity on the part of comparable specialists in every medium-sized community, a group that would number well into the hundreds of thousands. Or compare the number of Americans whose special training would cast them in leadership roles on such geographically based issues as Berlin, Vietnam, or the Congo with those whose specialties would accord them access to the channels of influence on regionally oriented domestic issues such as T.V.A., poverty in Appalachia, or the St. Lawrence Seaway. Again the latter might exceed the former by hundreds of thousands. The number of African, Asian, or European experts in the United States is infinitesimal compared to the ranks of those whose views would be sought or heeded on the question of developing the nation's resources.

Nor is the difference between the leadership structures of the two areas merely a matter of numbers. The roles comprising the domestic area are more widely dispersed as well as more numerous than are those forming the foreign area. Most domestic controversies are directly relevant to life at every societal level, from the national through the regional down to the smallest community. Consequently, such controversies are likely to activate the occupants of multi-issue roles at all these levels. Most of the issues encompassed by the foreign area, on the other hand, do not clearly bear upon day-to-day existence at every level. Rather, occupants of roles that have responsibilities of a nation-wide dimension—what we shall call the national leadership—are likely to feel the impingement of events in the environment much more extensively than are those whose

---

[42] As indicated below, a similar difference also prevails with respect to multi-issue roles even though it might seem that by definition both areas would activate roughly the same number of multi-issue leaders.

leadership roles are local or regional in scope.[43] Hence the pattern of leadership activity in the foreign area will ordinarily be substantially more concentrated than is the case for domestic issues. Recurring again to our imaginary wall map, lights will be twinkling in every hamlet of the society whenever domestic issues arise, whereas for foreign policy questions there will be bright glares of light in the centers of national leadership—in the national capital and in the seats of industry, finance, publishing, and culture—and darkness elsewhere.

This distinction can be readily illustrated. Consider, for example, American politicians and government officials. Those whose jurisdiction is confined to cities and states can be expected to participate in a variety of domestic issues. Such diverse questions as federal aid to education, water pollution, automation, civil rights, farm prices, urban renewal, and tax reduction are all likely to have repercussions within their constituencies. Thus, even if the national capital serves as the main site of the controversy, domestic issues are likely to require local politicians and officials to assert their opinions and to press for appropriate solutions.[44] Rare is the foreign policy issue, however, that will generate such behavior on their part. The local politician and official neither feel nor have an obligation to urge that the government follow a particular course in a Far Eastern crisis, nor are they obliged to insist that its stance toward a United Nations stalemate be altered. On the contrary, all the requirements of their roles orient them away from such matters and they may even be subject to electoral punishment or political reproach if they become too active in the foreign area. "Mind the community's business, not the nation's" constitutes a role limitation of which local politicians and officials are bound to be aware and which they can ignore only at their occupational peril. Stated in behavioral terms, the traffic of, say, city mayors who are brought to Washington, D.C., by domestic issues is a veritable deluge compared to that which is attracted by issues in the foreign area.

And much the same pattern prevails in other walks of life. Leaders of international labor unions are likely to be much more attentive to foreign policy questions than are their counterparts at the local level. Editors of small-town papers are much more inclined to restrict the space allotted to coverage of foreign affairs than are those with cosmopolitan audiences.[45] The heads of corporations with far-flung interests are likely to feel a much

[43] For an operational definition of the difference between national and local leadership, see my *National Leadership and Foreign Policy*, p. 7.

[44] Cf. Arthur J. Vidich and Joseph Bensman, *Small Towns in Mass Society: Class, Power, and Religion in a Rural Community* (Princeton: Princeton University Press, 1958), Chap. 8.

[45] Cf. Bernard C. Cohen, *The Press and Foreign Policy* (Princeton: Princeton University Press, 1963), Chap. 4.

greater obligation to be active on foreign policy issues than are local businessmen.[46]

Interaction Differences—In asking whether the foreign and domestic areas differ in terms of the patterns of interaction through which issues in them are sustained or resolved, two pattern variables seem especially useful. One is the *degree* of interaction, that is, the extent to which the parties to an issue act independently or in response to each other. The other is the *direction* of interaction, that is, the extent to which interaction unfolds vertically through hierarchical channels or horizontally among relatively equal actors. To anticipate the conclusion of our reasoning, differences between the two areas can be discerned with respect to both variables, with foreign policy issues tending to precipitate primarily vertical interaction, to a low degree, and domestic issues evoking mainly horizontal interaction, to a high degree.

Let us probe first the direction of interaction. Here empirical reality can hardly be mistaken. One cannot think of any society in which the task of making foreign policy is not assigned primarily to the executive branch of government. The need for decisive and unified action in coping with the external environment has led all political systems, democratic and authoritarian alike, to concentrate responsibility for foreign policy in the hands of relatively few officials. The need for this hierarchical arrangement has long been recognized in the United States and today the pre-eminence of the President in foreign affairs is as accepted a principle as any that is formally written in the Constitution. To be sure, exceptions can be cited, and later we shall have occasion to emphasize the existence of certain conditions that foster horizontal interaction in the foreign area. Generally speaking, however, the pattern is a pyramidal one in which interaction either converges upon or is responsive to the executive officials and agencies charged with maintaining control over the external environment. Whether the purpose be that of registering protest, exerting pressure, or proffering cooperation, citizens, groups, and legislative officials must turn to the executive branch for initiative and guidance.

The structure of the domestic area, on the other hand, is not nearly so hierarchical. Every segment of the society has some claim on the resources and relationships that distinguish it from its environment. Except in authoritarian systems, responsibility for making domestic policy is thus dispersed rather than concentrated, and accommodation rather than decisiveness is the paramount need.[47] Unity results from acquiescence in

[46] Some quantitative data bearing on this point can be found in Bauer, Pool, and Dexter, *op. cit.*, Part II.

[47] We except authoritarian systems from this analysis because presumably they are marked by a high concentration of authority and responsibility in both the

the foreign area, but only bargaining and coalition can produce it in the domestic area. Both in and out of government, therefore, horizontal inter-action must occur before domestic issues can be resolved. To be sure, some groups in the society are larger and more powerful than others and to this extent the interaction slants vertically. And it is also true that the executive branch is not entirely lacking in authority in the domestic area. Such discrepancies among groups and within officialdom are hardly notice-able, however, when compared to the hierarchical structure of the foreign area.

Another way of describing this difference is in terms of the useful distinction that Huntington has drawn between the executive and legisla-tive processes of policy-making[48] (or, to adapt his terminology to our perspective, the legislative and executive processes of issue-handling). Noting that under certain conditions decision-making within the executive branch "retains a peculiarly legislative flavor," Huntington emphasizes that the "legislative and executive *processes* of policy-making do not neces-sarily correspond to the legislative and executive *branches* of government," that instead

A policy-making process is legislative in character to the extent that: (1) the units participating in the process are relatively equal in power (and consequently must bargain with each other); (2) important disagreements exist concerning the goals of policy; and (3) there are many possible alternatives. A process is executive in character to the extent that: (1) the participating units differ in power (i.e., are hierarchically arranged); (2) fundamental goals and values are not at issue; and (3) the range of possible choices is limited.[49]

The relevance of Huntington's distinction to our discussion is obvious: interaction in the domestic area consists mainly of the legislative process, while issues in the foreign area are handled primarily through the executive process.

Having less of a need to fashion consensuses through bargaining and support building efforts than their counterparts in the domestic area, parties to foreign policy issues are bound to be correspondingly less impelled to interact with each other. They can, so to speak, move independently

foreign and domestic areas. Indeed, this is so virtually by definition: they are authoritarian precisely because hierarchical policy-making prevails in all walks of life. Yet, if our analysis of the domestic-foreign distinction is correct in this respect, it suggests that even in authoritarian systems the patterns of interaction in the two areas are not likely to be identical, that the claims of domestic groups cannot be totally ignored in such systems, and that the structure of the domestic area is bound to be at least slightly less hierarchical than that of the foreign area.

[48] Samuel P. Huntington, *The Common Defense: Strategic Programs in National Politics* (New York: Columbia University Press, 1961), Chap. 3.
[49] *Ibid.*, p. 146.

up the slopes of the pyramid of executive authority, whereas those involved in domestic controversies must respond to each other in order to join the issue and move toward their respective goals. Stated in terms of testable hypotheses, it seems reasonable to presume that the actors in the domestic area are more familiar with each other's identity and more conversant with each other's views than are those activated by foreign policy issues. Applied to the United States, one could hypothesize that for every White House Conference of national or regional leaders devoted to coping with a trend unfolding abroad, ten or more are convened on situations emerging at home.[50] It should be noted, however, that the lesser degree of interaction in the foreign area is not attributed to the aforementioned conclusion that this area contains many fewer roles susceptible to activation. We are talking about relative and not absolute degrees of interaction. Our reasoning is that the more hierarchical structure in the foreign area and the greater need for accommodation in the domestic area mean that proportionately more action will converge and overlap in the latter than in the former.

But there is another and, in view of the ensuing analysis, a more important reason for this difference in the degree of interaction. This is that foreign policy issues focus primarily on resources or relationships that are to be distributed or rearranged in the environment, whereas domestic issues involve mainly distribution and rearrangement among members of the system. Members of the system do not run the risk of forfeiting or relinquishing any possessions when they participate in a foreign policy controversy. They can, under such circumstances, suffer damage to their spiritual or psychic values, but nothing concrete can be taken away from them, since the resources or relationships at issue are located primarily outside the system. Foreign policy controversies, in short, do not require the participants to treat each other as rivals for scarce resources. What one actor or group gains, another does not give up. Each participant seeks to persuade the decision-making authority to adopt a particular solution, but none posits a solution that necessitates depriving other system members of some of their possessions or privileges. Thus, since there is nothing material to bargain over, the parties to the issue need never come together or respond to each other. Each can contest the issue independently and without regard for the others.

Let us cite some recent examples. Take the question of whether the United States should have given diplomatic support to Biafra or Nigeria. At least in the short run, it was not Americans who were likely to be affected by the outcome of the conflict. All those whose status and resources

50 See, for example, the cases cited in my *National Leadership and Foreign Policy*, p. 24.

could have been enhanced by the outcome, as well as all those who could have been deprived in these ways, were Nigerians. Some Americans may have been pleased by the outcome and some may have been disappointed, but none were likely to be poorer. Similarly, the question of United States involvement in Cyprus is primarily a matter of how Cypriote wealth and prestige should be rearranged; only secondarily, if at all, does it involve the reallocation of resources and status among Americans. Or consider the 1963 nuclear test-ban treaty. Neither the proponents nor the opponents risked a diminution of their resources or status. The welfare of the unborn may have been at stake, but like persons in the external environment, future generations are remote and unable to contest issues directly.

Domestic issues, on the other hand, unfold under conditions of scarce resources. The system itself encompasses all the resources that are to be allocated and all the relationships that are to be rearranged. What one actor or group gains, another gives up or fails to gain. There are only so many tax dollars that can be raised and only so many ways to spend them. And each dollar that is collected and disbursed results in loss to some and gain to others. Similarly, statuses have historical roots within the system and to change them is to deprive some of privilege and to provide it to others. Necessarily, parties to a domestic issue must view each other as rivals, as obstacles that must be confronted, refuted, thwarted, or accommodated in such a way as to permit satisfactory resolution of the issue. In short, even though their goals may be mutually exclusive, the actors in the domestic area are interdependent. They cannot avoid each other and continue to contest the issue. They must interact, if not on a face-to-face basis, then through actions that are explicitly in response to each other.

The civil rights issue in the United States is an obvious example of this process. Actual or proposed legislative, executive, and judicial action benefiting minority groups has involved a vast rearrangement of the society's resources and relationships. Some Americans, especially white Southerners, have correctly seen the issue as involving the loss of both material wealth and status privilege, while others, especially those in the affected minorities, have been equally accurate in their view that the issue promises them a gain in these respects. Whatever the outcome of the issue, therefore, great numbers of Americans will be directly affected and, in their own eyes, many will be poorer. Thus it is hardly surprising that the issue has stimulated interaction at all society levels, from the struggle for integrated schools in local communities to the contest for new statuses in the national legislature.

V. CONCLUSION

Summing up the analysis thus far, it seems clear that we have developed an affirmative answer to our original question of whether the foreign and domestic areas are distinguishable from each other. In terms of the motives, roles, and interaction sequences they activate, foreign and domestic issues do seem to differ in significant ways. The extent and nature of these differences are summarized in Table 17–3, which recreates Table 17–1 and adds the entries for each of the cells that our discussion has yielded.

Table 17 – 3   Characteristics of Foreign and Domestic Issues

		MOTIVES		ROLES		INTERACTION SEQUENCES	
		Intensity	Extensity	Number	Identity	Direction	Degree
Private citizens and groups	foreign issues	high	narrow	few	national leaders	vertical	low
	domestic issues	low	wide	many	all strata	horizontal	high
Government officials and agencies	foreign issues	low	wide	few	national	vertical	low
	domestic issues	low	wide	many	national and local	horizontal	high

There does remain, however, one unfinished task: that of relaxing our initial assumptions and inquiring whether the boundaries between the foreign and domestic areas are as rigid as we have presumed them to be. Again the answer seems clear. One can readily think of examples of foreign policy issues that unfold in ways descriptive of the domestic rather than the foreign area.[51] After all, it is virtually a truism that nations are becoming increasingly interdependent and that the internal life of no nation is entirely free from the intrusion of external factors.

In short, the distinctions we have discerned would seem to be generally valid, but there are major exceptions and the question is whether the deviations occur for systematic reasons, thereby permitting us to integrate them into our analysis. Once again a clear-cut line of reasoning suggests itself. The conclusion reached above, that domestic issues involve

---

[51] Although to a lesser extent, it is also possible to cite certain kinds of domestic issues (e.g., conservation) which would seem to consist mainly of characteristics ascribed to the foreign area. However, this point is tangential to our main concern and cannot be pursued here.

the allocation of scarce resources or the rearrangement of historic relationships while foreign issues do not, serves as a point of departure for a
train of thought that allows us to account for the exceptional issues and,
indeed, to predict their occurrence.

The crux of this synthesizing formulation is that some foreign policy
issues precipitate an exceptional degree of interaction that unfolds along
horizontal lines precisely because they involve, perhaps for a variety of
reasons, the utilization of a society's personnel and wealth. That is, certain
efforts to allocate resources or rearrange relationships in the external
environment cannot be carried out without domestic resources or relationships also undergoing change. The use or threat of force in the external
environment is an obvious example. In contrast to the more normal
procedure of relying on a handful of diplomats to restructure the environment through persuasion and negotiation, policies of force require a society
to dispatch its own troops and supplies abroad. Consequently, some
members of the society—say, the troops and those whose welfare suffers
as a result of the expenditure on military supplies—are deprived while
others—say, producers of military equipment—benefit. The area of controversy then widens as those who have an immediate stake in the policy
of force come to view each other as rivals. At this point the executive
process of issue-handling is no longer appropriate to the situation and
the outwardly directed policy comes to dominate the internal politics of
the society. The centrality of the issues of Indochina and Algeria in
postwar French politics is, *par excellence,* an empirical instance of this
process. Both issues came to dominate the domestic political scene in
France precisely because Frenchmen were having *their* resources and
relationships redistributed in Indochina and Algeria. In short, most foreign
policy issues may not involve the diversion of substantial resources from
the internal to the external environment, but some do and these are the
ones that exhibit the characteristics of domestic issues.

Other illustrations of this formulation are readily available from
recent history. Consider again the Nigerian situation. As has already been
implied, so long as the controversy over what diplomatic line the United
States should pursue in the situation involves deprivation only for some
Nigerian groups, participation in the issue within the United States is
confined to executive agencies of the federal government, some multi-issue
national leaders, and a few African specialists. Whenever there evolves
the possibility or fact of committing American transports, supplies, and
personnel to the situation, however, participation becomes more broadly
based, many members of Congress become aroused, and, in effect, the
issue is transferred from the foreign to the domestic area. Similarly, the
Berlin issue has moved back and forth between the areas as the consign-

ment of American troops and equipment has been raised and lowered. On the other hand, since the commitment of American resources to European defense would not be essentially altered by the proposed multilateral force, MLF has remained strictly a foreign policy issue insofar as its processing by the American system is concerned. For the European nations involved, however, the MLF proposal does require new allocations of men and material, and for these nations the issue has thus acquired domestic characteristics.

One other empirical case can usefully be cited to demonstrate the explanatory power of our interpretation that the manner of processing an issue is a function of the degree to which a society's resources or relationships are affected. We refer to Cohen's thorough account of the internal policy-making process through which the United States formulated, ratified, and formally adhered to the 1951 Japanese peace settlement.[52] The salient feature of this episode is that, contrary to all expectations, the conclusion of a conciliatory treaty with an archenemy of the 1940s did not provoke extended debate and intense activity throughout the country. It had been anticipated that lingering wartime hatred for the Japanese would foster widespread demands for a punitive treaty, but these never materialized and Cohen's one hundred-page account of the citizenry's reactions—in polls, the press, and interest group statements—makes for very bland reading indeed.[53] Only the question of fishing rights in the North Pacific stimulated a flurry of demands, interactions, and bargaining: members of Congress and fishing interests from the West Coast were so active that the original plan of including a single fisheries article in the peace treaty gave way to what Cohen calls "salt water politics" and was jettisoned in favor of negotiating a separate agreement —the North Pacific Fisheries Convention.[54] For Cohen the fisheries question is merely an exception. It emerges as a discordant note in an otherwise harmonious sequence that he ascribes to the skillful and careful way in which those responsible for obtaining foreign and domestic acceptance of the peace settlement—especially John Foster Dulles—mobilized support and diminished opposition. But our issue-area formulation suggests another interpretation. Although policy-making skills were no doubt operative and relevant, we would emphasize that most of the peace settlement dealt with the utilization of resources and the arrangement of relationships on the islands of Japan, that only with respect to fisheries were American resources at stake, and that therefore it is hardly surprising that the latter problem

[52] Bernard C. Cohen, *The Political Process and Foreign Policy: The Making of the Japanese Peace Settlement* (Princeton: Princeton University Press, 1957).
[53] *Ibid.*, Part II: "Public Opinion," Chaps. 3–6.
[54] *Ibid.*, Chap. 12.

was distinguished by the horizontal manner in which it was processed. In effect, the Japanese peace settlement was not a single situation. It was two situations, one falling in the foreign area and the other in the domestic area.

If our conception of the two areas and of the overlap between them sheds new light on past situations, it also allows us to predict the way in which future ones will unfold. So long as an issue focuses on some aspect of the external environment, and so long as none of the proposals to resolve it require more than the normal complement of foreign office personnel, then it is likely to activate relatively few national leaders and officials and their interactions are likely to be hierarchically patterned. However, once the focus of the issue shifts to aspects of the society itself, or once proposals to handle it necessitate the expenditure of societal resources or the alteration of societal relationships to supplement the work of diplomats, then relatively large numbers of citizens, leaders, and officials can be expected to make claims and counterclaims in a process of bargaining over its resolution. Indeed, in order to account for the exceptional issues that transgress the boundaries between the areas, we can pose our conclusion in terms of a single overall hypothesis: *The more an issue encompasses a society's resources and relationships, the more will it be drawn into the society's domestic political system and the less will it be processed through the society's foreign political system.*[55]

Note that we predict the way in which issues will unfold, not their outcomes. The foreign area would seem to be the more stable of the two and, accordingly, issues processed in it would seem likely to prove more integrative for the society than those processed in the domestic area. To comprehend the stability and integrative potential of an issue-area, however, is not to know how long an issue will endure or whose posture toward it will prevail. Process exerts some influence on outcome, to be sure, but it is equally true that the same process can yield a variety of outcomes, depending on the interplay of a host of variables that are not structural components of issue-areas. To predict outcome as well as process one would have to know the identity, capabilities, and aspirations

[55] Since the writing of the first draft of this chapter in January, 1965, the conflict in Vietnam has escalated considerably and the subsequent development of the issue in the United States has closely followed along the lines predicted by the hypothesis. Indeed, in this particular case domesticization of the issue bears some resemblance to an election campaign and all the innovative and frenzied activities that accompany such episodes: besides a rash of "teach-ins," the issue has precipitated an unusual (for a "foreign policy" issue) number of advertisements contesting the wisdom of escalation, a State Department "truth team" touring American campuses, a group of Congressmen holding "hearings" on street corners, and, in general, a highly consistent one-to-one ratio between the commitment of men and materiel and the involvement of citizens and officials.

of the participants in an issue; and to move to this plane of inquiry would be to descend from the theory-building level of issue-area analysis to the theory-constricting level of issue analysis, a step which we have already eschewed.

18 The Adaptation of National Societies: A Theory of Political Behavior and Transformation *

Never before has consciousness of the interdependence of national and international life seemed so pervasive. Sometimes proudly and oft-times painfully, national societies everywhere are either readjusting their external activities to their internal needs or rearranging their domestic affairs to facilitate their foreign commitments. Canada has reduced its contribution to NATO in order to devote more resources to its problems at home. Rhodesia has cut its last ties to Great Britain and isolated itself from world affairs in order to maintain the dominance of its white minority. Peru has altered its ties to the United States in order to satisfy the ambitions of a new leadership and the demands of a growing social unrest. Israel has adopted a tough policy toward its neighbors in the conviction that its socio-religious institutions will thereby be served. Commando groups demanding new and harsher actions toward Israel have emerged in the Middle East, pressing the Arab governments of the region to alter their activities abroad. Czechoslovakia has curbed its press and tightened its political structure in order to pursue a pro-Moscow orientation. And no less conspicuous, the United States has initiated efforts to diminish its involvement in Vietnam in response to demands for a reallocation of resources to domestic needs.

While the effort of national societies to achieve and maintain an internal-external balance is hardly new—years ago Walter Lippmann

* This chapter was originally published in 1970 by The McCaleb-Seiler Publishing Company of New York. The original version had an appendix in which operationalizations of the key variables were developed. This appendix had not been reproduced here due to space limitations. It can be found, however, in James N. Rosenau, *The Study of Political Adaptation* (London: Frances Pinter Publishers, 1980), Chap. 2.

noted that such a balance constitutes "the self-evident common principle of all genuine foreign policy" [1]—the self-conscious and pronounced preoccupation with these efforts on a worldwide scale seems unprecedented. It is almost as if the wave of independence movements that marked the postwar period has been replaced by a wave of "interdependence" movements in the present era—the demands for a new balance between domestic and foreign affairs. Just as the former was carried forward by a deepening mass awareness of national identity, so it now appears that the interdependence movements have gathered momentum through an increasing realization on the part of mass publics that the quality of life at home both shapes and is shaped by their governments' posture toward developments abroad. Ben Bella, Sukarno, Nkrumah, Dubcek, and Lyndon Johnson are perhaps the first political victims of the interdependence wave and Trudeau of Canada, Velasco of Peru, and Husak of Czechoslovakia the first to ride its crest, but it seems likely that the politics of national adaptation—of *explicitly* relating the essential economic, social, and political structures of societies to their external circumstances and conduct—will dominate world affairs for a long time.

Whatever the historic reasons for the emergence of adaptive politics on a global scale, and doubtless there are many, it is important to differentiate its various forms. To comprehend the dynamics of modern politics, we must see the interdependence movements as the complex phenomena they are. It is not enough to treat them as conflicts between isolationist tendencies, or as the products of a resurgent nationalism, or as expressions of a sharpened national interest. Concepts of this sort may have been useful in the past, but they are too simple as a basis for grasping the self-consciousness of interdependence that marks the present and is likely to mark the future. Nor is the view that modern technology is shrinking the world and making its parts more interdependent an adequate framework with which to comprehend the varied responses that are possible to the process of shrinkage. Such a perspective offers an overall description of central tendencies, but it sheds little light on the kinds of choices that societies are likely to make as their domestic and foreign affairs impinge ever more closely upon each other. In short, we are ill-equipped to analyze the politics of national adaptation and an attempt to articulate their major premises and forms thus seems imperative.

[1] Walter Lippmann, *U.S. Foreign Policy: Shield of the Republic* (New York, Little, Brown, 1943).

THE CONCEPT OF NATIONAL ADAPTATION

Considerable insight follows from an initial formulation that conceives national societies—like the single cell, the individual, group, or the organization—as entities that must adapt to their environments to survive and prosper. That is, if an entity is to maintain the boundaries that separate it from other entities, it must act toward the other entities in such a way to keep its essential structures intact. For the single cell, or indeed any living organism, this means, as an irreducible minimum, that the fluctuations in its essential structures must be kept within physiological limits. For the group or the organization, adaptation means that the fluctuation on its essential structures must at least be kept within legal limits. For a national society, adaptation means that fluctuation in the basic interaction patterns that sustain its social, economic, and political life must be kept within limits minimally acceptable to its members. Obviously the adaptation of the national society involves greater uncertainty than does that of other entities. The meaning and limits of fluctuations in its essential structures are not so clear-cut. While the failure of individuals, marriages, or business firms to adapt to their environments is readily determined and widely known (through death notices, divorce records, or bankruptcy proceedings), the points at which national societies fail to keep their essential structures intact are obscure and may vary as the society's values undergo change. Because they are always subject to redefinition, the limits within which the essential structures of societies may fluctuate are often the focus of considerable controversy, thus infusing the politics of national adaptation with an intensity and drama unknown to other entities.

Despite the difficulties inherent in assessing the fluctuations of societal structures, conceiving of societies as adapting entities provides the basis for constructing a useful framework to provide the interdependence of their domestic and foreign affairs. For the fluctuations in the essential structures of a society stem from a composite of three sources: from international developments and the society's success in coping with and benefiting from them; from trends at home and the society's success in absorbing them into its essential structures; and from the internal behavior whereby the society adjusts its institutions and values to meet the requirements of its external behavior and the demands of its environment.

Viewed in this way, a precise formulation of the activity conventionally called "foreign policy" is readily derived. Any external behavior undertaken by the government of any national society is adaptive when it copes with, or stimulates, changes in its external environment that contribute to keeping its essential structures within acceptable limits. A behavior is maladaptive when it copes with, or stimulates, changes in the external environment that change its essential structures beyond acceptable limits. By *essential structures* we mean those interaction patterns that constitute the basic political, economic, and social life of a national society. By *acceptable limits* we mean those points on a continuum between which the fluctuations in the essential structures do not prevent the society from maintaining its basic patterns or altering these patterns through its own choices and procedures.

The need for foreign policy arises, of course, out of the fact that the essential structures of societies cannot be kept within acceptable limits unless some kind of behavior is undertaken toward the environment. These structures cannot be sufficiently self-sustaining for all contact with the environment to be cut off. To be sure, most variation in the essential structures may result from the conduct of life within a society. The degree of social unity, the extent of economic prosperity, and the effectiveness of political authority can vary widely, even beyond acceptable limits, as a consequence of activities that never extend beyond the boundaries of the society. Strife among linguistic groups, strikes that lead to cutbacks in production and declines in employment, and prolonged civil wars exemplify internal trends that can push the basic social, economic, and political life of a society toward or beyond acceptable limits. Notwithstanding the impact of internal developments on internal structures, however, in the era of modern telecommunications and transportation, every society is dependent on its external environment. Some demands for commercial, fiscal, political, and cultural relationships originate in the environment and, correspondingly, some people and groups in the society need such relationships to maintain their political, economic, and social life. There will thus be a flow of people, information, and materials across the boundaries that divide the society from its environment; and while this flow can be minimized it cannot be prevented entirely, and it will affect the society's essential structures. Adaptive behavior is directed at controlling the extent and nature of this effect. Whatever may transpire within the society, the boundary-crossing flow of people, information, and materials must be so regulated that it contributes to keeping the essential structures within acceptable limits.

Under static conditions—that is, when little or no change is occurring at home or abroad—societies seek to maintain control over their environment by the routine procedures of commerce and the standard practices of diplomacy. Visas and passports are issued to regulate the flow of individuals and groups. Tariff and exchange rates are imposed to govern the flow of materials and money. Embassies and foreign offices are maintained to facilitate the flow of information and ideas. These are the day-to-day activities that achieve a minimum degree of adaptation and every society in the world engages in one or another form of them.

Modern life, however, is seldom static. Change within and among societies is virtually constant, so that the myriad routinized activities by which each society controls its ties to the international system are not sufficient to keep its essential structures within acceptable limits. The day-to-day activities contribute to adaptation, but they can be offset by a failure to cope with the demands for new boundary-crossing flows of people, information, and material that result from changes at home and abroad. Whether the change is domestic and involves altering essential structures and their acceptable limits, or whether it is foreign and poses potential threats to essential structures, it gives rise to demands on the adaptive capabilities of societies that routinized procedures cannot meet. Whatever the source of change, new arrangements have to be sought in the environment, and while the routinized procedures are adequate to maintain existing arrangements, they cannot foster new ones. Innovation is required, as well as allocating resources not previously used for adaptive purposes. Alliances may have to be built or broken, military moves threatened or made, diplomatic relationships severed or cultivated, foreign aid offered or sought, subversive and espionage activities initiated or countered, dignitaries sent abroad or received at home. Since these policy-making activities take place under changing conditions in which precedent may be weak and knowledge limited, they are not likely to be as consistently adaptive as the routinized ones. Perceptions of the change may be faulty, errors in judgment may be made, goals may be ambiguous, resources may be insufficient or not mobilized in time—for these and a host of other reasons societies are likely to engage in maladaptive as well as adaptive behavior in response to internal or external change.

FOUR PATTERNS OF NATIONAL ADAPTATION

Whether they prove to be adaptive or maladaptive, all foreign policy actions undertaken by a national society stem from at least one common source, namely, the need to keep essential structures within acceptable limits by achieving a balance between the changes and demands from within the society on the one hand and the changes and demands from its salient environment on the other. Four basic orientations toward the balance of internal and environmental demands are available. A society can attempt to keep its essential structures within acceptable limits by making them consistent with the changes and demands emanating from its present environment, giving rise to what we shall call *the politics of acquiescent adaptation*. Second, a society can seek to render its environment consistent with its present structures, thus engaging in what we shall refer to as *the politics of intransigent adaptation*. Third, a society can attempt to shape the demands of its present structures and its present environment to each other (i.e., by seeking to establish a desired equilibrium between them), behavior we shall designate *the politics of promotive adaptation*. Finally, a society can seek to live within the limitations that its present structures and its present environment impose on each other (i.e., by preserving the existing equilibrium between them), giving rise to what we shall call *the politics of preservative adaptation*.

For present purposes these four types of adaptation are conceived to be mutually exclusive. Empirical investigation may later dictate the need to relax this assumption of mutual exclusiveness and to posit societies as pursuing different types of adaptation in different issue-areas. To achieve theoretical clarity at this stage, however, it is useful to assure that a society pursues only one type of adaptation at a time. As indicated below, this assumption is supported by the conclusion that the four types are so fundamental that transformation from one pattern to another normally requires replacing one set of officials by another and, in the case of the shift from or to acquiescent and intransigent adaptation, the transition may well require a thoroughgoing social revolution, if not an international war. Stated differently, this fourfold breakdown refers to enduring patterns of adaptation and not to particular external behaviors—to the "eras" in a society's foreign policy and not to the specific situations in which it becomes involved.

Put in still another way, while the myriad foreign policy behaviors of a society at a given moment may be unrelated and even contradictory, they gain coherence through an underlying orientation toward basic changes that occur at home and abroad. Policies established at different times in the past may be contradictory, but when new internal and external situations arise the society will seek to cope with them through policies—old or new—that express whether it seeks to establish an acquiescent, intransigent, promotive, or preservative type of adaptive equilibrium between its essential structures and its external environment. It is not surprising or contradictory, for example, that even though Rhodesia is willing to engage in trade and tariff negotiations, it refused to bargain when the United Nations demanded changes in its racial policies. The former is a long-established practice, whereas the UN demands were a new aspect of the Rhodesian environment and thus compelled the Rhodesians to resort to their underlying orientation toward the relationship between internal needs and external demands. In other words, the key to which of the four adaptive orientations obtains at any moment lies in how societies respond to basic changes at home or abroad with which they have not previously been confronted.[2]

This is not to imply that foreign policy officials consciously connect every decision they make to the adaptive pattern they are seeking to achieve. Indeed, with a long-standing and widely used diplomatic rhetoric readily available, it is improbable that they are familiar with either the concept or the language of adaptation. That officials may not be conscious of the adaptive implications of each decision, however, does not imply that national adaptation is a predetermined process to which they unknowingly succumb. Officials must perceive and assess the changes unfolding at home and abroad, and their perceptions and assessments are conditioned by their individual needs as well as by the interplay of the internal and external demands emanating from the essential structures and environment of their society. Unlike cats, who automatically adjust their distance from a blazing fireplace to stay warm without getting burned, the adaptive mechanisms of societies are not unfailing. Some societies do get too close to the fires of world politics and begin to wither, while others remain too remote from them and begin to freeze. These adaptive fluctuations result from decisions made by identifiable human beings as well as from the events of world and national politics. The range of choice open to officials may be severely limited by the internal changes their society experiences and the external changes it is exposed to, but some choice necessarily underlies their actions, even if it is only the passive one of accepting the limitations that the internal and external changes impose upon each other.

In short, the type of adaptive balance a society seeks in any given era is conceived to be a basic premise—an organizing conception—that its foreign policy officials bring to every situation they face. They may not think in these terms and they may never have made an explicit choice among the four types of adaptation, but their thought processes are founded on and guided by one of the four orientations to how their essential structures and their environment do and ought to relate to each other, both in the immediate present and in the long run. Thus, while their explicit choices in, say, three specific situations may lead simul-

---

[2] Another clue is to be found in how societies respond when they are confronted with new and inescapable conflicts between external and internal demands. For example, just as Rhodesia's rejection of the U.N. demands revealed the presence of intransigent orientations, so did the Czechoslovakian response to the 1968 Russian intervention uncover the existence of an acquiescent orientation. Similarly, just as a promotive orientation was revealed in 1965 when President Lyndon B. Johnson decided to send his aide, McGeorge Bundy, to the Dominican Republic to cope with an unexpected uprising at the very time Bundy was scheduled to defend the Administration's policies toward Vietnam at a nationally televised teach-in, so did the same President's decision just before the 1968 election to call a half to U.S. bombing of North Vietnam reveal that the U.S. had undergone a transformation to preservative adaptation.

taneously to a military attack, a diplomatic concession, and a neutral stance, such discrepant behavior forms a consistent pattern viewed from the perspective of the adaptive balance being pursued. Table 18–1 suggests the relationship between the decision-making activities of officials

Table 18 – 1   The Nature of Decision-Making in Different Patterns of Adaptation

Patterns of adaptation	Demands and changes emanating from a society's external environment	Demands and changes emanating from the essential structures of a society
Acquiescent	+	−
Intransigent	−	+
Promotive	−	−
Preservative	+	+

and the four types of adaptive patterns to which their actions can conform.

The question arises as to how and when one of the four types of adaptation comes to prevail in a society. If officials do not necessarily make a conscious choice when they come to office or explicitly reiterate when they decide on a course of action in each situation, how does one type of adaptation emerge as predominant, and under what circumstances is it likely to change? Speculation about these important questions is best left until we have analyzed the distinctions among the four types more thoroughly, but it is perhaps useful to emphasize here that the processes whereby one or another of the types becomes and remains predominant are concrete and observable. Unlike the national interest—often cited as the basic premise of the external behavior of societies but to which can be attached as many symbols and meanings as there are officials, citizens, and scholars to interpret it—each of the four adaptive balances refers to specific links between societies and their external environments. A society's present structures are either tailored to present environmental demands, or the latter are tailored to the former, or some desired equilibrium between them is sought, or the existing equilibrium is allowed to prevail.

The consequences of each of the four types of adaptation for both the external behavior of societies and their internal institutions is elaborated below and summarized in Table 18–2. Here it can be seen that the four types do seem to lead to important differences in political behavior and form. It must be emphasized, however, that while the entries in each cell of Table 18–2 have been derived from the ensuing elaboration, they are extremely tentative and highly impressionistic. Their presentation in summary form is designed merely to suggest that different behaviors appear to result from the four types of adaptation. Obviously, operational measures of the variables constituting the rows of Table 18–2 need to be developed if the hypotheses represented by the impressionistic entries in each cell are to be subjected to an empirical test.

THE POLITICS OF ACQUIESCENT ADAPTATION

The prime characteristic of acquiescent adaptation is a readiness to adjust external behavior and internal institutions to the demands emanating from at least one segment of the environment (usually the nearest superpower). Societies that pursue this form of adaptation seek to live with rather than to moderate such demands. For a variety of reasons, their officials perceive themselves, accurately or not, as lacking the capacity to alter or offset the demands and thus they are not inclined to bargain with those who make them. Stated in game theory terms, they see themselves as participants in a zero-sum game in which they are bound to be the losers. The rationale for such a posture is that acquiescence to the demands that the society's external behavior follow certain basic lines will minimize the adjustments that must be made in its essential structures. The "satellite," the "banana republic," and the "penetrated system" are some of the terms used to depict societies committed to acquiescent adaptation. Recent history provides many concrete illustrations of this form of accommodation to the environment: the postwar readiness of Finland to follow neutralist policies dictated by the Soviet Union, the readiness of Czechoslovakia since 1968 to remain firmly within the Soviet bloc, the readiness of many Caribbean countries to vote with the United States in the United Nations.

It follows that the tasks of foreign policy officials in acquiescent societies are relatively easy. Ordinarily they need not agonize over the proper policy to pursue or the particular course of action to follow. Both the fundamental orientations and the specific decisions underlying their conduct of foreign affairs are predetermined because they are ready to heed the demands emanating from one segment of their environment. The officials need not, and indeed, dare not, be innovative or wide ranging in their policy making. The possibility of breaking old alliances or creating new ones is not theirs to consider. Nor do they initiate interventions in the affairs of other societies or use creative diplomacy to seek out new foreign markets or develop new sources of military or economic assistance. The scope of their concerns is necessarily narrow. As long as acquiescence characterizes their underlying posture toward

Table 18 – 2   Characteristics of the Four Types of Adaptation

	Acquiescent adaptation	Intransigent adaptation	Promotive adaptation	Preservative adaptation
1. Bargaining posture in the international system (and likely outcome of bargaining situations).	zero-sum (lose)	zero-sum (win)	nonzero-sum (plus)	nonzero-sum (minus)
2. Images of future change likely to preoccupy the society's officials.	short-run abroad	long-run abroad	long-run at home and abroad	short-run at home and abroad
3. Allocation of resources between foreign and domestic policy sectors.	priority given to domestic sector	priority given to foreign sector	often redistributed between foreign and domestic sectors	equal priority given to foreign and domestic sectors
4. Prime means by which foreign policy issues are ushered through the domestic political process.	avoidance	dictation	leadership persuasion	public debate
5. Scope of foreign policy concerns.	narrow	worldwide	variable	regional
6. Prime train of foreign policy rhetoric used by the society's officials.	subservient	ideological	normative	pragmatic
7. Attitude of masses toward leadership.	docile	supportive	apathetic	demanding
8. Character of the executive.	strong	preeminent	variable	weak
9. Character of the party system.	one party predominant	limited scope	variable	competitive
10. Role of the legislature.	weak	restricted	variable	strong
11. Role of the military in foreign policy.	nonexistent	maximal	variable	minimal
12. Reaffirming behavior.	extensive	nonexistent	infrequent	periodic
13. Innovative behavior.	nonexistent	extensive	periodic	infrequent
14. Interventionary behavior.	nonexistent	extensive	periodic	infrequent
15. Alliance behavior.	unchanging	minimized	variable	maximized
16. Foreign aid behavior.	negligible	extensive	variable	unchanging
17. Protocol behavior.	extensive	negligible	variable	unchanging
18. Central trend in flow of people (soldiers, diplomats, technicians, immigrants, tourists, students) across society's borders.	in	out	in and out (variable trend)	in and out (constant trend)
19. Central trend in flow of materials (arms, aid, trade, credit) across society's borders.	in	out	in and out (variable trend)	in and out (constant trend)
20. Central trend in flow of ideas (political, cultural, technical) across society's borders.	in	out	in and out (variable trend)	in and out (constant trend)

at least one segment of their environment, the officials concern themselves only with reaffirming the commitments and implementing the decisions required by and emanating from those segments of the environment they are responsive to. In short, their diplomatic rhetoric is one of subservience and their prime concern in foreign policy making will be the short-run changes that may occur in that part of the environment to which they are acquiescent.

Yet the politics of acquiescent adaptation is not free of difficulty. Foreign policy officials may not be faced with great challenges or tough decisions, but their domestic policy counterparts, responsible for keeping the essential structures of the society within acceptable limits, may not always find it easy to cope with the internal consequences of external acquiescence. Acquiescent adaptation can be sustained only if internal debates over foreign issues can be avoided and domestic publics remain docile about the conduct of external affairs. If some groups in the society begin to question the policies that flow from an acquiescent orientation, those in the environment demanding compliance will become concerned about whether the acquiescence will continue and thus add demands for restrictive domestic measures to their already existing demands for compliant external behavior. Unwilling to bargain with or otherwise contest the salient dimensions of their environment, the officials of acquiescent societies can do nothing but heed the external demands to maintain a tight control over internal politics. As a result, they are likely to be intolerant of dissent, or at least to try to confine it to a limited range of domestic issues. However, in an era marked by aroused mass publics and growing sensitivity to the interdependence of internal and external affairs, leaders may not readily avoid foreign policy issues or suppress dissent. Under certain circumstances, as in Finland, the leadership may permit several political parties to contest elections, while carefully screening the candidates, the parties, and the issues that compete for attention. Under other circumstances it may be necessary, as in East Germany, to resort to the more extreme practices of prohibiting opposition parties and directly controlling the mass media and the public activities of voluntary associations. Under still other circumstances the officials may decide to ride the interdependence wave and heed the aroused publics, in which case the society either undergoes a transformation to a new form of adaptation (as Czechoslovakia did in early 1968), or a new leadership committed to the acquiescent form and the rigid control it requires comes to power (as occurred in Czechoslovakia after the Soviet intervention in August 1968).

Other implications for domestic structure and policies follow from the nature of acquiescent adaptation. Not only, for example, does it require a party system in which one party is clearly predominant and a policy-making system in which a strong executive or cabinet is able, legitimately or otherwise, to insure that foreign policy issues are kept out of the arena of public discussion. Among its many other internal consequences are distinctly subordinate roles for the military elite and the legislature, albeit the members of both are not likely to be oriented toward acquiescence. In domestic policy, moreover, acquiescent adaptation is likely to permit and encourage a flow of persons, materials, and ideas from the segment of the environment officials acquiesce to, while prohibiting comparable flows from or to other segments of the environment.

It must be emphasized that acquiescent adaptation is not the equivalent of an isolationist foreign policy. Much depends on the nature of the environmental demands to which the acquiescent society is responsive. If the demands involve close adherence to the policies undertaken by a superpower, the society may have to participate in interventions, engage in the creation of new alliances, contribute to foreign aid programs, and indeed even go to war. Much of the postwar external behavior of the East European countries, especially East Germany and Bulgaria, reflect these nonisolationist forms of behavior. Of course, except when the demands on acquiescent societies require them to allocate their resources to foreign policy purposes, they normally give priority to the domestic sector. After all, it is precisely to preserve and enhance their essential structures that they are acquiescent with respect to the environment.

The foregoing is not to imply that geographic proximity to superpowers is the only source of acquiescent adaptation. Perhaps it is the paramount source (and in the ensuing analysis it is presumed to be the prototypic source), but cultural and economic dependence across more remote distances may also result in this type of adaptation. The external behaviors of certain African countries that were former British and French colonies are illustrative, as is the responsiveness of Far Eastern countries such as Japan, South Korea, Formosa, and Thailand to the lead of the United States during parts or all of the postwar period. Nor is this to say that geographic, cultural, or economic proximity necessarily result in acquiescent adaptation. On the contrary, recent history is replete with examples of societies located close to superpowers that either never adopted an acquiescent posture toward their environment or successfully defied the demands emanating from their environments and underwent transformation from acquiescence to another type of adaptation. Vietnam and Burma are societies that might be expected to heed the demands of a superior neighbor (China) but have never— or at least not through the first two decades of the postwar era—adopted an acquiescent posture, engaging instead in the politics of preservative adaptation. Similarly, Rumania's recent differences with the Soviet Union offers a good illustration of the ability of some societies to undergo transformation from acquiescent to preservative adaptation. And Cuba's posture toward the international system after its break with the United States in 1959 indicates that societies can even undergo trans- formation from an acquiescent to a promotive adaptation. In short, acquiescent adaptation is no more inherent in certain situations than is any other form of adaptation, thus posing the question of what combina- tion of variables is likely to conduce to a submissive stance toward the environment and what combination is likely to foster a transformation away from the politics of acquiescence. We shall return to this question below.

THE POLITICS OF INTRANSIGENT ADAPTATION

The central feature of intransigent adaptation is a readiness of a society to alter the environment to make it consistent with the demands inherent in at least one of its attributes. Intransigent adaptation means that under no circumstances will the society alter the salient internal attribute or attributes in response to demands emanating from the environment; on the contrary, its external behavior is addressed to making the environment accommodate to its internal attributes. The officials of such societies may exaggerate their capacity to achieve accep- tance in the environment, but the internal demands are so strong that leaders will not be deterred from seeking compliance abroad or from their unwillingness to make changes at home. Like their counterparts in acquiescent societies, but for opposite reasons, officials of intransigent societies are disinclined to bargain with their environment. Where the disinclination of the former stems from a readiness to accept external control over fluctuations in their essential structures, that of the latter is rooted in an unwillingness to accept any fluctuations, not even those induced internally, in at least one of their essential structures. Stated in terms of game theory, the officials of intransigent societies assume that they are participants in a zero-sum game in which they must be the winners. Their rationale for such a posture is that the internal attributes are too important to be the subject to negotiation. Present-day Israel, with its socio-religious institutions and unique history that predispose it to be aggressive in the Middle East rather than risk internal adjust- ments, is a good example of intransigent adaptation. So have been Rhodesia and South Africa, with their total unwillingness to undertake any alterations in their white-dominated social structures. These two African societies have not resorted to extensive military efforts to alter their environments, but their politics is that of intransigent adaptation in that they are unresponsive to the hostile societies and international organizations in their environments who demand that they alter their treatment of blacks. Hitler's Germany is another example of intransigent adaptation, albeit in this case the unbargainable internal demands sprung primarily from an individual and his small coterie of followers rather than from a major stratum or institution of the society.

In short, intransigent adaptation depends on the existence of a societal institution, norm, or group so powerful and inflexible as to make officials more responsible to its demands than to those from the international system. Indeed, while a variety of internal structures may perform this single-issue dominant role, it seems reasonable to presume this skewed, unyielding form of adaptation is likely to develop only in societies marked by a sharp imbalance in the salience and strength of their internal structures.

Whatever the sources of intransigent adaptation, the domestic politics it gives rise to are likely to be somewhat easier for officials to sustain than the domestic politics of acquiescent adaptation. Domestic publics are not likely to protest official unwillingness to accommodate to the environment or try to alter the priority given to foreign over domestic policies. The values underlying the societal attribute that makes foreign policy officials unwilling to bargain with their environment also predispose domestic publics to support the external behavior. The perceived essentially of the attribute to the society's existence is likely to make the intransigence abroad and the sacrifices necessary to its maintenance justifiable to most key groups. Consequently, while officials of acquiescent societies have a stake in encouraging docility and lack of public concern about foreign policy issues, those in intransigent societies have a stake in arousing their publics and keeping external problems constantly before them.

The above does not mean, of course, that the officials of intransigent societies submit the external problems to their publics for open debate. Officials see their solutions to the problems as inherent in the societal attributes regarded as so essential as to justify the intransigence. Hence the ends and means of foreign policy in intransigent societies are dictated to, and not debated by, the public. Officials may differ among themselves over tactical questions of when and how to be intransigent, but their shared commitment to the broad strategic posture of making the environment compatible with the demands of the society provides them with a compelling reason to prevent open discussion of their basic adaptive orientation. Their efforts to achieve compliance abroad can hardly be successful if the society appears divided internally. Indeed, the more unqualifiedly and manifestly supportive of the external behavior are its domestic publics, the more credible and therefore the more adaptive the society's unwillingness to bargain with its environment is likely to be. Thus public debate over policy goals cannot be tolerated even though public attention must be focused on them. To repeat, however, the politics of avoiding debate of and maximizing attention to foreign policy are not particularly delicate. The very societal attribute that underlies intransigent adaptation predisposes domestic publics to be unquestioningly supportive of whatever sacrifices their officials require them to make on behalf of foreign policy goals. From the perspective of the officials, therefore, keeping the public continuously aroused about external affairs serves both to support their demands on the environment and to divert attention from the possibility of relaxing the acceptable limits of fluctuation in the essential structures. Viewed in this way, it is appropriate that South Africans are not kept ignorant of the United Nations' demands that they end aparthied, and that Israelis arc not spared the details of Arab demands that their state be destroyed.

The domestic implications of intransigent adaptation, however, are not as clear-cut as the foregoing might suggest. Despite the dictatorial means by which foreign policy issues are ushered through the domestic political process, the intransigent society may not be otherwise authoritarian. Much depends on the nature of the societal attribute or attributes that underlie the intransigent adaptation. If the attribute encompasses virtually the entire society, as in Israel, then it is possible to have a competitive party system and open debate on domestic issues. The pervasiveness of the attribute allows such a society to maintain a consensus in support of dictatorial procedures in foreign affairs even as its various segments contest elections and dispute the allocation of the resources left over for internal distribution. On the other hand, if major groups of the society are not encompassed by the attribute or attributes that foster intransigent adaptation, as in the case of the Rhodesian and South African blacks, then the authoritarian method used to determine external behavior must also be used for policy-making in the domestic area. To do otherwise—to permit the groups not characterized by the salient societal attributes to contest elections and operate as an organized opposition—would be to allow for the possibility, if not the probability, that the acceptable limits of the society's essential structures would be redefined and a new type of adaptation thereby made necessary.

Whatever the ease with which officials are able to sustain intransigent adaptation, the external politics are extraordinarily difficult. As stressed in Chapter 10, altering attitudes and changing behavior abroad is the hardest of political tasks. The societies and international organizations that comprise the environment are not readily disposed to put their own internal demands aside in favor of demands made by the intransigent society. For this reason it might be concluded that in the long run the politics of intransigent adaptation are bound to fail. A society may enjoy short-run successes in seeking to make its environment compatible with its salient internal attributes, but eventually the resistance inherent in the contrary preferences distributed throughout the environment will become predominant and the intransigent adaptation will have to give way to one of the other adaptive orientations. For the officials of intransigent societies, however, such a conclusion is unthinkable. The societal attributes that lead them to seek compliance in the environment are too essential for the possibility of compromise to be considered. Hence, whatever the long-run reality, they become accustomed to asserting their non-negotiable demands and to coping with the hostility and resistance to which these demands give rise abroad. This means that their foreign policy concerns are likely to be worldwide in scope and their rhetoric ideological in character. The need frequently to proclaim and defend the justice and appropriateness of their internal structure will infuse their pronouncements with ideological fervor even though a coherent blueprint for the future may not be propounded. Such a rhetoric, however, will not dull their sensitivities to the need to cope innovatively with any developments abroad that may in the long run pose a threat to their essential structures. Where acquiescent societies cannot dare to be innovative or wide-ranging in their foreign policy, intransigent ones cannot dare to be otherwise. The environments of societies do not bend readily to their will. A substantial outward flow of persons, goods, and ideas must be maintained if the threats to essential structures are to be contested and support for their maintenance obtained.

Other characteristics of intransigent adaptation follow from the need to be both innovative and uncompromising. Presumably the officials of such societies are much readier than their counterparts in other societies to resort to intervention when circumstances abroad loom more threatening to their essential structures. Unwilling to bargain over the acceptable limits of these structures, the officials of intransigent societies must be ready to resort to military action if emerging threats to their structures cannot be offset in any other way. Israel's launching of the six-day war with Egypt and its behavior in the Middle East since that 1967 event are obvious examples of this point. Similarly, it seems likely that intransigent societies will be ever ready to develop new foreign markets and sources of economic and military assistance. On the other hand, it seems doubtful whether their external behavior will be marked by a predisposition to enter and break alliances, to reaffirm existing commitments, or to engage in the niceties of diplomatic protocol. Such foreign policy actions place too many limits on the capacity of an intransigent society to resort to new forms of external behavior when its efforts to induce change in the environment lag. To have formal allies or to reiterate the intent to abide by existing obligations abroad is to risk losing control over the salient internal attributes. Times change, and the officials of intransigent societies are bound to fear unanticipated circumstances in which the action required by any ally or a frequently affirmed obligation may necessitate unacceptable fluctuations in their essential sructures. Thus their diplomatic behavior will be marked by temporary coalitions and not permanent alliances, by reaffirmations of the importance of their essential structures and not of their international obligations. Even unqualified adherence to diplomatic protocol is potentially capable of requiring unacceptable compromises in the conduct of their internal affairs. South Africa's recent difficulties over whether to allow a Negro to enter their country as part of the American tennis team competing for the prestigious Davis Cup illustrates the extent to which intransigent societies are ready to ignore protocol if it conflicts with their essential structures.

It follows from the nature of the external behavior of intransigent societies that their military elites are likely to play prominent roles in their policy-making processes. The fact that such societies prefer to resort to military techniques of statecraft rather than compromise with their environments seems bound to give their defense experts a major voice in the conduct of public affairs. Similarly, to insure the innovation, flexibility, and single-mindedness of purpose necessary to intransigent adaptation, it is likely that a strong cabinet or chief of state will also characterized intransigent societies. Such societies may sustain multiparty systems and active legislatures under certain circumstances, but they are not likely to be structured to allow for any challenges to the preeminence of the chief executive in foreign policy.

Despite the role played by their military officials, the foreign policies of intransigent societies are not necessarily militaristic. While conflict must result from the unyielding insistence of the officials of such societies that their environments accept the external consequences of one or more of their essential structures, this insistence does not mean that their external behavior will be founded on violence. An unwillingness to bargain, for example, can mark their trade or cultural relations without escalating into issues where the use of armed force becomes relevant. If intransigent adaptation does not first undergo transformation into some other form, perhaps its inherent inflexibility will lead eventually to escalation in a military direction, but the postwar experience of South Africa suggests that the politics of intransigent adaptation can be pursued in nonmilitaristic ways for long periods. Again much depends on the nature of the internal attributes that underlie the unwillingness to bargain with the environment. The less the attributes pervade life in the intransigent society, the less the mutual relevance between them and the environment and thus the less likely are the officials to provoke developments abroad that escalate the military dimension of the society's external relations. On the other hand, when every aspect of the society's internal life is dominated by the narrowly defined essential structure, maintaining that structure will have widespread environmental consequences and the society's external relations are thus likely to be marked by military considerations. South Africa and Israel again offer a relevant contrast. The pervasiveness of Israel's socio-religious institutions presumably are part of the reason its external relations have been scarred by recurrent military conflicts, whereas the relatively limited sphere within which South African race relations have external consequences is surely a reason military escalation has not been a prime characteristic of its external affairs.

Although implicit throughout, one other aspect of intransigent adaptation should be clarified, namely, that the external behavior of intransigent societies is not rigid in every respect. Such societies are willing to bargain with their environments on a wide variety of matters. As long as a situation abroad is not perceived to be relevant to essential structures so narrowly defined as to prohibit fluctuation, the officials of intransigent societies are ready to back away from initial positions if the cost of adhering to them is not worth the gain. Thus a Hitler and a Stalin could afford to bargain with each other. Although each was the sworn enemy of the other, they could conclude a temporary non-agression pact not only because both found it expedient to postpone their ultimate clash, but also because the terms of the pact did not directly affect the internal structures that underlay their predispositions to engage in the politics of intransigent adaptation. But once an external situation is perceived to bear on the narrowly defined internal structure, the officials of intransigent societies view any cost as worth the gain of rendering the situation consistent with the requirements of the structure. Thus when the Nazis defined Czechoslovakians with German ancestry as part of the Third Reich, they laid the groundwork for an unbargainable position, as Chamberlain and the world discovered at Munich in 1938. While it may not always be immediately clear why some external situations are perceived as threatening to produce unacceptable fluctuations in a narrowly defined essential structure and some are not, the officials of intransigent societies are capable of both perceptions. Unwillingness to bargain over issues in one area is a defining characteristic of intransigent adaptation, but the external behavior of societies so oriented toward their environments is not necessarily marked by a stubborn refusal to negotiate in all areas.

THE POLITICS OF PROMOTIVE ADAPTATION

Freedom of choice for policy makers is the main characteristic of promotive adaptation. Officials with intransigent orientations toward their environment are subject to and responsive to intense demands from within their society; those moved by acquiescent orientations are subject to and responsive to intense external demands; and those with preservative orientations are the targets of irresistible demands from both within and without. The policy makers of promotive societies, in contrast, are not subjected to unyielding demands from either domestic or foreign sources and are thus relatively free to attempt to promote changes at home and abroad that will move toward a desired equilibrium between the essential structures of their society and its present environment. There are, of course, limits to this freedom. Neither the domestic nor the foreign scene is so pliable that officials can strive for any equilibrium they choose. Some equilibria may lie outside what is tolerated by the societies and international organizations in the environment, and others may require unacceptable fluctuations in one or more of the society's essential structures. If officials of a promotive society should attempt to establish these unacceptable kinds of equilibria, their society would either compel their ouster or undergo a transformation to another type of adaptation. Within the limits set by these unacceptable equilibria, however, the officials of promotive societies have considerable leeway to press for a new balance between their essential structures and their environments. Compared to their counterparts committed to other forms of adaptation, promotively oriented officials are neither exposed nor sensitive to intense demands from internal or external sources.

The desired equilibria that promotively oriented officials strive for are derived from their interpretations of the basic values and long-range goals of their society. Not impelled to action by immediate and unyielding demands, they are free to act in ways they believe are most likely to result in progress toward the desired state of affairs at home and abroad. This freedom means that they can make short-run bargains on behalf of their long-range goals with groups at home and societies abroad, sometimes giving in to one and sometimes to the other, but always in terms of a conception of how the bargains struck will ultimately promote change toward the desired equilibrium. Free to permit wide fluctuations in the essential structures of their society, promotively oriented officials can supplement their bargaining positions abroad by mobilizing new resources at home, and they can bulwark their internal bargains by retreating from external commitments. They are thus able to exercise a measure of control over the equilibrium that prevails between their society and its environment. In game theory terms, they can and do regard themselves as participants in a nonzero game in which the sum is always positive.

Perhaps the most obvious example of promotive adaptation is provided by certain large underdeveloped societies committed to a program of rapid modernization. The fact that they are under-developed means that their political institutions are not likely to generate a continuous flow of demands that curb the decisional freedom of their officials. But the fact that they are large relative to other societies in their region means that other societies cannot ignore their external behavior, thus giving their officials some flexibility in the conduct of external affairs. Finally, the fact that their officials are committed to a program of rapid modernization insures the existence of the motivation to promote a new equilibrium between their present environment and their present structures. Such a three-factor explanation seems to account for why Egypt, India, and Indonesia have exemplified promotive adapta-tion during most (if not all, in the cases of Egypt and India) of the postwar period.

The United States from the end of World War II until, say, the New Hampshire presidential primary in 1968 offers another example of promotive adaptation, albeit in this instance the desired equilibrium American officials sought to promote was more ambiguous than that sought by their counterparts in modernizing societies. Concerned about expanding welfare programs at home and building a more stable world abroad, American officials until 1968 promoted alliance systems, fought wars, provided economic assistance, and engaged in a variety of activi-ties designed to induce change abroad. Similarly, post-Stalin Russia and Mao's China, each with its own Communist version of a desirable kind of equilibrium between its essential structures and its external environ-ment, exhibited the readiness to bargain on behalf of new forms at home and abroad that is the defining characteristic of promotive adaptation. In other words, the value system underlying the desire to promote a new internal-external equilibrium need not be of a particular kind. It can be Communist or non-Communist, political or economic, Oriental or Occidental, as long as the values it embraces at least vaguely suggest changes that ought to be promoted.

Nor are promotive orientations necessarily confined to superpowers or large regional powers. Despite the examples cited, it is possible for a small, poorly endowed society to become dissatisfied with the politics of acquiescent or preservative adaptation and undergo a transformation to promotive adaptation. The new relationship to their environment that the officials of such a society seek to promote will not be as ambitious as those sought by large societies, but their behavior will nevertheless fit the pattern of promotive adaptation if they are both free to bargain with their environments and inclined to establish a new equilibrium. Cuba is an example of a small society that recently underwent transformation to the politics of promotive adaptation, and Tito's Yugoslavia offers proof that such societies can adhere to promotive orientations for extended periods.

Whatever the sources of promotive adaptation, the politics necessary to sustain it are perhaps easier than for any of the other adaptive orientations. While officials of promotive societies must be able to count on public support for the changes they seek to induce abroad, this task is greatly facilitated by the absence of strong demands on them. Their decisional freedom enables them to maintain support by redistributing the balance between domestic and foreign commitments whenever they discern incipient demands that may erode the public's confidence in their leadership. Hence, where officials of acquiescent, intransigent, and preservative societies must cope with foreign policy issues through avoidance, dictation, and debate, respectively, those of promotive societies rely on their own persuasive capacities. As long as they do not miscalculate the limits of the public apathy that underlies the lack of demands and is necessary to their decisional freedom, they can use resource redistribution at home to persuade the public to follow their lead abroad. The periodic stress on consumer and agricultural policies in post-Stalin Russia and the sporadic preoccupation of the Kennedy and Johnson administrations with fiscal and tax policies in the United States illustrates the internal redistributive activities that accompany promotive external behavior.[3]

While the internal politics of promotive adaptation are relatively easy to sustain if officials do not miscalculate the limits of public apathy, the qualification is important. The probability of miscalculation increases the longer that promotive orientations prevail in a society. That is, with the passage of time officials become increasingly confident of their capacity to lead domestic opinion even as they become increasingly involved in their efforts to promote change abroad. The convergence of these tendencies increases the probability that they will inaccurately assess the limits of public apathy and eventually underestimate the internal consequences of their external behavior. For example, despite its stress on redistribution through new fiscal and

---

[3] This is not to imply that domestic policies are knowingly or otherwise designed primarily to serve the purposes of foreign policy. Obviously the former spring predominantly from internal necessities and demands. The point is, however, that the domestic policies of a society are not undertaken in a vacuum, that to some extent they are conditioned and limited by its external undertakings. This overlap is what sustains the present wave of interdependence movements.

welfare policies, the Johnson Administration proved to be inept in calculating the limits of public apathy and the demands that emerged therefrom compelled an adaptive transformation in the United States after the presidential primaries of 1968.[4] Similarly, we can interpret the political demises of Nkrumah, Ben Bella, and Sukarno in the mid-1960s as brought about by erroneous assessments of the limits of acceptable fluctuation in the essential structures of Ghana, Algeria, and Indonesia. All three leaders carried their efforts to promote change abroad to the point where hitherto latent demands became manifest at home, and they were ousted from power. In at least two of these cases, adaptive transformations accompanied the leadership changes: the nature of Algeria's external behavior is less clear-cut, but both Ghana and Indonesia have engaged in preservative adaptation since the departures of Nkrumah and Sukarno.

These examples indicate that the political structures of promotive societies can vary considerably. The societies can be closed with single-party systems or open with two or more major parties. They can have active legislative institutions or formalistic ones. Their executive institutions can be organized along presidential or cabinet lines. As long as officials can persuade their publics to follow their lead in foreign affairs, the nature of all but one of their governmental institutions is irrelevant to the emergence and persistence of promotive adaptation. Only the variability of the role of the military elite can be clearly delineated. The periodic readiness, noted below, of such societies to enter new alliances and engage in intervening behavior to promote change abroad has the consequence of giving the military a fluctuating influence in the policy-making process. This influence rises during periods when promotive activities abroad are predominant and lessens when efforts to promote change at home become the focus of attention.

It follows that the external behavior of promotive societies is also variable. The scope of their foreign policy concerns vary as their resources are reallocated between external and internal needs and, consequently, so will both the direction and the flow of persons, materials, and ideas across their borders. To promote new patterns in their environments such societies periodically formulate innovative policies designed to break the existing patterns. On some occasions they may intervene in the affairs of other societies; at other times they may accommodate to them. Their alliance behavior is also likely to vary between

---

[4] Doubtless those responsible for formulating the Johnson policies would characterize their efforts in Vietnam as reflecting preservative rather than promotive politics. Clearly, however, fewer men and less bombings than were used in 1965-67 could have preserved the existing equilibrium in that part of the world. Thus the scale of the military effort in Vietnam in this period can be interpreted only as part of an attempt to promote a new, more desirable equilibrium.

efforts to promote new diplomatic ties abroad, during periods when their resources are mainly devoted to foreign affairs, and attempts to minimize their international commitments, during those times when their allocative process favors the domestic scene. Obviously, too, the freedom of choice enjoyed by their officials is likely to foster variability in their foreign aid and tariff programs. They will not hesitate to open up new markets or aid relationships abroad if such opportunities do not seem likely to generate external demands that curb their freedom of choice. Both the Soviet and American foreign aid programs since World War II have exhibited this combination of vigorous promotion of change when conditions permit and careful avoidance of involvement when they do not. To maintain their freedom to bargain with their environment, however, the officials of promotive societies will not, unlike their counterparts in intransigent societies, ignore the niceties of diplomatic protocol or the need to reaffirm their basic international obligations. To do so would be to risk a reputation for irresponsibility and untrustworthiness that would needlessly reduce their capacity to bargain innovatively, a capacity on which their orientation to the environment depends.

The rhetoric in which the officials of promotive societies conduct their external affairs is likely to be primarily normative. Their concern about promoting long-run changes at home and abroad that will result in new society-environment equilibria leads them to refer frequently to the goals that underlie their behavior. Yet this normative rhetoric is not likely to be ideological in tone, as is that of intransigent societies. The narrowly defined essential structures that underlie intransigent adaptation require the development of an all-encompassing and coherent blueprint that justifies the narrow range of acceptable fluctuation. In contrast, the greater leeway accorded officials of promotive societies relieves them of the need to espouse an inclusive ideology. The goals they promote abroad need not be related to each other nor to the specifics of their essential structures. Their rhetoric, however, will not be entirely pragmatic. As indicated below, a pragmatic rhetoric is characteristic of officials of preservative societies who, by definition, are preoccupied with making the best of immediate situations and are thus disinclined to refer to underlying principles and espouse long-range goals. The officials of promotive societies, however, are concerned about how the immediate circumstances of life at home and abroad may affect the realization of their long-term aspirations, and thus they are not likely to confine their foreign policy pronouncements to the pragmatic questions of how situations should be defused. Rather they are likely to talk about the permanent solutions and arrangements toward which the defusing of situations should be directed.

THE POLITICS OF PRESERVATIVE ADAPTATION

The overriding characteristic of preservative adaptation are the intense and conflicting demands emanating from both the domestic and foreign scene. These demands are so strong that the officials of preservative societies can achieve consistency between them by, in effect, bargaining them off against each other and preserving whatever equilibrium exists between their respective strengths. In this process of permitting the internal and external demands to impose limitations on each other the officials use their bargaining capacities to minimize the fluctuations in the essential structures of their society. Given the intensity of the demands, however, their freedom of choice is severely limited. Unlike their counterparts in promotive societies, officials of a preservative society cannot afford to bargain on behalf of long-run goals. The demands upon them are such that they must confine their efforts to preserving as much of their present essential structures and environment as they can. This means that short-run changes at home and abroad must be their prime concern. It also means, since the internal and external demands overlap and conflict, that they know they cannot satisfy them all and can only hope to maximize their accommodation to each other. In game theory terms, they know they are participants in a nonzero sum game in which the sum may be negative.

The postwar history of England is perhaps the classic case of preservative adaptation. The dismantling of its Empire, the effort to join the European Common Market, and the adoption of broad welfare policies at home are central features of a long process of readjustment in the balance between external commitments and internal needs that England has experienced since its capacity for promotive adaptation ended with World War II. Winston Churchill may not have wanted to preside over the dissolution of the British Empire, but in the late 1940s and early 1950s he and his successors discovered that the internal and external demands were so intense that only a perservative orientation was feasible. Although it is still too early to reach a clear-cut conclusion, it may be that the United States has undergone a similar transformation in recent years, perhaps culminating when the presidential primaries of 1968 revealed that the internal demands were no longer incipient and the promotion of change abroad no longer tolerable. Lyndon Johnson may not have wanted to de-escalate the American involvement in Vietnam, but by 1968 he and his successors developed a new set of adaptive orientations that could lead only in that direction. In a like manner the orientations and behavior of Indonesian and

Ghanaian officials shifted in a pronouncedly preservative direction after the political demises of the Sukarno and Nkrumah regimes revealed the inappropriateness of promotive orientations.

This is not to equate preservative adaptation with withdrawal from involvement in the international system. The foregoing examples have in common a retreat from external commitments only because the dynamics of preservative adaptation are most clearly revealed in the processes of contraction. Numerous examples could be cited, however, of preservatively oriented societies whose ties to their environment have remained essentially stable for long periods of time. Many Latin American, West European, African, and Asian societies are neither acquiescing to nor promoting new arrangements abroad, but are instead working, and bargaining, hard to maintain the prevailing balance between their internal and external needs. Indeed, it is likely that more societies will come to engage in preservative adaptation than in any other type because a strong sense of national identity inhibits acquiescence and resource limitations curb the emergence of intransigent and promotive orientations. Whether this line of reasoning can be extended to asserting that the long-run tendency of all societies is toward preservative adaptation is a complex question to which we shall return.

Although the politics of preservative adaptation are complicated by the need to allocate resources without sudden shifts in the prevailing balance, the task of preserving the existing equilibrium between internal and external demands is not difficult. Officials may have to cope with an endless series of momentary crises, but their ability to avoid succumbing to the excessive demands generated by crisis is considerable. Both groups at home and societies abroad know that the officials are subject to the demands of others as well as their own, with the result that the officials can effectively cling to bargaining positions somewhere between the two extremes. To be sure, particular sets of officials may not be able to restore the equilibrium when temporary imbalances develop between their society's domestic and foreign commitments, and the task of restoration may pass to a new set of officials who can use their newness in office and their lack of responsibility for earlier events to bring the internal and external demands back into balance. For this reason it can be hypothesized that cabinets fall or get reshuffled and parties lose favor or get regrouped more frequently in preservative societies than in any other type. Viewed from a larger societal perspective, the turnover in officialdom is a mechanism that facilitates the maintenance of preservative adaptation. In short, while the political careers of particular officials may not survive the ups and downs inherent in the politics of preservative adaptation, the task of sustaining this type of adaptation is not especially difficult for the society itself.

It follows, virtually by definition, that the politics of preservative adaptation are bound to be more open and animated than those of other adaptive orientations. The presence of internal demands too intense to be ignored means that leadership persuasion will not suffice as a technique for ushering foreign policy issues through the domestic process. Rather, public debate, invigorated by countervailing domestic and foreign pressures for resource reallocation, will doubtless mark policy making in preservative societies. Legislatures and political parties as well as private groups and nongovernmental organizations will thus be much more active and demanding than in societies oriented toward any of the other three adaptive forms. Certainly it is difficult to imagine a one-party system or a strong chief executive surviving in a society that remains preservatively oriented for a long time. If such institutions capable of maintaining tight control over policy making in the society should persist and successfully offset the demands that sustain the internal-external equilibrium, a transformation away from preservative adaptation seems bound to occur. As for the military in preservative societies, their influence seems likely to be minimal in comparison to intransigent and promotive societies. As elaborated below, preservatively oriented societies do occasionally become involved in foreign policy undertakings that require the deployment and use of, or at least the readiness to use, force. Thus, while the military ventures of such societies are not likely to be extensive or frequent, they cannot avoid training and maintaining at least a small officer corps capable of providing advice and leadership at high policy-making levels.

Given the readiness of preservative societies to live with rather than change the limitations inherent in their environments, the scope of their external behavior is not likely to extend much beyond their particular region. Global issues may sometimes be perceived as relevant to their internal-external equilibrium and the officials of such societies may even see some utility in playing a mediating or broker role in East-West conflicts. For the most part, however, their involvement in matters distant from their borders is likely to be peripheral and spasmodic. In direct contrast with their counterparts in promotive societies, preservatively oriented officials periodically reaffirm their preservative orientations and their intention to fulfill their international obligations, but only rarely are they likely to engage in innovative or interventionary behavior abroad. On the other hand, to maintain the constant flow of persons, materials, and ideas in and out of the society necessary to sustain the prevailing internal-external balance, preservatively oriented officials are not likely to engage in varying behavior insofar as protocol, tariffs, and foreign aid are concerned. The preservation of stability in their region may also require them to become extensively involved in establishing and maintaining alliances deemed necessary to regional security.

It follows that the rhetoric of preservatively oriented officials is likely to be essentially pragmatic in character. Concerned lest any of the situations at home or abroad disturb the prevailing internal-external equilibrium, such officials do not cast their behavior in the normative or ideological language of their promotive and intransigent counterparts. To talk of long-range goals is to run the risk of obscuring, and thus failing to cope with, the needs of the moment. Hence, policy makers of preservative societies tend to confine their rhetoric to the immediate dimensions and practical consequences of the situations toward which their external behavior is directed.

THE TRANSFORMATION OF ADAPTIVE ORIENTATIONS

Assuming that the distinctions among the four types of adaptation can be operationalized and empirical data bearing on the political processes that sustain them accumulated, two related lines of theoretical inquiry are worthy of further development. One arises out of the question of why one set of adaptive orientations prevails in a society rather than another. That is, what conditions must be present for a society to adhere to acquiescent, intransigent, promotive, or preservative orientations? Second, the foregoing analysis leads to the question of when and why transformations from one type of adaptation to another occur. That is, what kinds of changes have to unfold at home and abroad for a society to develop a new orientation toward whether the demands emanating from its environment should be accepted, contested, or altered? If hypotheses that probe these interrelated lines of inquiry can be formulated and tested, considerable light will be shed on the original question of why the present era is marked by a wave of interdependence movements, and perhaps on the more fundamental question of what processes allow most societies to adapt to their environments and lead a few to fail to survive.

While specific hypotheses relevant to these questions cannot be developed here, we can set forth some initial considerations. Implicit in the previous analysis are several broad hypotheses as to the nature and relative potency of the individual, governmental, societal, and systemic variables that foster and sustain each type of adaptation.[5] Table 18–3,

[5] Individual variables are those unique aspects of a policy maker's background, values, and talents that are not part of his official role requirements and that may vary from one occupant of the position to another. Governmental variables are the role requirements built into policy-making positions and many vary from one government to another. Societal variables are those unique aspects of a society's history, capabilities, institutions, and values that may vary from one society to another at one point in time or from one era to another for the same society. For more extensive definitions of these four clusters of independent variables, as well as elaboration of their utility as an analytic tool to explain the external behavior of national societies, see Chapters 6, 7, 16, and 17.

Table 18 – 3   The Relative Potencies of Four Clusters of Independent Variables as Sources of Four Types of National Adaptation

Relative potency to variable clusters	Acquiescent adaptation	Intransigent adaptation	Promotive adaptation	Preservative adaptation
HIGH	systemic	societal	individual	systemic societal governmental
LOW	societal individual governmental	systemic individual governmental	systemic societal governmental	individual

which classifies the four clusters of independent variables in terms of whether their relative potency is likely to be high or low in each type of adaptive politics, summarizes the hypotheses that can be derived from the foregoing pages. The rankings and classifications in each cell of the table are broad in scope and considerable elaboration and refinement are required before data can be gathered. Yet they do offer a point of departure for analyzing the transformation of adaptive orientations and the derivation of each cell thus needs to be briefly explained.

A geographical variable from the systemic cluster—the proximity of a much larger society intent upon imposing its will on its neighbors—is one of the two conditions necessary for the emergence and persistence of acquiescent adaptation.[6] The other is the absence in the adapting society of any highly potent societal, individual, or governmental variables. If a variable from any of these clusters should ever become as potent as the systemic variable and thereby restrain the latter's operation to another type of adaptation. When, for example, the Dubcek regime came to power in Czechoslovakia in early 1968 and allowed for a political and social transformation that greatly increased the relative potency of a number of societal and governmental variables, Czechoslovakia moved toward preservative adaptation until the systemic variable was restored to its relatively high potency with the Russian intervention of August 1968. Similarly, the emergence of new political forces in Panama led to an increase in the potency of some societal variables,

---

[6] As we saw earlier, under special conditions acquiescent adaptation may emerge and persist even in the absence of this geographical variable. These conditions are so exceptional, however, that to introduce them at this point would only obfuscate the analysis.

and that increase appears to have fostered preservative orientations toward the environment.

Although it is not as easy to specify precisely the variables that give rise to the emergence and persistence of intransigent adaptation, it is clear that two conditions are necessary to and sufficient for the operation of such an orientation. One is that a single variable from the societal cluster must be highly potent. The identity of this variable is difficult to specify. It may be the structure of a society's race relations (as in South Africa or Rhodesia), the uniqueness and pervasiveness of its socio-religious origins and institutions (as in Israel), the predominance of an ideological political party (as in Nazi Germany), or any one of a variety of other dimensions rooted in the historical experiences and structural characteristics of societies. The second condition necessary to intransigent adaptation is that relatively low potency must attach to the other societal variables and to all the individual, governmental, and systemic variables. If the potency of any of these should begin to approximate, and thereby constrain, that of the highly potent societal variable, then the intransigent orientations will be undermined and a transformation to another type of adaptation will ensue.

Two conditions are also necessary to and sufficient for the emergence and persistence of promotive adaptation. One is that relatively high potency must attach to a particular individual variable, namely, the presence of top officials who are inclined to promote changes at home and abroad that will result in a new and desired equilibrium between their society's essential structures and its environment. The second is that the potency of all governmental, societal, and systemic variables must be relatively low. If any of the latter should become highly potent and thereby operate as a check on the promotively oriented officials, or if the basic environmental orientations of the officials should for other reasons undergo change, then the politics of promotive adaptation will undergo transformation into some other kind.. Indonesia is an example. Whether its adaptive behavior subsequent to Sukarno's ouster is interpreted as resulting from high potency newly accruing to the societal variable that underlay the ouster, or whether it is seen as due to the presence of new officials who did not share Sukarno's interest in promoting new environmental ties, the fact is that the promotive adaptation that characterized Indonesia before 1965 has since given way to another type.

Three conditions are necessary to and sufficient for the emergence and persistence of preservative adaptation. First, relatively high potency must attach to various systemic and societal variables, thus preventing those from one of these clusters predominating over the other. Second, one governmental variable, the openness of the society's policy-making process, must be sufficiently potent to allow for the interaction between the various systemic and societal demands through which the existing equilibrium is preserved. Third, relatively low potency must attach to individual variables, so that no leaders come to power committed to and capable of avoiding or replacing the balance between internal and external factors. If any of these conditions do not prevail, then the society will undergo transformation to another type of adaptation. As already noted, for example, this happened to Czechoslovakia in August 1968, when the systemic demands upon it overwhelmed (through the Soviet military intervention) the societal and governmental variables that had sustained the politics of preservative adaptation. An example of what happens when the potency of societal and systemic variables begins to decline relative to that of individual variables is provided by the experience of Egypt. Before 1952 the conditions necessary to preservative adaptation prevailed in Egypt, but the accession to power of Nasser and other leaders committed to rapid modernization resulted in new forms of adaptive behavior. Likewise, if a society lacks an open policy-making process for mediating the systemic and societal demands, then either the systemic variables will predominate (as in Czechoslovakia), or a single societal variable will become relatively much more potent (as in South Africa), or the individual variable will emerge with greater potency (as in Egypt), developments that in any event result in some form of adaptive transformation. Still another possibility is the one that follows if the systemic, societal, and individual variables remain highly potent in the absence of a policy-making process capable of integrating them. Under these circumstances maladaptation, and possibly even extinction, rather than adaptive transformation, will occur as the society proves incapable of coping with the internal and external demands upon it. The collapse of France in 1940 is perhaps an illustration.

Assuming that the four rankings of the variables in Table 18–3 reflect stable patterns of national adaptation and that any of the other possible rankings would reflect transitions from one of the stable adaptive types to another, it is possible to speculate more correctly about the dynamics of adaptive transformations. As the numbered cells in Table 18–4 indicate, twelve different types of transformation may occur. If the rankings of Table 18–3 are superimposed upon the vacant cells of Table 18–4 to see which variables have to gain and lose relative potency for each transformation to take place, it becomes clear that some of the twelve possible transformations are more likely to occur than others—that, indeed, some of the twelve require an extremely unlikely convergence of social and technological forces. For example, for a society to go from an acquiescent to an intransigent form of adaptation (Cell 1 of Table 18–4) would simultaneously require a technological revolution that equalized its strengh vis-à-vis a nearby super-power and an internal upheaval through which one of its social institu-tions became more potent than both the external pressures and the other social structures of the society. The convergence of changes such as these seems so contrary to historical experience that it is reasonable to conclude that the probability of Type 1 transformations is zero. A somewhat similar conclusion can be reached about transformations from acquiescent to promotive adaptation. In this case it is based on the unlikelihood that a new group of officials will become so powerful in a society that they will be able to negate the will of a nearby superpower and promote a new internal-external equilibrium expressing their own aspirations. Since the adaptive transformation of post-Castro Cuba belies this conclusion, however, the probability of Type 2 transformations must be rated as somewhat greater than zero. On the other hand, the chances of Type 3 transformations occurring seem to be much greater than either of the other shifts from acquiescent adaptation. In an age of strong nationalist identities, the emergence of societal and governmental variables whose potency rivals external pressures is not unlikely. Rumania, Yugoslavia, Panama, and (briefly) Hungary and Czechoslo-vakia offer recent evidence that the probability of transformations from acquiescent to preservative adaptation is substantial.

Turning to transformations away from intransigent adaptation (the second row of Table 18-4), again two of the three alternatives seem quite improbable in contrast to the third. For an intransigently oriented society to shift to the politics of either acquiescent or promotive adapta-tion, the societal attribute sustaining its unwillingness to bargain with its environment would have to weaken to the point where either a nearby superpower or a group of new leaders would come to predominate in the society. Such changes, given the strength of the societal variable, seem so improbable that it is easier to imagine the failure of an intransi-gent society to adapt than undergoing either a Type 4 or 5 form of transformation. Certainly, for example, Israel is more likely to be destroyed by its environment than to acquiesce to it. On the other hand, it is not difficult to conceive of internal and external changes which interactively result in systemic, societal, and governmental variables equal to or greater in potency than the one societal variable that sustains the intransigent adaptation, thereby giving rise to a Type 6 transforma-tion to the politics of preservative adaptation. Change in the environ-ment could result in such a threatening situation that an intransigent society might find it necessary to begin to bargain. Or a readiness to bargain might result from an internal upheaval that drastically reduces the potency of the societal attribute that has underlain the uncompro-mising external behavior. If Israel should ever be unable to procure

Table 18 – 4   Twelve Types of Adaptive Transformation

Transformation from:	Transformation to:			
	Acquies-cent adaptation	Intransi-gent adaptation	Promotive adaptation	Preserva-tive adaptation
Acquiescent adaptation	—	1	2	3
Intransigent adaptation	4	—	5	6
Promotive adaptation	' 7	8	—	9
Preservative adaptation	10	11	12	—

military supplies abroad, or if its military superiority in the Middle East should be substantially undermined by the flow of arms to its neighbors, its officials may well move from intransigent to preservative orientations toward the region. Likewise, if a successful black revolution should ever occur in Rhodesia or South Africa, the conditions for a Type 6 transformation will have been established. Such a revolt would end the predominance of racial factors as a source of external intransigence and the new regimes would almost surely be inclined to preserve the new internal-external equilibrium that prevailed in the postrevolutionary situation.

Speculation about transformations away from the politics of promotive adaptation follows much the same line. The chances of change toward preservative adaptation (Type 9) seem much greater than toward the other two types (7 and 8). For a promotively oriented society to move toward acquiescent or intransigent adaptation, systemic or societal factors would have to undergo changes that normally take decades or centuries to unfold. Technological developments would have to greatly increase the superiority of a nearby society in order to facilitate a Type 7 transformation or one of the promotive society's social structures would have to acquire an importance greatly in excess of the others in the case of a Type 8 transformation. The seeming unlikelihood of such changes is in sharp contrast to the possibility of a Type 9 transformation. Here all that is required is that any of a variety of systemic, societal, and governmental variables become highly potent relative to the individual preferences of the officials who occupy the top policy-making posts. A number of variables can undergo such change in a matter of months or years. As we have already noted, for example, public unrest at home and resistance abroad can mushroom rather quickly if the efforts of officials to promote a desired internal-external equilibrium are based on miscalculations. Compared to Type 7 and Type 8 transformations, therefore, the probability that promotive orientations will change in a preservative direction seems very high.

Turning to transformations away from preservative adaptation (the fourth row of Table 18-4), here none of the three alternatives seems very likely. In particular, it appears doubtful that one societal attribute would ever become so potent as to overwhelm the systemic, governmental, and other societal variables that sustain a preservative orientation and thereby precipitate a transformation to intransigent adaptation. As indicated by the Israeli and South African cases, the societal attributes that sustain intransigent adaptation usually stem from the unique historical circumstances through which societies acquire a legal existence rather than from a slow evolution subsequent to their origin. If defeats in war and postwar peace terms are treated as the equivalent of national origins, this would also explain the rapid Type 11 transformation that Germany went through in the 1930s. Except for these rapid transformations associated with societal legitimacy, however, it is difficult to imagine that the kind of social change necessary for a shift from preservative to intransigent orientations could extend over a long time. Too many variables operate during slow evolutionary processes for the outcome to resemble a Type 11 transformation.

Since the shift from preservative to acquiescent orientations can result from experiencing the exercise of naked force, as Czechoslovakia did in August 1968, Type 10 transformations are perhaps somewhat more likely than Type 11. Obviously, however, this greater probability pertains only to those small preservatively oriented societies located close to a large regional power or a superpower. If the sample is enlarged to include all societies, the chances of such transformations occurring diminish considerably. Indeed, as previously suggested, in an age when national identity exerts a strong hold over people, it is conceivable that even some of the small, vulnerable societies would prefer, through a fight-to-the-death response to the nearby superpower, maladaptation and destruction to abandoning their commitment to preservative adaptation.

Similarly, it does not seem likely that the balance of systemic, societal, and governmental variables that sustain preservative adaptation could all undergo a diminution of potency that allowed for the emergence of officials sufficiently free of internal and external restraints to try to promote a new equilibrium consistent with their individual predictions. A Type 12 transformation would seem to require a coup d'etat or revolution that yielded a charismatic leader capable of ignoring the systemic and societal pressures that had sustained the politics of preservative adaptation. Nasser did it in Egypt after 1952 and so did De Gaulle in France after 1959, but these cases are exceptional rather than typical. Indeed, it could well be argued that they are only temporary examples, that both Egypt and France have since begun another transformation that is heading them back in a preservative direction.

CONCLUSION

The foregoing speculation is summarized in Table 18–5, which reproduces Table 18–4 with the addition of estimated probabilities in each of the cells. A pronounced tendency in the adaptive transformations of national societies can be discerned in the table. However a society may be inclined to adapt to its environment, the likelihood that it will move toward the politics of preservative adaptation is considerable once the processes of transformation are initiated. This is why, we would argue, the changing world scene presently amounts to a wave of self-conscious interdependence movements. Having become aware in the present era that a society's adaptation to its environment need not be permanent, mass publics and their leaders have precipitated social processes that, given the probability of occurrence of each type of transformation, seem to be leading all or most societies in the same direction. Preservative adaptation may not be an immediate requirement of national societies, but in the long sweep of history, it appears to be the ultimate outcome for most of them.

Table 18 – 5   **Estimated Probabilty of Occurrence of the Twelve Types of Adaptive Transformation**

	Transformation to:			
Transformation from:	Acquiescent adaptation	Intransigent adaptation	Promotive adaptation	Preservative adaptation
Acquiescent adaptation	—	1 nil	2 low	3 high
Intransigent adaptation	4 nil	—	5 nil	6 high
Promotive adaptation	7 nil	8 nil	—	9 high
Preservative adaptation	10 low	11 nil	12 low	—

19 Muddling, Meddling, and Modeling: Alternative Approaches to the Study of World Politics *

When paradigms crumble, they crumble very quickly. The slightest inroad into their coherence opens gaping holes and the collapse of each of their premises raises further doubts about their adequacy. Before long everything seems questionable, and what once seemed so orderly soon looms as sheer chaos.

Such a process of paradigm deterioration, I believe, is underway in the study of world affairs. And while this can lead to an exciting sense of venturesomeness, so can it result in enormous difficulties and confusion.

Thus these are hard times for those who theorize about world affairs and foreign policy. No sooner had we successfully come through several decades of enormous theoretical progress than the world which we began to comprehend manifested unmistakable signs of profound change, rendering our hard-won theoretical sophistication increasingly obsolete. No sooner had we replaced the "billiard ball" model of the realists with a differentiated state model that focused on decisional processes and the domestic sources of foreign policy than the competence of governments began to decline and their capacity to sustain effective foreign policies underwent further deterioration. No sooner had we moved significantly forward in understanding the dynamics of arms races and the premises of strategic theory than new problems of interdependence began to rival the older questions of diplomatic and military strategy as

* Earlier versions of this chapter were presented to the Seminar on Theories of International Relations and Theories of Knowledge, Department of International Relations, The Australian National University, Canberra, July 27, 1978, and the Conference on International Relations Theory, School of International Studies, Jawaharlal Nehru University, New Delhi, May 17, 1979, and published in K. P. Misra and Richard Smith Beal (eds.), *International Relations Theory: Western and Non-Western Perspectives* (New Delhi: Vikas Publishing Pvt. Ltd., 1979), Chap. 3. An abridged version is scheduled for publication in *Millennium: Journal of International Studies*, Vol. 8, No. 2 (1979). Reprinted with the permission of the Millennium Publishing Group, London.

issues on the global agenda. No sooner had we started to link the machinery of foreign policy formulation to the external behavior of states than a host of other important entities appeared on the world scene that were neither governments nor conducted foreign policies. And no sooner had we perfected new methodologies for analyzing decisions and tracing the pattern of events than relevant decisions and events began to spring from the behavior of multinational corporations and other types of nonstate organizations that could not be readily examined through the application of the hard-won methodologies.

In short, nothing seems to fit. Our great strides in theory and research during the 1950s, 1960s, and 1970s no longer correspond well to the world they were intended to describe. Authority has been too widely decentralized and societies too thoroughly fragmented to be handled by even our most refined concepts. Consider, for example, these recent events reported in the Los Angeles press:

> The Navahos and 21 other Western Indian tribes enter into discussions with the Organization of Petroleum Exporting Countries (OPEC) in an effort to get advice on the development of energy resources.

> President Sadat of Egypt takes his case to American Jews through a full-page advertisement in the *Los Angeles Times* and other U.S. newspapers.

> The University of Southern California and the government of Bahrein sign a contract in which the former agrees to provide the intellectual resources needed by the latter.

> Ministers of the Quebec separatist government undertake a series of tours of California in an effort to gain understanding and build support for their independence movement.

How does one analyze such developments? In what niches of the post-realist, differentiated, and multipolar state model can they be placed? The answer strikes me as obvious as it is distressing: such events have no home in our current formulations. We could, of course, discuss them as isolated, inconsequential, or transitory phenomena, a reaction that would then allow us to treat them as random incidents and to muddle through in spite of them. I doubt, however, whether we will long be able to muddle through our analyses as if basic and profound changes in the structures of world politics were not at work. The evidence that such transformations are underway seems too extensive to ignore. The Navaho may never get the aid they want. Sadat may never get the peace he wants, Bahrein may never get the guidance it seeks, and the Quebec separatists may never generate the private support abroad they desire; but aspirations, efforts, and activities of this kind seem likely to become more rather than less pervasive and salient in world politics. Or at least this possibility seems too great to justify an analytic posture of muddling through.

Another possible reaction to the indicators of underlying change involve acknowledging that structural transformations are at work and attempting to accommodate them by meddling with our current formulations. Indeed, this would seem to be the prevalent analytic posture in the field today. Aware that the dynamics of change are too extensive to dismiss, many analysts have understandably sought to tidy up their conceptual equipment to account for the transformations.[1] Explorations have been sought through emphasis on the mounting interdependence of groups and societies (hence Bahrein and U.S.C.), through stress on the proliferation of nonstate actors (hence the Navahos and the Quebec separatists), and though the notion that transnational relations have come to rival interstate relations as dominant features of the world scene (hence Sadat's appeal to American Jews). But such meddling will not do. The tidied up formulations are too ungainly to yield a deeper understanding. To posit greater interdependence is not to explain complexity. To allow for a much greater variety and number of significant international actors is not to account for the direction and pace of decentralization. To conceive of transnational phenomena as more salient is not to grasp what moves the course of events.

A third reaction to the presence of pervasive change is possible. Rather than preserving our current formulations either by dismissing the change or by absorbing it, we could treat it as so fundamental as to welcome the deterioration of existing paradigms and to warrant the construction of entirely new models. Such an analytic posture has been adopted by a few analysts who have gone well beyond tidying up and offered whole substitutes for the post-realist, differentiated, and multi-polar state model. Most notably, the underlying structural changes have been located in the context either of an issue paradigm that depicts the complexities of a decentralized world [2] or of a global society that subsumes and manages an ever more interdependent world.[3] But these

---

[1] For a succinct review of a variety of efforts to employ the meddling approach, see Kal J. Holsti, "A New International Politics? Diplomacy in Complex Interdependence," *International Organization*, 32 (Spring 1978), pp. 513-530.

[2] For example, see J. R. Handelman, J. A. Vasquez, M. K. O'Leary, and W. D. Coplin, "Color It Morgenthau: A Data-Based Assessment of Quantitative International Relations Research," a paper presented to the Annual Meeting of the International Studies Association (Syracuse: Syracuse University, 1973).

[3] Examples here are John W. Burton, *World Society* (London: Cambridge University Press, 1972), and Richard A. Falk, *A Study of Future Worlds* (New York: Free Press, 1975).

paradigmatic endeavors are also wanting. For the world appears to be both more decentralized and more interdependent, thereby requiring a paradigm that posits an overall global structure which imposes coherence on diverse issues without presuming the orderliness of a society.

PUTTING FIRST THINGS FIRST

The foregoing rests on two basic convictions that can usefully be explicated. One is that no amount of muddling or meddling through can prevent the collapse of a paradigm that has started to go. Thus I see no choice for us but to start afresh with the modeling approach. I shall return to the question of what this choice might involve.

Secondly, I am convinced that neither epistemological nor methodological problems are the source of our difficulties in the field today. The need to develop a new paradigm springs not from the failure of quantitative techniques or the insufficiency of qualitative modes of analysis. Rather our dilemmas derive from substantive sources, from the dynamics of change that are rendering the world ever more complex as the twentieth century nears an end. Whether one is inclined to rest inquiry on scientific practices, on Marxian dialectics, on historical-interpretive approaches, or on the methods of analytic philosophy, one still has to contend with the declining capacity of governments, the rise of new issues, the advent of new actors, and the many interactive effects that derive from mounting interdependence in an increasingly fragmented world. These substantive dynamics are at work no matter how we proceed. And they are not going to become any less perplexing if our methodological disputes are resolved and our epistemological differences clarified.

I suppose it is conceivable that some of the substantive dynamics lend themselves to greater clarification through one epistemology or methodology than another, but this would be hard to demonstrate and the energy invested in such a debate does not seem worth any gains that might result. Much more is to be gained, I would contend, by presuming that all the available epistemologies and methodologies have something to offer if more appropriate paradigms can be developed.

Such a presumption seems reasonable. The realist-idealist and science-nonscience debates have spent themselves, I think, and one senses that an acceptance—if not a tolerance—of diversity has set in. We in the international relations field probably contested methodological and epistemological issues more intensely, more stubbornly, and more thoroughly in recent decades than did those in any other area of political science, but thus we may also be able to move on more quickly. Or at least the philosophical and methodological debates now unfolding elsewhere in the discipline somehow seem antiquated. We have covered that ground and few among us still have a need to assert the importance of such matters.

I have wondered for a long time why methodological introspection seemed so much more endemic to the study of international relations than to other fields of political analysis. The answer would not seem to be in the recruitment process—in the kinds of combative personalities that are attracted to study international phenomena. Rather it is to be found, I think, in the elusiveness of international phenomena—in the great distances from which we must observe them and the tough cultural barriers through which our observations must pass.[4] But now it seems clear that these very difficulties are also an advantage, for they have inhibited the emergence of orthodoxy and encouraged the perfection of diverse methodologies.

This is not to say there is no need to be methodologically aware or epistemologically sensitive. Obviously such matters will continue to be important—if only because the advent of new nongovernmental actors may require the development of new techniques of analysis—and clearly inquiry will be more incisive the more sophisticated it is in these regards. But our hard-won tolerance of diversity does allow us to put methodological concerns in perspective and to converge on the central problem. This is, to repeat, the problem of theory, of constructing paradigms that more adequately account for the changing structures of world politics.

AN AMERICAN DISTORTION?

Reactions to earlier versions of the foregoing reasoning have made me keenly aware that the processes of pervasive change are not self-evident, that many observers do not perceive a need for new paradigms because they view the structures and dynamics of world politics as essentially undifferentiated from the past. The wealthy elites still dominate the working classes (say the Marxists), the superpowers still dominate the international scene (say the power theorists), and nongovernmental actors have always limited the capacities of governments (say the post-realists). The trends and developments that strike me as reflective of basic transformations, in other words, are seen by others

---

[4] For a useful discussion of this point, see Jeffrey Harrod, "International Relations, Perceptions and Neo-Realism," *The Year Book of World Affairs, Vol.* 31 (1977), pp. 289-305.

as peripheral, as mere perturbations in long-standing, deeply rooted historic patterns.

This criticism has been voiced primarily by nonAmericans, who contend that the perception of pervasive change is not so much an empirical observation as it is a conceptual bias of scholars.[5] The decline of the U.S.'s role in world affairs, supplemented by an inclination toward pragmatic and nonhistorical analysis that sometimes amounts to faddism, are said to have predisposed American students of international relations to be much too quick to treat marginal fluctuations as central changes and much too ready to ignore the possibility that things are the same as they have always been except for a substantial lessening of their country's influence over the course of events. It could be. The question of how much change constitutes basic change is more a conceptual than an empirical question. Or at least the empirical attempts to measure change have not yielded such clearcut and convergent findings as to promote widespread agreement on whether fundamental transformations are at work.[6] And surely American scholars have long been biased toward keeping their studies of world affairs consonant with their images of world affairs.[7]

To dismiss the indicators of change as an American bias, however, is to fail to confront the central question of whether world politics is undergoing transformation. Such a dismissal may even be expressive of a nonAmerican bias in which European and Oriental scholars presume that nothing basically new can ever develop because comparable events can always be found in history. To be sure, one can always identify incidents in the past that correspond in some salient ways to any present event. But history also records breakpoints, watersheds, transformations, redirections, and the like, with the result that the presumption of historical continuity can be just as prejudiced and self-

---

[5] For an analysis that emphasizes such a bias and argues that the changes are superficial in comparison to the continuities of world politics, see F. S. Northedge, "Transnationalism: The American Illusion," *Millenium*, 5 (Spring 1976), pp. 21-27.

[6] For some systematic attempts to assess the degree of structural change in the global system, see P. J. Katzenstein, "International Interdependence: Some Long-Term Trends and Recent Changes," *International Organization*, 29 (Autumn 1975), pp. 1020-1034; R. R. Kaufman, H. I. Chernotsky, and D. S. Geller, 'A Preliminary Test of the Theory of Dependency," *Comparative Politics*, 7 (April 1975), pp. 303-331; and R. Rosecrance, A. Alexandroff, W. Koehler, J. Kroll, S. Laquer, and J. Stocker, "Whither Independence?" *International Organization*, 31 (Summer 1975), pp. 425-472.

[7] Two observers, for example, note that the study of "international relations is an American invention dating from the time after World War I when the American intellectual community discovered the world. Like most American essays in regard to the world, it has been enthusiastic, well-financed, faddist, nationally-oriented, and creating more problems that it solves." Fred Warner Neal and Bruce D. Hamlett, "The Never-Never Land of International Relations," *International Studies Quarterly*, 13 September 1969), p. 283.

deceptive as the assumption that profound changes are occurring. Moreover, it is the very nature of paradigms that they are so encompassing as to be entrapping, preventing us from seeing their increasing inappropriateness because they are founded on premises that can absorb and explain any contradictions. This is why paradigms seem to crumble quickly once they start to crumble: when we finally break free of them enough to get an inkling of their inappropriateness, they are already far gone and thus appear to crumble quickly.

How, then, does one proceed? Assuming the problem is conceptual and not empirical, what presumption does one make as to whether profound changes are transforming world politics or whether deep-seated continuities are preserving the existing structure? My answer is already clear. I find it safer to proceed as if the changes are occurring than to treat them as peripheral. In this way we can at least allow for the evolution of a new paradigm which may, subsequently, prove insufficient because not that much change has occurred. But if we muddle or meddle through by stressing the deep-seated continuities, we run the risk of missing out on the prevailing dynamics of our field. I admit to being insufficiently grounded in history and I acknowledge the possibility that my perspectives are too grounded in American biases. Yet I find the indicators of change (such as those noted on page 535) to be so impressive and so pervasive that I cannot back away from the conclusion that trying to develop new paradigms is energy well expended.

SOME ESSENTIAL COMPONENTS OF NEW PARADIGMS

Having worked within the post-realist differentiated state model for nearly three decades, I am in no position to offer a new and coherent paradigm. To recognize the rapidity with which a paradigm crumbles when it starts to go is not to discern the outlines and basic premises of those that might evolve in its place. One is, of course, highly conscious of the reasons for the collapse, but these may point only to some of the essential components of a new paradigm rather than to the organizing assumptions and causal links that render it coherent and all-encompassing. A long period of disarray and tension may have to ensue before the essential components of a new paradigm are pieced together into a structured and parsimonious whole.

There is an exception to the lengthy process of paradigm replacement. If the reasons for the collapse of the old are consistent with the basic premises of a well-developed, existing paradigm that has not previously seemed competitive, then a ready-made alternative is at hand and the period of disarray can be avoided. If, for example, one became disenchanted with the differentiated state model because the behavior of the new actors and the dynamics of the new issues of interdependence appeared to stem from class conflicts that had not previously seemed so central, one might readily adopt the Marxist perspective. Such a shift to the Marxist paradigm strikes me as likely to be made by increasing numbers of international relations analysts in industrial democracies. The mounting of North-South tensions and the demands for a New Economic Order, not to mention the prominent role multinational corporations have come to play as rivals to governments in world politics, can readily be interpreted in a Marxist framework as the differentiated state model seems increasingly inappropriate. Moreover, since "Marx is capable of a wide range of interpretations . . . each perfectly consistent within itself," and since there are thus "many Marxes," [8] the handling of monetary crises, famine, trade imbalance, and many of the other new interdependence issues on the global agenda may be just as easily cast in one or another Marxist framework as any fledgling non-Marxist paradigm that may evolve.

I wish it was so simple. Building paradigmatic foundations is so arduous and tenuous that ready-made formulations as incisive as those to be found in Marx are tempting replacements. As I understand the four essential elements that the many Marxist formulations have in common,[9] however, the fit does not seem sufficient to yield to temptation. Though it surely needs to be done by many observers, this is not the place to undertake an analysis of how the dynamics of change may or may not be shaping a world that conforms to Marxist paradigms. Suffice it to note that I find too much diversity in the fragmentation of authority, as well as in the structures, social bases, and aspirations of the new nonstate organizations through whom the fragmentation is occurring, to accept the Marxist emphasis on class struggle as the prime motor of historical change.

So I, for one, need to start from scratch and undertake a search for the essential components of a future paradigm that accounts for an overall global structure which imposes coherence on diverse issues without presuming the orderliness of a society. But where to begin? How do we know the essential components of such a paradigm when we come upon them? What criteria should we use to select the building blocks of appropriate new models? My answer to these key questions is twofold. In the first place, we need to develop concepts that focus on dynamic rather than static phenomena, that are organized around the processes of interacting entities rather than their attributes. If we can construct the outlines of a world in which the course of events is

---

[8] Robert L. Heilbronner, 'Inescapable Marx," *The New York Review of Books*, Vol. XXV (June 29, 1978), p. 34.

[9] *Ibid.*, p. 35.

sustained by processes rather than actors, we need not fear that our paradigm will be rendered obsolete by the declining capacities of governments, the advent of new issues initiated by new organizations, the fragmentation of authority, or the growth of interdependence. For all these tendencies are processes, and they ought to be subject to investigation irrespective of whether they are maintained by states, bureaucracies, nongovernmental entities, or transnational bodies. Secondly, it follows that we need to begin with building blocks that are developed at such a high level of abstraction that they enable us to analyze the processes presently at work and any that may unfold in the future. Highly abstract concepts, moreover, can help free us from the differentiated state paradigm to the extent they involve new words, labels, and ideas that may inhibit our inclinations to fall back into old analytic habits.

But what processes should be the focus of our modeling effort? Here I derive the answer from what strikes me as the most elemental dynamic common to both the changes and the continuities at work in world politics, namely, that dynamic or set of dynamics whereby individual actions are summed and thereby converted into collectivities and then, at subsequent points in time, converted over and over again into more or less encompassing collectivities. Such dynamics underlie the emergence of new issues and actors, both those that result from the fragmentation of authority and those that stem from cooperative integration. And they also undergird the decline of old issues and actors as well as those that remain unaltered by changing circumstances. I shall refer to these most elemental dynamics as aggregative or disaggregative processes, since the summing of actions into more or less encompassing collectivities can be readily seen as transformations through which behavior is more or less widely aggregated.

To anticipate what follows, this line of reasoning leads to a world populated by a great variety of aggregations that are macro wholes summed out of micro parts. In this world some of the aggregations are formal organizations, others are loose coalitions, and still others are comprised of unorganized individuals whose actions sum to recognizable wholes; but all of them are subject to events or trends that alter their parts and thus the sums to which they cumulate. As a result, all of the aggregations are posited as either undergoing formation and leaderless or as established and led by authorized or self-appointed spokespersons who seek to mobilize the parts or otherwise articulate and advance their interests.

Although the ensuing analysis treats aggregation at a very high level of abstraction and as a series of never-ending processes, I would not claim that it is otherwise sufficient as a building block for a new paradigm. Such a conclusion requires a much more extended inquiry than is set forth here, not to mention the identification of the other building blocks out of which a viable conceptual structure can be fashioned. But at least this formulation is suggestive of what may be involved if we opt for modeling rather than muddling or meddling.

THE CONCEPT OF AGGREGATION

As indicated, an aggregation is conceived to be a whole (or macro unit) composed of parts (or micro units) whose actions are sufficiently similar to be summable into the whole, and an aggregative process refers to the interactions whereby such transformations occur. The smallest micro unit in world politics is the individual, but all aggregations of individuals—from two-person groups to nation-states to international organizations—can also be viewed as micro units if they are treated as parts of more encompassing wholes. All the aggregations, of course, can also be treated as macro units if there are no reasons to focus on how their actions are transformed into larger wholes. Thus, for example, bureaucratic agencies are macro units embracing individuals as micro units, whereas from a broader perspective the agencies are micro units embedded in such macro units as governments, large corporations, or international organizations.

But the important point is not that the varied collectivities of world politics can be viewed as either macro or micro units. Rather, for reasons developed below, the key to making a full break with the differentiated state paradigm and constructing new ones to replace it lies in the readiness to treat all collectivities as susceptible either to aggregative processes that transform them into larger wholes or to disaggregative processes that transform them from wholes into parts.[10] For these processes are nothing less than the causal flows in international relations, the dynamics through which action is initiated, sustained, redirected, or terminated on the world stage. Thus, whether one is concerned with a state's foreign policy, the population explosion, a balance of power, an arms race, the Third World's demands for greater equity, or a resource scarcity, its place in the larger scheme of world politics becomes more

---

[10] That the ensuing analysis deals only with aggregative processes is not meant to imply that there need be no concern about the causaol flows from macro to micro units. On the contrary, as noted elsewhere, the processes of disaggregation are also central to any paradigm-building effort. Aggregative and disaggregative processes, however, differ in certain key respects and I only have time here to probe the former. For an initial consideration of the latter, see James N. Rosenau, "The Tourist and The Terrorist: Two Extremes on a Transnational Continuum," a paper presented at the Annual Meeting of the International Studies Association, Washington, D.C., February 23, 1978, and the Workshop on Transnational and Transgovernmental Relations and International Outcomes, European Consortium for Political Research, Grenoble, France, April 8, 1978.

elaborately and more incisively manifest when it is viewed as the product of or a contributor to any or all of several aggregative processes.

Three aggregative processes strike me as specially fundamental. One results in *unintended* aggregations, another in *articulated* aggregations, and the third in *mobilized* aggregations, the differences among them being due to the ways in which their micro parts come together into macro wholes.

In the unintended process the micro parts are aggregated whenever the similarity of their parts is recognized but not acted upon (e.g., migrations), whereas in the other two processes recognition is accompanied by action on the part of spokespersons (e.g., immigration regulations). Leadership activities do not accompany unintended aggregations because the similar actions of their micro parts may stem from a variety of sources. Indeed, their similar actions may be undertaken for very different, perhaps even conflicting, private purposes. Yet, being the same, they are summable. These unintended sums may be recognized by journalists, scholars, and/or other observers who have occasion to take note of the separate but similar actions that comprise the aggregation in the course of performing their responsibilities. For reasons suggested below, however, the unintended aggregation is not the basis of action on the part of those who sum its parts through recognition. It is simply a structural feature of the world scene that may play a crucial if passive role in the course of events. A resource scarcity typifies an unintended aggregation. It results from individuals or groups consuming the resource for their own private reasons and, in so doing, creating a scarcity. None of the micro units intended the shortage, but their separate actions aggregated to such an outcome. The growing scarcity may have long been recognized by various observers, but it remains an unintended aggregation as long as their observations do not provoke action by spokespersons for other aggregations that have previously been converted into collectivities.

Frequently, of course, the actions of micro units are undertaken for similar purposes. If so, obviously they will also be similar in content and recognized as aggregating to a larger whole. Less obvious is that the similarity of the purposes of the micro units leads them to permit or select spokespersons to act on behalf of their summed actions. That is, the micro units intend—or at least allow—their aggregation and they intend for it to be recognized and organized in such a way that action can be continuously taken on behalf of their collective interests. It is this process that I refer to as an *articulated* aggregation. It is exemplified by the activities of multinational corporations, rebel movements, trade unions, professional societies, or international organizations, all of whose spokespersons seek to promote and preserve the concerns of their stockholders, members, followers, and any other micro units of which they may be composed. Most notably perhaps, an articulated aggregation is illustrated by the foreign policies of a state, which are framed and advanced by its spokespersons on the basis of the prior and continuing actions of its citizens that permit their aggregation into the state. The spokespersons and those toward whom their policies are directed presume that through aggregation they enjoy sufficient support of the citizenry—micro units—to articulate its interests. To be sure, on rare occasions the actions of foreign policy officials are lacking a support base and thus do not represent accurate summations of the micro units. But these exceptions also reveal the nature of articulated aggregations because they normally result in the ouster of the officials (as proved to be the case when Anthony Eden aggregated inaccurately and launched an English invasion of the Suez Canal in 1956 or when Lyndon Johnson did the same in 1965-67 and escalated U.S. involvement in Vietnam).

The third basic type of aggregative process occurs when the similar actions of microparts are stimulated by spokespersons who seek to sum them into a particular whole for a particular purpose. Normally an articulated aggregation is the focus of such efforts (as when states go to war or when some leaders of the Third World generate support among their colleagues in the Group of 77 to reinforce demands for a New Economic Order); but sometimes an unintended aggregation is the target of the stimuli (as when spokespersons for governments try to get people to conserve energy or when aspiring politicians attempt to seize leadership of a grassroots revolt against high taxes). Whichever may be the target of the efforts, it is the result of this process that I call a *mobilized* aggregation.

It is important to stress that the summing of the micro units of an aggregation into a macro whole is a process undertaken and sustained not by the micro units themselves, but by observers and/or leaders (i.e., spokespersons) who recognize, articulate, and/or mobilize them. The collective consequences of individual actions, in other words, only become aggregations when they are identified as cumulative sums. And they only become *politically relevant* aggregations when their sums are both identified and used by spokespersons to advance, resist, or otherwise contest claims vis-à-vis the community. Individuals might band together to press a claim, but even their concerted actions do not become those of an aggregation until their summed demands are articulated by their leaders and acknowledged by those of whom the demands are made. Spontaneous street mobs, organized protest marches, impulsive buyer resistances, or planned consumer boycotts, for example, do not become summed aggregations until the summing is experienced and reacted to as a collective action.

It follows that the relationship between the micro units of an aggregation and its macro spokespersons can vary greatly, from a tight, one-to-one relationship in which the latter do not act without the consent of the former to a loose, tenuous relationship in which the spokespersons need not be particularly concerned about the accuracy of their sums. Most aggregations are of the loose, tenuous type (thereby giving rise to the need for creative and effective leadership), but even here there can be great variety, depending on how well the leadership calculates, articulates, and mobilizes the sums.

Much more often than not the spokespersons are likely to be inaccurate in the sums they calculate, but their inaccuracies are rarely so serious as to provoke the micro units into collective actions that relieve them of their statuses as spokespersons. Tolerance of the inaccuracies is the norm partly because the calculation of objective sums tends to be impossible (if only because many articulated aggregations consist of parts, such as attitudes and motives, that are not readily quantifiable), partly because of the considerable leeway built into most processes through which summation occurs (i.e., most groups allow their leaders discretionary authority in asserting claims on their behalf), and partly because the links between the micro units and their macro spokespersons are so circuitous and cumbersome that the former are often unaware that the latter are acting on their behalf.

Usually, of course, macro spokespersons try to be as accurate as possible in the sums they calculate. The more accurate they are, the more they are likely to be in touch with their support base and thus the more effectively can they cite evidence supporting their claims. There may be times when the aggregated sums are intentionally exaggerated or underplayed for tactical purposes, but in the long run spokespersons have much to gain through maximizing the accuracy of their aggregated sums.

Whatever the accuracy with which the parts are summed, there is one sense in which inaccuracy is bound to occur: the aggregated whole is bound to be larger than the sum of its parts whenever the similar actions that comprise an aggregation are articulated or mobilized by its spokespersons and their assertions and activities thereby become the basis of issues in the political arena. At such points the needs and wants of the aggregation acquire an existence apart from its micro units. The aggregation becomes an entity unto itself, capable of pressing, resisting, bargaining, and accommodating demands, and in so acting its spokespersons render it into a whole that exceeds the sum of its parts.

USES OF THE CONCEPT

Crude as it may be, this initial formulation of the several types of aggregation can serve the paradigm-building task in a number of ways. One is that it leads itself to close empirical examination. The several aggregative processes consist not of hidden hands that somehow mystically transform individuals into collectivities. To be sure, the interactions of masses of people are so circuitous, complex, and subtle that they are not easily discerned. Nevertheless, in this formulation the ways in which micro units cumulate into macro units are concrete and identifiable; aggregation occurs when similar actions are recognized, summed, and articulated. Recognition and summation are manifest in birth rates, agricultural outputs, industrial production figures, election outcomes, trade patterns, and a host of other indicators that are regularly published or readily compiled; similarly, articulation is empirically manifest in the activities of spokespersons who continuously recognize and sum the aggregations for which they act.

Secondly, by conceiving of the collectivities that sustain world politics as aggregative processes rather than structural parameters, we allow for the dynamics of change at all levels of analysis and under all possible circumstances. Viewed as aggregations whose formation depends on the convergence of similar behavior, collectivities appear less as enduring constants and more as being in continuous flux. If we can discipline ourselves to see the world not as a cluster of nations, alignments, or publics, but as a cluster of ever-changing aggregative processes —of parts forming wholes, coming apart, reforming, and doing so in such a way that the wholes are sometimes roughly equal to the sums of their parts and sometimes greater than the sums—then we ought better to be able to pick up and rearrange the pieces of the paradigms that collapsed under the weight of pervasive change.

The capacity of the aggregation concept to render us more sensitive to the dynamics of change is especially relevant to the long-standing practice of viewing certain circumstances as the "realities" of world politics—as those deeper structures comprised of long-standing habits, cultural tendencies, economic imperatives, and sociological necessities entrenched in the environment that are beyond manipulation and yet profoundly condition what people do and how communities function. As considered here, however, all such "realities" are unintended aggregations that, being composed of recognizable parts, may be susceptible to manipulation (i.e., to transformation into articulated or mobilized aggregations). The energy problem, for example, is often posited as consisting of realities embedded in the interaction between the world's oil reserves and the consumption patterns of an industrial civilization. Recent efforts in the West to get people to change their energy utilization habits constitute an attempt to render an unintentional aggregation into a mobilized one and, notwithstanding the apparent failure of such efforts, it suggests the emergence of a readiness on the part of spokespersons to undertake manipulation of what not long ago had been regarded as unmanipulable. Much the same can be said about ocean problems, food shortages, currency fluctuations, and the population explosion. These are but a few of the many unintended aggregations that have lately become salient on the global stage as foci of endeavors to convert them into articulated or mobilized aggregations.

The ability to distinguish among the several aggregative processes, therefore, can greatly facilitate analysis as the world becomes more decentralized and as we search for ways of identifying those of its features that are becoming permanent and those that are undergoing fundamental change. It virtually compels us to reconsider the "realities" of world politics and assess the extent to which these collapsed with our paradigms. By viewing them as unintended aggregations rather than as deep-seated, habitual and immutable tendencies of people in a complex world, we at least allow for the possibility that altered circumstances may redirect the processes by which wholes get aggregated out of parts. For, to repeat, aggregations are processes composed of discrete and separable parts and, as such, they are susceptible to alteration, a characteristic which does not obtain if the same phenomena are viewed as fixed and permanent.

Fourthly, and relatedly, by treating aggressive processes as parameters of world politics, we put the individual person more centrally onto the global stage. Aggregations begin with and build upon concrete and identifiable individuals who, through recognized and articulated similar behavior, become groups, communities, governments, nations, international balances, and the like. Putting the person onto the global stage is important because the decentralization of authority, the fragmentation of societies, and the emergence of interdependence issues takes the origins and dynamics of politics into the homes and jobs where individuals make choices and undertake actions. The population explosion is perhaps the clearest example of how aggressive processes can be traced back to the individual level, but the relevance of the motorist, the banker, the farmer, the fisherman, and the terrorist to, respectively, the energy crunch, monetary instability, food shortages, ocean problems, and political upheaval is indicative of the large degree to which the structures of world politics have become even more solidly rooted in the soil of individual orientations and behavior. Indeed, the declining competence of governments can be traced partly, if not primarily, to mounting distrust of public institutions on the part of citizens.

A fifth advantage of this formulation is that it can hasten our break with any paradigm that relies on states as the prime sources of causation. By focusing on aggregations and their spokespersons, we allow ourselves to analyze varied behavior on the global stage without having to presume the importance of states or implicity ranking them as more significant than other types of actors. Indeed, this formulation enables us to get away not only from states as abstract actors, but also from the very notion of action being the product of any abstraction. As conceived here, action is located where empirically it originates and is maintained, i.e., in and by individuals. For the only actors in this formulation are the individuals who comprise aggregations and those who serve as spokespersons for them.

Sixth, the notion of spokespersons for aggregations offers the potential of a fresh approach to analyzing the policy-making process. Instead of being forced to treat such processes as bounded by the political and legal constraints of states, we can focus on the dynamics whereby the spokespersons experience, sum, assess, and articulate the interests of their aggregations and then interact with other spokespersons of other aggregations. Sometimes these interactions occur within governments (thus resulting in what are now called policy decisions), sometimes in bargaining between governments (thus giving rise to policy outcomes), and sometimes in the nongovernmental arena where political parties, interest groups, professional associations, and other groups compete for the support of citizens and the attention of officials. But mostly aggregations extend across the boundaries that separate agencies within governments, that divide governments from each other, and that differentiate governments from the private sector. Thus the consequences of mounting interdependence and fragmented authority are likely to be built into any analysis of what happens when spokespersons articulate and mobilize their aggregations.

A seventh reason why the concept can serve as a useful building block for a more appropriate paradigm is that its several types provide a uniform basis for analyzing any of the diverse issues that may be on the world's agenda at any moment in time. Any issue can be viewed as a problem posed by an unintended aggregation or as arising out of a competition among articulated or mobilized aggregations. Whatever its aggregative foundations, the issue can be dissected and probed by examining the dynamics—the motivations, presumptions, and/or habits —whereby the actions of individuals allow for and lead to their aggregation and the articulation of their collective needs and wants. Thus, despite the diversity of their contents, the structures, overlaps, and consequences of the prevailing issues can be contrasted and compared.

And, hopefully, such comparative analysis can lead to a more precise specification of a parsimonious typology of aggregative processes which, in turn, can facilitate the derivation of a few basic causal principles around which the beginnings of a paradigm can be organized.

It follows that the distinctions among the several types of aggregation should also better enable us to discern the similarities between the newer socio-economic issues spawned by mounting interdependence and the old military-diplomatic issues that continue to occupy prominent places on the global agenda. Presumably any new paradigm that evolves will have to surmount the inclination to treat the socio-economic issues as interlopers, as unconventional aspects of world politics that require special treatment. These new issues seem here to stay and we have to begin to treat them as integral parts of world politics. The differentiation among aggregative processes offers a means for achieving this analytic integration. It allows us to view socio-economic and military-diplomatic issues in the same context—as processes of aggregation that can undergo progression from the recognition through the articulation and mobilization stages of development. To be sure, since most socio-economic issues derive from the habits and patterns of millions of persons, they evolve in different ways and at different rates than do most military-diplomatic issues. Hence the former are much less subject to articulated aggregation than are the latter and they are also less susceptible to mobilization.[11] Nevertheless, viewing both types of issues as aggregative processes at least renders them comparable and enables us to contrast them in meaningful ways.

A final advantage inherent in the concept of aggregation is that it provides a means of observing how the global agenda is formed, with issues rising and falling, some crowding their way to the top of the agenda, some lingering on its periphery, and others never making it at all. By tracing how unintended aggregations are transformed into those that are articulated or mobilized, we can begin to see how activities at various levels of organization do or do not become linked with each other and, as a result, how the linked actions can culminate in a place on the global agenda. It will be recalled that whatever the most micro units of an aggregation—be they the purchases of citizens or the decisions of officials—they are not necessarily the basis for action once they are recognized and summed into a more encompassing macro unit. It can remain simply as an unintended aggregation recognized only by detached observers such as journalists and scholars. Even if such observers stress that the aggregation constitutes a serious social, economic, or political problem, it does not become a political issue if their warnings

---

[11] For a useful elaboration of this point, see R. L. Paarlberg, "Domesticating Global Management," *Foreign Affairs*, 54 (April 1976), pp. 563-577.

fall on deaf ears. Indeed, an unintended aggregation may even be recognized by public officials and not become a public issue. They may encounter the similar behaviors in the course of performing their responsibilities and merely take them for granted as a "reality" of the situation that cannot be altered. For years discrimination against minorities in the United States exemplified this circumstance. It constituted aggregate behavior that was recognized by disinterested observers and public officials alike, but virtually all concerned treated it as a given social condition.

In short, the conversion of an aggregation into a public issue occurs when its recognition is followed by spokespersons for macro units who have reasons to call attention to the similar actions of the micro units and to highlight the need to respond to their collective implications (say, the importance of the patterns formed by the purchases of citizens or the significance of the policy patterns formed by the decisions of officials). The spokespersons can speak on behalf of the aggregation or they can speak about it, contending that it enhances or threatens certain values. In either case, once an aggregative process thus enters the articulation stage, it can become controversial if spokespersons for different aggregations contest the claims made on its behalf. When enough spokespersons become involved, the aggregation becomes the basis of an issue competing for a place on the agenda of a political system. Stated somewhat differently, the articulation of an aggregation links it with actions at more encompassing levels of organization. Whether this occurs through the parts being mobilized to form a whole or simply through articulation of the interests recognized as the sum of the parts, the result is the same: the spokespersons precipitate processes of aggregation that can move through more and more encompassing levels until they pass beyond national boundaries and culminate in transnational and international activities.

Thus, for example, do votes become electoral mandates, and thus do the decisions of officials become the policies of governments. And so, too, do electoral mandates become societal demands and so do governmental policies become international conflicts. As the processes of aggregation move on from level to level, at some point their dynamics either wane or gather more force, with the result that the aggregation either fails to push its way as an issue onto the agenda of political systems or its urgency becomes unavoidable and it becomes an issue with which systems must cope. Having long been ignored by the spokespersons of most aggregations, discrimination against minorities in the United States followed such a pattern and eventually acquired status as a civil rights issue on the national agenda. And this particular aggregative process has continued to unfold to the point where it has now been pushed ever more securely onto the global agenda.

FROM BUILDING BLOCKS TO THEORY BUILDING

Whatever its many potential virtues, of course, the concept of aggregation is not in itself a sufficient foundation for a new paradigm. As formulated, it is just a building block, subject to any of a number of possible uses. If one is so inclined, for example, it could readily be integrated into a Marxist framework. Unintended aggregations could well be treated as instruments of the class struggle, unrecognized by both the dominant and the subordinate classes but nevertheless present as expressions of the latter's resistance to the former's control. Similarly, a Marxist would have no trouble viewing articulated and mobilized aggregations as reflections of imperialism, as the basis on which the ruling classes expand and secure their domination.

In short, necessary as the concept of aggregation may be to a new, non-Marxist paradigm, it is not sufficient to do the job alone. Other concepts are needed and so is the inspired creativity that can weave them together into a theoretical cloth. Among others, the concepts of role, authority, and legitimacy ought to be considered in this regard. The first can be viewed as the source of the similar behavior out of which aggregations are formed and the last two can serve as the stitching, so to speak, that links the micro parts of aggregations once they have been recognized and their interests articulated.[12] Developing these concepts for this purpose, however, will take some work. This is especially so in the case of authority. Although there is a vast and rich literature on the concept that ought to be consulted, it needs to be supplemented and enlarged with fresh thought. Virtually all the existing literature treats authority in a legal context, whereas the goal of the modeling approach is to free us of state-centric paradigms by allowing for aggregative processes that do not necessarily sum to relevant collectivities based on formal legal structures.[13]

As for the inspired creativity that can cement the building blocks into a coherent and parsimonious model, here one can only reiterate that modeling is preferable to muddling or meddling and urge that recourse to creativity be an endless commitment. The various types of aggregation need to be played with in our minds, imagined as responses

[12] For an initial effort to probe how the concept of authority might be used as a building for a new paradigm, see James N. Rosenau, "International Studies in a Transnational World," *Millenium*, 5 (Spring, 1976), pp. 1-20. An initial formulation of the role concept in this context can be found in my 'The Terrorist and the Tourist" paper (see note 10 above).

[13] For a cogent analysis that notes the difficulties inherent in applying the concept of authority to the nonlegal structures that sustain international phenomena, see Harry Eckstein, "Authority Patterns: A Structural Basis for Political Inquiry," *American Political Science Review*, 67 (December 1973), pp. 1142-1161.

to different conditions, fostering different outcomes, and governed by different lawful properties. And perhaps we should toy around with the possibility of treating the global agenda as an overarching structure that imposes coherence on diverse issues without presuming the orderliness of a society. A playful mind may not be enough to capture and discipline all the changes that are transforming world politics, but it surely is a necessary prerequisite to paradigmatic progress.

Bibliography of James N. Rosenau

1951

The Roosevelt Treasury
Editor. New York: Doubleday; xvi plus 461 pp.

1958

The Nomination of "Chip" Bohlen
New York: Hery Holt; 16 pp.

1959

"Senate Attitudes Toward a Secretary of State"
in J. C. Wahlke and H. Eulau (eds.), *Legislative Behavior*
(New York: Free Press), pp. 333–346.

1960

* "The Birth of a Political Scientist"
PROD 3 (January): 19–21.

1961

Public Opinion and Foreign Policy: An Operational Formulation
New York: Random House; vi plus 118 pp.
*International Politics and Foreign Policy: A Reader in Research
and Theory*
Editor. New York: Free Press; 511 pp.

KEY TO SYMBOLS:
* Also in this Revised Edition.
† Also in *The Study of Political Adaptation*.
‡ Also in *The Study of Global Interdependence*.

1962

　　"Consensus, Leadership and Foreign Policy"
　　　　SAIS Review 6 (Winter): 3–10.
　　"Consensus-Building in the American National Community: Some
　　　　Hypotheses and Some Supporting Data:
　　　　Journal of Politics 24 (November): 639–661. Reprinted in
　　　　John E. Mueller (ed.), *Approaches to Measurement in Inter-*
　　　　national Relations: A Non-Evangelical Survey (New York:
　　　　Appleton-Century, 1969). ⸍
　　"Convergence and Cleavage in the Study of International Politics
　　　　and Foreign Policy"
　　　　Journal of Conflict Resolution VI (December): 359–67.

1963

　　* Calculated Control as a Unifying Concept in the Study of Inter-
　　　　national Politics and Foreign Policy
　　　　Research Monograph No. 15, Center of International Studies,
　　　　Princeton University; 58 pp.

　　National Leadership and Foreign Policy: A Case Study in the
　　　　Mobilization of Public Support
　　　　Princeton, N.J.: Princeton University Press; xvii plus 409.
　　"The Functioning of International Systems"
　　　　Background 7 (November): 111–117.

1964

　　International Aspects of Civil Strife
　　　　Editor. Princeton, N.J.: Princeton University Press; vii plus
　　　　322 pp.
　　"Internal War as an International Event"
　　　　in J. N. Rosenau (ed.), *International Aspects of Civil Strife*;
　　　　45–91. Reprinted in George A. Kelly and Clifford W. Brown,

　　　　Jr. (eds.), *Struggles in the State: Sources and Patterns of*
　　　　World Revolution (New York: Wiley, 1970).
　　"Meticulousness as a Factor in the Response to Mail Question-
　　　　naires"
　　　　Public Opinion Quarterly XXVIII (Summer): 312–314.

1965

"Behavioral Science, Behavioral Scientist, and the Study of International Phenomena"
Journal of Conflict Resolution IX (December): 509–520.

1966

* "Pre-Theories and Theories in Foreign Policy"
in R. B. Farrell (ed.), *Approaches to Comparative and International Politics*, Evanston: Northwestern University Press, 27–92. Reprinted in W. D. Coplin and C. W. Kegley (eds.), *Analyzing International Relations: A Multimethod Introduction* (New York: Praeger, 1975).

"Transforming the International System: Small Increments Along a Vast Periphery"
World Politics XVIII: 525–545. Reprinted in Henry S. Kariel (ed.), *The Political Order: A Reader in Political Science* (New York: Basic Books, 1970).

1967

Of Boundaries and Bridges
Research Monograph No. 27, Center of International Studies, Princeton University, 66 pp.

Domestic Sources of Foreign Policy
Editor. New York: Free Press: xvi plus 340 pp.

* "Foreign Policy as an Issue Area"
in J. N. Rosenau (ed.), *Domestic Sources of Foreign Policy*, 11–50.

* "The Premises and Promises of Decision-Making Analysis"
in J. C. Charlesworth (ed.), *Contemporary Political Analysis* (New York: Free Press), 189–211.

* "Games International Relations Scholars Play"
Journal of International Affairs XXI (Summer): 293–303.

"Compatability, Consensus and an Emerging Political Science of Adaptation"
American Political Science Review LXI (December): 983*88.

1968

The Attentive Public and Foreign Policy: A Theory of Growth and Some New Evidence
Research Monograph No. 31, Center for International Studies, Princeton University; 48 pp.

"Political Science 221: Douglass College"
>   Vincent Davis and Arthur N. Gilbert (eds.), *Basic Courses in International Relations: An Anthology of Syllabi* (Beverly Hills: Sage Publications), 84–90.

* "Moral Fervor, Systematic Analysis, and Scientific Consciousness in Foreign Policy Research"
>   in A. Ranney (eds.), *Political Science and Public Policy* (Chicago: Markham), 197–236.

"Political Theory as Academic Field and Intellectual Activity"
>   Co-authored with Neil McDonald. *Journal of Politics* 30 (May): 311–44. Reprinted in Marian Irish (ed.), *Political Science: Advance of the Discipline* (New York: Prentice-Hall, 1968).

"Comparative Foreign Policy: Fad, Fantasy, or Field"
>   *International Studies Quarterly* 12 (September): 296–329

"The Concept of Intervention"
>   *Journal of International Affairs* XXII (Summer): 165–76.

* "The National Interest"
>   *International Encyclopedia of the Social Sciences.* New York: Crowell-Collier, Vol. 11, 34–40.

* "Private Preferences and Political Responsibilities: The Relative Potency of Individual and Role Variables in the Behavior of U.S. Senators"
>   In J. D. Singer (ed.), *Quantitative International Politics: Insights and Evidence* (New York: Free Press), 17–50.

1969

* *Race in International Politics: A Dialogue in Five Parts*
>   Monograph Series in World Affairs, University of Denver, Vol. 7, No. 2, 50 pp.

Linkage Politics: Essays on the Convergence of National and International Systems
>   Editor. New York: Free Press; xii plus 352 pp.

Contending Approaches to International Politics
>   Editor with Klaus Knorr. Princeton, N.J.: Princeton University Press; v plus 297 pp.

* "Toward the Study of National-International Politics"
>   in J. N. Rosenau (ed.), *Linkage Politics*, 44–63.

"Tradition and Science in the Study of International Politics"
>   Co-author with Klaus Knorr, in K. Knorr and J. N. Rosenau (eds.), *Contending Approaches to International Politics*, Chap. 1.

* "Intervention as a Scientific Concept"
   Journal of Conflict Resolution XII (June): 149–71. Reprinted in Richard A. Falk (ed.), *The Vietnam War and International Law*, Vol. 2 (Princeton, N.J.: Princeton University Press, 1969).

International Politics and Foreign Policy: A Reader in Research and Theory
   Editor. Revised edition, New York: Free Press; xx plus 740 pp.

1970

*† *The Adaptation of National Societies: A Theory of Political Behavior and Its Transformation*
   (New York: McCaleb-Seiler); 28 pp.

"Adaptive Strategies for Research and Practice in Foreign Policy"
   in Fred W. Riggs (ed.), *A Design for International Studies: Scope, Objectives, and Methods* (Philadelphia: American Academy of Political and Social Science), 218–245.

"Foreign Policy as Adaptive Behavior: Some Preliminary Notes for a Theoretical Model"
   Comparative Politics 2 (April): 365–89.

"Public Protest, Political Leadership, and Diplomatic Strategy"
   Orbis XIV (Fall): 557–71.

"Field and Environmental Approaches to World Politics: Implications for Data Archives"
   Co-author with Raymond Tanter. *Journal of Conflict Resolution* XIV (December): 513–26.

1971

The Scientific Study of Foreign Policy
   New York: Free Press: xv plus 472 pp.

"Public Opinion, Foreign Policy, and the Adaptation of National Societies"
   Societas I (Spring): 85–100.

1972

"*The Attentive Public in an Interdependent World: A Survey of Theoretical Perspectives and Empirical Findings*"
   Columbus, Ohio: Mershon Center; 116 pp.

† "Adaptive Policies in an Interdependent World"
   Orbis XVI (Spring): 153–73.

"Dissent and Political Leadership"
   Dialogue 5: 36–45.
Foreword
   Davis B. Bobrow, *International Relations: New Approaches*
   (New York: Free Press), vii-xv.
The Analysis of International Politics
   Editor with Vincent Davis and Maurice A. East.
   New York: Free Press; xii plus 397 pp.
* "The External Environment as a Variable in Foreign Policy
   Analysis"
   in J. N. Rosenau, V. Davis, M. A. East (eds.), *The Analysis
   of International Politics*, 145–165.

1973

International Studies and the Social Sciences
   Beverly Hills: Sage Publications; 147 pp.
The Dramas of Politics: An Introduction to the Joys of Inquiry
   New York: Little, Brown; xiii plus 250 pp.
† "Paradigm Lost: Five Actors in Search of the Interactive Effects
   of Domestic and Foreign Affairs"
   Policy Sciences 4 (December): 415–36.
"Mobilizing the Attentive Citizen: A Model and Some Data on
   a Neglected Dimension of Political Participation"
   (A paper presented at the Annual Meeting of the American
   Political Science Association, New Orleans.)
‡ "Theorizing Across Systems: Linkage Politics Revisited"
   in J. Wilkenfeld (ed.), *Conflict Behavior and Linkage Politics*
   (New York: David McKay), 25–56.
"International Studies in the United States: Some Problems and
   Issues of the 1970s"
   Yearbook of World Affairs, 1973: 401–16.
*"The Adaptation of Foreign Policy Research: A Case Study of
   an Anti-Case Study Project"
   Co-author with Philip M. Burgess and Charles F. Hermann.
   International Studies Quarterly 17 (March): 119–44.

1974

*Citizenship Between Elections: An Inquiry into the Mobilizable
   America*
   New York: Fress Press; xxxii plus 526 pp.
Comparing Foreign Policies: Theories, Findings, and Methods
   Editor. Beverly Hills: Sage Publications; xi plus 442 pp.

† "Foreign Intervention as Adaptive Behavior"
  in John Norton Moore (ed.), *Law and Civil War in the Modern World* (Baltimore: Johns Hopkins University Press), pp. 129–151.

The Transnationalization of Urban Communities: Some Data on Elites in a Midwestern City
  Columbus, Ohio: Mershon Center; 43 pp.

‡ *Success and Failure in Scientific International Relations Research*
  Final Report, National Science Foundation; 79 pp.

"The Final Examination as a Group Process"
  Teaching Political Science 2 (October): 65–77.

‡ "The Coming Transformation of America: Resistance or Accommodation?"
  World Studies I (Spring): 1–26.

‡ "Assessment in International Studies: Ego Trip or Feedback?"
  International Studies Quarterly 18 (September): 339–67.

"Comparing Foreign Policies: Why, What, How"
  in J. N. Rosenau (ed.), *Comparing Foreign Policies*, 3–22.

"Foreign Policy Behavior in Dyadic Relationships: Testing a Pre-Theoretical Extension"
  Co-author with Gary D. Hoggard in J. N. Rosenau (ed.), *Comparing Foreign Policies*, 117–150.

1975

* "Comparative Foreign Policy: One-Time Fad, Realized Fantasy, and Normal Field"
  in C. W. Kegley, Jr., A. G. Raymond, R. M. Rood, and R. A. Skinner (eds.), *International Events and the Comparative Analysis of Foreign Policy* (Columbia: University of South Carolina Press), 3–38.

* "External and Internal Typologies of Foreign Policy Behavior: Testing the Stability of an Intriguing Set of Findings"
  Co-author with George R. Ramsey, Jr., in P. J. McGowan (ed.), *Sage International Yearbook of Foreign Policy Studies*, Vol. III (Beverly Hills: Sage Publications), 251–68.

1976

World Politics
  Editor with Gavin Boyd and Kenneth Thompson. New York: Free Press; xii plus 754 pp.

In Search of Global Patterns
  Editor. New York: Free Press; ix plus 389 pp.

"Perspectives on World Politics"
   in J. N. Rosenau, A. Boyd, K. Thompson (eds.), *World Politics*, 1–11.
"The Study of Foreign Policy"
   in J. N. Rosenau, A. Boyd, K. Thompson (eds.), *World Politics*, 15–35.
‡ "Capabilities and Control in an Interdependent World"
   International Security 1 (October): 32–49.
"The Restless Quest"
   in J. N. Rosenau (ed.), *In Search of Global Patterns*, 1–9.
"Restlessness, Change, and Foreign Policy Analysis"
   in J. N. Rosenau (ed.), *In Search of Global Patterns*, 369–376.
"The Lessons: of Vietnam: A Study of American Leadership"
   Co-author with Ole R. Holsti. (A paper presented at the 17th Annual Meeting of the International Studies Association, Toronto, Canada.)
"Vietnam Revisited: A Comparison of the Recollections of Foreign Service and Military Officers of the Lessons, Sources, and Consequences of the War"
   Co-author with Ole R. Holsti. (A paper presented at the Xth Congress of the International Political Science Association, Edinburgh, Scotland.)
‡ "International Studies in a Transnational World"
   Millennium 5 (Spring): 1–20.
‡ "Intellectual Identity and the Study of International Relations, or Coming to terms with Mathematics as a Tool of Inquiry"
   in D. A. Zinnes and J. V. Gillespie (eds.), *Mathematical Models in International Relations* (New York: Praeger), 3–9.

1977
"Comparative Politics"
   Co-author with Robert R. Kaufman, in Donald M. Freeman (ed.), *Political Science: History, Scope, and Methods* (New York: Free Press), 45–83.
"Teaching and Learning in a Transnational World"
   (A paper presented at the First Assembly of the Institute for the Advancement of Teaching and Learning, California State University, Northridge.)
"Problem Recognition: Belief Systems of American Leaders"
   Co-author with Ole R. Holsti. (A paper presented at the Annual Conference of the International Studies Association/South, Columbia, South Carolina.)

"The Meaning of Vietnam: Belief Systems of American Leaders"
Co-author with Ole R. Holsti. *International Journal* XXXII
(Summer): 452–74.

† "The Adaptation of Small States"
(A paper presented at the Conference on Contemporary Trends
and Issues in Caribbean International Affairs, Institute of
International Relations, University of West Indies, Trinidad.)

* "Puzzlement in Foreign Policy"
The Jerusalem Journal of International Relations I (Summer):
1–10.

‡ "Of Syllabi, Texts, Students, and Scholarship in International
Relations: Some Data and Interpretations on the State of a
Burgeoning Field"
Co-author with Gary Gartin, Edwin P. McClain, Dona Stin-
ziano, Richard Stoddard, and Dean Swanson. *World Politics*
XXIX (January): 263–342.

1978

"Decision-Making Approaches and Theories"
Alexander de Conde (ed.), *Dictionary of the History of Ameri-
can Foreign Policy* (New York: Charles Scribner's Sons), Vol.
I, 219–228.

"Cold War Axioms in the Post-Vietnam Era"
Co-author with Ole R. Holsti. (A paper presented at the
Annual Meeting of the International Studies Association,
Washington, D.C.; revised for publication in Alexander
George, Ole R. Holsti, and Randolph M. Siverson [eds.],
International Systems Change, Westview Press.)

*Does Where You Stand Depend on When You Were Born? The
Impact of Generation on Post-Vietnam Foreign Policy Beliefs*
Co-author with Ole R. Holsti. Institute for Transnational
Studies, Monograph No. ITS 78–01; 94 pp.

‡ "The Tourist and the Terrorist: Two Extremes on the Same
Transnational Continuum"
(A paper presented at the Annual Meeting of the International
Studies Association, Washington, D.C.; translated into French
and published in *Etudes Internationales* X (June), 219–52).)

1979

American Leaders"
"America's Foreign Policy Agenda: The Post-Vietnam Beliefs of
Co-author with Ole R. Holsti in Charles W. Kegley, Jr., and

Patrick J. McGowan (eds.), *Challenges to America: United States Foreign Policy in the 1980s*, Beverly Hills: Sage Publications; pp. 231–268.

"Public Opinion and Soviet Foreign Policy: Competing Belief Systems in the Policy-making Process"
Co-author with Ole R. Holsti. *Naval War College Review* XXXII (July-August), 4–14.

† "The United States in (and Out of) Vietnam: An Adaptive Transformation?"
Co-author with Ole R. Holsti. *Yearbook of World Affairs*, 1979.

* "Thinking Theory Thoroughly"
in K. P. Mistra and R. S. Beal (eds.), *International Relations Theory: Western and Non-Western Perspectives* (New Delhi: Vikas Publishing House, Ltd.), Chap. 1.

* "Muddling, Meddling, and Modeling: Alternative Approaches to the Study of World Politics in an Era of Rapid Change"
in K. P. Misra and R. S. Beal (eds.), *International Relations Theory: Western and Non-Western Perspectives*, Chap. 3, and *Millennium: Journal of International Studies* 8 (2).

‡ "Toward a New Civics: Teaching and Learning in an Era of Fragmenting Loyalties and Multiplying Responsibilities"
(A paper prepared for the Annual Meeting of the American Political Science Association, Washington, D.C.)

"Vietnam, Consensus, and the Belief Systems of American Leaders"
Co-authors with Ole R. Holsti, *World Politics* XXXII (October).

1980

The Dramas of Political Systems: An Introduction to the Problems of Governance
North Scituate, Mass.: Duxury Press.

The Scientific Study of Foreign Policy (Revised and Enlarged Edition)
London: Frances Pinter Publishers, Ltd.

The Study of Political Adaptation
London: Frances Pinter Publishers, Ltd.

The Study of Global Interdependence: Essays on the Transnationalization of World Affairs
London: Frances Printer Publishers, Ltd.

Index

Fulbright, J. William, 208, 209, 471n
functional analysis, 102, 119
functional distance, 250-9
Furniss, Edgar S., Jr., 79n, 117n, 286n, 298n
fused linkages, 376, 387, 387n, 390, 397

Galtung, Johan, 55n
game theory, 121, 305, 311, 325, 509, 519
Gardiner, Robert K. A., 402n
Geller, D. S., 540
generalization, levels of, 17, 49, 59
general systems theory, 331
geographic variables, 512, 528
George, Alexander L., 105n
Germany, 75, 96n, 148, 148n, 149, 154, 267, 292, 336, 342, 391, 450-1, 514, 518, 529, 533
Geyer, Georgie A., 355n
Ghana, 374, 522, 525
Gilpin, Robert, 310n
global agenda, 536, 537, 542, 551, 554
Goa, 131
Good, Robert C., 120n
governmental variables, 54, 128, 131, 132n, 144, 363-7, 425-6, 445-7, 527, 528, 529, 530, 532, 533, 544, 550
governments, stability of, 57, 108, 112, 236, 535, 538, 543, 550
Graber, Doris A., 345n
graduate education, 3-7
Greece, 211, 391, 456
Grimshaw, Allen D., 84n
Gross, Feliks, 79n
Group of 77, 546
Guatemala, 48
Guetskow, Harold, 40n, 118n, 312n

Haas, Ernst B., 173n, 373n
Haas, Michael, 83n
Hall, David K., 105n
Halle, Louis, 79n
Halper, T., 105n
Halperin, Morton H., 45n
Halpern, A. M., 85n, 86n
Hamlett, Bruce D., 540n
Hammerskjold, Dag, 245
Hammond, Paul Y., 68n
Handleman, J. R., 112n, 537n
Hanessian, John Jr., 8n

Hanrieder, Wolfram F., 77n, 88n, 96n, 105n, 106n
Harding, Warren, 130
Harrod, Jeffrey, 539n
Hartz, Louis, 83n, 372n, 409n
Haviland, H. Field, Jr., 39n, 68-71, 68n, 69n, 70n, 155n
Heady, Ferrel, 82n
Heilbronner, Robert L., 542n
Hermann, Charles F., 105n, 106n, 107n, 214n, 222n, 232n, 320n, 329n
Hermann, Margaret G., 108n, 222n
Hero, Alfred O., Jr., 311n
Hevi, E. John, 411n
Hill, Norman L., 186n
Hilsman, Roger, 118n, 309n, 310n
historical factors, 317-22, 324, 325, 327, 329, 337, 531, 534, 538, 540-2
Hitch, Charles J., 124, 308n
Hitler, Adolf, 28, 284, 288, 292, 514, 518
Hitlin, Rona B., 106n
Hoffmann, Stanley, 304n, 312n
Hoggard, Gary D., 107n, 111n, 215, 215n, 217n, 419n
Holsti, K. J., 118n, 405n
Holsti, Ole R., 117n, 174n, 328n, 537n
Holt, Robert T., 83n, 310n
Honan, William H., 38n
horizontal analysis, 321-3, 326, 327, 329, 330, 337; political systems, 155n, 156, 157, 159, 159n, 160, 167n
Hovet, Thomas, Jr., 150n, 173n, 464, 464n
Hovland, Carl, 94
Howe, Irving, 482n
human behavior, 11, 40, 50; determinants of, 412-13; scientific approach to, 295-7
Humphrey, Hubert H., 208
Hungary, 131, 341, 343, 350, 353, 357, 442-3, 531
Huntington, Samuel P., 82n, 165n, 180n, 310n, 375n, 392, 493, 493n
Hurewitz, J. C., 374n
Husak, G., 502

idealism, school of, 12
ideology, 516, 523
imperialism, 345, 553